Exodus from Emp

EXODUS FROM EMPIRE

The Fall of America's Empire and the Rise of the Global Community

Terrence E. Paupp

Pluto Press
LONDON • ANN ARBOR, MI

First published 2007 by Pluto Press
345 Archway Road, London N6 5AA
and 839 Greene Street, Ann Arbor, MI 48106

www.plutobooks.com

British Library Cataloguing in Publication Data
A catalogue record for this book is available from the British Library

Hardback:
ISBN-13: 978-0-7453-2614-6
ISBN-10: 0-7453-2614-5

Paperback:
ISBN-13: 978-0-7453-2613-9
ISBN-10: 0-7453-2613-7

Library of Congress Cataloging in Publication Data applied for

10 9 8 7 6 5 4 3 2 1

Designed and produced for Pluto Press by Chase Publishing Services Ltd
Copyedited and Typeset from disk by Newgen Imaging Systems (P) Ltd, Chennai, India
Printed and bound in Canada by Transcontinental Printing

*This book is dedicated to Sparkey and
all of my friends*

Contents

Acknowledgments	xii
Preface	xiv
List of Abbreviations	xvii

INTRODUCTION 1
The Fate of Empires and the Rise of Community 3
The Collapse of American Democracy under the Mantle of Empire 7
Subordinating the Global South to the Empire 11
Liberating the Global South from Global Empire 14

1 FROM PRECEDENCE WE COME 19
Resistance to Global Empire is An Historical Constant 24
Alternatives to Hegemony 26

2 THE OCCUPATIONS OF EMPIRE 30
The Reign of America's Own Imperial Plutocracy 32
"World Order Values" versus the "National Interest" 34
The Private Powers of America's Global Empire 37
The Decline of American Democracy and the
Rise of Global Empire 38

3 WHEN THE "LAW OF THE LAND" BECOMES LAWLESS 61
Superpower Law—Superpower Syndrome 64
The "Federal Principle" of the New American Republic 66
From the Federal Principle to the Embrace of
"Radical Unilateralism" 67
The Definition and Dimensions of "Lawlessness" 68
Seeking American Democracy in the Shadow of Empire 71
The Birth and Evolution of "Democratic Despotism"
in the United States 73
Unprecedented: "Inverted Totalitarianism"
and "Managed Democracy" in the Service of Empire 75
Inverted Totalitarianism 76
The Transformation of America by its Plutocracy 80
The Dangerous Union of "Turbo-Capitalism"
and "Inverted Totalitarianism" 83
In Service to the Empire: Free Trade, Science,
Technology, and Militarism 86

The Re-Colonization of the Third World   94
Toward a Lawless Twenty-First American Century: The
   Collision of Law with Power Politics   98

4 CLASH OR CONVERGENCE?   100
The Moral Imperative to Realize Justice within the
   Global Community   103
An Alternative Discourse on the Uses of Power   104
The Moral Failure of the Citizenry in Global Empire   106
Building Global Community in the Shadow of
   "Imperial Overstretch"   107
Beyond the "Clash of Civilizations"   109
Global Integration, Nonviolent Resistance,
   and the Rise of Civil Society   110
The Inevitable Crumbling of a Deterministic Worldview   111
In the Name of Empire   113
Moving Beyond the Idolatry of Empire and the
   "Clash of Ignorance"   116
The Inseparable Nature of Power and Justice   118
Power in the Service of Justice   121
The Phenomenon of Global Violence   123
Building Fair Institutions for the Sake of Just Outcomes   127
A Global Ethic for a Global Community:
   The Convergence of International Law with the
   World's Great Religions   131
Evolving Trends in International Law   131
International Law as a Force in Restraining Empire   133
Evolving Legal Practices through "Universal Jurisdiction"   134
The Metaphysics of Global Justice: The Evolution and Rise
   of Global Community out of Moral and Legal Traditions   136
Nuclear Weapons versus a Humane International Order   137
From Nuclear Weapons to Global Warming   139
Moving Toward Global Liberation from Global Empire   141
Exiting the Global Empire   141
Establishing Practical Guidelines for Normative
   Human Rights Claims   143
The World's Great Religions as a Common Body of
   Authoritative Norms   145
Divine Providence and Nonviolence versus Empire   151
Confronting an Empire of Conflict   153
The Pathologies of Power versus the
   Affirmation of Human Dignity   156
Seeking the Common Good for the Global Commons   157
Transcending Sovereignty, Embracing Justice   160
The Moral Mandate of Inclusive Global Governance   160

Replacing the Power of the Global North within
   the Global South   162
Conclusion   165

5 THE HIDDEN POLITICS OF EMPIRE   172
Overt and Covert History   173
The Rise of Postmodern Fascism and Global Empire   175
The Hidden History of the US Global Empire in the
   Eisenhower/Kennedy Years   178
The Dysfunctions of the American System that Led to
   War in Vietnam   182
Bush's Dysfunctional Policy in Iraq   184
John Kennedy's Struggle against the US War Lobby
   over Vietnam   186
The Tortured Road to US Intervention in the Persian Gulf:
   The United States Creates another Pretext for War   188
Asserting America's Drive for Global
   Primacy: How the JFK Assassination and
   Warren Commission, the Attacks on 9/11
   and the 9/11-Commission Were Used to Open
   the Door for War and Close the Door on the Truth   191
Assassination-Politics: Reversing the
   Direction of US Foreign Policy   193
The Secret Way to War from Operation
   Northwoods to the Downing Street Memo:
   Justifying Wars and Fixing Intelligence   196
Reflections on the Collapse of
   Democratically Elected Leadership and
   the Hijacking of US Foreign Policy   199
An Imperial Presidency for a Global Empire   200
Fascism Comes to America   202
"Blowback"—The Unintended Consequences of US Foreign Policy 203
An Endless Struggle to Acquire Strategic Resources:
   American Planning for War without End from
   World War II to the Present   205
In the Shadow of Dallas: The Legacy of the Kennedy
   Assassination and the Road to War Without End   207
The Bush-2 Regime Designs an Energy
   Policy for Middle East Dependency   211
The Devastation of the Global Community by the US Global
   Empire: The Birth and Death of the Alliance for Progress and
   the Ascendancy of the IMF, World Bank, WTO,
   and the Western Banking/Financial Establishment   213
John Kennedy's "Alliance for Progress"   213
The Final Frontier of the US Global Empire   220

The Empire Strikes Back   221
Surrendering the "Commanding Heights" to the Market   225
The Accommodation and Abandonment of the Citizenry   225
Building a Post-Imperial America: Moving Toward
   an Inclusive Domestic and Foreign Policy   227
Finding a New Role in the World: The
   Nature and Purpose of a Post-Imperial America 230
National and Global Fascism in the Service of Empire   233
A "Global New Deal" for a Rising Global Community   235
Reflections on the Failures of the US Global Empire   238
Inclusionary Governance versus pro-Corporate Governance   239
Modern Extremism: Market Theology and the Rise of
   Theocratic States   242
Resurgent Militarism and the US Global Empire   244
The Downing Street Memo: Evidence of
George W. Bush's Search for a Pretext to go to War   247
In the Shadow of the Vietnam War   250
The Template of Conspiracy and Cover-up: The 9/11
Commission and Warren Commission as Mirror Images   253

6   CLAIMING "A RIGHT OF PEACE"   260
The Deterrence of Development Options for the Global
Community by the US Global Empire   261
A Global Community Requires Global Governance   264
The Predictable Effects of Socioeconomic Exclusion   266
The Legal Foundations for Claiming a "Right of Peace"   268
Claiming a "Right of Peace" Requires Inclusionary Governance   269
Centralizing the Claims of the Poor and Excluded in
   Global Development   270
Development Is Not Enough: Creating South-South
   Linkages to Remove Vulnerability and Exclusion 274
The Principles of Inclusionary Governance   276
Radicalizing Democracy: The Task of Bridging
   the Gap between Ideals and Demands   279
A Practical Strategy for Realizing Equality
   and Consolidating Democracy   280
Globalization, Poverty, and Inequality are Relational   283
The Washington/Wall Street Alliance: Leading the Way
   to Global Poverty   287
From Redesign to Replacement of the Neoliberal Framework   293
The Capacity of Social Movements to Confront
   the US Global Empire   297
Toward A Convergence of Global Struggles:
   The Basis for a North/South Alliance
   Against Neoliberalism   299

The Argument for Relief, Reparations, and the
    Forgiveness of Debt   302
Building a Counter-Hegemonic Alliance Across
    the Global Community   305
The Elements of a National/International
    Counter-Hegemonic Alliance   311
The Transformation of Latin America into a New Regional Power   315
Overcoming the Past   323
Placing the Empire on Trial: Establishing a
    Tribunal on the Crimes of the US Global Empire   325
The Future of Global Governance   328
"We the People"—The Voice of World Tribunals
    and Truth Commissions   329
The Foolishness of Empire and the Imperial Project   331
The Evolving Norms of a Rising Global Community   335

7   CONCLUSION   339
The Tribulations of Globalization and the Crimes of Empire   340
The United Nations' Millennium Development Goals: An
    Alternative Path for Globalization   342
"We the People": The Rise and Emerging Power of Global
    Civil Society   344

Notes   346

Index   417

About the Author   424

Acknowledgments

In the course of writing this book I have been able to reach back 30 years for the benefit of educational experiences and the contributions of professional friends and acquaintances. In that regard, I am grateful to all of the professors and colleagues that I have served with in the cause of progressive politics and peace. As a student, I benefited greatly from the liberal arts education I received at San Diego State University. In the early 1970s, I was engaged in both study and the anti-war movement with respect to Vietnam. My course of studies at the Lutheran School of Theology at Chicago allowed me to write my thesis on liberation theology in Latin America, as well as obtain a Master of Theological Studies degree. While attending the University of San Diego School of Law, I found my understanding of human and civil rights expanding under the guidance of Professors Sheldon Krantz in the area of prisoners' rights, Willard Wirtz in the area of labor law, and Roy Brooks in the areas of civil rights and employment discrimination.

In my professional life, I taught at a variety of community colleges and then went on to work for three NGOs. The Council on Hemispheric Affairs (COHA) is where I began as a research associate and now serve as a senior research associate. Its director, Larry Birns, has worked indefatigably across the decades in the task of monitoring human rights abuses and trends in Latin America. Headquartered in Washington, DC, the work of COHA serves as a constant reminder and resource to those who govern that US policies in Latin America, as well as those of the IMF and World Bank, have done more harm than good. I am grateful to Larry and to COHA for providing me with a forum during President Reagan's rampage of Central America in the early 1980s, as El Salvador was wracked by civil wars and CIA-trained death-squads while, at the same time, Nicaragua was subjected to US-sponsored terrorism at the hands of the CIA-supported Contras.

I also served for four years as the National Chancellor of the United States for the International Association of Educators for World Peace (IAEWP). I am grateful to its president, Dr. Charles Merceica, for the opportunity to build up the United States branch of an organization that is active in over 100 nations around the globe—dedicated to the tasks of advancing the cause of peace education, nuclear disarmament, protection of the environment, and the advancement of human rights.

During my term of office, I had the privilege of working in conjunction with the World Conference of Mayors for Peace on nuclear disarmament. I am grateful to the Mayor of Hiroshima, Mr. Tadatoshi Akiba, who serves as President of the World Conference of Mayors for Peace. I share their disappointment and contempt for the Bush-2 regime as it has actively worked to undermine the Nuclear Non-Proliferation Treaty (NPT). I share the same contempt for the Bush-2 regime's scuttling the 1972 ABM Treaty and the 1967 Outer Space Treaty in order to filter tens of billions of dollars into the coffers of its corporate supporters working on National Missile Defense (NMD) (Raytheon, TRW, Lockheed-Martin, and General Dynamics).

My work on the issue of nuclear disarmament has been enhanced by my professional association with Mr. John Burroughs, director of the Lawyers' Committee on Nuclear Policy. Under his guidance, I am working with the Association of World Citizens and the International Association of Educators for World Peace to distribute recently released copies of the Weapons of Mass Destruction Commission entitled, *Weapons of Terror: Freeing the World of Nuclear, Biological and Chemical Arms.*

I am grateful to Professor Bill Fitrakis who published my entire indictment of NMD in an edited collection on the subject—*The Fitrakis Files: Star Wars, Weather Mods & Full Spectrum Dominance.* I am also grateful to Mel Hurtig for generously quoting from my indictment in his book, *Rushing to Armageddon.* Finally, I am grateful to Marcus Raskin of the Institute for Policy Studies. Dr. Raskin published my essay entitled, "The Nuclear Crucible: The Moral and International Law Implications of Weapons of Mass Destruction" in his book, *In Democracy's Shadow: The Secret World of National Security.*

Last, but not least, I am grateful to the Association of World Citizens (AWC) and its president, Doug Mattern. The AWC is active in over 60 countries and involved with dozens of Nobel Prize Laureates in seeking nuclear disarmament and abolition. Working with the AWC has afforded me the opportunity to attend a week-long peace conference in Taiwan, the UN World Summit on Sustainable Development in South Africa, and a conference on global civil society in Geneva. Now, in my capacity as vice president for the AWC, I can return to writing and research on a more full-time basis. Due to this new role, I was able to complete my most current book, *Exodus From Empire.*

My professional life has been enriched by my association with Professor Richard Falk, Professor Bill Wickersham, and Professor Brian Foley. Their work and insights have contributed mightily to this book. I am especially grateful to Professor Falk for the many insights and suggestions that I received from him in the course of writing my first book—*Achieving Inclusionary Governance*—and the Foreword he wrote which graces its introduction.

I also want to take this opportunity to thank my publisher, Pluto Press, and its editor in chief—Mr. Roger van Zwanenberg. His appreciation of my book has allowed it to see the light of day. I also want to thank my friends who have done so much to enhance my life and encourage me over the course of this most recent effort. They are: Matthew Dawson, Curt Hatch, Jared Nelson, William Sims, and Rosemary Ferguson. For all of them, I want to express my deepest appreciation and gratitude.

Terrence E. Paupp
July 20, 2006.

Preface to *Exodus from Empire*

Within the United States all too few realized that the nation had transitioned from being a functional democracy into an empire. However, throughout the Global South (Africa, Asia, Latin America, and the Middle East) America's transition into an imperial force was abundantly clear. The US Empire's influence was experienced in the forms of direct military intervention, financial dominance, through economic hegemony, or a combination of all three. The economic model of neoliberalism has bankrupted many economies in the Global South or left them mired in a status of permanent debt repayment to the IMF and World Bank. In order to overcome this cruel oppression and exploitation, many nations throughout the Global South have sought to leave this system behind them and embark upon a path of genuine national and regional development. This phenomenon is what is intended to be conveyed by the title of the book, *Exodus From Empire*.

The Title: The Biblical account of the exodus from Egypt remains a powerful image for the oppressed leaving the bondage of an imperial system. The idea of embarking upon an "exodus from empire" conveys a sense of directionality about history as it evolves. The status quo can be overcome and the imperial bondage can be broken. In order to convey this notion, the book outlines the means and methods through which the US Empire has exercised its power in placing itself on a course toward world domination. Under the Bush-2 regime, the US Empire has used the doctrine of preemptive war to illegally invade and occupy Iraq. Yet, this move has only served to expose its failure and powerlessness to project and impose its imperial vision abroad. In the alternative, there has emerged a rising global chorus of opposition that has come from European allies, disaffected Arab and Islamic states, alienated social movements throughout Latin America, the bankrupted states of Africa, as well as from Russia and China. Hence, the subtitle of the book employs the words "failure" and "rise" to present the reader with a sharp contrast between the failure of the US Empire and the force of a rising Global Community in opposition to the US imperial drive for global hegemony.

The Terminology: As the US Empire spirals into greater financial crisis through rising deficits, the costs of maintaining bases and imperial garrisons, investments in the military-industrial complex, its own citizens have become the victims of a growing fascist state. The Patriot Act has been used to shred constitutionally guaranteed civil liberties. The National Security Agency has been allowed to collect billions of pieces of data on American citizens in order to monitor dissent. President Bush has claimed that the executive branch is all-powerful under the theory of the "unitary executive" and that both congress and the courts cannot curtail or restrain its actions or the sweep of its mandates. As a result, the American system of checks and balances has collapsed under the weight of empire. Abroad, torture is routinely employed in clear violation of US law and the Geneva Convention. Military tribunals have suspended the reach of civilian courts and constitutional protections in the course of conducting a "war on terror." In combination, all of these actions are expressions of the crumbling of the US Empire (*failure*).

In opposition to the US Empire, the peoples of the Global South, as well as Europe, China, and Russia are moving toward more inclusive forms of governance and resistance that place "Global Community" on the ascendancy (*rise*). In the past, the term "Global Civil Society" has been used to depict the idea of a cross-national world citizenship. By definition, *civil society* is representative of all aspects of a society that are nongovernmental. In contrast, the term *Global Community* incorporates the resistance of social movements throughout civil society *with* a change of their governments into what I have called the "Inclusionary State" and "inclusive forms of governance." Hence, the term *Global Community* serves to identify the growing trend toward putting new governments in place that are more inclusive in their decision-making processes and policies, reject the neoliberal economic model, and are opposed to the US Empire's attempt at hegemonic domination.

History is in the midst of changing. The change is predicated on the notion that the citizens of the Global South are part of a Global Community who can be viewed as a cohesive community of oppressed and exploited peoples who are seeking an "exodus from empire." As I use the term, it allows me to write of the peoples and governments of Asia, Africa, Latin America, and the Middle East, as well as Russia and China, coming together in a national, regional, and international *counter-hegemonic alliance* against the US Empire. We already see this process evolving in the 2006 political and economic alliance struck between President Morales of Bolivia, President Chavez of Venezuela, and President Castro of Cuba. It is also evident in the 2001-mutual security pact between Russia and China. Further, it can be seen in China's Africa-strategy insofar as Beijing has enjoyed considerable success in Africa, building close ties with countries from Sudan to South Africa, becoming a vital aid donor, and developing military relationships with many of the continent's powers. In short, the rise of Global Community is taking place in response to the aspirations of peoples for genuine national and international development.

The Thesis: If genuine national and international development is to be achieved, it can only be realized through a process of embarking upon an exodus from empire. International law's notion of the "equality of states" has been made into a mockery by the Bush-2 regime's assertion of absolute and unilateral power in international affairs. In the world of the Bush-2 regime, some states are "more equal than others." Such a view is characteristic of the imperial mind-set. It is a view that makes the world into a conflict-ridden war zone with no end in sight. For example, the Bush-2 regime has announced that the "war on terror" will go on for decades. This assertion is based on the fundamental feature of the power of global finance under US hegemony—its militarization. This reality is discovered in both the aggressive expansion of US military bases around the world, as well as by the growing presence of transnational corporations within the military-industrial complex.

On the economic side of the equation, the process of militarization is linked to globalization. In this world, the name of globalization is imperialism and imperialism is more openly enforced by war. Finance is at war against whoever tries to carry out or affirm autonomous development. The capitalist class can no longer retain its power except by war. Yet, the Global Community has increasingly rejected this historical trajectory as predetermined or inevitable.

Social movements have demanded more democratic constraints on their national governments. In turn, electoral outcomes around the globe have led to more progressive leaders and policies being placed into power that are at odds with the dictates of the US Empire. The regional alliances that have been developing in Latin America give concrete testimony to the fact that billions of people have decided not to allow the continuation of capitalism's economic and military dictatorship over their lives continue any longer. At the regional level, not merely economic alliances are being constructed, but clearly political ones as well—that have as their goal the end of dominance by the US Empire.

Not only have more democratically elected governments been installed, but accountability to the people now encompasses meeting the needs of the poor, protecting the rights of workers and labor, and expanding human rights claims by centralizing them in the national agenda. Similarly minded states are working with one another across the international spectrum. In short, an ever-expanding national-regional-international ·counter-hegemonic alliance to the US Empire is making possible an exodus from empire and the rise of Global Community.

List of Abbreviations

ABM   Anti-Ballistic Missile Treaty
ACLU   American Civil Liberties Union
AFTA   American Free Trade Agreement
ANC   African National Congress
AU   African Union
BWC   Biological Weapons Convention
CAFTA   Central American Free Trade Agreement
CFR   Council on Foreign Relations
CIA   Central Intelligence Agency
CISDL   Center for International Sustainable Development
CPA   Coalition Provisional Authority
CPD   Committee on the Present Danger
CTBT   Comprehensive Test Ban Treaty
DLC   Democratic Leadership Council
ECHR   European Convention on Human Rights
ELN   National Liberation Army
ES   Exclusionary State
FARC   Revolutionary Armed Forces of Columbia
FBI   Federal Bureau of Investigation
FISA   Foreign Intelligence Surveillance Act
FTAA   Free Trade Area of the Americas
GAO   Government Accounting Office
GATT   General Agreement on Trade and Tariffs
GDP   Gross Domestic Product
GNU   Government of National Unity
GRIT   Graduated Reciprocation in Tension Reduction
GTCE   Global Truth Commission on Empire
ICC   International Criminal Court
ICJ   International Court of Justice
ILO   International Labor Organization
IMF   International Monetary Fund
IR   International Relations
IRS   Internal Revenue Service
IS   Inclusionary State
ISI   Inter Services Intelligence
MDG   Millennium Development Goals
NAFTA   North American Free Trade Agreement
NAM   Non-Aligned Nations Movement
NATO   North Atlantic Treaty Organization

NEPDG	National Energy Policy Development Groups
NFZ	No-Fly Zone
NGO	Non-Governmental Organizations
NIEO	New International Economic Order
NLRB	National Labor Relations Board
NMD	National Missile Defense
NPT	Nuclear Non-Proliferation Treaty
NSA	National Security Agency
NSAM	National Security Action Memoranda
NSS	National Security State
OAU	Organization of African Unity
OECD	Organization for Economic Cooperation and Development
OSS	Office of Strategic Services
PNAC	Project for the New American Century
RMA	Revolution in Military Affairs
SAP	Structural Adjustments Program
SDI	Strategic Defense Initiative
SIDA	Swedish International Development Cooperation Agency
TINA	There Is No Alternative
TMD	Theater Missile Defense
TNC	Transnational Corporations
TRC	Truth and Reconciliation Commission
UDHR	Universal Declaration of Human Rights
UNDP	United Nations Development Program
UNRISD	United Nations Research Institute for Social Development
USSR	Union of Soviet Socialist Republics
WMD	Weapons of Mass Destruction
WOMP	World Order Models Project
WTC	World Trade Center
WTI	World Tribunal on Iraq
WTO	World Trade Organization

Introduction

Exodus from the Bondage of Empire

The path out from the bondage of empire must be rediscovered. If we fail to embark upon an exodus from empire we shall surely invite the fate against which Albert Camus warned of when he described those who supported the death penalty as both *victims and executioners*. The pursuit of empire becomes a version of the death penalty insofar as its pursuit often ends in both the death of imperial delusions and the death of thousands of victims caught in the vice grip of the imperial project. Empires have been notorious for their ruthless subjugation of peoples. After all, the imperial mentality is at odds with the recognition of human rights. Because the task of empire building is narrowly focused on the domination of people and their resources, the historical impact of empires on those peoples who are the objects of the quest for domination is one that is filled with tragedy.

The British experience in Kenya provides one such example. British settlers began displacing native Kenyans as early as 1900. The British appropriated the most fertile Kenyan land at the beginning of the twentieth century, precipitating an exodus of Kenyans to urban areas where poverty and discontent festered—especially among the Kikuyu people. In the economic depression that followed World War II, the ardent nationalism of the Kikuyu-based Mau Mau attracted new recruits at a pace that few could have imagined. A brutal war resulted between the insurrectionist Mau Mau and the colonial government. During that time, and in later historical accounts, there was a genuine dishonesty in failing to distinguish between terrorists and political insurgents. In the course of suppressing the Mau Mau revolt, Kenya's British rulers were responsible for thousands of unjustifiable killings, for gross abuses of both their own law and the laws of war, and for what are possibly the most brutal episodes of legal and physical oppression in twentieth century imperial history. The British, with the knowledge of both Winston Churchill and Harold Macmillan, committed untold atrocities against the Kenyan people, putting over 700,000 in prison camps and sending hundreds to the gallows without proper trial.[1]

The truth is that the Kikuyu rebels killed only 32 white colonists and that the real aggressors in this "dirty war" were the high-ranking members of the British government. From 1952 to 1960, the British detained and brutalized hundreds of thousands of Kikuyu—the colony's largest ethnic group—who had demanded their independence. In the eyes of the British colonizers, the men and women who fought in the insurgency were not freedom fighters but rather savages of the lowest order. The British felt justified, in the name of civilization, in crushing all those who challenged colonial rule, even if it meant violating their basic human rights. Later, in an effort to cover up this stain on its past, the British government ordered all documentation relating to detention and torture during its last days in Kenya destroyed. The destruction of these records should come as no surprise given the nature and extent of the British occupation. The British detained nearly the entire Kenyan population—some one and a half million people—for more than eight years. Inside the detention camps and barbed-wire villages, the Kikuyu lived in a world of hunger, fear, and death. Their only hope for survival was a full denunciation of their anti-British beliefs.[2]

In this regard, Britain's gulags in Kenya could be compared with the twenty-first century American occupation of Iraq and the nature of the US Global Empire's "war on terror." From its military base in Guantanamo, Cuba to "black sites" throughout Eastern Europe in old communist gulags, torture has been a tool of war for the United States. America's Central Intelligence Agency (CIA) and military have employed torture as a tool in their "war on terror." With the approval of President George W. Bush, Secretary of Defense Donald Rumsfeld, and Attorney General Alberto Gonzales, places of torture such as Abu Ghraib Prison have now entered into the historical lexicon of Bush's "war on terror." In reality, the US Global Empire's "war on terror" can be more appropriately understood as a *war of terror*. The policies of the US Global Empire, under the command of the leadership of the Bush-2 regime, are dramatically transforming both America, as a nation, and the nature of its Global Empire in both theory and practice. By removing all previous conventions and norms guiding State behavior, by its intentional abandonment of virtually all legal constraints on the use of power, by transforming the mission and purpose of American power in the world, under the leadership of the Bush-2 regime the United States has become the embodiment of what is implied by the term *rogue nation*.[3] By shredding the prohibitions against torture as contained in the Geneva Convention, of which the United States is a signatory, the neoconservative leadership of the Bush-2 regime effectively declared their own war of attrition upon international law, human rights treaties and covenants, the UN Charter, and the mandates of the US Constitution itself.[4]

THE FATE OF EMPIRES AND THE RISE OF COMMUNITY

All empires have two elements in common: first, their shared reliance upon oppression through militarism and, second, their shared capacity to inspire widespread resistance among those whom they seek to conquer, control, and exploit. To rediscover the path out from this bondage is to rediscover the truth that lies behind the first recorded exodus from empire—the departure of Hebrew slaves from servitude in Egypt's Empire. Its theme of liberation from oppression and imperial power has continued to be relevant through the centuries.

The exodus from Egypt was an historical event. It also remains paradigmatic for later generations. Infused within it are lessons that expose religious, political, economic, and social truths about the repressive nature of imperial power. In the twentieth century, Latin American liberation theologians often used the story of the *exodus event* as a powerful paradigmatic tool to preach and teach about a Judeo-Christian perspective on struggle in the world that would be shaped not only by the force of divine intervention but also by the free and conscious participation of human beings. In order to more accurately frame the sociological aspects of their political oppression, liberation theology employed a Marxist critique. When combined with a Marxist critique of their repressive and exclusionary societies, the liberation theologians of Latin America found that the exodus event gained a contemporary currency and vitality due to similar historical experiences in dealing with oppression.[5]

This viewpoint constitutes a method of understanding history. As a method, it has allowed many theologians on different continents and in different periods of time to more effectively comprehend the nature of political oppression and the moral duty to oppose it. For example, Howard Thurman (1900–1981) was one of the most respected and prolific religious figures of the twentieth century. As an African-American, the deep spirituality of the African-American community resonated within his psyche. After meeting Gandhi, he returned to the United States with a deep appreciation of the lessons of nonviolence. He also understood that self-actualized people are socially and psychologically whole. They cannot be whole if the socioeconomic and political structure under which they live is oppressive. That message resonated in the psyche of Thurman's most famous student, Martin Luther King, Jr. In their critique of racial, political, and economic oppression, both Thurman and King sought to use the strategy of nonviolence as a means to induce people of conscience to realize that noncooperation with an evil system is a moral imperative.[6]

Based on this perspective, King was able to develop a view of civil disobedience that made a distinction between just and unjust laws—*Any law that degrades the human personality is unjust*. Segregation and the Jim Crow laws that upheld this system of racial apartheid were unjust because it is a system that not only degrades the victims, but the perpetrators as well. To be truly liberated within American society requires that there be an interpersonal venture of cooperation and responsibility. Thus, while integration and liberation are analytically distinct, in practical terms they are inseparable.[7] With this perspective, both King and Thurman taught that it was necessary for America to embrace the *ideal community*—the *beloved community*.

Common themes in Thurman's and King's treatment of the actualization of community include: evil and sin as barriers to community, community as the norm and goal of the moral life, love as the means of actualization for community, and the nature and role of the moral agent in the creation of community.[8] Given these requirements for the realization of both national and Global Community, it is not difficult to see why King opposed the Vietnam War. The US Global Empire's war against the people of Vietnam was destroying the hope of building a just society in America just as it was destroying the underlying requirements for realizing a just Global Community. The tools of empire—war and violence—are thoroughly incapable of building just communities or building the necessary bonds of love between people to create community. Therefore, King made it clear that while the bombs that America dropped were dropped in Vietnam, they exploded in the cities of America. America's wealth and treasure was being diverted from the needs of the poor, the cities, and the task of building a just community for people of all races within the United States itself. The cost of empire exacted a heavy price upon both combatants and noncombatants. The cost of empire exacted not only a financial expenditure, but also an expenditure of moral and political capital. In the mid- to late 1960s it was becoming clear to many that the ever-increasing death toll of innocent Vietnamese civilians was a war crime in violation of the Nuremberg Charter. From King's perspective, the entire moral order—at the national and global levels—was under attack by the US Global Empire.

In 1965, under President Lyndon Johnson, the United States initiated a war of aggression against the people of Vietnam in the name of democracy. In 2003, the Bush-2 regime would launch another war of aggression in the name of democracy—this time against the people of Iraq. In so doing, the legal and moral dilemmas of empire are once again exposed. Some critics of the US Global Empire began to refer to its preoccupation with military force as the *Superpower Syndrome*. The term was meant to address the fact that from the Vietnam War era through the 2003 invasion of Iraq, the leadership of the US Global Empire never questioned their supposed right to exercise indiscriminate power in the service of maintaining and extending their empire. Rather, the architects of empire within the Bush-2 regime embarked upon a course to actualize their vision for *another American Century*.

The neoconservatives had already drafted their version for this world. Their outline for this undertaking is laid out in a document entitled, *Project for the Next American Century* (PNAC). To ensure American hegemony over the world for the next 100 years, the authors concluded that it would have to be a century under the military domination of the US Global Empire. And, once again, the contagion of war, like a disease, has been framed in global terms—a *global war on terrorism*. In the case of the Vietnam War, the leaders of the US Global Empire claimed that they were engaged in a global struggle against the forces of *godless Communism*. In the case of the Iraq War, the leaders of the US Global Empire claim that they are engaged in a global struggle against both a *godless version of Islam* and Islamic terrorists. Instead of embracing the goal of working toward *a postimperial America* (my term), this neoconservative clique came to power in order to dominate the executive and legislative branches of the US government. Bush's inner-circle viewed the world from the perspective that the twenty-first century would involve an inevitable *clash of civilizations*.

Yet, rather than defining the post 9/11 world as an era for the *clash of civilizations*, I have argued throughout this book that the twenty-first century is an era for the *convergence of civilizations* (see: Chapter 4, *Clash or Convergence?*). By the use of the word *convergence* I do not mean to imply that the unique aspects of the world's cultures or religions will collapse into one homogenized brand. Rather, by the use of the word *convergence* I mean to communicate the idea that an inherent commonality, contained in the world's greatest faiths and identities, will finally emerge. Despite their distinctiveness, these faiths and identities still have the capacity to point toward a common ground for discourse, reflective of a growing global consciousness of humanity's shared fate and shared concerns. It is this realization that gives rise to the phenomenon of convergence—of community in the midst of diversity.

The good news is that nations, faiths, and cultures do not have to evaporate in order for a global discourse to arise that embodies a spirit of acceptance, inclusion, and a more complete recognition of the worth and needs of *the other*. Common needs and challenges already provide the objective circumstances for this convergence to take place. For example, the challenge of global warming and climate change, the AIDS pandemic, the continuing threat of nuclear war, the dangers of terrorism (state-sponsored and group-sanctioned), higher degrees of inequality and poverty, all constitute a common environment for the convergence of peoples and nations to forge a sustainable Global Community.[9] In fact, the rise of Global Community is predicated upon such a convergence occurring. I would argue that this convergence has already been initiated as indigenous peoples have been responding the exclusionary nature of globalization and the clash of property rights versus human rights. Recognizing that the neoliberal order is unsustainable, indigenous peoples are in the process of working with other progressive social movements toward the transformation of the imperial global order.

Alternatives to empire, the International Monetary Fund (IMF) and World Bank are yet to be fully determined. Still, it is becoming increasingly evident that genuine alternatives will have to encompass the task of forging regionalized economic and political structures such as the European Union. In fact, progressive and indigenous social movements have already been joined in common cause by 15 European heads of state that condemned the US invasion of Iraq as illegal and asserted the primacy of the United Nations (UN) in the international order.[10] Throughout the 1990s and right up to the eve of the illegal invasion of Iraq by the United States in 2003, the UN has taken on the role of conflict prevention. Indeed, conflict prevention is a central goal of the UN system.[11] It is also a central prerequisite for building a sustainable Global Community.

The continually evolving bonds of Global Community may also be seen in the advances of customary international law norms in symmetry with the teachings and insights of the world's great religions. The convergence of an emerging international consensus around inclusive and humane world order values points toward a global desire to constrain and restrain the use of force.[12] The evolving bonds of Global Community may also be seen in new theoretical and practical approaches to development. Increasingly, human rights-based approaches to development are reinventing the entire concept of the role of human rights in the discourse on development. With a global recognition that the denial of human rights is invariably linked to impoverishment, vulnerability and conflict, UN agencies (UNDP, UNICEF), the Swedish International Development Cooperation Agency (SIDA), and international development agencies (Care, Oxfam), along with local grassroots non-governmental organizations (NGOs) and social movements, are transforming development practices. A new emphasis upon human rights is now linked to peace-building efforts in Northern Ireland. The practical solutions of rights-based approaches to legal and justice reform are responsible for advancing the reforms that benefit poor people. The human right to food and sustainable nutrition is contributing to strategies for combating infant malnutrition.[13] In short, the power of nonviolence, the growth of progressive social movements, and the unsustainable nature of the US Global Empire are all factors that point toward the rise of Global Community.

The idea that there are currently evolving bonds of Global Community is no longer a theoretical abstraction. It is an historical phenomenon. We may begin to trace these evolving bonds by appreciating the central role played by NGOs in the emergence of development of a comprehensive world polity. In this respect, a new *world polity perspective* may be contrasted to other approaches for understanding globalization, including world-system theory and interstate competition theory. What a *world polity perspective* provides is an assessment of transnational organizing. No longer are politicians, State bureaucrats, bankers and lenders, and multinational corporations the only actors on the global stage. So, in this respect, the work of NGOs in transnational organizing can be understood as part of an historical process for the purpose of creating global rules and norms. These norms and rules will change over time, but the important fact that remains is that transnational organizing will continue to have identifiable effects on social organization at the national and local levels. Some of the component elements of transnational organizing include environmental groups, women's rights organization, the Esperanto Movement, and the International Red Cross. Other emerging components of transnational organizing are found in technical and economic bodies, including development organizations, population policy groups, and international professional science associations.[14] Together, they form part of an incipient Global Community. The rising power of this Global Community may be at least in part attributable to the role that these NGOs play in helping to develop a world polity perspective.

THE COLLAPSE OF AMERICAN DEMOCRACY
UNDER THE MANTLE OF EMPIRE

At the dawn of the twenty-first century, America's experiment with democracy and constitutional government has largely collapsed under the mantle of empire. With the inauguration of the Bush-2 regime, the quality and degree of American democracy is not merely obscured, but purposefully repressed. The Patriot Act, illegal presidential wiretapping without benefit of court-ordered warrants, large scale domestic spying by the FBI and CIA, and a right wing ideological drift throughout the government and nation as a whole, has left the citizens of America as citizens of a democracy in name alone.

Some commentators have diagnosed a national malady that they have termed *attention deficit democracy*.[15] It has become an America where there is a rising level of ignorance among the electorate. Fear is produced by a constant mantra by members of the Bush-2 regime that America faces an imminent terrorist attack. Under Bush, America has become the breeding ground for a kind of *messianic democracy* that engages in deceit and the manipulation of foreign governments in the name of spreading democracy. It is rather ironic that after defeating totalitarian and fascist governments in the 1940s, the United States would begin to follow in the footsteps of those it had defeated and judged as war criminals at the Nuremberg and Tokyo Trials. Perhaps it is the price that must be paid when a democratic nation based on constitutional law and a system of checks and balances discards those benchmarks of democratic practice in order to become a National Security State and a Global Empire. It was a process that began as soon as World War II ended. Yet, it would not be until the Bush 2 regime that the United States would be fully transformed into a militarized Global Empire.

The end of World War II left the United States and the Union of Soviet Socialist Republics (USSR) as two superpower rivals struggling for hegemony. During the course of the Cold War, the nations of the global South were used as proxies and as battlegrounds for this rivalry to be played out.[16] The Korean War, Vietnam War, struggles for mastery over the resources of Africa, struggles for the markets of Latin America and Asia characterized the extent of this Cold War struggle. Terms such as *low-intensity conflict* were employed to describe wars throughout the Third World that were nonnuclear confrontations between the United States and USSR during the 50-year Cold War struggle. By the time the Cold War ended in 1989, the United States was the only Superpower left standing. In a spirit of triumphalism a new age dawned for the United States—its Global Empire would enter a new phase.

Capitalism had *defeated* socialism by outspending it on weapons of war in an unending nuclear arms race. Now, with the USSR out of the way, market capitalism was touted as the means to lift Russia, Eastern Europe, and the rest of the global South out of a financial *dark ages* and into a neoliberal dawn of wealth, development, and peace.[17] It was also a world in which the military bases and garrisons of the US Global Empire now spanned the globe, making it a global enforcer of American priorities. The newly empowered American Establishment sought to expand its global dominion beyond the constraints of a bipolar world and a policy of communist containment. The ideology of *America first* and an amorphous idea labeled globalization were embraced in order to sell a neoliberal economic model to the world. Empire and globalization would drive each other, influence each other, and feed off each other. The US Global Empire would use its financial clout to make the rules. The institutional task of making the "magic of the market" turn a profit for the corporations of the empire was augmented not only by the standard bearers in the Bretton Woods Institutions but also by the new rule makers for the global trading game in the World Trade Organization (WTO). If their rules were not followed, sanctions and penalties could be imposed, credit could be cut off, and in a worst case scenario the American military could be called into service in order to enforce the empire's commands. What this ultimately meant was that the Atlantic Alliance would no longer constrict the decision makers in Washington as they pursued their new version of America's foreign policy (see: Chapter 2, *The Occupations of Empire*).

The administration of President George W. Bush (hereinafter referred to as the *Bush-2 regime*) adopted a posture of conducting unilateral foreign policy abroad, while suppressing constitutional liberties at home. In the pursuit of the dream (delusion) of making the twenty-first century into *another American century*, the neoconservatives of the Bush-2 regime embarked upon dismantling international law in order to remove it as a restraining force upon their policies and conduct in the world. The 1972 Anti-Ballistic Missile Treaty was discarded by presidential fiat in early 2002 when Bush's executive branch decided that funding National Missile Defense (NMD) meant more to America's security—and corporate profits—than maintaining a viable nuclear nonproliferation regime. In much the same way, the Bush-2 regime withdrew its support from the Nuclear Non-Proliferation Treaty (NPT) in April 2004. Now, the administration and the Pentagon were free to talk about their new doctrine for planetary control by investing in new weapons systems for outer space, land, sea, and air—*full spectrum dominance*. This perspective has resulted in what some commentators have called *the Superpower Myth*—the idea that America could solve any foreign policy through military means.[18]

As inheritors of Britain's empire during the 1940s, one would have thought that American policymakers and leaders would have learned the lessons from the British experience. These lessons have clearly been forgotten, even though they remain relevant. In the early stages of World War II, the vast crescent of British-ruled territories stretching from India to Singapore appeared as a massive Allied asset. It served to provide great quantities of raw materials and helped present a seemingly impregnable global defense against the Axis. Yet, with a few weeks in 1941–1942, a Japanese invasion destroyed all of this, sweeping through south and Southeast Asia to the Indian frontier, and provoking the revolutionary struggles that would mark the beginning of the end of British domination in the East. It would result in the death of British rule in south and Southeast Asia.[19]

As the Bush-2 regime sought to extend its version of empire into the Middle East, it has had to confront the remnants of democratic dissent at home. Therefore, in order to stifle democratic dissent at home, the Bush-2 regime produced and, with a compliant Congress, imposed the so-called Patriot Act upon its own citizens in the aftermath of the events of 9/11. The Patriot Act was ostensibly put into place to combat the threat of domestic terrorism within the United States. However, its real effect amounted to nothing less than a direct assault upon Constitutional protections guaranteed to American citizens in the Bill of Rights. Further, the USA Patriot Act has had the effect of undermining the most basic principles of the Constitution with respect to the nation's war power by helping to invest the Executive branch with virtually absolute power. The shredding of America's system of checks and balances became one of the hallmarks of neoconservative governance in the Bush-2 regime. Further, by asserting the theory of the *unitary executive* (the theory that the Executive branch could declare and conduct a war on terrorism without regard to the system of checks and balances that mandates Congress and the Courts to be involved as coequal participants in such decisions), the Bush-2 regime actually advocates a centralized presidency. According to this view, power and accountability in government and in the Executive branch should be moved more toward the top, giving the president and his staff greater ability to make decisions themselves. Legal proponents of a strong unitary presidency usually do not outline a comprehensive policy defense of the legal position but rely more on doctrinal justifications and related policy arguments.[20]

The theory of the *unitary executive* fit easily into the power plays of the Bush-2 regime. Using doctrinal justifications and policy arguments instead of being constrained by a functioning democratic system of checks and balances, the Bush-2 regime has sought to hide executive abuses and unconstitutional actions under the rubric of an unending global war on terror. This approach has had the simultaneous advantage of ending democratic accountability within the homeland of the empire and eviscerating the role of international law in the empire's foreign policy and practices. Hence, torture is employed by executive fiat abroad in the Middle East and Europe, while illegal spying on American citizens, the jailing of enemy combatants without charges for years, and wiretaps without warrants characterize the Bush-2 regime's misuse of power at home.

In January 2005, relying on the theory of the *unitary executive*, President Bush declared that he had the constitutional right to order his administration to engage in illegal domestic surveillance and wiretapping under the rubric of *national security*. In the years after the events of 9/11 the National Security Agency (NSA), under Bush's orders, spied, wiretapped, and engaged in domestic surveillance to a degree unknown even in the Nixon years. Both Bush and his Department of

Justice not only admitted to carrying out these acts under color of law but also asserted that such a power was inherent in the Executive by virtue of the president's wartime authority as Commander-in-Chief.

In the foreign policy arena, the Bush-2 regime decided—even before 9/11—to invade the Middle East in order to secure its oil resources and to obtain a geopolitical advantage over potential rivals such as China and Russia (see: Chapter 5, *The Hidden Politics of Empire*). The Caspian Sea, the Persian Gulf, and oil rich states such as Iraq were areas seen as essential to making the twenty-first century into *another American Century*. This was the position of Zbigniew Brezinski, National Security Advisor to President Carter. In his 1997 book, *The Grand Chessboard: American Primacy and Its Geostrategic Imperatives*, Brezinski outlined a strategy that the Bush-2 regime and PNAC group endorsed as a blueprint for US foreign policy. A central premise in Brezinski's argument was to assert that while hegemony is as old as mankind, "America's current global supremacy is distinctive in the rapidity of its emergence, in its global scope, and in the manner of its exercise."[21]

When it comes to exerting US Empire's global supremacy, the general consensus among the elites of the US Global Empire seems to be that the American empire should do whatever it takes to "perpetuate America's own dominant position for at least a generation and preferably longer still."[22] In so doing, the fabric of international law was shredded by the Bush-2 regime at the same time that the constraints of constitutional government were removed by the aristocratic claims of a president who saw himself in the role of the *unitary executive*—as the titular head of the American National Security State. In this role, President Bush essentially embarked upon a role that he believed left him above the law and virtually unaccountable to congress, the courts, or the American people (see: Chapter 3, *When the Law of the Land Becomes Lawless*). The mantra of *national security* provided the same rationale for any action taken by the executive branch. In the task of extending the empire into *another American Century* the administration's ready reference to *national security* was touted out to provide a convenient justification for any executive action.

Having been spoiled by the luxuries of their consumer culture, most Americans were content to let the US Global Empire protect their way of life. For far too many Americans, it mattered little that the "American way of life" was largely made possible by their empire's continued exploitation, oppression, subjugation, and sacrifice of other peoples. The realities of hunger, poverty, and disease throughout the global South were all too easily blamed on the people and governments of the global South—without any regard given to the realities of their unequal power relationship with the US Global Empire. Very few Americans gave much thought to offering their blind adherence to an imperial system that countenanced even deeper economic and political divisions between peoples and cultures. After all, Americans lived in the *belly of the beast*. Why should they question the policies of their empire? The last thing that most Americans wanted was the burden of choice, the responsibility of having to choose between maintaining the status-quo through their tax dollars to the empire or, in the alternative, questioning and challenging the policies and practices that the US Global Empire was undertaking in their name.

SUBORDINATING THE GLOBAL SOUTH TO THE EMPIRE

At the dawn of the twenty-first century, structural hierarchies of exclusion and domination remain in place within the US Global Empire and throughout all too many of the nations of the global South.[23] The creation of such an international order was the result of the work of America's first generation of empire builders in the 1940s. The post-World War II period came to reflect the views of American elites and policymakers who were dogmatically committed to the idea that the resources of the global South ultimately belonged to the United States. After all, the United States was the *defender of the Free World*. The dominant status of the United States in world affairs was also seen by these elites as the necessary pre-condition to any kind of viable world order (see: Chapter 1, *From Precedence We Come*).

Yet, at the same time, the post-1945 world witnessed the Third World's revolution of *rising expectations*. Seeking freedom from colonialism would soon be understood as a natural consequence of the end of a world war that was fought to overcome totalitarianism, slavery by a foreign power, and imperial ambition. During the Cold War years, it would matter little to the peoples of the Third World whether the Soviets or the Americans wanted to impose their imperial ambitions on the nations of the global South. What mattered most to the peoples of the global South was the international recognition of their sovereignty, their desire for economic justice and development, an appreciation of their cultures and traditions, and their ability to peacefully coexist in a world that now lived under a nuclear sword of Damocles.[24] So, in the 1950s and again in the 1960s and 1970s, nationalist movements throughout the Third World actively sought to be non-aligned with either superpower.

As far as the people and leadership of the global South were concerned, the East-West conflict mattered, but so did overcoming the global disparities found in the North-South divide. Therefore, the Non-Aligned Nations Movement (NAM) and advocates for a New International Economic Order (NIEO) focused upon the Third World's exodus from the bondage of all empires and imperial quests. As early as the 1950s, the people of the global South wanted to have their rights to self-determination acknowledged by the United States and USSR.[25]

For the majority of citizens throughout the global South, the ideological system espoused by either of the Superpowers mattered very little. As it was expressed in various conferences among and between the leaders and representatives of Third World nations, the majority of nations and peoples throughout the global South were, without reservation, actively seeking to build a Global Community in which there would be a recognition of human rights attributed to entire groups of peoples rather than just to individuals. This catalog of rights included the rights to development, peace, a clean environment, and humanitarian assistance.[26] They wanted to bring an end to the dangers associated with an uncontrolled nuclear arms race. They sought an open discourse between the United States and the USSR that would be capable of sustaining the transition to a more peaceful global order. This more peaceful order would have to be premised upon the overcoming of gross inequalities, poverty, hunger, lack of educational opportunities, and the ever-present threat of war both within and between nations. In short, the primary goal for over two-thirds of humankind was to move the direction of international life away from a Cold War competition between two rival empires and toward the evolution of Global Community. Until that path became an objective possibility, the global consensus was that a path of nonalignment with *either* superpower was the most prudent choice for the peoples of the global South.

Unfortunately for the global South, the leadership of America's Global Empire in the 1950s and 1960s did not want nonalignment to become a part of the geopolitical equation. As Secretary of State John Foster Dulles saw it, the possibility of Third World states acting in unison would mean that the balance of power would drift toward the Soviets and leave the United States with diminished power. What was equally unfortunate was the US failure to give substance to the much-quoted but studiously ignored notion reflected in Article 28 of the Universal Declaration of Human Rights according to which "everyone is entitled to a social and international order in which the rights and freedoms set forth in this Declaration can be fully realized." The result of this failure is summed up in Philip Alston's observation: "The connotation of solidarity, of a duty to cooperate, and of the need for mechanisms to achieve an ongoing international redistribution of wealth linked to human rights obligations, have for too long been anathema to Western governments."[27]

For decades, many nations throughout the global South have fought wars of liberation from empire. As with America at its own founding, nations throughout the global South vehemently opposed the goals of empire builders. During the nineteenth century, Great Britain, France, and Germany had embarked upon colonial interventions into the global South in an attempt to control both the resources and peoples of Africa, Asia, the Middle East, and Latin America. On every continent where the empire builders appeared, liberation struggles emerged to confront them. However, in the aftermath of World War II, with the birth of the UN and the global reach of its Charter, it was clear that colonialism—as it was practiced—could not survive as a governing strategy for the empire builders. The UN's global structure of conflict prevention, the enforcement of human rights norms, and international law's continuing adherence to the norm of sovereignty, all combined to eliminate justifications for either colonialism or imperialism. Hence, the post-1945 period was to become the age of decolonization and anti-imperialism. The nations of the global South were supposed to be recognized under the banner of international law as having *sovereign equality* with the Great Powers.

Yet, on the road to the *New World Order*, the US Global Empire took on the imperial mantle from the British in 1945. Throughout the 1950s and 1960s, the United States presented itself as the defender of the *Free World*. The only problem was that the *Free World* was not really free—in the sense of civil and political liberties. Rather, the *Free World* contained US-sponsored dictatorships, as with Marcos in the Philippines, Samoza in Nicaragua, and the Shah of Iran. It was a world in which the door was held open for corporations and business interests that continually sought unbridled access to the nations of the global South in order to secure control over their natural resources, labor forces, and markets. In 2001, the Bush-2 regime began to use its *global war on terror* as an extension and new revised version of the *Free World* idea, insofar as the concept of an unending global war could easily mask the empire's abuses at home and abroad. The unhindered imperial project could then proceed without reference to law, human rights, the doctrine of sovereignty, or democratic constraints.

In the decades after the American exodus from Vietnam (1974), US-dominated institutions such as the IMF, World Bank, and WTO would attempt to manage the world economy, without having to call upon the military forces of the US Global Empire to enforce the imperial consensus. This strategy worked until the last half of the 1990s when the so-called *Washington Consensus*—the neoliberal economic model of the Reagan era—collapsed at the end of the Clinton presidency. When the Bush-2 regime took office in 2001, the process of globalization was incapable of maintaining or securing American global hegemony without the use of military force. Resource wars were already underway for the control of oil and pipelines throughout the Middle East. Both China and Russia were seen by elites in Washington as rivals for the world's dwindling energy resources.

The failure of the neoliberal economic model was evident throughout East Asia in the aftermath of the economic meltdown of 1999. The East Asian tigers became the victims of a domino effect linked to the forces of uncontrolled globalization and faulty neoliberal economic prescriptions. Additionally, Africa remained an economic basket case, with very few exceptions. Latin America, which had never really recovered from its decade of debt, was now locked into a downward cycle of increasing levels of poverty along with worsening socioeconomic inequalities. Despite Latin America's embrace of democratic governments, it was still relatively no better off. Angered and alienated citizens would continue to vote out previous governments, while social movements continued to demand concessions from the State and an end to neoliberal economic prescriptions which had failed them miserably.

At the dawn of the twenty-first century, Latin America was a continent still enslaved by IMF conditionality agreements that strangled economic growth and development. It was a problem that was further exacerbated by an uncritical reliance on the economic mantra of markets, privatization, and deregulation. By surrendering to the laws of the market without maintaining the ability of the State to intervene on behalf of the victims of the market, many Latin American nations witnessed a worsening of the degree of inequalities and poverty (see: Chapter 6, *Claiming A "Right of Peace": Moving Beyond the "Empire Syndrome"*)

No longer able to completely control the nations of the global South through its institutions of economic coercion (IMF, World Bank, US Transnational Corporations), the Bush-2 regime decided to rely predominantly upon its doctrines of resurgent militarism and preemption to reassert American hegemony. Armed with the doctrine of nationalism and resurgent militarism as its strategy of first choice, the Bush-2 regime embarked upon its version of how to capture the twenty-first century and make it into *another American Century*. The difference between the twentieth century period of American dominance and the projected twenty-first century period of American dominance was that the US Global Empire in the twenty-first century was willing to adopt a more fascist approach in attempting to maintain its hegemonic position (see: Chapter 2, *The Occupations of Empire*).

LIBERATING THE GLOBAL SOUTH FROM GLOBAL EMPIRE

For the advocates of human rights, for the sake of maintaining the integrity of the international law principle of the *sovereign equality* of nations, and for the goal of building a humane and inclusive global order, the only viable alternative to *another American Century* is the vision and promise of a rising Global Community. Throughout this book, I argue that the best strategy for realizing a rising Global Community would have to be one that was dedicated to abandoning neoliberal economic models, building strong South-South regional alliances, and incorporating the people power of social movements into a national/international counter-hegemonic alliance to the US Global Empire. Indeed, the power of a rising Global Community would be most dramatically and effectively manifested as the product of an emerging national/international counter-hegemonic alliance to the US Global Empire (see: Chapter 6, *Claiming A "Right of Peace"—Moving Beyond the "Empire Syndrome"*).

In what could easily be the most succinct preamble for any document announcing the nature of this counter-hegemonic alliance, Boaventura de Sousa Santos observes:

> Although neo-liberal globalization—the current version of global capitalism—is by far the dominant form of globalization, it is not the only one. Parallel to it and, to a great extent, as a reaction to it, another globalization is emerging. It consists of transnational networks and alliances among social movements, social struggles, and non-governmental organizations. From the four corners of the globe, all these initiatives have mobilized to fight against the social exclusion, destruction of the environment and biodiversity, unemployment, human rights violations, pandemics, and inter-ethnic hatreds, directly or indirectly caused by neo-liberal globalization.[28]

In short, there are two globalizations at work in our age. The first type of globalization is supportive of the US Global Empire and the imperial project. The second type of globalization is a reaction against the US Global Empire and supportive of a variety of constituencies and issues that make possible the realization of Global Community. To comprehend the difference between these two alternative paths of globalization is to begin to understand the core thesis of this book.

The main theme of my book—finding an *exodus from empire*—follows the general outline of analysis (as set forth above) by Santos. That is because our research and our perspective converge on how to define, conceptualize, and analyze the nature of the worldwide system of the US Global Empire. Additionally, we concur that another globalization is emerging—one that is accountable to human rights and human needs within a rising Global Community. Being able to grasp the role converging social movements in opposition to neoliberal capitalism makes it possible for us to recognize the reality that neoliberal globalization has come into open conflict with the agenda of emerging transnational networks and alliances. Throughout the global South, the poor, the unemployed, the disenfranchised and excluded are demanding that the *sovereign equality* of their nation within the Global Community be respected. It is no longer tolerable for the US Global Empire, the IMF and World Bank, or the WTO to dictate what their respective developmental paths will be in the absence of effective democratic representation.

This view embodies a recognition that is increasingly common among progressive thinkers around the globe. For example, Anne Orford has noted: "Economic globalization has made the fictitious nature of state sovereignty apparent to all but the most myopic observer of international relations and international law."[29] If state sovereignty is not an effective barrier to imperial intervention, then the entire world is simply left open to exploitation by the best-armed Superpower.

In Chapter 6, I detail how the financial axis of the empire, such as the IMF, World Bank, and WTO, operate in conjunction with the Washington/Wall-Street Alliance. I demonstrate how the purpose and conduct of these institutions is designed to facilitate the flow of wealth and resources out of the nations of the global South. As a consequence, the resulting collateral damage done by these institutions is to leave billions of people worse off than they were prior to the imposition of the neoliberal model and the destruction of their sovereignty.

The IMF and World Bank have had a significant impact on the policies of governments in those states seeking to make use of their resources in two ways. First, the IMF and World Bank influence government policy through the imposition of conditions on access to credits and loans.[30] Second, the IMF and World Bank do not comply with the obligation to ensure that the model of development adopted by states is one in which all human rights and freedoms can be fully realized.[31] Given this disempowerment of states, I outline a strategy for states, throughout the global South, to renew and remake their governments and societies in accordance with a model of governance that I have labeled the *Inclusionary State* (IS) (see: Chapter 6). The importance of the IS model is that the leadership of social movements, and all the major groups and classes within civil society, can finally be accorded a formal place at the table of decision making.[32]

My advocacy of an *inclusionary state* may be seen as a key component of an exit strategy from the US Global Empire and its institutions of exploitation. That is because the effect of World Bank and IMF policies is to strip the state of most of its functions, except for maintaining law and order while, at the same time, facilitating private investment. When a state becomes stripped of its power to engage in protecting the rights of its citizens, as well as the course and direction of its own economy, it then becomes transformed into what I have called the "*exclusionary state*" (ES).[33] It excludes the majority of classes and groups within the nation because the leadership of an ES state appears to address only the interests of international economic institutions and corporate investors. That is the bad news.

The good news is that as the effects of this kind of limited representation of interests becomes clear to labor unions, the unemployed, the victims of human rights abuses, and social movements in opposition to the neoliberal model, a transnational counter-hegemonic alliance against the US Global Empire is beginning to emerge. That is because the vulnerability, insecurity, and frustration of the people increases and with these symptoms of exploitation and a recognition of their ultimate cause. With rising levels of discontent comes a tide of global opposition in the form of violent protests, political destabilization, and the growth of populist nationalism. These are the societal consequences that emerge when ES in the global South appear to be accountable to only foreign investors, the IMF, and the World Bank.

Throughout this book, when I speak of an *exodus from empire*, I am also speaking of the need for the nations of the global South to embark upon an exodus from the influence, pressures, and coercion of both the IMF and the World Bank. Despite the fact that the *1997 World Development Report* spoke of the need to bring the state closer to the people, the reality was that there was no significant shift in the World Bank's commitment to policies of privatization and state restructuring based on a narrow model of economic development that continued to exclude the needs of the poor and human rights concerns. The situation is one that remains much the same as it was in the late 1990s when John Gray noted: "At the global level, as at that of the nation-state, the free market does not promote stability or democracy. Global democratic capitalism is as unrealizable a condition as worldwide communism."[34]

In this regard, some scholars have noted: "International institutions must make some changes in order to adapt to the human rights legal framework. But the institutions cannot change without a change in the international system itself, one of the main elements being the actual economic and financial system based on neoliberal rules."[35] So, despite the World Bank and IMF giving lip service to poverty reduction through new partnerships, we find: "The new poverty reduction partnerships are based on consensus and the idea of mutual interest among state and donor actors. The partnership idea is not far from new, nor is it politically neutral. Indeed … 'partnership' is commonly invoked when the more powerful party to an asymmetrical relationship feels threatened by impending hostilities and confrontation."[36] The impending hostilities and the dangers of widespread violent confrontations, feared by the IMF and World Bank actually emerge from a combination of factors. The two most evident factors are: (1) progressive social movements making new political advances within and between nations and, (2) the growing force of a national/international counter-hegemonic alliance in opposition to the US Global Empire.

Even in the face of these impending hostilities the IMF continues to deny that human rights protection is an area of activity with which it should legitimately concern itself. The IMF has remained adamant in asserting that the protection of human rights is outside of its scope and is a responsibility that remains the concern of individual governments. Yet, the very fact that it imposes conditionality requirements upon governments accepting its loans makes the IMF into a force that dictates the degree to which human rights will be protected and advanced or ignored. Even when the IMF considers the impact of its own policies, it still treats human rights as a matter that is outside of the Fund's mandate. It should be no wonder that there are impending hostilities against the IMF. It has been increasingly seen as just one more institutional bastion of Western power that continues to emasculate the right of the global South to embark upon a path of humane and inclusive development. It has effectively ignored the UN's Millennium Development Goals and protests against its conduct from the human rights community.

Despite the IMF and World Bank, and the militarism of the US Global Empire, the fact remains that the path toward the realization of Global Community, as well as humane and inclusive development, is more accessible than ever before in recorded human history. In large measure it is because the norms of a human rights culture have become universal. It is also because the failures and limitations of Global Empire are more apparent. Military force cannot generate global compliance to the demands of a Global Empire any more than a dictatorship can inspire the loyalty of those who are subjugated by it. Neither can an economic dictatorship, under the global guidance of the IMF and World Bank, result in a reduction of poverty and inequality or open the door for an *exodus from empire*. These insights have inspired people around the world to recognize that *Another World Is Possible*.

In January 2001, in Porto Alegre, Brazil, 20,000 activists, students, and film-makers assembled together in order to exchange ideas about confronting the US Global Empire. That was the birth of the now historic World Social Forum.[37] At the center of most of the discussions held at that time was the fact that the IMF and World Bank bear the greatest responsibility for the plunder of entire communities. That is also the reason why, throughout this book, I have gone to great lengths to make a connection between the Washington/Wall-Street Alliance of the US Global Empire and its primary financial institutions—the IMF and World Bank. In opposing the empire, an incipient national and international counter-hegemonic alliance must find alternatives to these forces. With the articulation of alternatives a global discourse can be accelerated that should lead to projects of emancipation and liberation—an *exodus from empire*.

At Porto Alegre, a general agreement was reached on the need for an alternative system of global governance. Some participants invoked the term *de-globalization* to describe this alternative. Walden Bello clarified the meaning of the term by noting that: "We are not talking about withdrawing from the international economy. We are speaking about reorienting our economies away from the emphasis on production for export and towards production for the local market."[38] At the top of his list, he suggested: "Drawing most of our financial resources for development from within rather than becoming dependent on foreign investment and foreign financial markets."[39] Following that fundamental principle, he added that it would be necessary to carry out long-postponed measures of income redistribution and land redistribution in order to create a vibrant internal market. Such a path would allow nations throughout the Global Community to de-emphasize growth and work instead toward maximizing equity in order to radically reduce environmental disequilibrium. Another benefit of taking this path would be strategic economic decisions would not be left to the market but make them subject to democratic choice. In furtherance of democratizing nations, the private sector and the state should be subjected to constant monitoring by civil society. Yet, for all this to take place and succeed, it will only be possible if it takes place within an alternative system of global governance. That alternative system is what I am calling Global Community.

In the four years since the first World Social Forum, the state of struggle against the US Global Empire has spanned the globe and encompassed the energies of millions of people. Social movements against neoliberal capitalist intrusion have sprung up throughout the Arab world, South Africa, East Africa, Australia, Central Asia, the Democratic Republic of the Congo, East and Southeast Asia, rural China, and throughout Latin America.[40] Social movements are a central part of a worldwide struggle, helping to accelerate the global process of creating an alternative system. When viewed in combination, these struggles are all part of a dynamic convergence between nations, cultures, and ideas (see: Chapter 4). The World Social Forum served as an important platform for opening the door to the creation of a counter-hegemonic globalization. Other examples of convergence may be cited in the form of a global anti-war movement, the trade union movement, and the struggles of over three billion peasants for a decent life.

A global mobilization against neoliberal hegemony has taken many forms, but it has a common objective—the defeat of Global Empire and the establishment of a viable Global Community.[41] The extent of this mobilization and the diversity of these struggles have just begun to be documented. Yet, it is undeniable that millions of people have become active in rejecting corporate globalization, the intrusions of Global Empire, and the IMF and World Bank. In all of these efforts, millions of people around the globe are developing alternatives to the current system.[42] They are actively engaged in a process that will lay the groundwork for an *exodus from empire*.

1
From Precedence We Come

The future is not a mere repetition of what has come before. We are haunted by our old concepts, ideologies, and our very nature. The influence of the past has not entirely dissipated from consciousness or memory. Perhaps that is one reason why postapartheid South Africa embarked upon a review of the atrocities of the old system through its Truth and Reconciliation Commission. In order to truly open the future for new possibilities, history must be dealt with, understood, and given meaning. In this important sense, the *past is prologue*.

Certainly, history seems to contain large segments of human experience that repeat the past. Everything from building global empires, to creating more peaceful communities, is expressed by and contained within the matrix of human imagination. The historical expression of these visions and aspirations is conditioned by the practical realities of time, place, and situation.

Throughout the history of civilizations the quest for either empire or community is a constant theme. Both empire and community represent a particular application of human power and purpose. Some scholars have attempted to categorize these two forms of governance into different kinds of experiments. The differentiations of these experiments have been expressed as tribal, imperial, and commercial.[1] Making such distinctions is vital to our understanding if we are to comprehend the implications of different kinds of social, economic, and political processes across time and civilizations.

The *tribal experiment* refers to domestic-scale culture (scale calls attention to growth thresholds, order of magnitude increases in the size of societies, and any new cultural features that are required to sustain larger systems). Tribal experiments are more inclusive. They do not operate as an *imperium* because no single person or dominant minority could direct it by gaining permanent control over the entire society.

The *imperial experiment* refers to societies that were much larger than tribal ones. In addition, strategic resources in the imperial world have historically been controlled by dominant political *imperia* (*imperia* is the plural of *imperium*, the Latin word for command over others, rule by an individual, or rule by an elite few). The danger of imperia is that when individuals are allowed to create increasingly expanding imperia, the fundamental human rights of others may be threatened. Hence, while an imperium can benefit society at large, its unlimited or unrestrained power is always potentially dangerous. Dangers arise when anti-democratic elites are interested primarily in their own self-aggrandizement of wealth, power, and control.

The *commercial experiment* refers to the phenomena of "globalization." Globalization embodies a practice of capitalism that separates the control of capital from producers and consumers. Under the auspices of the "Reagan Revolution" the nations of the poor South were increasingly relegated to the role of cheap producers of capital goods. Thanks to the Reagan roll back of the 1980s and the passage of North American Free Trade Agreement (NAFTA) in the 1990s, the consumers of the rich North became the beneficiaries of the new global stewards of sweatshop ownership and other labor-saving devices.

The commercialization of the world's networks of employment and investment has created a global market for transnational corporations. It concentrates power by co-opting the political processes of governments. The new global financial agenda seeks to produce and maintain "for profit" business enterprises regardless of the collateral damage done to the environment and workers of the exploited regions of investment and production. This phenomenon is the financial arm of America's "Global Empire." The operations of this empire exhibit high degrees of exclusion in its political and economic effects. The cost of "doing business" is at the expense of marginalized groups and nations that have been subordinated to the hierarchical structures of capitalism's Global Empire.

Despite historical differences between the aforementioned categories, as well as the attempt to neatly categorize the various experiments in global governance, there are strong linkages between the imperial and the commercial experiments. As Ellen Wood has commented, "older forms of imperialism depended directly on conquest and colonial rule. Capitalism has extended the reach of imperial domination far beyond the capacities of direct political rule or colonial occupation, simply by imposing and manipulating the operations of a capitalist market."[2] Some examples of the controlling reach of capital since 1945 are seen in the operations of the WTO, the World Bank, and the IMF. The controlling powers behind these organizations are Western governments and the corporations that they serve at the center of the capitalist world. Further, each of these institutions has been geared to drive the process of corporate globalization since the 1980s. In this regard, globalization drives empire just as the pursuit of empire sustains the process of globalization.

The majority of humankind remains excluded from the decision-making centers of the capitalist world system. The term "periphery" has been used to describe Latin America, Asia, Africa, and the Middle East in relation to the centers of global capitalism. The relationship between the northern and southern hemispheres has constituted the geographical dividing line between the rich nations of the North and the impoverished nations of the South.

The period of the 1970s was a short-lived period in which the Third World sought to assert itself against the nations of the North vis-à-vis the "Non-Aligned Nations Movement" (NAM). The period would be remembered as a brief interlude that promised a "North/South dialog." Despite the high hopes of those seeking progressive change in favor of the South there would be no reprieve. The nature of the dialog would be ultimately determined by the structure of America's "Global Empire" of immutable power relations. There would be no escape from the financial subordination of the South to the North that characterizes this system.

Given the power of capitalist classes to dominate and control landless workers, it would seem that a capitalist empire could simply rely on economic pressures to exploit subordinate societies. But this is not necessarily the case because "just as workers had to be made dependent on capital and kept that way, so subordinate economies must be made vulnerable to economic manipulation by capital and the capitalist market—and this can be a very violent process."[3] For example, just because the IMF has the financial power to impose loan conditionality upon Third World governments does not mean that the IMF enjoys political legitimacy. In fact, very often a social crisis emerges when recipient governments—as a condition of receiving the loans—are put in the position of destroying labor unions, exploiting the natural resources of the nation to service the repayment of the debt to the IMF, or are forced to cut funding for health, human services, and education.

The requirements of IMF conditionality, or *Imperial Capital*—in the service of *Global Empire*—may have the power to impose loan conditionality, but the entire notion of "conditionality" cannot be reduced to a simple economic equation. Neither can it be made into a quid pro quo arrangement that sacrifices the recognition and protection of people's rights. For, to sacrifice basic human needs, the aspirations of the oppressed and exploited, and to foreclose upon the exercise of democratic control over their own lives, means the death of human rights protections, the possibility for the creation of a viable *Global Community* or any other kind of humane community. The net result of excluding the voiceless creates a counterforce of violent opposition that will inevitably bring the excluded sectors of society to seek a greater measure of inclusion in State and local politics. The demand for distributive justice, socioeconomic inclusion, and real political power for the powerless is rising around the world. Hence, the rise of *Global Community* may be seen as a counterforce to the practices of the IMF, World Bank, WTO, the threat of "preemptive war," the processes of globalization, and *Global Empire* as these forces continue to take their toll upon the quality of the lives of the excluded.

The violence that has been unleashed by globalization is perhaps its greatest creation at the dawn of the twenty-first century. The combination of globalization and the spread of free markets (*in the name of democracy*) is a deadly force that has now accelerated beyond Africa, Asia, and Latin America to the Middle East. With America at the helm in this effort, the presidency of George W. Bush has launched the United States into Iraq with free markets and democracy on its lips, but with privatization on its mind. If Iraq follows the historical path taken by other nations, we will find that "the disturbing reality is that global markets, even if marginally 'lifting all boats', have consistently intensified the extraordinary dominance of certain 'outsider' minorities, fueling virulent ethnic envy and hatred among the impoverished minorities around them."[4]

In the case of Iraq, the potential danger for civil war becomes increasingly predictable, as the forces of US occupation and a client government exercise antidemocratic tactics while employing the rhetoric of democracy. In short, if the rhetoric and promises of democratic politics fail to create a more inclusive set of democratic practices and policies in government, in economics, in social and cultural life, then the fate of democratic legitimacy will be gone with the wind.

Despite the diversities that accompany human history, there are definite similarities between people's historical experiences under what I have called *imperial capital* and the North's historical quest for "Global Empire." It is this commonality of experience in reaction to *imperial capital* that has served to concentrate disproportionate wealth in the hands of a resented ethnic minority in every region of the world. In Africa, Asia, Russia, and Latin America, these *market-dominant-minorities*—Chinese in Southeast Asia, Croatians in the former Yugoslavia, whites in Latin America and South Africa, Lebanese in West Africa, and Jews in postCommunist Russia—invariably become targets of violent hatred.

In this context, it is not hard to understand that violent insurgencies are directed at an American occupation in Iraq since 2003. Because of the "outcast" nature of excluded groups, eliminated from the fruits of wealth, born from an imposed economic policy of privatization—as much as ethnic and religious differences—we find that collectively inspired groups of people have begun to forge communities that oppose all attempts to realize imperialistic ambitions. In short, at the heart of many social movements in opposition to America's "Global Empire," there is an effort to deny the legitimacy of privatization, of the trends toward even greater political, social exclusion, and economic subordination. In fact, there have been throughout the world many attempts to resurrect some variant of socialism to meet people's needs.

Whether we understand ourselves as realists or utopians is something that we must come to comprehend within the context of history. If we fail to see *the past as precedence*, then we shall be condemned in Iraq to watch the unfolding of a situation similar to that of what transpired in the former Yugoslavia where "the result of market liberalization and democratic elections was not prosperity and political freedom, but rather economic devastation, hatemongering, populist manipulation, and civilian-conducted mass murder."[5] Only the unreflective mind or the ideologically compulsive mind-set seeks to escape the task of developing recognition of the need to come to some kind of verdict on where we have come from in order to help us determine where we are going. In this regard, the so-called neoconservatives of the Bush-2 regime have conveniently failed to come to terms with realities and implications of history.

Within the rhetoric of the Bush-2 administration is the subtle attempt to start history at "ground zero." The attacks on 9/11 were like an arrow slicing through the Achilles heel of the United States, both physically and emotionally. The collapse of the World Trade Center induced a "shell-shocked" consciousness throughout the nation. As if by magic, the Bush administration successfully took advantage of the resultant fear by undermining both international law and the US Constitution. The officially sanctioned rhetoric of "protecting freedom" has been installed like a computer chip into the collective hard drive of American consciousness. The resulting foreclosure of people's capacity for critical analysis has been replaced by irrational patriotism and the indulgence of *group think*.

In the aftermath of 9/11, the phenomenon of *group think* has taken hold in the centers of power and throughout the media. It lies at the imperial center of America's attempt to create a Global Empire. The problem with "group think" is that it presents us with a predetermined conclusion as to what our historical truth should be. Because it lacks the component of critical self-examination it lobotomizes the capacity of citizens to question the government's rationales for war and peace. Therefore, the pronouncements of the Bush administration masquerade as the preordained word of some higher power that we need not question—and dare not question for fear of being called "traitors" or of giving "aid and comfort to the terrorists." By being caught up in the moment, in a state of constant emergency and fear, the average citizen is left with no real frame of reference. However, the reality of our current situation is that the historical present is still a product of precedence. That is why, for example, the Western legal tradition has stressed the role of precedence when interpreting cases or developing new laws to address new situations. While God may have the power to create *out of nothing*, humans are required to create meaning, rules, and understandings *out of something*. History needs to be remembered in order to reclaim the American Republic from the siren song of American Empire. America's role in funding the Taliban in the 1980s against the Soviet Union's occupation of Afghanistan needs to be understood as the precursor of much anti-American sentiment throughout the Middle East. The precedence of history serves to constitute and to create meanings, rules, and understandings. History is our common inheritance. It provides us with a basis on which to engage in some kind of shared discourse about where we have been and where we are going. It forces us to awaken from our historical amnesia.

History is also an inheritance with unresolved issues. Some progressive scholars have acknowledged that

> even if we look upon the Bush Doctrine as an anomalous historical detour in the development US foreign policy, even if we overlook all previous military interventions by the US, even if we ignore the many ways in which earlier administrations have stretched the principles of "liberal imperialism" to their utmost limits and beyond, the Bush phenomenon cannot be understood except as an extension, however extreme and ultimately self-defeating, of the logic inherent in US foreign policy at least since World War II.[6]

The US Global Empire has been historically wedded to the world of business. By being so intertwined, the politics of empire has influenced and shaped globalization. In turn, globalization and the business agenda of multinationals and corporate elites have shaped the world of imperial politics. Many American citizens still do not recognize this symbiosis. By embracing the Bush-2 regime's politics of fear, many Americans remain lock-in-step with a creeping fascism within the United States as President Bush declares that he has ultimate executive power as the "unity executive" and that he exercises power as he sees fit—beyond the constraints of a system of checks and balances. In his alteration of the constitutional order, he has claimed imperial powers as if he were an emperor. In this imperial mode, he declares himself to be nothing more and nothing less than a "war president." Yet, despite such dictatorial pronouncements, it is not as if we have learned absolutely nothing along the way. If historical experience has taught us anything, it is that violence and conflict and war are antithetical to building humane communities. It has also taught us that the path of nonviolence and realizing a global community is fraught with many hazards on the way to its achievement—from assassination to genocide, from economic coercion to imperial occupation. Still, the history of popular resistance to imperial capital and global empire—both violent and nonviolent—is an historical constant.

RESISTANCE TO GLOBAL EMPIRE IS
AN HISTORICAL CONSTANT

Resistance to global empire and the requirements of imperial capital (neoliberalism, privatization, and structural adjustment programs) are expressions of the search for a global community seeking new forms of governance that are more humane, inclusive, and democratic. Resistance to global empire is predicated upon the belief that humans are capable of a continuing commitment to building new frames of reference for cross-cultural understanding. That means not imposing a neoconservative definition of *democracy* that is authored by White House speechwriters. While it is true that the Arab countries are not changing much politically, it is equally true that the United States lacks credibility in the Arab world.

In light of this credibility gap, it should not be surprising that new frames of reference for defining democracy in the Arab world need to be left to the citizens of the Arab world. Recognizing this creative process as something that cannot be externally imposed discounts the claims made by the policymakers of Global Empire. Rather than following the dictates of the US Global Empire, it will be the interaction and engagement of the Arab world with the rest of the Global Community that will prove to be the most enduring force in not only defining democracy in that region of the globe, but also how well it fits with cooperative ventures and mutual dialogs throughout the rest of the world. Just as in the case of globalization there are diametrically opposed views. Those who define and practice globalization *from above* have a radically different agenda and diagnosis of its effects from those who define the effects of globalization *from below*. So it is with empire. The architects of the US Global Empire seek to present the image of a benevolent Goliath to the world. Those who resist the imperial fantasy have chosen the path of resistance to the occupations, invasions, and threats of the empire.

It is through the task of building understanding between peoples and their aspirations that the door is opened for the realization of our common humanity. It is through resistance to military intervention and economic privatization that a rising Global Community of people—regardless of nationality—are finding their common concerns delineated. Hence, resistance to global empire has as its corollary the desire to embrace an inclusive approach to economic development, as well as political cooperation between peoples, nations, and civilizations. Such a result represents an achievement that a global empire rooted in militarism and the culture of war could never produce.

The historical path of Global Empire travels on a different trajectory from that of Global Community. The path of Global Empire requires domination by force, exclusion, violence, and coercion. These are the requirements of global empire as it seeks to maintain its hegemony over suppressed alternative discourses, power-sharing arrangements, and inclusionary forms of governance. In short, the path of Global Empire is more often than not characterized by what may be called *global apartheid*, for it divides the interests of the rich from those of the poor, and it increasingly relies upon exclusionary forms of governance as a poor substitute for its lack of legitimacy. Inevitably, the practice of advancing a Global Empire will confront greater resistance and violence from those it calls "insurgents" or "dissidents." Yet, the dissidents and insurgents of these historical struggles are often seeking nothing more than a place at the table, a sense of interpersonal justice, and the practice of an inclusive politics which looks toward a resolution of differences instead of further obfuscation of what the real issues are.

American interaction with Asia, Africa, the Middle East, and Latin America, in the post-1945 period, began to expose the self-contradictions of America's liberal ideology. Washington invoked its version of liberal ideology in order to justify American intervention in the first place. The great terms and ideas of the Enlightenment: "freedom," "equality," "independence," and "self-determination" were all destined to become the elements of American policies and the dominant discourse for the authors of international law. Yet, the ideals of America's liberal ideology could not be realistically found in either its practices in the Third World or in the conditions of life as experienced by the peoples of the Third World. Immanuel Wallerstein has noted:

> The self contradiction of liberal ideology is total. If all humans have equal rights, and all peoples have equal rights, we cannot maintain the kind of inegalitarian system that the capitalist world-economy has always been and always will be. But if this is openly admitted, then the capitalist world economy will have no legitimation in the eyes of the dangerous (that is, the dispossessed) classes. And if a system has no legitimation, it will not survive.[7]

At the dawn of the twenty-first century, the world system is governed in both its economic and political life by a twofold reality. On the one hand, it is the reality of a neoliberal model of globalization. On the other hand, there exists the tyranny of the US Global Empire's struggle to maintain and extend its hegemony. Neither of these aspects of American power can be viewed as legitimate by most nations within the Global Community who are struggling to divorce themselves from the grip of this orbit.

In the years since the official end of the Cold War (1990), the United States has become what some have called "the lone superpower." Now, instead of having two superpowers compete for "spheres of influence," the one remaining superpower seeks worldwide domination. With the invasion and occupation of Iraq in 2003, the Bush administration has worked for corporate and financial sectors in the global economy to privatize the Middle East, while dividing the spoils of its military and economic conquest. The imperial order that the United States seeks to impose cares nothing for the voice of the vast majority in the Middle East. Rather, it seeks only to impose its neoconservative vision upon the region. In first and second terms of the presidency of George W. Bush the cracks in the imperial order are widening. Wallerstein has stressed the fact that:

> We live in a system in which there has been a continuing class struggle. We live in a system that has involved the steady polarization of the populations— economically, politically, socially, and now even demographically. We live in a system that has built racism and sexism into its structures from the outset. And of course we live in a system that has structured the very antisystemic movements that have challenged the legitimacy and viability of the system itself.[8]

William I. Robinson has come to a similar conclusion in the course of analyzing transnational conflict, globalization, social change, and the impact of privatization as an economic policy in Central America. He notes that:

> Privatization has taken on different patterns and forms depending on particular local histories and conditions ... Government itself has been privatized to the extent that numerous state functions have been transferred to the private sector and converted from a social (public) to a market (private) logic. Health, education, and others services have become "for profit"—meaning that these activities are reorganized not in order to meet human needs but in order to make money. Privatization results in pure market-determined distribution. Given the highly skewed structure of income distribution, the process tends to aggravate inequalities and social polarization. It has predictably sparked sharp conflicts.[9]

From this analysis, it follows that the antisystemic movements, which have arisen throughout the world to resist the hegemony of imperial capital and global empire, are opposed to the central economic weapons of imperial capital—privatization, neoliberalism, and structural adjustment programs. Hence, the "magic of the market," heralded by President Reagan at a 1981 meeting in Cancun, Mexico, is still a source of conflict and resistance as the Bush-2 administration seeks to control Iraq. The economic and political logic of the Bush-administration's drive into the Middle East is to see a Middle East pacified. What this means is that the Bush-administration wants to see the area brought into compliance with American ideological norms. This region would be policed by American soldiers so as to be counted on to produce plentiful supplies of oil and to accept the presence of a Jewish state in its midst. The problem is that "the ensuing collision between American requirements and a non-compliant world will provide the impetus for more crusades."[10]

ALTERNATIVES TO HEGEMONY

The price of global empire is the price of having to pay for perpetual war. It is, without overstatement, a war without end. It is a war on many fronts. The countries at the center of Global Empire will be forced to extract higher taxes from their citizens. At the same time, the center of this Global Empire will continue to run up huge deficits in order to pay for the imperial adventures. The social costs will, as always, be borne by the society at large. The benefits, as usual, will accrue to a small handful of companies and war-profiteers.

There are alternatives. However, the adoption of such alternatives will necessitate a profound change of fundamental doctrines in Washington. From military doctrines to financial doctrines, the authors of Global Empire have sought to expand the reaches of their domain, control, and influence. In the financial arena, the so-called *Washington Consensus* is one of many doctrines that have died since its inception. The Washington Consensus was dedicated to furthering the policies of neoliberalism, which were designed to open markets to financial speculation and getting government out of the business of currency and banking regulation. Then came the East Asian financial crisis and financial collapse of the late 1990s. Former chief economist for the World Bank, Dr. Joseph Stiglitz, became a leading critic of those IMF policies that were the driving force behind the Washington Consensus and the East Asian crisis. The alternatives that have since begun to emerge from that fiasco have given greater credence to the role of more hands-on government involvement, regulation and control of markets, and the banking establishment. Other alternatives point toward a greater focus upon the vulnerable, the poor, and the unprotected members of those societies who would be most adversely affected by the ensuing unemployment crisis emerging from such a major financial meltdown.

Yet, under current global conditions, the Bush-2 regime has continued to reject alternatives for a more humane, inclusive, and cosmopolitan world. For the Bush-2 regime, the purposes of military doctrines cannot be separated from the purposes of financial doctrines generated by the authors of Global Empire. There is an inherent overlap and continuity between the rule of force and the rules of finance that benefit those who author them. Insofar as the Western powers at the centers of capitalism both write and enforce the rules, the correspondence between financial purpose and military power becomes indisputable. However, those doctrines that are supportive of militarism, privatization, and the support of exclusionary policies and regimes cannot be maintained by force. The maintenance of exploitative frameworks of governance by privileged elites are doomed to create ethnic conflict (as with the US occupation of Iraq), exacerbate latent suspicions among different nations (India, Pakistan, China), and become potential arenas for genocide (Darfur in the Sudan, where the fight for oil revenues contributes to an ongoing genocide).

In the alternative, the practice of building and maintaining a nonmilitaristic, humane, inclusive, and democratic Global Community has the capacity for realizing all of the benefits that may be derived from cooperation, diplomacy, as well as an emphasis upon common values and a common morality that Richard Falk has termed "humane governance."[11] The emergence of humane governance means, in part, that we will have to redefine what human development and human security really means for the entire global community, as opposed to the interests of a privileged few (see: Chapters 4 and 6).

It is a central thesis of this book that we must produce fundamental alternatives that are centered upon our capacity to bring a greater correspondence between sustainable forms of development and sustainable forms of security. By investing our energies and talents into the realization of workable concepts and practices for development and security, global governance and the rise of a truly Global Community will be enabled to take on an inclusive political logic. I have termed this approach "inclusionary governance."[12] Inclusionary governance stands for the proposition that hegemonic efforts to reshape global politics in the imperial image will fail. The US Global Empire's attempt to dominate the globe will fail not only because of the rising costs of expansion, but by the inherent illegitimacy of the attempt itself. In the alternative, the strategy of inclusionary governance stands for the proposition that the benefits of voluntarily institutionalized cooperation throughout the Global Community far outweigh the costs of hierarchical domination under the rubric of US hegemony (see: Chapters 2, 3, and 6).

It is impossible to isolate one community from another. Communities are like an interconnected web. They are linked either by cooperation or conflict. The post-9/11 world has seemed to provide a convenient context for placing the proponents of the Islamic and Christian faiths at odds with one another. Whether calling the situation a *clash of civilizations* or demonizing the core tenets of the faith claims of the others' religion, the potential for a healing dialog has usually been replaced by ideological narrowness coupled with nationalistic fervor (see: Chapter 4).

However, the Islamic and Christian communities of the globe are more than religious categories or the foundation stones for a nationalistic credo. The teachings of these faiths comprise the psychological orientation of people, as well as the political commitments of individuals and groups. Contained with these faiths are points of human commonality that may open the doors of global understanding, global discourse, and global community. In this sense, these religious traditions may also be seen as instruments that form a part of the ideological self-definition of civilizations and cultures. The shared moral norms and sacred texts of all of the world's great religions represent a repository of hope, of guidance, and of inspiration for building a world of alternatives to the current structures of imperial power and arrogance.

As previously noted, it is impossible to isolate communities. One reason for this difficulty is found in the fact that new identities are emerging within all communities. These emerging identities are the product of many forces. There are dominant networks and subordinate networks both within and between societies. It is important to differentiate between the two types of networks and not merely say that a "network society" has emerged. While some scholars have written of a *network society*, other scholars criticize the idea of a *network society* for being too analytically separated from the harsh economic and political realities of globalization, the pursuit of empire, and the effects of neoliberal economics.[13] There are many variables that contribute to a *network society*. Among these variables are those forces that enjoy a privileged position in making and enforcing the rules within and between the networks. Alternatively, there are those who are permanently trapped in a subordinate position within these networks who are denied a democratic network, an inclusive economic order, and social equality. At the most basic level, the rise of Global Community will involve grappling with these questions of governance—as understood by the merger of developmental concerns with security concerns. Not since the early 1960s has the global community been presented with the opportunity to create a more egalitarian and less polarized social system at both the national and global levels.[14]

The great historical opening that has converged at the start of the twenty-first century involves coming to terms not only with the present system of neoliberal globalization, but also defining what kind of system will succeed our present one. In other words, we live in an era very different from that of the Reagan-Thatcher years. Prime Minister Thatcher declared, *There Is No Alternative* (TINA). By the late 1990s, progressive thinkers and movements around the globe declared, *Another World Is Possible*. These two viewpoints have been in contention over the period of the last 25 years. It is only now that the global community of nations is being afforded a critical window of opportunity to actually choose in what direction the human future will move. On the one hand, our future could simply maintain a pattern of hierarchical, exclusionary, unequal, and polarizing structures that are characteristic of the present system. On the other hand, our future could be placed on an entirely new historical trajectory. It would be one that is fundamentally more inclusive, more democratic, and more egalitarian. The tragedy of governance by Global Empire would be effectively replaced by the rising power of Global Community.

In turn, questions of global governance involve issues associated with the task of defining the purposes, values, and obligations of human life. Will human beings continue to be trapped by oppressive systems? Can the purposes and obligations associated with Global Empire be compatible with *sustainable economic development?* Or, do the demands of seeking Global Empire create *resource wars* between nation-states? Can the historical undertaking of Global Community be more effective in rescuing the natural environment and people's basic needs?

In short, we are caught between the historical legacies of pursuing Global Empire or seeking its alternatives. If we are to move beyond the abuses of empire, those abuses should be identified and dealt with as effectively as possible. At the core of the abuses of all empires is the practice and experience of fear. One dramatic expression of empires' use of fear as a means of control is torture. From Rome's use of crucifixion, to America's suspension of the Geneva Convention in the prison at Abu Ghraib (and elsewhere), torture has been one of empires' most valuable weapons—as well as a source of one of its gravest vulnerabilities.

All empires rule by fear. Fear is usually engendered by the possession of immense military power and the power over life and death that are associated with it. Military power exercises a primordial hold over the reptilian part of the brain that is characterized by aggressive behavior without reflection.[15] On the other hand, the course of building a Global Community that is committed to the realization of nonviolence charts a path that seeks to create humane forms of governance—demonstrating the power of the higher faculties of the human brain.

The movement towards a Global Community is one that is cross-cultural. It does not seek to divide the world into "haves" and "have-nots." It seeks distributional justice in economics and in the realm of political decision making. The rise of Global Community is an expression of humanity's collective desire to build a world of shared norms and common understandings within and between peoples. Shared norms and common understandings about what constitutes genuine security will be a critical first step and an ongoing process. In this critical regard, "the way to security lies less in achieving greater technological sophistication than in working toward a transformation of the spirit of our relationship with our potential adversaries."[16] With such a focus, it will be possible for the architects of the rising Global Community to begin their various tasks with the acknowledgement of our mutual vulnerability and common humanity.

As the historical path of South Africa's transition from apartheid to democracy demonstrates, the rise and eventual realization of Global Community, within a world of progressive national communities, is guided not by fear, but by love, empathy, and a firm commitment to practice inclusionary forms of governance. The rise and eventual realization of Global Community liberates people from their isolated roles, cultures, and political affiliations. Its promise has the capacity to reveal a common citizenship not only with other people in distant lands, but those in close proximity to our own condition.

2
The Occupations of Empire

The logic of state security has created a cycle of violence and preparation for violence in the international system which hinders the development of policy for a durable peace—whether national, regional or global.[1]

David Held

Democratization is not itself an assurance of decency or moderation, but can be both abusive and abused. The quality of a given democracy depends on the direction and orientation of civic life. This direction and orientation can be vulnerable to manipulation by militarist and market forces, as well as by pressures generated in relation to globalization from above ... It would be erroneous to draw anthropological lessons from such historic failures of democracy and claim human nature to be flawed, or inevitably aggressive. Rather, one may draw constitutional and socio-political lessons that acknowledge that concentrations of power are normatively unwieldy, regardless of political orientation, and tend to be highly susceptible to various kinds of decay and manuipulation.[2]

Richard Falk

Throughout history, there have been many overseas empires. As Europe began to expand outward, both Spain and England extended their reach to the New World and beyond. Some political and economic theories have described this outward reach as "imperialism." Central to these economic theories of imperialism is the view that particular individuals and sectors within society benefit from expansion and outreach. Until historian Paul Kennedy authored his book, *The Rise and Fall of Great Powers*, little attention was paid to the consequences of this outward expansion, which Kennedy termed, "imperial overstretch."[3]

At the time that Kennedy wrote his book, the Reagan administration was in office and pursuing a massive military build up. It sponsored a series of counter-revolutionary wars in Africa, Central America, and Asia. These interventions constituted imperial attempts to counteract the defeat of the United States in Vietnam and other parts of the world. At the same time, US economic preeminence appeared to be threatened by the dynamic economies of both Japan and Western Europe. At the turn of the millennium, it seemed that Professor Kennedy's argument of imperial overstretch was largely irrelevant. His argument was seen as irrelevant because America's conventional forces were not over-deployed. There were limited interventions in Somalia, Haiti, and with the Bosnian Serbs, but the United States was largely at peace with the world. At least it seemed irrelevant until the rise of the administration of George W. Bush in the year 2000.

Under the leadership of a second Bush administration, the United States became divorced from its historic post-1945 consensus with respect to multilateralism. It also failed to give even tacit acknowledgment to the relevance of international law. Replacing the post-1945 consensus were the Bush-2 doctrines of unilateralism and preemptive war. Professor Kennedy's assessment of "imperial overstretch," as a concept, would be reestablished as the second Bush administration undertook a unilateral modus operandi. By 2003, the US Global Empire had inaugurated wars that were being waged in both Iraq and Afghanistan. The UN was ignored. With the exception of Great Britain, European allies were marginalized. The Bush-2 regime had invested in political capital in support of policies that furthered a resurgent militarism.

The preoccupations of the Bush administration from 2000 to 2003 were about to find their material realization in the invasion and occupation of Iraq. The dreams and imperial preoccupations of neoconservative policy elites would finally seek to be actualized by the authors of the *Project for the New American Century* (PNAC) in the aftermath of the Clinton years. The document's primary authors, Paul Wolfowitz and Donald Rumsfeld had approached the Clinton administration with their findings, only to be ignored. George W. Bush would return the previously exiled planners of the PNAC back into office. Under the leadership of Rumsfeld and Wolfowitz, the Pentagon's organization, strategy, and tactics would undergo a thorough reworking—a true "revolution in military affairs" (RMA).

The PNAC document was primarily dedicated to how to accelerate the militarization processes of the American government in order to achieve what the Pentagon called *full spectrum dominance* (domination over land, air, sea, and space). The agenda of this program included the removal of the United States from the legal restraints of the 1972 ABM Treaty. The weaponization of space was to be opened for financial profit and military dominance under the auspices of a program called *National Missile Defense* (NMD)—formerly labeled the *Strategic Defense Initiative* (SDI), or to its critics, "Star Wars."

In anticipation of the global resistance to US attempts at achieving global hegemony, the planners in the Pentagon and throughout the military-industrial complex were gearing up for the new demands of maintaining an American Empire. When troop strength alone would not be enough, when financial pressures and threats would not be sufficient, when rival hegemons (perhaps China) would resist the imposition of the American imperial will, it would then be resolved by a space armada of weapons in conjunction with an on-the-ground Theater Missile Defense (TMD) system, equipped with strategic nuclear capabilities (or so the planners thought).

There has been a progressive militarization of US policy ever since the end of the Vietnam War. This is especially the case with regard to US policy as it relates to the Middle East at the dawn of the twenty-first century. The militarization of the American economy as well as its foreign policy had acquired a momentum to which the events of September 11, 2001 only added. The tide of this militarization of US foreign policy would find further expression in the Bush administration's construction of an imperial plan driven by neoconservative hawks. As Roger Burbach and Jim Tarbell observed, "Their rhetoric promoted the virtues of spreading liberal democracy across the planet. But the reality of their actions revealed that they were fundamentally intent on advancing the narrow interests of an imperial plutocracy that plunders the planet's resources regardless of the political consequences."[4]

THE REIGN OF AMERICA'S OWN IMPERIAL PLUTOCRACY

It is the limited vision of the American imperial plutocracy that serves to constitute a politically powerful preoccupation with a very narrow set of interests. More ominously, I call the antidemocratic and illegal work of this imperial plutocracy "the hidden politics of empire" (see: Chapter 5). If there is a proclivity within the American body politic for fascism and/or fascist-like policies, it will most likely emerge out of the hidden politics of empire for it is in the dark corners of concentrated power and wealth that unaccountability reigns supreme. In the absence of public knowledge and without the benefit of a system of checks and balances, the political process is easily corrupted according to the dictates of private interests.

Since the invasion of Iraq by the Bush administration in 2003, it is difficult, if not impossible to speak of a true national interest (that is comprehensive in nature and in furtherance of the interest of the country as a whole), much less invoke the concept of a larger human interest that takes into account the rest of humanity. By definition, a truly comprehensive national interest would take into account the concerns of all major groups, interests, and parties within the body politic of American society. It would be the product of honest debate and a mutually arrived at consensus. Further, it would have clear goals and objectives. None of these elements can be used to describe the nature of the Bush administration's march to war against Iraq. Rather, between 2003 and 2006 there has been revelation after revelation of President Bush's intent to invade Iraq despite his early assertions to the contrary. The Bush-2 regime primarily relied on its arsenal to create "weapons of mass deception." Such a conclusion is appropriate when the threat of terrorist "mushroom clouds" and an unproven arsenal of "weapons of mass destruction" would be cited as the ultimate rationale for war—only to later be proven fallacious.

Additionally, the Bush administration's incapacity to comprehend the role of diplomacy and negotiation is indicative of an imperial hubris that has begun a process of victimizing itself by virtue of its imperial delusions. The delusions of what the American Empire is actually capable of carrying out are the first cracks in a façade of force, serving to expose its real vulnerability. The abuses of empire are an expression of its actual weakness and its capacity to be brutal, cruel, and inhuman (such as the endorsement of torture as a state-sanctioned tool in the *war on terror*). By relying on the employment of torture, engaging in the practice of ignoring diplomacy, and exhibiting the arrogance associated with setting a one-nation agenda in opposition to the UN (within a world of states that constitute a global community), the fact remains that the United States cannot act alone without consequences. Throughout the 1990s, in order to mitigate the abuses of empire, the Clinton administration relied primarily upon economic models and strategy to advance US interests without troops. The Clinton administration's strategy was to hide the force of US military power under the rubric of "globalization."

Under the Clinton administration, it was assumed that the economic model of neoliberalism would connect the community of nations through the power of globalization. However, by the time of the presidency of Bush-2, that grand hope was dashed upon the rocks of the East Asian financial crisis, the failure of African and Latin American states to effectively meet their debt obligations to the IMF, and the negative effects of a growing resistance to the rules and methods of the WTO. Hence, while globalization had connected and affected the world, only American military force could keep it from coming unglued from the orbit of US power and influence.

Globalization has unlocked a developing system that is global in scope. As an historical process, globalization has exhibited different effects and outcomes that vary from region to region, continent to continent, nation to nation. Its uneven nature has produced sectors of great wealth and deepening poverty. The inequality factor that is emerging from this process has increased the numbers of excluded people both within and between nations. Should the evolving global system prove tyrannical or inhumane, all of humanity will be left as the ultimate loser. Yet, the Bush-2 regime continues to seek American hegemony of this system—a system in decay. Some have argued that America's hegemonic decline might yet be reversed. Yet, the revival of American hegemony has become very problematic. On this matter, Thomas McCormick has noted that, "globalization seems to have reached its likely limits, and militarization seems too blunt an instrument to be effective save in special instances ... So it may well be that no strategic choice is likely to sustain American hegemony over the long term."[5] Assuming that this diagnosis is largely correct, it follows that the search for alternatives is more than necessary. The diagnosis of an inevitable decline for the US Global Empire does, however, make possible an examination of where there are movements and efforts underway to build a viable Global Community.

Concern over the fate of the long term leads us back to examining the concept of what constitutes the *national interest*. Even if we take a very narrow definition of what constitutes the national interest, Robert Johansen was correct when he observed that

> The highly acclaimed concept of the national interest is not scientifically determined. It is a cluster of goals and strategies derived from more fundamental values ... This includes maintaining sovereign control over a defined territory and population. The competitive accumulation of military power, and, secondarily, of economic resources, are the principal means for pursuing the values of security and prosperity.[6]

What Johansen has described is the Bush-2 regime's proclivity for a "go-it-alone" approach in the world that obviates any serious consideration of growing global poverty and hunger, the threat of global warming, the depletion of natural resources, and the quality of our food, water, and air. Rather, the plutocracy that sets the standards, goals, and objectives for the US Global Empire is dedicated to global dominance through resurgent militarism. Why? The plutocracy assumes that resurgent militarism guarantees the accumulation of military power while, at the same time, it makes possible short-term hegemonic control over other people's natural resources.

Beyond this traditionally narrow definition of what constitutes the national interest, is an alternative. The alternative is not less scientific or less empirically oriented than the defenders of the traditional definitions. In fact, "an un-traditional orientation may simply mean that one endorses a slightly rearranged hierarchy of values."[7] By changing the hierarchy of values by which a nation pursues its conception of the national interest, it is possible to develop an alternative framework for decision making. This is an extremely important point. Decision making is at the heart of governance. President Kennedy once said that, *to govern is to choose*. The priorities embraced by Bush and the neoconservative hawks represent more of a "cult" within the American government than a group of rational decision makers. Hence, the distortions that are characteristic of America's use of its power in the world are representative of what I call the *occupations of empire*. The imperial mind-set is occupied with a set of choices divorced from any real capacity to consider untraditional alternatives. Untraditional alternatives are vital and important because they contain the capacity to take the first steps toward an *exodus from empire*.

"WORLD ORDER VALUES" VERSUS THE "NATIONAL INTEREST"

We must begin to question the choices that an imperial plutocracy has made with regard to the pursuit of not only American security, but the security of the world as well. In that regard, some scholars have developed a set of alternative concepts that rearrange the hierarchy of values exhibited within the traditional definition. New scholarship has produced a more inclusive set of values that they call, *world order values*. These world order values include the following: "(1) peace without national military arsenals, (2) economic well-being for all inhabitants on the earth, (3) the universal human rights and social justice, and (4) ecological balance."[8] One need only imagine how radically such a revolution in values could easily change the course of the world's history. I would argue that the correspondence between "world order values" and action in accordance with the dictates of those values is the ultimate corrective to the occupations, vulnerabilities, and abuses that characterizes empire building.

These *world order values* envision the rise of "Global Community." By giving primacy to the health of the global commons, the environment would no longer be at the mercy of a narrowly driven corporate agenda "for profit." By giving primacy to the pursuit of peace, the hypocritical equation of pursuing war in the name of peace would become obsolete. By giving primacy to human rights and social justice, the supportive structures and motivations for terrorists and terrorism would be curtailed if not entirely eliminated. By giving primacy to the realization of economic well-being for all inhabitants on the earth, there would no longer be a situation where over 2 billion people live on less than a dollar a day. Therefore, the closer that we move toward the untraditional category of *world order values* the closer we will move toward the rise of "Global Community."

Clearly, what separates the traditional definition of the national interest from the alternative vision of the human interest provides us with two dramatically contrasting sets of values, priorities, and policies. Let us take the example of what has happened in the early twentieth century as a result of decisions made with respect to the destabilizing impact of oil production itself. In the Middle East, the risk of disorder and conflict is heightened as ruling elites work to monopolize the distribution of oil revenues. With the rest of the population mired in poverty, the divide between the privileged and the disadvantaged can easily coincide with tribal or religious differences. As a result of this division, violence is a likely outcome. Yet, the predictability of this outcome has not, in any fundamental way, altered the decision-making processes that affect the future of American energy behavior or the policies of America's client regimes in the Middle East.

Given this analysis, Michael Klare has noted that,

> four key trends will dominate the future of American energy behavior: an increasing need for imported oil, a pronounced shift toward unstable and unfriendly suppliers in dangerous parts of the world; a greater risk of anti-American or civil violence, and rising competition for what will likely prove a diminishing supply pool.[9]

Klare maintains that, "only by subjecting these policies to close and careful scrutiny ... and by devising alternative energy strategies will it be possible to avoid either the perils of dependency or the unconscionable costs they incur."[10]

At this point in history, we should ask ourselves how we could avoid the perils of dependency and unconscionable costs. I maintain that the failure of *Global Empire* is a direct consequence of patterns of decision making based upon traditional notions of what constitutes the national interest. Wars for natural resources, especially oil, are not in the long-term interest of the people of the United States or the rest of the world. The threat of such wars constitutes one of the many "occupations of empire." For the pursuit of Global Empire prioritizes military values even as it strangles the federal budget and deprives the citizens of the United States of decent schools, health care for all, and needed improvements in its infrastructure. The pursuit of Global Empire also represents an occupation of the American neoconservative mind-set and elite that has retained an alliance with corporate and oil interests to the exclusion of the concerns and values of most of the American people and most countries on the planet.

America's imperial plutocracy, representative of the interests of the oil industry and large corporations, is based upon a hierarchy of values that need to be dramatically rearranged in reference to the needs of the larger global community; namely the cause of peace, the health of the environment, and the protection of human rights. In making such an alteration of policy decisions, the advocates of *world order values* maintain that, "the human race is the important constituency to consider in policymaking. The world's people should benefit from policy decisions. The traditional approach gives priority to the people of one nation."[11]

Yet, even in the narrow context of just one nation there is the danger of giving monopolistic banks and industries associated with the military-industrial-complex priority over budget outlays and political preferences that result in the exploitation and subordination of many different groups and classes. Such a result is clearly antidemocratic. It is an expression of the exclusionary nature of politics in the service of a narrowly defined national interest that leaves one asking the question:

> Whose national interest? It is interesting to note on this matter that, Lenin drew on this theme, identifying monopolistic banks and industries as the key culprits behind imperial expansion. Central to these economic theories of imperialism is the notion that certain individuals and sectors within society benefit from expansion. Even if empire leads to a net economic loss for the state, it is nevertheless pursued because the benefits associated with imperialism accrue to a select few, while the costs of expansion, administration, and defense are more evenly distributed through the population in the form of taxation.[12]

Nowhere is Lenin's thesis more dramatically borne out than in the imperial onslaught of neoliberalism and privatization in Iraq. The Iraqi Constitution prohibits the privatization of vital economic assets and forbids non-Iraqis from owning Iraqi firms. If left in place, the Iraqi Constitution would frustrate the Bush administration's reconstruction plans insofar as US corporations were supposed to be the beneficiaries of the country's natural resources under the ideology of a new "Open Door." Therefore, in September 2003, the Bush administration quickly set about appointing a "Coalition Provisional Authority" (CPA) that overturned the existing laws on ownership. The US administrator of the CPA, Paul Bremer, codified the privatization of state-owned resources in his "Order-39" which legalized foreign ownership of "Iraqi banks, mines, and factories." It also permitted the complete repatriation of profits from Iraq.

Lenin's thesis is not a new one. It was discussed in Grant McConnell's 1966 classic work, *Private Power and American Democracy*.[13] It was prefigured in, *The Power Elite*,[14] by C. Wright Mills. In fact, it has reverberated in the progressive literature of economics and political science with even more intensity since the Vietnam War years (1964–1974). Further, this thesis has been expanded to encompass the American foreign policy establishment's search for "endless enemies." Published in 1984, Jonathan Kwitny's book, *Endless Enemies: The Making of an Unfriendly World*,[15] critiqued the emergent path of American foreign policy in the middle of the Reagan years. His thesis lays out facts and examples of where the betrayal of America's fundamental principles would ultimately create a *blowback* effect. In short, he exposed how America's interventions in the Third World actually destroy democracy and defeat its own best interests. His book prophetically argues that we actually ruin the countries we go in to help—destroying the very values we seek to secure—and we corrupt ourselves in the process.

In the early 1970s, the Nixon administration illegally widened the conflict in Vietnam in Laos, Thailand, and Cambodia. Nixon and Kissinger paved the way for Pol Pot to come to power in Cambodia and subsequently unleashed what would be called "the Auschwitz of our generation." In this same period, the Nixon administration conspired with a Chilean military junta to overthrow the democratically elected government of Salvador Allende, thereby creating a bloodbath in which thousands of Chileans died under General Pinochet's dictatorship. In 1994, the Clinton administration failed to adequately reinstate a semblance of democracy in Haiti under President Jean-Bertrand Aristide. In 2004, the Bush administration simply invaded Haiti and sent Aristide into exile for opposing Washington's wishes for the region.

THE PRIVATE POWERS OF AMERICA'S GLOBAL EMPIRE

American interventions (invasions) throughout the Third World have usually led to the destruction of the autonomy of nations, and the corruption of their governments by turning them into client states. What has also been destroyed by these interventions are the international legal systems' concept of and respect for sovereignty, self-determination and autonomy (the issue of law and the Bush administration will be addressed in Chapter 3). American interventionism in the Third World violates international law as it intrudes on the autonomous self-government of nations. National development is halted and often reversed as the United States works to install governments in Third World nations that collude with the United States to create a "proper investment climate" for US-based corporate interests. Profits, not people, are the bottom-line preoccupation of the architects of Global Empire.

As Transnational Corporations (TNC) have penetrated the markets and governments of Third World nations, subordinating them to the interests of the North's mechanisms for creating the "magic of the market," the WTO, World Bank, IMF, and finance capital worked havoc by employing the doctrine of neoliberalism, structural adjustment programs, and imposing the practice of privatization. The communities of these nation-states were excluded from the decision-making processes of their own governments, while the entire nation would eventually become subordinated to the mandates of international capital. In the process, what was also corrupted were the ideals of a democratic America as the practice of "Global Empire"—representative of private power—uplifted the market as the ultimate arbiter of all values (thereby producing a capacity to know the price of everything and the value of nothing).

The authors of American foreign policy cannot serve two masters. They must choose between two competing sets of values. One set of values *serves* the "Global Community" while the other *exploits* it. Values that serve the Global Community are what have been referred to as *world order values*, *humane governance*, and *inclusionary governance*. Values that serve the Global Empire are the traditional values associated with a class-bias that remains accountable to the North's financial and political elites at the expense of the majority of people throughout the global South. Further, limiting the definition of the national interest to merely encompass concerns with US national defense and national security issues, removes larger concerns from the table; such as labor rights, environment standards, and the constitutive elements of sustainable development. Under the economic model of neoliberalism, all of the values of the Global

Empire have one primary focus and purpose—to serve global capitalism by extending and dominating global markets.

Marcus Raskin notes: "Global capitalism is meant to replace or absorb traditional cultures into the global market economy."[16] The reign of *global capitalism* is synonymous with the reign of *Global Empire* insofar as they are mutually supportive of each other. The reality of this union between capital and empire makes a bastard of democracy because it transforms what was once a "democracy" into an "oligarchy." The problem with oligarchy is that it is not only antidemocratic, but is also irresponsible. It is irresponsible because it wields power without reference to a knowledgeable public. The people become divorced from the realities of genuine facts and knowledge. As this collective ignorance expands, the practice of democracy becomes not merely problematic but virtually impossible. Yet, such an outcome serves the oligarchy. For such a condition removes the possibilities for broad-based dissent, debate, and civil disobedience.

THE DECLINE OF AMERICAN DEMOCRACY
AND THE RISE OF GLOBAL EMPIRE

C. Wright Mills was prophetically accurate when he observed that "Two things are needed in a democracy: articulate and knowledgeable publics, and political leaders who if not men of reason are at least reasonably responsible to such publics."[17] Mills discovered that in post-1945 America, leaders would become less and less responsible to the public and more dedicated to the *higher circles* of power. They were not *representative men*, for their powerful positions were neither based upon merit nor informed by intelligent public debate. Rather, they came to serve in what Mills called, *the American system of organized irresponsibility.*[18] This system has also been called the National Security State by its proponents, the National In-Security State by its detractors. In January 1961, it was referred to as the Military-Industrial Complex. Presidents Truman and Eisenhower presided over the rise of the military-industrial complex (a term coined by Eisenhower himself in his *Farewell Address* to the nation).

In 1961, the inauguration of John F. Kennedy would provide the nation with a set of alternative views and values to the National Security State. Kennedy was sensitive to the demands and nature of Third World nationalism. He was open and responsive to new leaders coming to power that shared a commitment to democratic principles and human rights. Kennedy was not the kind of leader inclined to intervene in Third World nations with American combat troops. He resisted the pressures by members of his own government—his own advisors, the Pentagon, the CIA. Because of this stance, Kennedy encountered opposition from the Joint Chiefs of Staff by virtue of his continuing veto of their plans for intervention in Laos and Vietnam with American combat troops. He favored negotiated settlements and he refused to commit American combat forces to Southeast Asia. In this respect, the pressures of the Cold War did not encourage him to endorse or support plans for Global Empire.

Recognizing the dangers inherent in the nuclear arsenals of the superpowers, Kennedy sought to minimize the risks of having to reach that *hour of maximum danger*. Rather, as expressed in his inaugural address, he sought to create a new balance of power *where the strong are just, the weak secure, and the peace preserved*. In line with pursuing such a course, he designed policies that were to be supportive of social reform under the Alliance for Progress (a social reform foreign policy of the Kennedy administration that was dedicated to land redistribution, replacing dictatorships with democratic governments, and the expansion of educational opportunity throughout Latin America). All of this ended with Kennedy's assassination in 1963 (Chapter 5, *The Hidden Politics of Empire*). The Kennedy years were a short thousand day interlude between aggressive empire building and Kennedy's innovative attempt to create a more peaceful world. The Nuclear Test Ban Treaty of 1963, Kennedy's plans for a phased withdrawal from Vietnam, the support given to democratic governments and withdrawn from dictatorships, all made the Kennedy presidency a unique departure from the practices and plans of the traditional American establishment.

In the aftermath of the assassination of President Kennedy, the course of American foreign policy lost its moral authority. Its strategic integrity was sacrificed in the quagmire of Vietnam. Artificial doctrines such as the *Domino Theory* served as distractions and justifications for an oligarchy committed to the demands of the war machine. Democratic accountability slipped away on the shoals of *Executive Privilege*. Fear-based explanations, such as the *Domino Theory* (if Vietnam fell to the Communists, so would the rest of Asia), were used to supplant reason. While still constitutionally protected, dissent increasingly became equated with disloyalty and even treason.

The truth of the Vietnam War remained sealed off from public scrutiny. The truth remained hidden within the classified National Security Action Memoranda (NSAM) of the Kennedy years, and was contained in a series of classified documents that came to be known as *The Pentagon Papers*. The Johnson and Nixon administrations served the interests of finance capital, oil men, and the military-industrial complex on the domestic front, while expanding the Vietnam War into Laos, Cambodia, and Thailand, on the international front (in that time period these actions were called *incursions*). The public was intentionally divorced from critical sources of knowledge and information that would be necessary to hold the National Security State accountable. It was during this time that the irresponsibility of the men in power abandoned democracy, as they laid the foundation for an oligarchy in the service of empire.

Vietnam became the first of many imperial projects that would follow throughout the lives of successive administrations. A traditionally narrow conception of the national interest would be left to the men of power—the servants, architects, planners, and warriors of Global Empire. In many respects, the American occupation of Iraq represents the perfect expression of a traditionally bound concept of the national interest. It promotes the promise of stability and the introduction of democracy into a region largely unfamiliar with its practice. Yet, the unfolding of increasing resistance and insurgency unmasks the folly and limitations of an ideologically imposed agenda. The escalation of violence and the threat of civil war fail to support the justifications for the intervention and the rationales for a continuing occupation.

An *untraditional approach* to defining the national interest finds new expression in *world order values*. Martin Luther King, Jr., observed: "Injustice anywhere is a threat to justice everywhere." If the *untraditional approach* were to be invoked in the service of American foreign policy, the entire neoliberal regime would collapse and the Pentagon budget would be radically slashed. Further, reliance upon the use of military force would be replaced by diplomacy and discourse. Invoking this path would serve to create a new world in which Global Community could flourish for it would render the processes of global cooperation, peaceful engagement, and democratic enlargement more attainable. As for the United States itself, it would find itself on the path to becoming a post-Imperial America.

Let us contrast the traditional approach of US foreign policy with *world order values*. Within the category of economic well-being, traditional US foreign policy argues that military spending is more important than promoting the economic and social well-being of the world's poverty-stricken people. In contrast, the proponents of world order values argue that military spending distracts from the effort to eliminate world poverty and the general achievement of economic and social well-being.

The *traditional approach* to meeting the demands of the national interest finds itself locked in the dead-end of *war without end*. To engage in a failed policy of *war without end* is the consequence of reliance upon a traditionally constructed understanding of what constitutes genuine security. It is the view that the past is forever prologue, that there are no alternatives for a *realist*, and that it is only *utopian* to believe that another world is possible. Such are the basic beliefs of the cynics and hawks who seek to govern America's Global Empire. It is their "realism" that makes them confident that militarism is the only guaranteed path to a continuation of American hegemony. They also recognize that American hegemony would have to be enforced.

It is understandable that they would only be able to anticipate global resistance to the imposition of American hegemony and domination. Resistance is the predictable consequence of imposing power on those who wish to be free. Hence, the advocates and architects of American's Global Empire are destined to incite a global revolution. Inadvertently, they are assisting the rise of Global Community—a community forged in opposition to such an empire. In this scenario, the cynics and the hawks have set the stage for their own demise.

International relations in the twenty-first century may go one of two directions; either in the direction of continuous war or in a direction that emphasizes cooperation coupled with the pursuit of peace. Professor Marcus Raskin has summed up the two trajectories with great insight in observing:

> If the century is dominated by conflict, it will be a terrifying time. Even a benign Pax Americana will not be able to contain threats, ethnic and religious wars stemming from hatred, and partition that may result in the subjugation of minorities within a geographic boundary ... American military planners and warrior-minded presidents present preemptive military activity as the way to keep "stability" or preempt attacks on the United States. Those who exercise control over the various forms of state violence will be seen as altogether necessary and rational.[19]

Throughout the remainder of this chapter, I shall delineate how the traditional approach of giving priority to the people of one nation (pursuing only its narrowly defined ideas of what constitutes the national interest, defense, and security) serves to expose: (1) the vulnerabilities of empire, (2) the abuses of empire, and (3) the occupations of empire (intellectual paradigms, ideological justifications, the geographical occupation of sovereign nations, a limited conception of "security"). In combination, I will argue that these three categories serve to explain the failure of Global Empire. Correspondingly, I will highlight the contrasting vision of the rise of Global Community as an antidote to the fantasies of trying to build a Global Empire under the rubric of a *Pax Americana* that is the product of an oligarchy and grounded within a narrowly defined conception of what constitutes the *national interest.*

The Vulnerabilities of Empire

Our starting point in assessing the vulnerabilities of the United States, as an empire, must begin with a question: *When did the United States stop being a democracy (or a republic) and begin its transformation into an empire?* The answer to this question is important for a variety of reasons. It is impossible to arrive at a synthesis between democracy and empire. Following Hegel, we may argue that democracy is a political thesis, while empire is its antithesis. Unification between the two is not possible in either theory or practice. A democracy is founded upon a set of practices, values, and policies that are antithetical to the pursuit of empire. True democracy strives toward an inclusive political community and an inclusionary state. Alternatively, empire strives toward domination, hegemony, and oligarchy in the service of an exclusionary state.

In light of this conclusion, we are forced to address two interrelated questions. The first question is: *Where and when in the historical time-line did the transformation from democracy to empire begin?* The second question is: *How did a revolution in national values and global strategy transform the American republic into a would-be empire, thereby condoning the diminishment of democratic ideals, constitutional protections, and the rule of law?*

Approaching the first question, we find that various scholars have posited different historical starting times or events for the transformation of the United States from a republic to an empire. Some believe "the new American empire has been a long time in the making. Its roots go back to the nineteenth century; when the United States declared all of Latin America its sphere of influence and busily enlarged its own territory at the expense of the indigenous people of North America, as well as British, French, and Spanish colonists, and neighboring Mexico."[20] Then, at the edge of the twentieth century came the Spanish American War. It launched the United States into the business of setting up military bases around the globe, starting with Central America, various islands in the Caribbean, Hawaii, Guam, and the Philippines.

Other scholars have traditionally delineated America's historical turning point from a republic into an empire at the close of World War II.[21] In 1940, Roosevelt demanded from Churchill "a blank check" on all of Great Britain's transatlantic possessions. Great Britain had become an American client state.[22] With the decolonization of the British Empire, the United States emerged from the war as the inheritor of a colonial legacy that would be re-labeled, the "Free World." The freedom of the so-called Free World should not be confused with political freedom, civil rights, or human rights. Within this "Free World" there were dictatorships and tyrants. Those leaders were useful because they made their markets and economies open to the needs and requirements of US capital, multinational corporations, and the US military. Maintaining commercial access to and investment in foreign markets was always at the heart of the imperial enterprise.

Following World War II, the United States was determined to prevent the extension of socialist alternatives or of communist influence. Asia, Latin America, and Africa would become the battlegrounds for a Cold War. An informal empire of American client states was created throughout continental East Asia as well as Southeast Asia.[23] The great expectations associated with the informal American empire inspired Washington's policymakers to begin a process of "over-committing" the United States to support "free peoples who are resisting attempted subjugation by armed minorities or by outside pressures."[24]

Both the pledge and the process of such a commitment continued through the period of America's involvement in the Vietnam War and beyond. In fact, it may be argued "those who chart America's course do so with a clearly defined purpose in mind. That purpose is to preserve and, where both feasible and conducive to US interests, to expand an American imperium."[25] Therefore, *in answer to the first question posed*, we could argue that it was the Truman presidency that marked the critical historical juncture when the United States began its transformation from a democracy into an empire. In fact, on the domestic front, America started to become a *National Security State* under Truman's watch as the Cold War reshaped both the domestic and foreign affairs of the nation.

Approaching the second question, we may argue that America's transition from the values of a republic to the pursuit of empire was a transition forged within the governing bodies of the American-Imperium and its policymakers. The transition was largely based on a desire for economic and political supremacy of global affairs. The leaders of an embryonic American Empire were primarily concerned with opening global markets. As their predominant concern, it led them to regard a commitment to global openness as central to their strategy for success. At the center of this strategy for global openness was a desire to remove barriers that would inhibit the movement of goods, capital, ideas, and people.

Through NATO, contractual agreements with Germany, and a security treaty with Japan, the United States forged a configuration of power within the industrial core of Eurasia. America's leadership assumed that by supporting multilateral trade and helping to promote economic growth the US geopolitical preponderance would be automatically secured. As a result, America's leadership failed to see what would become a costly Cold War. Exaggerations and overestimations about the Kremlin's intentions and the nationalist upsurge throughout the Third World allowed US policymakers to misconstrue the unfolding of a rising Global Community.

By the 1970s, the cracks in the empire were beginning to appear. The tragedy of the Vietnam War (1964–1974), the waste of money on the arms race with the

Soviet Union, the wars on the periphery of the Third World from El Salvador, Nicaragua, and most of Central America to those fought in Nigeria, the Congo, and throughout South Africa would prove to be the undoing of America's margin of economic superiority. By the 1990s and certainly at the dawn of the twenty-first century, it is clear that Japan, Germany, and the European Union, as well as China and India, were powers on the rise—prepared to eclipse the United States and its claim to world domination. In short, America's leadership gambled and lost when it decided in the late 1940s that its ultimate objective would be the creation of an open and integrated international order based on the principles of democratic capitalism, with the United States as the ultimate guarantor of order and enforcer of norms.[26]

Within this understanding lies insight into one of the greatest vulnerabilities of the American empire as it seeks to be a global empire. *Therefore, in answer to the second question, it can be argued that:* (1) The diminishment of democratic ideals and the rule of law is a necessary consequence of embarking upon global empire and the domination of capital. The redefinition of America's global strategy placed the United States on a militaristic path. Militarism in the service of empire is inherently at odds with democratic ideals and democratic constraints. *On a global scale, we may also assert that*: (2) The demands and requirements of Global Empire are antithetical and hostile to the demands and requirements of a functional Global Community.

It is impossible to have a seamless "open-ended international order" measured by American standards. This is because of the inherent uniqueness and diversity of global cultures, economies, and political systems. This insight brings us to a fundamental realization about the inevitable vulnerabilities of empire. As we have already noted, one such vulnerability is the failed synthesis of empire and democracy. Democracy stands for representative civic ideals, while empire stands for the rule of an oligarchy that sees itself as responsible only to itself.

The vulnerabilities of Global Empire in an interdependent world

In an interdependent world, a peacefully functioning Global Community is truly impossible when subjected to the competing demands of Global Empire. The practices of Global Empire transcend the barriers and prohibitions of international law. In so doing, the effect of these practices allows the power of imperial rule to embark upon a dismantling of all of the elements essential to maintaining human community. The impossibility of a functioning Global Community in contention with the claims of Global Empire arises on all possible policy fronts: environment; human rights and social justice; economic well-being; peace. For example, in the area of human rights, the architects of the American Empire have maintained that the United States should never decrease its military spending in order to eliminate inequity. Alternatively, the proponents of a peaceful Global Community have consistently stated that maintaining the present levels of military spending by the United States undermines global peace by perpetuating inequities of wealth, privilege, and opportunity.

The radically conflicting policy goals and global objectives that divide these two camps comprise the epicenter of a struggle between two different worlds. The proponents of Global Empire have sought to determine the nature of the global contract. Alternatively, the proponents of an inclusive Global Community have sought to remake the global contract through inclusive decision making at every level—through multilateral means, through balanced decision-making processes, and through forms of diplomacy and negotiation that recognize the growing interdependence of the world's economy.

Unfortunately, like President Truman, President George W. Bush demonstrated a parochialism that caused him to disregard contrary views, whether they were the views of allies or potential foes. Instead of broadening the political environment in which the US citizenry can operate, Bush has tried to shrink it under the presumed legal authority of the USA Patriot Act—just as Truman's leadership intensified the ideological fervor of anticommunism. Just as Truman narrowed the channels for policy choices and waged a long-term global Cold War—Bush has followed a similar course in the name of conducting a global "war on terrorism." Given the nature of these choices, we can argue that the second Bush presidency has pursued a path wherein "militarism and imperialism threaten democratic government at home just as they menace the independence and sovereignty of other countries."[27] Despite these trends, the Bush administration "seems not to grasp the relationship between its military unilateralism and the collateral damage it is doing to international commerce, an activity that depends on *mutually beneficial* relationships among individuals, businesses, and countries to function well."[28]

A similar argument was made as early 1990 with the collapse of the Soviet Union. In his book, *Bound to Lead,*[29] Joseph Nye put forward a thesis regarding the nature of power itself. He argued that the nature of power has changed as the world has become more interdependent. In this new world, both Non-Governmental Organizations (NGOs), as well as TNCs have acquired more power. Because of these realities he argues that the real challenge for the United States is how to manage a transition to interdependence. Nye concluded with the finding that all of the attention being given to US national decline only served to obscure the real challenge of transitioning to a more interdependent world. Certainly his conclusion gives at least some credence to the idea that there is a rising Global Community. However, the Bush-2 regime rejected the challenge of transitioning to a more interdependent world. Instead, it chose the path of militarism—a US Global Empire was to be put in place by military force, not consensus. In the immediate aftermath of September 11, 2001, the Bush-2 regime would swing the focus of policymakers away from interdependence toward a projection of American power—primarily through the exercise of unilateralist military imperialism.

However, in assessing the choice of the United States to embrace and become a Global Empire, Richard Falk has asserted "the idea of a global empire administered from Washington is also a dead end. It rests on a premise of permanent militarization and submission of other constellations of power and influence."[30] The problem is that throughout world history the perception of such imperial ambitions has "generated a reactive formation among states—alliances to defeat, or at least contain, the quest for global empire. There is every reason to suppose that the remainder of the world will not accept, without mounting some sort of resistance, this American bid to establish such a global empire."[31]

Given this analysis, the question becomes: *How and why the United States should change course and embark upon an exodus from empire?* The question is critical for it allows us to recognize that our current course is not *inevitable*, that the future remains open, that hegemonic enterprises are historically condemned to either failure or forced transitions, and that imperial ambitions are able to go only so far and no further. With this in mind, we turn our discussion to the challenge of beginning an *exodus from empire*.

Exodus from empire by relinquishing hegemonic/imperial ambitions

The world at the close of the Cold War and with the onset of globalization has become an increasingly multilayered and multicentric world. Unfortunately, the elite policymakers of US foreign policy have so narrowed the conceptualization of what is in the national interest that they remain committed to an expansionary economic policy that simply creates new capital that seeks a home overseas—or in dubious fiscal schemes on Wall Street (Enron). At the same time, radical free-market policies (neoliberalism and privatization) have depressed the incomes of working people in both the global North and the global South, while wealth continues to concentrate in the hands of a plutocracy. It is an economy that may be described as exhibiting overproduction, overcapacity, and overaccumulation.

The real solution to this crisis can be stated simply: wages in both the Third World and among the working classes in the North must rise. A narrow focus on the problems of poverty and austerity is no longer sufficient. What is needed is a clear recognition that without growth Third World countries can neither service their debts nor prevent political upheaval. In First World countries, wages must rise as well, and the corporate "outsourcing" of jobs must end. Hence, for both First and Third World nations, an inclusive form of governance needs to come into play that is capable of replacing the logic of Global Empire and corporate capital. Essentially, this means that a US "grand strategy"—based upon economic and political expansion must be replaced because it is inherently fluid, unstable and volatile. A perfect example of this phenomenon is the US/Mexico crisis over immigration. The passage of NAFTA led to declining wages on both sides of the border. The corporate interests that engineered NAFTA became the same interests that tore over 500 industries out of Mexico when cheaper labor markets were created in Asia. The proverbial "race to the bottom" was made possible by corporate decisions that transferred jobs overseas, thereby leading to greater unemployment in Mexico which also served to accelerate immigration across the US/Mexico border. On the US side, business interests silently welcomed undocumented workers that would not be offered health care benefits, decent wages, or become a tax liability.

In this environment there is not a cohesive national interest because various ruling classes are involved in a conflict-ridden struggle to decide what the grand strategy of the US Global Empire should become in relationship to the demands of international capital and finance. Despite the reality that the lives of billions of people will be affected by these decisions, as far as the plutocracy is concerned the majority of the people on the planet never even enter into this equation. It is for this reason that the

> idea of global politics calls into question the traditional demarcations between the domestic and foreign, and between the territorial and the non-territorial, found in modern conceptions of 'the political'... Global problems highlight the richness and complexity of the interconnections that now transcend states and societies in the global order.[32]

A global politics for a Global Community has the capacity to embrace "world order values." Such a global politics would serve to overcome the deficiencies of traditional national interest formulations and, at the same time, assist the historical process of embarking upon an exodus from empire. The rise of a viable Global Community and a post–Imperial America is dependent upon such a global politics because the boundary between foreign and domestic has been increasingly eclipsed by the forces that set globalization into motion. If those forces can be made accountable to a global politics that is democratic, it would be possible to shape national and international policies that serve to enhance inclusive forms of governance. In contrast, the Bush Doctrine centers its considerations on what the policy elite of neoconservatives in Washington want for the world. By failing to see an emerging global politics of interdependence and interconnectedness, the Bush administration remains locked in a position of refusing to abandon the demarcations between domestic and foreign.

Regardless of the difficulties and uncertainties that will inevitably accompany such a re-orientation of values, priorities, focus and resources, a "decentering" from the pull of the US Global Empire is both needed and essential to move toward a more peaceful world. While the process of "decentering" is likely to be a dangerous and awkward one, "the major players of today's world order may well have to imagine and create a world beyond hegemony—perhaps some more collaborative entity to perform hegemony's essential role of being stabilizer to an otherwise unstable system."[33] A more collaborative entity would be made up of institutions, individuals, groups, and cooperative norms that are formulated in such a way that greater adherence would be given to the task of addressing the problems of the entire Global Community—not just some privileged sectors of it.

The failure of Global Empire and its reluctance to alter course toward a process of decentering from unilateralist militarism could easily result in "a high-risk rivalry, wasteful of resources, endangering catastrophic warfare among state actors, and shifting priorities of policymakers away from human rights, environmental sustainability, and equitable development."[34] The course of unilateralist militarism has already created another difficulty for Washington policymakers. In the case of Iraq, as previously had been the case in Vietnam, popular resistance to foreign interventions has increased and multiplied. In this regard, it is ironic that the Bush administration's expressed desire to bring democracy to the Middle East has resulted in a popular expression of democratic aspiration through resistance to empire. According to some scholars, "The Iraq War was the point at which neo-conservative ideology became fully operational. It no longer depended on the lifeblood of academic symposia at Washington think tanks. It had the full might of history's most powerful military force at its disposal."[35]

Military force alone has never been sufficient to be the final arbiter of political outcomes. In fact, when military force has been coupled with particular conceptions of empire, the two have often wound up embedded in a strategic culture that can place severe constraints on the ability of policymakers and elites to undertake strategic adjustments. The failure to undertake strategic adjustments exposes one of the great vulnerabilities of empire and empire building. Given the recalcitrance of the Bush administration to question its imperial adventure in the Middle East, it is doubtful that either democracy or the rule of law will see the light of day in the daily lives of average people throughout the region.

The resistance to foreign control in the Middle East is a matter of historical record. Part of the lack of recognition of the inevitability of such resistance can be traced to older histories of the Western subjugation of the Middle East. The focus of these earlier works was primarily centered upon how this region fit into the overall process of European expansion, while "considerably less attention has been paid to the degree of resistance that this process engendered, and to the stubborn perseverance and changing forms of this resistance."[36] The failure of most Western scholars and leaders to fully comprehend the lessons of the history in this region has contributed to not only misunderstandings about the cultures, but also the inevitability of guerilla resistance to foreign control and occupation.

The vulnerabilities of empire in a democratic order

Charles A. Kupchan's book, *The Vulnerability of Empire* concluded with a last chapter entitled, "Grand Strategy and Peaceful Change: Avoiding the Vulnerability of Empire." Kupchan posited that several factors account for the more moderate and self-limiting behavior of democratic states. The four factors are as follows:

1. First, democratically elected elites do not need to rely on external ambition to legitimate their rule.
2. Second, the free exchange of ideas that takes place in democratic polities is likely to expose and undermine fallacious strategic concepts.
3. Third, because democratic societies are less monolithic in political and ideological terms than autocratic ones, opposition parties and interest groups are almost always ready and willing to take the lead in pushing alternate policies whenever setbacks or incoming information discredits reigning strategic concepts ... A monolithic political and ideological environment left elites entrapped in a strategic culture of their own making.
4. Fourth, democratic forms of governance, because they provide for the regular turnover of leaders, moderate processes of entrapment.[37]

None of these four criteria actually apply to the situation that the United States currently finds itself in. To begin with, it is not that the aforementioned points do not have relevance in a particular context, because they do. The problem is that the circumstances associated with elite planning by the neoconservatives who took power, serve to cancel out the relevance of these points. For example, the legitimacy of Bush's presidency was already in question given the disputed election of 2000. Also, the administration seemed to simply drift until the terrorist attacks of September 11, 2001.

As to the second point, both internally and externally, the Bush administration was not noted for engaging in a free exchange of ideas. Secretary of State Colin Powell was largely frozen out of the final discussions and consultations with regard to going to war with Iraq. Various agencies of the government had conflicting interpretations and ideas about the validity of certain strategic concepts being advanced by the neoconservative agenda. The UN was halted and blocked in its efforts to determine whether or not weapons of mass destruction were even present in Iraq. The dialog that normally would take place between members of the NATO alliance was frozen out of consideration by preordained plans that were largely accepted without question throughout the executive branch. Finally, in the aftermath of the country's war hysteria and the passage of the USA Patriot Act, dissent became equated with treason (see: Chapter 3).

As to the third point, while democratic societies are usually less monolithic in political and ideological terms, the right wing direction of the United States has been increasing in both influence and power ever since the presidency of Richard Nixon. In assessing the ideological commitment of the neoconservatives, some authors have argued that they constituted a new political interest group that exhibited tremendous reticence about their true objectives. This is a very important criticism of the neoconservatives, "namely that they have not come clean and are not coming clean with the country."[38] If the citizens of the democracy are entitled to the truth, they are certainly entitled to hearing truth-based presentations by their government. It seems that, "on Iraq, deception had the upper hand ... If there is a case to be made, the governments and advocates within governments should make it truthfully rather than using the techniques of mass persuasion we thought we were banning from the world when we broke down the Berlin Wall.[39] Unfortunately, the Bush administration followed in the steps of Leo Strauss who has been credited with developing the philosophy of mass deception.[40]

As to the fourth and final point, Kupchan argues that because democratic forms of governance provide for the regular turnover of leaders, it follows that this turnover would serve to moderate processes of entrapment. In the context of American decision making in the Middle East, that particular assumption is not borne out in the history of the twentieth century. To begin with, American foreign policy was never the same after King Ibn Saud of Saudi Arabia met with President Franklin Roosevelt in 1945 and pledged a steady oil supply in return for US protection. Ever since that time the United States has propped up many dictatorships throughout the Middle East and North Africa. These states include Iran, Iraq, Syria, Lebanon, Jordan, Turkey, Saudi Arabia, Afghanistan, and Pakistan.

Two full decades before September 11, 2001, President Jimmy Carter decided that the Persian Gulf region would be placed in the uppermost tier of US geopolitical priorities. From 1945 to 1979, the primacy of US policy in the Gulf region has simply been to ensure stability and American access to oil. That strategy minimized overt US military involvement. All of that changed in 1980. In the aftermath of the Iranian revolution and the Soviet invasion of Afghanistan, the strategic centrality of the entire Persian Gulf region rose in prominence because of how these two events directly threatened the West's oil supply.

President Carter concluded that the United States had to assume a central role in determining exactly what changes the United States would or would not accommodate in the Persian Gulf. In his State of the Union address, the president announced the Carter Doctrine: "An attempt by any outside force to gain control of the Persian Gulf region will be regarded as an assault on the vital interests of the United States of America, and such an assault will be repelled by any means necessary, including military force."[41] According to Andrew J. Bacevich, "From Carter's time down to the present day, the doctrine bearing his name has remained sacrosanct."[42] In light of this history, the general consistency and policymaking from the time of Carter to the second Bush presidency discounts the assertion that a regular turnover of leaders helps to moderate processes of entrapment. In the case of US involvement in the Persian Gulf, from administration to administration, an increasingly militarized American commitment has been the hallmark of every administration since Carter, regardless of party.

This short analysis of the vulnerabilities of empire has begun the process of revealing how a narrowly defined idea of what constitutes the national interest may in fact be highly detrimental to the genuine aspirations, security, and interests of the entire nation. In keeping with the thesis of this book it begs the question, stated at the outset: "Is an exodus from empire in fact preferable to the vision of the neoconservative's dream to establish a global American empire?"

In the shadow of the second Iraq War, the damage done to the integrity of American democracy on the domestic front seems to have a correspondingly tragic impact upon the hopes for the realization of democracy on the international front. The process weakening the balance of power within the American government had been prophetically foretold throughout the work of C. Wright Mills in the late 1950s. Writing on the collapsing scheme of the "balance of power" within the American government, he concluded,

> it is not merely a framework within which contending pressures jockey for position and make politics ... There is no effective countervailing power against the coalition of big businessmen ... Those having real power in the American state today are not merely brokers of power, resolvers of conflict, or compromisers of varied and clashing interest—they represent and indeed embody quite specific national interests and policies.[43]

While describing the birth of a whole new set of institutional arrangements for the practices and centers of power within the American government, Mills went even deeper in his attempt to reveal the ideological core driving the bureaucratic changes. At the ideological core of this process he identified "quite specific national interests and policies." The clash of interests envisioned within the texts of the Federalist Papers was to be mitigated by the separate but equal centers of power located in the executive, congress, and judicial branch. Now, the force of these countervailing powers had all collapsed, victimized by a new situation in which "administration replaces electoral politics; the maneuvering of cliques replaced the clash of parties."[44] Nowhere is this phenomenon more evident than within the hawkish clique of neoconservatives who guide the foreign policy of the second Bush administration.[45]

In the spirit of C. Wright Mills, my critique of the new American empire identifies a similar culprit as the driving-force of its intentions, purposes, and policies—*a national interest divorced from the larger human interest*. The national interest of the Bush-2 regime is content to abandon the constraints of the Geneva Convention and give authorization to the practice of torture. The Bush-2 regime has found it convenient to withdraw from international treaties on arms control, such as the ABM Treaty of 1972, so that it could embark upon the weaponization of space under the rubric of *National Missile Defense*. The Bush-2 regime betrays the majority of America's citizens as it depletes funding for national health care, education, housing, eliminating poverty, and job creation as it rewards its corporate backers who are predominantly oil men, weapons dealers, polluters, and pharmaceutical companies. In short, the second Bush-2 regime fails to even advance a democratically inclusive national interest. It is totally devoted to a minority of powerfully placed centers of wealth that pillage both the citizens of America and the citizens of the globe.

The larger human interest takes many shapes and forms. In part, it is expressed in international law, treaties, covenants, as well as through the UN, NGOs, and social movements. The Global Community, to which I refer, is the sum total of a larger collective human interest that presents itself as a powerfully rising force against the imperial pretensions of the Bush-2 regime. The larger human interest knows no borders. It comprises "world order values" that are inherently opposed to a world based on war and conquest. The Charter of the UN begins with a firm commitment to prevent war, advance peace, and work toward the peaceful resolution of international disputes. Those commitments are commitments to the larger human interest. Those commitments are the most basic elements of the foundation on which a rising Global Community can emerge.

The authors of the US Global Empire have boxed themselves into a paradox. On the one hand, they engage in the pursuit of empire and imperial projects in order to promote global security while failing to recognize that such a pursuit is actually antithetical to humanity's global aspirations for genuine human rights, security, and peace. If the leadership of the Bush-2 regime reviewed history, they would learn a lot about the Spanish Empire from the late fifteenth to eighteenth centuries. The Spaniards established the most extensive empire the world has ever known. Its reach extended from Naples and the Netherlands to the Philippines. However, the measure of its real success was not predicated upon brute force. Its power and its conquests proved to be deceptive in terms of explaining its actual successes. Spain's rise to power was actually made possible by the collaboration of international business interests, including Italian financiers, German technicians, and Dutch traders, in the task of setting up networks of contact ranging across the world's oceans. At the height of its apparent power, the Spanish Empire was in reality a global enterprise in which Spaniards, Portuguese, Basque, Aztec,

Genoese, Chinese, Flemish, West African, Incan, and Neapolitan all played an essential role. In the final analysis, it was this diversity of resources and peoples that made Spain's power so overwhelming. Yet, in the end, its reliance upon war and conquest brought the empire to ruin. Writing in the 1640, Diego Saavedra Fajardo ruefully commented: "If Spain had spent less on war and more on peace, it would have achieved world domination, but its greatness has made it careless, and the riches that would have made it invincible have passed to other nations."[46]

The human suffering that was incurred by the Spanish Empire (1492–1763) resulted in a corresponding hatred for the empire by the rest of the world community. Like the American response to those individuals and nations practicing Islam, the question became: "Why do they hate us so much?" In answer, through the lens of the historian, Henry Kamen suggests: "Like Americans and Russians of the twentieth century, the Spaniards had to learn to live with universal hatred ... Protected by their own view of how the world should be run most Spaniards were incapable of seeing that there was a price to be paid for their imperial role."[47]

The history of imperialism involves the creation of great human suffering. The reality of this suffering cannot be reduced to Pentagon authored terms such as *collateral damage*. For the human costs, sacrifices, and sufferings that are borne by all people—as a consequence of empire's imperial project—will eventually have to be dealt with in terms of their harmful effects. While this notion may not be easily calculated with mathematical efficiency, it can be measured in terms of a moral equation of sorts. What this means is that the most developed countries are usually the ones to engage in imperial adventures. It is they who are the chief upholders of the *might-makes-right* principle. Their imposition of this principle undermines the very democratic principles that they have said was their goal to realize in the developing countries.

There are results to be reckoned with when it comes to the infliction of human suffering and the abuses of empire. In this critical respect, the recognition of the abuses of empire serves to reveal another of the many vulnerabilities of empire. Having embarked upon an overview of some of the various vulnerabilities of empire, we now turn to a specific discussion of the abuses of empire.

The Abuses of Empire

Conceptually speaking, the abuses of empire are both *internal* and *external* The abuses of empire are internal to the extent that national elites of empire impose within their own sovereign borders policies and practices that abuse citizen and noncitizen alike. For example, the limitation or the suspension of constitutionally guaranteed rights for its citizens creates an atmosphere of disregard for the rights of citizenship itself. The denial of political, social, and/or economic inclusion, as well as civil protections to minorities and excluded groups, becomes a denial of benefits and protections to be afforded to all people by virtue of their human rights. The abuses of empire are external to the degree that they are carried out beyond the sovereign entity of the homeland of the empire, but are carried out in its name, nevertheless. The foreign policy of the empire transports its domestic abuses abroad, without fear of constitutional or other legal restraints upon its actions. In turn, abuses carried out abroad will eventually find their way back home to their point of origin. The moral calculation is circular—those who live by the sword shall die by the sword.

Practically speaking, the abuses of empire are fluid between the internal and external contexts in which they occur. The abuses of empire, whether internal— as with the Native American tribes of North America—or external—as with the people of North and South Vietnam (1964–1974), or the Iraqi prisoners at Abu Ghraib, become a part of a common history of the genocidal nature of imperial ambition and the demands of empire. Insofar as human rights abuses in one sphere (nation or region) become actualized in another sphere (nation or region), the common thread between them is that there is a *modus operandi* of criminal conduct. Imperial ambition opens the door for war crimes and crimes against humanity. It is the very character and nature of such imperial projects that leads them into a moral quagmire from which they cannot emerge with clean hands. The moral quagmire becomes a political *crisis of legitimacy*. Without legitimacy, the imperi- al quest is doomed to eventually collapse under the heavy weight of its own con- tradictions and the various forms of resistance that it will engender among its victims. Additionally, there will probably be a "blowback" effect, where the sins of empire that are committed abroad return to the homeland of their imperial origin.

The internal and the external contexts in which the abuses of empire emerge are covered over with a host of justifications, rationalizations, and ideologies—all designed to support the imperial project. The ideology of conquest will produce the justifications for genocide, while the imperial demands of empire can then rationalize the genocide as *Manifest Destiny*, *National Security*, or some other "doctrine" (Truman, Nixon, Carter, Reagan, Bush-1, Clinton, Bush-1 and 2). Whatever label is applied, these are imperial doctrines that serve a dual role—first, they justify the commitment to and expenditures for imperial conquest; second, they are undertaken to achieve what a particular constituency or coalition of powerful constituencies want to achieve in the name of the *national interest*.

In his book, *A Little Matter of Genocide: Holocaust and Denial in the Americas, 1492 to the Present*, Professor Ward Churchill addresses the fact that

the situation of Native North Americans … remains much as it has been since the moment the Old World predator landed in this hemisphere. Liquidated to the extent deemed necessary or convenient by the invader … we are maintained alive at all primarily as a matter of utility by our colonizers, and then only in a form considered acceptable to them. No amount of humanitarian rhetoric, demographic sleights of hand, or deformity and denial of history can alter the substance of these essential realities.[48]

Furthermore, this process has not ended. Rather, "the genocide which has been perpetrated against the indigenous people of this continent is an experience unpar- alleled in its scope, magnitude, and duration … it is a process which is ongoing."[49] From the Senora to the Arctic, North America's indigenous peoples have been dispossessed of nearly all of their original territory, with the residue—about 2 percent— held under a colonial "trust" authority by the United States and Canada. Ironically, the presumable useless fragments of geography set aside to keep Native Americans out of sight and mind have turned out to be some of the most resource-rich on the planet. Given these facts, Native Americans should be among the most affluent sectors of the population. Instead, they are the absolute poorest. The reason for this paradox is clear: "the riches of North America's indigenous nations continue to be channeled into the settler's economy."[50]

The abuses of empire and the goals of the imperial project know no bounds or limits when it comes to saying one thing and doing precisely the opposite. Since the founding of the American Republic, a predominantly white elite has governed the decision-making processes of government and defined the quality of governance. The highly exclusionary character of this style of governance has left minorities of every kind—women, Native Americans, African-Americans, the young. All of these constituencies have been effectively deprived of representation in the halls of power. A predominantly privileged white elite has managed to develop "legal means" to repress, to exclude, and to enslave entire peoples and groups (*discrete and insular minorities*).

The threat of the *tyranny of the majority* was constitutionally addressed with the passage the 13th, 14th, and 15th Amendments. In particular, it was with the *equal protection* clause of the 14th Amendment that the weight of socioeconomic and sociopolitical dominance by a predominantly white majority was balanced against a judicial test of *strict scrutiny* in areas where minorities had been at an historical disadvantage. However, outside of the protections provided to persons by virtue of their citizenship as Americans, the victims of empire were to remain relegated to the status of slaves or, in the parlance of Bush-2 administration doublespeak, *enemy combatants* (not to be afforded either *due process* or the protections of prisoners of war pursuant to the Geneva Convention).

A thesis statement regarding the abuses of empire

Historically, the task of nation building exhibits many of the same traits associated with the task of empire building. Both these historical tasks have employed ruthless, contradictory, hypocritical, and murderous means to achieve their respective ends. In the case of nation building, the initial tasks involve deciding which groups will be included within the nation's power structure—with the full rights of citizenship—and who will be excluded (deprived of the full rights of citizenship). Understood in this way, citizenship may be seen as an institutional mechanism for establishing boundaries of inclusion or exclusion in the nation-state.

Usually, the process of exclusion leads to a mobilization of the excluded group(s) to seek inclusion—or at least demand to have their rights recognized. At the international level, the recognition of a right to self-determination and respect for national sovereignty are central to the realization of national independence. The expression of independence means freedom from the instruction of colonialism, exploitation, occupation, or foreign intrusion into the nation's life without the consent of its people. The independence sought is primarily expressed through the eventual realization of self-determination and sovereignty. The goal is to achieve independence from either great power manipulation or the imperial projects of Global Empire. The ideal nature of global citizenship (within the community of nations) should find its actualization in its ability to draw a clear line between national self-determination versus the claims of Global Empire. However, in practice, the lines between the world of sovereign nation-states and the intrusions of Global Empire are often blurred. For example, in the multilateral system of the early twenty-first century, the instructions of the US-directed IMF, WTO, and World Bank have created a true global crisis of legitimacy. These multilateral institutions have claimed to pursue universal interests—such as poverty reduction. In reality, poverty has widened, inequality has deepened, and socioeconomic exclusion from the promised benefits of global markets all remain in place as the only universal realities for the vast majority on the edges of the Global Empire. These are the conditions that constitute the realities of the *New World Order*.

In short, the destabilizing effects of corporate-driven globalization—supported by the US Global Empire—have successfully excluded not just indigenous people, but also the workers, the poor, and middle classes of every nation. Global levels of poverty have been increasing since the 1990s, resulting in over 2 billion people living on less than a dollar a day. Further, the financial disparities effectuated by globalization account for widening gaps within and between nations, thereby signaling not only a growing lack of equality but also raising serious questions about the legitimacy of the global system itself. As a consequence of these trends, the anger of the excluded has begun to find expression through violence, terrorism, and a growing opposition to the intrusions of Global Empire.[51]

Hence, my thesis regarding the abuses of empire emerges even more clearly: The abuses of empire conducted internally (within the homeland of the empire) are manifested in the abuses that the empire conducts externally (on the international stage).

There is a corollary to this thesis: The abuses of empire conducted externally (on the international stage) will be manifested domestically (within the homeland of the empire) in terms of a "blowback" effect from those abuses.

To see the inherent linkage between the abuses of empire internally and externally is of vital importance. For if we are to fully grasp the domestic and foreign policy of President George W. Bush, the interaction and linkage between the internal demands of empire and the external functions of empire must be understood and seen clearly. Therefore, in order to comprehend the current imperial project of the US Global Empire, it would be helpful to briefly turn back to the internal realities of American life and law. On the one hand, if the American empire is truly governed by law—understood as "justice for all," "equal protection," the protection and extension of political and civil rights—then it must produce just outcomes. On the other hand, if the American empire is actually using a corrupt form of legalism to justify its abuses at home and its imperial adventures abroad, then both the citizens of the United States and the citizens of the world have a moral and a legal right to resist and actively oppose such an unjust global order.

Take, for example, the treatment of Native American Indians by the US government. By tracing the evolution of federal Indian law, Professor Ward Churchill has shown how the premises set forth therein not only spilled over to non-Indians in the United States, but were also adapted for application abroad. There is a connection between the nature and purpose of the domestic laws of the United States and the application of the principles of the domestic laws as the United States moves into the international arena.

On this point, the United States is readily distinguishable from other countries, Chief Justice John Marshall opined in 1803, because it is a "nation of laws, not of men." Churchill takes Marshall at his word by exploring how the United States has consistently employed a corrupt form of legalism as a means of establishing colonial control and empire. In his book, *Perversions of Justice: Indigenous Peoples and Anglo-American Law*, he demonstrates how this *nation of laws* has so completely subverted the *law of nations* that the current US-dominated international order ends up like the United States itself—functioning in a manner diametrically opposed to the ideals of freedom and democracy it professes to embrace.[52] (It is a theme that will be explicated further in Chapter 3.)

From this perspective, we can identify the trajectory of America's imperial logic from its earliest expressions all the way to the present *New World Order*. The reality presented by the history of American law and power is that this *new world order* is not that much different from the *old world order* (except for the fact that the evolution of military technology and weaponry has refined the means of waging wars). Beyond the differences wrought by advancing military technologies there are few real differences.

The *New World Order* is new in the sense that there are increasing pressures from globalization. These pressures include the internationalization of the economies of the global North, the penetration of multinational corporate power and finance capital into the markets and economies of the global South, and the application of a neoliberal economic model onto Third World nations (i.e., Thailand, Mexico, Argentina, Indonesia) designed to replace the sovereign rule of those nation-states with the dictates of the IMF, WTO, and World Bank. With this economic penetration has come a sharpening of class differences on a global scale. Still, in the final analysis, "the basic rules of world order remain as they have always been: the rule of law for the weak, the rule of force for the strong; the principles of 'economic rationality' for the weak, state power and intervention for the strong."[53] Our question about whether American life and law is governed by a concept that actually results in *justice for all* must be answered in the negative. Our question as to whether American law is using a corrupt form of legalism to justify its abuses at home and its imperial adventures abroad must be answered in the affirmative.

The Imperial Dynamic of Empire

Insofar as America's imperial wars impact not only upon the invaded and occupied nation-states, but also upon the quality of life in the homeland of the empire, there is an emerging symmetry between foreign and domestic policy. It may be referred to as the *Imperial Dynamic* (my term). The effects and the interplay of this imperial dynamic have been seen before in recent history. Commenting upon this dynamic in the case of the Vietnam War, Dr. Martin Luther King, Jr., wrote: "It challenges the imagination to contemplate what lives we could transform if we were to cease killing. The security we profess to seek in foreign adventures we will lose in our decaying cities. The bombs in Vietnam explode at home; they destroy the hopes and possibilities for a decent America."[54] The Bush-2 regime's invasion and occupation of Iraq invites a similar analysis. As of March 2006, the war in Iraq costs $271,160,098,800.

Martin King recognized the *Imperial Dynamic* for what it was—a war system in the service of militarism and the US Global Empire's socioeconomic domination of the global South. In response to America's culture of militarism, King called upon all people to become *maladjusted* to a socioeconomic order that deprived the many of the necessities of life while, at the same time, it allowed luxuries for the few. Like Gandhi, he opposed militaristic practices that are embedded within a Global Empire which engages in the self-perpetuating use of violence in the service of an expanding empire. There are many faces to this imperial violence. It is evident in the conduct of the torture and prisoner abuse scandals that has characterized the *War on Terror*. In the first year after the US invasion of Iraq, torture memos and reports, written by US Government officials, came to the world's attention. In order to establish a legally viable argument to justify harsh interrogation techniques and procedures, the Bush administration began to pave the way for practices previously forbidden under both US law and intentional law.[55]

In the years since Martin King's assassination, numerous commentators and scholars reflecting on his legacy agree "long before globalization was in mode he knew that a global system, dreamed of by corporate imperialists, would harmonize standards across the globe down to the lowest common element. Social responsibility would be regarded as inefficient in a global free market and demands for a living wage would be a targeted source of inefficiency and purged wherever possible."[56] Under the auspices of the US Global Empire, the economic premises of neoliberalism (as expressed in its "Washington Consensus" policy model) failed to reduce poverty and inequality, or to promote economic growth and financial stability. The fact that this record is the result of failed policies appears to be beside the point to Washington Consensus insiders. Precisely because it does not matter to them demonstrates that "this is the corruption of moral sentiments on a global scale."[57] The policies embodied in the Washington Consensus are just one example of the many abuses of empire. The mandates of the Washington Consensus were conducted primarily through economic channels with the institutional support of the US Treasury Department, the White House, the IMF, WTO, and World Bank. That experiment ultimately failed in the 1990s. The failure and collapse of the neoliberal economic model created disasters in Argentina, Indonesia, and East Asia. In order to gain a longer perspective on this failure, it will be necessary to look at some historical precedents.

The American Empire and the roll back of progress in the Third World

Historically, the battle lines have been drawn for generations between the aspirations of Northern nations at the core of the capitalist empire and the resistance of Southern nations—originally united in the 1970s under the ideology of the New International Economic Order (NIEO).[58] The NIEO was proposing "a substantial redistribution of wealth and power from North to South."[59] This effort collapsed in the 1980s with the election of Ronald Reagan. The right wing foreign policy elites of the Reagan administration developed a strategy toward the South that was designed to bring an end to the NIEO. This strategy was called "roll back."

The goal of "roll back" was to transform the nations of the South into free-market economies. The polarized social structures that emerged—on a global scale—resulted in class cohesion at the top, fragmentation in the middle, and atomization at the bottom.[60] In this period, the "structural adjustment programs," of the IMF inaugurated the reign of what would become known as neoliberalism (the promotion of trade liberalization, deregulation, and privatization). In this task, "they served as the principal mechanism for disciplining the economic aspirations of the South."[61]

On the military side of the equation, the Reagan administration engaged in the invasion of Grenada, the intervention in Lebanon, and support for the "contras" against the Sandinistas in Nicaragua. In its secret war against Nicaragua, the CIA mined the harbors of Nicaragua, in violation of international law. The issue was brought before the World Court by Nicaragua, but the Reagan administration failed to participate and refused to acknowledge the jurisdiction of the court. After being condemned for the mining by the Court, the response of the Reagan administration was to refuse to recognize the legitimacy of its jurisdiction.[62] (In this regard, it might be argued that the refusal of the Reagan administration to recognize the legitimacy of the World Court helped to set a precedent for President Bush-2 ignoring the jurisdiction of international law as prelude to his 2003 invasion of Iraq.)

In the aftermath of the World Court's ruling on the Nicaragua case, a major scandal broke which almost led to the impeachment of President Reagan. With the president's support, the United States engaged in trading arms for hostages held by Iran. The CIA and members in Reagan's own cabinet then retained part of the proceeds from these undercover sales in Swiss bank accounts where the secret money funded the guerilla activities of the Nicaraguan Contras (a counterrevolutionary group that Congress—pursuant to the Boland Amendment—had specifically forbidden the administration to support). The US Congress appointed Judge Lawrence E. Walsh as the Independent Counsel in the Iran-Hostage Investigation. Judge Walsh and his associates successfully prosecuted many senior officials, and obtained an indictment of Secretary of Defense Caspar Weinberger, all of whom were eventually pardoned by President George Bush, Sr., in the waning days of his presidency.[63]

On the economic side of the North-South equation, the Reagan administration "did chart new territory ... launching comprehensive economic counterinsurgency campaigns to undermine those state assisted capitalist regimes that had served as the base for such challenges as the New International Economic Order."[64] This was the legacy inherited by succeeding US administrations—both Clinton and Bush-2.

Under Clinton, the structural adjustment programs of the IMF were repackaged as *globalization*—designed to accelerate the elimination of barrier to investment and the lowering of tariffs. The logic behind the globalization strategy was the idea that with a more rapid integration of the South into the global economy, it could be "designed to widen the arena for exploitation by transnational capital" which, in turn, "was critical for northern economies trying to escape the dilemmas of their own stagnation."[65] Within the developed nations of the global North, Clinton embarked upon so-called *Third Way* policies. Clinton's Third Way policies were hailed as combining a pro-business stance with social responsibility. This approach appeared to be vindicated by the fall in both inflation and unemployment. Yet, in reality, the apparent successes of the Clinton years were based on antilabor policies, the stagnation of real wages, deregulation of financial markets, and an historically unprecedented stock market boom. Even before the events of 9/11, there were indications that the "Clinton bubble" would burst and collapse into recession. The response of Bush-2 was to give massive tax breaks to the super-rich, introduce more antilabor measures, and work to cut social spending at both the federal and state levels.[66]

Both Clinton and Bush applied free-market principles and policies only very selectively within the United States itself, when such policies have benefited the interests of big business.[67] Still, the strategy has been applied much more harshly throughout the South. For example, these policies have led to financial ruin in Argentina, financial meltdown in East Asia, as well as increasing numbers of sweatshops and widening levels of poverty. These facts stand as testaments to an inherently flawed economic model.

With the collapse of both the Washington Consensus and the neoliberal model of globalization, the Bush-2 regime has revived the policy of "roll back," thereby making American militarism the centerpiece of a revived US attempt to achieve global domination through Global Empire. With this in mind, we now turn to our last section, dealing with the occupations of empire in its historical, military, and socioeconomic aspects.

The Occupations of Empire

The occupations of empire have a long series of precedents throughout history. Ancient Egypt and Rome, Spain, France, Great Britain, Germany's Third Reich, and now the United States are all examples of the occupations of empire. Their sociopolitical and socioeconomic pedigrees differ, but not their record of human carnage and waste. Each of these empires has exemplified a form of imperialism—seeking military domination and financial benefit through the occupations of empire.

Reflecting on the occupations and preoccupations of empire, J. M. Coetzee captures the essence of efforts to realize imperial dominion. In his novel, *Waiting for the Barbarians*, he writes:

Empire dooms itself to live in history and plot against history. One thought alone preoccupies the submerged mind of Empire: how not to end, how not to die, how to prolong its era. By day it pursues its enemies. It is cunning and ruthless, it sends its bloodhounds everywhere. By night it feeds on images of disaster: the sack of cities, the rape of populations, pyramids of bones, acres of desolation. A mad vision, yet a virulent one ... [68]

There are many ways to dissect Coetzee's depiction of empire. All of them are relevant to comprehending what is involved with the concept of the "occupations of empire."

First, there is the imperial dialectic of empire: *to live in history and plot against history*. Empire attempts to live on eternally, never grasping the fact that decline and fall are historically inevitable. Empire dooms itself to live in this paradox. Instead of accepting the inevitable shifts in history and recognizing the need to adapt to changing times, the imperial project of empire engages in denial; it acts as if there is no end. As noted at the start of this chapter, Professor Paul Kennedy wrote of the phenomena of *imperial overstretch* as a way of diagnosing the terminal nature of empires when they expand and seek continuous expansion without taking into account the necessities of contraction and adjustment to new realities. On this point, historian Geoffrey Parker turned to a concept in the field of evolution to explain the ruptures in history caused by empires and imperial expansion. In his book, *Success Is Never Final: Empire, War, and Faith in Early Modern Europe*, he writes: "I find very attractive the controversial 'punctuated equilibrium' model of human evolution advanced by Niles E. Eldredge and Stephen J. Gould: an underlying tendency towards balance, with occasional 'events' causing a drastic change that destroys the prevailing equilibrium and produces other compensatory changes until a new balance emerges."[69] So, one argument that emerges about the occupations of empire is, in their various forms and effects, these occupations ultimately result in the destruction of the *prevailing equilibrium* of international order, thereby producing anarchy or a shifting *balance of power*. While it is more common for political scientists and historians to employ the term *balance of power* to describe the risks, liabilities, and costly effects of empire and imperial overstretch, the point is that drastic changes in the exercise of power produce drastic reactions.

Second, there is the imperial preoccupation with how to "prolong" empire. Professor Jeffrey W. Taliaferro in his book, *Balancing Risks: Great Power Intervention in the Periphery*, has investigated two interrelated questions: (1) "Why great powers often initiate risky military and diplomatic interventions in peripheral regions that pose no direct threat to them; especially when they may risk confrontations with rivals in strategically inconsequential places?" And (2) "Why do powerful countries behave in a way that leads them to entrapment in prolonged, expensive, and self-defeating conflicts?" His conclusion is that senior officials are driven by the refusal to accept losses in their state's relative power. So, instead of cutting their losses, these leaders often continue to invest blood and money into failed interventions into the periphery.[70] In this regard, empires both "live in history and plot against history." But, by their plotting how to avoid their inevitable death, empires consign themselves to death (or at least permanent reduction in their power) by engaging in avoidance behavior regarding the central realities that they must face at a particular historical moment of transition. Nowhere is the phenomenon more apparent than in the refusal of the Bush-2 regime to deal with the global economic realities of the twenty-first century. The facts surrounding US production and trade point to serious vulnerabilities.[71]

Third, the occupations of empire destroy civilian populations. The carnage associated with imperial occupations is extensive and seems to know no boundaries. Samir Amin writes: "The militarist program adopted by the United States now threatens all people. It is the expression of the logic adopted by Hitler—to change social and economic relations by military force in favor of the master race of the day."[72] Given the military dominance of the United States, it certainly does have the short-term capacity to deliver massive blows "with few immediate risks and costs," but—over the long-term—"blowback follows a more protracted, tortuous, uncertain path: local attacks on US targets, proliferation of 'incidents', popular movements, terrorism, sabotage, guerrilla insurgency, and simply mounting general revulsion toward US power wherever it is experienced."[73] This assessment reveals rising tides of revolt and opposition, both within the United States and around the world, to the occupations of empire. It is reflective of a process—of an evolutionary movement in global consciousness. It can be traced to the end of the Vietnam War and the birth of the *Vietnam Syndrome*— a moral and political opposition to undertaking imperial wars in Third World nations. In this regard, both national and global consciousness has been moving toward what John Foster has termed "*an Empire Syndrome*"—a global opposition to the efforts of the American ruling class to expand the American Empire.[74]

This insight about *an Empire Syndrome* represents more than the traditional *balance-of-power* analysis. Rather, as discussed earlier, it is representative of truth within the *punctuated equilibrium* model. It helps to bring into sharper focus the dynamic qualities unleashed by the occupations of empire. It allows us to take the "long view" instead of a short-term snap shot. This longer view provides us with insights into both the fragility of empires and the corresponding desire of those unwillingly subjected to their rule to engage in resistance, to mount insurgencies, and to conduct guerilla warfare.

In conjunction with global resistance to empire, there is a corresponding claim of all people to have a recognized *right to peace*. Obviously, such a right will not emerge automatically. It will be the evolving product of a *Global Reconstruction*. Marcus Raskin has argued:

> Reconstruction in the international sphere must sustain emphasis on international laws of liberation and social and economic justice in many different venues that directly engage the citizenry. Just as there are domestic laws and assumed rights protecting individuals against murder, similar rights grow out of an already existing international law such as the Nuremberg judgments, which held against the crime of aggressive war and crimes against humanity. The crimes of genocide, rape, and pillage are predicates for the conclusion that people have a right to peace.[75]

At the dawn of the twenty-first century, expressions of this global resistance reveal how the fight for compensatory change in the international order accounts for the rise of Global Community. In this struggle, the rise of Global Community is being worked out in new alliances and forms of human solidarity against the intrusions, interventions, and failures of Global Empire.

3
When the "Law of the Land" Becomes Lawless

The fact that democracy continues to be invoked in American political rhetoric and the popular media may be a tribute, not to its vibrancy, but to its utility in supporting a myth that legitimates the very formations of power which have enfeebled it. The actual weakness of democracy is the consequence not of frontal attack but of a judgment that democracy can be managed and, when necessary, ignored.[1]

Sheldon S. Wolin

The peculiarity of Superpower and of empire is that they have no formal constitution in the sense that their structure and authority are prescribed and circumscribed beforehand. Their powers are viewed as outside the scheme of legitimation bestowed by constitutionalism and hence exempt from its constraints ... The dynamics of Superpower are far stronger than those of earlier empires because it is conjoined with the dynamics of globalizing capitalism.[2]

Sheldon S. Wolin

It is difficult to escape the conclusion that the drift of US policy is toward US dominance of the international system. In a sound legal system rules apply equally to all. In a system of politics, rules need not apply to those states with military and economic strength not only to defend themselves but also to assert themselves.[3]

John Burroughs

Although rules do not provide unequivocal answers to all puzzles they do provide tentative answers to many puzzles, and although they cannot unequivocally prescribe or forbid particular acts they do delimit ranges of conforming and nonconforming conduct.[4]

Terry Nardin

How is it possible for the "law of the land" to become lawless? There are numerous possibilities. The "rule of law" is often cited as a principled depiction of how the United States is governed and governs itself in relation to other nations. After all, America did begin as a republic with a constitution that set limits upon the authority of the state. The protection of individual liberties against the intrusions of an officious state was a fundamental ideological norm in the era of 1776.[5] As traditionally understood, law's dominion under the US Constitutional scheme is to restrict government from overreaching. The powers of government are to be subordinated to the "law of the land."

However, government's subordination and accountability to the "law of the land" may be fundamentally altered if the government itself is altered. In other words, when a government that is founded as a republic or democracy transitions into some other type of governance, it exercises different powers than the powers vested in it within the original scheme or framework. An alteration of government in response to crisis may produce a different constitutional outcome than the outcome that was originally projected by the authors. In light of this insight, some scholars have distinguished between the *Normal Constitution* (protective of individual rights) and a *Crisis Constitution* (hostile to individual rights and friendly to the unchecked power of government officials).[6]

The danger posed by the *Crisis Constitution* is that it has a tendency to override the *Normal Constitution*, and allows for the exploitation of the fears and passions associated with a national emergency. In this situation, a state of national emergency may be invoked as justification for the rule of some politically influential elite.[7] In such a world, the interpretation and application of "law of the land" would come to reside in the hands of "elites who could manipulate the dominant ideology."[8]

In the aftermath of the attack on the World Trade Center on 9/11 the US Government was placed into a crisis mode. In response to the perceived threat of terrorist attacks, a crisis mentality took hold of the Bush administration that was used to foist an already militaristic agenda on the American public. Using the imagery of external threat as its primary focus, the Bush administration was enabled to accomplish two alterations with regard to governmental powers and functions.

First, in an atmosphere approaching a "state of emergency" or a "state of siege" the Bush administration pushed a constitution-altering document through the congress called the USA Patriot Act. It contained a laundry list of powers that the FBI and CIA wanted to have at their disposal for years. Now, in the wake of 9/11, it was policy. No longer would the Bill of Rights act as a prohibitive barrier against the intrusions of a growing domestic police state.

Second, in an atmosphere of crisis, the whole direction of foreign policy shifted from a defensive to an offensive posture. Whether or not there was evidence to support the allegations, the sovereign nation of Iraq was deemed to be culpable in the 9/11 attacks. Regardless of the fact that the Bush-2 administration and its PNAC members had advocated the overthrow of the Hussein regime in Iraq for years prior to the events of 9/11, the Bush administration started to alter, fabricate, and manipulate both intelligence and evidence to fit their scenario of why Iraq was a culpable entity in the war on terror. In light of this chosen path, the path to war was a predetermined outcome and a political inevitability. All of these things transpired because there was an alteration of the US Government by the Bush administration. These alterations have been of such a magnitude that their effect was to produce a different constitutional outcome than the constitutional result that would have obtained in more "normal" circumstances.

In addition to the alterations made by the "crisis constitution" of the Bush-2 regime, the application of the law has been manipulated by the Bush-2 regime's ideological agenda. On the domestic side, the rule of law has been reduced to endless debates on abortion and the rights of the unborn, opposition to gay marriage, significant curtailments on the right to protest governmental decisions and actions, and a "state of siege" mentality in a war on terror that is codified in the USA Patriot Act. In short, the domestic side of the US legal regime has been taken hostage by right wing Christian fundamentalists, right wing ideologues, and the national security bureaucracy. On the international side, the rule of law was swept away as the President's chief legal counsel and Attorney General advised the White House that the prohibitions against torture in the Geneva Convention were "quaint," and did not apply to the conduct of the US war on terror. The foreign policy establishment of the Bush-2 regime was captivated by the doctrine of *preemptive war* as a means of going on the offense and not limiting itself to the defensive use of war—as a legal and constitutionally sanctioned response to national crisis.

Following 9/11, the executive branch unleashed both the FBI and CIA from previous legal constrictions of their respective mandates. The CIA and FBI could now avoid the need to seek judicial warrants if the suspects under consideration were deemed to be "terrorists." In the post-9/11 era the Bush-2 administration decided that privacy issues were now to be considered an unnecessary appendage to civil liberties. The government argued that it was justified in approving extra-constitutional means to fight a terrorist enemy.

Among the casualties of war one could count the 4th Amendment of the Constitution as warrantless wiretaps were approved by the President. The NSA was authorized by the president to spy on American citizens despite the prohibitions put in place to protect against this kind of abuse. Refusing to consult the congress to update the Foreign Intelligence Surveillance Act (FISA), the president simply decided to claim absolute executive power in making the determination. His constitutional theory used to support this exercise of power was the theory of the *unitary executive*. Additionally, the president lifted a previous executive order banning assassination as a tool of US foreign policy. Regardless of the cost and despite the sacrifice of civil liberties, the Bush-2 regime was determined to go its own way. Unilateral action had come to define the actions of the Bush-2 regime on both the foreign and domestic fronts. The executive branch sought to be free of control from the congress and the courts. Therefore, it effectively worked to make both moot. A constitutional crisis had been set into motion. The system of checks and balances was not merely endangered—it was almost dead.

In an atmosphere of fear, the congress surrendered its war power to the Bush White House, relinquished its constitutional oath to uphold the constitution by sanctioning the USA Patriot Act, and gave virtually unconditional support to the president in all matters pertaining to war and peace. Traditional civilian courts and constitutional protections were shoved aside to make room for military tribunals, the kidnapping and interrogation of terrorist suspects through a procedure known as "rendition," and the suspension of all legal norms regarding the use of torture from Guantanamo Bay to Abu Ghraib and beyond. Furthermore, if war was what was required to deal with Iraq, then the UN would be casually shoved aside and a doctrine of "preemptive war" would be put in its place. How did all of this come to be?

SUPERPOWER LAW—SUPERPOWER SYNDROME

Since 1945, America has been in the process of transitioning from a "federal principle" into a militarized society and global empire. The final nail in the coffin of the American republic came with the aftermath of the collapse of the Soviet Union in the period of 1989–1990. The collapse of the USSR meant that the United States would become the only remaining global Superpower with both the imperial capacity and imperial ambition to dominate the globe militarily and economically.[9] Beginning with the second Bush presidency in 2001, the United States made its final turn on the path toward becoming a full-blown empire.

Two of the primary mechanisms that account for this turn are as follows: (1) the Bush Doctrine of "preemptive war," under the rubric of unilateralism and, (2) the passage of the USA Patriot Act that served to emasculate the Bill of Rights and transfer primary legal authority on matters of war and peace from the congress and judiciary to the executive. By investing almost absolute power in the White House and the national security bureaucracy, the system of checks and balances was virtually annihilated. Military courts were given the power to detain terrorist suspects under the rubric of *enemy combatants*. Removed from the constitutional protections of due process and the protections of the Geneva Convention regarding torture, a whole new path was charted for the US intelligence agencies as well as the Pentagon. In this radically new national and international environment, what used to be considered the *law of the land*—as well as international law and custom—had been eclipsed by a transition from democratic accountability to unconstrained and unrestricted executive authority—supposedly emerging from the "inherent powers of the president."

The shifting legal terrain that allowed the Bush administration to embrace the practice of torture with respect to *enemy combatants* also allowed for unilateral interventions in the Middle East based upon the principle of power, not the principles of law. The power principle began to replace the rule of law principle prior to 9/11, with the collapse of the USSR. At that time, Washington already had its eye on the Muslim oil-producing region of Central Asia, as a natural extension of the already US-dominated Gulf. While it is true that the scramble for the resources of Central Asia had accelerated over the decade of the 1990s, its full momentum would not really begin until 2001. As the Bush-2 regime continued to shift its rationale for invading and occupying Iraq, it would increasingly move toward spreading the reach of its military doctrine. Hence, while the Bush administration began by talking about failed UN sanctions and failed UN mandates, it proceeded to rely on unsubstantiated allegations about Iraq's possession of weapons of mass destruction (WMD). By the time that the WMD argument crumbled, the new rationale was to become democracy promotion throughout the region, while the administration continued to support dictatorships in Egypt, Saudi Arabia, and elsewhere.

As radical as these shifts have been, it is not as if earlier presidents did not previously use the powers of the executive to intervene in foreign nations without benefit of at least the façade of fidelity to the "rule of law." In the case of the Vietnam War, under the pretext of self-defense, President Lyndon Johnson initiated a *police action*, similar to the actions taken by President Truman in the context of the Korean War. The legal authority for the 1964 transfer of the congressional war power to the executive branch came in the form of the *Gulf of Tonkin Resolution*. The resolution was little more than a fig leaf for the power to wage war in the absence of an actual declaration of war, as required by the Constitution. During the administration of President Johnson, rule by the principle of executive power was in the process of eclipsing the rule of law. By the time that President Nixon entered the White House, the growth of the imperial presidency was evolving so quickly that the rule of law was almost swallowed up, but for the Watergate scandal.

The substitution of power for the *rule of law* is a complex dynamic. It is not only a political, economic, and military dynamic—it is a psychological dynamic as well. When the principle of power replaces the rule of law in international affairs, the entire world becomes deeply affected and vulnerable to the abuses of unconstrained power. In short, the triumph of the principle of power, as the principal means of achieving an objective without reference to law or diplomacy, becomes a standard mode of operation—a syndrome. As noted by Robert Jay Lifton, the psychological dynamic can begin to account for a transubstantiation of legal principle into the exercise of raw and unconstrained power—resulting in what he calls the "Superpower Syndrome." By invoking the term "Superpower Syndrome," Lifton means to communicate the idea that there comes to be a national mind-set that is put forward by a tight-knit leadership group and that the invocation of this mind-set takes on a sense of omnipotence.

An example of the mind-set of imperial omnipotence can be seen in the writings of Thomas Donnelly, a past executive director of the PNAC. The PNAC is made up of the same group of neoconservatives that rose to top leadership and decision-making posts in the Bush-2 regime. In an essay entitled, *What Is Within Our Powers?—Preserving American Primacy in the Twenty-First Century*, Donnelly asked: "... in a globalized, sole-superpower world, what are the outer walls of the city? What are the limits of political obligation and organization, particularly in matters of security and war?" Donnelly's answer is that

> our political ideals, which we hold to be universal and alienable, drive us onward and outward. If we no longer understand them as perfectly self-evident we do not shrink from the effort of realizing them. Our economic resilience, our military might, the tranquility of American domestic democracy, the racing energy of our high and low culture combine to define a remarkably robust Pax Americana.[10]

The implications arising from this sense of omnipotence demonstrate that "while the US refusal to join a legal regime does not equate with a rejection of international law, it is arguable that in those instances in which the United States is an indispensable party for the formulation of international law, any unilateralist stance by the United States could be tantamount to the single superpower impeding or opposing the development of that law." Should that be the case, "it is arguable that, under the administration of George W. Bush, the United States increasingly sees itself as an absolute sovereign whose favored position could be compromised by the concept of international community—and thus by many aspects of international law."[11] As we shall see throughout the chapter, this is especially clear in the area of security-related treaties that the United States has either failed to ratify or refused to meet its obligations under.

In the early part of the post-1945 era, the process of checks and balances was already beginning to be altered. America envisioned itself as the protector of the *Free World*. Like Great Britain at the height of its power, the sun never set on the American empire. Its military bases spanned the globe. Its strategies for conducting the Cold War turned it into a Superpower that would be capable of standing down another Superpower—the Soviet Union. In this new world, the *law of the land*, as embedded within a constitution written for the exigencies of the eighteenth century, was now viewed by the men of power as incapable of addressing the security needs of the twenty-first century. The constitution that the men of power had sworn to "preserve, protect and defend" upon their entry into office had become an obstacle to their imperial agenda. In this regard, the movement of the United States toward a *universal empire* or a Global Empire should be measured against the historical yardstick of the *federal principle* that conceived the new American republic.

THE "FEDERAL PRINCIPLE" OF
THE NEW AMERICAN REPUBLIC

According to some scholars,

> the word "*federal*," is one that must be used with some caution, since it now carries meaning and connotations distinctly at odds with the understanding of the eighteenth century ... In the eighteenth century ... the term "federal" then comprehended constitutionalism and diplomacy alike ... At the root of the federal principle, as then conceived, was the idea of a covenant ... That ideal proposed itself as a means of contending with the opposing specters of international anarchy and universal empire, and as offering a solution to the baffling question of how to secure international order in a system of sovereigns prone to collective violence and unilateral action.[12]

When understood as being conceived in terms of a covenant, the federal principle may be seen as synonymous with the ideas of promise, commitment, undertaking, the idea of cooperation, reciprocity, mutuality, and predictability.[13]

With the dawn of the Cold War, the American state would act *for reasons of state*, no longer fully accountable to the *law of the land*. Nor would the American state see itself as accountable to the federal principle. Rather, through the creation of new institutions within the executive branch, the direction of US foreign policy would abandon the federal principle when it judged such an abandonment to be feasible. Hence, the UN was relegated to the role of referee in the Cold War while the two Superpowers fought for *spheres of influence*. The UN Security Council was convened in October of 1962 to deal with the Cuban Missile Crisis, but it was ignored as the United States waged war on the peasant populations of South Vietnam, Cambodia, Laos, and Thailand.

With the close of World War II, new institutions, such as the CIA, were designed by the US foreign policy establishment to act as a global counterforce to the Soviet Union's grand design for world revolution. Emerging out of the Office of Strategic Services (OSS), Allan Dulles became the CIA's first director, while his brother, John Foster Dulles, was chosen to head the State Department. Working in tandem, the Dulles brothers helped to forge the basic tenets of Cold War policies. These same tenets would largely carry over into a post-Cold War World. The overthrow of foreign governments, the sanctioning of assassination as a means of altering governmental leadership and policies, and undermining progressive social movements that opposed corporate rule and military solutions, were all an integral part of the CIA's agenda. In turn, the Pentagon's projection of power turned the *arsenal of democracy* into a permanent arrangement with the weapons industry—thereby transitioning the defense of the nation into a *military-industrial complex*. Following suit, the executive branch of the United States evolved into the American *National Security State* (NSS). Within the context of fundamental ideological shifts and bureaucratic perceptions of new security needs, a new way of holding and exercising power was evolving. The holding and exercise of power would become increasingly unaccountable. In fact, the term "imperial presidency" is quite revealing for it describes not only the almost limitless power of the president, but an imperial (imperialistic) agenda as well.

The path that the NSS embarked upon exposed "the peculiarity of Superpower and of empire." Neither embodiment of the nation's power in the form of Superpower or empire was entirely accountable to a formal constitution "in the sense that their structure and authority are prescribed and circumscribed beforehand."[14] Hence, as empire and as Superpower, the exercise of US power became increasingly freed from its constitutional moorings and was unaccountable to congressional oversight. Unlike the democratic state, the NSS was not to be exposed to the vast array of conflicting societal pressures. In this new world, the NSS was removed from the democratic requirements of review and accountability to its own citizens. This layer of protection came in the form of *plausible denial*. This new doctrine was invoked by the NSS in fear of the formal institutions of democratic governance being able to reveal activities carried on under the newly cloaked mandate of "National Security." Hence, by divorcing the exercise of state power from the constraints of law, law's domain would increasingly recede in practical importance in the decades to follow. Insofar as the powers of empire were viewed as outside the scheme of legitimation bestowed by constitutionalism, the powers of a Superpower were treated as exempt from its constraints.[15] In this way, the *law of the land* became lawless, both domestically and internationally.

FROM THE FEDERAL PRINCIPLE TO
THE EMBRACE OF "RADICAL UNILATERALISM"

During the first term of Bush-2, the United States embarked upon a path of radical unilateralism. It was radical because it disposed of a basic adherence to an international security-related treaty regime. What was discarded on the international front during the period of 2001–2004 included: (1) US failure to comply with the

NPT disarmament obligation by reason of the failure to make disarmament the driving force in national planning and policy with respect to nuclear weapons; (2) The Comprehensive Test Ban Treaty (CTBT) remains locked within the Republican dominated Senate Foreign Relations Committee, with the Bush administration opposing its ratification; (3) The Anti-Ballistic Missile Treaty (ABM) which limited missile defense to two sites in each country was unilaterally withdrawn from in late 2001 because the Bush administration wanted to pursue NMD without treaty restrictions; (4) The United States withdrew from the Biological Weapons Convention (BWC) on grounds that are suspect at best and do not stand up to serious scrutiny; (5) The United States keeps company with Russia, China, Iraq, Iran, North Korea, Burma, India, Pakistan, and Cuba by its refusal to join the Treaty Banning Antipersonnel Mines; (6) The United States has effectively withdrawn from both the United Nations Framework Convention on Climate Change and the Kyoto Protocol, designed to deal with rising concentrations of greenhouse gases in the earth's atmosphere; (7) The United States has refused to ratify the Rome Statute of the International Criminal Court (ICC) despite the fact that as of July 27, 1998, 120 countries voted to adopt it.

Taken in combination or individually, the aforementioned list of Bush-2 administration noncompliance with an evolving international security-related treaty regime is both reckless and irresponsible. Because it conflates its own self-importance with law itself, the Bush-2 administration has so corrupted US standing in the world with respect to withdrawal from security-related treaties or noncompliance with them, it has exposed itself as being an administration that is inherently lawless.

THE DEFINITION AND DIMENSIONS OF "LAWLESSNESS"

To comprehend the range and scope of what is implied by the term "lawless," the *Oxford Dictionary and Thesaurus—American Edition—1996* defines the term as: *adj.* 1. having no laws or enforcement of them. 2. disregarding laws. 3. unbridled, uncontrolled—lawlessly, *adv.*; lawlessness, *n*.- 1. anarchic, anarchical, anarchistic, chaotic, disorderly, unruly, unregulated. 2. unlawful, criminal, felonious, illegal, illicit, larcenous ... dishonest, corrupt ... 3. unbridled, uncontrolled, unconstrained, unrestrained, unchecked, undisciplined, wild, unruly, rogue ... out of hand or control.

All of the qualities and traits enumerated herein came to define the nature of the United States as a Superpower and as an empire. The lawless nature of the United States as a Superpower may be seen to have legal, psychological, and political dimensions. We shall take each of these in turn.

The Legal Dimensions of the United States as a Superpower

As noted above, the United States during the course of the second Bush presidency has opted out of compliance and/or ratification in at least seven separate legal arenas. Most notably, this phenomenon is a glaring reality in the area of security-related treaties. This result reflects a conjunction of legal, political, moral, and psychological arrogance. For example, the refusal to sacrifice some part of its sovereignty as a Superpower for the greater good of the Global Community demonstrates an utter lack of restraint with regard to its power and the effects of exercising that power.

> Some scholars have noted that: Treaties by their very nature involve some sacrifice of sovereignty. In exchange, treaty regimes contribute to nation and global security in important ways, including: (1) articulating global norms; (2) promoting and recognizing compliance with norms; (3) building monitoring and enforcement mechanisms; (4) address the likelihood of detecting violations and effectively addressing them; (5) providing a benchmark for measurement of progress; (6) establishing a foundation of confidence, trust, experience, and expertise for further progress; (7) providing criteria to guide states' activities and legislation, and focal points for discussion of policy issues.[16]

In sum, the contribution to national and international security by going down the aforementioned path creates great benefits for the entire Global Community insofar as, "over the long term, treaty regimes are a far more reliable basis for achieving global policy objectives and compliance with norms than 'do as we say, not as we do' directives from an overwhelmingly powerful state."

Compliance with the objectives of international treaties is not just a matter of black-letter law. Rather, treaties that address the security concerns of many nations should not be ignored by the veto of one. Norms and values are at the heart and center of every treaty we have discussed. These norms and values are an expression of an evolving legal regime of customary international law and the principles that form the core of all of the world's great religions. When understood in this manner, we may argue that the intersection of law and religion in international law, customs, and treaties represents the mandate of a rising Global Community.

Unfortunately, the Bush administration has effectively divorced itself from a treaty regime that would enhance the rise of Global Community. Instead, the Bush administration embraced the pursuit of Global Empire. By choosing the path of empire, it effectively assumed the title and designation of being a *rogue nation*— a label previously used in reference to Third World states that refused to comply with US demands and expectations. Now, the situation is dramatically altered. The United States has so distanced itself from the rule of law that it is viewed around the world as a rogue state by virtue of its abandonment of international treaties, customs, and norms.

The Psychological Dimensions of the United States as a Superpower

Sheldon S. Wolin, Emeritus Professor of Politics at Princeton University, has given significant attention to the psychological aspects of a Superpower as it acts without reference to the constraints placed upon the exercise of its power. Historically, the lawful exercise of power was carried out in reference to the scheme of legitimation bestowed by constitutionalism. Put in psychological terms,

> Superpower might be described in Freudian terms as ego driven by id (basic power drive) with only mild remonstrance from a weak superego (norms or

conscience). Superpower flaunts the ego in a cavalier disregard for its allies, renounces treaty obligations when it finds them confining, refuses to enter into international agreements or to join international agencies and tribunals when they impose limitations on its freedom of action (sovereignty), and asserts its right to invade or wage war against any country that it deems dangerous.[17]

Certainly the Bush administration's abandonment of the ABM Treaty, the Kyoto Treaty, CTBT, and the NPT may be seen as the result of a basic power drive that is divorced from international norms and the moral conscience of peoples around the globe. In this sense, the American version of Global Empire has placed itself at odds with those global forces, social movements, and nations that are seeking to build a Global Community.

Similarly, Professor Robert Jay Lifton, Visiting Professor of Psychiatry at Harvard Medical School, has defined the *Superpower Syndrome* as "a harmful disorder." He states: "I use this medical association to convey psychological and political abnormality. I also wish to emphasize a *confluence* of behavior patterns: in any syndrome there is not just a single tendency but a constellation of tendencies."[18] While each of these tendencies can be identified separately, "they are best understood as manifestations of an overarching dynamic that controls the behavior of the larger system, in this case the American national entity."[19]

Further, he argues that a dynamic takes shape "around the American collective mindset that extends our very real military power into a fantasy of cosmic control, a mindset all too easily tempted by an apocalyptic mission."[20] He sees the larger syndrome as that of unilateralism. Such a conclusion is especially the case as the dynamic of the Superpower Syndrome relates to war making, the use of military technology, and a sense of entitlement. It includes a belief in the right to decide who may or may not possess weapons of mass destruction. Finally, underlying all of these symptoms, there is the presence of a religious vision dedicated to ridding the world of evil and thereby bringing about a purification of it both politically and spiritually. The problem with ridding the world of evil is a mixed bag in the political realm because looking at US actions over the past 50 years it is impossible to discern any consistent definition of evil.[21]

The Political Dimensions of the United States as a Superpower

In the aftermath of the events of September 11, 2001, there has been a sea change in the political, intellectual, moral, economic, and social climate of America. How much of this sea change may be attributed to the media, government, propaganda, public and elite ignorance, or calculated misinformation is open to debate. However, there remain from the days of the founding of the American republic the old polarities of the unionist paradigm—international anarchy and universal empire.

On one end of the spectrum, in the category of *international anarchy*, we find the elements of total war, Cold War, détente, and alliance. In this situation, there is no single superpower capable of enjoying global hegemony. Rather, international anarchy is spawned from competing interests that are on a quest to capture enough spheres of influence so as to undermine all other competitors in search of the victory that comes with achieving domination over the entire international system. Underlying all these elements—total war, Cold War, détente, and alliance systems—is conflict.

At the other extreme side of the spectrum, in the category of *universal empire*, we find the pursuit of hegemony and dominance. With only one superpower, no effective opposition exists that can act with enough singular power to resist the strategies and policy designs of the remaining superpower. Further, with the drive for universal empire as the primary unifying principle of superpower action in the world, only grassroots insurgencies, guerilla warfare, social movements, and other forms of resistance are available to those who are the objects of domination by the imperial strategists. Even allies of the superpower are left out in the cold with respect to their capacity to influence the ultimate outcome as conceived by the architects of empire. Under these conditions of superpower hegemony there remains a fundamental choice—either to revolt against imperial dominance, or to submit to it.

In between these extremes is the middle ground on which the American republic was founded and the ideal to which it aspired—the realization of *a federative system*, composed of a society of states at the international level and a federal union at the national level. Ideally, it would be a system designed to promote cooperation and multilateralism—ideals that lie at the heart of a viable Global Community. The relevance of these different strategies for governance has become even more apparent at the dawn of the twenty-first century.[22]

SEEKING AMERICAN DEMOCRACY
IN THE SHADOW OF EMPIRE

The possibility for a different kind of American democracy is especially true in the context of the evolution and application of the "law of the land." It is also true in the general context of American culture, politics, economic outlook, and conceptions of what constitutes the *common good*. For example, the ideal of *equality* in a *land of opportunity* is often cited as a central component of the American dream. Yet, as John Dewey once remarked, the idea of equality becomes dangerous when it is widely praised but empty in practice.

Tocqueville had made a similar point about democracy in America at the dawn of the republic. In reviewing the historical record, some scholars have identified and commented upon Tocqueville's concern with the possibility of the republic being turned into a *democratic despotism*. On this point, Professor Wolin has commented upon this warning: "if democracy failed to cultivate participatory forms that engaged politically the energies of the ordinary citizen, political populism would be displaced by a cultural populism of sameness, resentment, and mindless patriotism, and by an anti-political form he labeled 'democratic despotism'."[23] Certainly, the presidency of Bush-2 has relied heavily on blind patriotism to overlook or forgive the fact that no weapons of mass destruction were found in Iraq. Domestically, the administration relied on both the fear and resentment toward Muslims to lend credence to the suspension of civil liberties for certain groups and minorities in a "time of terror." Also, in appeals to his voting base, President Bush would rely on the populism of sameness, found among Christian-right evangelicals, to produce his electoral majorities. All of of these trends reflected a form or expression of *exclusionary governance*.

An alternative model to "democratic despotism" and "exclusionary governance" is outlined in my book, *Achieving Inclusionary Governance*. At the heart of my thesis, I make a critical distinction between various forms of governance based upon the degree to which they are either exclusionary or inclusionary. By examining the policies of states, the degree to which they allow for significant citizen participation in the actual decision-making processes of the nation, and their approach to issues of poverty and social justice, it becomes possible to assess how "democratic" and "inclusionary" a nation-state actually is.[24] With this in mind, let us turn to a short review of the US record in the twentieth century and early twenty-first century, in order to discern the gradual defacement and impairment of the *law of the land* in America's national and international life.

On the domestic front, the excesses of the McCarthy years would reappear in Nixon's Watergate scandal and through George W. Bush's USA Patriot Act. The threat of a developing American *police state* could be glimpsed in disguised references to martial law in times of "emergency," echoing the Latin American version of a *state of siege*.[25] The growth of America's *prison-industrial-complex* exposed not only the inequities of a class divided society, but the degree to which the law of corrections had been corrupted by the Reagan revolution's emphasis upon economic "privatization" and its own ideologically driven version of what constitutes "law and order." Both the growth and ideology of the *prison-industrial-complex* remained intact under the rule of both the Republican and Democratic parties.[26]

On the international front, the anarchical character of international relations would be exposed in the US sponsored and supported overthrow of the Chile's democratically elected Allende regime and its replacement with the right-wing terror of General Pinochet's military junta.[27] America's alliances with Europe would strain and crumble as an unchecked second Bush presidency ignored the UN and NATO in its decision to undertake unilateral action against Iraq. The United States Congress would continually abdicate its constitutional role—in a system of *checks and balances*—to restrain presidential war making. With the congressional surrender of its power to declare war, it opened the floodgates of international lawlessness by its de facto endorsement of the Bush Doctrine.[28]

In the aftermath of the events of 9/11, the Bush administration embarked upon a lawless path to legitimize the US Global Empire's destruction of national sovereignty under the rubric of *preemptive war*. The congress had removed the restraints of the *War Powers Act*, which had been intended to circumscribe the president's power to place American troops abroad for more than 90 days without future congressional authorization.[29] The congressional surrender of its constitutional obligations resulted in the resurrection of the *Imperial Presidency*, and with it the potential for war without end. In short, the congressional abdication of its responsibilities to restrain the executive resulted in adding new dimensions to the president's foreign policy quiver of arrows.[30]

A similar result obtained on the domestic front, further aggravating the potential for even greater abuses of civil liberties as both the FBI and the CIA were granted new powers under the USA Patriot Act.[31] Basically, the act allows for the state-sanctioned sacrifice of civil liberties in the name of fighting the *war on terrorism*. As a consequence, the dual effects of the NSS with respect to national and international law were continuing to exert a tremendous influence upon the demise of democratic control and governance. An unchecked *Imperial Presidency* would linger long after Nixon.

THE BIRTH AND EVOLUTION OF "DEMOCRATIC DESPOTISM" IN THE UNITED STATES

A resurgent *imperial presidency* would also account for the drift toward draconian solutions to domestic social problems that could no longer be addressed by weakened democratic institutions. By 2004, wealth inequality between social classes widened, millions more Americans fell below the poverty line. In the absence of federal intervention health care, costs zoomed out of control. At the same time, the wealthiest 1 percent of the population received a $1.4 trillion tax break from the Bush administration. American corporations engaged in *outsourcing* jobs to low-wage markets in Asia and Latin America, while the office of Homeland Security was charged with turning the United States into a "Fortress America."

As democratic institutions have weakened, a central question remains: *Where can we identify the institutional sources of governmental lawlessness in the power structure of the United States?* In response, I would argue that C. Wright Mills was the first scholar to describe in detail the inner workings of power within and between the corporate rich, the warlords of the military, and the political directorate. He described this combination of relationships as the workings of a *power elite*. The idea of the power elite, he argued,

> rests upon and enables us to make sense of (1) the decisive institutional trends that characterize the structure of our epoch ... the several coincidences between economic, military, and political institutions; (2) the social similarities and the psychological affinities of the men who occupy the command posts of these structures ... ;(3) the ramifications, to the point of virtual totality, of the kind of decisions that are made at the top, and the rise to power of a set of men who, by training and bent, are professional organizers of considerable force, and who are unrestrained by democratic party training.[32]

C. Wright Mills' identification of the vital importance of *the command posts of these structures* is critical in understanding how the *law of the land* became lawless. Mills identified the primary institutional sources of this lawlessness. The political directorate, the corporate rich, and the warlords of the military would now embark upon a path that was protected by concentrated power, divorced from any real effective scheme of checks and balances. Historically, such concentrations of power have demonstrated a unique proclivity toward authoritarian and totalitarian styles of governance.[33] Following Mills, regarding the transition "from" a representative democratic state in the service of the rule of law "toward" the lawlessness of a centralized and unaccountable State in the service of the power elite, my thesis may be articulated as follows:

> With the centralization of power in the *command posts* of the military, the polit-
> ical directorate, and the offices of the corporate rich, the door of American state
> governance was opened for a transition of power from democratic accountabil-
> ity to the exercise of "unrestrained lawlessness in the name of law" (my term).

With the sabotage of congressional oversight, the surrender of the congressional
war-making power, and the congressional corruption of the *power of the purse*,
there is little incentive to abide by the letter or even the spirit of the law. Laws
could be rewritten or introduced to accommodate the requirements of the
command posts of the power elite. In other words, the *buying of the congress* has
led to the constitutional disempowerment of the congress, as well as its ethical
corruption in conjunction with a culture of lobbyists.[34]

The military-industrial complex was enabled to gain an increasingly larger slice
of the budget while, at the same time, members of congress could create more
Pentagon-related jobs in their districts. In turn, the corporations would become the
beneficiaries of new tax breaks, while congress turned a blind eye to "costs overruns." It mattered little to the command posts that this process of governance ran
up the taxpayers' bill for weapon systems that either did not ultimately function
or took longer to produce than originally promised.[35]

The political directorate of the power elite would take their cues from their corporate backers. Congressional priorities would consistently find their articulation
in judgments set out by the warlords in the military-industrial complex. Democratic
debate, public discourse, and informed consent would be replaced by the rubber-
stamp of almost automatic congressional approval with little internal dissent. Both
the warlords and the business elites worked in concert by subverting democratic
debate and citizen representation.

Increasingly, average citizens, labor groups, and environmentalists were
becoming political obstacles to the corporate agenda. Should their voices be
granted an inclusive role in the writing and the implementation of international
treaties and accords dealing with issues of trade and comparative advantage, a corresponding reduction in profits would severely diminish the "businessmen's
incentive." One glaring example is in the conduct between Canada and the United
States with regard to the negotiations involving Free Trade for the Americas.[36] By
the time Mexico was incorporated into a new North American Free Trade regime
under NAFTA, both environmental and labor protections were placed into
non-enforceable "side agreements" which left the progressive agenda scuttled
while multinational corporations and their political allies reaped the rewards.[37]

The corporate rich would continually influence both the warlords and the
political directorate. In the shadow of democracy, both business and the warlords
would prosper. By taking refuge in the sanctuary of the NSS, these powerful special interests would be protected by the power elite in the command posts. The
American economy came to be characterized as a series of hegemonic relationships between individual corporations and between the industrial and financial
sectors. Within this matrix, financial firms, in particular money market commercial banks, stood at the peak of this hierarchical arrangement.[38] The profits of the

Superpower's empire would be dispersed to those well positioned within this system of *lawlessness in the name of law*. As a consequence of this internal shift of power and influence within the government, citizen apathy, disempowerment, and disenfranchisement would become the barometer to measure the death of democratic accountability and the rise of power, greed, and wealth in the command posts of Global Empire.[39]

Through this *power elite*, the United States—as both Superpower and empire—asserted itself not by reference to the rule of law, but despite the rule of law. No longer circumscribed by the restraining concepts of conforming and nonconforming conduct, the foreign policy of the United States gradually entered into a state of lawlessness. The assassination of heads of state—euphemistically referred to by the CIA as *executive action*—was an accepted policy of the American government, until exposed by the Church Committee in the early 1970s.[40] Criminal and illicit schemes that interlinked weapons, drugs, and off-the-record financial accounts characterized the hidden history of the Vietnam War in Southeast Asia's "Golden Triangle."

In the aftermath of the Vietnam War, the decade of the 1970s found the United States engaged in unconventional wars in Central America, the Middle East, and Africa. By altering the legal definition of war, it was the hope of the US foreign policy establishment that US-sponsored counterinsurgency and antiterrorism campaigns would not be subject to constitutional constraints. By the mid-1980s the same strategy was employed by the Reagan administration as it swapped arms for hostages in Iran and supplied weapons and money to the Contras in Nicaragua in violation of the Boland Amendment.[41] The Iran-Contra Affair could have led to the impeachment of President Reagan—however the president's popularity at the close of his second term allowed him to avoid it.

No sooner had the Soviet Union collapsed and the Cold War ended than the Pentagon declared a new threat existed. In place of a competing Superpower, the Pentagon was now preoccupied with rising Third World powers equipped with chemical and nuclear weapons. The US Global Empire's search for enemies would now have to focus on new dangers, threats, and nations. The new object of American foreign policy makers was to control what they euphemistically called *rogue states*—North Korea, Libya, Iran, and Iraq. This *rogues' gallery* was Washington's creation to justify levels of military spending that were nearly as high as they had been during the Cold War. The United States—as the only remaining Superpower—had to allege that *some* credible threat existed so as to justify the continuation of such high military expenditures. Ironically, in early 2003, the second Bush presidency turned the only remaining Superpower into a *rogue nation* when it sanctioned the doctrine of *preemptive war* so as to allow for the United States to unilaterally invade and occupy Iraq.[42]

UNPRECEDENTED: "INVERTED TOTALITARIANISM" AND "MANAGED DEMOCRACY" IN THE SERVICE OF EMPIRE

Since early 2003, the war in Iraq has so monopolized public attention that an insufficient amount of consideration has been given to the *regime change* that is taking place in the Homeland. The overthrow of Saddam Hussein was the only kind of "regime change" the US media cared to discuss with the American people. The alteration of America's constitutional protections under the Bill of Rights was given a back seat to the perception of threat that lingered in the aftermath of the events of 9/11. In this context, the Bush administration's promise of delivering democracy to the Middle East has all but totally obscured the fact that both democratic practices and institutions are being diminished in the United States. As I pointed out in Chapter 2, my thesis regarding the abuses of empire stated:

> The abuses of empire conducted internally (within the homeland of the empire) are manifested in the abuses that the empire conducts externally (on the international stage). *The corollary to this thesis is that*: The abuses of empire conducted externally (on the international stage) will be manifested domestically (within the homeland of the empire) in terms of a "blowback" effect from those abuses.

In this context, the *blowback* effect of America's projection of power abroad has diminished the role and power of the citizen.[43] Professor Sheldon Wolin observed:

> Consider how odd it would sound if we were to refer to "the Constitution of the American Empire" or "superpower democracy". The reason they ring false is that "constitution" signifies limitations on power, while "democracy" commonly refers to the active involvement of citizens with their government and the responsiveness of government to its citizens. For their part, "empire" and "superpower" stand for the surpassing of limits and the dwarfing of the citizenry.[44]

The practice of *unrestrained lawlessness in the name of law* had previously been the hallmark of totalitarian regimes. As defined by Aaron Friedberg: "Totalitarian states are ... more likely to be able to pursue ambitious force postures and strategies and extensive power-creating programs, even when they are not at war. In liberal democratic regimes, on the other hand, with representative governments, institutionalized protections for individual rights, ideologies that emphasize personal liberty, and varied, vibrant civil societies, the state will be exposed to an array of conflicting social pressures."[45] All of these definitions and assumptions changed in the aftermath of September 11, 2001.

INVERTED TOTALITARIANISM

What Mills had warned about with regard to the "power elite" was now taking hold as the predominant political reality within the United States. In this regard, Sheldon Wolin notes: "What is crucially important here is not only the expansion of governmental power but the inevitable discrediting of constitutional limitations and institutional processes that discourages the citizenry and leaves them politically apathetic."[46] Wolin states: "I want to go further and name the emergent political system '*inverted totalitarianism*.' By inverted I mean that while the current system and its operatives share with Nazism the aspiration of unlimited power and aggressive expansionism, their methods and actions seem upside down."[47] Wolin cites the example of the Weimar Republic, before the Nazi seizure of power. At that time the "streets" were filled with totalitarian-oriented gangs. In contrast, within the United States the streets are where democracy is most alive. Now, "the real danger is with an increasingly unbridled government."[48]

With respect to *democracy in the streets*, one need only recall the *Battle of Seattle* in 1999 to comprehend the force of the power of the people aligned against the WTO. Opposition to a neoliberal free-trade agenda was challenged by the excluded people in the streets calling for fair trade and inclusion in decision making about policies that shape their lives. Additionally, "democracy in the streets" was seen in the expression of popular resistance to the elites gathered at Davos, Switzerland, as the people protested at the annual meeting of the World Economic Forum.[49]

While opposition was centered on the polices of the WTO, the 1999 street demonstrations in Seattle would be the first shot heard around the world of a global uprising against all of the undemocratic or antidemocratic institutions of Global Empire. While the anti-war demonstrations of the late 1960s were worldwide in scope, the late twentieth century was beginning to witness a rising consciousness that specifically targeted corporate rule and abuses. Resistance to global corporate rule would also produce public participation in alternative forums with agendas aligned with the proponents of Global Community—such as the World Social Forum held in Porto Alegre in early 2001.

The people of the world, who are both members of the Global Community and the victims of Global Empire, realize that the instruments of empire (WTO, IMF, World Bank, CIA) are embodied within institutions that reflect the singular desire of the United States to dominate the people of the globe—whatever the cost. Knowing this fact and seeing its implementation has begun to energize a global resistance movement. Whether it is peasant farmers in Mexico or Brazil, social justice advocates in Asia or Africa, or progressive political groups in Europe or the United States itself, there is a common desire to oppose the agenda of Global Empire. In this regard,

at the global level, sheer military force without legitimacy and without political alliances is a hollow reed for the empire to rest on. The debacles in Iraq and Afghanistan have proved that coalition-building and consensus are more critical than military force in holding an empire together. When Washington launched two demonstration wars, it ended up teaching two valuable lessons to the global South: that it is possible to stand up to the empire, and that effective resistance in one part of the empire weakens the empire as a whole.[50]

At the same time, there is a corresponding desire to build a Global Community of people that makes governments accountable to practicing the mandates associated with human rights, protecting the natural environment instead of leaving it at the mercy of corporate polluters, closing down the hidden business deals of weapons manufacturers that make children into soldiers in wars around the globe, and ending the disgrace of sweatshops that are designed to exploit the poor in the name of free trade. In all of these areas of challenge, it is the people themselves who are making the difference. They share a common aspiration and a common goal, which is to overcome the injustices of a bitter age and to oppose the fascist-like policies contained within the imperial drive of the United States. For they recognize that the nature of such a drive for domination can only result in their exclusion from the possibility of living a decent life and passing along to their own children the hope of a better tomorrow. It is for this reason that the promise contained in working for the creation of a Global Community, region to region, locality to locality, takes on a moral force.[51]

While economic and political considerations may be the means to achieve this Global Community, the fact remains that the forging of this community is the product of conscience, moral commitment, and a singular human aspiration to embrace genuine freedom—not the false freedom of the privatized market economy. Ultimately, this effort is defined by a common sense of dignity and worth among and between human beings who have seen enough of war, hate, and aggression. Increasingly, these human tragedies are understood as an avoidable consequence, not an inevitable result of fate or of history. Rather, they are seen as the product of exclusionary power elites who focus their policies on the pursuit of Global Empire. The antidote is now recognized as centered within a combination of moral, social, cultural, political, and economic principles that are inclusive and place the value of human dignity at the center of all major considerations. These inclusive principles embrace the influence of local, national, and international movements that are in the process of contributing to the rise of Global Community as a means to seek a newer world.[52]

The inclusive premise of all local, national, and international movements is the realization that the real enemy with which they must contend is located within the elite governing circles of the United States—not among the people. Insofar as they largely understand the source of their oppression, they realize that their enemy is the US power elite that have acted so irresponsibly that they have made the citizens of the United States prisoners in their own land. As Marcus Raskin has noted, "over fifty years of war and Cold War left the body politic prone to information authoritarianism, in which the corporate or government official has virtually unlimited access to the individual, such as credit history, education, personal history, and medical information." Raskin has also observed that, "the national security state's standard of need to know access, which compartmentalizes information from different parts of the government as well as the public, is another perversion that prevents access needed for deliberation. Obviously, this problem will grow starker as people are prepared to cede their own space for reasons of security."[53]

Wolin concurs with Raskin on the drift toward *information authoritarianism* and the march toward *inverted totalitarianism* when he observes,

thus, the elements are in place: a weak legislative body, a legal system that is both compliant and repressive, a party system in which one party, whether in opposition or in the majority, is bent upon reconstituting the existing system so as to permanently favor a ruling class of the wealthy, the well-connected and the corporate, while leaving the poorer citizens with a sense of helplessness and political despair, and, at the same time, keeping the middle classes dangling between fear of unemployment and expectations of fantastic rewards once the new economy recovers.[54]

Many specific examples abound to support Wolin's critique. For example, the US Senate passed a draconian revision of the US Bankruptcy Code in early March 2005 that allows for creditors to still recover vast amounts of cash from those already declared bankrupt. The average citizen is politically emasculated of genuine representation in the congress, as corporate lobbyists buy special legislation for the special interests that they represent. Unemployment under Bush-2 has been on the rise ever since he entered the White House due to "outsourcing" American jobs to Third World nations and the embrace of an economy increasingly devoted to militarism. Correspondingly, the size of the federal deficit swallows up the capacity of the economy to generate higher wages, making greater indebtedness and reliance on credit the backbone of the economy at the expense of the average citizen and worker. Hence, average citizens are economically emasculated of having a viable opportunity to improve their living standards. Additionally, at the beginning of his second term, Bush-2 embarked upon a dismantling of the last element of the FDR years by launching an attack upon Social Security by trying to push for private accounts in its place. Such a scheme would only enrich the corporate elite on Wall Street, while handing the citizen-taxpayer a bill of over $2 trillion to cover the cost of making the transition.[55]

In short, the effects of *inverted totalitarianism* are felt within the United States among a large number of people at every class level and every station of life. In the aftermath of the passage of the USA Patriot Act the people have seen the creation of a culture hostile to dissent. In this climate of fear, civil disobedience has come to be viewed by the "powers that be" as an expression of treason to the state. Under fascist-like policies such as *rendition* to another country by the CIA to interrogate suspected terrorists or their allies, these and other extra-constitutional and un-constitutional uses of state authority by the Bush administration have served to illustrate the hypocrisy of a "new world order" that promises democracy abroad, while denying its application at home.[56]

In other situations, the USA Patriot Act has been invoked to mandate placing people in jail without reference to either due process or equal protection. In some respects, this situation brings to mind the challenging days of Martin King's leadership of the civil rights struggle. His call to nonviolent opposition to segregationist laws became the strategy through which the old order of American racial apartheid would eventually crumble. Those laws built upon the foundation of Jim Crow era segregation were challenged by African-Americans who sat at lunch counters reserved for "whites only," used rest rooms reserved for "whites only," and took freedom rides to desegregate bus lines that were reserved for "whites only." Once challenged, the offenders of these apartheid laws spent time in jails, were beaten, and sometimes killed. The lawlessness of an unjust racial order took a terrible human toll. Ultimately, their sacrifices and suffering would be redeemed in the Civil Rights Acts of 1964 and 1965, as well as a host of US Supreme Court cases dealing with expanding the range of the 14th Amendment's equal protection clause.[57]

Looking back at the 1960s, the period should be remembered as a strengthening, not a weakening of constitutional protections. It would be an era that defined the progressive movement of American democracy under the "rule of law." By 2001, the *inverted totalitarianism* of the Bush-2 regime had changed the state's adherence to both civil and human rights principles. A period of regression set in around 2001 that reflected an utter arrogance of power toward political opponents, overseas allies, and established norms of national and international law. In so doing, America's domestic and foreign policy would be altered as well.

Perhaps the most telling aspect of the American drift toward totalitarian solutions has come in the Bush-2 regime's choices on how to conduct its version of the war on terror with respect to the treatment of prisoners of war. In the immediate aftermath of 9/11, President Bush issued an executive order for "terrorist suspects" to be tried before military tribunals. The president's decision to remove "due process" from these trials opened the door to contested constitutionality. It further exacerbated strained relations with the judiciary as the door was opened to other executive-sanctioned abuses regarding the treatment of prisoners when they were deemed to be "enemy combatants" and not subject to the protections afforded by the Geneva Convention. The entire issue broke wide open with revelations about prisoner abuse in Iraq at the prison in Abu Ghraib, as well as the detainment facility at Guantanamo Bay, Cuba. The Red Cross had raised questions about the treatment of prisoners as early as 2003. The criticisms lodged by the Red Cross were soon to be followed by Amnesty International when it depicted these prisons as the American version of Russian "gulags." The response from President Bush on June 1, 2005 was that these criticisms offered by Amnesty International came from a group of "people who hate America."

THE TRANSFORMATION OF AMERICA BY ITS PLUTOCRACY

Some scholars have argued that the transformation of America, under the Bush-2 regime, is the legacy of Reaganism. Reagan and his foremost disciple George W. Bush have created a plutocracy where the United States is no longer a government of the people, by the people, and for the people, but is ruled by the wealthiest individuals and corporate America. The combination of weakened government institutions in conjunction with the massive corporate fraud of Enron and other large firms have robbed the nation.[58]

Other scholars have argued that citizen disaffection in the Trilateral democracies (the United States, Japan, Europe) is not the result of a frayed social fabric, economic insecurity, the end of the Cold War, or public cynicism—they believe that the trouble lies with governments and politics themselves. They think that the sources of the problems include governments' diminished capacity to act in an interdependent world and a decline in institutional performance. In combination with new public expectations and the media, there has been a sea change in consciousness that has altered the criteria by which people judge their governments.[59] These perspectives are more of the centrist variety. In keeping with the political climate of the Clinton years, neither hard left nor hard right philosophies would be a significant part of mainstream discourse. Centrist strategies would be invoked to win elections as well as promote new social policies, such as the *Third Way*. The transformation of economic policies from left wing progressive to center required a shift from the "commanding heights" of the state to the "commanding heights" of the market. In order to accommodate this ideological transition, the centrist strategies of the Democratic Leadership Council (DLC) in the United States, and the government of Tony Blair in Britain, conspired together to form a mutually supportive coalition that could advance the cause of the corporate agenda at the expense of political parties and social movements that were oriented more to social justice concerns than the "bottom line" of corporate governance.

Still other scholars, edging closer to a more radical critique, have stressed social and cultural causes of dissatisfaction with the US government, the polarization of the political parties, the evolving scope of government, and the erosion of mass loyalties to long-established hierarchical political parties.[60] The most radical critique of the Bush-2 regime's regressive shifts come from a sociological perspective that sees centralized power and vested class interest as ultimately determinative of what direction the leadership of the United States takes. It is an updated version of C. Wright Mills *power elite* thesis.[61] These scholars envision the salvation of democracy surviving "in the form of liberal constitutionalism, and also in the form of a multiplicity of new social movements and political associations that promote inclusivity, mutual respect, and democratic deliberation."[62] This more hopeful vision requires a populist president who would "propose an international charter that adds a new dimension of moral authority to our foreign policy by setting our sights on a higher state of unity within the global community.[63] Such a populist trajectory is more in keeping with the ideals and claims of building a Global Community and abandoning the militarist ideology that sustains the advocates of Global Empire and the PNAC.

The challenge for those who seek to abandon the project of Global Empire and embrace the work associated with building a Global Community is to be found in the current state of affairs created by the Bush-2 regime. For example, "there are increasing signs of rebellion at the US state level against the limitations of international law."[64] Looking toward the future, some scholars have suggested that there are two possible future scenarios:

> The first scenario envisages the United States increasing its adherence to the rule of law in international affairs. The second would see the United States draw back further from the international legal order and rely primarily on the application of national law and procedure and on unilateral action to resolve international problems.[65]

Should the United States retreat to the application of national law in its relationship to the rest of the world, forsaking its adherence to international legal norms, the irony of recent history is that if the USA Patriot Act had actually been in effect when Nelson Mandela and the African National Congress (ANC) were fighting the white apartheid government of South Africa, both Mandela and the ANC would have been labeled as being a part of a terrorist organization.[66] In other words, under Bush-2, the act of seeking social justice and human rights protections has become illegal (pursuant to the definition of "terrorism" contained in the USA Patriot Act). What constitutes the definition of terrorism is so vague that anyone who strongly resists the government and its policies can, on a technicality, be considered to be a "terrorist." The definition of what constitutes "terrorism" is so wide that the government and its lawyers can drive a bus through it. The tragic conclusion to be drawn is that, in the murky legal world of "inverted totalitarianism," the power elite's intention is to protect the powerful and to terrorize the powerless.

In this sense, the USA Patriot Act is as much an inversion of the moral code of every major religious faith as it is also an inversion of the most basic premises of a constitutional democratic order or an evolving international law regime. Such an outcome is a demonstration of what transpires when the law of Global Empire's "power elite" becomes lawless. By protecting the powerful and victimizing the powerless, the criminality of state lawlessness exposes itself for what it really is. These actions of America's Global Empire constitute a projection of an imperial project that is divorced from principles that are the foundation for Global Community. Concern for the common good of this inclusive community resides in the values of justice, peace, security, and coexistence. These values are enjoyed through participation in a common body of authoritative practices.

In contrast, by virtue of its unbridled assertion of unilateral decision-making power, the will to dominate the world without reference to a common body of authoritative legal practices serves to illustrate the fact that the managers of Global Empire are conducting the *business of empire* in a manner that is hostile to the foundational norms of Global Community. The *business of empire* is little more than the doctrine of *might makes right*—unchecked, unconstrained, and unrestrained by the norms of international law. The resulting decline of world order may be attributed to the absence of respect for "world order values." By expressing contempt for the values of justice, peace, security, and coexistence, the managers of Global Empire have effectively disrupted the international processes for a stable social order. A stable social order is only possible where there exists widespread toleration for a great diversity of basic beliefs and values. A stable social order is also predicated upon an attitude of deference to common rules of mutual accommodation. Without such deference, the anarchic character of the ensuing global disorder may be attributed to the authors of an American Global Empire that is both dishonest and corrupt.

Recognizing this history makes it incumbent upon American citizens, as citizens within the American empire, to oppose state practices that demonstrate state lawlessness in the name of law. In that regard, for those who oppose unilateral war in violation of the UN Charter and international law; for those who oppose the flagrant disregard of the prohibitions against torture as outlined in the Geneva Convention; for those who oppose the abuse of the international law of human rights; and for those who are offended by US officials discarding the demands of domestic law (including the 8th Amendment's prohibition against cruel and unusual punishment), the hour has arrived for protest and resistance. Supported by whatever tools are left in the American legal arsenal, it will be necessary to mount legal challenges and actions against the Bush-2 administration.[67] Such efforts to confront the Bush-2 regime have already been undertaken by the American Civil

Liberties Union (ACLU) and various human rights groups within the United States. In the alternative, *inverted totalitarianism* will have won the day within the United States and captured the future for the power elites of Global Empire.

THE DANGEROUS UNION OF "TURBO-CAPITALISM" AND "INVERTED TOTALITARIANISM"

To maintain its hegemony, at home and abroad, the Global Empire will have to rely on big business—multinational corporations and transnational corporations—to economically subdue the billions of people who are to be the new global peasants and serfs in the service of the empire. Characteristic of this elite-planned world order is a global situation of widening income differentials in exchange for not-so-rapid growth. The conclusion that can be drawn from this analysis is that a neoliberal agenda matched to an antidemocratic political order is designed to be global in scope and ruthless in character.

Given this conclusion, we may put forth the following thesis: "The union of *turbo capitalism* with the practice of *inverted totalitarianism* will, if unrestrained, destroy the prospects for building and maintaining Global Community." It will have the capacity to do this by allowing "turbo-capitalism" to advance in an unrestricted manner, thereby becoming the driving force that leads to the disintegration of societies—leaving an elite number of winners and a mass of losers. These trends are made even more apparent by business strategies that involve the outsourcing of jobs from high-wage labor markets into low-wage labor markets. In this scenario, "the resulting social breakdown must then be countered by harsh laws, savage sentencing and mass imprisonment, to remove from circulation disaffected losers."[68] Hence, the ultimate consequence of this process will be a disintegrating world of global societies characterized by an endless series of civil wars. These wars will not come about because of differences of language, religion, or even nationality. Rather, such wars will be the result of these elements in combination with doctrines that hold that such differences are intolerable. The doctrine of America's Global Empire, under Bush-2, is a doctrine of "intolerance" ("if you are not with us, you are against us"). It is this lack of tolerance that exists at the heart of all forms of fascism—whether "inverted" or not.

There are numerous examples of *inverted totalitarianism*. Many of these examples center on the role of *big business*. Under Nazi rule, the subordination of business to the regime was a central premise. In contrast, corporate power within the United States has become predominant in the political establishment. Nowhere is this phenomenon more evident than within the Republican Party.[69] Under the second Bush presidency the Republican Party, with the assistance of the right wing, has radicalized the corporate agenda to such a great extent that neither young nor old are immune to the dictates of concentrated wealth and power in the fields of health care, education, labor, and the environment.

As *big business* works in concert with a neoliberal model of privatization, deregulation, and business-friendly allies in the political directorate, the insidious workings of *inverted totalitarianism* seeks to transform what is left of a free society into a variant of the extreme fascist regimes of the past century.[70] This insight has recently been expressed by a number of critics of the Bush-2 regime—most prominently, Robert F. Kennedy, Jr. In his book, *Crimes Against Nature*, Kennedy writes:

> my *American Heritage Dictionary* defines fascism as "a system of government that exercises a dictatorship of the extreme right, typically through the merging of state and business leadership together with belligerent nationalism." Sound familiar? The rise of fascism across Europe in the 1930s offers plenty of lessons on how corporate power can undermine democracy. While the United States confronted its devastating depression by reaffirming its democracy ... Spain, Germany, and Italy reacted to their economic crisis in a very different manner. Industrialists forged unholy alliances with right-wing radicals and their charismatic leaders to win elections in Italy and Germany, and then flooded the ministries, running them for their own profit, pouring government money into corporate coffers, and awarding lucrative contracts to prosecute wars and build infrastructure.[71]

Both the political and corporate agendas of the American power elite have now merged. In this respect, the corporate world of power is most representative of the dynamics of unconstrained and unrestricted *turbo-capitalism*. Writing about the Bush-2 regime, one cannot help but to draw this conclusion as an objective assessment. The economic dynamic of *turbo-capitalism* has been merged with the political dynamic of *inverted totalitarianism*. Again, Robert F. Kennedy, Jr.:

> The president and his cronies have taken the conserve out of conservative. Instead of rugged individualism, they've created a clubhouse that dispenses no-bid contracts to Halliburton. They talk about law and order while encouraging corporate polluters to violate the law. They proclaim free markets while advocating corporate welfare. They claim to love democracy while undermining open government. They applaud state rights and local control, but they are the first to tear up local zoning laws and bully states into lowering environmental standards to make way for corporate profit taking. They exalt property rights, but only when it's the right of a property owner to use his property to pollute or destroy someone else's.[72]

Nowhere is this trend more evident on a global scale than in the areas of free trade and American militarism. The agendas of both corporate and military planners are dedicated to a common strategy and a common goal: *expansionism*. *Expansionism* is their common denominator. For trade to be profitable for the titans of corporate capitalism there must be on an ever-expanding corporate capacity to conquer new markets and retain a competitive advantage against all would-be contenders. The focus upon expansion applies to the Pentagon's mission of domination through militarism.

In an age of *resource wars* for oil and markets, the architects of Global Empire believe that American domination is the only way to bring *security* to the enterprise of maintaining empire.[73] After all, it is necessary to keep American centers of consumerism and profit making ever thriving. It is also necessary to pay attention to the geographic dimensions of US strategy in conjunction with the operational aspects of US security so as to guarantee that the protection of oil fields and the defense of maritime routes remain secure for the requirements of Global Empire.[74] Therefore, it has now become the unending mission of American forces to dominate regions and resources. Because it is an unending mission, it will never be a "mission accomplished." According to various scholars, this strategy reveals the fact that "while the military can do little to promote or enhance financial stability, it can play a key role in protecting resource supplies."[75]

The strategy that has been outlined by the Pentagon divides the world into five regional "unified combatant commands." The Southern Command covers Latin America, the Pacific Command and Central Command cover the strategically important regions of Western and Central Asia, respectively. The European Command presides over NATO's forces. The role played by these commands has been likened to a modern-day proconsul—in the tradition of the warrior-statesmen who ruled the Roman Empire's outlying territory. In the person of these proconsuls, the orders and legalistic mandates of the empire would be expressed.

In this sense, the US Global Empire, like its Roman predecessor, has made its own law superior to that of any other. Its claim to authority over conquered nations is the final word. Some scholars have suggested that this is the perspective of "empire's law." It is unique from ordinary conceptions of law insofar as "empire's law" is "an assertion of a constitutional superiority backed by the power of violence. Empire's law overrides all other legal orders."[76] The following table outlines the main assertions of "empire's law":

The New Constellation of Legal Norms Within Empire's Law

---

1. Within the empire, all laws are not equal.
2. There is no international law deriving from the UN Charter that can be interpreted as applying to prevent the United States (as empire's politico-military center) from undertaking unilateral action to maintain or establish the global political conditions necessary for the proper functioning of the empire's activities.
3. All international laws supporting empire's fundamental interest in the unrestrained movement of capital across territorial boundaries shall be inviolable, and shall be enforced through international enforcement agencies.
4. All laws at the national or subnational levels that aim to preserve and protect the political, economic, and cultural needs of empire shall be inviolable, and must be respected through effective enforcement by the relevant authorities.
5. All laws that seek to preserve national or subnational self-determination in matters pertaining to the conduct of the empire's activities are repugnant to the idea of empire's law and shall thereby be non-enforceable by reason of unlawfulness, and shall instead be subject to harmonization to facilitate the smooth progress of the empire's activities.

Source: Jayan Nayar, "Taking Empire Seriously: Empire's Law, People's Law and the World Tribunal on Iraq," *Empire's Law: The American Imperial Project and the "War to Remake the World,"* edited by Amy Bartholomew, Pluto Press, 2006, p. 314.

IN SERVICE TO THE EMPIRE: FREE TRADE, SCIENCE, TECHNOLOGY, AND MILITARISM

It has been said that trade follows the flag. That statement is even more accurate in the twenty-first century than it was in the nineteenth when Europe's imperial powers circled the globe and proceeded to carve up Asia, Africa, Latin America, and the Middle East. The US Global Empire has evolved to a point where it is capable of coordinating the terms of trade, the scope of investment in research and development for new technologies, and working to assemble various new forms of military capabilities that can reach into space for the purpose of maintaining US hegemonic control on earth. In order to explicate these interlinked categories as they function in the service of empire, we shall examine trade, technology, and militarism in turn.

Terms of Trade under Hegemony and Domination

In the arena of free trade, the early 1990s witnessed congressional authorization for international trade treaties, such as the NAFTA, placed on *fast track*. Fast track is a device used to limit debate on corporate-produced legislation. International lawyers have now taken the place of legislators in forging trade agreements, writing the words, and addressing the penalties for noncompliance. The complexities of international trade are compounded by the convoluted and esoteric nature of the language of international commerce. In combination, these features of treaties authored by corporate free-trade advocates have effectively scuttled democratic control over the subject matter of trade and those affected by it. The same approach was adopted in the spring of 2001 as President George W. Bush affirmed in Quebec City strong US support for a Free Trade Area of the Americas (FTAA). It is a corporate-friendly agreement that its critics describe as "NAFTA on steroids." Aside from support from the United States, Mexico, and Canada, it is generally acknowledged that among the rest of the nations in the Western Hemisphere the passage of the FTAA will be a hard sell "to overcome the resistance of entrenched 'losers'."[77]

Due to the fact that one-sided free trade defines the tactics, strategies, and methods of Global Empire, it is inherently flawed as a vehicle for social justice concerns. In this respect, some scholars have aptly noted: "redesign of the FTAA negotiating process itself is a first priority for strengthening democracy in regional governance. If the current negotiating process proceeds without such redesign, the prospective FTAA will likely undermine democratic governance in the hemisphere."[78]

The necessity and desire for expansionism remains an integral part of the capitalist dynamic. The military and political component of this program is summed up by the terms "hegemony" and "domination." As already noted in Chapters 1 and 2, the ascendance of neoliberalism has, since the early 1980s, provided the planners of Global Empire with a set of economic beliefs that subordinates all social and development considerations to the demands of private capital and the world market. To this end, the doctrine of neoliberalism has given great ideological force to global campaigns to deregulate, to privatize state-held industries, and to liberalize trade and investment. All of these policies are integral to what has transpired under NAFTA.

These same policies are also integral to the dynamic behind the proponents of FTAA. The problem with the strategy is that "the inroads of global economic integration have made it ever more difficult for Mexico to orient its economy to provide primarily for the needs of its own population."[79] By acceding to the economic demands of globalization by restructuring economic policy to make the country more attractive to foreign investors and traders, Mexican government officials have failed to regulate the national economy in the interests of the people. In short, "the old development strategies based on satisfying the demands of the domestic market have been gradually abandoned."[80]

The adoption of NAFTA by the Mexican government signaled more than just the abandonment of old development strategies. It also resulted in a fundamental change to the Mexican Constitution. In late 1991, President Salinas proceeded to amend Article 27 of the constitution. The amendments included the termination of land redistribution and a host of other rights.[81] The changes that were made opened the door to more than merely an "economic reform"—they signified an historical retreat from more fundamental concerns about the character of the land and how natural resources were to be used and appropriated. Specifically, with the changes to Article 27, the government terminated its long-standing commitment to land redistribution and "made land more of a commodity and less of a national resource to be used for socially productive purposes. By favoring the individual over the social or communal, and financial over moral considerations, the state released itself from its responsibility to promote the common good."[82]

The resulting changes that came with the alteration of Article 27 did not have an immediate impact. Rather, the changes would come with the full-scale adoption of neoliberal measures that placed market forces in control of people's destiny, while relegating social concerns to the side. As a result, maintaining food security, absorbing rural labor, halting out-migration, preserving cultural values, and fostering rural development would be effectively abandoned.[83] Under Salinas, the Mexican state became a more "exclusionary state," relegating the victims of neoliberal policies to even less choices and hope than they had before.[84]

In the years since, every US administration has sought to capitalize on the gains made in Mexico and extend the Mexican model to the rest of Latin America. However, this is not to say that Washington's policies have not met with resistance from Latin America's leaders and people. President Juan Carols Wasmosy of Paraguay vowed "not to let economic factors prevail over the destruction of our national patrimony, because I am committed to respect it and enforce respect for it …" Also, Alberto Fujimori of Peru stressed the challenge of poverty:

We must not only protect the environment and our nonrenewable resources, but also eliminate a factor that renders the problem unmanageable: abject poverty. This is the starting point. The dynamism of poverty promotes a survival strategy and this entails an extremely high cost. The poor have no recourse other than to use the resources at hand, and thus, in some cases, they grow things such as coca leaves that are marketable and in high demand.[85] Added Eduardo Frei of

Chile: "There cannot be sustainable development with the high level of poverty that exists in cast areas of our continent."

By the end of the 1990s, a decade of environmental activism had produced only mixed results. It turned out that agenda setting was the most dramatic achievement. Popular consciousness was rising. Active lobbying for provisions in treaties and laws took on a more forceful urgency. The NGOs expanded in conjunction with citizen groups. In this new political context, environmental issues rose to a more prominent position on the inter-American docket.

In the early part of 2002, the Bush-2 regime was not merely pursuing the hoped for passage of its more expansive trade policies for Latin America. It was also covertly plotting the overthrow of the government of Hugo Chavez—the democratically elected president of Venezuela. Chavez's policies conflicted with neoliberal orthodoxy, because they were oriented toward social reforms that would help the poor, the environment, and labor. His policies were also intensely nationalistic. He courted friendships with the labor-oriented president of Brazil and with Fidel Castro. Chavez also happened to be the president of a nation with vast oil reserves that were coveted by the Bush regime.[86]

The Technology and Geopolitics of Oil

The 2001 National Energy Policy lists eight countries whose oil reserves are of potentially great advantage to the United States. Professor Michael Klare refers to these countries as "the Alternative Eight."[87] The eight countries are: Mexico, Venezuela, Columbia, Russia, Azerbaijan, Kazakhstan, Nigeria, and Angola. These countries all have proven reserves, export and production capacity, and are non-Persian Gulf oil producers. Yet, "as a response to America's energy dilemma" the Bush-2 plan that relies on these alternative countries for US needs will succeed only if:

> (a) there is sufficient oil outside the Gulf to significantly reduce our dependence on the Middle East; and (b) we can get that oil while avoiding the sorts of dangers and liabilities we now face there. In reality, *neither* of these conditions holds true ... the non-Gulf suppliers do not have enough petroleum to permit a substantial reduction on our reliance on Persian Gulf oil, yet they present a very high risk of American entanglement in regional strife and disorder.[88]

Many of these alternative suppliers "are developing nations with rising populations and ever-increasing domestic demand for oil."[89] To rely on these countries is ultimate folly. Reliance on the US Global Empire's ability to coerce the *Alternative Eight*, or to invade, intervene, or threaten them, is the result of denial and delusion.

Despite the realities of a new age with new demands, America's failure to confront the challenge of finding an alternative to reliance on foreign oil is an attempt to repeat the past as adequate precedent. By pursuing its intention to build and extend a US Global Empire in order to secure its continued worldwide dominance, it has revealed the fact that its policymakers and apologists are caught in the rip currents of the past. This dead past is part of an earlier era in which geopolitical factors were the primary focus in shaping the strategic outlook of the 𝗇 At the dawn of the twenty-first century, such a perspective is severely with the new challenges of a new age.

In this respect, America's attempt to create its own Global Empir contempt for the evolving *rule of law* in international affairs. Intern customs, and norms have been ignored as the Bush-2 regime h "disregard the legal equality of sovereigns and reinstate such concep ed membership and broad rights to use force that were so charact international legal order 50 years ago. Indeed this past order would been considerably more amenable to hegemonic aspirations than th al law of today."[90] Yet, America's attempt to recreate the hegemony time is not only at odds with the twenty-first century's regime of inter it is at odds with the realities of limited resources and the need to sustainable development, the creation of alternative energy sources enlightened attitude toward the protection of the environment.

The US failure to embrace these progressive moves and its failu key security-related treaties has resulted in the Bush-2 regime aba the evolving system of international law and the broader human inte nation on earth. The failure of the US Global Empire is exemplified tion of the "rule of an evolving system of international law" that is the aspirations of the rising Global Community. As expressed by Nic the 1990s, various US scholars sought to redefine international law individuals, a liberal international law, in which only states with liberal structures deserve protection against intervention or the right in international law making." The inherent danger of such a view is realization that such a redefinition "might lead to a world divided int the most civilized in the center, the half- and non-civilized at the per a corresponding gradation of rights."[91]

RAVEN

USED BOOKS

52-B JFK STREET
HARVARD SQUARE
617. 441. 6999

If this course were pursued, it would close off the development of a Community because no truly global community could exist on the sha of a gradation of rights. The Global Community rests on the assuran its constituent members enjoy an equality of membership—not a system of hierarchical exclusion or limited incorporation. Hence, i international law, the equality of membership within the Global Con odds with the idea of an international gradation of rights and the sp of Global Empire.

We can discern two trends on the international stage. First, there is the expansion of international law and its emerging order of inclusiveness. Second, there is the increasing politicization of international law. This second trend represents the pull toward greater inequality and is representative of a past history where the reach of international law was not as extensive as it has become in the post-1945 era. Historically, "the rules of sovereign equality were compatible with the needs of powerful states because of some very specific factors, among them restrictions on membership in the international community and the limited reach of the international legal order."[92] All of this changed in the twentieth century. The growing writ of the UN—as an international body seeking to democratize a widely divergent expression of views within the global commons—was chartered with a very inclusive mandate. Reinforcing its mandate were the legal findings contained in the Nuremberg Charter. The idea of what constituted "crimes against humanity" now had greater salience and relevance to policymakers in light of the Nazi holocaust.

However, in the aftermath of the US defeat in the Vietnam War and the rise of the NAM (representative of Third World states seeking autonomy from Northern capitalist intrusion), "the United States has sought to reverse this trend by reintroducing distinctions among members and reducing the scope of the prohibition on the use of force."[93] By exemplifying its fidelity to the masters of global corporate control, the policymakers of the US Global Empire found it convenient to make distinctions among member states that would leave them in a subordinated position to the whims of Washington. Therefore, the terms *rogue states* and *axis of evil* came to dominate Washington's discourse. It was a strategy highly dismissive of international law and the true nature of an evolving Global Community.

The American strategy for this approach to the world was already mapped out at the end of World War II. It was a view that was succinctly articulated in 1948 by George Kennan as well as some of the other architects of the fledgling US Global Empire: "We have 50 percent of the world's wealth, but only 6.3 percent of its population ... In this situation, we cannot fail to be the object of envy and resentment," noted George Kennan in 1948. "Our real task in the coming period is to devise a pattern of relationships which will allow us to maintain this position of disparity," said the then Director of Policy Planning of Department of State. "We should cease to talk about the raising of the living standards, human rights, and democratization. The day is not far off when we are going to have to deal in straight power concepts. The less we are then hampered by idealistic slogans, the better."[94]

According to Professor William I. Robinson, it may be argued that Kennan's candid statement "emphasizes that the strategic objective of US foreign policy during the Cold War was less battling a 'communist menace' than defending the tremendous privilege and power this global disparity of wealth brought it as the dominant world power ..."[95] Robinson's argument is that behind the façade of *democracy promotion*, the policy has been designed more to retain the elite-based and undemocratic status quo of Third World countries than to encourage mass aspirations for democratization. While US policy is more ideologically appealing under the title of *democracy promotion*, it does nothing to reverse the growth of inequality and the undemocratic nature of global decision making. For example, by 2004, once the Bush-2 regime was forced to admit that its primary rationale for the 2002 invasion of Iraq was without merit (no findings of weapons of mass destruction), it switched its rationale for a continuing US-led occupation to an old and time worn ideological fixture of American foreign policy—*democracy promotion*.

Under the rubric of promoting democracy, the US Global Empire has conspired to bring trade and technology into harmony with financial control, hegemony, and domination. Correspondingly, when trade and technology are not sufficient by themselves to maintain the imperial order, then the weapons of war—from outer space to air, land, and sea are being coordinated to solidify the hold of the power elites. This brings us to the final link in the chain of the US Global Empire—the doctrine of *full spectrum dominance*.

Full Spectrum Dominance: From Trade and Technology to Weapons in Outer Space

As we have already discussed, the US reliance on oil resources, whether from the Middle East and Persian Gulf States, or from the *Alternative 8*, reveals the fact that its hegemonic designs are predicated upon the exploitation of the world's natural resources and the subordination of its people. In the decades since 1948 (with Kennan's admission about US strategic goals), and in the decades since 1968 (the year that marked the turning point for global opposition to the US war in Vietnam), global resistance to the US war machine and the *Wall Street-Treasury-IMF Complex* has been growing.

Globally, it has become increasingly evident that both the US military and the US financial order have conspired together so as to maintain a *New World Order*— an order representative of the US hegemonic ambition to maintain global apartheid. It is little more than a world of poverty amidst plenty.[96] In this regard, the *New World Order* looks a great deal like the *Old World Order*—widening circles of poverty, greater global disparities in wealth, growing inequalities both within and between nations, and rising levels of violence,

On this point, David Harvey has noted:

> resistance towards and resentment of the powers of the Wall Street-Treasury-IMF complex are everywhere in evidence. A worldwide anti-globalization movement ... is morphing into an alternative globalization movement with a lot of grassroots support. Populist movements against US hegemony by formerly pliant subordinate powers, particularly in Asia (South Korea is a case in point) but also now in Latin America, threatens to transform grassroots resistance into a series of state-led if not intensely nationalist resistances to US hegemony. It is under these conditions that anti-imperialism begins to take on a different coloration which, in turn, helps define more clearly within the United States what its own imperialist project might have to be if it is to preserve its hegemonic position. If hegemony weakens, then the danger exists of a turn to far more coercive tactics of the sort we are now witnessing in Iraq [97]

In this regard, the militarist ideology of the Bush-2 administration embodies a totalizing drive for power—not dissimilar to the ideological notions of the Nazi party as it advanced the ideology of *Lebensraum* (the territory which a nation believes is needed for its national development). In much the same spirit as the Nazi claim to *Lebensraum*, the Pentagon in its document, entitled *Vision for 2020*, set out its goal to realize *full spectrum dominance*. As expressed in the Pentagon's *Joint Vision 2020* the term meant: "Full spectrum dominance—the ability of US forces, operating unilaterally or in combination with multinational and interagency partners, to defeat any adversary and control any situation across the full range of military operations." The roots of this vision may be traced back to its

Nazi legacy—a legacy that includes names such as Wernher von Braun, a guru of the cult of space. His legacy links the Nazi dream of world dominance with its most recent incarnations in the American dream of Global Empire. We find in von Braun a man who "oversaw the creation of the V-2 rockets that served as Hitler's Vengeance Weapons, of the US Army's long range ballistic missiles, and of the NASA Apollo spacecraft that carried astronauts to the moon."[98]

The Nazi dream of world domination can be seen in its most recent historical incarnations within America's grand strategy for achieving *full spectrum dominance*. It is a dream that is not isolated to the late von Braun and a few militarists in the Pentagon. Rather, the election of Ronald Reagan signaled the end of US efforts to even pretend that American space activities would be dedicated to peaceful purposes. Under the guidance of Edward Teller (another Nazi immigrant from the Third Reich) and Retired General Bernard Schriever, the Reagan administration adopted a plan to seize the "high ground" through military superiority in space. It was labeled the *Strategic Defense Initiative* (SDI). It would soon be euphemistically referred to by its critics as *Star Wars*.

The evolving technology for SDI was far from perfection. In fact, the promise of SDI failed when put to the test every time. Yet, based largely on the reputation of Teller, the *father of the hydrogen bomb*, the SDI experiment would continue to unfold along with the expenditure of billions of dollars going to Raytheon, Boeing, TRW, and Lockheed-Martin. They all rested their faith on Teller's theories about SDI, especially those that had been "crucial in establishing in the mid-fifties that H-bombs could be made small enough to fit in the nose cone of Schriever's ICBMs."[99]

, Edward Teller's career, from the time he left the Third Reich right through his career in the United States, reflected the fact that he was a strong advocate for military solutions to every strategic challenge. In this self-appointed role, Teller had the almost unique distinction of being a vigorous opponent of every arms control agreement ever signed between the United States and the USSR. This included his opposition to the 1963 Test Ban Treaty and the 1967 Outer Space Treaty. By the time of the Reagan administration, Teller's pet project was demonstrating the feasibility of basing high-energy lasers in space as part of a global missile defense system.[100]

Teller's vision of such a global missile defense system would be revived after his death during the presidency of George W. Bush. The Bush-2 regime called its version of the program: *National Missile Defense* (NMD). The Pentagon has already spent $22 billion on space weapons research—although no one can be quite sure since much of it is financed out of a classified black budget. Some specific programs were to have been cancelled. Equally likely, they may merely have been renamed. Given the military spending binge since 9/11, it should be no surprise that in May 2005 the Congress approved an overall spending bill for the Pentagon that came to over $491 billion. That sum is more than the combined defense budgets of the 15 next largest military powers. In this competition for Pentagon dollars, despite NMD-testing failures in California and Alaska, US planners have recommitted themselves to switch their focus to space—even though an effective space-based system could cost up to $1,000 billion.[101]

New goals for the US military include placing weapons into outer space. In total disregard of the 1967 Outer Space Treaty, and in the shadow of Bush's unilateral withdrawal from the 1972 ABM Treaty, the United States seeks *full spectrum dominance* of the globe through the exertion of its military power in outer space. Divorced from UN control or any mandate, custom, and/or norm from the field of international law, the United States under Bush-2 has made it clear that it intends to embark upon the militarization of the heavens—another attempt at creating an Americanized vision of *Lebensraum*. Space is already in the service of the military with satellites that gather data, speed communications, and conduct electronic eavesdropping. But these are not weapons in the accepted sense of the word. What the Pentagon seeks for its NMD program is an altogether different matter. For example, killer satellites, which the United States has been developing, are aimed at destroying an enemy's satellites. Also, the Common Aero Vehicle (CAV) is a hypersonic craft that is launched in mid-air and swoops from space, hitting targets up to 3,000 miles away with conventional weapons.

Another weapon is the Hyper-Velocity Rod Bundle, nick named "rods from God." It consists of tungsten bars weighing 100 kg or more and designed to be deployed from a permanently orbiting platform—able to hit terrestrial targets, including buried targets, at 120 miles a minute, 7,200 mph, with the force of a small nuclear weapon. In conjunction with these weapons, the Bush-2 regime is actively examining a new type of weapon—the Robust Nuclear Earth Penetrator (RNEP), designed to attack underground targets. The problem is that it would have to be a massively contaminating weapon to be effective.

Free trade, science, technology, and militarism are now working in perfect combination *in service to empire*. Nowhere is this collaboration more evident than in the Pentagon's *Vision For 2020* that unabashedly proclaims the military's mission in outer space as nothing less than: "Dominating the space dimension of military operations to protect US national interests and investment—Integrating Space Forces into war-fighting capabilities across the full spectrum of conflict." To this end, the authors of *Vision For 2020* emphasize the role of *global partnerships* because these kinds of partnerships augment military space capabilities *through the leveraging of civil, commercial and international space systems*.

On this matter, the *SIPRI-Yearbook 2002: Armaments, Disarmament and International Security* observed:

> Space-based systems are becoming an increasingly important component of military power, above all for the United States. The USA is currently investing billions of dollars annually in development and deployment of a wide range of new precision-guided weapons which are revolutionizing the conduct of warfare. These weapons rely heavily on an integrated "system of systems" that combines intelligence, communications, navigation and other military space systems.[102]

It is for this reason that "the issue of the 'weaponization' of outer space has reappeared on the arms control agenda."[103]

Given this trend it is essential that the issue of space weapons reappear on the arms control agenda. The Bush-2 regime has set the stage for a probable return to *balance-of-power* politics, insofar as the destabilizing effects of an arms race in space is quite likely. Such a result remains too grave for humanity to overlook. In that regard, such a discussion would have the efficacious effect of forcing the Global Community and the US Global Empire into a serious discussion that would "consider the gains to national security to be found in an international regime banning space weapons," thereby altering history by working "to encourage other states to join a regime opposing the deployment of space weapons."[104]

However, given the attitude of the Bush-2 regime toward the CTBT, NPT, the Outer Space Treaty of 1967, and its unilateral withdrawal from the ABM Treaty of 1972, it is dubious that the administration would be inclined to alter its current course unless forced to do so by objective limitations that are inherent in advancing the weaponization of space. Three such limitations have been identified: (1) high cost; (2) considerable susceptibility to countermeasures, and; (3) the availability of cheaper, more effective alternatives.[105]

In order to accommodate a perspective that would take the aforementioned points into serious consideration at the policy level, it would have to be acknowledged that the US Global Empire is unmanageable and counterproductive to both the national interest and the human interest. A genuine alternative policy prescription would have to include a renunciation of the basic tenets of the current investment in NMD and TMD.

Correspondingly, such a change in perspective would mean that the current group of neoconservatives would have to fundamentally alter both their current socioeconomic and sociopolitical path. Additionally, an alteration in policy of this magnitude would also have to address taking the nuclear missiles of both Russia and the United States off "hair trigger alert" status, thereby foreclosing on the danger of an accidental launch of nuclear weapons and/or a failure of operational safety. Given the scope of this agenda for peace, neoconservatives would have to alter their most sacred doctrines. In short, the adoption of a new reality and a new paradigm supportive of Global Community would have to be embraced.[106] Such a turn of events is highly unlikely as long as the Bush-2 regime remains in office.

THE RE-COLONIZATION OF THE THIRD WORLD

Ever since the end of the Cold War, a small group of militarists, neoconservative policymakers and intellectual apologists have endorsed, promoted, and invoked the grand design of an American-dominated world order. Some of them called it "the unipolarist imperative." Instead of reducing military expenditures, their contention was that such spending should be expanded. The events of September 11, 2001 became their *Pearl Harbor moment* to galvanize public and bureaucratic support for their imperial vision (see, Chapter 5). The intellectuals who acted as agents for this agenda include: Paul Wolfowitz, Colin Powell, Charles Krauthammer, Joshua Muravchik, William Kristol, Robert Kagan, and the contributors to the PNAC.[107]

While a retreat from this agenda is unlikely to come from the neoconservatives themselves, it must be argued that a change of direction is the only way in which an exodus from empire can be peacefully achieved. It is also the only way that the rise of global community could begin to be realized without tremendous difficulty and opposition. Around the globe, anti-war sentiment against the US occupation has continued to gain momentum, as well as resentment toward the policies of a Bush-2 regime that consistently relegated *the opinions of mankind* to less than a second-rate status in its foreign policy calculations.

Still, neoconservatives, such as Robert Kagan, insisted that the problem with realists was that they were "professional pessimists" and, contrary to the realist view of the world, the United States is founded on universal principles that should remain second to none. Therefore, when those principles are under siege, indifference to the violation of America's universal ideals was not only dead wrong it was also un-American. According to the neoconservative perspective, in order to avoid a return to the ideologies of the 1960s or the 1930s, "an authentically American foreign policy would reject amorality and pessimism; it would refuse altogether to accept the notion of limits or constraints."[108] This neoconservative view largely comprised the myths of empire. As has often been the case with the myths of empire, an endless piling on of reinforcing claims demonstrates the use of ex post facto justifications rather than a revelation of serious strategic assessments.

The neoconservative refusal to accept the notion of limits or constraints goes a long way toward explaining the Bush-2 administration's reluctance to embrace international law. The doctrine of preemptive war is a prime example. In this regard, the neoconservative agenda places the United States on a collision course with the finding at the International Tribunal at Nuremberg which stated: "individuals have international duties which transcend the national obligations of obedience imposed by the individual state. He who violated the laws of war cannot obtain immunity while acting in pursuance of the authority of the state if the state in authorizing action moves outside its competence under international law."[109]

Cracks in the US Global Empire are already evident. Some scholars have noted:

> On many issues there is active resistance to the United States, simply because it is the most powerful state today. Recent evidence of this resistance can be found in the decisions of world society to proceed with major initiatives despite the open and vehement opposition of the United States. Consider the agreement to move forward with the obligation of the Kyoto Protocol to the Framework Convention on Climate Change, the adoption of the Rome Statute for the International Criminal Court, the almost universal acceptance of the Ottawa Landmines Convention, and the opposition of the latest version of "Star Wars" (the so-called missile defense shield) even by the closest military allies of the United States.[110] In early 2005, Canada's parliament voted against NMD. Although it was a high priority for the Bush-2 regime, the Canadian people and their leadership rejected it.[111]

When these various forms of resistance and opposition to the US Global Empire are viewed in combination, it shows that one of the greatest vulnerabilities that the United States faces is one that flows from a global crisis of legitimacy. The neoconservatives have either failed to recognize this fact, or chosen to ignore it. Rather, they remain preoccupied with threats coming from potential military or economic rivals—the traditional sources of power. Because they have committed themselves to identifying and eliminating military and economic threats to the future of US supremacy in the world, they have failed to see that their own approach of lawless crusades for supremacy has exposed their greatest Achilles heel—a crisis of legitimacy.[112]

A crisis of legitimacy goes far in helping to explain the broad-based global opposition to a US-dominated Global Empire. The very states that were created by colonialism in the twentieth century were the result of the Great Powers creating fictional divisions and utilizing existing ones. In reality, the West manufactured false states with artificial boundaries and engaged in mixing nationalities. These imperial powers then proceeded to set them off in opposition to one another—and then engaged in exploiting them all. In the 1960s, Egypt's leader, Gamel Abdel Nasser attempted to reintegrate the Arab world and to pursue independent nonaligned policies. His efforts were met with condemnation from the West—especially from the United States.

By the early 1970s, Washington began to reap results from a sustained campaign by the CIA to establish working relationships with key Arab client regimes from Morocco and Jordan to Saudi Arabia and Iran. Regardless of the horrific human rights records in these states—some of the most repressive and undemocratic in the world—the United States made its alliances with these states so that it could secure an ever-growing supply of inexpensive oil. The policy has remained in place through the Bush-2 regime. According to one scholar: "To this day, the Western powers under the leadership of the United States continue to prop up the same illegitimate regimes created in the 20th century in contradiction to basic humanitarian and democratic principles to fulfill strategic and economic interests."[113]

Even after the demise of colonialism, Western interests continued to mold postcolonial states. Imperialism continued in an indirect form through the ability of the United States to forge working alliances with ruling cliques in the postcolonial states. So, while decolonialism was supposed to signal a reversal of the West's continuum of empire building, it actually signified its rehabilitation through more subtle and entrenched forms. It was subtle because the practice of imperialism continued not through direct control, but through the manipulation of regional surrogates. The CIA's covert arm employed secretive methods and strategic interventions. The new imperialism was more entrenched because the appearance of independence through decolonization "veiled the extent to which domestic structures were still ordered to meet Western interests."[114] However, the veil has often been ripped down. For example, in the late 1970s the fall of the Shah of Iran demonstrated the contradictions inherent in client leadership and brutal surrogates for the US Global Empire. The Shah of Iran used his secret police to terrorize his own people while he made deals with Nixon's Secretary of State, Henry Kissinger, to raise the price of oil so that he could buy more arms.

The Nixon administration gave its blessing to dismantling democracies in Chile and the Philippines and installing dictatorships. The US Global Empire was caught between two conflicting goals: a disdain for colonies and its desire for control. The contradiction was reproduced on a global scale. The struggle to contain Communism in the Cold War era led to the idea that the mission of the United

States was to build democracies around the world. It was a convenient justification for US intervention in the sovereign affairs of foreign states.

However, the effort to extend Philippine formal democracies failed in most places in East Asia, such as South Korea and Vietnam. The 1970s were a turning point when authoritarian regimes dismantled democratic practices in Chile and the Philippines. By the late 1980s, the United States removed its support from these dictatorships. It did so not from an inherent disdain for dictatorships but rather "it did so because they proved incapable of imposing stabilization and free market policies demanded by the IMF and the World Bank. They lacked the legitimacy to foist those measures on their subject populations."[115] Still, the crisis of the US Global Empire did not end with the imposition of democracy because "the democratic governments that displaced authoritarian regimes faced their own dilemma. ... It soon became clear that what the multilateral agencies wanted them to do was to use their democratic legitimacy to impose structural adjustment programs."[116]

The logic of the US Global Empire is burdened by an impossible task—to keep a system going forward that is inevitably going to continue to be in a state of decline and fragmentation due to its reliance on uncontrolled growth and the unsustainable use, and depletion of the planet's natural resources. When coupled with rising populations, more pressure to produce more energy and a dwindling base of fossil fuels, the fact remains that the imminent threat of unending resource wars does not augur well for achieving a peaceful twenty-first century. Also, the extent, duration, and sacrifices called for by the war on terror—as contemplated by Washington—have been officially extended to the following countries: Iran, Iraq, Somalia, Sudan, Lebanon, Syria, Libya, Georgia, Columbia, Malaysia, Indonesia, the Philippines, and North Korea. In January 2000, the Pentagon released a document entitled *National Military Strategic Plan for the War on Terrorism* which called for 20 to 30 years of war on a variety of states and anti-US groups.[117]

The combination of fighting a global war on terrorism, decades of resource wars, the dwindling of natural resources, the rising levels of population growth, and the lack of political legitimacy for the imperial project under US dominance, all point toward interrelated difficulties for the continuation of the US Global Empire and the aspirations of a rising Global Community. Given these trends, it seems relatively safe to assume that the contradictions contained in the imperial project of Global Empire point to its ultimate failure. Without a fundamental change in course, it is difficult to imagine that military strength alone is capable of dealing with this constellation of challenges.[118] Military solutions are not what are required for achieving "human security"—broadly understood.

In summary, the *Wall Street-Treasury-IMF Complex* has unleashed an American dominated globalization process that seeks a continued effort to secure an economic *Lebensraum* through the US-dominated institutions of the IMF, WTO, and World Bank. The *Pentagon-CIA-White House Complex* have unleashed a military agenda for global domination that seeks a continued effort to secure a military and political *Lebensraum* through a policy and program dedicated to the realization of *full spectrum dominance*. In short, the *power elite* of the US Global Empire remains prepared to go to any lengths that they perceive as necessary in order to make the twenty-first century into *another American Century*.

TOWARD A LAWLESS TWENTY-FIRST AMERICAN CENTURY:
THE COLLISION OF LAW WITH POWER POLITICS

If the Bush-2 regime represents anything besides a stubborn adherence to a right wing agenda, it is found in its contempt for the rule of law in international affairs. By deciding to fabricate evidence to justify a war with Iraq, effectively blocking the work of UN inspectors in Iraq before the official onset of the war, the Bush-2 regime has effectively demolished the legal standard embodied by the concept of sovereign equality. By shoving aside any genuine concern with the opinions of other states, the Bush-2 regime has glorified a form of Global Empire building that is supportive of an unequal hierarchy of states and the prerogatives of law of power. Further, its actions have been justified by the architects of Global Empire as an expression of American military power in service to a vague and ill-defined pursuit of Middle East freedom and "spreading democracy."

The confluence of democracy promotion with balance-of-power scenarios and global strategies designed to ensure superpower dominance is a deadly mix. To begin with, it guarantees international instability with respect to leading states such as Russia and China. Even US allies throughout Europe are at odds with a US position that seeks hegemonic advantage at the price of long-term stability and mutual cooperation. Both allies and potential adversaries can now share a similar disdain for America's Global Empire without having to apologize for finding agreement from states that used to be rivals. Europe, China, Russia, and parts of Latin America find themselves in mutual agreement over their mutual contempt— the designs, policies, and strategies of the US Global Empire.

The Bush doctrine on spreading freedom and democracy collapses the concept of the defense of freedom into the expansion of freedom. The *defense of freedom* has been depicted in and through the Bush-2 regime's launching of a "war on terror." The *expansion of freedom* has been characterized by the Bush-2 regime as central to its historic mission. Both characterizations are more mythology than policy. If the initial fury over the attacks on 9/11 were to be used as a rationale for a war on oil-producing countries in the name of fighting terrorism, then so be it. If the long-term struggle to secure military bases and US hegemony over rich oil-producing regions was required, then the idea of *expanding freedom and democracy* has been viewed as a propaganda tool that could be marshaled to provide an explanation and a rationale for military adventures around the globe. Even an ill-conceived war of aggression against Iraq would be characterized as a war in defense of freedom.

While the search for WMD launched the US war against Iraq, the US occupation of Iraq has been sustained by the idea of spreading freedom and democracy. In reality, it has been the spread of economic efforts to privatize the Iraqi economy that has been at the heart of the occupation. Along with the need to protect Iraq's oil pipelines against disruption by terrorist attack and insurgents, the US military has been given an assignment that US Secretary of Defense Donald Rumsfeld admitted could last 12 years. In short, while US access to dwindling oil supplies has been the primary driving force behind neoconservative policymakers in Washington, the ideological fig leaf of *democracy promotion* would be employed and heralded as the most newly conceived justification for the occupation of the oil-rich territories of the Persian Gulf and the Caspian Sea.

Since 2001, new American military bases are continuing to be constructed by special arrangements with host governments throughout the Persian Gulf and the Caspian Sea region. The US goal is to establish a permanent presence in these regions so as to cut off intrusions by Russia or China that might cripple US access to dwindling sources of oil. In this scenario, by maintaining that its military presence in the Persian Gulf region, the architects of the US Global Empire claim that they are merely embarking upon a benign foreign policy that is designed to extend and expand freedom and democratic institutions. Ostensibly, this extension of freedom will come through regime change, voting, and a semblance of democratic reforms. However, the reality of popular insurgencies, the threat of civil war, and the inherent instability of fledgling democratic states fails to provide little substantive credence to an argument about extending the domain of freedom. In reality, the geostrategic reasons for America's imperial expansion are never far from the consciousness of those in power. The men of power remain aware of how the great game is really played. Hence, the pursuit of the national interest remains, as ever, a great power rivalry between potential hegemons.

Along with these imperial arguments, the neoconservative policymakers of the Bush-2 regime maintain that there is an alleged right that America is entitled to in the world by virtue of its exceptional role in history. Neoconservatives in the Bush administration also maintain that the US Global Empire owns an entitlement to exceptional treatment, because it alone can lay claim to a special mission in the world. Such a faith is the most recent expression of the ideology of American "exceptionalism." One of the problems that arise from this view is found in the realization that it is inconsistent with the principle of the sovereign equality of nations. If America is exceptional among the nations, then it is no longer to be judged as an equal among other equals. Rather, it allows America to be transmuted into a Global Empire that allows for the domination of all other states by the decrees of US policymakers. In short, the doctrine of American exceptionalism is supportive of a belief in international hierarchy in which sovereign equality has to be abandoned as a principle of international law. Therein lies the danger of a lawless twenty-first American Century.

4
Clash or Convergence?

The Emerging Unity of
Religions and Civilizations

Unfortunately, the September 11 attacks appear to have eclipsed the hopeful democratizing tendencies of the 1990s. The attacks give rise to a strengthened marriage of economic and state power—taking the unprecedented form of a non-territorial, counter-terrorist crusade that wields its interventionary authority throughout the world and seeks to perpetuate and extend this role of global security through the exercise of monopoly control over the militarization of space and oceans. Only the great world religions have the credibility, legitimacy, and depth of understanding to identify and reject the idolatry that seems to lie at the core of this American project of planetary domination.[1]

Richard A. Falk

Because the systems view of mind is not limited to individual organisms but can be extended to social and ecological systems, we may say that groups of people, societies, and cultures have a collective mind, and therefore also possess a collective consciousness. We may also follow Jung in the assumption that the collective mind, or the collective psyche, also includes a collective unconscious. As individuals we participate in these collective mental patterns, are influenced by them, and shape them in turn. In addition, the concepts of a planetary mind and a cosmic mind may be associated with planetary and cosmic levels of consciousness.[2]

Fritjof Capra

Identities at all levels are constructed by establishing order and security within a radically impermanent and interdependent world ... To create order, we exaggerate differences between peoples, create dichotomies between "us" and "them," and reify these into fixed and independent entities set off from one another by imputedly intrinsic and insurmountable differences. Fostering intense and distorting emotional attachments, these fixations provide the basis for strong identification with our group and antagonism toward the other.[3]

William S. Waldron

In view of the failures of America's attempt to impose its vision for a Global Empire on the world, there is a need to identify an alternative to its destructive cadence. Previous chapters have outlined many, if not most, of the major failings of America's imperial project. Yet, what remains to be addressed is the fact that these failures are as much moral failures as they are failures of a military or economic nature. In this regard, my reference to the word "failure," is not meant to imply merely a failure of American military might to repress people. Neither is it meant to refer only to economic failures, such as rising levels of poverty and inequality in First and Third World nations. Rather, I mean to expand the idea of the failure of Global Empire to encompass the idea of moral failure—a betrayal of ethical standards embodied in the world's great religions, the normative ethics and the demands of an evolving regime of customary international law, and the ideals of freedom and democracy in a post-Enlightenment era.

The moral failure of Global Empire is attributable to its political architects and its intellectual apologists and collaborators. The intellectual foundations for the current imperial project may be traced to the neoconservative authors of the PNAC (*Project for the Next American Century*). The intellectual foundations for empire extend beyond the works of neoconservative authors and their ideological allies. Our analysis should attempt to reveal all the major sources that constitute an ideological justification of empire. In particular, we need to examine the work of Professor Samuel Huntington. He is the author responsible for the now famous (infamous) *clash of civilizations* thesis. The argument of this chapter runs counter to his thesis. My counterargument to Huntington's thesis is an argument for the *convergence of civilizations*.

I will argue that a *convergence of civilizations* is an historical trend that is currently in the process of evolving. It is largely due to the intersection of an evolving concept of customary law that subordinates even the most powerful of states to its normative demands and the moral mandate that emanates from the world's great religions. Both international law and the central teachings of the world's great religions share some basic elements in common. Religion provides the foundations for a more compassionate and empathetic approach to suffering than is provided by economic thinking. Economic thinking (capitalistic) is single-mindedly dedicated to efficiency, profits, growth, and radical individualism. Religion provides a foundation for the long-term stewardship of the environment, including the norms of sustainability and resource management. A religious orientation toward the environment provides a commitment to avoiding environmental decay and ecological collapse. The moral mandate emanating from the teachings of the world's great religions opened the diplomatic door to forgiveness and the reconciliation of peoples, as exemplified by the work of South Africa's Truth and Reconciliation Commission (TRC).

In short, the symbiosis of the normative dimensions of international law and the moral teachings of the world's great religions can act as the vehicle for the actualization of Global Community. These shared elements constitute a unity. It is a unity that is discernible amidst the global diversity of cultures and nations. It is a unity made possible through shared values. It is a unity that transcends rules and rule-based thinking. While rules are often formed by a dominant party and capable of breeding resentment, we find an opposite result obtains with regard to shared values. Therefore, because there are universal norms and values that are held in common by the evolving regime of international law and the moral traditions of the world's great religions, I will argue that there exists a basis of understanding from which we can identify an historical process that I am calling the *convergence of civilizations*. Due to the global impact and normative force of this evolving legal and moral consciousness, we are enabled to speak of a rising Global Community without the danger of sounding utterly utopian.

Hence, my argument is the counter-thesis to both a *clash* of civilizations and the idea that a Global Empire can exercise *domination* over all civilizations. Both the notions of *clash* and a political project based upon achieving *domination* reflect the moral failure of status quo thinking. In other words, the *realist* school of international relations (IR) thought—centered around concepts of *balance of power*, and a continuing *war of all against all*,—are reflective of a status quo paradigm that falsely claims to have captured the "realities" of global life. However, the realist paradigm fails to capture the full range of potentialities contained in international affairs. Because the realist paradigm seeks to provide an explanatory framework that is overtly deterministic, it only creates the illusion of the historical inevitability of contending global powers in persistent and unremitting conflict. What it fails to grasp is the ever-changing nature of human beings and their capacity to transcend the experiences and practices of the past.

While the world's great religions teach and promise transcendence and transformation, the realist paradigm constructs an artificial prison in which humanity continues to return to some new variation of its past experiences. The central issue is human freedom and the capacity for choice versus blind adherence to a fixed set of identities of assumptions. The central question is: "Will human beings make their identity into a prison?" That is what the realist paradigm and the *clash* thesis attempt to do because the categories that they seek to create are confinements that place limits on what individuals and nations can or cannot accomplish. It is intellectual surrender.

In contrast, by rejecting the idea that people belong in rigid prisons of allegedly decisive identities the *convergence of civilizations* thesis celebrates human freedom and creativity. The exercise of human freedom allows for the interjection of transcendent values into history—thereby transforming human history, institutions, and experience. Instead of being trapped in rigid categories, I argue that humans share a plurality of identities. In support of this proposition, I am arguing that both the world's great religions and the norms of evolving customary international law represent a convergence of moral and intellectual agreement on the nature of this pluralism. This pluralism needs to be protected and respected. For it is the ethical, political, moral, and legal foundation of a viable Global Community.

Our duty to other human beings may not necessarily be linked only to the fact that we share a common human identity, but also to our sense of concern for them irrespective of any sharing of identity. To break loose of the categories that trap us in the cages of stagnant identities and frozen categories, is to experience the liberation of the mind and spirit that comes from a sense of solidarity with one another. The Western values of tolerance and liberty are the historical products of a particular civilization and the evolution of its identity. These norms are an achievement. Yet, the ultimate value of these norms on the world stage resides in their capacity to transcend the categories in which they were forged. The contemporary relevance of these norms will be found in new global applications—in forms of human solidarity that transcend nation-state, tradition, and political allegiance.

Hence, the *convergence of civilizations* thesis that I am proposing is not pointing toward a convergence of identities, but to a shared appreciation of our various identities—under the conditions of pluralism. Ultimately, the *convergence of civilizations* is discovered in the experience of solidarity with one another. This is the platform on which the promise and realization of Global Community can be freely forged. The intersection of evolving strains of customary international law along with the moral traditions of the world's great religions presents us with a picture of unity in diversity—a Global Community. As such, this intersection represents a shared morality based on human rights, human dignity, and human action that can ultimately be dedicated to serving the human interest as a whole—regardless of nation or nationality. If we fail to serve the larger human interest, then we have embarked upon a path of "moral failure."

The various elements of our current moral failure include: (1) the moral failure to reduce national and global poverty; (2) the moral failure of states to protect and extend the reach of human rights; (3) the moral failure to protect the natural environment; (4) the moral failure to extend the rights, freedoms, and values set forth in founding statements and documents of the UN. In combination, these moral failures may lead to a "clash" between peoples, but it is not because there is something inherently wrong with these civilizations or religions. Rather, the *clash* emerges as a consequence of moral failures listed above. Until humanity's common moral center is discovered and respected for its capacity to forge a new vision for Global Community, it is clear that the old vision of the old order will persist.

Should the human community invoke the will and shared vision to reverse course on these moral failures, then it will be possible to witness the rise of Global Community and a corresponding decline of Global Empire. Therefore, an *exodus from empire* is predicated upon finding a shared moral center that underlies the inherent unity of peoples amid diversity. The discovery of this shared moral center emerges from universally held values. These values have the capacity to drive and inspire a new vision for global order because these values support and sustain fidelity and respect for our common human interest. The discovery of the shared moral center constitutes the basis for *convergence*.

THE MORAL IMPERATIVE TO REALIZE
JUSTICE WITHIN THE GLOBAL COMMUNITY

In the mid-twentieth century, the first universal acknowledgment of humanity's moral center was expressed in the Universal Declaration of Human Rights. Therefore, in this discussion, I will use as my starting point the moral principles for global governance as outlined in the Universal Declaration of Human Rights, Articles 25 and 28: *Everyone has the right to a standard of living adequate for the health and well-being of himself and of his family, including food, clothing, housing, and medical care. Everyone is entitled to a social and international order in which the rights and freedoms set forth in this Declaration can be fully realized.*[4] In light of the language of Articles 25 and 28, it is significant to note that the shared moral perspective of the authors clearly recognizes the need of the international community to create a "social and international order" in which the aforementioned rights and freedoms can be actualized. This insight has the force of a moral imperative. As a moral imperative, it calls for national and international accountability to a higher standard as opposed to a narrowly defined national interest. In this regard, my first thesis statement is as follows:

> The logic of America's Global Empire is completely at odds with the moral imperative to create a social and international order that is capable of sustaining the elements that constitute a humanely (justly) ordered Global Community.

By placing profits before people, a fundamental shift of the moral paradigm has enabled the architects of the US Global Empire to play a shell game with the lives of billions of people. The neoconservatives who inhabit and control the agenda of the Bush-2 regime not only disregard the lives of billions of people—they remain in a state of denial about the human costs perpetrated by the Global Empire. Critical scholars examining the neoconservatives and their agenda have noted:

> By calling for the end of class conflict, they implicitly leave their wealthy patrons in control. They refer to egalitarian illusions as if the ideals of equality that America is built upon are unattainable. By leaving the decision to go to war in the hands of the political elite, they forsake the government of "*we the people*" and institute a regime that pursues policies that cater only to the needs of the imperial establishment.[5]

Choices made and designed for the imperial establishment can only work to undermine and eventually eliminate the moral imperative to create a socially just and humane order—both within the United States and around the world. That is because the nature of their choices and decisions are inherently exclusionary—representative of the priorities and paradigms of the power elite in the service of the imperial project.

In the alternative, the introduction of a moral imperative makes a demand that policies be shaped to advance humane and inclusive forms of governance. Inclusive and humane forms of governance are normatively equipped to undermine the imperial projects of Global Empire. By endorsing the idea of unity in diversity, the claims of a rising Global Community place the architects of Global Empire on the defense. Why? Because both the claims and demands arising out of this moral imperative reflect the aspirations and choices of the excluded majorities of peoples in First and Third World nations.

AN ALTERNATIVE DISCOURSE ON THE USES OF POWER

The discovery of an alternative discourse is found not only in the *uses* of power, but also within a thoughtful consideration of the *consequences* of power in the shaping of humanity's future. For example, the moral imperative that "the service of human needs should be the guiding principle for major economic and political decisions, rather than the maximization of national power or corporate profit,"[6] lays a creative foundation for developing a Global Community characterized by cooperation and an increased sense of solidarity. This perspective is also a revolution in values. The principle of placing people before profits is a value—not a rule. Rules can be disputed, but values guided by shared moral principles travel on a higher level than the pursuit of profit for the sake of profit.

Cooperation and solidarity are expressions of inclusive forms of humane governance that transcend nationalism and a traditionally narrow definition of what is in the national interest. Inclusive forms of humane governance are antithetical to the claims and agenda of the imperial project of Global Empire. Insofar as the concepts and practices of cooperation and solidarity are inherently capable of transforming the worlds of political and economic life, they represent a threat to the exclusionary practices of domination and repression that characterize the status quo of America's imperial project. The advocates of empire, by virtue of their insistence that the UN will lead to tyranny, show no faith in humanity. In fact,

by implying that the growth of American military power was a fluke, they ignore the century-long drive by corporate America to construct a military used to open doors to resources around the world. Finally, by promoting the pre-emptive use of military power, they promote a wanton military force that plays upon the fear-mongering that has been used to sell the use of military power for centuries.[7]

In this regard, my second thesis statement is as follows:

The *clash of civilizations* is nothing more than an ideological construction for proceeding with business as usual. The *clash* thesis is a cruel hoax that is employed to justify huge expenditures on a so-called *war on terror* while continuing to wage *war on the weak*.

The failure to understand the moral consequences of Global Empire ultimately results in a failure to comprehend the devastation wrought by poverty, exploitation, and the unequal treatment of people in the international arena. The march of corporate-styled globalization has demonstrated that "downsizing, corporate restructuring and relocation of production to cheap labor havens in the third world have been conducive to increased levels of unemployment and significantly lower earnings to urban workers and farmers ... According to the International Labor Organization (ILO), worldwide unemployment affects one billion people, or nearly one third of the global workforce."[8] These results are in large measure attributable to globalization. Such results are also the consequence of what I have termed *exclusionary governance*.[9] When major social groups, parties, and interests are purposefully divorced from decision-making processes that affect their lives, an anti-democratic form emerges that I call: *exclusionary governance*. It is through exclusionary governance that the tyranny of the global marketplace finds its ultimate expression in following the dictates of the neoliberal agenda.

The imperial agenda of corporations and empire serves to explain how the global corporation minimizes labor costs on a world level. We find that "real wages in the third world and Eastern Europe are as much as 70 times lower than in the United States, Western Europe, or Japan: the possibilities of production are immense given the mass of cheap impoverished workers throughout the world."[10] These realities are not merely economic, political, and social. These realities also constitute deeply moral issues that have a blowback effect upon the citizens in the homeland of America's Global Empire. On this point,

> there is a serious democracy deficit ... in the affluent countries, whose citizens have not approved, and for the most part do not even understand, very important foreign policies and international practices that are conducted and upheld in their name ... Democracy involves the fulfillment of not only important rights, but also of important responsibilities of citizens. To the extent that citizens abandon their responsibility to control the power that is exercised in their name, their country is less than fully democratic. Most citizens of the affluent states are abandoning this responsibility, insofar as they choose to understand very little about how the vast quantities of imported resources they consume are acquired and about the impact that the terms of such acquisitions have in the countries where these resources originate.[11]

THE MORAL FAILURE OF THE CITIZENRY
IN GLOBAL EMPIRE

By failing to understand where these resources originate, the majority of citizens within the affluent states suffer from a corresponding failure to understand the role of the IMF, WTO, World Bank, and multinational corporations. After all, these are the leading institutions of the Global Empire responsible for maintaining such a state of affairs. When average American citizens blame the poor of the Third World for their own poverty, they exhibit an ignorance of the fact that "the restructuring of the world economy under the guidelines of the Washington-based institutions and the World Trade Organization (WTO) increasingly denies individual developing countries the possibility of building a national economy."[12]

The WTO, in accordance with the dictates of macroeconomic policy, "transforms countries into open territories and national economies into 'reserves' of cheap labor and natural resources."[13] When coupled with the structural adjustment programs of the IMF, the affected countries find that their state apparatus is undermined, industry for the internal market is destroyed, and national enterprises are forced into bankruptcy.[14] These particular institutions, with the support of the US government, have made possible many of the great social, political, economic, and environmental disasters of the late twentieth and early twenty-first centuries—not the least of which has been the elimination of minimum wage legislation, the repeal of social programs, and a general diminution of the state's role in fighting poverty.[15]

At this point, it should be more than clear that American propaganda about the "miracle of the market" has effectively obscured the real causes of global poverty, global conflict, and the sources of terrorism. This is the case because America's Global Empire is supported by a hegemonic discourse—reinforced by the Western media. Yet, buried underneath a mountain of disinformation, the fantasies of right wing think tanks, and an industry of governmental and corporate sponsored propaganda, it remains vitally important to recognize that there are various submerged and alternative discourses. The Global Community has at its command the force of international law, the moral codes of the world's great religions, and the lessons of history. All of these sources of wisdom, persuasion, and intellectual achievement represent an alternative consciousness that is at odds with the Global Empire's arsenal of theories supportive of exploitative financial capital and the neoliberal model.

America's Global Empire is in large measure maintained by its betrayal of the Bretton Woods Agreement of 1944. America's broken mandate with respect to the Bretton Woods Agreement has resulted in the United States forsaking the very foundations on which the system was originally predicated—"economic reconstruction" and the stability of exchange rates. Instead of keeping faith with the spirit of the Bretton Woods mandate of 1944, the Reagan administration radically altered national and global economics in the decade of the 1980s. The Reagan years ushered in a decade of debt for Latin America, Asia, and Africa while using the IMF and World Bank to contribute to the destabilization of national currencies and ruining the economies of developing countries.[16]

BUILDING GLOBAL COMMUNITY IN THE
SHADOW OF "IMPERIAL OVERSTRETCH"

There many reasons for the appearance of numerous cracks in the imperial project. In fact, there is a virtual catalog of problems associated with just the notion of *imperial overstretch*.[17] While the concept of *imperial overstretch* is valid, I believe that it is an incomplete assessment. In order to obtain a comprehensive assessment it will be necessary to take into account the complexities of an evolving world order that is connected to an evolving human consciousness. Within the process of collective thinking, "we create a world of culture and values that become an integral part of our natural environment ... Social institutions evolve toward increasing complexity and differentiation, not unlike organic structures, and mental patterns exhibit the creativity and urge for self-transcendence ..."[18] In this regard my third thesis statement is as follows:

Global Empire is incapable of change because it is premised upon retaining power, domination, and hegemony, while Global Community can only emerge by continuing to evolve in reference to humane values and inclusive norms. Therefore, the emergence of Global Community is predicated upon the self-transcendence of cultures as they converge toward a condition of unity in diversity. The nature of this unity is not a reification of the past through ritual and domination—it is the embrace of uniqueness and the willingness to adapt in relationship to other diverse cultures.

The mere exercise of raw power cannot be a substitute for ideas, beliefs, and values. Imperial power in the service of the status quo is ultimately destructive to both those who exercise it as well as those who are the victims of it. Poverty and inequality are the twin children of the US Global Empire's marriage to processes and institutions of exploitation. In this imperial word, there is a shredding of people's personal dignity and worth, while relationships between individuals and cultures are disfigured through the continuing legacy of racism, hierarchy, and socioeconomic subordination. In this respect, "the world of neo-liberal capitalism rolls on its usual course. The dominant fact about this world is not the 'war against terrorism', but the remorseless growth of poverty and inequality."[19]

In the Western framework, technocratic forms of knowledge have been employed largely for military conquest and/or economic efficiency and profit. Yet, the science that lies behind these endeavors is dehumanizing. It is a form of science that allows, permits, and encourages technology to sit in judgment on itself, divorced from a moral criterion. Recognizing this situation exposes the weaknesses and vulnerabilities of a science based upon reductionism. It exposes the true nature of empire and opens the doors of perception to see the failures and limitations of the imperial project even more clearly. Only ignorance and huge investments in propaganda, combined with an insular nationalistic outlook, can hope to sustain the illusions and distortions of the *might-makes-right* principle.

On this very point, some scholars have already alluded to the "writing on the wall" that attends the imperial project because:

> it is hard not to believe that this is a world heading for catastrophe. The "war on terrorism" can contribute materially to this process. The assertion of naked American military power will feed the hatred and despair that helped to produce the 9/11 atrocities in the first place. The geopolitical instability and Great Power rivalries that the conquest of Iraq has promoted will encourage states large and small to look for weapons and tactics that will give them an edge against the Pentagon ... Nemesis awaits the 'democratic imperialists' in the Pentagon, as it did earlier conquerors. The only question concerns the form that retribution will take. Will the imperial war machine finally fall by bringing on the great catastrophe that market capitalism has long been secreting within itself, in the process of destroying the rest of us, and perhaps the earth itself as well?[20]

The maintenance of the imperial project depends upon adherence to the illusion that different peoples and cultures are separated by insurmountable differences. The façade of the empire's legitimacy is premised upon unsubstantiated claims of cultural and religious clashes followed by a perceived necessity for the imperial project. In order to expose the illegitimacy of the imperial project, it is essential to see beyond illusion and unsubstantiated claims that arise more from ideological loyalties than from objective analysis. In the category of unsubstantiated claims, I place the argument of Samuel Huntington—that a *clash of civilizations* is to be expected as an inevitable outgrowth of the cultural and religious differences between Western societies and Islamic and Asian societies. In contrast,

I argue that the illusion of insurmountable differences may be little more than a distorted mental map that provides a prolific breeding ground for fear, hostility, and resentment. However, such a mental map is not adequate to sustain the long-term requirements of a functional Global Empire. Therefore, it is essential to recognize that there is no historical doctrine of predestination that would make a *clash of civilizations* inevitable.[21]

BEYOND THE "CLASH OF CIVILIZATIONS"

Huntington's argument is centered on the notion that the most important countries in the world come from radically different civilizations and cultural backgrounds. From this starting point, he somehow makes the leap to asserting that broader wars will arise "between groups and states from different civilizations."[22]

My question is: "Why is conflict inevitable between states from different civilizations?"

Could we not make an opposite argument that the twentieth century represents a history of international political integration? Could we not argue that there is a movement toward *convergence* instead of *clash*? Could we not further posit the idea that the learning-to-learn experiences with international political integration have widened, deepened, and expanded human nature and consciousness to such a degree that differences between and among civilizations and cultures are becoming less extreme? Could we not further argue that in the process of discovering our common humanity, common interests, and shared areas of common concern (such as global climate change) that there are ever-expanding possibilities for building a viable Global Community? Could we not argue that the period from the late nineteenth century to the early twenty-first century has marked the rise of an international civil society? Could we not also identify an increasing reliance on non-violence as a method for enacting political changes as well as regime changes?

My answer to these questions is in the affirmative. It is an affirmation that is partially premised upon the realization that since the early nineteenth century there has been an evolving trend in building international political organizations. It is an affirmation premised upon the growth of nonviolent methods, movements, and strategies that gave definition to Russia's people's strike of 1905, India's movement for self-rule under Gandhi, Poland's release from communist domination by the demonstration of workers' power through the "Solidarity" union, the resistance of Denmark and the Netherlands to Nazi rule, the American campaign for civil rights under Martin King, South Africa's campaign against apartheid by Nelson Mandela, as well as the rising democratic tide in China, Eastern Europe, and Mongolia.[23] Underlying all of these examples is the realization that a moral mandate was used to encourage the convergence of people under principles that recognized unity in diversity, the centrality of human rights, and the sanctity of preserving human dignity.

In the category of the evolution of international political organization we find that the Concert of Europe was succeeded by the League of Nations, and the League of Nations was succeeded by the United Nations. While the UN has not always been the most effective provider of collective security, "it has made great strides since the end of the Cold War" and "ended the stalemate in the Security Council."[24] In the category of economics, for better and for worse, the forces of globalization and the integration of separate groups of national capitalists into a single global capitalist class had led to the formation of the Trilateral Commission and the Group of Seven. The conclusion that can be reached is that these developments support the notion that more is going on at the global level than the formation of "a club for statesmen."[25]

The growth of global governance has been augmented by the development of civil society, at both the national and international levels. By definition, civil society is composed of many nongovernmental actors—religious groups and institutions, trade unions, universities and colleges, and a variety of many other civil associations. Civil society is a sphere of associations (voluntary associations), social movements, and forms of public communication. For analytical reasons, civil society should be differentiated from both a political society (made up of parties, political organizations, and parliaments/congresses) and an economic society (composed of organizations of production and distribution, firms, cooperatives, and partnerships). Both political and economic societies remain directly involved with state power because they seek to control and manage it. In contrast, civil society can subordinate the struggle for state power to the evolution of patterns of normative integration and open-ended communication.[26] In contrast to Huntington's thesis about an inevitable *clash of civilizations*, my argument is as follows:

The combination of international political integration (such as the European Union, the United Nations), the rise of civil society (which has expanded the intellectual and geographic boundaries of normative integration and open-ended communication), as well as an increasing reliance upon the methods and strategies of nonviolent resistance (the ouster of Britain from India, the dismantling of Jim Crow laws in the American south, the breakdown of apartheid in South Africa), has allowed the door to be opened for the rise of Global Community.

GLOBAL INTEGRATION, NONVIOLENT RESISTANCE, AND THE RISE OF CIVIL SOCIETY

Since the end of the Cold War, some Americans have tried to depict the early twenty-first century as a moment of change and transition to a new age by invoking various titles for it, such as: *the end of history*, the *clash of civilizations*, the birth of *another American century*. I will argue that all these conceptualizations of world order and disorder are essentially fragmentary elements of a larger reality. Further, I will argue that these various conceptualizations represent a snap shot in history that freeze-frames a particular moment in time. Therefore, to fixate on a particular moment would be to make it into an absolute. Such a fixation would have the effect of transforming a moment in historical time into a deterministic mind-set. Such a fixation would indulge the temptation to take an impermanent situation and translate its temporal significance into the illusion of a fixed ideological reality (such as the inevitability of a *clash of civilizations* or Bush's nationalistic crusade about a nonending *war on terrorism*).

To yield to such a temptation would result in a closure of our minds to other alternative worlds of human possibility, experience, and collective action.[27] Therefore, it is possible to argue that the trends associated with global political integration of the world have opened the door for a new set of historical alternatives to the status quo. I shall argue that with the rise of civil society, humanity can exert a collective power that can act as a counterweight to the imperial project of neoliberal capitalism and US militarism. Finally, I shall argue that the power of nonviolent resistance constitutes a force that can reach critical mass and evolve a capability for giving birth to a more humane and inclusive global order. To argue otherwise would be to close off all considerations of alternative worlds. It would make the *clash of civilizations* a self-fulfilling prophecy. Such a possibility arises not from any inherent truth-claim in Huntington's thesis, but rather a collective surrender of moral responsibility for the choices, directions, and policies that are undertaken in the name of the people or "national security."

Such a surrender of moral responsibility is the product and result of *empire's law*. Empire's law is "an assertion of a constitutional superiority backed by the power of violence. Empire's law overrides all other legal orders."[28] Given this perspective, it would seem that the potential for *clash* is really the product and result of imperial rule. Acting through its administrators, the imperial directors of the empire seek to impose their iron will on the rest of the world. It is their "law" that overrides all other legal orders and belief systems—thereby inviting war, violence, and perpetual conflict. If this is an accurate depiction of the imperial reality, then the *clash thesis* is merely a prediction concerning the reaction of people in the global South to the tyranny of empire. In contrast to *empire's law* we can assert an alternative—a people's law perspective. A *"people's law perspective* of resistance against empire's rule would begin with a series of demystifications necessary as a first act of repudiation."[29]

1. Despite attempts to claim the opposite, there exists no inviolable right, on the part of the powerful, to govern, rule, order, the weak.
2. Regardless of the ideological claims being advanced, there exists no unifying or unified civilization consensus on the naturalness of a corporate-dominated, militaristic imperialism as comprising the common values, truths, visions of human futures that prescribe a universal course for humanity's social evolution.
3. Notwithstanding attempts to convince otherwise, there exists no preordained rationale for eternal truth of inevitability, regarding forms of socially constructed orders that form the institutions of governance, including the form of "law."

THE INEVITABLE CRUMBLING OF
A DETERMINISTIC WORLDVIEW

From the standpoint of international law and politics, the Westphalian rubric of international order is no longer adequate to describe present realities. It was inaugurated in 1648, intended to designate a state-centric, sovereign-oriented, territorially bounding framing of international authority. It was structured to identify a hierarchically structured world order shaped and managed by dominant or hegemonic political actors. At the close of the twentieth century that order was in decline.

The end of the Cold War was supposed to signify its final demise. However, while the old system cannot be resuscitated, the geopolitics of America's imperial project seeks to revive its basic pathology under the rubric of an American-dominated Global Empire. This is the worldview in which Huntington's thesis resides with its dire prediction of an inevitable *clash of civilizations*. This negativity is "complemented by other tendencies associated with corporate and apocalyptic globalization, but it is offset to varying degrees by the energies associated with civic and regional globalization."[30]

I have previously identified the rise of civil society as a hopeful precursor to the rise of Global Community. Further, I have listed its twin companions: *international political integration* and the employment of *nonviolent strategies and methods* to overcome the repressive dynamics of America's drive toward Global Empire. From the viewpoint of some progressive scholars, this means "encouraging receptivity to bolder thinking about the goals of the struggle against these darker forces—including a reevaluation of the spiritual message of the great world religions and the possibility of constructing human security on a foundation of nonviolent politics."[31]

The promise of an emerging Global Community, devoid of an inevitable *clash of civilizations*, also stands in radical contrast with other dead-end forecasts, such as Francis Fukuyama's contention that the end of the Cold War marked *the end of history* (a restatement of Daniel Bell's *end of ideology* thesis). In the alternative, the idea of an emerging Global Community offers testimony to a new beginning for human history—a quantum leap in overcoming the stifling influence of a singular Western identity imposed on the world by American weapons of war. Such a view removes the necessity of Huntington's other argument that—with the United States in decline—America must be ever vigilant about maintaining its Western identity—"which he believes is important to the maintenance of both Western civilization and global capital. This vigilance ... has a cost: the reduction of the already 'thin' democracy in the world."[32]

It would be a terrible disservice to the future if we were to artificially draw an imaginary line in the sands of history and say, "*This far, but no further.*" Such a deterministic and/or fundamentalist approach to contemplating the human future does little to serve the cause of truth, the desire for peace, or the evolution of consciousness. All too often, deterministic views have led to forms of false consciousness—the idea that the unfolding of history itself is in some way preordained. If this is the horizon of all human possibility, then it should not be difficult to conclude that a deterministic view of history can only betray the maturation of our individual beings and our collective identities in the shifting sands of history.

The comfortable assurances of fundamentalisms and the uncritical nature of deterministic thinking are inadequate foundations on which to either build or maintain viable civilizations and enlightened societies. This is especially the case when viewed in the context of history and the stream of civilizations that have flowed through its tributaries. Civilizations and empires have collapsed under the weight of their flawed assumptions about power and its limits, unexpected turns taken by human stresses placed upon the natural environment, and religious dogmatisms that remain disconnected from human reflection and experience.

For the architects and the power wielders of Global Empire, it may seem appropriate to rely upon imperial ideologies that set out to prove their self-revealed "truths," or set out to provide imminent verification of their claims. In reality, ideologies are little more than provisional belief systems. As such, they are incapable of acting as an adequate substitute for principled reasoning, objectivity, or a sustained and scholarly study of difficult and complex issues. While ideas and beliefs matter, the important point that needs to be remembered is that they must evolve and be modified or replaced in the face of new knowledge, the accumulation of wisdom, and a utopian longing for an alternative discourse. If either the architects of Global Empire or the authors of a rising Global Community fail to come to terms with the inherent limitations of the status quo, they will find themselves taking two steps backward instead of one step forward. Old battlegrounds are not the appropriate place to wage new struggles.

The struggles of the present age require new modes of thought for new ideas— not old wineskins. New forms and expressions of an interconnected human consciousness demand the transcendence of the boundaries of the past. These new expressions of consciousness comprise the collective human aspiration for a world devoid of needless poverty and endless war. As such, the rising new consciousness of Global Community requires a resurgence of those human traits of courage, integrity, and purpose that can sustain a viable vision that operates through new forms of cooperation. In this new world, reliance upon the easy assumptions of a deterministic worldview may be invoked to achieve a temporary appeasement with the uncertainties of history, but it cannot resolve or confront the challenges that those uncertainties bring.

Yet, such a deterministic view seems to be the underlying theme of Huntington's thesis on the inevitable *clash of civilizations* insofar as it assumes that there is a constant and seemingly permanent threat of war. It seems that the real agenda behind this view is to diminish the trend toward increasing democratic participation in the world. It does so because it seeks to exclude other nations, peoples, and groups, from having an inclusive role to play in global rule making, decision making, and our collective sociopolitical evolution.[33] To embark upon a path of *exclusionary governance* would be antithetical to the rising culture of Global Community as it seeks to replace the hegemony of economic systems of global repression—such as the "triangular division of authority" among the IMF, the World Bank, and the WTO.[34] In short, the deterministic argument for maintaining America's drive toward creating a Global Empire remains intent on protecting American power and hegemony as an end in itself.[35] This seems to be borne out throughout the work of both neoconservative policy makers and the intellectual apologists of the imperial project.[36]

IN THE NAME OF EMPIRE

At every level the imperial project is unremitting and unapologetic. For example, President Bush and his neoconservative policymakers embarked upon a campaign to destroy the UN by nominating John Bolton as US ambassador to the UN. In response to his nomination, 62 former American diplomats signed a letter in early April 2005 urging the Senate to reject Bolton's nomination. After all, in 1994 it was Bolton who declared: "There is no such thing as the United Nations." He also said: "The Secretariat building in New York has 38 stories. If it lost ten stories, it wouldn't make a bit of difference." Bolton's career is also distinguished by his successful campaign to prevent the US Senate from ratifying the CTBT, thereby clearing the way for increased testing for nuclear weapons. As the Bush regime's undersecretary of Defense, he was instrumental in the 2002 withdrawal from the ABM Treaty and the administration's renunciation of the International Criminal Court (ICC). When Bush announced that he was taking the United States' signature off the ICC treaty, Bolton hailed the event as *the happiest moment* of his government service. He also opposed the conventions on land mines, child soldiers, and small arms. Earlier in his career, he aided and abetted the cover-up of the Iran-Contra scandal.[37]

In addition to the Bush-2 regime's contempt for international law and the UN, the administration's foreign policy toward certain independent oil-producing nations has been revitalized. This is especially the case with respect to a policy of US aggression toward Venezuela. Not since the days of Nixon and Kissinger attempting to overthrow the democratically elected government of Salvador Allende has the US government become so involved with the rise of black ops, propaganda, and dirty war tactics. The Bush-2 administration made it clear that Venezuela would be a target for Washington.[38]

The US State Department used every major US media outlet to condemn President Hugo Chavez by calling him a "threat to democracy" or alleging that the Venezuelan Government provides refuge and collaborates with "terrorist" groups, such as the Columbian FARC and ELN. Formerly clandestine destabilization campaigns would now be transformed into an open campaign by a Bush-2 regime seeking the chance to openly intervene in Venezuela in order to remove Chavez from power. The campaign would be undertaken under Bush's infamous banner declaring war on the *Axis of Evil*. Relying on its right wing allies in the media, the Bush regime's friends, in the April 11, 2005 edition of the ultra conservative magazine, *The National Review*, placed an image on the cover that showed President Chavez in military fatigues alongside Cuba's Fidel Castro with the byline, "The Axis of Evil ... Western Hemisphere Version."

The very term, "axis of evil," provides another example of an ideological process of decoupling truth from history. The term was originally applied to Iran, North Korea, and Iraq. However, with the occupation of Iraq underway, the Bush-2 regime apparently feels that it can replace one country with another country in the *axis of evil*.[39] In short, the *axis of evil* idea serves an ideological function as a source of justification for the next preemptive war, the realization of the vision of *full spectrum dominance*, and the triumph of America's Global Empire in a war without end. The idea of an *axis of evil* also neatly connects to ungrounded speculation about the inevitability of a *clash of civilizations*. After all, this is the defining clash that will decide whether or not the twenty-first century will be *another American Century*. If the twenty-first century is to become *another*

American Century, then the *war on terrorism* must be an ongoing enterprise. This is despite the fact that the end of the Cold War was supposed to usher in the *end of history* with the collapse of communism in Russia and the triumph of the market economy going global. After all is said and done, we are left with the impression that work of the intellectual apologists of the imperial project is never done.

For example, Francis Fukuyama's *end of history* argument is reflective of a triumphalist viewpoint that celebrates the collapse of communism in Russia, while celebrating the US virtues of free-market capitalism in the service of a neoliberal model of economics. Samuel Huntington's thesis on the *clash of civilizations* masks political and economic conflict while it privileges a paradigm of cultural conflict. The neoconservative proponents of *another American century* seek to perpetuate the hegemonic supremacy of the United States in its quest for *full spectrum dominance*. What all of these labels share in common is a US-centric preoccupation with the prospect of global dominance and hegemony. The challenge for humanity is to move beyond the neoconservative *Project for the Next American Century* (PNAC). To do so, large segments of humanity must discover their common bonds.

Beyond religious divisions, beyond the hubris of self-centered cultures and the economic pillars of privilege that are attempting to sustain the unsustainable, beyond the distortions of temporary political alliances, and beyond the incessant propaganda of the corporate media culture, there is an escape from the disease of the Global Empire's single vision. The escape from the trap of single vision politics will find its embryonic rumblings in the prayers, efforts, strategies, tactics, and enduring faith of those who can embrace the possibility of transcendence by reopening the metaphysical issues of the politics of the last two centuries.

From the seventeenth century forward, the horizons of Western thought have expanded toward an even closer union between scientific rationality and technocratic solutions to human problems. At the same time, the moral, existential, and metaphysical approaches to issues of *ultimate concern*—as expressed in the theological work of Paul Tillich—have receded into the background of history and Western philosophy. In fact, by the middle of the twentieth century, the West had largely become a post-philosophical culture. The nature of this technocratic, consumer-oriented, and rationalistic enterprise has increasingly treated human beings as little more than automatons in the capitalist marketplace. As such, the person has become expendable, replaceable, just another factor in the cost of production.

In contrast, the new politics of Global Community will be a religious politics. Not a religion of the churches, but rather a religious politics in the oldest and most universal sense—which is a vision born of transcendent knowledge. In embracing this vision, it will be necessary to reject the idolatry spawned by the imperial project of Global Empire. The extension of a vision born of transcendent knowledge will reveal the nature of the *clash of civilizations* as the *clash of ignorance*—an ignorance that remains actively at work because of the failure to acknowledge the interdependence of the Global Community and the moral force of the transcendent vision behind it.

MOVING BEYOND THE IDOLATRY OF EMPIRE
AND THE "CLASH OF IGNORANCE"

The aforementioned depictions and labels regarding America's Global Empire reflect a great deal about an ideological adherence to current power arrangements within the national and international status quo. In contrast, the revival of the metaphysical issues of human life and purpose has the capacity to restore what has been lost. The elements of a transcendent vision allow us to view the course of human history as a movement toward the convergence of cultures and civilizations. As such, these elements constitute the traits of a new and evolving global order. They represent new trends that are the building blocks of a viable Global Community. Diverse global perspectives, progressive social movements, and the claims of the world's great religions may now be understood as alternative paths away from an embrace of empire. The reintroduction of a transcendent vision for actualizing a cooperative world order opens the door for international law, the world's great religions, and progressive social movements to forge a new world centered upon the values of justice, cooperation, and mutual respect. These are the elements that I have sought to identify under the rubric of *a rising of Global Community*.

The quotations that introduce the beginning of this chapter, taken from Falk, Capra, and Waldron, all constitute radically different perspectives from the authors and defenders of the status quo. Falk rejects the hegemonic project of America's Global Empire as little more than an exercise in *idolatry* as America's Global Empire seeks to exert *monopoly control over the militarization of space and oceans*. Capra's reference to Jung gives greater interpretive weight to the *collective psyche* and *collective mental patterns*. He believes that not only individuals but also entire societies and cultures reveal the workings of a *planetary mind* that can act as the ultimate power shaping humanity's future. Waldron warns of the dangers wrought by *distorting emotional attachments* that *exaggerate differences between people* and how these attachments and fixations provide the basis for *strong identification with our group* ("united we stand"), while creating an*tagonism toward the other* (the "clash of civilizations").

In fact, Waldron's point about creating antagonism toward the other may be seen as nothing less than imperial hubris. The hubris of empire, evident in its quest for domination, is an enterprise that necessarily seeks to establish strong group identifications. In turn, strong group identifications eventually lead to an exaggeration of differences between people. While the architects of empire and their intellectual apologists would like to depict differences between people and civilizations as "empirical truths," "fundamental to human nature," and/or a "product of history," the fact remains that such differentiations are cultural constructions. As cultural constructions, in the Western world, they are the product of a combination of factors—the scientific method and enterprise as it has evolved since the seventeenth century, the union of the political state with the technocratic state, the logic of reductionism taken to the extreme. For with the rise of "quantifiable man" there has been a corresponding "undoing of political community."[40]

Of the many failures of Global Empire, chief among them is the fantasy that it can dominate the world with technological precision—laser-guided missiles, the employment of stealth surveillance aircraft, and precision bombing that allegedly avoids "collateral damage" (the death of innocent civilians). All these weapons and technologies constitute a gold-plated arsenal—unnecessary weapons at unnecessarily high prices. Cost overruns accompany the purchase of these weapons systems, while the national deficit skyrockets into trillions of dollars. Technocratic planners in the Pentagon fuel the work of scientists within the military-industrial complex with the fantasy of a militarized science capable of global domination. Together, they offer a false sense of security while, at the same time, acting in concert to produce another marketing tool for the arms lobby in congress. In reality, the fantasy of an effective militarized science fails to produce genuine global security. Rather, it fuels global resentment, stirs interstate conflict, and destabilizes entire countries. In short, the promise of global security turns out to be a lie. This lie became more than evident in the war in Vietnam (1964–1974) and in the first Gulf War in 1991. It is now manifestly evident in the Iraq war launched by the Bush-2 regime.

By 1992, Ramsey Clark, former Attorney General of the United States, upon his return from his fact-finding mission in Iraq, founded the Commission of Inquiry for the International War Crimes Tribunal to gather testimony from survivors and eyewitnesses around the world. In his book, *The Fire This Time: US War Crimes in the Gulf*, he brings the evidence together to form a scathing indictment of US activities in the Persian Gulf. His findings and those of the tribunal reveal war crimes against civilians, Washington's continuing effort to control the Middle East, the desecration of the environment, almost countless violations of human rights, the trashing of the United Nations Charter and the US Constitution, and an early 1990s plan for US dominion over the Gulf.[41] Similarly, the Bush-2 regime's invasion and occupation of Iraq has followed a similar course. The major difference is establishment of a permanent force of occupation in Iraq, with more military bases, coupled with an effort to privatize Iran's national economy, and sanction an ongoing process of war-profiteering by private companies.

To begin to comprehend the logic and depth of the imperial project, it is necessary to show how the union of scientific *objectivity* severs the connection between issues of moral concern, on the one hand, and the military and technological means associated with waging the wars of empire on the other. Theodore Roszak notes:

> Objectivity involves a breaking off of personal contact between observer and observed; there is an act of psychic contraction back and away from what is studied for the sake of a sharp, undistracted focus. In contrast, moral unselfishness means to identify with the other, to reach out and embrace and feel with. Far from being a contraction of the self, here we have expansion, a profoundly personal activity of the soul. At its warmest and most complete, this expansive relationship of self to other becomes love, and issues forth gracefully in compassion, sacrifice, and magnanimity. And these, not any sort of rational calibration of intellectual precision, are the secret of peace and joyous community.[42]

In light of the intellectual and spiritual scope of Roszak's diagnosis of the technocratic mind-set in the service of empire, the distinction between Global Empire and Global Community becomes clear at its most fundamental core. The imperial project of Global Empire employs a Robert McNamara-like precision, or a Donald Rumsfeld-like failure to have any form of personal connection between the observer the and observed. Instead of considering the massacre of civilians as a war crime, the victims are objectified into collateral damage. Instead of comprehending the fact of resistance to invasion and occupation as a natural expression of nationalism and a defense of sovereign rights, the opponents are labeled as "insurgents" and their cause is called an "insurgency"—which deprives their opposition of being understood as a moral challenge to an immoral situation.

The same moral and intellectual disconnect may be seen in the work of the intellectual apologists of empire, who posit the inevitability of intercivilizational conflict. Huntington's *clash of civilizations* thesis ignored the ideological and economic aspects of what global politics would look like as it entered its post–Cold War phase. Huntington's clash thesis *objectified* the world's peoples with terms such as *civilizational identity*. The tone of his thought is belligerent and looked at civilizations as totalities, rather than seeing them as evolving through their own internal dynamics.

By ignoring the plurality of every civilization, Huntington exhibits a cognitive failure to comprehend the modern cultural need to establish the definitions or interpretations of each culture. Such objectification commits one of the greatest sins of intellectual life—a presumption to speak for a whole religion or civilization. Further, by retaining a picture of global politics from the Cold War years—*'the West versus the rest'*—Huntington has painted with too broad a brush. The effects of his view are inflammatory. By placing the imperial project of America's Global Empire in the context of the vocabulary of apocalypse, he prepares the reader for a war without end rather than embracing the transcendent vision of a rising Global Community, capable of sustaining a peaceful interdependence.

THE INSEPARABLE NATURE OF POWER AND JUSTICE

Edward W. Said effectively critiqued the "clash of civilizations" thesis on two key points. First, he found the thesis inadequate on the grounds that it mainly revealed imperial self-pride (associated with empire). Second, he found the thesis was antithetical to comprehending the "interdependence of our time" (Global Community). In his article entitled, *The Clash of Ignorance*, Said noted:

> These are tense times, but it is better to think in terms of powerful and powerless communities, the secular politics of reason and ignorance, and universal principles of justice and injustice, than to wander off in search of vast abstractions that may give momentary satisfaction but little self-knowledge or informed analysis. "The Clash of Civilizations" thesis is a gimmick like "The War of the Worlds", better for reinforcing defensive self-pride than for critical understanding of the bewildering interdependence of our time.[43]

Said's critique of Huntington accomplishes two things at once. He identifies the inequalities and disparities arising from unequal power relations between nations and communities (within the context of empire) while, at the same time, identifying the moral issues arising from unequal power relations by reference to the universal principles of justice and injustice (within the context of global interdependence). By returning our attention to the realities of power, Said alerts us to the effects of unequal power relations in numerous contexts. At the same time, he pays attention to the need to invoke the universal principles of justice and injustice as we assess these situations as more than just imbalances of power. Imbalances in power serve to expose imbalances in the way a set of values is prioritized. Unequal power relations give rise to the strong giving greater weight to domination over the weak. Conversely, the weak (the victimized) seek to rectify the imbalance by struggling to prioritize universal principles of justice in order to off-set the disparaging effects of uncontested power relationships. Recognizing this reality returns us to a more fundamental core set of values in human relations.

By giving greater attention to moral, ethical, and religious concerns about the use of force, the deprivation of human rights, the exploitation of peoples, and the nature of governance as more than merely an economic or political enterprise, we are alerted to the reality that global governance in the service of empire disserves both the universal principles of justice and the Global Community. Global Empire takes the name of morality and justice in vain, for it has not made itself ultimately accountable to them. Rather, Global Empire is predicated upon the extraction of wealth and the exercise of dominance—irrespective of the moral consequences of its imperial endeavors. Its reliance upon *technique* supplants moral concerns, thereby devaluing the dignity and worth of the person. The *techniques* of imperial domination employ a militarized science in service to a neoliberal economic model. The model is used to subjugate the indebted nations of the global South. Attendant to this model is the infamous phrase—*debt-for-nature-swap*. The resource exploitation of the global South constitutes a pillage of Third World countries which has led to deforestation, pollution, political and economic disempowerment, and the theft of Third World resources.

The alleged *legitimacy* of Global Empire is attained through the smoke and mirrors of propaganda, political rhetoric, and the labels its apologists apply as empty explanations for the absence of justice. In this regard, the *clash of civilizations* thesis is a disservice to the cause of peace, the struggle for justice, and the evolving convergence of international cooperation through common values, and a shared moral ethic that is reflected in law and culture. The "clash thesis" sets up an artificial separation between the aspirations of all peoples versus the ideological agenda of neoconservatives, neoliberals, and the military strategists of empire. It is a disservice because it fabricates the illusion of legitimacy without embodying the substance of legitimacy. Legitimacy is not the result of domination by military force or coercion, but arises out of a reverence for life that takes seriously the inclusive nature of moral and ethical principles that are universal in scope and demand. Legitimacy is the by-product of the application of power united with moral and ethical practice in all realms of life—including the political, economic, and social.

The universality of the principles of justice and injustice serves as the ultimate critique upon the question of whether the exercise of power (in the name of Global

Empire) has created a form of humane governance or inhumane governance—or failed to do so. If the enterprise of Global Empire fails that test, then it would be safe to conclude that it lacks legitimacy. Such a conclusion is objectively reinforced by the necessity of having to employ military force as a substitute for diplomacy, negotiation, and intellectually honest political discourse. If the gap between powerful communities and powerless communities is not being narrowed by the imperial project, then there is—by definition—universal injustice. Hence, Said's juxtaposition of powerful and powerless communities is one critical aspect of the human reality that lies behind Huntington's alleged *clash of civilizations*.

Said's analysis demands that we pay attention to the universal categories of justice and injustice. For with the perception of injustice, there is a natural response to meet injustice with violence. In the alternative, by embracing the movement toward the realization of justice, there is a showing of good faith, an adherence to principle, and an ethical commitment to make right the perceived wrongs and injustices. In short, such a movement lays the groundwork for a *healing of civilizations* (my term) instead of setting up the conditions for a *clash of civilizations*. I use the term "healing of civilizations" in order to communicate the idea that the victims of the imperial project are in need of liberation and release from the disease of empire. Empires seeking the expansion of their raw powers create the disease of exploitation, which in turn diminishes the person and the human personality. Without liberation from the disease of empire, both the victims and the executioners of imperial policies will be swallowed up in wars, violence, and destruction. There is no other endgame for empire.

In the alternative, movement toward the realization of justice is the moral force that lies behind the rise of Global Community. This movement can be discerned in the establishment of TRC that have been set up in Latin America and South Africa. The mechanism of the TRC has been effectively used to acknowledge past criminality without relying on punitive and vindictive responses. In this regard, the need for reconciliation and forgiveness is not only foundational in the teachings of the world's great religions, but also for the establishment of a nonviolent Global Community. I would argue that it will be necessary to set up a global TRC to deal with the abuses, illegalities, and crimes of Global Empire (a topic to be addressed in Chapters 6 and 7).

In short, the movement toward the global realization of justice constitutes the foundational ground on which the judgment of Global Empire will eventually come to rest. In this regard, the denial of human rights by the strategists and apologists of empire stands under judgment not only by the laws of man (Geneva Convention on Torture and international human rights treaties and covenants), but also by the transcendent moral judgments of the world's great religions. While the abuses of Global Empire under the Bush-2 regime have been undertaken in reference to a "war on terrorism," the terrorism of this war has produced even greater harms than the original injustice that was used to justify the *war on terrorism* in the first place (9/11).

The war on terrorism may have begun with an act of vengeance, but the response to it was a response "in kind"—a crusade of conquest in the name of an inevitable *clash of civilizations*. In truth, the *war on terrorism* has been the product of a preplanned imperial drive for the oil of the Middle East and Persian Gulf. Its inauguration was premised upon the events of 9/11—used as a pretext for war. The "war on terror" has become a "war of terror"—supported by ensuing mythologies associated with a host of contradictory ideological explanations (from "regime change" to "bringing democracy to the Middle East"). From the threat of a "mushroom cloud" to allegations regarding arsenals filled with weapons of mass destruction, from humanitarian justifications for war to a US-sponsored crusade for "democracy promotion," the horrors of war have only been matched by the pitiless process of war profiteering, the imposition of a neoliberal model of privatization, and by a massive civilian genocide directly resulting from the carnage of a US-dominated occupation of Iraq.

In this context, the *healing of civilizations* must be the product of coming to terms with the human agonies produced between the drive for vengeance, on the one hand, and the need for forgiveness on the other. The healing power of reconciliation can only be realized by first confronting the truth—as demonstrated by South Africa's TRC. Therefore, the lies, murderous practices, and tortured legal reasoning of the Bush-2 regime—with respect to the suspension of the Geneva Convention and the corresponding torture of prisoners and "enemy combatants"—constitute a few of the many truths that must be exposed before the crimes of empire can be dealt with, rectified, and eventually healed.

Establishing an inclusive moral and legal regime of this order will necessarily have to be premised upon the categorical removal of old patterns and organizations based upon exploitation, exclusion, and the violation of human rights. Whether the forum for this global venue of inclusive participation will be found in a World Parliament or within a reorganized UN, what is clear is that the rise of Global Community will have to be predicated upon bringing the excluded and the victims to the table.

The days of sanctioning the imperial domination of one nation over other nations must be brought to an end. The reasons for this conclusion range from the immediacy of the crises that humanity confronts. These crises include—but are not limited to the following: expanding global poverty, widening gulfs of inequality within and between nations, global climate change, wars for dwindling resources, and the continuous exploitation of the environment. In all of these realms, there is the need to apply a global ethic, a shared moral vision, a universal set of humane values that can make powerful demands in conjunction with sufficient powers to realize those demands.

POWER IN THE SERVICE OF JUSTICE

Properly conceived, a cross-cultural cosmopolitan order must be premised upon power in the service of justice. Power in the service of justice is interpersonal, intercivilizational, and intra-civilizational. The application of power in the service of justice allows for the *healing of civilizations* and identities because it substitutes in a renewed human consciousness that is capable of radically reconceiving the nature and purpose of both human purpose and global order. The idea of a rule-based global order is not an adequate starting point—because global order without a universal value to transfigure it is governed by the law of expediency. The last days of the British Empire supply a clear example of this logic: "When Britain no longer ruled the waves, it waived the rules." Hence, a new global consciousness that is framed by a shared set of moral values allows humanity the chance to change history by reframing its understanding of the human interest and the quality of human purpose.

In the New Testament tradition, its authors invoke the Greek word, "metanoia" in order to point toward the possibility that individuals may experience a radical change of consciousness. On a global basis, the "collective unconscious" of which Carl Jung wrote is "metanoia" writ large. It signifies the capacity of a transcendent vision to remake human history. By radically altering the direction of history, a radical change of consciousness represents a genuine threat to empire—all empires. It is a threat because individuals and entire peoples are empowered to break out of the boxes of domination, conformity, and an uncritical acceptance of the status quo.

Only the establishment of a transformed and transforming order is capable of maintaining humane and inclusive forms of governance—for it subordinates power to the role of serving the greater good as opposed to being an end in itself. The mere acquisition of power for the sake of power becomes an insatiable drive for dominance and domination. Power becomes illegitimate when divorced from justice. When power becomes separated from an attempt to approximate the claims of justice, power loses its moral bearings and purpose. Therefore, power and justice must remain inseparable because the legitimacy of one is dependent on the presence of the other. Unless power and justice exist together, they are morally at odds with one another.

The claims of Global Empire are antithetical to the maintenance of peaceful communities insofar as peaceful communities are not the products of domination, force, or exploitation. Peaceful communities, both within and between states, are able to strike a healthy balance between the exercise of power, on the one hand, and respect for the constant need to realize justice, on the other. In this regard, the idea of a rising Global Community should be understood as a collection of powerful local and national communities, sustained by mutual respect, common wisdom, and a shared set of understandings reflective of common aspirations. Such a world is only possible under conditions considered to be just. In that respect, it is the realization of justice through the morally conditioned exercise of power that brings legitimacy and strength to the Global Community.

With this in mind, we can make an effective distinction between the exercise of imperial power in the service of one civilization (empire) *versus* the desire for and practice of universal justice throughout a collection of national communities (the Global Community). As national communities remove themselves from the claims of Global Empire, the *exodus from empire* constitutes both a moral renunciation of empire and the embrace of an inclusive commitment to human unity, interdependence, and mutual obligation. The international *exodus from empire* discards the notion of a predetermined or predestined "clash of civilizations" by embarking upon a global project of *healing civilizations* of their individual and collective wounds. In this sense, a Global Community is now free to emerge so that the claims of power and the demands of universal justice will be enabled to counterbalance one another. In this regard, the disparities found in unequal power relationships may be overcome. I will now turn to a brief summary of these two interrelated matters.

First, Said's critique serves to highlight the divergence between the agenda of Global Empire and the rising power of Global Community. His insightful juxtaposition of *powerful and powerless communities* reminds us of the historical disjunction between Western dominance over Third World peoples. His insight also points to the current dichotomies ushered in by an age of neoliberal globalization. The disparities between the social classes within and between nations are highlighted by the situation of displaced peasants from Mexico to Asia, from Africa to South America. It is also a condition highlighted by the global growth of sweatshops and other forms of exploited labor. Within the US Global Empire's own borders, over 10 million Mexican immigrants demand that their contributions as workers not be criminalized by proposed harsh immigration laws that would make them felons. Both in the United States and around the world, millions of people are part of powerless communities. The promise of a rising Global Community predicates its rise on its capacity and willingness to incorporate the excluded, exploited, and disadvantaged into a new moral, political, social, and economic order. It is an order that must be predicated upon universal justice norms, shared moral values, and inclusive forms of governance.

Second, by introducing the importance of an ethical and moral perspective, Said liberates us from analyzing categories of socioeconomic relations in isolation from other considerations to a discourse of shared moral considerations. He acknowledged that if a rising Global Community was to be viable, it must exhibit adherence to values that embody and incorporate cross-cultural understandings regarding the *universal principles of justice and injustice*. These principles allow us to see the interrelatedness of unequal power relations and the attendant phenomenon of global violence. To be enabled to understand and to feel the strife brought about by injustice—for both individuals and groups—allows us to open the doors of communication and action to an honest appraisal of unequal power relationships under the conditions of globalization in the service of Global Empire.

THE PHENOMENON OF GLOBAL VIOLENCE

By definition, the maintenance of Global Empire is premised upon unequal power relationships. Due to this design, it is virtually inevitable that violence, wars, and conflict would follow as a predictable consequence of these kinds of arrangements. During the mid-1970s, progressive scholars began to search for a late twentieth century alternative to global governance that would have the capacity to avoid the pitfalls created by unequal power relationships and global violence.

Throughout the 1970s, a combination of factors could be credited with the renewed interest in studying this dynamic, ranging from the end of the Vietnam War to the claims made by the NAM. While the Cold War still played a pivotal role in considerations about unequal power relationships, the primary impetus came from Third World nations seeking to build a New International Economic Order (NIEO). A case in point is found in the work of Professor Ali Mazrui. In his capacity as director of the African section of the World Order Models Project (WOMP), sponsored by the Institute for World Order,[44] he wrote about his vision of *a world federation of cultures* from an African perspective. It was an effort to identify and help to mitigate the problem of unequal power relations and the violence evoked by them. His solution centered on values and strategies that could begin the process of enacting justice on a global scale. With a global justice strategy in place, he argued that it would be possible not only to mitigate the causes of violence both within and between nations, but also to address the root dynamics of injustice within nations before they achieved global proportions. In short, he viewed the dynamics of a nation's domestic tensions and domestic pathologies as the point of a "ground zero" from which international conflicts emerged. In order to properly understand the dynamics of international conflict, he argued that international conflict could be best understood as an externalized arena for conflict that arose from cultural and social deficiencies *within* nations, not between nations (as Huntington would have us believe).

Almost 30 years prior to the events of 9/11, Mazrui centered his attention on the importance of the role that social justice concerns play on the international relations stage. He started with the assertion that the problem of world peace is a problem that begins with the internal dynamics contained within domestic cultures. So, his argument maintains that within individual countries there are domestic cultures and social groups divided by unresolved tensions. These tensions are largely the product of social injustice *within* civilizations, not *between* them. Unresolved tensions arising from social injustice become externalized and will be manifested on the international stage. The start of World War I provides an example of this phenomenon. Yet, the resultant international wars should not be understood as a *clash of civilizations*, but as a consequence of *clashes within civilizations* that becomes externalized. As violence takes hold at the international level, it should then be seen as an externalized consequence of the violation of social justice or the denial of economic welfare within particular sovereign nation-states.

However, the task of defining exactly what constitutes a working definition of "social justice" adds a further complication to the equation. This is because the ideal of social justice is relative to particular cultures. Therefore, the culture-bound narrative of social justice binds it to a more subjective standard than the more objective and measurable elements of economic welfare or enumerating specific strategies that can lead to a reduction in violence. Mazrui wrote: "Social justice as an ideal is more relativistic, more culture-bound, than either economic welfare or the question of what constitutes a reduction of violence." Yet, he went on to observe:

in a sense, social justice is prior to economic welfare and minimization of violence. Welfare will not be equitably distributed, nor violence be averted unless justice is done or is in prospect. From the point of view of evolving a more desirable world order, a basic *clash* which needs to be resolved is precisely this one between the primacy of social justice as a value and the extent to which it is culturally relative.[45] (Italics are mine)

Clearly, the *clash* that Mazrui identified was not one between civilizations. Rather, the clash was between universal demands for justice *and* those power centers of particular cultures that failed to make social justice a primary concern in shaping policy. By leaving the value of social justice out of the power equation, social justice would be reduced to little more than a culturally relative factor. Mazrui's proposed solution to the dilemma was to argue that culture itself had to be made less "relative." For the sake of an evolving Global Community, this would mean moving beyond cultural differences and promoting what he calls "some degree of cultural homogenization on a world scale"[46] (what I have called *Global Community*). Only by accomplishing the transition toward such a unified global system, subject to the primary value of social justice, could humanity develop a world order "capable of yielding both widespread economic welfare" and a "widespread retreat from violence."[47] Mazrui concluded that: "A cultural world with the Western heritage at the top is a world of a cultural hierarchy, when what is really needed is a world *federation of cultures*."[48]

With the world of the twenty-first century currently subjected to a cultural hierarchy that places America's Global Empire at the top of the cultural pyramid, it is no wonder that military force is the only way to guarantee even its short-run endurance. Insofar as America's Global Empire cares little for realizing social justice, the value of global social justice has been so dramatically minimized that it is virtually nonexistent. The tragic nature of this conclusion becomes abundantly clear when we recognize the fact that

> the development of global institutions has led to the development of *"entrenched rights"* for global corporations and financial institutions. The process of enforcing these international agreements at national and international levels invariably bypasses the democratic process. Beneath the rhetoric of so-called "governance" and the "free market", neo-liberalism provides a shaky legitimacy to those in the seat of political power.[49]

> The crisis of legitimacy that attends the enterprise of both Global Empire and neoliberalism opens the door for the world's great religions, competing ideologies, and submerged socioeconomic and sociopolitical discourse to further undermine the power claims of the imperial project.

Washington's rhetoric about spreading democracy is turning back upon itself with a vengeance, because the hypocrisy of saying one thing in international affairs and doing another is increasingly unacceptable to the majority of the world's people. Hence, the international discourse of human rights law, over 50 years in the making, has opened a political and a religious door for the critique and condemnation of Global Empire. From a political view, the politics of Global Empire is nothing less than exploitation while, from a religious view, it is a violation of human dignity and the belief that the rights of man come not from the generosity of the state, but from the hand of God. Therefore, to privilege US-backed corporations and financial institutions with *entrenched rights* while denying basic human rights to billions of the world's people, can be construed as an enterprise that is both illegitimate and a blasphemy of the most wretched kind.

If radical elements of the Islamic faith view the actions of the United States in foreign affairs as the actions of the infidel, then the clearest explanation for such a reaction is the fact that US corporate and financial interests have debased and offended not only the sovereign rights of Islamic countries, but added insult to injury by viewing everything through the tunnel vision of profits and materialism.

The exclusionary nature of *entrenched rights* for corporate and financial institutions makes a mockery of any claim by the advocates of Global Empire that they are "spreading democracy" to the Middle East. In fact, there is a tragic self-delusion that accompanies the imperial project and those who serve it. In his 1980 study on the guiding forces behind US foreign policy, Robert Johansen discovered that

> the need to serve vested economic and political interests distorted the perceptions of the most astute officials ... The bureaucratically-reinforced, nationalist version of reality produced psychological and material incentives to seek further US advantages through competition with other nations. These incentives drowned out any inclination toward recognizing a global human interest. Unable to look beyond the statist, Westphalian image of the world, US leaders were ill-equipped to guide the international system toward the twenty-first century.[50]

A focus upon maintaining and extending the Global Empire makes violence inevitable. This is largely because the way in which violence is framed by US policymakers is inherently distorted. Because their agenda is premised on achieving "full spectrum dominance" all that is left is a concern with the rule of force and the expectation of counterforce.

What US policymakers have ignored is the fact that the phenomenon of violence includes the violence of poverty, hunger, disease, and war itself. Therefore, in their eyes, the *clash of civilizations* becomes little more than a self-fulfilling prophecy. According to Thomas Pogge, "Global institutional reforms could solve these problems through international law or treaties by creating a source of investment capital to foster economic development in the poorest regions, and by creating global minimum standards for working conditions. I conclude that explanatory nationalism and the moral worldview based on it do not fit the real world ... Current policies of the rich countries contribute to poverty and unfulfilled human rights in the poor countries and thereby inflict severe undue harms on many. These harms could be dramatically reduced through even relatively minor international reforms."[51]

The issue of economic justice is one of the central pillars of Global Community. It is also an issue of great contestation with the US Treasury Department, the WTO, the IMF, and World Bank. These US-financed institutions of Global Empire have worked to achieve global profits for corporate and financial interests who care little for the values of distributive justice, the eradication of poverty, and the cause of genuine national development among the nations of the Third World.[52] Yet, it is precisely in the context and work of these institutions where the issue of economic justice can best be addressed. In this forum, there are two questions in particular that need to be asked: "Are these institutions fair and neutral?" And, "Are their outcomes fair?"

BUILDING FAIR INSTITUTIONS FOR
THE SAKE OF JUST OUTCOMES

From an institutional perspective, some scholars have worked on the assumption that fair institutions will, by definition, lead to outcomes that are just. The preconditions of institutional fairness are premised on the following background conditions: (1) fair institutions (equal treatment, institutions that would be universally accepted); (2) fair equality of opportunity (non-discrimination in employment and access to social positions); (3) fair prior distribution of productive assets; (4) fair opportunity to develop one's human talents (fair access to education and health); (5) free bargaining by all agents concerning the terms and use of labor and capital.[53] In the real world, institutions such as the WTO, IMF, and World Bank have not been fair. Their agenda is not neutral (it is mainly pro-corporate and anti-Third World). Hence, their policy outcomes are neither fair nor just. For those who remain excluded by Western-produced rules of trade and commerce, the plight of the Third World's poor either remains the same or even worsens. For example, the record of the World Bank's performance demonstrates a long-standing inability to uplift the global poor.

The reports produced by the World Bank are not adequate to help or assist the global poor in their day-to-day struggles. Some have argued that "This failure arises from an initial analytical failure to define the characteristics of the poor accurately, but is exacerbated by the report's fuzzy and inadequate recommendations concerning the institutional reforms that are required to enable the poor not merely to participate in decision-making … but more important to oppose and to struggle more effectively against those political forces that oppress them."[54] By following the directives of the US government and its corporate backers, the World Bank is not capable of producing a fair or accurate strategy that is geared to actually combat poverty. For if the Bank were to produce an intellectually honest and critical strategy for eliminating global poverty, such a strategy would place it into conflict with the very forces that direct and fund the Bank's activities throughout the Third World.

The human costs of maintaining this Global Empire are too great for the global poor. They are also too great for the citizens of the empire who are required to bear the tax burden and the sacrifice of its young soldiers in its service. The instrumentalities of military force have been placed at the disposal of corporate and financial interests. Alternatively, Global Community is a collective effort that calls upon all nations, cultures, and civilizations to develop new patterns of trade, production, empathy, shared values, common goals, and cooperation in meeting the goals of global fairness and the alleviation of global poverty. In practical terms, the sustainable development of a Global Community is predicated upon giving support to democratizing trends, practices, and policies. This is especially important in facing the widening gaps between classes and nations with respect to inequality. Radical inequality is the antithesis of democracy. Where there is a weak or nonexistent set of democratic institutions there is a corresponding lack of justice. Democracy and justice reinforce one another. Democracy united to the claims of justice brings about new forms of social empowerment. Social movements tied to political parties devoted to democratic principles have the capacity to reduce and eventually eliminate radical inequality.

The issue of trade provides a tremendously relevant example of how democracy and justice reinforce each other, enabling them to function as agents for global justice. In this regard, "the goal is not to stop international trade. In appropriate circumstances and under the right conditions, international trade can support local economic development, provide needed goods that cannot be produced domestically, and create jobs." This is important because "recognizing the potential of trade, there is a need for a set of principles to serve as the basis for a different kind of trade policy, one under which the benefits of trade might flow primarily to the countries and communities most in need."[55]

Unfortunately, the status quo is predicated upon the maintenance of an unequal and unjust order. That is why whether we are talking about the World Bank or international trade, a reinvention of these arrangements cannot be expected to come *from within* the centers of Western power. A reinvention of these arrangements and unequal power structures must be imposed *from without*. Pressures from outside the system have arisen when members of the Global Community have united in protest against these arrangements—as with the "Battle of Seattle." The WTO was forced to listen and to make some concessions to the global protest. In the absence of such a reinvention, the same dysfunctional path will be taken and result in the same tragic results for the majority of the world's poor and oppressed.

Reductionism versus Cultural Convergence

It is possible to avoid the crushing inevitability of a *clash of civilizations* by working to harmonize cultures through a convergence of commonly held principles and values. Some of these values are reflected in international law, some of these values are found in the world's great religions. In either case the scope of these values transcends the limited categories imposed by centuries of Western domination and, more recently, by America's Global Empire. According to Mazarui,

> our perspective on world order puts a special premium on cultural convergence, partly derived from the conviction that a shared pool of values constitutes consensus. The reform of the world in the direction of greater social justice, enhanced economic welfare, and diminishing prospects for violence, requires human consensus behind some core values. The world of tomorrow can either be tamed through outright force or through shared values. And the shared values are what constitute cultural convergence.[56]

The cage in which the architects of Global Empire have placed themselves, as well as the rest of the world, is the cage of *categorization*. The very categories in which neoconservative policymakers and their intellectual apologists think are actually prisons of thought. The neoconservative paradigm has made its authors prisoners of their own thought, divorced from the possibility of achieving a more peaceful world through the convergence of shared cultural values, the embrace of common human aspirations. The cracks in the neoconservative paradigm for global domination are also apparent in Huntington's thesis. On this point,

Amartya Sen, winner of the Nobel Prize in Economics in 1998, has noted:

> The thesis of a civilizational clash can be ideologically linked with a more general idea that provides the methodological foundation of the "clash thesis." This concerns the program of categorizing people of the world according to some single—and allegedly commanding—system of classification. To see any person wholly, or even primarily, as a member of a so-called civilization (in Huntington's categorization, as a member of "the Western World," "the Islamic world," "the Hindu world," or "the Buddhist world") is already to reduce people into this one dimension. The deficiency of the clash thesis, I would argue, begins well before we get to the point of asking whether the disparate civilizations (among which the population of the world is forcefully portioned out) must necessarily—or even typically—clash. No matter what answer we give to this question, by even pursuing the question in this restrictive form we implicitly give credence to the allegedly unique importance of one categorization over all other ways in which people of the world may be classified.[57]

The maintenance of Global Empire is predicated upon maintaining artificial categories that divide the world's people, civilizations, laws, religions, and cultures into an "us" versus "them" dichotomy. In many ways, it represents an ugly embodiment of the West's seventeenth century experiment with reductionism. The advent of science and its ascendancy in the seventeenth century escaped the laboratory and have been applied to social affairs. The result "has been the grotesque model of politics reduced to quantity and formula and, accordingly, of life robotized."[58] Categorization and reductionism go hand-in-hand. The emphasis of quantification lies at the heart of this enterprise.

When the US military and the Pentagon attempt to quantify the effects of their precision weapons, they invoke terms such as *collateral damage* to describe civilian death due to imprecise technology. The categorization of destruction has become a science of its own. Yet, the Western tendency to reduce everything to quantifiable categories extends beyond the battlefield to the global marketplace. Free markets are never really free. The free-market system of the US Global Empire enjoys the benefits of state protectionism while preaching a different message abroad. Hence, free markets are hailed as an economic force for spreading prosperity. Yet, they cannot deliver prosperity without state intervention on their behalf in a world where they must compete for advantage in the global marketplace.

In reality, the age of globalization has done more to spread poverty than wealth—inequality rather than democracy. The global financial architecture has been largely left in the hands of the IMF. Today, the IMF is a failed institution. From its undemocratic decision-making structure to its structural adjustment programs, it has set poor countries on a course for crisis and bankruptcy.[59] The IMF and the Pentagon are just two institutions that may be singled out as examples of dominant social structures that are wedded to the mind-set of seventeenth century reductionism. The intellectual linkage between reductionism and categorization is an important one to make. It is important because the linkage reveals flaws in theory and in practice that account for the failure of Global Empire. Reductionism and Global Empire share an overweening desire to dominate, they both seek quick and simple answers to complex problems, they both suffer from the disease of a *single vision* that lends itself to easy categorization and to an idolatry of domination and control that turns what is alive into a mere thing.[60]

In short, reductionism is found in the interplay between science and technocracy. The maintenance and extension of America's Global Empire relies on both. In fact, we can argue that the entire thesis about a "clash of civilizations" is nothing more than an attempt at compartmentalization and categorization designed to reinforce America's imperial domination as an end in itself. That is because the US Global Empire's primary focus is upon nothing less than domination for the sake of profit maximization.

Further, both science and the technocracy have been politicized. The Bush-2 regime has sought out scientific findings that support its goals and discards valid science that conflicts with it—such as the science that supports global warming. Science that is supportive of the Kyoto Treaty becomes a threat to the agenda of the Global Empire. If a strong international treaty were to be passed (such as the Kyoto Treaty), then the profits of oil companies and car manufacturers would decline. However, when science discounts the validity of NMD, it is ignored by the Bush administration. As a result, entire debates are effectively dominated by propagandized categories in which American citizens are expected to "debate" the truth and relevance of public policies without the benefit of valid science. The citizens of empire are thereby trapped in a technocratic and ideological box. The ideological fixations of neoconservatives are presented in ways that glorify militarism and discount the value of genuine scientific findings—free of distortion.

Freedom within the context of Global Empire actually stands for the "freedom to be ignorant." Ignorance of the crimes of empire, the deceptions of empire, and the actual agenda of empire reduce the integrity of the average American's thought to rubbish. In this vast wasteland patriotism declares: "United We Stand." Hitler's "fatherland" has been reborn in the Bush regime's "homeland." Preemptive wars are justified in the name of defending the fatherland/homeland (Poland in 1933—Iraq in 2003). International law is discarded in favor of nationalistic pride (Nazism for Hitler's Germany—Unilateralism for Bush's America). Racial subordination is employed to create a targeted group for collective hate and prejudice so as to give greater legitimacy to the expansion of state power (in Hitler's Germany, an extermination program against the Jews of Europe—in Bush's America a racial profiling program targeting Muslims, Arabs, and those who practice Islam, coupled with the use of torture in prisons from Abu Ghraib to foreign nations where the Geneva Convention is ignored). The constitutional rights and protections of citizens are eliminated in response to a "national crisis" (Hitler burned the Reichstag, declared himself Fuhrer, and destroyed the remnants of the Weimar Republic—Bush passed the USA Patriot Act with a compliant US Congress, set up Military Tribunals to try suspected terrorists without the protections of "due process" and "equal protection," and employed torture as a tool in the "war on terror"). On an international scale, the US Global Empire employs militarism not only to justify preemptive wars in Third World nations, but also to service a declining national economy. Domestically, within the United States, those who dissent from officially sanctioned categories of thought and action are labeled "traitors and terrorists." In fact, living under the cloud of the USA Patriot Act creates a political climate where dissent against the empire is reduced to the category of treason.

The highly restrictive nature of categorization acts to suffocate the freedom, sovereignty, and self-determination of all elements of Global Community that chose to avoid the rubber stamp of an American imprimatur. On this very point, Abraham Maslow once wisely observed that if behavioral scientists would pay attention to the whole human situation before them in their research, they would see that the predictability they seek is sharply offensive to their subjects. And *that* is a supremely significant finding, is it not? "When I *can* predict what a person will do," Maslow states, "somehow he feels that it implies a lack of respect for him … as if he were no more than a thing. He tends to feel dominated, controlled, outwitted. I have observed instances of one person deliberately upsetting the predictions simply to reaffirm his unpredictability and therefore autonomy and self-governance."[61]

A GLOBAL ETHIC FOR A GLOBAL COMMUNITY:
THE CONVERGENCE OF INTERNATIONAL LAW
WITH THE WORLD'S GREAT RELIGIONS

The rise of Global Community is largely predicated upon the desire of the world's people for autonomy and self-governance. Opposition to domination is the predominant characteristic of the early twenty-first century. It is an opposition born of the disappointments and tragedies of the last two thousand years. The evolution of substantive norms are still being codified and practiced in the fields of international law, the transcendent norms of the world's great religions, and the nature of an increasingly interdependent world that seeks unity around shared values—the values of a global covenant for a Global Community. In short, global human consciousness is at a breakthrough point. The dynamic convergence of an evolving set of normative traditions from the realms of international law to the world's great religions has created the possibility for all humanity to enter into a new age. This new age is not defined by terrorism. Instead it is an age defined by an expanding domain of tolerance, communication across the boundaries of civilizations, and fixed identities. It is also an age in which the development of a shared discourse of rights and responsibilities is continuing to rely upon transcendent norms and shared moral values. It is a new age prepared to give birth to a global covenant for a Global Community. In order to explicate the inauguration of this new era, I will now turn to an examination of shared values and norms evolving in the field of international law, the understandings of the world's great religions, and the creative process of an emerging global covenant that can act as a normative bridge between civilizations.

EVOLVING TRENDS IN INTERNATIONAL LAW

International law in the age of America's Global Empire has been not merely restricted in its application, but ignored and rejected outright as a normative constraint upon the actions of the Bush-2 regime. Yet, international law is substantively dedicated and directed toward one primary goal: the imposition of constraints even upon the most powerful members of international society. The centrality of this goal highlights a very practical concern—"if the 'rule of law' means anything, it must imply the ability of a society to rein in the entirely self-interested impulses of the powerful."[62] However, there is a problem with implementing this idea.

The idea of the *rule of law* is trapped between two contradictory views. *The first* maintains that customary international law can only fill its constraining function when it is married to a consent-based theory of law that privileges the role of sovereign and equal nation-states. *The second view* highlights the role that customary law can play in giving rise to norms that may not be supported by all-powerful states, or even by the most powerful nation-state.[63] The idea contained in *the first view* does a disservice to history and to truth. *The first view* is little more than a legal fiction insofar as there never has been a world of "sovereign and equal nation-states." World history demonstrates that since 1648, the continents of Africa, Latin America, and Asia have been forced to play a subordinate role in the global system. Colonial rule was followed by neocolonialism. Imperial rule was followed by neo-imperialism.

The nineteenth and twentieth centuries reflect a history of non-equal nation-states. The so-called Third World is the subordinated Global South. It has been (as Chapters 1–3 have demonstrated) a set of unequal states located on the "periphery" of global capitalism, with Europe, the United States, and Russia, exercising hegemony over most of the Global South for over 100 years. At the dawn of the twenty-first century, the reality of a world of non-equal and non-sovereign states remains. The US-dominated institutions of the IMF, WTO, and World Bank have financially invaded and captured entire nations and regions for corporate exploitation. The US Global Empire follows a worldview of its own making—divorced from the realities of over two-thirds of humankind. This conclusion leads to my fourth thesis statement:

> What is at stake in the global battle between Global Empire and Global Community is the continuation of the global primacy of an all-powerful state—versus—the needs of a rising Global Community.

From an international law perspective the elements of the argument between the two aforementioned views on the "rule of law" reflects a divergence between an imperialistic perspective and an anti-imperialistic perspective. What we see at play between these two contradictory views is a consent-based theory of law which is not universally binding on all states—*versus* an evolving customary law that gives rise to norms that need not be supported by all-powerful states in order to possess ultimate sovereign authority over state conduct in the global arena.

According to the *first view*, relied on by the Bush-2 regime, we see the centrality of the nationalist view of an all-powerful sovereign state. It is a view that attempts to trump the evolving international view that holds that even an all-powerful state must be subject to evolving international norms of conduct and the values behind those norms. The Bush-2 regime still clings to an imperial arrogance that declares: *Whatever the United States wants to pursue, the United States will pursue—regardless of what other nations prefer or what the evolving norms of international law command.*

Historically, adherence to the *first view* has been understood to mean that all nations—even the all-powerful ones—must give their consent before international law becomes binding. This view also stands for the idea that by unilaterally opting out of an international law regime endorsed by the rest of the world, the United States can go its own direction in international affairs. On this basis, the Bush administration has opted out of established security-related treaties or refused to ratify new ones (as discussed in Chapter 3). While giving lipservice to the idea that nation-states are equal and sovereign, the Bush administration exercises its superpower status as a sufficient justification for making the US Global Empire the ultimate sovereign among sovereigns. Therefore, with or without the support of international law, with total disregard for even the basic norms, customs, and diplomatic arrangements of the past, the Bush-2 regime has created the doctrine of "preemptive war" as a strategy to pursue its "war on terrorism." Underlying this pretext is the blatant pursuit of a self-chosen set of US nationalist priorities on the international stage. The employment of this approach explains how the Bush-2 regime was able to embark upon the invasion and occupation of Iraq without feeling obligated by the constraints of international law or the United Nations Charter.

The adoption of the *first view* regarding the "rule of law" represents the inherent limits of the concept of the "rule of law." In light of the *first view* we discover that in the age of the US Global Empire, "international society as such—that inclusive society of states, or community of communities, within which all international association takes place—is not a purposive association constituted by a joint wish on the part of all states to pursue certain ends in concert. It is, rather, an association of independent and diverse political communities, each devoted to its own ends and its own conception of the good, often related to one another by nothing more than the fragile ties of a common tradition of diplomacy."[64] In a world of independent and diverse political communities, there can be no recognition of the interdependent character of a true Global Community. In place of a world of interdependence and accountability there now remains only the drumbeat of the unilateral cadence of Global Empire. Under *the first view*, it remains free of the rule of law so that it can embark upon a path of savaging the globe to carve out its domination over those resources that it deems essential to keep its own privileged position of dominance. The law of the empire is "rule *by* law" as it picks and chooses which laws to abide by and those that it will ignore.

INTERNATIONAL LAW AS A FORCE IN RESTRAINING EMPIRE

Despite assertions of unilateral power, there exists an alternative international law perspective that is growing in legitimacy among the nation-states of the Global Community. The alternative view is found in the assertion that "the role of *opinio juris*, has been reconceived, so that the concept now serves to buttress the assertion that States can be bound by customary law to which they do not consent." For this reason, "the United States does not and cannot play a uniquely dominating role in the shaping of customary international law even though its material power is preponderant in contemporary world society."[65] If the United States cannot dominate the shaping of international customary law that means that "the US hegemon is precluded from effective dominance even in areas central to its perceived interests, and despite its overwhelming material power."[66] Therefore, the decline of the *first view* (as a strictly consent-based theory of law for the global rule of law) is a victory for those who stand in opposition to Global Empire. The decline of the *first view* is a victory for those who act as advocates for a rising Global Community of interdependent and coequal states. Having come to this point in the discussion, we need to ask: "Why is this result the dominant trend in international law?"

The *first view* has been placed in a free fall of decline for two principle reasons. First, it has undermined advances made in progressive areas of international law such as human rights and environmental protection. Second, the *first view* is in decline because the idea of formal equality among nation-states masks substantive inequality in power relations.[67] Therefore, progressive scholars have begun to focus more on *consensus-based decision making* in intergovernmental forums.

Progressive jurists and scholars have suggested that an evolving *community consciousness* can displace individual consent in the formation of specific norms.[68] *Therefore, we can set forth the following thesis statement*: The rise of Global Community—operating in association with this second view of the "rule of law"—demonstrates that there are fundamental changes with respect to the formation and operation of customary law. What this ultimately means is that, "even though it is overwhelmingly materially powerful, the United States alone cannot prevent modifications to customary international law." Therefore, "despite persistent US objection to a new or changing rule, the rule can change, and can bind the United States along with all other States."[69] In short, the reign of brute force sanctioned under *the first view* is slowly being replaced by *the second view*—the power to persuade—for legal power lies in the capacity to persuade. If the architects of the US Global Empire fail to understand the need to practice and participate in the global art of persuasion, the United States will simply fail to partake in a legitimate process of law creation.[70]

Raw material power and brute force are not an adequate substitute for persuasion, linked to the pursuit of the common good. An inclusive Global Community demands more than a weak international law standard that can be discarded when an all-powerful state seeks to impose its own will without reference to global norms and the embodiment of those norms in customary international law. In this regard, the dawn of the twenty-first century marks an historical turning point where "the common good of this inclusive community resides not in the ends that some, or at times even most, of its members may wish collectively to pursue but in the values of justice, peace, security, and coexistence, which can only be enjoyed through participation in a common body of authoritative practices."[71]

EVOLVING LEGAL PRACTICES THROUGH "UNIVERSAL JURISDICTION"

Reflective of the international trend among nations toward participation in a common body of authoritative practices is the advent of *universal jurisdiction*.

As with the case of evolving norms in the field of international customary law, we now find that the historical definitions of sovereignty, jurisdiction, and territory are evolving beyond the narrow limits of the sovereign states—including the most powerful among them. Universal claims about what constitutes the common good are increasingly centered upon universal values that are shared by all humanity—whether as embodied in the world's great religions, as codified in international law, or as emerging in a common body of authoritative practices which are shared by all twenty-first century communities. In order to assure the continued successful evolution of these current trends, an inclusive Global Community demands more than a weak international law standard that can be unilaterally discarded by powerful states, or states seeking to dominate international affairs through the brute force of military hegemony and threat of force.

By centralizing the values of peace, justice, security, and coexistence, we discover that the evolution of international law, in congruence with the moral codes and sacred texts of the world's great religions, demonstrates an orientation toward the strengthening of Global Community. Further, the merging of common principles between an inclusive and human rights oriented international law standard with the traditional moral codes of the world's great religions has started to both reflect and create a realignment of global consciousness. If human rights have acquired both a legal and moral force, then it is unprecedented in human history. A shared moral vision and shared moral values are in the process of becoming a transcendent power above the claims of empire. This new development means that human rights claims can begin to act as significant curtailment upon the unbridled ambitions embodied in the pursuit of Global Empire.

Such a result also points to the fact that human rights claims—as embodied in evolving international law standards—are also claims that are evolving in conjunction with the traditional moral codes of the sacred texts of the world's great religions. The union of international law standards with the normative force of the moral codes of the world's great religions will be developing a capacity to begin the process of establishing a bulwark of opposition against the architects, apologists, and collaborators of Global Empire. Such a principled opposition to empire will be necessary in order to overcome the violence propagated by empire. If there is a "clash," it is not a clash between civilizations, but rather between the nonviolent agenda of an emerging global community and the violent agenda of empire builders.

Today, the new trend in international law is that those who are guilty of "crimes against humanity" must be held accountable to the entire Global Community. This is applicable to the weakest states and to the most powerful of states. Traditionally, sovereignty, jurisdiction, and territory have been closely linked. This linkage has allowed for all kinds of criminality—war crimes, crimes against humanity, genocide, and torture—to go unpunished. If a sovereign chose not to extradite an individual to face charges for such crimes, he could claim sovereign impunity. If the sovereign chose to argue that the laws of his nation governed all those within the borders of his state, then national jurisdiction would be used to ignore the claims of international jurisdiction.

With late twentieth century innovations in international law,

the theory of universal jurisdiction transcends national sovereignty, which is the historical basis for national criminal jurisdiction. Two propositions can be identified to justify this. The first is *the normative universalist position*, which recognizes the existence of certain core values that are shared by the international community. These values are deemed important enough to justify overriding the usual territorial limitations on the exercise of jurisdiction. The second position is a *pragmatic policy-oriented* one, which recognizes that occasionally there exist certain shared international interests that require an enforcement mechanism not limited to national sovereignty[72]. (Italics are mine)

Both the normative and pragmatic features of the emerging doctrine of universal jurisdiction find their justification and their roots within the matrix of different cultures, different times, and different religious traditions. To recognize these historical realities is to begin to understand why the early twenty-first century marks a turning point for global culture as it moves toward the realization of Global Community and a rejection of the Global Empire's claims to impunity. Remaking history involves dismantling the current paradigms of empire and the "clash thesis." From this analysis, the following thesis statement emerges:

The clash between the advocates of Global Empire and the advocates of Global Community is the genuine "clash" that has ushered in the twenty-first century. Interestingly enough, it is clearly not a "clash of civilizations," for the advocates of Global Community reside in every single civilization on the planet.

Every civilization on the globe has representative members and groups who oppose the unilateral actions of any Global Empire that puts the welfare of the Global Community at risk. The global commons is not the single prize for any one nation or group of nations to dominate and exploit. The global commons is an interdependent and unified whole.

THE METAPHYSICS OF GLOBAL JUSTICE:
THE EVOLUTION AND RISE OF GLOBAL COMMUNITY
OUT OF MORAL AND LEGAL TRADITIONS

Scholars have noted "the universalist normative position can be traced to metaphysical and philosophical conceptions arising in different cultures and at different times. For example, in the three monotheistic faiths of Judaism, Christianity, and Islam, full sovereignty rests with the Creator. Transgression of the Creator's norms confers the power to enforce religious laws by the religious community, irrespective of any limitations in place or time."[73] With this perspective, it is easy to discount any presumed validity for the *clash* thesis insofar as the universality of norms across cultures provides a more legitimate argument for a shared ethics among nations.

In addition to the metaphysical and philosophical unity found in the shared moral codes of the world's great religions there also exists a conceptual basis for uniting the normative aspects of cross cultural experiences with Global Community—it is at the intersection where customary international law and shared morals merge. The political life of the Global Community has already been changed due to the rediscovery of shared legal and moral arguments that are supportive of humanitarian intervention. From this perspective, it is possible to see the evolution of a complementary legal, ethical, and moral convergence in the service of human rights. The point of convergence is found in the commitment to defend the dignity and worth of the individual person, regardless of nationality, race, religion, gender, or political loyalty.

From the standpoint of international law, universal jurisdiction is based strictly on the nature of the crime committed. Certainly, the Torture Convention would make heads of state legally accountable for crimes of state. Hence, the crimes of America's Global Empire and its collaborators, such as General Pinochet and his use of state terror in Chile would open the door to a world where there is *justice without borders*.[74] It is also a world that could open the door to the prosecution of high-ranking civilian heads of state, such as former US Secretary of State, Henry Kissinger, who helped to orchestrate the CIA-sponsored coup that overthrew the democratically elected government of Salvador Allende and installed General Pinochet and his junta in 1972.[75]

Since the late twentieth century, the hatred that is directed at the US Global Empire from every corner of the globe is related to particular situations and events, such as those that transpired during the Nixon administration in Chile, Vietnam, Laos, Thailand, and Cambodia. In fact, one of the original articles of impeachment against President Nixon involved lying to Congress about extending the use of force into other nations without congressional authorization or knowledge. Nixon's imperial presidency, of which Kissinger was an integral part, exemplified the ability of America's National Security State to act no better than the Nazi regime that was condemned at Nuremberg. Yet, the Nuremberg Charter of 1946 remains as the primary legal standard against which the acts of all states must be judged. As the American government's foreign policy has proceeded under the rubric of "National Security" and acted *for reasons of state*, the legacy of the Nuremberg Charter has served to inspire the global movement toward the establishment of universal jurisdiction.

NUCLEAR WEAPONS VERSUS A HUMANE INTERNATIONAL ORDER

The current evolution of universal jurisdiction has proceeded in conjunction with respect to the treatment of crimes based on conventional and customary international law sources. Serious international crimes include the following: (1) piracy; (2) slavery and slave-related practices; (3) war crimes; (4) crimes against humanity; (5) genocide; (6) apartheid and torture.[76] As important as the expansion of universal jurisdiction is in the aforementioned areas, it needs to be expanded if we are to see a viable Global Community emerge in conjunction with a viable human future. A viable human future means a future without nuclear weapons. The logic associated with maintaining a Global Empire requires nuclear weapons, the promise of a viable Global Community demands that they be abolished.

In 1996, the International Court of Justice (ICJ) ruled that nuclear weapons were illegal and their indiscriminate effects would create a human disaster of genocidal proportions. Hence, at the dawn of the twenty-first century, it should be argued that an agreement to abolish nuclear arms and all other weapons of mass destruction is the sine qua non of any sane or workable international system. Based upon this precedent, it should be universally recognized that no humane international order could rationally justify dependence upon a threat that could potentially extinguish humanity. The logic of abolition remains as the real alternative to the logic of empire. Still, the Bush-2 regime, at the start of its second term, has continued to push for a new generation of nuclear weapons—including "bunker busting bombs." Instead of complying with the ICJ ruling, the Bush-2 regime has ignored its mandate completely. Further, it has refused to participate in the process of ratifying the CTBT and the NPT. Instead, the Bush-2 regime has engaged in perpetual saber rattling against North Korea and Iran, arguing that they do not have a right to nuclear weapons and should not fear a preemptive strike by the United States against their nuclear facilities.

The tragedy of the postwar 1945 era is found in the realization that the crimes of America's Global Empire have continued unabated. Not only has the United States continued to pursue building and basing nuclear weapons, it has continued to aid criminal regimes and their authoritarian dictators. As long as these leaders kept their nations and markets open to US-based multinational corporations, the United States was all too willing to look the other way. If the US State Department was critical of human rights abuses that did not necessarily mean that the US Defense Department and Pentagon had to follow suit with the criticism.

For example, in the case of Chile under Pincohet, as well as US conduct in Southeast Asia during the Vietnam War (1964–1974), and US crimes in Persian Gulf Wars (I) and (II), crimes against a host of nations throughout the Global Community multiplied. Specifically, the abuses of America's Global Empire have included war crimes throughout Asia, Latin America, and the Middle East. In Cambodia, the Nixon Doctrine sanctioned genocide, torture, and a multitude of crimes against humanity. The transparent and flagrant employment of criminal conduct in the pursuit of US policies were crimes committed at the behest of the leaders of America's Global Empire in order to further advance the empire's perceived national interest. Crimes were given euphemistic labels in an attempt to maintain the façade of America as the *defender of the Free World*. Ultimately, however, the self-definition of what constituted the "national interest" turned out to be little more than a game of labels designed to help the United States and its collaborators escape criminal jurisdiction in the pursuit of its particular geopolitical goals and objectives. In order to avoid a continuation of this historical humanitarian catastrophe, it will be important for the Global Community to enforce its normative and value-oriented focus on justice, cooperation, and peace with an authoritative legal set of guidelines. This is especially true with respect to the threat of nuclear weapons.

Robert S. McNamara, former Secretary of Defense under President John F. Kennedy, knows how close the world came to a nuclear apocalypse during the 1962 Cuban Missile Crisis. In 2005, he has stated that he believes the United

States must no longer rely on nuclear weapons as a foreign policy tool. To do so is immoral, illegal, and dreadfully dangerous. He notes that what is shocking about today, more than a decade after the end of the cold war, is that the basic elements of US nuclear policy are unchanged. From this observation, he has asserted that to launch weapons against a nuclear power would be suicide. To do so against a nonnuclear enemy would be militarily unnecessary, morally repugnant, and politically indefensible. Therefore, he concludes that the United States must move promptly toward the elimination—or near elimination—of all nuclear weapons.

Similarly, Robert Johansen notes, "it is imperative to construct a normative basis for international transactions to insure that through inadvertence or moral callousness we do not create a system that eventually destroys our highest values."[77] Certainly, the use of nuclear weapons would constitute the ultimate destruction of our highest values for it would destroy life itself. In order to be faithful to a morally normative basis for international transactions, the Global Community's first priority must be to turn moral callousness into a moral commitment that supports the abolition of weapons.

FROM NUCLEAR WEAPONS TO GLOBAL WARMING

In this regard, with coequal urgency, it will be necessary for citizens of the Global Community to address the problems associated with climate change (global warming) and other threats to the earth's environment. The founder and former president of the World Resources Institute, Professor James Gustave Speth, has addressed the urgent nature of the challenge noting: "Today, the transition to a globalized world is progressing rapidly. But the transition to a sustainable one is not. Some believe that globalization is a prime reason for the failure to realize sustainable development. Others argue that globalization can and should advance the transition to sustainability."[78]

Whether globalization is the ultimate culprit or not, the evolving norms of customary international law and the concerns of the world's great religions with man's stewardship of the earth, demand that the Global Community gives greater attention to the maintenance, sustainability, and care of God's creation. Such a worldview constitutes a moral mandate as well as a political, social, economic, and cultural responsibility. With increased calls for environmental sustainability, it is clear that global consciousness has been moving toward a point of international convergence. Whatever relevance the "clash" thesis retains, it is best summed up in the inherent clash between the corporate drive for profits at any cost and the moral demand to protect the earth.

The exclusion of most of the Global Community from US decision making on nuclear abolition and environmental issues has contributed to a global crisis that is breaking wide open as we enter the twenty-first century. In light of this unsavory history, it is necessary to renew and reformulate state practices and the international order in accordance with humane principles. It should be the first priority of the United States, in conjunction with the Global Community, to undergo the task of advancing normative requirements in state policies and practices so that we can move toward the attainment of the common good. In this regard, throughout the course of my own writings, I have continually stressed the importance of distinguishing between the policy choices and value-orientations of *inclusionary states* versus those of *exclusionary states*.[79]

As we look at the entire context of an evolving Global Community, my own research and writings have led me to believe that the approaches and values associated with the practice of inclusionary governance are essential to developing a humane world order. The reason for this assertion is found in the realization that the strategies, values, and policies of inclusionary governance serve to address not only the need for adherence to an already established human rights legal regime, but also serve to build a strong international framework for developing policies and practices that advance the socioeconomic rights of all classes, nations, and groups (see: Chapter 6).

With power comes accountability. The power of the US Global Empire has been wrongly focused on military and economic domination of the globe, rather than addressing the interrelated challenges of poverty, war, environmental degradation, and the threat of nuclear annihilation. From a moral point of view, all of these challenges are equally important and should be addressed simultaneously. Yet, the most immediate threat that can be most easily addressed is ending global poverty; for poverty remains at the epicenter of all these other difficulties. The Global Community must act to end poverty on a global scale, while it also works to respond to the challenge of climate change and global warming. This is one of the primary goals of the *UN Millennium Development Report*. Yet, like so many initiatives of its kind, it remains ignored within the highest counsels of the American government.

There are many reasons for the American government to discount the UN Millennium Goals—especially those that relate to the reduction and elimination of poverty. Such a goal automatically discounts traditional fixations upon a narrowly defined national interest, balance-of-power considerations, and unipolar power concepts. The abolition of poverty, like the abolition of nuclear weapons, means bringing an end to the culture of the NSS, as well as the multinational corporations that benefit from the hunger and powerlessness of nations, not to mention the $900 billion annual trade in conventional weapons. In short, to seek to diminish the power of the NSS means to threaten the enterprise of Global Empire itself.

Insofar as the imperial project feeds off global poverty and inequality, serious undertakings to move toward global social justice and reduce the spread of armaments mean drastic cuts in the profits of the war industry. As contradictory or as paradoxical as this assertion may sound, it is grounded in empirical studies. For example, by keeping the global poor in a condition of subordination to the United States, especially in resource-rich nations such as Venezuela with its oil reserves, the American NSS assumes that it is able to keep the nation "in line" with American energy needs. However, President Hugo Chavez has been unwilling to bend to the Bush Doctrine of "fall in line with imperial directives." Despite a Bush-supported coup in 2002, President Chavez was not overthrown. Yet, Venezuela fears it may face a US-sanctioned preemptive war in the name of "fighting terrorism."

MOVING TOWARD GLOBAL LIBERATION
FROM GLOBAL EMPIRE

In both the socioeconomic and sociopolitical realms of global life, there is a need to reorder priorities so that a genuine liberation of mind and spirit, human needs, and humane aspirations can be actualized. In this regard, there is an attendant moral mandate to alleviate human suffering and to realize social justice. The enactment of this moral mandate becomes the means through which the poor, the powerless, and the excluded can live in hope of seeing the day when their liberation is actualized. In order to actualize this liberation there is another factor that needs to be introduced into the equation. It is found in the power created through the union of a binding and authoritative international legal order with the underlying shared moral codes of the world's great religions. My argument regarding the promise of liberation is summed up in the following interrelated thesis statements:

Thesis Statement A: The actualization of this global liberation will require the evolution of a binding, authoritative, and universal international law and legal system that works in conjunction with the moral codes of the world's great religions and divergent cultures. What underlies both the legal and moral systems is the universal claim of human rights, human dignity, and human worth as the primary consideration for political, economic, and social action.

Thesis Statement B: Under the rubric of a Global Community conceived in this manner, the claims of Global Empire will either be diminished or ruled out altogether. An exodus from empire is made possible by the rising force of a Global Community predicated upon "unity in diversity." In order to be effective, this global unity will have to be predicated upon the union of a normative consensus and practical means and strategies for the actualization of this consensus.

Thesis Statement C: In the final analysis, the strength and viability of this union of normative consensus and practical strategies can only truly be realized through a cooperative dedication to realize a Global Community centered around human rights, human dignity, and human worth. The development of such a capacity among nations is essential if humankind is ever to engage in the task of governing a global culture that is mutually beneficial. Guided by norms of social justice, cooperation, and shared values, the Global Community can finally embark upon an *exodus from empire.*

EXITING THE GLOBAL EMPIRE

The aforementioned principles of Global Community are diametrically opposed to the logic of Global Empire. One thrives on the diminishment of the other.

The pursuit of Global Empire exacerbates destructive trends and policies at every level. By abandoning security-related treaties, such as the Kyoto Protocol, the United States placed itself on a collision course with both human welfare and nature. To constrain the US Global Empire, the Global Community needs to develop a strategy of opposition that allows for a normative convergence of peoples and cultures in opposition to the imperial drive for domination. Such a convergence has the capacity to create a global mandate that can provide the incentive for continuing resistance to imperial domination in all of its forms. The capacity to wage global resistance against the intrusions of empire will require a "counter-hegemonic alliance" throughout the global South. South-South regional cooperation and alliances are essential to this strategy (see: Chapter 6). Nonviolent strategies will be required that are capable of building economic and political alliances of mutual assistance throughout the global South. New trading partners and trading blocs will have the capacity to neuter and defang the empire's current hegemonic hold over billions of people. Also, shared moral values will have to be employed in order to carry the long-term burden of both global trans-formation and global resistance.

Following the logic of the above-stated thesis statements, I would argue that the main conclusion to be drawn is as follows:

> *Global resistance to Global Empire will require the active employment of a global moral code to provide the framework for an* "exodus from empire."

In this context, a global moral code is necessary to bring about the normative convergence of law and religion. Implementing this code in practice will require the same kind of dedication and endurance that brought down the system of racial segregation that divided apartheid South Africa. Such a legal and moral code is the only way to bring about an end to global apartheid—understood as the division between the extremely rich and the extremely poor, the included and the excluded, the powerful and the powerless.

The challenge facing global resistance movements to Global Empire is the same challenge that is encountered by (1) *global humanism* (Robert Johansen), (2) *humane governance* (Richard Falk), (3) *cosmopolitan democracy* (David Held) and (4) *inclusionary governance* (Terrence Paupp). The precise nature of the challenge is found in the fact that normative orientations and value-oriented approaches to global governance desperately need to discover and to build the objective mechanisms for implementing normative claims through state policies (both interstate and intra-state). Too often, there is the failure to realize human rights, dignity, and worth because there is a radical disjunction between normative prescriptions and their implementation.

More often than not, the powers of states are not congruent with the will of their own people, not to mention the 6 billion person membership of the Global Community. Consequently, the political will and resources needed to strengthen the rights and legal protections of the most vulnerable are ignored. It is now clear that it is a false hope to believe that the employment and deployment of state power will somehow automatically mirror the same objectives embodied in these normatively based and value-oriented approaches. State power is primarily con-cerned with the maintenance of its own power—as an end in itself. Alternatively, a source of genuine hope is found in the co-creative union of normative human rights claims and the teachings of the world's great religions on how best to make more receptive the human mind and heart for the full embrace and practice of human rights through mutual respect.

ESTABLISHING PRACTICAL GUIDELINES FOR
NORMATIVE HUMAN RIGHTS CLAIMS

In the furtherance of justice and human rights, the dignity and worth of the person must be seen as the core value of an emerging Global Community. The importance of uniting the *normative universalist position* (found in universal jurisdiction) *with* the *pragmatic policy position* (taken by states) remains absolutely critical to the integrity of establishing practical guidelines for the realization and enforcement of normative human rights claims. The practice of universal jurisdiction must be one that is able to unite shared moral values and norms with pragmatic policies. This assertion points to the discovery that "it is necessary to have guidelines for the application of this theory in order to avoid jurisdictional conflicts, disruptions of world order, abuse and denial of justice, and to enhance the predictability of international criminal law. Supplying these guidelines has been the purpose of the Princeton Project on Universal Jurisdiction."[80]

The Princeton Project on Universal Jurisdiction was formed to contribute to the ongoing development of the law in this area. The Project was convened at Princeton University in January 2001. It comprised an assembly of scholars and jurists from around the world. They sought to develop a consensus around evolving principles of universal jurisdiction. On January 27, 2001, they arrived at a final text that consists of 14 principles.[81] The authors and advocates of the principle of universal jurisdiction agree that in its present state, the doctrine looks like a checkerboard. Yet, they also hope that the Princeton Principles, or a set of revised and redefined principles, "will in time garner consensus among scholars and, ultimately, among governments. Then an international convention should be convened so that guidelines on universal jurisdiction can become positive international law."[82]

In the quest for justice, the quest for clarity should not eclipse universal efforts to effectively implement international law principles. Too often the quest for justice has remained at the theoretical, philosophical, and/or theological level. If justice is to be realized in history, it must be concretized in specific institutional mechanisms that are capable of following specific strategies, politics, and procedures. These elements are necessary to bear the weight of what is required by and for humans if they are ever to achieve real justice. In this regard, the good news is that concerns with clarity have not hampered the progress of the International Criminal Court (ICC). The criminal law jurisdiction of the court is clearly mapped out in reference to the principles of justice and state accountability that have evolved through customary international law.

Additionally, from the standpoint and perspective of the world's great religions, the rising moral force of Global Community is directly related to the process and progress of international law. As international law evolves, it incorporates shared cultural norms and principles from the sacred texts of the world's great religions. Through the interplay of law and principles, the precedents of customary international law are made over into a global juridical consensus. As such, the emerging consensus promises to be an effective antidote to the abuses of war criminals and the lingering tragedy of war crimes. This insight leads to my next thesis statements regarding the promise of liberation from the bondage of empire:

Thesis Statement D: The convergence of civilizations—not the clash of civilizations—is the most pressing need as humanity begins to forge an *exodus from empire*. The nature of this exodus will entail the building of unprecedented forms of national and global cooperation. It will be reflective of the intersection of evolving norms of customary international law with the moral codes and shared moral values contained in the texts of the world's great religions.

Thesis Statement E: Through the development of unprecedented forms and practices of legal and normative global governance, a global consensus can emerge that strengthens and activates political, social, and cultural mechanisms for the advancement of human rights and human liberation. The realization of such a convergence of human purpose and consensus has the capacity to heal nations (from nuclear weapons abolition to dealing with the problem of climate change). With this consensus in place, new institutional mechanisms will be equipped with binding legal authority. Effective global mechanisms for human liberation will need to be put in place so that the Global Community can effectively embark upon a final *exodus from empire*.

In furtherance of this process, the jurisdictional reach of the ICC has been augmented by enabling statutes that were adopted primarily in response to international obligations to implement various conventions adopted since World War II, such as the Geneva Convention.[83] In the aftermath of the Abu Ghraib prison scandal, with the revelation that the Pentagon and CIA have transferred detainees and *enemy combatants* to other nations so as to try to escape the prohibitions on torture embodied in the Geneva Convention, it becomes clear that as the reach of universal jurisdiction is extended in conjunction with that of the ICC, it will be more difficult to play shell games with the Bush-2 regime's revived practice of employing torture as a tool in war.[84]

Despite the assertions of White House lawyers in the Bush-2 regime, the Geneva Convention is not just a "quaint artifact of the past."[85] Eventually, the weight of international law will come crashing down upon imperial hubris. Just as the judgment on the Third Reich was hammered out through the Nuremberg Charter—with its detailed definitions and condemnations of war crimes and war criminals—so too the blowback effects from the Bush-2 regime's so-called *war on terror* could easily come back with a vengeance upon Bush's White House, the Pentagon, and CIA.

One of the great benefits of the Princeton Project was to bring about the recognition of the need for legislative reform in many countries to address the significant limits on the exercise of universal jurisdiction by almost all states. Since the Princeton Project on Universal Jurisdiction began in 2001, there has been significant progress in many countries in broadening the scope of the universal jurisdiction. In fact, "a system of international criminal justice has begun to emerge in which both international criminal tribunals and national courts have an important and mutually reinforcing role to play in the enforcement of international criminal norms."[86]

If the United States should ever finally be able to divorce itself from its Global Empire and return to the principles on which the republic was founded, national courts, international courts, and international tribunals will have a great deal of state-sponsored criminality to adjudicate. Such a result is not without precedent. As Telford Taylor, the US Chief Counsel at Nuremberg observed in his book, *Nuremberg and Vietnam: An American Tragedy*: "prior to Nuremberg the individuals against whom the laws of war had been enforced were, for the most part, ordinary soldiers or officers of middle or low rank. At Nuremberg and Tokyo, on the other hand, nearly all the defendants stood at or near the top of the military or civilian hierarchy."[87]

Even more directly and personally, Taylor posed to his readers the following question: "More generally, are the people of the United States able to face the proposition that Jackson put forth in their name, and examine their own conduct under the same principles that they applied to the Germans and Japanese at the Nuremberg and other war crimes trials?"[88] At the conclusion of the book, in his reflections on America's conduct in the war in Vietnam, Taylor asked: "How could it ever have been thought that air strikes, free-fire zones and a mass uprooting and removal of the rural population were the way to win 'the allegiance of the South Vietnamese'? By what mad cerebrations could a ratio of 28 to 1 between our investments in bombing, and in relief for those we had wounded and made homeless, have even been contemplated, let alone adopted as the operational pattern?"[89]

After cataloging the moral, political, and legal failures of the US prosecution of the war in Vietnam, Taylor lamented:

> And so it has come to this: that the United Nations Charter is invoked to justify our venture in Vietnam, where we have smashed the country into bits, and will not even take the trouble to clean up the blood and rubble ... Somehow we failed ourselves to learn the lessons we undertook to teach at Nuremberg, and that failure is today's American tragedy.[90]

By merely changing the reference of the country from Vietnam to Iraq, the same analysis and conclusions could be reached in the year 2005.

THE WORLD'S GREAT RELIGIONS
AS A COMMON BODY OF AUTHORITATIVE NORMS

Francis Cardinal Arinze, the head of the Pontifical Council for Inter-religious Dialogue, wrote in his book, *Religions for Peace: A Call for Solidarity to the Religions of the World*: "To promote overall human development is to prepare for peace. Excessive inequalities among peoples in the economic, social, and cultural fields arouse tension and are a threat to peace. Peace and prosperity are the goods that belong to the whole human race."[91] In the midst of America's war in Vietnam, James Douglas, a professor of religion, made a similar point in his book, *The*

Non-Violent Cross: A Theology of Revolution and Peace. Douglas argued: "Any political or economic system which can preach an ideological crusade against the poor, punctuating it with napalm and TNT, or can tolerate worms in the stomachs of children, deserves not allegiance but uprooting."[92]

Contained within these critiques is a convergence of Christian thought and tradition on the subject of peace and liberation. It represents a convergence of political thought and a political/revolutionary ethics that began in the early 1960s with the *Theology of Hope* movement under the pen of the German theologian, Jurgen Moltmann. Moltmann sought to convey a theological view that linked radical political liberation from oppressive socioeconomic and political structures with spiritual liberation. As the *theology of hope* became a new theological paradigm it also became a movement. Some called it a *political theology* while others considered it to be a retrieval of the ethical core of the Judeo-Christian message. Its strongly prophetic tone inclined it to become supportive of progressive social movements in the 1960s.

As both a new movement and a strongly articulated ethics of engagement, it served to explicate the claims of Christ's teachings about the "Kingdom of God" with political movements attuned to the same set of core beliefs about love, interpersonal justice, and opposition to structures that denied the dignity and worth of the person. From the standpoint of Judeo-Christian ethics, the *theology of hope* came equipped with a revived message centered upon liberation stories contained in the Old and New Testaments. Eventually, as the decade of the 1960s moved toward an end, the theology of hope took on a strident revolutionary tone and became increasingly integrated into the worldview and belief structures of Third World theologians, especially in Latin America. Its transmigration from Europe to Latin America also served to provide the theology of hope with a new label: *liberation theology*.

The liberation themes of the Old and New Testaments were discovered in the "exodus event" and in Christ's "Sermon on the Mount." For example, the theological meaning that lay behind the "exodus event" was analogized to an exodus from the socioeconomic and political structures of oppression found in twentieth century Latin America. Also, the crucifixion of Jesus represented the suffering, torture, and torment of the poor and left wing political opponents of right wing military dictatorships throughout the Latin American continent. In this atmosphere, the theology of liberation was a *theology from the underside of history*. In other words, it was written and preached from the perspective of the poor and the oppressed. Liberation theology had become attuned to and in solidarity with the struggles experienced by landless peasants, the isolated urban poor, and the socially marginalized and excluded masses of Latin America. Its ethical focus upon the transcendent claims of the *Kingdom of God* soon became a call for universal liberation—a liberation that gave ethical justification to the moral obligation to shake off the chains of their national dictatorships—as well as the interventions of a US Global Empire that supported these dictatorial regimes.

With respect to these themes, Elsa Tamez, wrote a volume entitled, *Bible of the Oppressed*. She asserted: "The oppressors are thieves and murderers, but their ultimate purpose is not to kill or impoverish the oppressed. Their primary objective is to increase their wealth at whatever cost. The impoverishment and death of the oppressed are a secondary consequence."[93] In order to make her point, she cited the biblical narrative of the *Book of Exodus* in order to describe the enslavement and exploitation of the workers: "Therefore they set taskmasters over them to *afflict* [*'anah*] *them with heavy burdens*; and they built for Pharaoh store-cities, Pithom and Raamses" (Exodus 1:11). The word here used for 'afflict', namely *'anah*, might well be translated 'enslave'."[94]

Also attributed to the Egyptians was the practice of genocide: "the next step in Egyptian oppression was the murder of children. The king gave the midwives the following order: 'When you serve as midwife to the Hebrew women, and then upon their birth-stool, if it is a son, you shall kill him; but if it is a daughter, she shall live.' (Exodus 1:16)."[95] In Tamez's summary on the forms and methods of oppression used in the Egypt of Pharaohs, she notes:

> Oppressors are idolaters who follow false gods that can lend an aura of legitimacy to their actions; Yahweh, the God who demands that justice be done because he is himself justice and love, will not serve their purpose. The oppressed are the impoverished, the slaves, the day laborers, the widows, the resident alien, and the orphan. All are poor and lack both social standing and power.[96]

Given this perspective, liberation theologians throughout Latin America were able to produce a contemporary interpretation of the *Book of Exodus*. In doing so, they saw "capitalism as a system" that "does not permit existing resources to be directed to the satisfaction of needs, because the purpose it imposes upon them is the augmentation of capital."[97] Because this is the objective case of oppression in Latin America, Jose Miranda argued that: "Capitalism has seized the resources of humanity and physically kills millions of human beings day by day with hunger, or leaves them lifelong mental defectives."[98] In Miranda's view, whether death comes suddenly or slowly is irrelevant—it still constitutes genocide.

Significantly, the interpretations of Latin American liberation theologians are not geographically, theologically, or politically confined to a particular region, faith, or political agenda. For example, Islam acknowledges Judaism and Christianity as its forerunners in a single religious tradition of revelation-based monotheism. Islam also preaches equality, justice, and human dignity. These ideals have all played an historical role in the sixteenth century German Reformation undertaken by Luther, the eighteenth century revolutions in America and France, and are connected to various expressions of "liberation theology" as developed in Latin America, Africa, and Asia.[99]

The tenets and practices of Islam embrace pluralism—as exemplified in the traditions of *ijtihad* (interpretation), *ijma* (consensus), and *shura* (consultation). Acknowledging these pluralistic traits in Islam paves the way for asserting that "politicized Islam is not a monolith; its spectrum is broad."[100] Hence, like Latin America's liberation theology and social movements,

> many of today's Islamic movements are trying to adapt the tenets of the faith to changing times and circumstances. In their own way, some even resemble

Catholic "liberation theology" movements in their attempts to use religious doctrine to transform temporal life in the modern world. The more accurate word for such Muslim groups is "Islamist". The term is growing in popularity in Western academic and policy-making circles, since it better allows for the forward-looking interpretation, and often innovative stances that such groups assume as they seek to bring about a reconstruction of the social order.[101]

For those who have adopted the "clash" thesis, the human future is one of inevitable barbarism.[102] For those who adopt the "convergence" thesis, the promise of Global Community is achievable because the normative forces of international law, the principles of the world's great religions, and the driving force behind national and global social movements, are an alternative historical future that ruptures the claims of imperial thinking and the associated delusions of empire.[103]

For Muslims, there are many proactive groups seeking nothing less than an Islamic reformation. This revolution centers on questions of how best to modernize and democratize their political and economic systems in an Islamic context.[104] Its answers cannot be imposed from the outside. The advent of late twentieth century mass communications, improved education, and the intercontinental movement of peoples and ideas stimulated an impulse toward reform. Tens of millions of Muslims have been incorporated into a debate of global proportions.

The momentum toward reform began in the 1980s as secular ideologies succeeded colonialism. Yet, "variants or hybrids of nationalism and socialism ... failed to provide freedom and security to many people in the Muslim world."[105] The politics of global upheaval have contributed to the unfolding of a new consciousness that seeks inclusive practices in the realms of politics, economics, and ideas so that decision making and the formation of opinion is no longer a function of the elites from a Global Empire or their collaborators in repressive authoritarian state structures. As with the leaders of the sixteenth century Lutheran Reformation, the Islamic Reformation and its non-fundamentalist reformers "want to strip the faith of corrupt, irrelevant, or unjust practices that have been tacked on over centuries ... they want to draw on Islam as both a justification and a tool for political, social, and economic empowerment."[106]

This sense of empowerment comes not from adopting the ideological approach of terrorist doctrines, but upon the realization that love, empathy, and the realization of peace provide the basis for a convergence and healing of both civilizations and the individuals within them. On this point, Harun Yahya maintains that the real ideological moorings of terror are to be found in the secularist and relativist doctrines of the twentieth century. He maintains that modern terrorism's ideological foundations go back to Social Darwinism and the materialist tendencies derived from it. Hence,

people exposed to this indoctrination believe that life is a field of struggle and that only the strong survive ... Man, and in fact, the entire universe, are both products of chance. Therefore, no one is responsible for his actions to anyone else. These and similar ideas inevitably coax people into leading an animalistic form of life, where ruthlessness, aggression and violence are regarded as acceptable or even virtuous.[107]

In the alternative, he argues that "anyone sincerely opposed to terrorism should show the same empathy for the thousands of innocent victims it has slaughtered—not only at the World Trade Center, but in attacks in Japan and Spain, in East Turkestan and Indonesia, in the massacre of more than half a million Hutus in Rwanda, in the murder of defenseless people in Palestine, Israel, and all across the globe."[108] His argument is an argument in support of the idea that there is a growing global convergence of thought around the principle that "no idea can prevail by means of violence, oppression and cruelty; and despotism can never triumph."[109]

Taking his point further, I would argue that the means of violence, oppression, cruelty, and despotism adopted and practiced by the architects, advocates, and apologists of Global Empire can never triumph. The revival of the crusader mentality in the Bush-2 regime in Afghanistan and Iraq is antithetical to "fighting terror" because it "employs terror"—terrorizing the powerless, the poor, the dispossessed. The Bush-2 regime is guided by its own Christian fundamentalism mixed with the orthodoxy of militarism.[110]

Fundamentalism is not one of the world's great religions—it is an approach to interpretation. Its followers hold the view that their scriptures are the literal, unchanging, and eternally manifest truth of their God. Contained within this worldview is a strict adherence to an unquestioning faith in a divine will that cannot be apprehended by reason, critical thought, or doubt—only absolute obedience can express adequate reverence for the divinity. Hence, fundamentalisms of either a Christian or Islamic variety assert one truth, one way, and one answer. Within this view, Church and state are obliged to operate in sync. In the United States, if the nation's political leadership fails to demonstrate a similar commitment to core right wing beliefs, then the State's leadership finds itself admonished by fundamentalism's true believers to admit its "sin" and fall in line with the "Word." If the faithful, who may be moderates or even liberals, cannot find their place in this cookie-cutter theocracy, then they are to be branded as misled, far from the truth, and deserving of only God's judgment and vindictive wrath. If vengeance only belongs to the Lord, then the extremist segments of fundamentalism's loyal followers have appropriated this godly wrath onto their own political, social, and cultural agendas by claiming their "right" to act in His name and on His behalf. In short, the fundamentalism of the fundamentalists slowly replaces God with a golden calf. In place of God, they make a substitution of Him with their own ideological agenda. In so doing, fundamentalists have hijacked the language and spirit of faith in order to further their own less-than-divine purposes, beliefs, and attitudes.

Islamic terrorists and fundamentalists have a great deal in common with the policies and ideological fundamentalism of the Bush-2 regime. The mentality of one mirrors the mentality of the other (hence, Edward Said's reference to a clash of ignorance). For example,

a terrorist may learn by heart all of the fundamental sources behind his beliefs. Yet such a person is still unaware of the one evident truth that will bring him happiness and inspiration, both in this world and the next. That's because all his life, he's been educated in radical ideologies, in the context that the idea of life is a battleground in which only the strong survive, where violence and oppression are the only means of survival. Anyone resorting to terrorism, no matter what his religion, race, or nation, must understand that he/she is acting under the influence of a misleading philosophy, that in the final analysis stems from materialist and Darwinist thinking—though it sometimes poses as a religious idea.[111]

What is important to recognize is that both political fanatics and religious fundamentalists in the West and in the Middle East are caught up in an endless cycle of violence. By succumbing to the temptation of trying to demonize the *other*, an opportunity is lost for genuine self-interrogation or self-reflection. As a result of taking the path of extremism without reflection, of ideology without critical reflection, the peaceful resolution of conflict is replaced by belligerent threats, hostile actions, and a descent into terrorism. Quite often, the irrationality of terrorism often rises out of the psychological and spiritual pain of loss suffered by those who have had loved ones or friends die as a result of unjust political circumstances. Certainly the Israeli–Palestinian conflict fits into this typology. Suicide bombers, the voluntary sacrifice of the young for the sins of the old, all reflect a descent into blind hatred—a hatred that is also traceable to US policies in the region.

With Israel acting as a US proxy in the Middle East, Palestinian and Arab anger finds its most violent expression among the powerless—the disenfranchised who live and die without hope. In the *clash* of fundamentalisms, the *clash* deafens dialog and deadens sensibilities. As a consequence, opponents on both sides adopt uncritical assumptions about some alleged "static essence or identity" in "the other." Such a result only serves to strengthen the inclination of masses of people to ignore history. Some scholars have noted that

> what distinguishes the critiques of clash theorists ... from other critics, from within and without Islam, is the consistent inability either to find anything to criticize in the contemporary policy or attitudes of the civilization they consider their own or to find anything of interest or value in the worlds they consider to belong to the backward other, in this case, the Arab and the Muslim Middle East.[112]

In the final analysis, an "us" versus "them" dichotomy emerges not just from a few fanatics in the world, but that "conflict-driven fundamentalism induces others to identify with the homogenous, monotonic 'we' in which the individual and group affirmation becomes possible only through the destruction of the other."[113] The desire to engage in the destruction of the "other" helps to explain the prevalence of violence, war, and terrorism. What we are witnessing is a problem with conflicting identities. One scholar has referred to this phenomenon as the *affliction of identities*.[114]

The central problem arising from such disfigured thinking about the *other* is that it either destroys and/or distorts relationships between individuals and groups. From the perspective of the Old Testament,

> relationships are constitutive of life itself; through relationships all things are woven together like a spider web. Interrelatedness is a basic characteristic not

only of the God-Israel; (and God-world) relationship but also of the very nature of the created order. Human sin ripples out and affects the entire creation (see the linkage between human violence and the nonhuman in Hosea 4:1–3). To live in a relational world inevitably means that every creature will be affected by every other; each individual is involved in the plight of all. Violence perpetrated anywhere reverberates everywhere through this relational structure of life, leading to even further violence.[115]

DIVINE PROVIDENCE AND NONVIOLENCE VERSUS EMPIRE

The Judeo-Christian tradition teaches that God's will for humanity is life without violence. Yet, because of God's committed relationship to the world, he cannot force compliance with the divine will. Therefore, God's efforts to end violence are marked by both constraint and restraint in the use of power.[116] This consciousness of divine providence, constraint, and restraint also underlies the theological message of Dr. Martin Luther King, Jr. On May 17, 1957, Dr. King spoke about the fact that the African nation of Ghana acquired its independence from British colonial rule. In King's first national address, which was given before the Prayer Pilgrimage, he stated that these developments were the work of divine providence: "we proudly proclaim that three-fourths of the peoples of the world are colored. We have the privilege of noticing in our generation the great drama of freedom and independence as it unfolds in Asia and Africa. All these things are in line with the unfolding work of providence."[117]

In the same address, he discussed the presence of evil in the world. He saw that political and spiritual evil worked through Global Empire and "Caesar" (a reference to the imperialistic state). King acknowledged:

Evil may so shape events that Caesar will occupy a palace and Christ a cross, but one says that same Christ will rise up and split history into A.D. and B.C., so that even the life of Caesar must be dated by His name. There is something in this universe that justifies Carlyle in saying, "No lie can live forever." There is something in this universe that justifies William Cullen Bryant in saying, "Truth crushed to earth will rise again." There is something in this universe that justified James Russell Lowell in saying:

'Truth forever on the scaffold
Wrong forever on the throne
Yet that scaffold sways the future
And behind the dim unknown stands God
Within the shadows keeping watch above his own.'[118]

King's spiritual consciousness clearly informed his political consciousness. From the issue of racial discrimination to the war in Vietnam, King's message called the Global Empire to accountability—at home and abroad. In 1960, King spoke of the rising tide of racial consciousness and the problem of racial discrimination when he noted:

> The great challenge facing the nation today is to solve this pressing problem and bring into full realization the ideals and dreams of our democracy ... The price that America must pay for the continued oppression of the Negro is the price of its own destruction. The hour is late: the clock of destiny is ticking out. We must act now! It is a trite yet urgently true observation that if America is to remain a first-class nation, it cannot have second-class citizens. Our primary reason for bringing an end to racial discrimination in America must not be the Communist challenge ... The primary reason for our uprooting racial discrimination from our society is that it is morally wrong. It is a cancerous disease that prevents us from realizing the sublime principles of our Judeo-Christian tradition. Racial discrimination substitutes an "I-it" relationship for the "I-thou" relationship. It relegates persons to the status of things. Whenever racial discrimination exists it is a tragic expression of man's spiritual degeneracy and moral bankruptcy. Therefore, it must be removed not merely because it is diplomatically expedient, but because it is morally compelling.[119]

It is not difficult to take King's analysis of domestic power relations (racial discrimination) and apply the same analysis to power relations throughout the US Global Empire. The United Nations Development Program in its *Human Development Report, 2003: Millennium Development Goals—A Compact Among Nations to End Human Poverty*, made it clear that "poor countries face constraints that can only be eased through policy changes in rich countries."[120] The same perspective was set forth in King's last book, *Where Do We Go From Here: Chaos or Community?* Prophetically, King wrote: "A genuine revolution of values means in the final analysis that our loyalties must become ecumenical rather than sectional. Every nation must now develop an overriding loyalty to mankind as a whole in order to preserve the best in their individual societies."[121]

King's message, like that of the United Nations Development Program's *Human Development Report (2003)*, stressed the importance of building a sustainable Global Community. King argued that the growth of militarism was certain madness for it only contributed to the self-perpetuating use of violence in the development of the US Global Empire.[122] In opposition to empire, King emphatically embraced both national and global movements to bring about the realization of Global Community. On the issue of opposition to empire, he explicitly: "called for a world-wide fellowship that lifts neighborly concern beyond one's tribe, race, class and nation ... for an all-embracing and unconditional love for all men. This often misunderstood and misinterpreted concept has now become an absolute necessity for the survival of man."[123]

The combined dangers of annihilation by nuclear weapons, the threat of racial and ethnic strife, the debilitating effects of poverty and the violence spawned by the recognition of "relative deprivation" constituted the basis for King's articulation of a moral mandate to seek ways in which the international community could begin to adopt paths leading to the realization of Global Community. The legacy and moral mandate of the world's great religions were part of King's answer to the gathering storms created by America's militarist approach to global problems. On this point, King observed,

> When I speak of love, I am speaking of that force which all the great religions have seen as the supreme unifying principle of life. Love is the key that unlocks the door which leads to ultimate reality. This Hindu-Moslem-Christian-Jewish-Buddhist belief about ultimate reality is beautifully summed up in the First Epistle of Saint John:
>
>> "Let us love one another: for love is of God:
>> and everyone that loveth is born of God, and
>> knoweth God. He that loveth not knoweth not
>> God; for God is love … If we love one another,
>> God dwelleth in us, and his love is perfected in us."

Let us hope that this spirit becomes the order of the day. We can no longer afford to worship the God of hate or bow before the altar of retaliation. The oceans of history are made turbulent by the ever-rising tides of hate. History is cluttered with the wreckage of nations and individuals who pursued this self-defeating path of hate.[124]

CONFRONTING AN EMPIRE OF CONFLICT

Samir Amin, in a provocative essay entitled *Confronting the Empire*, castigated the brutality of the US program's imperial attempt to loot the resources of the planet.[125] Amin attributes the historical choices of the US imperial project to "the mantras of vulgar economic, the single-minded focus on maximizing the financial profitability of dominant capital in the short term, putting the military at the disposal of this capital, and de-linking this capital from any system of human values."[126] What this process really means is that the type of globalization that assists the US Global Empire to advance is a predatory one—it denies human rights, it eliminates social welfare provisions and institutions in First and Third World nations, and creates a larger number of poor people while the gulf of inequality continues to widen. Alternatively, there is a struggling alternative to predatory globalization. The alternative stands for the proposition that with a change in the nature of policies both social insurance and egalitarian redistribution need not be foreclosed upon. The problem is that single-minded focus on competition for resources and a neoliberal economic model has bastardized the integrity and humane governing potential of American foreign policy.[127] It does so by centralizing the material facts of a nation's existence—"its physical capabilities, technological achievements, geographical location … as the final arbiters of political outcomes."[128] If we were able to decentralize those material facts, it would be possible to achieve different political and economic outcomes. Hence, the alternative to predatory globalization places primary value on universal human rights, sustainable development, the elimination of poverty, and the need to bring about the death of neoliberal models. This alternative represents a growing counter-hegemonic alliance throughout the Global Community to the US Global Empire and its neoliberal economic agenda. Adherents to the neoliberal of capitalism continue to treat the identities, interests, legal norms, and values as preexisting and fixed.[129] Yet, the reality is that these kinds of norms "derive exclusively from rational egoistic choice."[130]

The decision makers in the US establishment are trapped. They exist in a bureaucratic culture that transforms them into little more than agents for a paradigm premised upon rational egoistic choice. In their role as agents for empire, they are limited in both the choices they make and the worldview that they adopt. The agents of empire, both in and out of government, are trapped by their allegiance to a set of preexisting preferences in the service of capitalist institutions.[131] By betraying its own national origins in one of the world's great religions—the Judeo-Christian tradition—the US Global Empire has betrayed itself. The adoption of an institutional, rationalistic, egoistic paradigm has served to emasculate both the credibility and freedom of choice of the world's only remaining superpower.

The commitment to a long-term struggle for oil was made by the Bush-2 regime despite the fact that: there is insatiable demand for energy throughout all the world's economies; there is an inadequate supply of energy; and there is only the promise of an intensifying struggle over energy resources in the decades to come. The US decision to invade and occupy Iraq demonstrates that the US foreign policy establishment believes that control of the country would provide the United States with great advantages in any coming struggle over Persian Gulf energy with competitors like China. On this point, Professor Michael T. Klare has concluded that

> once a problem like energy security has been tagged as a matter of national security, it passes from the realm of economics and statecraft into that of military policy. Then, the generals and strategists get into the act and begin their ceaseless planning for endless 'contingencies' and 'emergencies.' In such an environment, small incidents evolve into crises, and crises into wars. Expect a hot couple of decades ahead.[132]

The neoconservative viewpoint, as exemplified in the writing of Robert D. Kaplan, finds that the early twenty-first century focus is balanced between concern over the control of oil from the Middle East, on the one hand, and the rising competitive power of China, on the other hand. For example, in the June 2005 issue of *The Atlantic*, the cover story is entitled, *How We Would Fight China*.[133] Ominously, he predicts "the idea we will no longer engage in the 'cynical' game of power politics is illusory, as is the idea that we will be able to advance a foreign policy based solely on Wilsonian ideals."[134] Kaplan's pessimism about the United States never being able to escape the "cynical" game of power politics is never explained by him—it is taken as a given. All that Kaplan does is label an alternative to power politics as "illusory." As with other intellectual apologists who write to further the idea of the intractable and imminent hegemony of the United States as it begins *Another American Century*, Kaplan omits the possibility that widespread political support for an alternative scenario may shift the United States and the world onto a different path.[135] Widespread support for an alternative scenario is what an "exodus from empire" contemplates. It is present in many forms: an emerging left wing turn in the national political life of most Latin American nations, a growing global counter-hegemonic alliance to the empire, the articulation of alternative sets of values that conflict with a neoliberal agenda and paradigm.

In 1971, Professor Richard Barnett authored a classic study on American foreign policy entitled, *Roots Of War: The Men And Institutions Behind US Foreign Policy*.[136] Barnet acknowledged the fact that

the dependence of the American economy upon foreign raw materials or upon war production means that certain foreign policy options are for all practical purposes foreclosed. The United States cannot disarm, significantly lower the defense budget, or relax economic warfare against commercial competitors, nor can the American businessmen halt the restless, exploitative search for economic opportunities abroad *unless the economy is managed in a very different way* (Italics are mine).[137]

Barnet uses the word "unless" in order to point to an alternative path—a path that leads away from Kaplan's nightmare scenario of power politics without end. Barnet suggests that the alternative path involves both a moral and a political demand that is coupled with a willingness to prepare "to build a society rooted in the politics of peace."[138] At the dawn of the twenty-first century, the foreign policy options of empire must change in order to adjust to an international counter-hegemonic alliance to the US Global Empire. If that change is not done willingly, it will be forced upon the United States by a Global Community of nations and social movements dedicated to making an exodus from empire.

It is obvious that Kaplan and other neoconservatives, as well as the bulk of "realist" scholars, reject the alternative as "out of hand" and branding it as "illusory." Yet, even among realist theorists there is an argument gaining in strength and currency that "America's relative power position has been slowly and inexorably eroding for several decades."[139] From the realist perspective, the Cold War bipolarity produced incentives for Western cooperation. Under the conditions of the Cold War, the consequences of the decline of America's hegemony were not fully felt. However, the end of the Cold War exposed institutional decay and conflict in the West. Therefore, the central thrust of these realist theorists is that "relations among Western states will return to the patterns of the 1930s and early 1940s, in which the problems of anarchy dominated: economic rivalry, security dilemmas, arms races, hyper-nationalism, balancing alliances, and ultimately the threat of war."[140]

In contrast to the realist scholars, the *balance-of-power* theorists believe that the United States will not face a frontal assault from potential rivals. They come to this conclusion based on the belief that the US position in the world—as the engine of economic globalization—constrains other major states from resorting to traditional balancing strategies.[141] According to this view, China, Russia, Japan, the European Union, and India, are precluded from mounting an effective opposition to US hegemony. Therefore, most balance-of-power theorists believe that all potential competitors are incapable of effectively using either force or economic sanctions against the US Global Empire. In sum, most balance-of-power theorists believe "state behavior in the contemporary era does not correspond to traditional hard balancing as depicted in realist theories."[142]

Now that we have given a quick overview to realist theorists, balance-of-power theorists, and neoconservative thinkers, it seems as though the answers of the past will not suffice in coming to terms with the real world of the twenty-first century. Therefore, we must ask ourselves: *Where does this analysis leave us with regard to assessing the possibilities for the advocates of a hegemonic US Global Empire versus the advocates of an inclusive Global Community?* The answer cannot be provided in response to a simplistic "either/or" question. To begin to chart an answer, it has been suggested that we go back a few decades, to the last 50 years of the twentieth century. In that 50-year period, the United States played a unique role—the role of an institution builder that was serving not just its own needs, but also serving the needs of others. In other words, many of its political and economic acts were forged out of a moral criterion of service to the global community of nations. Some examples of this phenomenon may be cited. They include Cold War alliances like ANZUS, SEATO, and CENTO. For good or for ill, the institutions that the United States built included the UN, IMF, World Bank, GATT, OECD, NATO, and the WTO. According to Josef Joffe, "the United States bestrode the world as provider of public goods that cemented America while serving the needs of others. Previous hegemons were in business for themselves."[143]

The above-cited analysis is good—as far as it goes. The problem is that it must go much further to be accurate in its totality. Otherwise, we are left with a simplistic "either/or" response to a complex question. For we know that these institutions have contributed a great deal of misery to the world's peoples by virtue of the profit motive as the ultimate value and the drive for greater accumulation and wealth at the expense of human rights sustainable development. Therefore, I will argue that we should take our lead from Dr. Paul Farmer, and look at what he calls the "pathologies of power."[144]

THE PATHOLOGIES OF POWER VERSUS
THE AFFIRMATION OF HUMAN DIGNITY

Dr. Farmer contends that violations of human dignity "are not to be accepted merely because they are buttressed by local ideology or longstanding tradition."[145] In sharp contrast to Huntington's "clash" thesis, Farmer takes an interdisciplinary approach to find the cause or causes that lead to violations of human dignity. Relying on insights gathered from anthropology, as well as sociological and historical perspectives, he asserts "these disciplines permit us to ground our understanding of human rights violations in broader analyses of power and social inequality."[146] Also, by going beyond a purely legal view of human rights, he concludes that the aforementioned disciplines assist in forming a context in which to comprehend the *pathologies of power*. He concludes that "social inequalities based on race, ethnicity, gender, religious creed, and—above all—social class are the motor force behind most human rights violations. In other words, violence against individuals is usually embedded in entrenched structural violence."[147]

At this point, the complexity of our answer is about to match the complexity of the question. For example, while Joffe has argued that in the period of 1945–2000 the United States was a global institution-builder and assisted in serving the needs of others, he neglects to mention how these very institutions also engaged in structuring social inequalities into nations and among nations—thereby creating antagonisms between social classes as a by-product of capitalist exploitation and the violence associated with entrenched structural violence. For example, Farmer notes that with the progress of globalization and its adherence to Washington's economic doctrine of neoliberalism—including the ideology and practice of privatization, deregulation, and placing the market above the state in decision making, we find that "the withdrawal of states from the basic business of providing housing, education, and medical services usually means further erosion of the social and economic rights of the poor."[148] On this same point, other scholars have noted:

> With the world's resources controlled by a few hundred ... global corporations, the life-blood and the very fate of humanity is in the hand of transnational capital, which holds the power to make life and death decisions for millions of human beings ... Any discussion of "democracy" under such conditions becomes meaningless ... The burning challenge of our time is how to wrest such enormous power away from transnational capital and its agent, the transnational elite. This challenge amounts to no more or less than how to democratize global society.[149]

SEEKING THE COMMON GOOD FOR THE GLOBAL COMMONS

The evolving norms of international law and the teachings of the world's great religions, as well as historical experience, teach that service to maintaining the "common good" of the global commons is the most reliable way in which to achieve genuine security. Genuine security is never the product of military force and violence. For those approaches can only breed resentment and violence. Genuine security is premised upon a moral and legal foundation that centralizes the spirit of the "golden rule" in international life. On this very point, Professor Robert Jackson reminds us "modern international society is based on principles and practices of mutual accommodation—not at its extremities but at its foundations."[150] Jackson's emphasis upon the principles and practices of *mutual accommodation* in international society is important because "the normative foundation of international relations is pluralistic and ... it must be so to accommodate the assorted civilizations and cultures of the globe whose values may be inconsistent, divergent, incompatible, or even mutually antagonistic."[151] In Jackson's view, mutual accommodation (what I have called "convergence") is possible if we move beyond a crippled state-centric approach to international relations and embrace a "global covenant."

By definition, "the global covenant should be understood as an institutional response" to the twin international realities of "human diversity and human imperfection." Given these two limiting conditions, "human diversity separates people into different personalities and collectivities. Human imperfections, on the other hand, unite people via their shared intellectual frailties and common moral deficiencies." Against this background, Jackson defends the moral and legal foundations of the global covenant: normative pluralism, political anti-paternalism, international law, and political virtue. Using this conceptual approach, he argues that these are the qualities that "are justified as serviceable international norms that come to grips with the unavoidable realities of human diversity and human imperfection."[152]

Normative pluralism is a serviceable international norm because "pluralism repudiates the alleged moral anarchy of a multicivilizational world. It affirms the possibility of mutual intelligibility, recognition, communication, and interaction between people of different civilizations."[153] Contrary to the *clash* thesis, there is a genuine hope and possibility for the convergence of civilizations. At the heart of the matter is the question of human conduct. Imperfect human beings have created this international order. Only imperfect human beings can attempt to improve it. The task of improving this global order, so that it can move toward a genuine Global Community, will require both agreement upon and adherence to shared norms of conduct. In this respect, "the international conduct prescribed by the global covenant ... is simply the norms, practices, and institutions of civility that apply to human relations within the international sphere which often cut across civilizations."[154]

In its political dimension, "the global covenant ought to be understood as a constitutional arrangement that seeks to accommodate human diversity while trying to uphold common humanity. It gives institutional expression and substance to pluralism."[155] In other words, by rejecting the notion of an inevitable clash of civilizations, human beings can move toward a convergence of action in a spirit of civility. In giving serious attention to the need for civility, as opposed to the doctrinal absolutism of the neoconservatives who run the US Global Empire, it is possible to develop an appreciation of the pluralistic nature of the Global Community and, in so doing we can argue that an *exodus from empire* is possible. Obviously, such an *exodus from empire* will require the abandonment of "exclusive, excluding, and ethnocentric principles of recognition based on the standards of Western civilization. That is what de-colonization involved and indeed required."[156] On the basis of this interpretation, I would argue that principled opposition to the US Global Empire becomes a moral mandate. Adopting this position becomes necessary insofar as people around the world should be afforded the right to protect their political independence from unwarranted interference by either their neighbors or superpowers.[157]

Yet, according to Jackson, the global covenant he envisions "does not provide any escape from the vast differences of power and wealth between sovereign states. It is not an insulation against global market forces."[158] In my view, such a result is too limited a victory for the kind of Global Community that is being advocated in this book. Therefore, while I agree with Jackson's formulation of a global covenant that represents an encompassing normative framework, I disagree with his assertion that "it would be a familiar category mistake to condemn the global covenant for not keeping globalization at bay" because "that would be mistaking independence for autonomy."[159] I disagree with this assertion because it fails to secure the very sovereignty of independent political communities that he says a global covenant is dedicated to maintaining. Such a view also consigns the normative claims of social justice and global justice to the periphery of concern, thereby eliminating the possibility that a viable moral mandate for human rights and global transformation can ever realistically take effect.

Jackson's attempt to make a semantic distinction between "*independence*" and "*autonomy*"—branding it as "a familiar category mistake"—fails to take into account the nature of the real world. It is almost as if we were back in the days of the Reagan administration listening to the US ambassador to the UN attempting to make a distinction between *totalitarian dictatorships* and *authoritarian dictatorships*. In the real world there is no practical difference—dictatorships are dictatorships. So too, empires are empires—regardless of the ideology of the superpower that seeks to extend its imperial grasp. If this is true, then it follows that reliance upon the juridical concept of sovereignty fails to provide the protections for a viable global democratic order, a viable global covenant, or a viable Global Community.

The fact is that sovereignty fails, in both theory and practice, if it neglects to protect the self-determination of local and national communities by failing to hold the state accountable to protect its own citizens from the ravages of global finance, the intrusions of predatory globalization, or from the negative effects of environmental pollution made possible by negligent transnational corporations. Also, the concept of sovereignty fails if it neglects to protect the global workforce from outside interference. An example of such unwarranted interference is IMF-imposed *structural adjustment policies* that are placed upon both nation-states and their populations. In fact, sovereignty fails as a viable concept for global governance when it fails to comprehend the most basic truth about sovereignty itself: "it is not a natural fact of international life. Instead it is politically contested and has variable political effects."[160]

In reality, the juridical concept of sovereignty is not well equipped to deal with the realities of either globalization or Global Empire. Therefore, the task of constructing a Global Community is one that cannot afford to be built upon the weak and inconsistent historical track record of juridical sovereignty. The reason that the concept of sovereignty cannot be trusted is because placing a heavy reliance upon it only serves to further emasculate national and global accountability to the normative claims of progressive world jurisprudence. I argue that the evolving norms of customary international law need to be centralized to a higher degree so that the substantive content of humane values, shared moral values, and the larger human interest can achieve greater influence in accordance with the normative claims of progressive world jurisprudence. If we leave the governance of the global order to a sterile and empty shell called the doctrine of sovereignty, then the powerful will simply maintain an international hierarchy of exploitation and domination at the expense of billions of lives that have been effectively disempowered.

TRANSCENDING SOVEREIGNTY, EMBRACING JUSTICE

If an evolving Global Community is to be realized, it must be equipped with widely shared ideas, norms, and values from which it can effectively develop institutions and mechanisms that protect the poor and most vulnerable peoples on the planet from exploitation. This cosmopolitan order requires adherence to the claims of peace, justice, protected liberty, guaranteed rights, clearly defined authority that is circumscribed by law. This order must also provide minimum standards of well-being—not as ends in themselves but as conditions for the public order and health of the Global Community. If that means we have to redefine terms and concepts so that our theory of governance corresponds to our practice of governance, then so be it. For example, if we want to democratize the global order, then the "misconceiving of democracy makes necessary its re-conceiving. Especially over the last two centuries, we have learned that the transformatory effect of *democracy* is not merely a matter of institutions or a particular distribution of social power. The central ideal of democracy is better expressed as *nomocracy*, the rule of *nomos* (the law), rather than merely the rule of those who claim to represent the people (*demos*)."[161]

Since 1945, a vast international public realm has been formed through the piecemeal cooperation of governments, "determining the lives of all human beings everywhere."[162] In short, a largely unaccountable concentration of social power coexists with the power of transnational industrial and commercial corporations. The global agenda has been forged by sovereign states in collusion with vast empires of corporate wealth that span the globe. The US Global Empire itself operates in service to the dictates of a conglomerate of influence peddling. As an alternative to this system, a variety of scholars have asserted that "the need is apparent and urgent for a presence of the nomocratic ideal at the level of international society, acting as an enacting and enforcing instrument of universal ideals of justice and social justice. But the full ... power of law can only operate at the level of all-humanity within an international society whose high values it enacts, including the values of justice and social justice."[163]

My argument about the nature and claims of a rising Global Community has more in common with the views of Richard Falk, Terry Nardin, and Philip Allott. From this perspective, the states system constitutes an obstacle to global human solidarity. I do not share the optimism exhibited by Jackson's embrace of the existing nation-state system.[164] After all, a nation that is also a superpower can easily rely on its nation-state status as a shield against the normative claims of human rights treaties, covenants, and the mandates of international law. By hiding behind the mask of national sovereignty, a superpower can continue to conduct the violent business of Global Empire with impunity.

THE MORAL MANDATE OF INCLUSIVE GLOBAL GOVERNANCE

By definition, imperial domination is antithetical to the universal claims of international law as well as the normative claims of the world's great religions.

Therefore, the central problem that accompanies the state-centric view is that by inflating the importance of the nation-state, the state-centric view acts to legitimate the strengthening of what I have called *exclusionary states* and *exclusionary governance*. Exclusionary governance destroys the basis for building either a national or a global human rights culture because governance by ES is predicated upon hierarchy; domination; inequality; and the attendant injustices that flow from these forms of exclusion.[165] In contrast, the path of *inclusionary governance* and the development of the "inclusionary state" (IS) follows a normative path which accentuates the centrality of human rights law, covenants, and treaties as the benchmarks for a rising Global Community that places the meeting of basic human needs and the common good at the center of its agenda and priorities.[166] With respect to the importance of inclusion as a normative priority in international life, Professor Richard Falk has argued "even inclusivity that is bounded by culture and religion rather than by world identities could induce positive trends toward regional political arrangements, thereby weakening the regressive sides of a statist world order."[167]

Contained with the idea and practice of *inclusionary governance* is an outline for a new paradigm for the international legal system. In my work, I have extended the reach of a new paradigm to incorporate the recognition of socioeconomic rights into the legal systems, policies, and practices of both the national state and the international community. Similarly, according to Allott, "the new paradigm of the international legal system is a new ideal of human self-constituting" and has three leading characteristics.[168] The first characteristic is that "the international legal system is a system for disaggregating the common interest of all humanity, rather than merely a system for aggregating the self-determined interests of so-called States." Hence, he discounts traditional notions of the national interest when they are antithetical to realizing global justice. The second characteristic is that "the international legal system contains all legal phenomena everywhere, overcoming the artificial separation of the national and international realms, and removing the anomalous exclusion of non-governmental transnational events and transactions." From this perspective, NGOs can aspire to greater prominence on the international stage as they advance concerns addressed by humanitarian efforts as well as struggles for human rights and social justice. The third characteristic is that "the international system, like any legal system, implies and requires an idea of a ... society with its own self-consciousness, with its own theories, values, and purposes, and with its own systems for choosing its future, including a system of politics."[169] In my view this is an argument that incorporates the ideas of both independence and autonomy. I think that independence and autonomy can be mutually reinforcing stances, depending on how they are balanced.

Based upon the above-cited analysis, I would argue that Allott's new paradigm for the international system and its three defining characteristics all converge on the idea that a rising Global Community is within our grasp. In fact, he himself says as much in the conclusion to his essay: "The idea of international society, the society of the whole human race and the society of all societies, takes its place at last, centuries late, within the self-constituting of international society, that is to say, as an essential part of the self-creating and the self-perfecting of the human species."[170] Allott's emphasis upon the concepts of the *self-creating* and *self-perfecting* aspects of the human species gives rise to genuine hope for the actualization of a Global Community. These themes are not new. These themes resonated throughout the 1950s, 1960s, and early 1970s in the works of Julius K. Nyerere, Kwame Nkrumah, and Frantz Fanon. They are themes that have continued to echo in the late twentieth century and early twenty-first century in the works of Amartya Sen and Walden Bello.

REPLACING THE POWER OF THE GLOBAL NORTH WITHIN THE GLOBAL SOUTH

The names of Nyerere, Nkrumah, Fanon, Sen, and Bello, all represent a view from the South—a view that emerges from those peoples and societies that have been victimized by empire and its economic tentacles. In other words, these are names that are representative of many voices from the *underside of history*—the neglected, the excluded, the dispossessed, the disenfranchised, the victims of the imperial projects of Global Empire. Collectively, their voices point toward a consciousness of opposition to empire. In their opposition, they offer a critique of the imperialistic policies of the North as well as a new vision of what the Global South may be destined to become.

For example, in a 1958 essay entitled, *The Algerian War and Man's Liberation*, Frantz Fanon asserted: "The process of [the] liberation of man, independently of the concrete situations in which he finds himself, includes and concerns the whole of humanity."[171] Fanon saw the struggle against colonialism as the "exploitation of man by man." It was a global problem and a global challenge. If Africa was to be for Africans, then the achievement of Africa's independence from colonial interference would ultimately be discovered in the context of global solidarity and struggle with other liberation movements seeking to shake off their own colonial chains. If liberation from colonialism was to be finally achieved, he asserted that it "is in the national struggle against the oppressor that colonized peoples have discovered, concretely, the ... interdependence of the liberation movements."[172] In this regard, the struggle for liberation certainly contained political, military, and cultural components. Yet, out of these three arenas of contestation, Fanon maintained that the struggle for national culture was central to the liberation struggle. It would be a substitution of humane values in exchange for the imperial values of empire.

In Fanon's last book, *The Wretched of the Earth*, finished in 1961, he asserted: "We believe that the conscious and organized undertaking by a colonial people to re-establish the sovereignty of that nation constitutes the most complete and obvious cultural manifestation that exists ... The struggle itself in its development and in its internal progression sends culture along different paths and traces out entirely new ones for it."[173] Fanon believed that the struggle defined new values and that it did not mean an automatic return to one's old culture once the struggle was over. Rather, the struggle for freedom against colonialism is one that "aims at a fundamentally different set of relations" between people and for that reason "cannot leave intact either the form or the content of the people's culture. After the conflict there is not only the disappearance of colonialism but also the disappearance of the colonized man."[174]

In updating Fanon's critique of the struggle for freedom against colonialism to the struggle for freedom against the US Global Empire, we can argue that the disappearance of empire would constitute a defining moment in human history. With the rise of Global Community, the door would be opened to an interdependent world free of intrusions by empire and its imperial ambitions dedicated to the domination of others. By embracing this vision, the vision of the "self-creating" and "self-perfecting" of the human species becomes attainable. In the words of Fanon, "A nation which is born of the people's concerted action and which embodies the real aspirations of the people while changing the state cannot exist save in the expression of exceptionally rich forms of culture."[175] Similarly, the advent of a rising Global Community, as it evolves and eclipses Global Empire, cannot exist but for its capacity to embrace a rich and vibrant global culture.

Once the interference of empire is finally overcome, there are possibilities for the re-discovery of the Global South's own unique culture and political agenda. The new world of the Global South is predicated upon its potential to build a new regional politics on the continents of Africa, Asia, and Latin America. For example, in the summer of 2001, Libyan leader Colonel Muammar Gaddafi arrived at the Organization of African Unity (OAU) conference in the Togolese capital of Lomé. He had come to present a new initiative to the continent's leaders—replace the OAU with the African Union (AU), modeled along the lines of the European Union. This initiative was based upon the recognition that in order to compete in a tough global environment, Africa needed to create its own strong institutions. Africa's heads of state unanimously endorsed the text for the creation of the AU with an executive assembly, a fixed parliament, a central bank, and a court. Gaddafi's dream was coming true. The African continent was heading toward its future as the new USA—the United States of Africa.[176]

In the spirit of the NAM in the early 1970s, current trends throughout the Global South are moving toward the embrace of a Global Community that is capable of becoming immune from the attempted domination of Global Empire. By severing its strangling ties to the US Global Empire, the nations of the Global South can begin the process of recovering their own culture, their own unique set of political identities, and forging new economic ties and alliances through regional South-South cooperation. All these efforts are being undertaken in the first decade of the twenty-first century for the sake of realizing genuine national and regional development. I refer to this phenomenon as a *national/international counter-hegemonic alliance* to Global Empire (see: Chapter 6).

Instead of having the wealth of the Global South hauled off to the centers of monopoly capital in the North, new forms of South-South cooperation and institutional organizations can guarantee that essential resources and wealth can be used in Africa, Asia, and Latin America, for domestic and regional development and meeting basic human needs. For over 50 years, this has been a dream in the making. Going back to 1964, one of the first proponents of this dream, Kwame Nkrumah, noted that "Neo-colonialism is a greater danger to independent countries than is colonialism ... To allow a foreign country, especially one that is loaded with economic interests in our continent, to tell us what *political* decisions to take, what *political* courses to follow, is indeed for us to hand back our independence to the oppressor on a silver platter"[177] (*Italics already in text*). In 1974, writing on the eve of the Non Aligned Conference, the President of Tanzania, Julius K. Nyerere, wrote:

> The fact is that our political independence depends upon the degree of our economic independence, as well as the nature of our economic development depending upon our political independence. These things are interlinked in the modern world. And because of their interdependence, our economic relationships with one another, and individually with the Great Powers of the world, are matters with which the Non-Aligned Conference must be concerned.[178]

As it turns out, Nyerere was prophetically accurate. Between the 1990s and 2005, the interlinked nature of economic relationships and political dependence demonstrated that while the liberation of finance capital promised economic development, it usually delivered severe instability. The promise of the NAM in the 1970s never materialized. It was "rolled back" by the low-intensity conflicts of the Reagan era. Corporate capitalism was dedicated to retaining what Nyerere termed *neocolonialism*. For the financial wizards of the IMF, World Bank, and the corporations of the global North, it was termed *neoliberalism*. In the new world order of neoliberalism, "financial liberalization, like trade liberalization, was a fundamental tenet of neo-liberal doctrine that served as the ideology of corporate-driven globalization."[179] Corporate-driven globalization worked hand-in-hand with the US Global Empire. They are two faces of the same coin. Therefore, if the process of globalization is to be reclaimed for the peoples of the Global South, then it is a new kind of globalization that must sever the dominating links of neoliberalism, US-backed corporate agendas, and the vice grip of the IMF, WTO, and World Bank. In short, the kind of globalization that the Global South requires for its own independence and the well-being of its peoples is going to have to be forged in regional alliances—a new South-South paradigm of cooperation and development. It can and will come about only if the Global South is successful in carrying out a strategy that I have termed a "National-International Counter-Hegemonic Alliance" to Global Empire (see: Chapter 6).

Ignoring the earlier warnings by Nyerere, Fanon, and Nkrumah, many nations in the South bought the sales pitch that came with the neoliberal model. According to Bello, "Through financial liberalization, Third World nations were promised [that] their private sectors would get the capital they needed for development, in exchange for a just return to foreign financial investors."[180] Instead of getting what was promised, these Third World nations soon discovered that "speculative investors were not interested in nurturing strategic sectors of the economy, like industry and agriculture. Rather, they were there to play the stock and real estate markets."[181] The result was not a *clash of civilizations* but rather a *clash of currencies*. The Argentine economy collapsed in 2004, just as the Mexican economy had collapsed in 1994. Every aspect of Third World economic life was affected from the time of the Third World debt crisis in the 1990s to the Asian panic of 1997. By the dawn of the twenty-first century, Argentina was next in line to suffer the results of Northern speculators operating under the guise of neoliberal doctrine.

According to Bello, "Imperial efforts to transform the South over the last two decades embrace every aspect of Third World economic life. Moreover, they foreclose any significant development except along lines that favor northern interests."[182] Therein lies the difficulty with the current global situation at the dawn of the twenty-first century. The primary problem facing the world's peoples is that northern interests—in the arenas of oil, corporate power, and the military industrial complex—seek to continue with "business as usual." Hence, the transforming power of the UN and the rising aspirations of the world's peoples are being actively blocked by the architects of Global Empire. In order for the Global Community to overcome the blockages and resistance of these northern interests, it will have to confront the various forms of resistance to change head-on.

CONCLUSION

In light of the above-cited critique, the two central points on which I want to conclude this chapter are as follows: (1) That an "exodus from empire" is not only an objective need for humankind to achieve peace, it is more specifically a necessary prerequisite for the actualization of peace and prosperity for the Global South. The prospects for genuine national development throughout the Third World, as well as the reclamation of cultural identity and national purpose, remain predicated upon opposition to acquiescence or subordination to the dictates of the US Global Empire. (2) That the "clash of civilizations" thesis is an illusion because it relies on artificial categories and constructs to create lines of difference where there need not be any. Rather, the evolution of international law, in conjunction with growing adherence to the principles of the world's great religions, points to a *convergence* of civilizations and peoples. Such a convergence is not merely a product of globalization. Rather, it is a product of the *normative convergence* of international law, the principles from the sacred texts of the great world religions, and the emerging features of a global culture that is not the property of any one nation.

I will conclude this chapter with a summary of the findings that come out of my *clash or convergence* analysis. These findings constitute my recommendations regarding the construction of a viable alternate strategy for global governance that can help to effectuate an *exodus from empire*. It is hoped that these recommendations may contribute to efforts to supply the basis for a global ethics for a Global Community. Therefore, they should be understood as my attempt to address the most egregious aspects of conduct that the US Global Empire has engaged in without restraint or accountability to the larger Global Community. In order to rectify the damage done by the actions and conduct of the Global Empire, the following recommendations are offered.

The Democratization of the Global Community

The de-structuring of social inequality, both within and between nations, is essential to bring about a democratization of the Global Community. The task of global democratization will have to embody both normative and political dimensions. The normative features of global democratization will include, (but are not limited to) the following: the rule of law; a shared devotion to values that advance the common good—in reference to both the evolving norms of customary international law and the teachings of the world's great religions. To this end, the policies and practices of national and global governance should be evaluated in reference to the degree to which they exhibit inclusive traits that further the values of human dignity, rights, and self-determination.

Replace Neoliberalism with Inclusionary Governance

The ideology, doctrine, and economic model of neoliberalism must be abolished. It needs to be abolished for both practical reasons and moral reasons. Because neoliberalism seeks to give all power to the "magic of the market" (and corporate powers that shape markets), neoliberalism deprives the State of its ability to represent all classes of people, especially the poor and excluded. The market cannot protect or extend either sociopolitical rights or socioeconomic rights. Only the State can do that. In broader terms, neoliberalism allows for citizens to be disenfranchised—both in the market place and in the political arena. Additionally, neoliberal ideology only promotes the entrenchment of the ES. By following its doctrinal logic, the neoliberal model will only allow for the weakening or destruction of environmental protections, a diminishment or elimination of the rights of labor unions, and the destruction of State policies to protect the poor and vulnerable. Therefore, only the development of the IS can advance policies that support the protection of the environment, the rights of labor unions, and develop State policies that can protect the poor with social safety nets while—at the same time—embarking upon a dismantling of those societal mechanisms that reinforce social inequality. In short, the restoration of national and global citizenship, as well as global democratization, is predicated upon the removal of the neoliberal agenda. Given its supporting role to the expansion of a US Global Empire, the ideology of neoliberalism must be discredited and abolished so that both America and the world can embark upon an *exodus from empire*.

Insofar as neoliberalism seeks to embark upon state re-structuring through the imposition of exclusionary forms of governance, its approach is antithetical to building inclusive and humane policies at the national and international levels. In this respect, neoliberalism contributes to outbreaks of national and global violence. It contributes to the revival of ethnic hatreds by using the market as a means to bring about social and political exclusion. By denying participation in the decision-making processes of national life, millions of people are treated as pawns in a profit-seeking game of neoliberal economics. By virtue of its antidemocratic nature, neoliberalism fails to provide for needed services in employment, health, and education. By virtue of its adherence to strategies that enhance privatization and deregulation, neoliberalism engages in promoting political and economic strategies that emasculate the ability of States to serve a majority of their citizens.

Further, neoliberalism may be faulted for failing to make adequate provision for adequate housing, sanitation, clean water, and other quality of life necessities. With such results, it is not difficult to make the case that the neoliberal model is antithetical to realizing the common good at either the State or global level. Rather, it serves the interests of global financial capitalism without reference to the effects it has upon the majority. Neoliberal models are focused upon serving the interests of political and economically well-placed minorities. Hence, the ensuing violence that transpires where its strategies and prescriptions have been adopted constitutes a foreseeable risk for States that adopt it. It can be concluded, therefore, that it is antidemocratic, exclusionary, and antigrowth as far as the recognition of the human rights and the self-determination of peoples is concerned.

In the alternative, the approach of inclusionary governance provides institutional strategies, policies, and practices that are supportive of a more egalitarian and normatively just social order. By eliminating the arbitrary forms of social, economic, and political exclusion that are incorporated into the practice of neoliberalism, the prescriptions of inclusionary governance supply the institutional mechanisms for moving toward the peaceful resolution of disputes and conflicts, a truly incorporative national and international strategy to eliminate poverty, and create participatory avenues that lead to democratic outcomes in decision making (see: Chapter 6).

The Convergence of Socioeconomic Rights with Political Rights

The democratization of the world's resources can bring an end to resource wars as well as the ideological and economic theories that support policies that lead to global violence (balance-of-power theories, realist theories, the "clash" thesis, the neoliberal model of economics). Democratization on a global scale should not merely encompass the formation of various forms of political democracy that are limited to the recognition of civil and political rights. Rather, global democratization should be undertaken with a view toward expanding socioeconomic rights in conjunction with an effort to embark upon building inclusive forms of governance.

The Foundational Normative Principle for Global Community

The guiding principles and values for the Global Community must be informed by the teachings of the world's great religions in conjunction with the evolving norms of international customary law. In this regard, the *golden rule* of *do unto others as you would have them do unto you* constitutes the foundational principle for building a nonviolent, just, and peaceful world order. Ideally, the rules, customs, and norms of international law can continue to be synthesized with the principles of the world's great religions.

In practical terms, the national and global application of these moral and legal principles provides an adequate foundation from which the United States should begin its *exodus from empire*. True, it will be a challenge to contest the legitimacy of a traditionally defined national interest so that a global human interest can be discovered and pursued. Yet, it can be accomplished. After all, the national interest of South Africa was once defined in reference to the system of apartheid. Since 1990, South Africa has been transformed into a democratic parliamentary democracy that is inclusive in the form of representation it has chosen (not a "winner-take-all" arrangement, but proportional representation).

Blending the norms of an evolving regime of international customary law with the claims of the world's great religions will involve finding a subjective and objective place for "normative convergence" (my term). What I mean by *normative convergence* involves an acknowledgment that both international law and the shared moral norms of the world's great religions complement and reinforce one another in giving dignity, worth, and reverence to all peoples and all forms of life. Humanity's duty to be good stewards of the global commons means fidelity to environmental protection. From the standpoint of religion and culture, *normative convergence* intends to bring attention and reverence to Buddhists, Muslims, Christians, Hindus, and Jews in a multicultural world. Recognizing that no one religion is the supreme repository of all truth, the truth of each may be seen as a valued identity in its own right. Within this pluralism there also exists a common thread that has the capacity to produce global unity and community—certain shared moral values. These values have a greater capacity to inspire the hearts and minds of people than merely producing another rule-based regime that is open to further contention and debate. Rather, by centralizing these shared moral values (which are also articulated in the evolving norms of customary international law); it is more likely that policy choices, as well as political and economic decisions, will be made in accordance with those shared moral norms.

From the standpoint of political and social life, the pluralism of the Global Community represents an appreciation of the fact that many of the West's predominant cultural traits, such as tolerance, may be found in each of the world's religions—thereby doing away with the artificial separation suggested by the phrase: *the West versus the rest*. Recognizing and acting upon this *normative convergence* moves us toward a Global Community that protects persons and the environment by placing the value of both above the mindless search for greater profit for profit's sake. In place of the profit principle, the rising Global Community can be guided by the principles of mutuality, reciprocity, and service to others. In this sense, the foundational principle of the *golden rule* is prologue to the birth of a Global Community. Clearly, the victory of the people of South Africa over apartheid is testimony to the force of this principle in action. When we observe the democratic defeat of apartheid at the polls, combined with the subsequent work of South Africa's TRC, the transformational power of legal and religious norms becomes apparent.

Enforcing International Legal Norms and Moral Mandates

The problem of enforcement is one of the greatest impediments to actualizing the claims of legal norms and moral mandates regarding human rights, the protection of the environment, the avoidance of war, and strategies for advancing the nonviolent resolution of differences and conflicts. The mere presence of laws on the books, the establishment of legal constraints, and the moral mandate to justify efforts to realize justice is not enough, in and of itself, to cure the ills of failed forms of human governance. Yet, without the moral force of law and the complementary mandates of the principles contained within the world's great religions, humanity would be largely powerless to reverse course and plan for an *exodus from empire*.

If the advocates of empire refuse to be held responsible for their crimes, it is incumbent upon the Global Community to ensure that responsibility and accountability for the crimes of empire be addressed. In this regard, at least the majority of the world's nations have demonstrated their commitment to justice by having ratified the Treaty of Rome and have become accountable to the jurisdiction of the ICC. Only the United States remains as the major exception to participation in an emerging Global order. For fear of allowing the US Global Empire and its leadership to be placed in judgment by the Global Community, America's national leadership has absented itself from the controlling norms and judicial force of the ICJ as a restraining institutional mechanism upon state power and its abuses in the international arena. The great task for the Global Community in the twenty-first century will be to make the US Global Empire accountable for its acts of omission and commission (see: Chapter 6).

For example, when the US Global Empire has omitted its moral and political obligation to sustain life by rejecting the use of nuclear weapons and has instead continued to invest in a new generation of nuclear weapons, it is at this point that the empire has committed an act of terrorism. The threat of force and use of force in the form of nuclear weapons is abhorrent to both jurists and many Christian theologians. Yet, the Bush-2 regime has hidden behind its dubious doctrine of "preventive war" in order to justify its contemplated use of nuclear weapons against Iran.

During the Reagan years, America's Catholic bishops wrote a pastoral letter condemning the planned use of nuclear weapons, as well as the inherent destructive capacity of such weapons, as immoral and antithetical to the maintenance of God's created order. In turn, in 1996, the ICJ declared that nuclear weapons were illegal on the same moral grounds. In coming to this conclusion, the findings of the 1946 Nuremberg Charter were often cited in order to bring attention to the deaths of millions of innocent civilians. Under the Nazi regime, these deaths were a product of indiscriminate genocide throughout Europe. Under the nuclear weapons regime of the post-1945 Cold War era, the potential for planetary suicide and nuclear fall out would condemn most—if not all—of the human race to death.

Nuclear annihilation would be the ultimate *crime against humanity*. Neither the principles contained within the law of human rights, nor the commands of God (the focus of any religious faith) could possibility be reconciled with nuclear annihilation. As the Global Community looks for guidance toward an evolving synthesis of law and religion, it can overcome particular theological differences by concentrating energy and effort upon areas of common agreement that already exist. The abolition of nuclear weapons is a central issue of global concern where the synthesis of international law and religious principles can be easily merged. In this merger of legal and religious principles, a global mandate for the elimination of nuclear weapons has the capacity to insist that the United States rediscover the American Republic and bring the American Empire to the bar of justice and international accountability. At the present time, the only ingredient lacking is political will.

The Presumption of an Interdependent Globe

Both international law and the world's great religions presume that the world is united and interdependent. Therefore, if a particular nation or group of nations allow themselves to become *rogue nations*—not subject to the dictates of law or morality, then the collective will of the Global Community can eventually bring the offending nation into compliance or contribute to its eventual collapse. Take, for example, the history of South Africa in the late twentieth century. The racial state of South African apartheid had effectively consigned the black majority to an undemocratic subservient status as citizens. Even the domestic laws of the apartheid order were not considered legal by virtue of the fact that they lacked a common core of standards and values that failed to comply with either international law or the common moral sense of the Global Community. Therefore, working through the UN, as well as the congresses and parliaments of nation-states, the world united to place South Africa under a ban—a nation under sanctions and subject to disinvestments. Sanctions were used to bar trade with the apartheid government just as disinvestments strategies weakened South Africa's ties to entrepreneurs from Wall Street and multinational corporations. The end result of imposing a global policy of disinvestments and sanctions was the collapse of the South Africa's apartheid government. Should the Global Community embrace a similar strategy with the US Global Empire, the debilitating effects of currency shifts, trade imbalances, and the calling in of loan debts on the US deficit could have the impact of at least changing the policies and practices of Washington's most grievous offenses toward the rest of the world community.

Removing Global Imbalances by Abandoning Militarism

The US Global Empire will have to come to recognize that its failure to provide public goods on a global scale will escalate into envy and fear—thereby leading to violence and terrorism. Its current reliance upon militarism is not a program for humane, cosmopolitan, or inclusive forms of governance. Should the architects fail to change their current course in their manufactured "war on terror," the untenable nature of their global enterprise will eventually unravel. Given the fact that the polices of the US National Security bureaucracy have not changed for decades, regardless of administration, it remains highly unlikely that such a change will occur—at least voluntarily.

Ultimately, the anger of the American people and the pressures of the world's citizens will have to be brought to bear upon the elite corporate interests and military-industrial forces that currently control the US government and govern the direction of its policies. The last time that a US president acted independently of this bureaucracy was in 1963. The fate of that president met with assassination in Dallas, Texas. The regicide of 1963 transformed the trajectory of history. The bright promise of the Kennedy years was replaced by a collusion of eastern establishment of old money with the new wealth being generated in the southern rim— from Florida and Texas, to Southern California—where the defense industries of the military-industrial complex were in the process of expanding. The southern rim was destined to enjoy a massive shift of wealth through new federal dollars brought to it by the Pentagon for future wars throughout the Third World. The Southeast Asian war (1964–1974) and the Persian Gulf Wars (1990–2006 and beyond) are both the products of policies sought by this ruling group. In the election years of 2000 and 2004, the oilmen of Dallas succeeded in having one of their own installed in the presidency. The Iraq war and the so-called *war on terrorism* have served to make war-profiteers of them all (see: Chapter 5).

In moral terms, as the citizens of the United States begin to contemplate their *exodus from empire*, there should be a corresponding recognition of a newfound willingness to embrace a moral code that appreciates the principle: "Do good for others in order to do well for yourself." Such a mandate advances the common good of the global commons, while maintaining the integrity of one's own house. A sampling from the texts of the world's great religions serves to underscore this point:

The Primary Themes of the World's Great Religions

---

1. *Confucianism:* Do not do to others what you would not like yourself. Then there will be no resentment against you, either in the family or in the state. Analects 12:2
2. *Buddhism:* Hurt not others in ways that you yourself would find hurtful. Udanda-Varga 5:1.
3. *Christianity:* All things whatsoever you would want that men should do to you—do you so to them—for this is the law of the prophets. Matthew 7:1.
4. *Hinduism*: This is the sum of duty; do naught onto others what you would not have them do unto you. Mahabharata 5,1517.
5. *Islam:* No one of you is a believer until he desires for his brother which he desires for himself. Sunnah.
6. *Judaism*: What is hateful to you, do not do to your fellowman. This is the entire Law—all the rest is commentary. Talmud, Shabbat 3id.
7. *Taosim*: Regard your neighbor's gain as your gain, and your neighbor's loss as your own loss. Tai Chang Kan Yin Pien.

In the final analysis, service to others is the primary value that has the capacity to guide and maintain a viable Global Community. In contrast, adherence to a narrowly defined national interest and reliance on militarism in order to achieve that national interest is not only immoral, but a death sentence for a Global Empire that seeks to endure on such a foundation.

5
The Hidden Politics of Empire

From the New Frontier to the Final Frontier

There is no credible aggressive new power that can provoke the breakdown of the US-centered world system, but the United States has even greater capabilities than Britain did a century ago to convert its declining hegemony into an exploitative domination. If the system eventually breaks down, it will be primarily because of US resistance to adjustment and accommodation.[1]

Giovanni Arrighi

As the optics through which consumer-country energy "security" is viewed in the powerful consumer countries have changed over the decades, something that has remained constant is the instability and insecurity their strategies have engendered. Russian concerns over the US dominance of Central Asia are intensifying. The potential for serious clashes of interests between China and the US over third-party energy supplies is growing. From the Caucasus through the Persian Gulf and across the Sahel to West Africa, the "arch of instability" that corresponds with an arch of oil and natural gas reserves and transit routes has become a justification for interventionism that is guaranteed to exacerbate tension and promote conflict.[2]

Toby Shelley

... it seems national security has been quite deliberately sacrificed by Western governments, especially the United States and the Untied Kingdom, throughout the post-Cold War period to secure not the nation but rather the interests of the corporate-military-industrial complex ... The consequence is an ever-deepening vicious circle of escalating insecurity and intensifying police-state powers on a national and international scale: a guaranteed recipe for the emergence of a new form of postmodern fascism[3]

Nafeez Mosaddeq Ahmed

Short of uncovering the proverbial "smoking gun," no seamless explanation as to the "who" and "why" of Dallas is possible. Ideally, the time for uncovering answers to these questions was forty years ago, had the Warren Commission enjoyed the full cooperation of government agencies and a clear mandate from the Johnson White House to pursue the truth no matter where it led. Instead, "settling the dust" of Dallas as quickly as possible was the course the executive branch settled upon ... The government did not want to delve into the heart of darkness of the Kennedy assassination because it feared what it might uncover ... that his assassination was carried out by powerful and irrational forces within his own government.[4]

Gerald D. McKnight

OVERT AND COVERT HISTORY

Networks of Western financial, corporate, banking, military, and political elites have actively worked for generations to subordinate their own national citizenry while making the citizens of Third World nations mere subjects to their imperial reign. These hidden networks of power are fundamentally unaccountable to meaningful democratic influence. Since the 1950s, the entire *Military-Industrial-Intelligence Complex* has hidden covert plans that are illegal and even undertaken, as throughout the Kennedy years, in violation of presidential directives or without the president's knowledge.

Certainly the history of America's CIA comes to mind as a perfect example of a power structure that is fundamentally unaccountable to meaningful democratic influence or control. Since its formation at the end of World War II, the CIA has charted a course that has sometimes acted independently of US presidents—as well as at their behest. Suffice it to say that the CIA has often been actively working to accomplish the disempowerment of US citizens, while simultaneously covertly acting to disenfranchise the rest of humanity from having a voice or a vote in the direction of either their personal lives or their own nation's future.

The hidden hand of the CIA has been instrumental in the overthrow of governments, the assassination of heads of state (*Executive Action*—a CIA euphemism for the assassination of a head of state), and as a covert force designed to keep the door of foreign nations open to be available markets for US goods and investment opportunities. In the furtherance of the goals of the US Global Empire, the CIA has faithfully served as the covert hammer of policymakers. Alternatively, the IMF, World Bank, and WTO have undertaken more overt forms of hammering. Still, the same mixture of lies, deception, and hidden agendas are characteristic of all four Western-led agencies. In each of these institutions, the hidden politics of empire are at work.

As always, the only issue that has ultimately mattered to these networks is the attainment and maintenance of power. As Hans Morgenthau observed in his classic work, *Politics Among Nations*: "Domestic and international politics are but two different manifestations of the same phenomenon: the struggle for power."[5] In his view, the struggle for power is manifested differently in the two spheres "because different moral, political, and social conditions prevail in each." The degree of social cohesion, cultural uniformity, technological unification, and hierarchic political organization all combine to create a domestic order that is "more stable and less subject to violent change than is the international order." From this perspective, he concluded, "all history shows that nations active in international politics are continuously preparing for, actively involved in, or recovering from organized violence in the form of war."[6] This description of national and international power remains largely accurate as far as the visible (overt) politics of the US Global Empire are concerned. Yet, it is not an accurate description of the hidden (covert) politics of empire for it is a view that fails to account for "a sprawling network of overarching criminal and financial interests."[7] What is common to both criminal and financial interests is that they possess overt and covert capabilities.

What has most dramatically changed since Morgenthau offered his assessment of national and international politics is the almost complete internationalization of the corporate-military-industrial complex and what Ahmed calls "the criminalization of Western power."[8] It is a phenomenon that has led to the corruption of Western democracy and a crisis of legitimacy. Since the 1970s, the Trilateral countries have all suffered from what Jurgen Habermas has called a "*legitimation crisis*." With the Bush-2 regime in 2000, the Western Alliance crumbled as the doctrine of "preemptive war" effectively preempted both diplomacy and the rule of international law. While this trend did not begin with the Bush-2 regime, it has come to penetrate into the domestic structures of American society more broadly than ever before in the nation's history. Both the White House and the congress have abdicated their respective constitutional duties and oaths of office in the furtherance of following the agenda and the dictates of the architects of the US Global Empire. The hidden politics of the Council on Foreign Relations (CFR) continues to shape the views and influence the decisions of policymakers in government. The hidden politics of corporate boardrooms often conjoin with the agenda items discussed in White House cabinet meetings. Perhaps no clearer example is found than in the Task Force on Energy, headed by Vice President Dick Cheney, where the minutes of the meetings are still sealed, still secret, and sanctioned as private business—not public business—by the US Supreme Court itself.

Even the judiciary, from the federal bench to the Supreme Court, has sanctioned the creation of new layers of secrecy, opening the door for clandestine decision making and covert operations. This growing culture of secrecy has engendered new forms of immunity for the protection of government secrets—thereby depriving American citizens of need-to-know information that makes democratic discourse possible and informed consent a genuine possibility. The Supreme Court and federal judiciary have also aided and abetted a diminishment of civil liberties through the auspices of the USA Patriot Act, turned a blind eye to state-sanctioned torture in the "war on terror," and effectively transformed a right wing ideological agenda into the litmus test for judicial candidates seeking legal appointments.

Both the Republican and Democratic parties have been in a long decline in reaching this historical juncture. It has been an almost 40 year decline. Since the 1963 assassination of President John F. Kennedy, the nation and the world have been placed on an entirely new path—a path that was opened up by his assassination.[9] As with the events of 9/11, Kennedy's death opened the door for dramatic policy reversals—especially in the realm of foreign policy. After Kennedy, major policy reversals came with regard to the issue of Vietnam and the commitment of American troops to Asia, the future of the Alliance for Progress in Latin America, the federal government's tax policies with respect to American oil companies (*the elimination of the* "oil depletion allowance"), the role of the Federal Reserve system, the interests of the Wall Street elite versus the larger public interest, the nature of détente toward the USSR and Cuba, the future of nuclear arms testing and reductions, and the future of the Atlantic Alliance.[10]

A similar shift in US foreign policy took place in the aftermath of 9/11. The door was opened to the invasion and occupation of Iraq, the curtailing of domestic dissent under the guise of the USA Patriot Act, a neoconservative assault on democracy and justice, enormous transfers of wealth from the poor and middle class to the super-rich, an expansion of war-profiteering, and an alliance with Wall Street accompanied by White House calls for the privatization of Social Security.[11] In many respects, the Bush-2 regime continued to follow in the footsteps of his father, George Herbert Walker Bush. Where Bush Sr. had helped with the looting of the Savings & Loans—covering up and protecting many of the perpetrators of the scandal—so too, Bush Jr. did his best to protect his friends at Enron as the financial meltdown made it into one of the largest financial scandals in the nation's history.[12]

Both the Kennedy assassination and the events of 9/11 share many elements in common. These elements point us toward the need to examine and comprehend the *hidden politics of empire*. The very structures of Western power itself, from both a domestic standpoint to the evolving shape of the international system, reflect a conspiracy at work to achieve Western dominance for particular elite groups and coalitions—regardless of the cost or sacrifice. Within this *hidden politics of empire* we shall find the actual forces and reasons for decisions that have led to wars, assassinations, dubious financial arrangements, and criminal activities that have not merely undermined but have virtually destroyed American democracy.[13]

In the years since the Kennedy assassination, the structures of Western power have been dramatically altered. Among the alterations in the conduct and structures of Western power we can list the introduction of American combat troops into Vietnam in 1965, the Watergate affair, and the subsequent resignation of President Richard Nixon, the Iran/Contra Affair of the Reagan/Bush-1 years, the Savings & Loan scandal of the Bush-1 regime, and the Bush-2 regime's falsified intelligence on Hussein's Iraq and the American occupation of Iraq.[14] This is only a partial list. This list represents only some of the major milestones in a history that has yet to be exposed. We have an incomplete record of all the events, decisions, and people at work in shaping the still hidden politics of empire.

THE RISE OF POSTMODERN FASCISM
AND GLOBAL EMPIRE

What is not so hidden is that both in the United States and Great Britain, the concept of national security in the post–Cold War period has increasingly subordinated the genuine welfare and security of British and American citizens to the status of Third World citizens—expendable in both war and peace, subject to unconstitutional treatment, and groomed to adopt the role of obedient servants. In this new world, the role of the average citizen is one where he/she is to be uncritically subservient to a new form of postmodern fascism. In both First and Third World nations the drift toward an embrace and practice of postmodern fascism is clear and already evident. Examples abound of the transformation of the United States from an ostensibly democratic nation to an antidemocratic national security state.[15]

Since the events of 9/11, the tragedy of that day has served as a convenient pretext to launch a "war on terror." It has become a war filled with war profiteers both in and out of government. The reality is that *war on terror*" was launched by another kind of *"Pearl Harbor event*"—in the form of the events of 9/11.[16] Since 9/11, an elite leadership and membership within the US Global Empire has rewarded its corporate and military CEOs and allies while, at the same time, it has been actively working to re-structure, strengthen, and reinforce America's declining global hegemony.

Even more fundamentally, the Bush-2 regime is confused about how to go about reconciling its approach to its geopolitics with its approach to geoeconomics. Writing in the CFR magazine, *Foreign Affairs*, Jeffrey Garten has noted:

> President Bush has frequently voiced his commitment to spreading democracy and free markets around the globe. For him, democracy and capitalism have the same goal: human liberation. But the administration needs to reflect on whether simultaneously pushing open politics and open markets is realistic. If US rhetoric is out of step with its behavior, the United States will be seen as hypocritical and purely opportunistic. That is what is happening now. If the Bush administration is so committed to liberty broadly defined, for example, why has it been so timid in criticizing China for its failure to democratize? Why has it remained almost silent as Russia's Prime Minister Vladimir Putin has eliminated political opposition and a free press? Why has it been so skittish about pursuing political openings in Saudi Arabia? The answers are obvious: in each case, stability and economic ties are more important to the Bush administration than real democracy, because the latter carries with it the dangers of radical political change and destabilization. That may in fact be a realistic calculation. But in any case, Washington needs to reconcile the inherent tensions between its geopolitical and its geo-economic aspirations."[17]

The threat to America's global hegemony in the Middle East has allowed for the collusion of the United States with Israel in a bloody genocide and occupation of Palestine with the use of American weapons of war. Previous bans on the use of these weapons involved their use for defensive purposes only. Since the Bush-2 regime took office, these weapons have been engaged in offensive operations with no justifiable defensive purpose in mind. The goal has been one of extermination, intimidation, and the exercise of raw power by using the *war on terror* as a cover for other reasons of state. Since the 2003 war against Iraq was launched, the United States and Israel have come to share a broader regional agenda. This regional agenda is designed to strengthen Israel as a forward base of American influence and military power. As such, Israel has been charged with carrying out the larger US regional objectives in the Middle East, including: reshaping Middle East politics, suppressing anti-American resistance, and solidifying the US hold on the region and its petroleum wealth.[18]

While both the United States and Israel claim to be democratic states, in practice their domestic and foreign policies are not truly democratic because their domestic polities are antidemocratic in function and their foreign policies are not subject to accountability by national courts or international tribunals. For example, many top officials in the Bush-2 regime, such as Richard Perle and Paul Wolfovitz, are closely linked to the Israeli right wing. This has led to a considerable confluence of policy agendas between the United States and Israel from 2001 to the present. In the case of Israel's war on the Palestinian Authority, the United States excused Israeli brutality against the Palestinian people by declaring it a war of self-defense. The Bush-2 regime has not even asked Israel for minor concessions. Rather, when it came to the illegal and ongoing settlement activities in the occupied territories, both Rumsfeld and Perle called the actions the legitimate spoils of war.[19] Hence, war crimes now flourish where the rule of law once restrained the barbarous inclinations of public leaders and the hidden interests of invisible elites, lobbies, and special interest groups.[20]

Since 9/11 a hidden elite in the United States has embarked upon a national and international program that runs on two policy tracks—parallel to one another. On one track, the nature of social cohesion in the domestic arena is less a matter of allowing for democratic choice than of protecting an imprinted and state-sanctioned cultural uniformity under a banner of *United We Stand*. After the events of 2001, the nature of America's social cohesion and cultural uniformity exists mainly as a consequence of induced fear, not the result of an enlightened democratic discourse. The Department of Homeland Security has come into being to monitor domestic dissent as much as to protect American citizens against future terrorist attacks. In response, progressive groups such as the American Civil Liberties Union are more likely to sue the Justice Department, the Department of Defense, and the White House, rather than to uncritically accept significant breaches of constitutional protections by government officials. In this regard, progressive critics of the Bush-2 regime recognize that the USA Patriot Act can be seen as being a useful tool for a governing elite and its coalition membership that seeks to stifle dissent, shred civil liberties, and maintain a climate of domestic fear.[21]

On the other track, the less stable international environment remains subject to violent change, thereby inviting a similar response from Washington's elite. International law and the Geneva Accords are remolded and reconfigured by the Department of Defense and the Department of Justice in order to declare that international conventions against torture and human rights protections for "detainees" are nothing more than "quaint artifacts" from the a past that no longer retains any relevance in the "war on terror." In this atmosphere, Amnesty International has been more inclined to speak of Guantanamo Bay as an *American Gulag* rather than to accept the Pentagon, Defense Department, and Department of Justice's endorsement of torture as an appropriate tool in the "war on terror."[22]

The hidden politics of empire has sanctioned both torture and assassination as appropriate tools for the task of maintaining American hegemony in the international arena. These activities of the US Global Empire comprise the dark side of state terrorism. State terrorism contains within its arsenal of tactics a moralizing war myth that is coupled with the dehumanization of the enemy, an emphasis upon only the terror tactics of the other side, and a policy of insisting that responsibility for terror tactics be attributed to the enemy.[23] In this atmosphere, the perceived threat of international terrorism has reduced the citizen of the empire to little more than a tax-paying cog in the international war machine that sanctions the assassinations of both alleged terrorists and democratically elected heads of state that refuse to cooperate with the larger economic and political agenda of the US Global Empire. It is within this matrix of power and influence where the hidden and covert politics of empire direct and control its internal domestic life as well as its external and overt manifestations.

THE HIDDEN HISTORY OF THE US GLOBAL EMPIRE IN THE EISENHOWER/KENNEDY YEARS

In any attempt to introduce the hidden history of the US Global Empire it is necessary to begin with a description of the nature of its economic system. It is necessary because a basic understanding of the economic structure and requirements of America's Global Empire helps to explicate the nature of its hidden power structure and the foreign policy implications that stem from it. To begin with, America's capitalist system involves not just the management and investment of vast concentrations of wealth. Vast fortunes and concentrated wealth existed in other ancient empires, feudal Europe, and other class-divided societies. What is unique about capitalism is its perpetual need to engage in the dynamic of accumulation and expansion.[24] This is the dynamic that dominates the American economic order and its leadership. In this regard, "the Western powers under the leadership of the United States continue to prop up the same illegitimate regimes created in the twentieth century in contradiction to basic humanitarian and democratic principles, to fulfill strategic and economic interests."[25]

For the US Global Empire, its primary concerns are with strategic and economic interests—for that is the overriding dynamic that drives its domestic politics as well as its approach to foreign policy issues. To understand this basic reality is to comprehend the most fundamental reality of the US Global Empire—to stand still is to decline not only in relative terms, but in absolute terms as well. According to Mark Curtis,

> the fundamental aim of the most powerful Northern states and their allies has been clearly outlined in the planning documents of the postwar period: control over the international economy and the world's economically most important regions, including raw material supplies and markets, in a system which benefits their business elites and confers great power status, having the effect of subordinating the people and resources of the Third World to these basic priorities. The poor are also expected to bear the main burden of adjustment to global crises in the system such as low commodity prices, the debt crisis and devaluations.[26]

The costs and burdens that capitalism has placed upon the people of the poor South—throughout the Third World—has been well documented over the decades. Andre Gunder Frank has referred to this situation as the "development of crisis and crisis of development." Writing in 1980, a full 25 years before the word "outsourcing" entered the popular lexicon, he observed:

> To provide these low wages and indeed to reduce wages from one country to another competitively, as each tries to offer more favorable conditions to international capital, requires political repression, the destruction of labor unions and/or the prohibition of strikes and other union activity, the systematic imprisonment, torture, or assassination of labor and other political leaders ... In fact, the whole state apparatus has to be adapted to the Third World role in the new international division of labor.[27]

In order to grasp the larger picture conceptually, it would help to refer to the centers of power in the nations of the North as the "metropoles" and the nations of the South as those on the "periphery" (on the periphery of the political and economic centers of power and decision making). With this in mind, Henrik Spruyt has argued: "Many empires ... find their roots in the benefits that they yield to specific segments within polities. Beyond the purview of the state, individuals and groups pursuing their own narrow interests draw the metropoles further into imperial expansion."[28]

Imperial expansion whether in the case of US involvement in Vietnam, (1965–1974), or in the case of the Bush-2 regime's preemptive war against Iraq (2003), reflects a misunderstanding of nationalism and the nationalist sentiments of people. Nationalist sentiments include the strong desire of a people to defend their sovereignty, to defend and realize their human rights, and protect their own self-chosen path of development. All of this was foreclosed upon when President Lyndon Johnson launched a war of aggression against North Vietnam. The same error was repeated when President George W. Bush invaded Iraq, began an occupation, and mislabeled nationalist opposition to the American presence an "insurgency."

Throughout his presidency, John F. Kennedy was opposed to the pursuit of these narrowly defined imperial interests. In the case of Vietnam, he clearly understood that the "American assumption that the United States would do better than the French in defeating Vietnamese aspirations for a unified independent country rested on the arrogance of a modern superpower battling a so-called backward people."[29] In fact, Kennedy's message to his advisors was that US military involvement was to be a last resort.[30] Basically, Kennedy believed that "if the conflict in Vietnam were ever converted into a white man's war, we would lose the war the way the French had lost a decade earlier."[31] Kennedy's reluctance to involve the United States in Vietnam was so great that he "also resisted making a categorical commitment to saving Vietnam."[32] During his first 10 months in office, he had made it clear that he doubted the wisdom of expanding US involvement in the fighting.[33] At the heart and center of Kennedy's reluctance to become militarily engaged in Vietnam was his fundamental recognition that the United States would be perceived as fighting an Asian war merely to reestablish colonial control over Vietnam.[34]

In light of all of the debates about military options in Laos, Kennedy's fears about escalation were confirmed. It was clear to him that no military strategy "could compensate for the chronic weakness of indigenous anticommunism." Therefore, "if this assumption could be generalized throughout Southeast Asia, then the American position had to be recognized as being irredeemably weak."[35] The Joint Chiefs of Staff disagreed. On January 13, 1962, the Joint Chiefs sent to the president their most strongly worded memo yet on the strategic importance of Southeast Asia and Vietnam, in particular. Clearly, "The memo was extraordinary. In it the Chiefs described the stakes in Vietnam as incredibly high, and said they had done all they could under the restraints of the president's program. They then offered their views ... as to what should be done should his program fail. Their solution, of course, was to send US combat troops to Vietnam ..."[36] It was their last discourse on the subject until *after* Kennedy's death in Dallas.

The US Government's policy on Vietnam was dramatically altered only *after* Kennedy's assassination. In a National Security Action Memorandum (NSAM-111), issued on November 22, 1961, Kennedy's final decision against intervention in Vietnam was arrived at after all the arguments for it had been put forward. As the record reveals, "it was the major Vietnam decision of his presidency, drawing as it did a line that he never crossed."[37]

The record also reveals "the assassination of John F. Kennedy and the entrance of a new president into the White House dramatically increased the distorting effects of the aggressive role of national security advisors on Vietnam policy."[38] Throughout his presidency, Kennedy would seek diplomatic solutions to problems that could escalate into war. The problem that Kennedy faced was that he was at war with his own national security bureaucracy. In fact, "Kennedy's efforts to initiate diplomatic contacts with Hanoi were resisted by the national security bureaucracy in the firm belief that South Vietnam was a place where the United States could and should effectively exert its power."[39] Had Kennedy's preference for a diplomatic solution been given a chance, it is likely that the United States would have had a greater opportunity to shape the political outcome in Vietnam. Instead, the national security bureaucracy, the Pentagon, and the CIA combined to undermine Kennedy's approach, open the door for a purely military solution, and thereby block the possibility of a diplomatic compromise.[40]

Diplomacy was Kennedy's chief political weapon in the Cold War, but it certainly was not at the top of the list for either national security bureaucracy or the economic interests behind it. Rather, financial profit for the few was a primary motivating factor of the first order when it came to America's "shadow government." In the shadows were the men in power positions in business, banking, finance, oil, and the military-industrial-complex who supported only military expansion, involvement, and solutions to the problems of the Cold War. This perspective is what placed Kennedy into conflict with his own bureaucracy. Negotiated settlements meant more to JFK than the financial gain of a small network of steel titans, oil barons, and arms dealers in the military-industrial-complex. In 1962, he was able to get US Steel to back down from a price increase and roll back prices to the level of an earlier agreement made with labor. In 1963, he planned to submit to the Congress in 1964 a proposal that would end the oil depletion allowance for the oilmen. At the close of 1963, he committed himself to opening trade with Cuba and beginning a withdrawal from Vietnam.

Kennedy's approach to global governance was an exception to the standard rules of the game. He was able to comprehend the necessity for building a global community to deal effectively with a world of nuclear weapons states where the dangers of nuclear proliferation and war loomed large. Familiar with the poverty and plight of Third World nations he was sympathetic with the emotions that drive nationalist movements. His experience at the Bay of Pigs left him unconvinced of the ultimate wisdom of the domino theory or the judgment of the Joint Chiefs of Staff and the CIA. His experiences led him to place a premium on an ability to read a crisis—the sources of its urgency, the interests of those involved, and the options available to them. The dangers and pressures of the Cold War required a readiness to focus on primary interests and, if necessary letting go of those that were of secondary importance.

After the 1962 Cuban Missile Crisis, he was painfully aware of the need to develop military options carrying a minimal risk of escalating into a catastrophic war. In short, Kennedy learned how to engage in forms of activity that signaled resolve without projecting an image of recklessness. All this led Kennedy to adopt what became known as a policy of *graduated reciprocation in tension reduction* (GRIT) or *flexible response*. These alternatives to relying on military answers to political problems allowed him to move forward in crises one step at a time, raising at each stage the pressure on his opponents, probing their will, exploring opportunities for a settlement even while preparing to up the ante. This approach characterized his method in dealing with awkward clients, such as Diem, as well as with dangerous adversaries in the Kremlin. Kennedy employed this method because it best expressed his conviction that it was the only sane way to manage the Cold War and avoid a nuclear war.

Despite Kennedy's record of success in seeking and achieving peaceful and negotiated settlements (Laos and Berlin in 1961, and the Cuban Missile Crisis of 1962), his method and principles of governance did not survive his assassination. His vision for a nonnuclear world through a "graduated reciprocation in tension reduction" (GRIT) and an evolving nuclear nonproliferation regime, his hopes for the Alliance for Progress in Latin America which emphasized land reform and a redistribution of wealth, his commitment to overcome poverty at home and abroad, and his determination to rein in powerful elite interests both in and out of government, all died with him in Dallas.

Apparently, the truth about the exercise of American power in the twentieth and twenty-first centuries is that while motives and mechanisms may change over time, the US Global Empire has largely remained true to its ultimate concern: the fate of the American economy in general and its elite's interests in particular. Such an approach leaves little room for concerns with socioeconomic justice, correcting the harsh effects of the market on the poor and middle class, or bringing about needed structural and substantive changes in health care, education, and government.

Kennedy's commitment to building a genuine American democracy and expanding its substantive achievements around the globe was simply not a goal shared by other elites in the American establishment. In fact, as Michael Klare observed,

the immediate motives behind expansion of *America's invisible empire* and the actual mechanisms of control have changed through the years. Nevertheless, the relationships forged between the United States and its overseas dependents have followed a consistent pattern: each linkage is designed to meet some current need of the American economy while further securing the dependent status of the colonial economy ... *The United States needs unhampered access to and control of overseas trade to serve as a market for the products of American industry ... as an outlet for the surplus of US investment funds, and as a source of raw materials and cheap labor* (Italics are mine).[41]

Similarly, Peter Dale Scott has noted that "the policy concerns of a relatively small and economically powerful CIA financial establishment" were critical in shaping the policies of the US Global Empire throughout the 1960s. In his assessment of that period, Scott's analysis could easily apply to the conduct of the Bush-2 regime's march to war against Iraq. However, in order to see the linkage between the American escalation in Vietnam from 1965 to 1968 and the invasion of Iraq 40 years afterwards, it is necessary to expose the dysfunctions of the American system that led to the Indochina war. For it is in the dysfunctions of the American system itself that the seeds for war are planted and grown to fruition.

THE DYSFUNCTIONS OF THE AMERICAN SYSTEM THAT LED TO WAR IN VIETNAM

In Professor Scott's list of systemic and structural dysfunctions in the American system he highlights the following: "the scandals and irregularities, the private usurpations of the nation's political processes, the repeated distortion of decision-making by contaminated 'intelligence', the draining of a weakened domestic economy for ruthless profit-making abroad."[42] These were the central systemic and structural dysfunctions that led to the Vietnam War. These elements also account for the success of the conspiracy to assassinate Kennedy and its cover-up. Since the truth was never exposed regarding the assassination or crucial decision making on the road to war in Vietnam, these same systemic and structural dysfunctions have not only remained in place but have grown like a cancer throughout the American government.

Certainly the revelations about how the Bush-2 regime worked to manipulate intelligence regarding Iraq, connived with Enron and Halliburton to engage in price gouging schemes and the awarding of no-bid contracts from the Pentagon, the stealing of the 2000 presidential election (and probably the 2004 election in Ohio), the revelations in the Downing Street Memo that expose Bush's commitment to go to war with Iraq before securing congressional authorization or establishing viable evidence to make the case that war would be the "last option," are all examples that point to a dysfunctional, antidemocratic and unaccountable system.

Sharing Professor Scott's perspective about the evolution of the US Global Empire under conditions of systemic and structural dysfunction, Carl Boggs has observed that "in this transformed setting—corporate, globalized, militarized—politics has degenerated into a mix of narrow interest-group maneuvers, bureaucratic intrigues, and electoral rituals, even while *corporate and military priorities remain largely unchecked in a context where Empire takes on a logic of its own*"

(Italics are mine).[43] With the removal of effective checks and balances within the American government, the corruption and decline of accountability and the salutary effects of democratic politics have been lost. In place of checks and balances, a *power elite* (C. Wright Mills) have united in a broad-based coalition of interest groups. Their advocacy is designed to advance Global Empire. The nature of this advance is to be undertaken from the core centers of the Northern capitalist countries and taken into the periphery of the Third World.

In this regard, it becomes possible to understand why the advocates of Global Empire have too much to loose "if the metropole decides to retreat from the periphery. Moreover, given that concentrated groups as business and landed interests can more readily overcome collective action problems than diffusely organized groups, they have a distinct advantage over social actors who favor disengagement. Consequently, these groups will try to prevent territorial dissolution by any means—some within the constitutional rules of political competition, others outside those rules (through coups d'etat, even assassination)."[44] Since 1963, American politics has at crucial moments become *government by gunplay*.

Fundamental alterations of the foreign policy of the Kennedy years were undertaken in every succeeding administration. Among these changes were the lowering of barriers between private interests and the public business. The priorities of domestic elite coalitions linked to multinational corporations succeeded in emasculating the Alliance for Progress and moving the priorities of the trade regime from the General Agreement on Trade and Tariffs (GATT) to the North American Free Trade Agreement (NAFTA). By the summer of 2005, the passage of the Central American Free Trade Agreement (CAFTA) could be characterized as NAFTA on steroids.

What this brief historical review demonstrates is that the struggle for both world markets and *spheres of influence* are integral ingredients to the success or failure of global capitalism, in general, and the future of the US Global Empire, in particular. As far back as the Eisenhower administration, American policymakers were preoccupied with the question of who would control Asia.[45] Its markets, its raw materials, its peoples, were all components in a calculus of geopolitics and economics. Also, during the 1950s,

> as more and more Asian and African nations began moving toward independence and a non-aligned, neutral bloc began to emerge, Secretary of state Dulles took a strong public position against neutralism ... NSC policy statements embodied the principle that neutralism—defined not simply as non-alignment but as a willingness even to entertain diplomatic relations with Communist powers— was dangerous. Under Eisenhower, the American government—including both the State and Defense Departments and the CIA—generally tried to support factions within emerging nations that would unequivocally reject contacts with Communism and support the West throughout the world.[46]

Such was the nature of Washington's *democratic option* for emerging Third World states and their nationalist aspirations. As long as they would side with the West in the Cold War struggle, they could maintain their neutrality. It was, of course, utter hypocrisy on the part of the US Global Empire and the financial establishment behind it. Further, the position taken by the Eisenhower administration had serious effects in Indochina. For "although the Geneva Accords of 1954 forbade Laos, Cambodia, and South Vietnam to join any military alliance, the Eisenhower administration nonetheless expected them to maintain firm opposition to Communism."[47]

The same US government policy of recalcitrance toward neutralism and nonalignment characterized US administrations from Nixon to Reagan. In the 1970s, dozens of nations throughout the Third World sought to develop South-South economic and political ties that would separate them from the superpower struggle over their own nation's futures. Both the United States and the USSR used the Third World as a battleground involving "low-intensity conflicts" in order to gain control over natural resources, labor markets, and establish spheres of influence. The response of many Third World countries was to join the NAM. By 1980, the Reagan doctrine toward the Third World was *"roll back"*—an effort to roll backwards the gains made by NAM and reassert US hegemony over the Third World. Reagan's version of democracy promotion in Latin America was to keep the civil war going in El Salvador at the same time he conducted his own state-sponsored war of terror on the socialist government of Nicaragua.

Keeping Central America safe for multinational corporate investment and financial exploitation were the twin goals that grounded US foreign policy in Central America. Only the intervention of President Oscar Arias of Costa Rica in the late 1980s rescued Central America from even more years of internecine civil war and US military intervention. By the end of Reagan's term, El Salvador was still recovering from the terrorism of US-trained "death squads" (later termed *death-squad democracy*). Also, Nicaragua was finally granted a reprieve from the bloody work of CIA-trained Contras who had committed hundreds of human rights violations while conducting a US-sponsored war on terror against the socialist government of Daniel Ortega (in violation of the Boland Amendment).

Since the invasion of Iraq in 2003, the Bush-2 regime has employed a similar strategy throughout the Middle East. Instead of fighting Communism, the US Global Empire has declared that it is fighting a *war on terrorism*. In the name of national and international security, the Bush-2 regime has pursued military options to the exclusion of almost every other option. It has only been with regard to the issue of Iraqi sovereignty and the challenge of establishing long-term stability in the region, that President Bush has launched a democracy promotion campaign in the Middle East to deal with a growing insurgency, increasing resistance to what is generally perceived to be an illegitimate American occupation, and what many in the Arab world believe is an attempt to usurp Islam and its culture by a forced infusion of both American culture and Western values—not to mention Anglo-American control over Iraq's natural resources.

BUSH'S DYSFUNCTIONAL POLICY IN IRAQ

By actively engaging in its own brand of *democracy promotion* the Bush-2 regime contends that democracy can spread American values and improve US security.

The same justifications and rationalizations were made during the course of America's involvement in Vietnam—in the administrations of Eisenhower through Nixon. American policymakers in the national security bureaucracy wanted to make the case that by bolstering a client regime in South Vietnam the United States could manage an ally that would deny South Vietnam to the Communists. The euphemism employed at the time was *self-determination*.

Similarly, the Bush-2 regime argues that it seeks to deny Iraq to terrorists groups and/or Islamic extremists by installing a regime that is elected and ostensibly democratic. Yet, as of January 2005 elections were held that resulted in a representational imbalance among contending Iraqi factions and did little to halt the bloodshed brought by daily terrorist attacks. As of September 2005, the Iraqi constitutional drafting process had broken down. Adding to the difficulties, major social groups and political actors had been excluded by the process. Complicating the matter of democracy promotion still further is a nebulous notion of what constitutes freedom, democratic inclusion, and how long it would take for a Western conception of these qualities to be realized. All these realities "begs a fundamental question: *Is it true that the more democratic a country becomes, the less likely it is to produce terrorists and terrorist groups?*" (Italics are mine).[48] In addition to this question we need to ask: *"Even if democracy were achieved in the Middle East, what kind of governments would it produce?"* (Italics are mine).[49]

While predictions are never certain, the provisional answer is that the course new democratic governments will take anywhere in the Middle East seems likely "to produce new Islamist governments that would be much less willing to cooperate with the United States than are the current authoritarian rulers."[50] Based upon this assessment, it is clear that Washington probably would not like the governments that Arab democracy would produce. In fact, "history indicates that legitimate democratic elections in Arab states would most likely benefit Islamists."[51] In that regard, the so-called insurgents and Islamists of twenty-first century Iraq share many of the same nationalist sentiments that were held by both the North and South Vietnamese when the French and then the Americans occupied their nation. Yet, perhaps a different historical analogy may be more pertinent in assessing Iraq's constitutional process.

As of September 2005,

> the Iraqi constitutional process has the potential to repeat the understandable but disastrous strategy of Oslo—reach agreements on vague and high-sounding principles, but leave the tough questions for a later date, when developments on the ground will (it is hoped) invest the reconciliation process with enough momentum for compromises on issues that were off the table at the start. In addition to the abject failure of the Oslo method of conflict resolution, it is hard to imagine Sunnis, who have lost so much they have little left to lose, Shites, who have gained unprecedented power and have little reason to compromise, and Kurds, most of whom want an independent Kurdistan … making the hard compromises that would be necessary to secure a united and peaceful Iraq. And so the Osloification of Iraqi politics—and escalating cycles of violence—will likely be the reality for the near future.[52]

Additionally, the call to return to the purity of the principles and teachings of Islam further fans the flames of resistance to an occupation by the US Global Empire. Religion and politics have become inseparable. Just as with South Vietnam's struggle with the Buddhist crisis of 1963, the Iraq of 2005 faced the difficulty of trying to reconcile the fact that many elements of Iraqi society remain excluded, fearful of the evolving nature of the political process, and unsure whether the principles of Islam can be preserved throughout the course of a major social, economic, and political transformation. None of these issues have been seriously addressed by the Bush-2 regime as it has proceeded with its program of *democracy promotion*. Rather, the Bush program believes that if it can have periodic elections take place, then elections alone will be enough to guarantee a semblance of legitimacy for any future Iraqi regime ("demonstration elections"). The same hubris is evident in the Bush-2 regime's attitude toward the drafting of a constitution. All that matters to the Bush administration is the end result of a constitution being put on paper—not what the long-term effects will be of the constitutional design or its long-term prospects for producing stability, legitimacy, or a sense of justice among all groups within Iraqi society.

JOHN KENNEDY'S STRUGGLE AGAINST THE US WAR LOBBY OVER VIETNAM

In the case of South Vietnam in 1963, President Kennedy faced a situation that had been inflamed by religious issues about what constituted a properly ordered Confucian/Buddhist society, as well as the problems associated with Diem's reliance upon political repression in the face of declining legitimacy. The Buddhist crisis of 1963 presented South Vietnam's president with a fundamental challenge to his legitimacy. Like the Shah of Iran in the 1970s, Diem ignored the degree of outrage among the citizenry—especially those elements whose religious affiliation and beliefs left them offended, alienated, and excluded by the policies and practices of their nation's leader. Diem's fatal flaw was that he constantly ignored Buddhist demands and grievances.

In late 1963, Diem's recalcitrance to deal with the Buddhists' demands would literally ignite a revolution against his regime. A 73-year-old Buddhist monk named Thich Quang Duc burned himself to death at a street corner in downtown Saigon—protesting Diem's corruption of the country. Historians have agreed

· Diem's road to ruin had begun a long time before Quang Duc struck the match that ignited the Buddhist revolution, but the fire from that single glow did more than any other event to engulf the regime ... Diem now had to deal with the Buddhist demands which were consistent with a central theme of Vietnamese history: the restoration of the basic moral and social values of a Confucian society that, in this instance, the Ngo family had corrupted beyond repair. Heaven had mandated a revolution requiring Diem's demise.[53]

The religious fervor of the Buddhist revolution represented a desire on the part of the excluded to seek changes in the laws and the government. But this was not because they wanted to hold political power. Rather, "the overarching number of

Buddhists claimed no interest in political power and demanded changes in Saigon's leadership because it had violated the moral and ethical precepts of a just and orderly Confucian society."[54]

In many respects, the grievances voiced by the leadership of both Islamic clergy and Al-Qaeda throughout the 1990s and early twenty-first century reflect a similar dissatisfaction with the political and social direction of their respective societies—from Saudi Arabia to Egypt, from Iran to Pakistan, from Iraq to Lebanon. The principles and values of Islam are seen as being sacrificed to American and British intervention in the Middle East with the compliance of their respective governments and national leadership. The historical parallels between the South Vietnam of 1963 and the Iraq of 2005 are closer than many commentators in the mainstream media have dared to acknowledge.

The United States had installed Diem as president of South Vietnam in the 1950s. From the start he was problematic for the Americans to deal with, but even more difficult for his own people to deal with because of his general compliance with US interests, the crony capitalism that his family and friends indulged in without remorse, and his own brutal style of exclusionary leadership. As a result, in the South Vietnam of late 1963, a historic shift was occurring: "the new generation of young Buddhists began to shift from social criticism to political activism."[55] In this atmosphere, militant youths marched around the old citadel section of Hue, chanting "Down with Catholicism" and "Down with the Diem Government". There was even a student banner that welcomed martyrdom: "Please Kill Us."[56] Diem's response was to simply increase his repressive tactics. When McNamara made his case that the "political deficiencies" in Diem's government would damage the war effort, and presented the "tangible evidence" of the seriousness of the crisis, "Diem rebutted the points in some detail and displayed no interest in seeking solutions or mending his ways."[57] Throughout the Kennedy years, JFK used a variety of strategies to encourage Diem to move in a more inclusive direction in his governing style so that his problems with domestic dissent would diminish. Diem ignored the president even when threatened with American withdrawal.

By October 2, 1963, Kennedy had decided to begin the American withdrawal from Vietnam—in opposition to his advisors.[58] In fact, there was little doubt that Kennedy was moving toward a total withdrawal from Vietnam when he left for Texas in November 1963.[59] In large measure this decision was an inevitable outcome for him insofar as "never in Kennedy's thousand days in office did he stray from the principle that the war was South Vietnam's to win or lose."[60] It was only Kennedy's assassination that brought the process of pursuing the American withdrawal to a halt.

In October of 1963, Kennedy had approved a withdrawal plan in National Security Action Memorandum 263. It formalized his presidential decision to have all American troops out of Vietnam by early 1965. Between November 20th and 24th a policy reversal of Kennedy's withdrawal plan was hatched in NSAM 273. It was a policy reversal of the Kennedy withdrawal plan, authorized by President Lyndon Johnson only two days after Kennedy's assassination in Dallas. According to Professor Scott, "*NSAM 273, it seems clear, was an important document in the history of 1964 escalation, as well as in the reversal of President*

Kennedy's late and ill-fated program of 'Vietnamization,' by 1965. ... It also suggests that the Kennedy assassination was itself an important, perhaps a crucial event in the history of the Indochina war" (Italics mine).[61] In the final analysis, the Americanization of the war in Vietnam was not inevitable, as some have claimed. Rather, the United States went to war in a manner that was unique in American history. The historical record demonstrates "Kennedy had maintained that only the South Vietnamese could win the war and repeatedly resisted the demands for bombing North Vietnam, sending combat troops, and taking charge of the war: *Johnson adopted all three measures"*(Italics are mine).[62]

The reluctance of President Kennedy to commit combat troops to Vietnam was seen in the Pentagon and CIA as not only a decision that threatened to let the dominoes fall, but an act of treason by a head of state in securing his own nation's national interest. In addition, the October 1963 signing of the Nuclear Test Ban Treaty was seen as a looming loss of power and wealth for those who derived their profits from the Cold War and investments in the military-industrial complex that supported it. Given the seriousness with which Kennedy was moving toward détente and a peaceful resolution of difficulties with the USSR through negotiation, compromise, and a willingness to live with a socialist government in Cuba, any continuity of Kennedy's policies would spell ruin for certain elites. From the perspective of Kennedy's enemies, the long-term effect of Kennedy's policies would be to ultimately restructure or destroy many capitalist enterprises involved in the Cold War who benefited not only from its continuation but also its expansion.

From the perspective of some elites in the Pentagon, CIA, finance, banking, and oil, Kennedy had to be removed by any means necessary. Only with a change of presidents could these various parties and interest groups begin to thrive again. Both the conspiracy to assassinate Kennedy and its cover-up were essential to consolidate the political legitimacy of Lyndon Johnson.[63] With these two goals accomplished,

> an entire Cold War status quo in Washington was preserved along with Lyndon Johnson. Surviving with him were Johnson-allied power-movers in the Democratic Party like Edward Bennett Williams ... Vietnam and Cold War hawks like Dean Acheson and Clark Clifford (the architects of containment), a dependent tribe of military-industrial lobbyists like Fred Black and the two Murchison employees Robert Thompson and Thomas Webb (a former assistant to J. Edgar Hoover). It was this power base for the Vietnam War whose power was preserved by the assassination; and key elements of it survived to play a similar, equally hidden role in Watergate.[64]

THE TORTURED ROAD TO US INTERVENTION IN THE PERSIAN GULF: THE UNITED STATES CREATES ANOTHER PRETEXT FOR WAR

The US national security bureaucracy—since the early twentieth century—had centralized the importance of access to raw materials and markets as predominant considerations in making foreign policy. Only in the thousand days of John F. Kennedy did a US president dare to question the absolute centrality of these assumptions. The dangers associated with a potential nuclear war tempered Kennedy's thinking and policies. This was not the case with his advisors or with the US national security establishment. By 2001–2006, this unaltered strategic framework was used by the White House and the CIA to manipulate intelligence so as to influence policy outcomes. In the period of 2001–2003, the focus had shifted from Southeast Asia to Central Asia, from a well-designed global Cold War to an amorphous *war on terror*. The strategic framework used by US planners placed access to natural resources and markets at the top of the list. All other political and economic considerations would ultimately be subordinated to this strategic framework.

Starting in 2002, American power would be exerted covertly in illegal "no-fly zones" (NFZs). The Bush-2 regime had secretly decided to free the use of American power from the constraints of the congressional war power in the US Constitution, reliance on a UN resolution, or any other international authority. Ominously, in a December 2002 article in *The American Prospect* entitled, "Persian Gulf—or Tonkin Gulf?—Illegal 'no fly zones' could be war's trip wire," Robert Dreyfuss noted:

> no UN resolution or other international authority exists to legitimate the NFZs, which are currently the scene of an intensifying air-to-ground firefight between an armada of US and British war-planes and an ineffectual Iraqi defense system. The British-American presence over Iraq is a case of might makes right, and Iraq's feeble attempts to defend its skies are justified under international law. Yet the NFZs are immeasurably more explosive now because a unilateral US interpretation of UN Security Council Resolution 1441, adopted on November 8, provides a pretext for launching the war that President George W. Bush wants.[65]

In furtherance of this goal, the US national security bureaucracy was placed in the hands of Bush's neoconservative elite in 2001. With the US Supreme Court's appointment of George W. Bush as President, the road was cleared for the neoconservative policy elite and their right-wing ideologues to inaugurate the goals outlined in their 1990s study entitled, *Project for the Next American Century*.

Beginning in 1991, the experience of the Persian Gulf War and planning for *Operation Steppe Shield* were indications that the US military was planning for a long-term operation modeled on Operation Desert Shield. The goal was to establish a network of permanent US military bases in the region. This had already been accomplished at the end of the first Gulf War in Saudi Arabia, Kuwait, and Iraq. The new and expanded goal was to extend US war planning into Afghanistan, which was widely recognized by US officials as the gateway to Central Asia and the Caspian. By opening this gateway, the architects of the US Global Empire believed that they were opening the door to global primacy. All that would be needed was an excuse for the invasion. The events of 9/11 and the official explanation of those events provided the pretext for war.

The actual motivation for the wars in both Afghanistan and Iraq can be traced to a geostrategy for American primacy outlined in a 1991 CFR study entitled,

The Grand Chessboard: American Primacy and its Geostrategic Imperatives.[66] The author of the study, Zbigniew Brezinski, had served as President Carter's national security advisor. Brezinski's CFR study, representative of the elite banking, financial, political, and military elements of the American establishment made clear that US interests in Eurasia had to be "sustained and directed" and that US involvement in the Central Asian region was to be primarily dedicated toward securing these interests.[67] He declared that Central Asia had historically been the center of world power for over 500 years. In that regard, he argued that the key to controlling Eurasia lies in establishing control over the republics of Central Asia.

The only remaining question is: "Who will be in control?" The US answer to that question is obvious—especially as it has been engaged in the militarization of the Eurasian corridor with the foreign policy goal of undermining its competitors in the oil business including Russia, Iran, and China.[68] In this task, under the Bush-2 regime, "the US oil giants have gained direct access to the planning of military and intelligence operations on their behalf. This has been achieved through the powerful Texas oil lobby, resulting in the appointment of (former) oil company executives to key defense and foreign policy positions."[69] The Bush family has run oil companies since the 1950s, Vice President Dick Cheney spent the 1990s as CEO of Halliburton, National Security Advisor Condoleezza Rice sat on the board of Chevron, and Commerce Secretary Donald Evans was the CEO of Tom Brown, Inc. (a natural gas company) for more than a decade.[70]

From Brezinski's perspective, Russia and China are the two main powers bordering Central Asia that might threaten US interests in the region. Therefore, if the United States were to maintain its primacy in the region, it would have to manage and manipulate the "lesser" surrounding powers (Ukraine, Azerbaijan, Iran, and Kazakhstan). Only in this way could the US Global Empire have sufficient counterweights to any Russian and/or Chinese actions that might threaten control over the oil, gas, and minerals of the republics of Central Asia (Turkmenistan, Uzbekistan, Tajikistan, and Kyrgyzstan). At the heart of the entire analysis is a preoccupation with one primary concern: the maintenance of US global dominance. In that regard,

> the Anglo-American oil companies are intent upon taking over the Russian oil companies and excluding Russia from the Caspian Sea basin. At the same time, the Anglo-American groups are clashing with the Franco-Italian consortium, which in turn has ties to Russian and Iranian oil interests. The militarization of the Eurasian corridor is an integral part of Washington's foreign policy agenda. In this regard, America's quest to control the Eurasian pipeline corridors on behalf of the Anglo-American oil giants is not only directed against Russia, it is also intended to weaken competing European oil interests in the Transcaucasus and Central Asia.[71]

The tortured road to American intervention in the Persian Gulf and Central Asia was mandated as necessary a full seven years before President George W. Bush began his wars against Afghanistan and Iraq. The overarching mandate is laid out in the conclusion to Brzezinski's book, *The Grand Chessboard*, where he asserts: "The time has come for the United States to formulate and prosecute an integrated, comprehensive, and long-term geo-strategy for all of Eurasia. This need arises out of the interaction between two fundamental realities: America is now the only global superpower, and Eurasia is the globe's central area. Hence, what happens to the distribution of power on the Eurasian continent will be of decisive importance to America's global primacy and to America's historical legacy."[72] His great fear for the future of America's global primacy comprised two interrelated elements: "averting global anarchy and impeding the emergence of a power rival."[73]

ASSERTING AMERICA'S DRIVE FOR GLOBAL PRIMACY: HOW
THE JFK ASSASSINATION AND WARREN COMMISSION,
THE ATTACKS ON 9/11 AND THE 9/11-COMMISSION
WERE USED TO OPEN THE DOOR FOR WAR AND
CLOSE THE DOOR ON THE TRUTH

Given the centrality assigned to the maintenance of US dominance as the ultimate national security priority, it is clear that neither the elites of the American establishment nor the architects/apologists of the US Global Empire would let any consideration stand in the way of their achieving their primary objective. Therefore, what I have called "the hidden politics of empire" involves one primary mandate: *A willingness to undertake any shocking action that could serve as a pretext for war in order to secure their economic interests.* This mandate leads to the following conclusion—which is also the thesis of this chapter:

> *Just as the Dallas assassination of JFK and the Gulf of Tonkin incident opened the door for a ground war in Southeast Asia, so too the 9/11 attacks on the World Trade Center and the Pentagon opened the door for war in Afghanistan and Iraq and beyond.*

The 9/11 attacks were no surprise to the men at the center of the US Global Empire. As early as 1993 the Pentagon commissioned an expert panel to investigate the possibility of an airplane being used to bomb national landmarks.[74] In 1994, after the first World Trade Center (WTC) bombing, one of the experts on the aforementioned Pentagon panel wrote in the *Futurist* magazine that the WTC was a likely target of an "airplanes as weapons" terrorist attack. As early as 1994, the Pentagon was aware not only of an "airplanes as weapons" plot against the WTC but was specifically concerned about the possibility of such a plot being implemented in the form of "multiple, simultaneous operations."[75] By 1995, the entire US intelligence community became aware of the fact that al-Qaeda was planning such an operation that would target not only the WTC, but also a wide number of other key buildings in the United States.[76]

Within the period of 1996–2000, there was a rising tide of terrorist alerts.[77] By 2000, the US intelligence community had no doubt about Osama bin Laden's plans to conduct a terrorist attack on US soil.[78] Approximately 12 days before the 9/11 attacks, the United States received an authoritative warning from Egyptian intelligence about an imminent terrorist attack within the United States (in fact, the warming was personally sent by Egyptian president Hosni Mubarak).[79] Hence, the CIA's failure to disseminate crucial information about the impending attacks and of known al-Qaeda terrorists operating in the United States leads to some awkward questions such as: "Why were their names not placed on a terrorist watch list according to normal protocols?"[80] The answer to that question is even more troubling when we discover that there is an alarming pattern here of extensive US intelligence surveillance of a number of al-Qaeda operatives with confirmed records of terrorist activity on various watch lists, nonetheless being able to freely pass in and out the United States without restrictions.[81] In fact, according to Justice Department officials, it has been estimated that more than 50 people were likely involved in a plot that required extensive communications and planning to pull off. Yet, the conspirators continued on through their planning and preparation for the attacks unhindered and feeling unthreatened by law enforcement.[82]

In summary, after reviewing these facts, one is left with the idea that the success of the 9/11 attacks was more of a failure of state policy than an intelligence failure. On this point, the British intelligence analysis newsletter, *Jane's Intelligence Digest*, argues that the 9/11 "intelligence failure" was not in reality the result of mere structural incompetence among US intelligence agencies, but rather of the explicit political decisions made by those at the highest political echelons of the Bush-2 regime.[83]

If the aforementioned body of evidence is factually sound, then the following conclusions can be reached with certainty:

> The US intelligence community had sufficient information of an impending al-Qaeda attack, but was unable to undertake preventive action. This data strongly suggests ... that a deliberate decision had been taken by the highest political echelons in Washington to turn a blind eye to accurate intelligence on the impending al-Qaeda terrorist attacks. In other words, the intelligence failure was the inevitable culmination of carefully imposed blocks that restrained agencies from acting on the very clear intelligence received. Those blocks were used for improper political reasons. The Intelligence failure did not pertain to a blinded bureaucracy as such. Indeed, the intelligence community had been struggling against awkward, bizarre, and inexplicable obstructionism originating from the highest levels of government. The failure was therefore a consequence of US government policy.[84]

Under the Bush-2 regime, US government policy was concentrated upon preserving US hegemony over the Middle East and Central Asia because together, these two regions hold over two-thirds of the world's oil and natural gas reserves. In fact,

> after Saudi Arabia, Iran and Iraq are respectively the second and third largest oil producers in the region. Both Iran and Iraq, in accordance with their local interests, are fundamentally opposed to the US drive to secure unimpeded access to regional resources. Iran, for instance, has been attempting to secure

its own interests in Afghanistan and Central Asia, thus coming into direct conflict with regional US interests.[85]

The primary purpose of the Bush-2 regime's war on Iraq was to replace Saddam Hussein with a compliant new regime. After enjoying short-term success in the 2003 Gulf War, Bush declared "Mission Accomplished," but the real mission was only beginning. In order to eliminate other potential regional threats to US hegemony in the region, the Bush-2 regime has also been actively contemplating invasions of Iran, Syria, and other nations.[86]

The *hidden politics of empire* have been at work for decades in keeping the truth about American foreign policy from its own citizens. To keep the American people in the dark about the truth of the JFK assassination, long-term planning for the Vietnam War, another potential invasion of Cuba (*Operation Northwoods*), the true purposes behind the military invasion of the Middle East and Central Asia, and the function of the Anglo-American alliance in furthering Western hegemony into the twenty-first century with endless wars, the Warren Commission and the 9/11 Commission fulfilled their respective duties and their ultimate purpose—to cover up evidence of conspiracy and allow the foreign policy elite of the United States to do what they will.

In assessing the performance of the 9/11 commission, it has been noted:

> The conventional version of events officially espoused by the US state and slavishly repeated by the media and academia fails to account for or explain them. The publication of the findings of the Joint Congressional Inquiry into 9/11 and the Staff Statements and final report of the National Commission has only served to whitewash and ignore many ... salient anomalies ... while avoiding the placement of blame on high-level administration policies.[87]

The cover-up of the truth regarding both the 9/11 attacks and the circumstances surrounding the Kennedy assassination should be understood as manifestations of a policy that has been conducted in the same manner for decades. The 9/11 Commission and the Warren Commission share a great deal in common when it comes to keeping the hidden politics of empire hidden.

ASSASSINATION-POLITICS: REVERSING THE DIRECTION OF US FOREIGN POLICY

The history of the United States in the twentieth century, especially at the close of World War II, opened up a host of unacknowledged programs involving the CIA, drug traffickers, and elements of organized crime that span the globe, including Indochina, Columbia, and Afghanistan.[88] The roots of the Cold War allowed for the growth of linkages between large corporate and banking interests, the ever-expanding American intelligence apparatus, and the international petroleum cartels that were lined up with a bevy of military brass and Mafia chieftains against the policies of the Kennedy brothers. From this perspective, "the death of Robert Kennedy, like that of his brother John, was neither an accident nor a misunderstanding. Both crimes bore the signature of frangible bullets. Both murders were the work of a few men desirous of maintaining the political, social, and economic situations and philosophy of another era."[89]

The planning for Kennedy's execution and the cover-up was elaborately planned. For example, a thorough examination of the hidden post-assassination medical evidence involving President Kennedy's autopsy, X-rays, and witness statements, prove that Kennedy was killed by frangible bullets, otherwise known as dum-dum bullets, or exploding bullets. This means that the ammunition explodes upon impact when it enters the body.[90] The use of this kind of ammunition in combination with the lack of standard protection afforded to the president as a matter of official protocol insured that his murder would be guaranteed. The conspirators made sure that Kennedy was left devoid of any real protection. According to Colonel L. Fletcher Prouty,

> An assassination especially of the chief of state can always be made easier and much more predictable if his routine security forces and their standard policies are removed and canceled. The application of this step in Dallas was most effective. A few examples serve to underscore this phase of the concept:

> 1. The President was in an open, unarmored car.
> 2. The route chosen was along busy streets with many overlooking high buildings on each side.
> 3. Windows in these buildings had not been closed, sealed, and put under surveillance.
> 4. The Secret Service units and trained military units that were required by [standard] regulations to be there were not in place. As a result there was limited ground and building surveillance.
> 5. Sewer covers along the way had not been welded shut.
> 6. The route was particularly hazardous with sharp turns requiring slow speeds, in violation of protection regulations.[91]

With this review of the breakdown of presidential security in Dallas, we can begin to grasp the true nature of the covert and operational side of the hidden mechanisms and mechanics (assassins or "operatives") of empire. The hidden politics of empire involves conspiracy and cover-up. This is a form of hidden politics that requires cover-ups to continue on into the future. Why? Because the hidden politics of empire, once exposed, reveal major policy reversals through undemocratic means and for the achievement of undemocratic ends. Knowledge of this *hidden politics of empire* reveals the true nature of policy choices made by those who are dedicated to private interests, not the public welfare. The hidden politics of empire reveals the covert dominance of elites within the American Establishment who believe that they can remove a president that they disapprove of with total immunity from discovery and prosecution.

It is a story that goes back to Ancient Rome and the forces behind the assassination of Julius Caesar. On this point it is clear that, as with just about every ruling class in history, the Roman nobility reacted fiercely when their interests were infringed upon, especially their untrammeled "right" to accumulate as much wealth as possible at the public's expense. If not their only concern, accumulation was a major preoccupation. In a word, the nobles were less devoted to traditional procedures and laws than to the class privileges those procedures and laws were designed to protect. They never hesitated to depart from their own "hereditary constitution", resorting to acts of bloody repression when expediency dictated. They treated egalitarian reforms and attempts to democratize the Republic's decision-making process as subversive of republican rule.[92]

Kennedy's style of inclusive governance had threatened the wealthy elite of the nation.[93] Kennedy sought universal health care, fought for raising the minimum wage, was genuinely committed to workers' rights and job creation, supported equal pay for equal work, stood up against the steel companies and the oil barons, used the power of the federal government to protect the civil rights of African-Americans, introduced revolutionary civil rights legislation to the Congress in 1963, and sought to end the oil depletion allowance and tax breaks given to offshore accounts. His foreign policy was predicated on approaching problems in stages—moving first to diplomatic solutions and negotiated compromises in order to avoid military confrontations.

Residing at the very heart of the *hidden politics of empire* in the Kennedy years are the following inconvertible facts:

JFK was elected power, they—the Establishment—hereditary. He was public authority, they private power. He spoke for the nation, they for the empires of private wealth and property. He looked forward to continued use of governmental institutions to advance the interests of the people within and outside the United States. They looked to a world in which diminished state power would leave them to dominate a global corporate system free only in the sense of lacking interference from democratic authority. Kennedy sought peace through progress, the Establishment sought peace born of the submission of their opponents. Kennedy encouraged people to think of the United States as a Democratic Republic that needed alert and active citizens. The Establishment promotes a cynical withdrawal into a self-oriented passivity and indifference. Kennedy was the Establishment's nightmare. He was the one, the President or Monarch whose first commitment was to the many, not the few. He was winning—democracy was working. They killed him.[94]

The assassination of President Kennedy was a prerequisite for the Anglo-American Establishment to achieve its primacy objectives, which were diametrically opposed to Kennedy's foreign and domestic policies. The primary objective of the US Global Empire, vis-à-vis the worldview of the Establishment, was to maintain US Global dominance at all costs. Not only was it necessary to have a strong military to repress the aspirations of billions of people throughout the Global Community, but also a strong military meant very high profit margins for

---

The Hidden Politics of Empire

(A)	The Primary Objective	Maintain US Global Dominance
(B)	The Primary Mandate	Undertake any action for war
(C)	JFK Assassination and Gulf of Tonkin	Indochina War/Vietnam War
(D)	9/11 Attacks on WTC and Pentagon	Afghanistan/Iraq War
(E)	Purpose of the Warren Commission	Cover-up
(F)	Purpose of the 9/11 Commission	Cover-up

---

their investors on Wall Streets and those who owned and managed the companies that did billions of dollars worth of business with the Pentagon and CIA.

The primary mandate of the Establishment was to have a president, congress, and bureaucracy that would be compliant enough to take the nation to war under any set of circumstances should their foreign investments be placed at risk (as through nationalization, nationalist movements, or superpower competition). In the Establishment's view, the US Constitution was little more than *a scrap of paper* (a statement originally attributed to Allen Dulles, but also attributed to George W. Bush). If they determined that the nation's Constitutional mandates, system of checks and balances and needed to be overridden, they would arrange to have it done. After all, in their view, Constitutional restrictions on the nation's war power could be removed by providing the American people with a pretext for war. Under certain conditions, they believed that a pretext could and should be created. They felt that it was their class right to make that decision—whenever the elites of the US Establishment determined it was necessary. The fact that Kennedy did not agree with them on this, as well as other issues close to their hearts and interests, was just one more element in writing Kennedy's "death warrant." After all, David and Nelson Rockefeller, as well as the Texas oilmen, had all appealed to Kennedy to reverse his policies over a three-year period, but he had refused. Over the course of Kennedy's legendary "thousand days" they had determined in private conversations and meetings that his recalcitrance would not be tolerated. The captains of industry and finance had an empire to run—by any means necessary.

THE SECRET WAY TO WAR FROM OPERATION NORTHWOODS TO THE DOWNING STREET MEMO: JUSTIFYING WARS AND FIXING INTELLIGENCE

By undertaking state-sponsored conspiracies and cover-ups, the architects of the US Global Empire have engaged in continuous planning and preparation for wars of aggression since at least the early 1950s. Both Eisenhower and Nixon were engaged in planning for the invasion of Cuba long before Kennedy was elected President. Once elected, Kennedy worked to prevent a nuclear war with the USSR over Cuba. In defiance of Kennedy, both the CIA and the Joint Chiefs sought to provoke a war.

Declassified secret documents reveal that top levels of the US military proposed carrying out acts of terrorism within US cities in order to drag the United States into a war against Cuba. In his book, *Body of Secrets*, James Bamford revealed what he called "the most corrupt plan ever created by the US government. In the name of anticommunism, they proposed *launching a secret and bloody war of terrorism against their own country* in order to trick the American public into supporting an ill-conceived war they intended to launch against Cuba" (Italics are mine).[95]

The basic outlines of this plan are similar to some evidence that has surfaced surrounding the 9/11 attacks. In 1962, the Joint Chiefs embarked upon a highly secret and illegal plan

> codenamed *Operation Northwoods* … which had the written approval of the Chairman and every member of the Joint Chiefs of Staff, called for innocent people to be shot on American streets; for boats carrying refugees fleeing Cuba to be sunk on the high seas; for a wave of violent terrorism to be launched in Washington, DC, Miami, and elsewhere. *People would be framed for bombings they did not commit; planes would be hijacked.* Using phony evidence, all of it would be blamed on Castro, thus giving Lemnitzer and his cabal the excuse, as well as the public and international backing, they needed to launch their war (Italics are mine).[96]

The JCS had collectively made a judgment about the Kennedy brothers. In the view of the Chiefs, the Kennedys had "gone soft" on fighting communism. Not only had the president denied the intervention of American forces to rescue the 1961 Bay of Pigs operation, but he and Robert Kennedy had ordered General Lansdale to drop all covert activity and anti-Castro activities that were under a Lansdale supervised program called "Operation Mongoose."[97] In desperation, the JCS recommended to McNamara that bombings, false arrests, and hijackings would be the most convenient way to start a war with Cuba.[98] By March 13, 1962, Lemnitzer conducted meetings on Operation Northwoods with his covert action chief, General Maxwell Taylor—Kennedy's own military representative. Three days later, the president assured him that the United States would never use overt military force in Cuba.[99]

In the aftermath of all these rejections, Lemnitzer tried to destroy all copies of the relevant documents on the operation in fear of a congressional investigation.[100] Yet, some detailed plans for the operation survived. The reason for the survival of these documents is that plans had been drawn prior the Kennedy inauguration by officials in the Eisenhower/Nixon administration. Additional plans had been developed since that time. So, "even after Lemnitzer lost his job, the Joint Chiefs kept planning 'pretext' operations at least into 1963."[101]

In retrospect, the newly discovered documents on Operation Northwoods provide evidentiary support to the long-held suspicion that the 1964 Gulf of Tonkin incident—the spark for the Vietnam War—was "largely staged or provoked by US officials in order to build up congressional and public support for the American involvement."[102] In any case, it is damning evidence that top officials in the US government were more than capable of such deceit. Such damning evidence has also become available with respect to FDR's foreknowledge about the Japanese attack on Pearl Harbor, as revealed in Robert Stinnett's book entitled, *Day of*

Deceit: The Truth About FDR and Pearl Harbor. In other words, the basic plan or *modus operandi* for establishing a pretext for war has existed from administration to administration. The explosion that blew up the Maine was probably staged in order to start the Spanish American War, just as Pearl Harbor, Operation Northwoods, the Gulf of Tonkin incident, and the 9/11 attacks were most likely allowed to proceed with the intention of taking the United States to war.[103]

Based upon this existing history and implicit circumstantial evidence, there is a great likelihood that the assassination of President Kennedy may have been an outgrowth of a collaboration between right-wing and extremist elements in the Pentagon, CIA, and the oil industry. Each particular group had its own agenda, but for the sake of removing Kennedy, they could come together in a coalition to assassinate the president and then proceed with their own private agenda. As far as the Pentagon was concerned, Kennedy simply did not understand how to win the Cold War militarily. In this regard, "Dallas was the consequence of extremist Cold War elements who were convinced that Kennedy was a 'no-win' leader when it came to the 'Castro problem' and therefore had to be removed from office before the communist government in Cuba could be uprooted."[104]

What the hidden events of 1963 also reveal is that the problem of the CIA's unrestricted covert operations was not limited to Cuba. In June 1963, Kennedy had delayed authorization for *any* action against North Vietnam. Yet, "North Vietnamese and right-wing US sources agree that in this very month of June 1963 covert operations against North Vietnam were resumed by South Vietnamese commandoes." These actions "had the approval of General Harkins in Saigon, but not ... of President Kennedy."[105] It was as if a shadow government worked behind the scenes of official Washington without specific authorization from the elected civilian leadership. Under these circumstances, President Kennedy was being marginalized by the insubordination of his own bureaucracy.

The evidence suggests that in late 1963, "covert operations were beginning to escape political limitations, both internal and international ... established during the course of the Kennedy Administration."[106] Further, the available evidence shows that "covert operations may have been escalated in defiance of the President's secret directives."[107] This internal bureaucratic and military defiance to Kennedy was evident in the manipulation of intelligence in order to influence public policy. A significant source of defiance is discernable in the role played by the Director of the CIA, John McCone. Those elements in the US government who wanted to go to war in Vietnam were determined not to let a "weak president" stand in the way of how they thought the Cold War struggle against Communism should be waged. The difference between Kennedy's NSAM 263 (favoring an actual withdrawal of American forces), and NSAM 273 (a joint product of the Pentagon, CIA, and some elements of Kennedy's own inner-circle), points toward serious inconsistencies and contradictions between pre-assassination and post-assassination Vietnam policy. In this drama, the Pentagon Papers seem to indicate "someone is being carefully protected by the censorship of NSAM 273, and by the concealment of the way in which the assassination of President Kennedy affected the escalation of the Indochina war. It is almost certain that McCone, perhaps the leading hawk in the Kennedy entourage, played a role in this secret policy reversal."[108]

REFLECTIONS ON THE COLLAPSE OF
DEMOCRATICALLY ELECTED LEADERSHIP AND
THE HIJACKING OF US FOREIGN POLICY

In the absence of democratic accountability and a viable system of checks and balances, appointments to top-level positions in the executive branch demonstrate that those who are chosen for those posts are either multimillionaires who are well connected to Corporate America, or ideologues carrying out an antidemocratic agenda. As the Bush-2 regime has demonstrated, environmental and energy politics have been taken hostage by a Republican war on science that intentionally distorts the dangers of global warming and climate change as well as mercury both in vaccines and in water supplies, rivers, and oceans.[109] The neoconservative influence in the Bush-2 regime is especially felt in the arena of foreign policy. However, the American foreign policy establishment, both the Republican and Democratic elements of it, has largely been taken over by elite think tanks and Establishment centers of thought—as is the case with the Council on Foreign Relations.[110]

Alternatively, the democratic impulse is alive and active wherever deliberative democracy is employed to solve practical problems.[111] Deliberative democracy dramatically opens up the possibility for progressive changes in popular preferences. As those preferences become materialized in votes, shifts in the power of ideas and shifts of office holders become inevitable. Rather than being a prescription for democratic collapse, deliberative democracy rescues the public business from private abuse and miscalculation. In that regard, scholars have now determined that democratic collapses are caused less by changes in popular preferences than by the actions of political elites.[112] Until the glaring imbalances of undemocratic power and purpose are redressed, the US Global Empire will remain on a rampage until it either breaks under the weight of its own contradictions or is challenged by a competing power or coalition of powers.

Having briefly reviewed the hidden history of the US Global Empire that has led to this *New World Order*, (or more properly, New World Disorder), it is possible to understand some of the fundamental reasons why the United States has taken an imperial course over the last 40 years, conducted cover-ups of state crimes, and hid the evidence of complicity by high-ranking Establishment figures, and corporate leaders in the military industrial complex. A review of the publications and speeches of various Establishment elites over the last 50 years provides a source of primary evidence to support the allegation that America's ruling elites are, for the most part, unrepentant imperialists at heart. Elite distrust of democracy has been clearly expressed in the workings of both the Council on Foreign Relations and the Trilateral Commission, as well as a host of right-wing conservative think tanks.

Both the Warren Commission and the 9/11 Commission, in their findings and conclusions, facilitated the work and goals of the American Establishment. Both commissions succeeded in conducting cover-ups of state crimes by hiding incriminating evidence of complicity in these crimes by high-ranking governmental officials, as well as banking, financial, and corporate giants. In short, these two commissions assisted a handful of the managers of the US Global Empire to escape criminal prosecution for their murderous conspiracies. As a consequence, both the American people and the people of the world have been betrayed. Once freed of the constraints of law and constitutional restraints on the use of power, the imperial elite and their political managers in Washington had effectively started their march down the path of empire—with an *imperial presidency* at the helm.

AN IMPERIAL PRESIDENCY FOR A GLOBAL EMPIRE

Attempts to rein in an antidemocratic imperial presidency have been short-lived. In 1972, the US Congress overrode President Nixon's veto and passed the "War Powers Resolution." It was the beginning of a congressional effort to rein in the war-making power of the chief executive so that no commitment of American troops could be extended beyond 90 days without further congressional authorization. Its importance, as I stated in the conclusion to my 1987 law journal article on the resolution:

> The mandate of the War Powers Resolution reaffirms Congressional power and the Congress' rightful authority to terminate the interventionist policies of an American-Imperium. The effects of the Cold War created an unconstitutional assumption: that Washington's Executive establishment could act in the arena of foreign policy oblivious to legal standards that did exist and were enforceable. Yet, because those standards were not enforced, there was "a presumption of legality to the illegal."
>
> A humane role for American democracy must evolve and may evolve in a framework of mutual compliance with the laws of the land and the international community. The War Powers Resolution is more than mere restraint on the prerogatives of the Executive. It should also provide a basis for the actions and the policies of the Executive. When Congress endorses the actions of the President, it must be able to do so knowing that the Constitutional requirements have not been circumvented. Congressional consultation allows political integrity to be manifested in the consultative-process. It acts as a bar to impropriety and poor judgment. It serves to legitimate Presidential action as it also works to assure allies and allay fears of indiscriminate action without reflection. In sum, it restores Constitutional principles to their rightful preeminence.[113]

As my article demonstrates, the War Powers Resolution had been repeatedly violated in the Reagan years. By October 16, 2002, it died under the pen of President George W. Bush, who had just received congressional authorization to do whatever he wanted to do with Iraq.

In late 2002, the members of Congress abandoned both their responsibility and their oath of office under the US Constitution by abandoning the Congressional war power to the discretion of President George W. Bush. The war-making power had again been unconstitutionally transferred from the Congress to the Executive. In so doing, the hidden politics of empire regarding the impending invasion of Iraq were destined to remain in the closet of state secrets, immune from public scrutiny or congressional oversight. According to Professor Peter Irons,

> With every House seat and one-third of the Senate at stake in the November elections, Bush had carefully timed his invasion campaign. On October 2, he submitted to Congress a proposed resolution, authorizing him to employ military force against Iraq ... The resolution cited as justification for its blank-check grant of power all three of the president's repeated charges against the Iraqi regime, including the "brutal repression of its civilian population", its 'capability and willingness to use weapons of mass destruction against other nations and its own people", and its role in "supporting and harboring terrorist organizations'. The House approved the resolution by a vote of 296 to 133, and the Senate followed with the even greater margin of 77 to 23. Virtually all of the House dissenters were Democrats who held safe seats and thus faced little risk of electoral reprisal, while only a single Senate Republican, Lincoln Chafee of Rhode Island, opposed the resolution, which President Bush signed on October 16, 2002.[114]

As with the passage of the war resolution authorizing Bush to employ military force against Iraq, the passage of the USA Patriot Act in the days after 9/11, demonstrates that the Congress ceded to the Executive branch more legal authority than it was entitled to possess. In this regard, "the soul of the Patriot Act is a blind trust in the arbitrary power of federal agents and federal officials. The Bush-Ashcroft steamroller persuaded the legislative branch of government to largely cede both its own role and that of the judicial branch in the American system of checks and balances."[115] By virtue of the congressional surrender of civil liberties on the domestic front, and its surrender of its war power on the foreign front, the Congress of the United States left the vast majority of the American people un-represented.

Domestic policies on the subject of terror are now streamlined to reflect foreign polices on the international front. From employing torture on terrorist suspects to labeling people with the amorphous title of *enemy combatants*, the Bush-2 regime has opened the door on a host of governmental abuses that would no longer allow for dissent, questioning, or debate. A new era of super-patriotism had eclipsed the Bill of Rights, and with those rights the public's right to know what its own government is doing and why. As a consequence of this development, a new era of secrecy threatens the possibility of democratic governance and accountability. According to Professor Geoffrey Stone,

> Excessive secrecy has been a consistent feature of the Bush administration, ranging from its refusal to disclose the names of those it detained after September 11 and its narrowing of the Freedom of Information Act, to its unprecedented closure of deportation proceedings and its redaction of "sensitive" information from tens of thousands of government documents and Web sites. Some degree of secrecy in the interest of national security is, of course, essential, especially in wartime. But the Bush administration's obsessive secrecy effectively constrains oversight by both the press and the public and directly undermines the vitality of democratic governance.[116]

FASCISM COMES TO AMERICA

The issue of a constitutionally guaranteed right to privacy under the 4th Amendment—versus an expansive view of presidential power in a time of terrorist threat and war in Iraq and Afghanistan—broke into the open in December 2005. Shortly before Christmas 2005, it was revealed that President Bush had authorized the NSA to wiretap and spy on American citizens without first obtaining a warrant from a court. As the year of 2006 began, Congressional leaders were vowing to hold a hearing on the matter. A constitutional crisis was starting to emerge that would invariably resurrect issues associated with how the United States was led into the Iraq War and how the USA Patriot Act was increasingly seen as a domestic threat to the integrity of America's civil liberties.

In the aftermath of the 9/11 attacks, the Bush-2 regime has purposefully and effectively begun to build more layers in the foundation for an American Global Empire. The reason for this approach to governance should be clear in light of the foregoing discussion on the War Powers Resolution and the USA Patriot Act. No political unit is better equipped to undertake such an approach to foreign policy than an empire. The main reason for this assertion is that an empire, whether operating directly or indirectly, would not be subject to democratic constraints. Additionally, in order to maintain the kind of long-term hegemony that the architects of the US Global Empire seek, it is also necessary to put into place imperial garrisons and bases that can be depended upon for decades to ensure order and stability in key strategic regions of the world. At home, it is necessary to control the news and the media, keep a lid on domestic dissent, and invoke the claim of national security in order to maintain absolute secrecy.

With the passage of the new "anti-terrorist" legislation, the USA Patriot Act now criminalizes peaceful anti-globalization protests. Demonstrations against the IMF, WTO, or World Bank, are now considered "a crime of domestic terror." Under the USA Patriot Act, "domestic terrorism" includes any activity which could lead to "influencing the policy of a government by intimidation or coercion."[117] Under this Nazi-like cloud of intolerance resides an expanded police and spying power for the FBI and CIA. The US intelligence community is, in many respects, more in fear of what American citizens are up to than the terrorists who are supposed to be after them.

A major reason for this empowerment of the FBI and CIA comes from the neoconservative orientation of the Bush-2 regime. The neoconservative view agrees with Trotsky's idea of a permanent revolution. In the neoconservative mind-set, the US government should conceptualize the war on terror as a permanent war. Equipped with an image of a permanent, unending, and enduring war on terrorism, the neoconservative view demonstrates a conscious willingness to suspend constitutional freedoms and protections. From this perspective, the official view of how the law should now be employed makes law's past precedents both impractical and *quaint*. Certainly, after public revelations about the unrestricted use of torture techniques at Abu Ghraib prison and Guantanemo, the new atmosphere of fear mixed with a desire for revenge has afforded some neoconservatives the chance to express this view publicly. The boundaries established by the Geneva

Convention on Torture and the protections of the US Constitution are to be suspended. Now, they assert, the war on terrorism is a war without boundaries. A similar contempt for the nation's declared enemy had been expressed by some in the American military in World War II—as when, in an internal memorandum in January 1942, Admiral William D. Leahy, chair of the Joint Chiefs of Staff, wrote that "in fighting with Japanese savages all previously accepted rules of warfare must be abandoned."[118]

In the period of 2001–2006, the Bush-2 regime would transform Admiral Leahy's attitude into State policy for the new war on terrorism. The CIA and Pentagon were about to be authorized to take torture to the legal extremes and beyond. The new Bush-approved policies would transcend all previous legal boundaries when it came to the question of the use of torture techniques. In its own tortured logic, the Bush administration relied on its legal counsel in the Department of Justice and CIA to guide it through the murky waters of legal prohibitions against torture techniques so that it could employ torture techniques with virtual impunity. In the name of fighting terrorism, the Bush-2 regime began to engage in its own brand of terrorism around the globe.

"BLOWBACK"—THE UNINTENDED CONSEQUENCES OF US FOREIGN POLICY

Along with periodic changes in the rules of warfare, a strategy of setting up imperial garrisons and bases around the world has been the long-term goal of US military planners since World War II. Still, as geostrategic priorities shift throughout time, so will the basing requirements of the empire. Hence, the Pacific-Asian basing strategy has now a diminished emphasis insofar as the Persian Gulf and Eurasian arenas are the empire's primary concern at the dawn of the twenty-first century. Such a strategy requires new wars and new enemies. Former allies in the proxy war against the Soviets in the Afghanistan of the 1980s (al-Qaeda) have, since the events of 9/11, now been transformed into the enemies of the American Empire in the "war on terror."[119]

Comprehending the evolution of this history is important, for it reveals the *blowback effect* of foreign policy. Throughout the 1980s, CIA covert support to the "Islamic Jihad" (*or holy war against the Soviets*) operated indirectly through the Pakistani ISI. Operating under President Reagan's National Security Directive 166, which authorized increased military aid to the Mujahideen. The secret Afghan war had a new goal—to defeat the Soviets in Afghanistan through covert action. It was hoped that the ultimate result would be a Soviet withdrawal. To that end, the CIA, using Pakistan's ISI also played a key role in training the Mujahideen. In fact, the CIA-sponsored guerilla training was integrated with the teachings of Islam. Wahabi fundamentalists set up the madrasas (schools). Most of the funding came through Saudi Arabi. From these schools, which could be numbered in the thousands, the germs of the Taliban emerged.[120] The dominant themes that were taught at these schools were "that Islam was a complete sociopolitical ideology, that holy Islam would be violated by atheistic Soviet troops, and that the Islamic people of Afghanistan should reassert their independence by overthrowing the leftist Afghan regime propped up by Moscow."[121] In the after-math of the Soviet withdrawal from Afghanistan, it would be difficult to turn off these Pakistani-CIA-trained terrorists. The problem of closing down this kind of enterprise is what former CIA Director Allen Dulles called a *disposal problem*— in reference to the anti-Castro Cubans after the disaster at the Bay of Pigs.

In the early 1980s, the Reagan administration had a two-pronged strategy in advancing the "Islamic Jihad"—one was to destabilize the pro-Soviet government in Afghanistan, while the other was to destroy the Soviet Union itself. US policy makers reasoned that if the Soviet Union could be bankrupted by a Vietnam-like war in Afghanistan and, at the same time, economically drained by attempting to keep up with American spending on the arms race it was only a question of time before the USSR would fall apart.

In what would become the last decade of the Cold War, the struggle of two superpowers for spheres of influence in the Third World also remained an impor-tant goal. After all, it was the natural resources of Afghanistan that drew the Soviets into their war in the first place. *Business Week* magazine reported in its September 29, 1980 issue:

> Hunger for Afghanistan's important and strategic minerals was an incentive for the Soviet invasion and attempt to annex Kabul to the Soviet Bloc. This can be surmised from a three-year old geological study by Russian experts ... .The report makes clear that Afghanistan possesses a broad spectrum of minerals, in addition to its well-known oil and natural gas deposits, which the Soviet Union and the Communist block badly need.[122]

In an inset, the editors of *Business Week* included a map of Afghanistan show-ing where its reserves of copper, oil, gas, bauxite, beryl, iron ore, fluorspar, coal, and chrome were located. What the map did not reveal was Afghanistan's rich trade in opium. In fact, "the multi-billion dollar revenues of narcotics are deposit-ed in the Western banking system. Most of the large international banks—togeth-er with their affiliates in the offshore banking haven—launder large amounts of narco-dollars. Therefore, the international trade in narcotics constitutes a multi-billion dollar business of the same order of magnitude as the international trade in oil ... geopolitical control over 'the drug routes' is as strategic as oil pipelines."[123]

When viewed from the perspective of the *hidden politics of empire*, a common theme emerges from an examination of US foreign policy in the twentieth and twenty-first centuries: both drugs and oil have been at the center of profit-making, colonial adventures, and geostrategic imperatives. On May 28, 1939, Secretary of State Cordell Hull observed: "Great as are the material resources with which our country is endowed, they are not sufficient to enable us as a nation to meet the needs of our people."[124] Hull's observation came at an historical juncture when "the United States' rapid transition from an agrarian society to an industrial powerhouse in the early 20th century fundamentally transformed its international economic position."[125]

Hull's views not only shaped American foreign policy for decades to come, but his views also contributed to an American foreign policy that would result in the "blowback effect"—negative consequences arising from imperial adventures to secure strategic resources and set up military bases to secure them against all potential competitors. In a certain sense, Hull's perspective, later adopted by Roosevelt, Truman, Eisenhower, Johnson, Nixon, Carter, Reagan, Bush (1) and (2), shaped some of the underlying assumptions about America's definition of its geostrategic imperatives and how best to achieve them. The only twentieth century president to disagree with Hull's unconditional approach was John F. Kennedy.

AN ENDLESS STRUGGLE TO ACQUIRE
STRATEGIC RESOURCES: AMERICAN PLANNING FOR
WAR WITHOUT END FROM WORLD WAR II TO THE PRESENT

As the century progressed into the early 1930s, the Roosevelt administration was beginning to express concerns of its own about the availability of "strategic" materials—meaning that they were "essential to national defense." In 1933, "the War Department published its Revised Industrial Mobilization Plan, which addressed the problem of raw material scarcity. The War Department classified twenty-six different primary products as 'strategic'."[126] By late 1941, a confidential State Department analysis entitled, *Japan versus the United States*, concluded that the nation could not afford to have its military and industrial capacity left "at the mercy of Japan" lest the world balance of power shift irrevocably.[127] This perspective would continue to exercise powerful influence over US policy in Asia. In July 1949, "the National Security Council concluded that in pursuing control of Southeast Asia, 'the Kremlin is, of course, motivated in part by a desire to acquire SEA's resources and communications lines, but its immediate and perhaps even greater desire is to deny them to us'. The State Department warned in 1951 that 'the fall of Indochina to communism would also pave the way for aggression against Indochina's neighbors', who supplied '80 percent of the free world's supply of natural rubber and half of its tin. The loss of these resources would be serious to the free world and would enormously increase the military capabilities of the Communist bloc'."[128]

The aforementioned viewpoints are not just attributable to the State Department and National Security Council. These views were endemic to the military culture of the Pentagon and the national security bureaucracy as a whole. The historical record of 1961 demonstrates that "the US national security bureaucracy had come to regard the maintenance of the political-military status-quo as a vital interest."[129] Maintaining the status quo also meant rejecting "neutralism" anywhere in the world. This was the bureaucracy that Kennedy inherited from the Eisenhower administration. It was also endemic to a CIA bureaucracy. The CIA warned, just a few days before Kennedy took office, that unless reversed, the trend toward neutralism in the developing world would result in the West losing both the support and the resources of many nations in the Third World. To prevent such a trend from going any further had become the primary mission of national security officials who were committed to resisting such an outcome— whether that trend was to be initiated from Third World states or from President Kennedy himself.[130]

Once inaugurated, Kennedy began what would be a three-year bureaucratic war with the Joint Chiefs and the CIA. Kennedy's decisions on the Bay of Pigs, the Cuban Missile Crisis, the issue of US involvement in Vietnam and Indochina were all subject not only to criticism from within his administration, but outright insubordination. A 2005 study on civil-military relations examines the Pentagon and the Presidency from FDR to George W. Bush. By far, Kennedy's presidency had the most contentious, difficult, and antithetical clash of cultures recorded in that time frame. In sum, the military viewed Kennedy as a president who constantly violated military culture. In turn, Kennedy viewed the chiefs as "political Neanderthals unequipped to function in the world of politics and diplomacy."[131]

Politics and diplomacy means the ability to think seriously about negotiating, reach a political settlement, and finding and maintaining effective diplomatic channels. A national security bureaucracy rooted in the Cold War upon designs for building a *New World Order*, will probably be recalcitrant toward any other option than a military option—combined with geostrategic considerations. To come to that realization is to come to the point where it is possible to comprehend the distinctiveness of the presidency of John F. Kennedy—especially with regard to the issue of Vietnam. On November 21, 1963, less than 24 hours before he was assassinated in Dallas, Kennedy told Michael Forrestal, the NSC staff specialist on Southeast Asia,

> that he wanted to start "a complete and very profound review of how we got into this country; what we thought we were doing, and what we now think we can do". ... In light of the increased risk of rapid decline of the Saigon government and Kennedy's abiding interest in the diplomatic option, these conversations appear to indicate that he was now thinking seriously about negotiating a political settlement in South Vietnam before the situation had deteriorated too far.[132]

If we contrast Kennedy's approach to world affairs with those of George W. Bush, the differences could not be more dramatic. In June of 1963, Kennedy's speech at American University made clear that the America he envisioned in the world would not seek a *Pax Americana* that would be imposed on the world with American weapons of war. It required Kennedy's assassination to reverse the pledge that he made at American University. Lyndon Johnson and Richard Nixon engaged in Vietnam War spending that actually cost the United States $30 billion a year beyond the normal spending costs of maintaining a national defense. Inflation and unemployment followed. As the Vietnam War budget expenditures rose, the number of unemployed civilians in the labor force declined. The national debt grew while the real growth of GNP slipped downward, well into the 1970s.

Defense contractors and private research and development for the Pentagon, combined to create an emerging form of socialism—referred to as "state capitalism." It characterizes part of the war industry and leads to the kind of war profiteering that characterized the Vietnam War years and currently characterizes the years of the Bush-2 regime since its invasion and occupations of Iraq and Afghanistan. Since 2001, the hidden agenda behind Bush's declaration of an *"axis of evil"* (Iraq, Iran, North Korea, Libya, and Syria) is to create a new legitimacy, opening the door for a "revitalization of the nation's defenses," while also providing various justifications for direct military interventions by the US in different parts of the world. Meanwhile, the shift from civilian to military production pours wealth into the hands of defense contractors at the expense of civilian needs.[133]

As in Lyndon Johnson's experience with the unraveling of the Vietnam War, the 2005 assessment of the US Empire's ability to win a war in Iraq is in doubt. The cover story for *Time*, September 26, 2005, is headlined with a question: *"Iraq: Is It Too Late To Win the War?"* The violence of the insurgency continues to grow unabated. Further, Iraq experts in the intelligence community believe the proposed constitution could heighten the chances for an outright civil war.[134] A US senior retired military official is quoted at the conclusion of the article as saying: "We have never taken this operation seriously enough ... We have never provided enough troops. We have never provided enough equipment, or the right kind of equipment. We have never worked the intelligence part of the war in a serious, sustained fashion. We have failed the Iraqi people, and we have failed our troops."[135]

The officer's gloomy assessment is strikingly similar to historical assessments of the 1966 situation in Vietnam. According to one historian:

Rather than adapt to the political-economic-military realities of the war, Westmoreland, Wheeler, and Sharp were, in essence, forcing the president to choose between a politically difficult, if not impossible, escalation, or continued stasis. Since Johnson was no more likely than the brass to reevaluate the war or his commitment to the RVN, and was, if anything, more aware of the domestic ramifications of both escalation and failure, America's service chiefs had put the ball into the White House's court. With American forces unlikely to attain success in Vietnam, civilian and military leaders were scrambling to avoid blame in Washington.[136]

Further, in both the case of Vietnam and that of Iraq, the fundamental questions about why the United States intervened at all were never truthfully addressed in public by official Washington. Neither was an "exit-strategy."

IN THE SHADOW OF DALLAS: THE LEGACY
OF THE KENNEDY ASSASSINATION AND THE ROAD
TO WAR WITHOUT END

In order to open the path to long-term goals such as access to raw materials and resources for energy, the architects of the US Global Empire will always require a pretext for future wars, a loosening on the restraints of democratic accountability, and developing a culture of secrecy within government. The pretext allowed the architects of the US Global Empire to remove the last remaining obstacles to their plans for achieving US global dominance. The last remaining democratic constraints on the road to war were severed.[137] In the case of the Kennedy assassination, the door was opened for a possible attack on Russia and/or Cuba in retaliation for the assassination. It also made possible the entry of a new president who did not share Kennedy's reluctance to commit American combat troops to Southeast Asia. In either scenario, the architects of the US Global Empire were prepared to launch a war.

First, the scenario involving a re-invasion of Cuba was the Cold War dream-war for highly placed officials such as Desmond FitzGerald and William Harvey in the CIA, the Chair of the JCS, General Lyman Lemnitzer, and other right-wing elements in the military intelligence communities. Collectively, they expressed the view that Kennedy's 1962 "no-invasion pledge" to the Cuban government was tantamount to giving Castro an intolerable degree of sanctuary.[138] Additionally, just a few days before his trip to Dallas, Kennedy instructed William Attwood to travel to Cuba in order to initiate a normalization of relations with Castro's government by offering to lift the US embargo. In so doing, Kennedy hoped that the "fruits of such a détente would be the satisfaction of wooing Castro away from the Soviet orbit and shifting the domestic balance of power within Cuba away from hard-liners such as Raul Castro and Che Guevara."[139]

For the hard-liners in Kennedy's administration, such as the CIA stalwarts in the Harvey-FitzGerald faction, they were still determined to get revenge for the Bay of Pigs with a re-invasion of Cuba. These CIA men also let their anti-Castro exiles know what Kennedy intended to do. For these reasons, it has been suggested "Kennedy may have crossed his Rubicon when he gave the green light to Attwood and a policy of accommodation with Cuba's leader."[140] In terms of the Kennedy conspiracy itself, "as soon as Oswald was charged with Kennedy's murder, the CIA surreptitiously launched a disinformation campaign in the national press to convince the public that the assassin was linked to the Castro government."[141] In such a highly charged atmosphere, such an allegation—if believed—could have served as a pretext for war. If the United States went to war over Cuba on such a trumped up claim, it might also have resulted in World War III.[142]

Second, the desire to have Kennedy removed from the presidency so that the United States could go to war in Vietnam and the rest of Indochina supplies the other interrelated motive for the Kennedy assassination conspiracy and cover-up (an outline of this scenario has already been discussed throughout this chapter). Suffice it to say that "the assassination of John F. Kennedy and the entrance of a new president into the White House dramatically increased the distorting effects of the aggressive role of national security advisors on Vietnam policy."[143] It is also important to re-emphasize the fact that Kennedy was virtually alone and isolated in his government by virtue of his opposition to introducing US combat troops to a land war in Asia. Kennedy's abbreviated presidency is a record of a leader who was constantly at odds with the CIA, JCS, and right-wing elements throughout the government, corporate America, Wall Street, and the radical right.

Ominously, "by the time Kennedy entered the White House high officials in the Defense and State Departments and the White House Office of National Security Affairs, as well as the JCS were asserting their primacy in making Vietnam policy … That pattern became openly more pronounced over the course of 1961."[144]

In Kennedy's first year as president he carried out his own policy regarding the neutralization of Laos. Key officials in all of the aforementioned departments "were outraged that Kennedy was making an end run around them. Many of them considered that he was selling out a US ally to the Soviet bloc."[145] Then, in November 1961, Kennedy tried to compromise with the hawks in his administration on the issue of combat troops in Vietnam, "but he made it clear that he would approve the use of combat troops only under diplomatic circumstances that every-one knew were prohibitive. That decision shocked his national security advi-sors."[146] Three years later, in November 1963, he was determined never to introduce US combat troops into Vietnam and began the planning for the phased withdrawal of all American advisors by early 1965. The historical record is also clear about the fact that "in late 1963, as conflict with the Administration intensi-fied over Vietnam, Cuba, and the future of the Cold War, the various fronts merged into a polarized contest between the supporters of the President and of the Vice-President."[147] At that moment in time he was assassinated. With Kennedy's death, the growth of the imperial presidency would exceed all past imagined boundaries under the tutelage of Lyndon Johnson and Richard Nixon.

It became the primary job of the Warren Commission to dispel any rumors or evi-dence of conspiracy. The Warren Commission was given not merely a mandate to investigate the assassination of President Kennedy, but the official conclusion as well—a lone assassin was to be found responsible for the murder. As a consequence of adopting this foregone conclusion, the responsible individuals and groups involved in the planning, conspiracy, and cover-up avoided exposure and prosecution.[148]

After the assassination, the national security bureaucracy and some of his clos-est advisors were allowed to reverse his policies—without question or debate. A silent transfer of power was made possible once the gunshots of Dallas ceased to echo. The dramatic policy alterations and reversals between Kennedy's NSAM 263 and Johnson's NSAM 273 regarding US intentions for Vietnam (signed by Johnson just 48 hours after the assassination), is a sinister historical fact that is not even acknowledged within the Pentagon Papers. After all, Kennedy had attempt-ed to reshape US foreign policy. He wanted to move US foreign policy away from the neocolonialist and imperialist policies that were romanticized by Establishment figures like John J. McCloy and Allen Dulles.

Kennedy had traveled to Asia as a US Congressman and as a US Senator. In his Senate speeches and his book, *The Strategy of Peace*, he discussed the difficulties of fighting in Asia where the enemy is simultaneously everywhere and nowhere. Yet, even more fundamentally, Kennedy identified the revolutionary struggle from colonial rule in Asia with the experience of the American Revolution. What he acknowledged was that it was wrong to confuse the fight against Communism with a nationalist revolution seeking to shake off former colonial masters. Kennedy's visionary hopes and policies for the image and the substance of American foreign policy were designed to make the United States more than a replacement power for French and British colonial policies in the Third World. In Asia, Africa, and Latin America, new and younger leaders were coming to power that did not share the fears and suspicions of the past. As one of those young leaders, neither did he.

Dulles and McCloy represented the views of Wall Street. As members of the traditional Establishment, they wanted: (1) economic stability (Kennedy sought to stimulate the economy and move it in a more equitable direction); (2) trade and markets (Kennedy wanted cooperation and investment); (3) maximizing the freedom of personal interests (Kennedy sought national progress through science, technology, education, and opportunity).[149] In the final analysis, McCloy was an agent of powerful cliques based in inherited wealth. McCloy was Chairman of the Council on Foreign Relations. He also served as head of one of the Morgan-Rockefeller network's most important banks, the Chase Manhattan.[150] In 1964, both McCloy and Dulles were called on by President Johnson to serve on the Warren Commission—charged with the task of investigating the murder of John F. Kennedy—their sworn enemy. It was even more ironic that Dulles, the man whom Kennedy had fired as CIA director after the Bay of Pigs fiasco, was now a formal member of an official government commission dedicated to the task of investigating the forces responsible for Kennedy's assassination.

As the Warren Commission was completing its work, the US Constitution's war power was in the process of being transferred from Congress to the Executive vis-à-vis the Tonkin Gulf Resolution. With its enactment, the Tonkin Gulf Resolution provided Lyndon Johnson with the ability to commit American troops to the quagmire of Vietnam. At the same time he consigned over 3 million Asians to die as a result of US military actions in a land war and air campaign of carpet bombings (that exceeded all of the tonnage dropped in World War II) throughout North and South Vietnam. Under Nixon, the war was illegally extended into Laos, Cambodia, and Thailand. With Nixon's withdrawal strategy of "Vietnamization," (South Vietnamese be trained to take the place of American soldiers), all that changed was the skin color of the war's body count—fewer Americans, but more Asians.[151]

Despite the success of keeping secret the Kennedy assassination conspiracy and cover-up, the ugly manifestations of that transfer of power have continued to surface and trouble every successive presidential administration. The democratically elected government was overthrown by a conspiracy and the new *officially installed* government covered up the true nature of the crime—as well as the Mafia's role and the governmental and Establishment officials behind it. The crime was whitewashed by an official cover-up that included forged assassination photos and films, forged autopsy pictures, and eventually the involvement of *The Journal of the American Medical Association* (1992), attempting to lend support to the Warren Commission's conclusion that Oswald "acted alone." All this proceeded despite the fact that there remains a conflict in the medical evidence between the doctors at the Bethesda Naval Hospital and the doctors at Parkland Hospital in Dallas. The medical reports from Bethesda and Parkland recount totally different descriptions of the president's wounds and probable trajectories.[152]

In November 1963, an illegal and violent transition of power was undertaken by men who were hostile to the constraints and requirements of constitutional government in the United States. President Lyndon Johnson worked throughout 1964 to reverse his predecessor's foreign policy goals in Latin America and Vietnam. Domestically, he failed to act on Kennedy's pledge to remove the oil-depletion allowance from the US Tax Code. Rather, oil interests, banking and financial groups, and the military were about to reap gigantic private profits from their participation in the Vietnam War. As the war began to drain the financial resources of Johnson's *Great Society* the problems of poverty and unemployment were addressed at the margins, while the structural problems remained endemic to the system.

An enormous transfer of wealth was leaving the Northeast (*called the rustbelt in the Reagan years*) as the federal budget began to reflect the political changes resulting from the Kennedy assassination. Now, instead of addressing the problems of poverty and unemployment, the federal budget was directed to companies and corporations throughout the southern rim of the United States (from Florida, through Texas, and into Southern California). Among the beneficiaries of governmental largesse were aerospace firms and corporations. Lockheed Martin, Boeing, Raytheon, and TRW would reap enormous windfall profits as they were contracted by the Pentagon to work on NMD, the fantasy of Edward Teller and Ronald Reagan. It was all part of the way that the domestic game of empire was played.

It was a world in which white collar crime would bring rewards to top executives as they engaged in managing cost overruns. It was becoming a socioeconomic world in which corporate fraud would be given a slap on the wrist by the Department of Justice and the GAO, and routinely ignored by the Pentagon. On the other hand, common criminals wound up imprisoned for life on the legal shoals' new sentencing guidelines that required *mandatory minimums* and *three strikes* legislation. The *prison-industrial-complex* was starting to warehouse the poor, the minorities, and the excluded of American society. The compassion for the oppressed that resonated during the decade of the Kennedy brothers and Dr. King was now effectively silenced.

Increasingly, the hidden power structure of corporate interests that had been tied to a permanent war economy began to mutate in the successive decades. The Nixon-Kissinger supported overthrow of the democratically elected government of Salvador Allende in Chile, the illegal bombing and subsequent genocide in Cambodia, the Watergate scandal, the Iran/Contra Affair, the Savings & Loan Scandal, and the corporate thievery and collapse of Enron are all examples of the mutation of private power, privilege, and wealth in the American political economy. Yet, nowhere has this trend been more documented than with regard to the petroleum industry.[153] And, in no other administration has the power and influence of big oil been greater on both foreign and domestic politics and policy than in the Bush-Cheney administration.

THE BUSH-2 REGIME DESIGNS AN ENERGY
POLICY FOR MIDDLE EAST DEPENDENCY

To develop a new plan for a new era, the National Energy Policy Development Groups (NEPDG) was created by the President George W. Bush and Vice President Cheney. Only 4 months into his administration, Bush ordered the group to complete its work by May 2001.[154] As NEPDG began its work in February 2001, it had one of two choices. First, the United States could continue consuming increasing amounts of petroleum and pay the price for a greater dependency on imports. In the alternative, the second choice would enforce strict energy conservatism, encourage the use of fuel-efficient vehicles, and promote renewable energy resources.[155] No one doubted which path the Bush-2 regime would choose—especially with Dick Cheney at the helm.

After meeting with 109 representatives of energy firms between January and May 2001, (including Chevron, Texaco, Exxon, Mobil, and Enron), NEPDG chose to perpetuate dependency.[156] This decision automatically triggered demands for an increase in the defense budget insofar as "the authors of the NEP were perfectly aware how vulnerable the global oil trade is to serious disruption, especially in the Persian Gulf."[157] The only real question that arose was "whether America was prepared to assume the endless and inescapable bloody task of policing overseas oil zones."[158] The answer would come in the days immediately after September 11, 2001. For the events of 9/11 would provide the Bush-2 regime with a pretext for war in the Middle East. The US takeover of Central Asia would start in October 2001. For "as soon as the bombing campaign commenced, the Bush administration began pursing the principal interests that had motivated its pre-9/11 regional war plans."[159]

The presidents who have followed Kennedy have all been obedient to the mandates of the oilmen and the requirements of the petroleum industry in all the US government's geostrategic discussions. Instead of presidential leadership, the nation has been introduced to successive presidential scandals, including President Nixon's near impeachment (the product of Watergate). During the presidency of Jimmy Carter, while there were no major scandals, there was the development of the Carter Doctrine, which anticipated the use of US forces in taking over Middle Eastern oil fields as a matter of national security. Since the birth of the Carter Doctrine, its basic principles have been increasingly incorporated into US government policy, thereby turning the US military into the guardians of private oil reserves or, in the alternative, the force to take them away from those who own them through a permanent occupation of strategic fields throughout the Middle East. In the 1980s, President Reagan sought to avoid possible impeachment hearings as a result of the political minefield of the Iran-Contra Scandal. Out of the scandal came the Iran/Contra Report as well as the report of Special Counsel, Lawrence Walsh. Indictments were eventually handed down, but President George W. Bush pardoned former Secretary of Defense under Reagan and other top-ranking officials—in fact, some have been appointed to key positions in the George W. Bush administration. In both the case of Watergate and Iran/Contra, the major perpetrators were pardoned and large segments of the truth remained buried. Following in the footsteps of the Warren Commission, the conduct of the US government had become *government-by-damage-control*.

By the time of the presidential election of 2000, not even the voters would ultimately matter. George W. Bush would be installed (not elected) by the US Supreme Court into the office of President of the United States.[160] The legacy of the Kennedy assassination left a power structure in place wherein the special interests of Texas dominate and rule in American political life.[161] George W. Bush is a product of this culture. In his worldview and in his policies he is the heir of the

Southern conservatives who once dominated the right wing of the Democratic Party. The combination of repressive economic policies, religious fundamentalism, and aggressive militarism has long characterized the state of Texas. Now it threatens the future of the United States and the world.[162]

THE DEVASTATION OF THE GLOBAL COMMUNITY
BY THE US GLOBAL EMPIRE: THE BIRTH AND
THE ASCENDANCY OF THE IMF, WORLD BANK, WTO,
AND THE WESTERN BANKING/FINANCIAL ESTABLISHMENT

Beginning in 1965 and continuing unabated through the 1990s, the US Global Empire has ravaged the Third World with endless wars, low-intensity conflict, opposition to land reform, and numerous struggles for strategic resources. With the most recent phase of this period, commencing with the Bush-2 regime in 2001, the history of the last four decades can be seen as virtually littered with the debris of what could have been an ascendant and peaceful Global Community. It has been eclipsed by the lawless exercise of raw power (both militarily and financially) of the US Global Empire.[163]

As investments in the American war machine have grown, needed funding has been drained away from debt relief in Africa and Latin America.[164] This has been especially the case in Latin America where Latin American elites could usually count on US tolerance toward economically regressive and even politically authoritarian regimes.[165] The one recent exception to this approach was President John F. Kennedy's program—the Alliance for Progress (the *Charter of Punta del Este*—1961). Kennedy recognized that social and institutional reform must precede economic growth, for economic growth cannot be an end in itself.

JOHN KENNEDY'S "ALLIANCE FOR PROGRESS"

Under Kennedy's direction, the Alliance represented an historic effort to unite the economic, political, and social aspects of development. In other words, it did not begin and end with a purely economic prescription that would only serve the interests of landed oligarchs in Latin America and US investors and businessmen. Kennedy's Alliance was dedicated to poverty alleviation and social justice through genuine land redistribution, helping the urban and rural poor, stimulating progress in education, health, and housing. Kennedy's approach was a working, inclusive, and democratic effort to begin building a nonexploitative Global Community throughout the Americas. That spirit and direction died with him in Dallas. It would be left to his brother, Robert Kennedy, to articulate the meaning and purpose of the Alliance as it was originally conceived. As Kennedy gave voice to the original purposes of the Alliance, he also voiced his own and often more radical description of its goals. In doing so, Robert Kennedy made clear his opposition to a political and economic status quo that was supported by both Latin American oligarchs and the American power structure that was dominated by President Lyndon Johnson and David and Nelson Rockefeller.

Writing in 1967 about his late brother's intentions for the Alliance, Robert Kennedy asserted: "There is no such thing as 'pure' economic development in Latin America. Development depends on change—on new balances of wealth and power between men. Economic development requires hard political decisions; it depends on political leadership, political development, and political change."[166] This view was not shared by the enemies of the Kennedy brothers, as "when David Rockefeller observed in 1966 with great satisfaction that the Alliance for Progress was no longer what it had been under Kennedy, he was indicating that the challenge to neo-colonialist economic policy was gone ... Kennedy's intention to pursue government to government coordination for development purposes and his determination to avoid using military force to subdue nationalist forces in the Third World caused the Establishment to view him as the major problem in world affairs."[167] The same Establishment hostility that was directed at John Kennedy was directed at Robert Kennedy during the last 4 years of his life. It was understandable because Robert had become even more radical and revolutionary in his identification with the disaffected, the poor, the angry, and the powerless than his brother John. This is also what made Robert Kennedy everything that Nelson Rockefeller was not. The battle lines had been drawn: Kennedy, the US Senator from New York, was at war with Nelson Rockefeller, the Governor of New York.[168]

By 1968, while Nelson championed the "new military in Latin America" and was vigorously working to protect his economic interests in Standard Oil throughout Latin America, Robert Kennedy was supporting popular dissent and rebellion among the poor, farmers, and disaffected peasants in the provinces of Ecuador and Peru. With Peru's nationalization of Standard Oil and its subsequent political drift to the left, some in the Establishment would blame liberals like Senator Robert Kennedy. For others, blame turned into hatred. The "new politics" that Robert Kennedy embodied went beyond the New Deal liberalism of the past. Kennedy was innovative because he viewed his era as revolutionary. Therefore, revolutionary times demanded revolutionary answers. In this new era, as the Rockefellers and Lyndon Johnson remained wedded to the past, the assumptions and prejudices of a bygone era allowed them the comfort of exercising power without reflection. For those who did reflect, think, and imagine a different kind of world, the words of George Bernard Shaw took on a new poignancy: "Some men see things as they are and say why? I dream things that never were and say, why not?" Many leading members of the American Establishment did not want to hear those questions— much less the answers.

As early as 1965, Kennedy had made comments on his tour of Peru about the most fundamental challenge to the sovereignty of the nation of Peru: Standard Oil. Kennedy believed that as long as fair and just compensation was given to Standard Oil, the nationalization of Peru's own resources was a decision that should be left to the people of Peru. To the CIA and the Rockefellers, this stance was unforgivable.[169] Despite the fact that Kennedy supported nationalization, as long as there was just and fair compensation, the reality was that Kennedy's comment sent shockwaves down the spines of oil executives and embassy officials.[170] Despite the anger of the US Establishment, Kennedy stayed on the offensive, challenging the Peruvians to act for themselves:

> I think that the action is up to you people. President Kennedy had to act against some large American firms: Argentina has cancelled its oil contracts; years ago Mexico nationalized its oil, and what happened? It is up to you not to get overwhelmed and to act according to your interests and according with what you consider is most convenient. And nothing can happen, as nothing happened before.[171]

Robert Kennedy's attitude toward the Establishment was hostile. Both the factions of the Democratic Party that supported LBJ and the moderate Republicans who supported Nelson Rockefeller were opposed to many of the policies pursued by the late president. In this political climate, the Rockefellers and President Johnson opposed Robert's efforts to update, radicalize, and expand the Kennedy legacy into the late 1960s. A tremendous cleavage of opinion divided the elites of the American Establishment. The Kennedy brothers were determined, in the words of the Old Testament prophet Isaiah, "to undo the heavy burdens and let the oppressed go free." The Establishment, represented by David and Nelson Rockefeller, as well as Lyndon Johnson, remained determined to leave the burdens alone and not worry too much about oppression in the Third World. The battle between the two camps would not end until an assassin's bullet would take Robert Kennedy's life in June 1968, after claiming victory in the California primary for the Democratic presidential nomination.

The Kennedy brothers, serious about spreading democratic institutions and extending the benefits of social justice investments (health, education, and housing), opposed Latin America's oligarchies, while Johnson and Rockefeller supported them (on behalf of the Establishment's business interests). The Kennedy brothers sought social reform and agrarian reform, while Johnson and Rockefeller opposed these reforms, fearing their economic and political repercussions. The continent's peoples and democratic sectors recognized the Kennedy brothers as allies, friends, and a hope for change. The Kennedy brothers saw the continent's poverty as the greatest threat to its people and to the stability of the entire Western Hemisphere. Johnson and Rockefeller saw the continent's peoples and democratic sectors as a threat to their business interests—especially their oil interests. Perhaps that explains the fact that "when Vice President Lyndon B. Johnson became president, he abandoned the Alliance for Progress and returned to the hard line of interventionism and 'big stick' policies."[172] Johnson's action was a major policy reversal of Kennedy's program and the hopes generated by the Alliance. Additionally, Johnson and various American business elites had a hidden alliance with the local oligarchies of Latin America and they were all determined to launch a *counter-reform.*

A 1970 historical assessment of the Alliance was published by Ernest Feder entitled, *"Counter-reform"* (a reference to the opposition of Latin American and US business interests that Kennedy's program engendered). In the article, he notes:

> Given the undeniable existence of a highly conflictive inequality in the distribution of economic and political power in the rural sector and its obvious threat

to political stability and continued US hegemony, the best approach to avoid an upheaval was to guide land reforms into controllable channels through appropriate international agreements and mechanisms. This seems to have been the goal of the Charter Punta del Este (1961), the foundation of the Alliance for Progress. *The Charter is a remarkable, almost revolutionary document ... it spoke with frankness of the place of social and institutional reforms in the process of development.* Development was not any more a purely economic matter—of more capital investments, of slightly improved price and credit policies, of more efficient marketing channels or better farm management—but a function of fundamental changes in basic institutions. *Economic growth had to be preceded, not only accompanied, by social reforms as the new basis for an economic growth take-off.* (Italics are mine).[173]

From the time the Alliance was launched in 1961, "the Charter clashed almost at once with US business which looked at land reform of any shape or kind as a threat to US interests and investments abroad and as subversive."[174] As far as these conservative US business interests, right-wing reactionaries, and oligarchies were concerned, the Kennedy brothers were subversives. Viewed in this light, the old money of America's elite Establishment viewed the Kennedy brothers as "traitors" just as much as the American right wing did—but for different reasons. Hence, "counter-reformists" emerged on the US home front with a veiled criticism of the Alliance that was veiled in the language of needed "technical reforms" and other devices. The intent of the counterreformists was "to create false problems or delay land reform ... In retrospect, it now seems that there was a deliberate, subtle campaign to talk land reform to death; to take the steam out of the progressive dogma of the Charter; to shift attention from the main to marginal aspects; to belittle the real issues or put them in a false light."[175] The main conclusion that can be reached is "the truth seems to be that land reform in Latin America threatens the whole infra- and supra-structure of American economic hegemony in the hemisphere."[176]

The years since 1963 would be characterized by a retreat from the ideals, policies, and hopes that the Alliance engendered. The ideals of representative democracy, social and economic inclusion and participation, would not be sustained without committed leadership in the United States or in Latin America itself. The dictatorships of the 1970s came out of a general fear of revolutionary change. Repression was seen by some sectors of Latin America's ruling and middle classes as the only way to guarantee social peace and their nation's security. On the other hand, the poor and popular sectors saw revolution as the only way to alter institutions that cared nothing for them or their miserable condition. As a result of this dialectical tension, large sectors of the population opted for the perceived shelter of the authoritarian state.[177]

Yet, what can be said about the nature and effect of the actual policies of the Alliance and their implementation is very commendable. At the beginning of the Alliance, most of Latin America's borrowing went into relatively productive enterprises. In Brazil, dams, power stations, and roads were built. In Argentina, the money went into automobile plants, new farmland, and housing. In Mexico, roads, communications, schools, and housing were all paid with project-oriented loans. However, "the period that began with so much promise soon deteriorated into huge fiscal deficits and public mismanagement as money poured in and the Alliance for Progress disintegrated in the wake of the Vietnam War."[178] As noted earlier in this chapter, the American intervention in Vietnam was the decision of Lyndon Johnson and the national security bureaucracy—not a decision made by Kennedy. Similarly, after the Dallas assassination, Johnson gutted the Alliance. Johnson appointed Thomas Mann to head up Latin American Affairs. As a result, historian Arthur Schlesinger, Jr., explicitly stated: "The Alliance for Progress, in the hands of Johnson and Mann, was undergoing a basic transformation—so much so that the historian must talk of two Alliances for Progress. Another program by the same name now struggled on after the political and social components of Kennedy's Alliance—i.e., its heart—had been removed."[179]

It became Mann's job "to liquidate two of the three goals of Kennedy's Alliance—structural reform and political democratization—and to convert much of what remained into an instrument for North American corporations."[180] With Lyndon Johnson and Tom Mann in charge, Standard Oil of New Jersey and the rest of the business community were welcomed back to the White House and the US government. The Rockefellers and Johnson were serving their business constituents very well. In many respects, Juan Bosch of the Dominican Republic summed up the change best when he observed: "The vitality and spirit with which John Kennedy had imbued the Alliance died with him in Dallas."[181]

The Dallas assassination brought about a revolution in Washington and throughout the Western Hemisphere. As Lyndon Johnson dismantled John Kennedy's Alliance, he did so in conformity with the dictates of US business in general, and the Rockefellers in particular. The Johnson administration was aware that in early 1963 the editor of *Fortune* magazine, Charles J. V. Murphy, attacked most if not all of Kennedy's policies. Murphy called Kennedy's idea of stimulating general economic progress through government action—especially on a global scale—"a wearied assumption." In reality, it is an idea of recent origins. *Actually, what Kennedy's policies toward the Third World represented was "an energetic effort on Kennedy's part to break the United States away from a truly 'wearied' and morally exhausted policy of suppressing economic progress elsewhere in the world in the interest of preserving global power for the Anglo-American Establishment."* (Italics are mine).[182] With this in mind, Murphy had "admonished the president for engaging in economic negotiations on a nation-to-nation basis, which bypassed the international financial community."[183] Murphy's criticism of Kennedy reflected the views of the financiers who believed that they—rather than elected representatives—should organize the world's economy and its direction.

In 1962, as the threat of nationalization increased for US businessmen and investors, business leaders demanded that the US Treasury guarantee their private investments from losses from nationalization. The battle over the issue continued well into 1967. At a 1967 conference in Punta del Este in Uruguay, birthplace of the Alliance, the participating governments could not agree upon a trading agreement between the United States and its southern partners. Robert Kennedy suggested that the United States was the problem. US companies feared nationalization by unstable governments. Out of fear, they would not make long-term commitments to the countries in which they operated. Robert recognized that the most difficult problem facing US business was expropriation. He argued that for American companies to gain real security in their investments they had to be willing to surrender control of them to the local authorities. "What Kennedy advocated was US companies giving up 51 percent of their shares in a foreign venture to local shareholders. In this way, the success of a company's project would be in the interest of the local authority and therefore more secure. In Mexico this arrangement was already being tried with notable success."[184]

Neither US companies, nor the Rockefellers and their allies, wanted to give up anything. Rather, they wanted more. Therefore, they attacked Robert Kennedy as they had his brother. They had consistently urged the Kennedy brothers to follow the lead of the International Monetary Fund (IMF). In direct conflict with the announced goals and polices of the Alliance for Progress under Kennedy, the IMF demanded that borrowing countries adopt an austerity program and open their economies to foreign takeover. In other words, US companies wanted a complete reversal of the Kennedy proposal and sought instead to make their business agenda the official US government policy.

From the late 1960s through the East Asian Crisis of the late 1990s, the IMF demanded *loan conditionality* (i.e., conditions to be met to qualify for further lending).[185] The elements of this approach involve "abolition or liberalization of foreign exchange and import controls; currency devaluation; domestic anti-inflation measures ... [the] elimination of government subsidies, elimination of price controls; and greater hospitality to foreign investment."[186] The IMF and the business interests of the American Establishment won the battle (note: a more detailed discussion of the IMF and World Bank policies will be outlined in Chapter 6). Yet, their victory has left a situation where "IMF conditionalities are still a major source of conflict between indebted countries and the Anglo-American financial elite ... Those IMF policies are widely viewed as a substitute for colonial domination."[187]

On this exact theme, Joseph Stiglitz, former chief economist for the World Bank and Nobel Prize winner in economics has written: "In the United States, in the recession of 2001, both Democrats and Republicans agreed on the need for a fiscal stimulus to restore the economy; yet throughout the developing world, the IMF forces contradictory fiscal policies on countries facing downturns—just the opposite of the mission for which they were created."[188] The *hidden politics of empire* reveal the hypocrisy that lies at the heart of the financial elite who lead and guide the Anglo-American Establishment. By demanding that Third World nations adopt the strict guidelines of IMF conditionality agreements, the primary banks and lending institutions of the West foreclose upon the possibility that these countries will ever experience genuine national development. Rather, the policies of the IMF have guaranteed the development of underdevelopment.

Stiglitz notes

what is clear is that there is disappointment in the policies that have been pursued for the past two decades, the policies focusing on liberalization, privatization, and stabilization which collectively have come to be called the Washington Consensus ... Even in those countries which have seen significant growth, a disproportionate share of the gains have gone to the better off, the upper 30 per cent, or even the upper 10 per cent, with many of the poor actually becoming worse off.[189]

In part, these results are the objective consequences of deliberate actions—as in the case of Argentina, where "debtors are being put on notice that there will be serious consequences to default."[190] Given this historical track record of the two decades between 1980 and 2000, Stiglitz comes to the conclusion that "the rules of game have been designed for the most part by the advanced industrial countries, for their own interests, and often do not serve well the interests of the developing world, and especially the poor."[191]

These decades of debt and austerity represent a complete reversal of US policies inaugurated when President Kennedy declared the 1960s the decade of development. Through the Alliance, the *decade of development* was designed to be guided by "development aid, low-interest loans, nation-to-nation cooperation, and some measure of government planning." This was replaced after Kennedy's death by an economic program that was designed "to create a financial relationship that operated to keep underdeveloped countries in the position of being backward exporters of raw materials. This was not JFK's idea of the purpose of loans, nor was it his goal to perpetuate the backwardness of Third World nations."[192]

The difference between the worldview of the Kennedy brothers versus the worldview of the American Establishment (as represented by David and Nelson Rockefeller and Lyndon Johnson) is best summed up by the distinction I have referred to as between the US Global Empire and a rising Global Community. The Kennedy brothers, in opposition to the wealthy centers of Western capitalism, sought to establish an era of Global Community, characterized by foreign aid and long-term loans/low-interest government loans. Contrary to this policy, seeking to circumvent Kennedy, financial leaders in the Establishment aimed at realizing three basic goals: (1) reduce government control of foreign investment; (2) turn Third World economies into export-oriented economies so that they could earn money to service or pay the debt; (3) offset the inflationary pressures that had been brought on in the 1970s and 1980s by high-energy prices and high interest rates being mandated by the IMF demands. Complicating the plight of Third World nations even more was a June 1979 announcement from David Rockefeller that rising energy prices could be expected to severely limit economic growth.

In 1980, Rockefeller addressed 200 top bankers and government officials at an IMF conference in New Orleans in order to warn debt-ridden nations "the major banks would not be able to extend new loans to help borrowers cope with the recent 150 percent increase in oil prices."[193] Rockefeller, a banker and an oilman, represented an era and a coalition of interests that had little concern for the fact that their policies were devastating the Global Community and most of the people who were trying to survive within it. Of Rockefeller's policies and the historical trends emanating from them, it can be said that "throughout the underdeveloped nations, charges were made against the IMF and, implicitly, the same people and institutions with which Kennedy had been at odds."[194] The Third World's struggle with Kennedy's enemies has continued in all the years and all the presidential administrations since 1964—right up to the 2005–2008 presidency of George W. Bush.

The neoconservatives of the Bush-2 regime have continued to build on the Rockefeller legacy through their own uniform neoconservative version of the Washington Consensus. Structural adjustment programs have been extended to the transition countries of Eastern Europe and the former Soviet Union. Watching the process unfold, some observers have gone as far as accusing the IMF and WTO of being the cause of terrible poverty, exploitation, and war. Yet, it is still the American government that has the biggest voice in the WTO "whose rules are widely seen as stacked against developing countries."[195] To have such a critical view of the United States, which is reflected in most of the opinion polls taken around the world, demonstrates that it is a view that has become the dominant perception of most nations in the Global Community of the early twenty-first century. It is further testimony to the abject failure of the US Global Empire and the ruling cabal behind it.

THE FINAL FRONTIER OF THE US GLOBAL EMPIRE

Starting in the 1970s and culminating in the US invasion of Iraq in 2003, the geostrategic imperatives of the architects of the US Global Empire turned American soldiers into a permanent occupying force in the Middle East and throughout Eurasia. The history of the process that led up to the occupation of Afghanistan and Iraq in 2003 spanned a period of about 20 years. It can be argued that the process dated back to the late 1970s, when President Carter faced the Iranian hostage crisis and uncertainty about the ability of the United States to maintain access to Persian Gulf oil. Given the economic interests of US oil firms and commercial banks in the regions of the Middle East, the Iranian Revolution was a cataclysmic event. Not only did an anti-US regime in the region threaten the interests of leading capital-intensive US-based foreign investors, but it also coincided with the rise of many other left wing and revolutionary movements throughout the Third World. The simultaneous rise of revolutionary movements in Central America, from El Salvador to Nicaragua, led to increased calls from investors and US elites to expand the US military budget. During the last two years of the Carter administration labor-intensive firms with investments in Central America joined with capital-intensive firms invested in the Middle East to demand higher levels of military spending.[196]

Not surprisingly, none of these groups could reach an agreement on either the amount or purposes of the military budget increases. To fill the intellectual void right-wing organizations and think tanks emerged that shared a commitment for increased military spending. The most significant organization of its kind at that time was the Committee on the Present Danger (CPD). In many ways, its membership, sources of support, and general purpose was a forerunner of the *Project for the Next American Century* (PNAC). The CPD was financed by a wide variety of US multinational corporate interests. They all shared a common interest and a common stake in foreign investments. The common denominator for them all was their vested interest in making their profits from their business dealings in the oil industry and with the managers in the Pentagon, at the hub of the military-industrial-complex.[197]

Domestically, the effects of imperial overreach and the over-extension of American power throughout the Persian Gulf has already started to undermine the US economy. As with the costs of the Vietnam War, the costs of war and occupation in Iraq are very high. After all, a permanent war economy is an investment strategy predicated upon waste, for it provides a few huge defense corporations with great profits while draining Social Security, emasculating jobs and wages, and running up historic deficits. These are the predominant characteristics of the US economy under the leadership of George W. Bush. Yet, the fact remains that these realities are just a short list of where American society is now vulnerable. Because of its many vulnerabilities, the US Global Empire may be headed toward its final frontier.

THE EMPIRE STRIKES BACK

Since the end of World War II, the vulnerability of America's economy was really not apparent until the early 1970s when the government sought to boost growth by adopting an expansionary fiscal policy (more spending combined with lower taxes) and encouraging a weakening of the dollar. By 1978, this strategy reached its limits as inflation began to rise.[198] Inflation was also a consequence of Lyndon Johnson's decision not to raise taxes in 1968 to pay for the extra costs of the Vietnam War because, had he done so, he would have had to admit he was running an illegal war without a legitimate declaration of war from the congress. By the time that Ronald Reagan entered the White House in the early 1980s, the balance of power between employers and workers was about to tip in favor of the employers. The National Labor Relations Board (NLRB) worked to reinforce the policies of the Reagan administration—policies that were designed to weaken workers' rights.[199] With the weakening of workers' rights came a commensurate lowering of wages. The response of working America was to work longer hours and have many households start producing a two-wage earner income. This new trend continued from the Reagan years to the Bush-2 years, leaving middle-class Americans both overspent and overworked. It also left them with a crisis in pay due to lowered wages and the claim (myth) that America's corporations were "downsizing." Deliberate political choices had been made throughout the Republican administrations of Regan, Bush-1, and Bush-2 that would result in a furthering of the inequality gap between rich and poor. It would be a policy that reflected the real goal of the owners and managers of capital.[200]

In 1993, Kevin Phillips completed a book that forecast dire times ahead for America's middle class. He documented in detail what had happened to the middle class since the 1970s in disposable income, earnings, home values, job prospects, public services assets and net worth, pension safety, and health insurance. He concluded that the next generation's chances for enjoying the same rising living standards as their parents were dismal, at best. Such an outcome was not the result of adverse global trends, as many in corporate America had argued, but rather was the result of deliberate political choices.[201] By 1996, the cover story of *US News & World Report* concurred with Phillips' dismal assessment for the future of the middle class entitled, *Is The American Worker Getting Shafted?—The Assault On The Middle Class.*[202]

Just one year after publishing *Boiling Point*, Kevin Phillips published a sequel entitled, *Arrogant Capital: Washington, Wall Street, and the Frustration of American Politics.*[203] Phillips describes Washington as a city mired in bureaucracy, captured by the money power of Wall Street, and dominated by 90,000 lobbyists and 60,000 lawyers, and the largest concentration of special interests in history. In Chapter Four, he notes that if the "collaboration between government and finance was unprecedented in the twentieth century United States, so was the scarcity of insistence on the kind of financial reform typical of a post-speculative era—the regulatory accomplishment of both the Progressive and the New Deal eras." In fact, not only was an historical cycle of reforms abandoned, both politics and public policy were at the mercy of both Republican and Democratic financiers.[204] Phillips admonished his readers not to look to overt criminal behavior in measuring the influence of the financiers. Rather, he argued

> we should attach much more importance to the favoritism shown the financial sector in perfectly legal ways—from the S & L bailout itself to the Fed's interest rates cuts, George Bush's persistence in calling for capital gains tax rate reductions, Bill Clinton's top economic policy appointments, and the bipartisan Washington willingness to let corporations raise their profits and stock prices by large workforce lay-offs.[205]

Two points from Phillips analysis deserve a few more moments' attention: (1) how the favoritism shown the financial sector was expressed and demonstrated in "perfectly legal ways" and; (2) "the bipartisan Washington willingness" to stand back and let corporations engage in "large workforce lay-offs." Both of these developments serve to represent an historical rupture between the era of the Kennedy brothers and the American presidencies that were to follow.

To begin with, the first point that needs to be stressed is that by the year 2000, whether your family made $30,000 or $300,000 a year, you were being robbed because the IRS and other institutions had been systematically corrupted—under both Republicans and Democratic administrations—to serve the needs of people who make millions.[206] The financial sector was shown favoritism, in "perfectly legal ways," yet this very favoritism worked to effectively undermine both the positions of the middle class and the poor even more than before. Over 50 million Americans are now given the dubious label *the working poor* while more families, under the Bush-2 regime, have fallen below the poverty line. As usual, the hardest hit and least able to defend their interests are the most vulnerable—America's children.

Second, the collusion between the Democratic and Republican parties is the other major element of historical significance. After losing the White House for 12 years to the Republicans (two terms under Reagan, one term to Bush-1), the

Democrats decided to become *centrists*. In so doing, they lost their historical identity as fighters for labor and the middle class—selling out to Wall Street financiers,
arms dealers, and multinational corporations seeking a quick buck through
inflated profit margins resulting from rigged international trade agreements such
as NAFTA. Both labor rights and environmental protections were reduced to
unenforceable "side agreements" as the deal on NAFTA closed. Investors, financiers, Wall Street, and multinational corporations would soon be going to the
cheap labor markets of the Third World. This change in investment outlook resulted in the "outsourcing" of American jobs, an increase in the US unemployment
rate, and *a race to the bottom* for many millions of the earth's people. In fact, Karl
Marx's dire prediction about late capitalism turning the world into *a global
sweatshop* was coming true. Despite the harsh realities of the US Global Empire
and its financial barons' proclivity for exploitation by either one-sided trade agreements or military force, the trend has accelerated under the Bush-2 regime. For
example, on the issue of trade agreements, the Central America Free Trade
Agreement (CAFTA) extended the exploitative reach of NAFTA from North
America to all of Central and South America.

In a major study of the centrist politics of the Clinton years entitled, *Dead-
Center: Clinton-Gore Leadership and the Perils of Moderation*, historian James
MacGregor Burns recounts that "Democratic base voters were best described as
confused, disappointed, and angry. Labor was upset with the President and congressional Democrats for their support of NAFTA. Unions had withdrawn their
support and money from the National Health Care Coalition after the NAFTA
fight, further weakening the already tepid effort for the President's plan."[207] What
is the lesson about the "hidden politics of empire" on the domestic front of the
United States? It is this: That the interests of working families have gradually been
sacrificed to the corporations. How did this happen? Although capitalism is the
most productive system ever devised, it also tends to generate deep economic
inequalities and encourage the pursuit of profit at the expense of all else.[208]
Following the gospel of "free trade," and using it as a mantra, both political parties
chose to ignore the fact that "free trade predicated exclusively on wage competition is entirely unacceptable and represents a major threat to mass prosperity in
America and Western Europe."[209]

The threat of frozen wages is certainly an economic concern. For example,
as wages have remained stagnant, the issue of what constitutes a *living
wage* has come to the forefront of grassroots American politics. A living-wage
campaign is now a campaign that is national in scope, promising to emerge as
the most interesting and underreported grassroots enterprise since the years of
the civil rights movement.[210] Yet, even more than that, the grassroots movements
points to a larger national need—the need to formulate a larger and more comprehensive national response to the challenges faced by working families.[211]
The lack of attention given to the problem is next to incomprehensible given
the fact that as early as 1994 and 1995 scholars were writing and publishing
about a *jobless future*[212] and about *the end of work*.[213] However, the inattention
to the problem is not incomprehensible once one realizes that the same IMF
and World Bank policies of neoliberalism and privatization that have been used

to exploit the Third World had been applied domestically within the American *homeland*.

Privatization and the private plunder of our common wealth—America's national commonwealth—poignantly depicted as the *silent theft* of our day and generation—characterizes the nature of a financial system built upon a creed of exploitation.[214] In this *silent theft* perhaps one of the most glaring abuses of corporate power has been the abuse of the nation's publicly held natural resources. Yet, the reach of privatization does not end at the edge of nature's frontiers because it constitutes a desire for increasing acquisition that is insatiable. The reach of privatization absorbs nature, the wealth of the commons, and those sources of public knowledge that are necessary to protect the public from *silent theft*—thereby leaving the majority of the citizenry vulnerable.

Corporate power, privatization, and economic downsizing are the sources of centralized power that systematically engage in a massive public plunder by *downsizing democracy*—that is, taking the powerful idea of a collective citizenry and transforming it into a concept of a personal autonomous democracy.[215] In the world of *downsized democracy* we discover that the legislative branch itself has encouraged a shift from active participation in the political process to litigation, lobbying, and term limits. Citizens have been pushed to the periphery of political life while narrow special interest groups—largely comprising faceless members drawn from mailing lists—have come to dominate state and federal decision making.

The largest of the special interest groups that has come to dominate state and federal decision making is the World Trade Organization (WTO). It has also simultaneously sought to exert undue influence over the domestic policies that national governments adopt throughout the Third World. The WTO has literally acted as "a further infringement on the sovereignty of national governments."[216] Both developing and developed countries have felt its effects. Like its sister organizations, the IMF and World Bank, the WTO seeks to assert its undemocratic rule-making authority to infringe on the democratic autonomy of people in First and Third World nations in order to further advance its version of privatization (including intellectual property rights) vis-à-vis a discredited neoliberal economic doctrine. This is the new global "triangular division of authority" which has unfolded between the IMF, World Bank, and WTO.[217] The end of this authority is nowhere in sight.

Analysts have predicted that WTO pressures will build on developing countries from September 2005 onward. This prediction is attributable to the fact that at a July 2005 meeting of the WTO, held to revive negotiations on international trade, the meeting ended without any results. Therefore, as of the fall of 2005, the surmise is that there will be more intense talks from September forward and that developing countries should prepare to face great pressures from the developed countries to pry open their markets.[218] In this global environment, most Third World nations are literally flying blind, not fully cognizant of their place in an historical process that dates back to the early 1980s. The Reagan *roll back* of the Third World gains had the effect of stimulating a new wave of global poverty through increased debt. Therefore, the challenge currently facing Third World nations is compounded by the fact that "the manipulation of the figures on global poverty prevents national societies from understanding the consequences of an historical process initiated in the early 1980s with the onslaught of the debt crisis. This false consciousness has invaded all spheres of critical debate and discussion on the 'free market' reforms."[219]

SURRENDERING THE "COMMANDING HEIGHTS" TO THE MARKET

The critical debate on free market reforms was temporarily resolved by an historical process—also initiated in the early 1980s—in which the State and its welfare functions were surrendered to the "magic of the market" (Reagan's phrase). The battle for what had come to be known as the *commanding heights* was nothing less than a control for power over not just individual nation-states, but the governance of the entire global economy. Would the State or the market become the victor and emerge triumphant?

In a 1998 study entitled, *The Commanding Heights*, author Daniel Yergin noted: "Where the frontier between the state and market is to be drawn has never been a matter that could be settled once and for all, at some grand peace conference." Rather, "this frontier is not neat and well defined. It is constantly shifting and often ambiguous. Yet, through most of the century, the state has been ascendant, extending its domain further and further into what had been the territory of the market."[220] Up until the advent of the so-called *Reagan Revolution*, in many of the industrial countries of the West and in large parts of the developing world, the model was the *mixed economy*. The State would still play a dominant role, but not completely be able to stifle or eclipse the market mechanism.

THE ACCOMMODATION AND ABANDONMENT OF THE CITIZENRY

Historically, the primary goals of the State involved providing equity, maintaining the general welfare, expanding opportunity, and working to guarantee a decent way of life. In order to achieve those goals, governments "sought to capture and maintain the high ground of their economies—the *'commanding heights'*."[221] The last two decades of the twentieth century would rewrite history with a gigantic reversal of fortunes for those Left and progressive movements that had struggled for a more equitable and fair economy. In the early 1980s, with the neoliberal revolution of Reagan and Thatcher, the newly packaged and market-friendly ideology of neoliberalism ushered in a decade of debt for the Third World. It also represented a massive scaling back of the welfare state in the United States, and a corresponding rise in power of the Federal Reserve that loosened the triangular global financial forces of the IMF, World Bank, and WTO.

Social justice and welfare concerns, agreements with labor to seek a full employment economy, access to universal health care and quality education for everyone, all became the agenda of the past. Instead of fighting to maintain the Left and a socially progressive agenda, there came in its place the policies of privatization, deregulation, and structural adjustment programs. These were the new ideals that would reign supreme under the banner of the *Washington Consensus*. The Third World and the First World were now placed squarely at the mercy of the neoliberal agenda.

As in the period of reconstruction after World War II, in the wealthy industrial centers of Western capitalism, "large segments of the population would be accommodated, and would be led to abandon any more radical vision under a rational cost-benefit analysis."[222] What is most damning about this analysis is the realization that "once its institutional structure is in place, capitalist democracies will function only if all subordinate their interests to the needs of those who control investment decisions, from the country club to the soup kitchen."[223] The subordination of the larger human interest, in both the economies of North and South, placed the American middle class at the mercy of those multinational corporate interests that had been plundering the Third World for decades. The poor and middle classes of both the Northern and Southern hemispheres, East and West, were now more captive than ever before to the uncertainty of the markets, the vicissitudes of corporate decisions on investments and where to locate plants, the private determination of wages, and the objectives for global governance derived from an aristocracy of wealth. Whether the average American realized it or not, the age of multinational capitalism, driven by the financiers and managers of the capitalist system, would replace the centers of political and economic decision making by placing the corporate boardroom's worldview over and above the worldview of those in the halls and deliberative chambers of democratic governments. What became even more evident and disturbing was the realization that the rule makers in Washington (charged with the regulatory framework of capitalism) and the deal makers on Wall Street (the managers and financiers of corporate wealth) had struck a bargain that would continue to favor the privileged and exclude just about everyone else.

By the mid-1990s, some journalists and news commentators recognized the human reality that "cutting a program is like bombing a settlement."[224] Social Science scholars, such as Frances Fox Piven and Richard A. Cloward wrote of "the breaking of the American social compact." They recognized that "institutions reflect power, and they enhance power. Patterned rules and practices are constructed by those who have power, with the aim of stabilizing power over time." Still, the stabilization of power is difficult to maintain because "while power is solidified by institution-building, it is not frozen."[225] This insight was recognized by the cover story of *Business Week*, November 20, 1995 entitled: *Rewriting the Social Contract: Welfare, Medicare, and Social Security. As federal entitlements get cut, a vast economic adjustment is coming*. The authors of the article acknowledged, "GOP fervor goes way beyond what most Americans expect." The authors outlined what they called *The War on Entitlements*—listing the safety net for the poor, Medicare, farm subsidies, Social Security.[226] With graphic honesty, the Editorial was entitled: *The De-Entitling of America.*[227]

A Pulitzer Prize-winning team of reporters, Donald Barlett and James Steele, offered their assessment of the US economy in their book, *America: What Went Wrong?* As they saw it, part of the intentional dismantling of the middle class involved shifting the tax burden from the rich to middle class, thereby inaugurating a grim era for the middle-class tax squeeze. In addition, disappearing pension funds and pension raiders had begun to rewrite America's economic history along with a bandwagon effort to force along the process of deregulation, plant closures, lucrative business bankruptcies, and an expanding pattern of exporting jobs.[228] About four years later, Barlett and Steele updated their critique of a failing economy in their next book, *America: Who Stole the Dream?*[229] Their focus shifted even more to the global economy as they analyzed the dynamic of importing goods and exporting jobs, the new math of free trade, and the decline and fall of American manufacturing. They wrote about how the workforce was being retrained for nonexistent jobs while, at the same time, being conditioned to learn to earn less. The nexus between layoffs and a growing health care crisis was exposed as another element in a corporate cycle of pillage that sent jobs abroad (now referred to as "outsourcing") while helping out the corporate bottom line by removing the high cost of offering health care coverage to the workers in the companies and corporations.

An extended company of like-minded people would engage in a similar diagnosis of the American economy. Derek Bok, the President Emeritus of Harvard University, completed a study in which he examined five areas that he believed to be of paramount importance: economic prosperity, quality of life, opportunity, personal security, and societal values.[230] He showed that America had performed poorly when compared with other industrial nations. When it comes to providing adequate health care at a reasonable cost, educating young people for high-skilled jobs, alleviating poverty and urban blight, and reducing crime, the US record has been dismal. Other scholars who have commented upon the same five areas that Bok highlighted have not only shared his views, but have also expanded upon the reasons for America's failure and how it differs with Europe's successes.[231] A primary feature that accounts for the difference between America and Europe is how US policymakers have underestimated the role of social policy. Even more important is the European idea of *social exclusion* as a category worth investigation, study, and attention. While poverty may be defined "as a situation of deprivation due to lack of resources" there is a corollary to that which is

> lack of resources carries with it lack of access (exclusion from) the basic social systems (market for goods and services, labor markets, health system, social security system, educational system, financial system, etc.); it may result or lead to exclusion from systems of social relations ... and may, ultimately ... imply the loss of the system of references (identity, self-esteem, autonomy, etc.).

Therefore, the greatest challenge is to move toward "the reduction of inequalities (relative)" and that the reduction of such inequalities "is one of the goals of social policy and an indicator of social quality in Europe."[232] This insight has great significance for building a *post-Imperial America*.

BUILDING A POST-IMPERIAL AMERICA: MOVING TOWARD AN INCLUSIVE DOMESTIC AND FOREIGN POLICY

If America is to finally deal with the root causes of its social fragmentation, growing inequalities, and economic decline, it must do as Europe has done—learn to deal not only with poverty, but also create and formulate a public policy that can adequately address the issues associated with poverty and its close connection to the phenomena of social inclusion and social exclusion.[233] As it forges a new relationship with the rest of the world, a *post-Imperial America* must begin to work toward a rejection of its historic reliance on militarism and strive to re-democratize its institutions and policy patterns so as to build an inclusive democratic framework for governance both in the United States and around the world.

Only by establishing a more intimate correspondence between America's own quest for social and economic justice within its own borders can America's role in the world be transformed into a foreign policy that places justice and human rights concerns over and above a narrowly defined elite-sanctioned *national interest*. Certainly in the area of jobs and employment, a developing policy of socioeconomic inclusion requires an end to radical wage and tax disparities. As a *post-Imperial America* goes abroad, its goals should include developing an inclusive approach to fair and just wages throughout the global South. Both can benefit by increasing wages and the standard of living at home and around the globe. In fact, I am arguing that only by developing a complementary global wage structure will it be possible for the global South to move toward genuine development and growth with a *post-Imperial America*. Should that not be the case, the global South should create more South-South linkages so that its current dependence on an exploitative economy—fashioned in the image of the US Global Empire—can be completely severed.

A *post-Imperial America* must reject the policies, practices, and rationales that have characterized the *hidden politics of empire*. A *post-Imperial America* must learn to embrace the dynamics of a rising Global Community in which America no longer engages in the fantasies of global domination that have characterized the thoughts and policies of the architects of a US Global Empire. In its place, a *post-Imperial America* needs to find a path toward political, economic, social, and spiritual liberation for both its own people and the peoples and governments of the rest of the world. The path of a *post-Imperial America* would constitute nothing less than a total reversal of the present course being taken by the US Global Empire. By contemplating an alternative future, it should be clear that the path of a *post-Imperial America* is a revolutionary proposition and a revolutionary goal. Taking such a path is worthy for those who believe that liberation from imperial rule is the only way to re-democratize America and, at the same time, supply the necessary means to achieve an interdependent, human rights oriented world under the rule of law. In this fundamental sense, it becomes feasible to think of a post-Imperial America working in conjunction with the global South toward the realization of a more economically equal and inclusive Global Community.

In short, the direction of a *post-Imperial America* is a path that is to be taken by those who reject the *hidden politics of empire* and seek, in its place, the promise embodied in the dream of a rising Global Community. Instead of building a twenty-first century international order supportive of the principle of interdependence, the US Global Empire has actively promoted exclusionary policies and practices—all designed for the purpose of cementing its alleged global hegemony. This is what has characterized the Bush-2 regime's conception of superpower predominance. However, continued reliance upon exclusionary forms of governance is too slender a reed on which to place the weight of an empire.

The strength and viability of any viable international order is ultimately predicated upon the recognition of mutual respect, interdependence, and mutual cooperation. The longevity of the post-World War II international order can be derived from the fact that the international treaty system that evolved under the auspices of the UN was committed to a shared developmental design for the world. The UN Charter speaks of inclusive purposes, inclusive goals, and the evolution of an inclusive framework of governance for an interdependent world. The UN Charter does not contemplate endorsing superpower hegemony at the expense of evolving norms of customary international law, or respect for the faiths embodied in all of the world's great religions, or the realization of building international institutions and mechanisms capable of maintaining and enforcing the peace. It is, therefore, antithetical to the UN Charter for the US Global Empire to act as a rogue force in international affairs, undermining the legacy and ongoing work of over 50 years of international governance through interdependent and accountable international bodies.

Alternatively, the sanity of making a commitment to an inclusive, interdependent, and interconnected Global Community opens the path to ending global inequalities, injustices, and internecine wars. With such an achievement, nations are empowered to participate as coequals in an interdependent world. Such a world provides the opportunity to strengthen the UN; it serves to advance the work of progressive and humanitarian NGOs; and it offers support to a host of newly created international institutions (the International Criminal Court, Truth and Reconciliation Commissions, and various Tribunals) that are committed to realizing national and individual accountability for war crimes and crimes against humanity.

In a *post-Imperial America*, support for the International Criminal Court (ICC) would have to be automatically forthcoming. Unlike the Bush-2 regime, the role of a *post-Imperial America* in the world would seek to promote a world governed by international law instead of playing the role of the lone superpower acting in defiance of it. A *post-Imperial America* would seek to revive and extend international compliance with the Nuclear Non-Proliferation Treaty (NPT). In short, a *post-Imperial America* would actively support efforts to enhance the practice of global justice under the auspices of the ICC, honor its treaty commitments, oppose wasteful spending on bunker-busting nuclear bombs, and undertake unprecedented steps toward controlling and eliminating the global trade in conventional arms.

With the decline and eventual demise of the US Global Empire, both America and a rising Global Community can embark upon a new historical trajectory—removed from the political and economic prison of militarism. Both the Global Community and a *post-Imperial America* can dedicate their fortunes and their hopes to developing vibrant communities at the local, national, and international levels. One of the first steps in this new direction has been suggested by Professor Gar Alperovitz, as outlined in his book, *America Beyond Capitalism*. He argues that the basic outlines of an achievable and community-sustaining vision are quietly taking shape—as vision that offers far better market-based ways to use

America's vast wealth to realize equality, democracy, and liberty. In the book's conclusion, he admits that "little has been said in the preceding pages about global issues and international relations," but the reason he gives for this neglect is that "America is unlikely to play a different role in the world until it is a different America."[234] This insight is truly fundamental in coming to understand the relationship between a *post-Imperial America* and realizing the potential for a rising Global Community.

In large measure, this insight explains why I have taken the last few pages to discuss the social and economic problems that the United States faces—for it is more than just a review of the internal problems of a struggling Global Empire. The social and economic problems faced by the United States from 2001 onward are directly connected with the exploitation of the global South by the institutional structures and policies of the *Wall Street/WTO/IMF/ World Bank complex*. Until the interplay between the global North and the global South is more completely understood and appreciated, the more unlikely a sudden or progressive transformation in human relations will be. Therefore, it is essential for the sake of a rising Global Community to be incorporated into the concerns and policies of a *post-Imperial America*. This will require of the United States a commitment to get its domestic house in order so that it can better serve in its new role as a positive and constructive force in international relations.

FINDING A NEW ROLE IN THE WORLD: THE
NATURE AND PURPOSE OF A POST-IMPERIAL AMERICA

It is important to comprehend the failures of the US Global Empire and why they have occurred and continue to occur. Additionally, it is just as important to comprehend the possibilities for that future time in history when the US Global Empire collapses in upon itself, due the weight of its murderous contradictions, actions, and policies. We need to ask important questions in anticipation of that event: What will be the shape, the nature, and the purpose of a *post-Imperial America*? What role should a *post-Imperial America* play in the world? How will that difference translate into practice as a *post-Imperial America* embarks upon serious efforts to meet the needs and challenges of a rising Global Community? These are the primary questions that reside at the heart of this book (as well as Chapter 6). Still, these issues should be briefly addressed here, at the close of our analysis of the *hidden politics of empire*.

The Fate of the Global North is linked to the Fate of the Global South

First, taken together, the record of America's decline since adopting neoliberal policies in the 1980s and its current neoconservative drift under the Bush-2 regime, clearly demonstrates that the fates of billons of people in the North are linked to the billions in the South. A common destiny links the global North and the global South. For example, just as globalization has destabilized American communities, it has done the same throughout the global South. In this respect, the general impact of trade and imports on jobs and wages has devastating effects on both sides of the global Northern and Southern frontiers. In the United States between 1992 and 1999, trade had a net negative impact on unemployment. Increased trade hurt American workers and communities because it involved new imports entering the American market and directly displaced American producers.[235]

Similarly, under NAFTA, labor wars have opened up on the US/Mexico border.[236] For Mexicans who have entered the United States, many are unable to afford rent on wages of 30 cents an hour. As a result, people who have been locked into this socioeconomic trap have been hospitalized with pneumonia from sleeping on the floor where they work. Yet, groups such as the Workplace Project have helped immigrant workers in the underground suburban economy. Vulnerable workers came together to demand safe wages and working conditions. In so doing, many undocumented workers won a series of victories, included a raise of 30 percent for day laborers and a domestic workers' bill of rights. In this process, they have transformed themselves into effective political participants.[237] Many of these struggles are not as historically recent as globalization, but the problems of people in these situations have been exacerbated by globalization. In the case of the "illegal alien," historical studies have revealed that this label represented a new legal and political subject whose inclusion in the nation was a social reality but a legal impossibility—a subject without right and excluded from citizenship.[238] In far too many Third World nations a similar set of conditions obtain. These conditions are often worsened by globalization and debt as in the case of Argentina in 2001–2004, struggling with the impossibilities of IMF conditionality loans, unequal distribution of social wealth, and lingering poverty mixed with trade imbalances. The issues of social inclusion and social exclusion, as already noted, are a burden in Europe, the United States, and other nations around the globe.

The main tasks for a *post-Imperial America* will be to rectify these injustices within its own borders and simultaneously address its historical injustices outside of its own borders—in its trade agreements and treaty relationships with nations throughout the Third World. In the last analysis, our common fate is undeniable. It is the recognition of that reality which links us together inextricably. For workers in both the First World and the Third World, the same oppressive forces that have guided the actions of national and multinational corporate rule have been at work for decades. These oppressive forces, once hidden, have just been made more apparent under the conditions of globalization as labor's bargaining power has been reduced. There has also been increased labor market volatility. Insofar as globalization has impacted upon the national economic policy of individual states, there has been a corresponding global weakening of welfare state throughout Europe as well. In summary, these oppressive forces have brought about a weakening of democratic self-governance.[239]

Workers and their families have struggled against the agenda of ruthless Wall Street financiers and managers in every nation around the globe. These hidden and unaccountable forces are the real sources of political and economic powers that have thoroughly corrupted America's political and taxation system.[240] These same forces have been at work for decades in the tasks of refining their exploitative skills on the people and governments of the Third World. Now these policies have a "blowback" effect of their own—as they come back to undermine and destroy American and European communities (note: my earlier discussion about the

Kennedy brothers battling Wall Street, the Rockefellers, oilmen, and the IMF was prolegomena to this very point).

Trade and Investment Policies Must Benefit the Citizenry of both the Global North and the Global South

Second, in practice, a *post-Imperial America* will have to admit that current international trade and investment policies do not benefit the global South or the citizenry of the global North. The reality of the international trade regime under the US Global Empire is that "except under tightly defined conditions, such rules (enforced in Geneva by a World Trade Organization (WTO) that has only very abstract and indirect accountability to democratic publics) essentially forbid labor and environmental laws at either state or federal levels from being stronger than 'international standards' if they restrain trade."[241] In this context, *international standards* may be understood as *Wall Street/WTO/IMF/World Bank standards*. These are standards that do not facilitate comprehensive or independent national development.

The nations of the global South are not the intended beneficiaries of trade or investment (vis-à-vis the WTO). In fact, in terms of how this policy affects the global South, it has become clear that economic integration and free trade do not drive successful development—especially when financial liberalization is added into the equation. In the case of East Asia (the crash of the late 1990s) and throughout Latin America (Brazil, Argentina, Chile), there is plenty of evidence to show that financial liberalization (designed to attract investment) is often followed by a financial crash.[242] Hence, thanks to the trends associated with globalization and augmented by the Wall Street/WTO/IMF/World Bank complex, we discover that the destruction of local and national communities is an almost inevitable result throughout the global South.

Neoliberal Globalization Increases Global Inequality

The correlation between the social, economic, and political fate of the citizenry in the global North and the global South can best be understood by the following equation: "Globalization increases Global inequality and Destabilizes Communities in the Developing World, Leading to Increased Downward Pressure on Wages in the Developed World."[243]

During the Kennedy years, both America and the world were presented with a radically different path for social, political, and economic development. It was a highly inclusive path of governance at every level. A central emphasis of the Kennedy brothers, Martin Luther King, Jr., Malcolm X, and the civil rights movement, centered upon attacking poverty by providing the poor and near poor with decent jobs and rising wages, the removal of barriers associated with structural racism and racial subordination. It was only their assassinations (combined with the reassertion of the policies of the old elites in the American Establishment), that effectively put an end to the possibility of a US-led revolution of power and idealism throughout the world. The politics of *roll back* began with LBJ in the Vietnam War. It was accelerated by Nixon with coups in Chile and his escalation of the Vietnam War throughout all of Indochina—Laos, Cambodia, and Thailand.

Those men in the American Establishment who used assassination as a political tool to regain their influence also used international financial institutions to re-colonize the lives of billions of citizens across the global South.

Conservative and right-wing ideologues had decided

> the instruments chosen for rolling back the South were the World Bank and the International Monetary Fund. The project represented an interesting transformation particularly for the World Bank, which had been vilified by the *Wall Street Journal* as one of the villains responsible for weakening the North's global position and accused by the right of promoting Socialism in the Third World through its loans to southern governments. But the ideological right-wingers seeking the closure of the bank were restrained by pragmatic conservatives who wished to use it, instead, as a disciplinarian.[244]

NATIONAL AND GLOBAL FASCISM IN THE SERVICE OF EMPIRE

Since the late 1960s, both the people of the United States and the world have witnessed the abject failure of America's major political parties to deal with either domestic or international poverty. Instead, both political parties failed to carry on the causes and the fight initiated by the Kennedy brothers and Dr. King. Instead of adopting their legacy and idealism, both of America's political parties succumbed to endless experimentation with neoliberal economic prescriptions and a neoconservative brand of militarism (re-mixed with a resurgent neoliberal dose of privatization and deregulation).[245]

Not only have the neoliberal economic prescriptions of deregulation, privatization, and downsizing the labor market served to subordinate wages and workers' rights in Third World countries, these policies have also augmented the march of a right-wing political trend within the Third World and the United States to dispense with democratic constraints by inserting a fascist protocol by which the governing elites govern. For example, within the United States itself, military and political training provided at the School of the Americas (aka, the *School of the Assassins*), involves educating Latin American military officers in the use of strategies and tactics for political repression and state authoritarianism. The fascist nature of this kind of training has blown back into the United States and its own national security bureaucracy with a frightful intensity. Under the post-9/11 Bush-2 regime, this fascist legacy has endangered the maintenance of America's own civil liberties. It has done so through the USA Patriot Act and through the expanded powers of the CIA, FBI, NSA, and military intelligence.

For many centuries—up to the last decades of the twentieth century—Latin American states encouraged their elites and military to defend *la patria* (the nation) at the expense of human rights and civil liberties. These Latin American states were governed by what has been described as *regimes of exception*— because these regimes withdrew the normal constraints on constitutional protections and, for legal reasons, simply declared that an internal state of war exists. Other euphemisms for this practice are imposing a "state of siege" and declaring a "national emergency." Even before its 1976 coup, Argentina's elected government declared a "state of war against terrorism."[246]

In a declared state of war against terrorism, "internal wars and regimes of exception change the rules; civil liberties and rights are suspended. Protection of human rights, as defined in international treaties or natural law, succumbs to the law of war and to the fundamental rights of all states to preserve their own existence." Yet, "this right of states to preserve their existence does not unambiguously supercede international treaties on human rights."[247] Under the presidency of George W. Bush, the United States has regularly taken action with respect to various treaties— of which it was a party—that were not consonant with some of the most fundamental rules of the law of treaties. For the Bush-2 regime to disregard the legal effects of signature, as well as the binding effects of treaties to which it is a party, constitutes the most flagrant attempt to obstruct the functioning of treaty regimes.

In the post-9/11 era, the Bush-2 regime has invoked the newly passed USA Patriot Act in order to create a *state of emergency* within the United States. Under the conditions of a "state of emergency," all kinds of extra-constitutional abuses are allowed. For example, the CIA has been granted virtually unlimited power by the Executive to engage in sanctioned efforts to detain, kidnap, or torture alleged terrorists. This power also extends to transporting terrorism suspects and flying them to foreign nations that have no legal restrictions against torture under the euphemism of a *rendition*. These policies reflect the increasingly fascist nature of the Bush-2 regime (see below, the 14 common threads of fascism, especially #2: "disdain for the importance of human rights").

The Bush-2 regime's obsession with national security exposes other areas of national life to fascist tendencies. The result is that American democracy is experiencing *collateral damage* in its civil life, media culture, nationalist calls to support militarism in foreign adventures throughout the Middle East—and wherever else oil constitutes a natural resource. Lawrence W. Britt, writing in *Free Inquiry Magazine*, delineated 14 "common threads" of fascism:

1. Powerful and continuing expressions of nationalism.
2. Disdain for the importance of human rights.
3. Identification of enemies/scapegoats as a unifying cause.
4. The supremacy of the military/avid militarism.
5. Rampant sexism.
6. A controlled mass media.
7. Obsession with national security.
8. Religion and ruling elite tied together.
9. Power of corporations protected.
10. Power of labor suppressed or eliminated.
11. Disdain and suppression of intellectuals and the arts.
12. Obsession with crime and punishment.
13. Rampant cronyism and corruption.
14. Fraudulent elections.[248]

The fascist drift of American life, under the auspices of the US Global Empire, endangers all of the world's citizens. In turn, the citizens of the United States must come to realize that their own fate is linked with the fate of the Global Community. It will be in the interest of the citizens of a *post-Imperial America* to admit the failures and crimes of its Global Empire. Only by confronting this reality will America be able to begin to place the progressive and productive energies of the United States into a global process of cooperation with the Global Community and begin to participate in a global process of rebuilding and healing.

The current trends indicate two factors. First, the Global Community, especially those nations that constitute the global South (as a rising force and power) are capable of making their own trade agreements and regional arrangements with or without the United States. Second, regional economic cooperation throughout the global South is the wave of the future. It is a future that can also do better without the World Bank and the IMF. The United States has retained a veto power within the IMF and World Bank that has often thwarted the will of 183 other nations on earth. This antidemocratic power needs to be eliminated for the future well-being of the entire Global Community—especially throughout the global South.[249]

A "GLOBAL NEW DEAL" FOR A RISING GLOBAL COMMUNITY

In this new century, the United States should participate in a constructive and reconstructive manner with a rising Global Community—dedicated toward realizing what President Kennedy called a "grand and global alliance, north and south, east and west," joined in common purpose and united by a shared commitment to end poverty, disease, and war itself. A *post-Imperial America* must differentiate itself from the history of its predecessor—the failed US Global Empire. It must renounce its false premises, as well as its failed policies. If the search for truth, reparations, and global reconciliation should require the employment of global tribunals, truth and reconciliation commissions, or access to and use of the ICC, then so be it, for in the final analysis, the *hidden politics of empire* demonstrates that since the end of World War II, the US Global Empire has struggled against diversity, nations seeking neutrality and/or nonalignment, and autonomous national development throughout the Third World (with the exception of Kennedy's Alliance for Progress & the Peace Corps).

In the 1990s, both President Clinton and British Prime Minister Tony Blair briefly experimented with *Third Way* politics in order to protect their corporate constituency while, at the same time, attempting to engage in a cooptation of labor, leftists, and progressives by getting them to back off from their criticisms of the Clinton-Blair turn toward the right.[250] In America, the *New Democrats* were products of the post-Reagan Democratic Leadership Council (DLC), intent on gaining back the White House and the Congress, but little else. The liberal and progressive policies of the Kennedy-King years were deemed as unacceptable to both the elite establishments of the Democratic Party and the Republican Party. In the new age of the 1990s, Clinton and Blair attempted to build a bridge between past and future by adopting a balancing of class and economic interests that they called the *Third Way*.

It was a politics that presented itself as a centrist experiment that would try to preserve what was best from the policies of the welfare state when the welfare state was at its political end. Its demise had begun with Reagan and Thatcher, but that demise would not be fully ratified until Clinton and Blair moved their respective governments further to the right. The *Third Way* was an ideological experiment that failed for a variety of reasons. It could not bring the results it promised in terms of building a fair and just society in any of the Western democracies where it was supposed to have that effect. Rather, it simply underscored the reality that, with the decline of the welfare state, there was no effective framework in place for building a societal commitment to social justice or economic fairness. Rather, the divisions between the wealthy and all the rest would now grow at an even faster rate. Inequality would rule the day, both within the former welfare states and throughout the Third World. Finally, the experiment with the *Third Way* would be totally eclipsed with the US Supreme Court's appointment of George W. Bush to the presidency in 2000.

Of all that has been accomplished in the years of the Bush-2 regime, what stands out the most is the reality of a widening inequality gap between those who have and those who have not. It is no longer just a national phenomenon, it is a global one that has accelerated at astronomical proportions.[251] Therefore, if the promise contained in the historical rise of global civil society is to be realized in the years ahead, it will be necessary for the Global Community to adopt policies that are specifically designed to close the gap between the widening inequalities that have developed within and between nations over the last 40 years. To that end, it has been suggested that a *Global New Deal* be formulated within the normative framework of human rights. After all, since the end of World War II, the international community at the UN has "successfully defined, articulated, and elaborated the content of international economic and social human rights. The *Global New Deal* is an attempt to fulfill these basic economic and social human rights."[252] The specific elements of the *Global New Deal* comprise seven main points:

1. Promote economic equality.
2. Finance global public goods.
3. Hear the victims' voices.
4. Maintain ecological balance.
5. Prioritize the rights of racial and ethnic minorities.
6. Prioritize women's rights.
7. Inhibit militarism.[253]

All of these issues will be addressed and expanded upon next in Chapter 6. For now, suffice it to say that such a series of developments will require the assistance, support, and involvement of a *post-Imperial America*. The successful unfolding of this *Global New Deal* will also necessitate the development and evolution of regional bodies and nation-state groupings that are dedicated to genuine national development. These developments should be augmented by the UN and its human rights treaty-regime. Additionally, all of the above-referenced undertakings should be undertaken in conjunction with the evolution of South-South alliances that can meet national developmental goals while, at the same time, serve to advance the larger requirements of a rising Global Community. In other words, it is now clear that national economies throughout the Third World should finally be able to real-ize their historical aspirations for nonalignment with exploitative corporate capitalism—whether from Europe or the US Global Empire and its Wall Street/ IMF/World Bank/WTO complex.

In this endeavor, the greatest burden and the greatest challenge will ultimately be in the hands of the global citizenry. In one of the first major struggles of this contest, in both First and Third Worlds, the citizenry must claim their authority over corporations by adopting the principle that *companies should serve the public good*. The recognition and enforcement of this principle applies equally to the current manifestations of the US Global Empire, a *post-Imperial America*, and to every nation within the Global Community. To this end, it has been suggested that the following initial steps be taken:

1. Crack Down on Corporate Crime.
2. Rein in the Imperial CEOs.
3. Shore Up the Civil Justice System.
4. Regulate in the public interest.
5. Trust-Busting in the New Century: Start With the Media.
6. Get Corporations Out of Our Elections.
7. Reclaim the Constitution.
8. Subordinate Corporations to People.[254]

Through all the twists and turns that history has in store for the human future, what remains essential to recognize is the global devastation wrought by the reality of neoliberalism's inhumane tradition and its conspiracy with neoconservatism's fantasy of global domination. Multinational corporations have been the primary leaders in both creating and pushing the advancement of a global neoliberal agen-da. There is little doubt that the role that corporations have played in this global drama is an extensive one. It is a role that has relied on the US military and nation-alistic fervor to sustain a corporate plan that resonates with globalization's mantra of privatization, deregulation, and profit maximization. The most recent expression of this role and the policies used to accelerate its path to these goals takes us to the doctrine of preemptive war. War serves as both the means and the ends to realizing vast profits and political control for those who run the US Global Empire.

Both endless wars and the financial exploitation of the vast and excluded citi-zenry of the earth are the bastard twins of the US Global Empire. It is an empire that has been placed on the trajectory of a global rampage. Recent history has demonstrated that a corporate-driven economic plan for national and global pri-vatization, deregulation, IMF structural adjustment programs—combined with the dynamics of a permanent war economy—can only continue to accelerate the decline of the United States as a democratic nation. Despite its claims to be a benevolent force in world affairs, the US Global Empire still relies on militarism— a visible force to carry out its agenda. The visible use of force and reliance upon force is designed to assist the empire in enforcing its hegemonic position. Yet, as it employs military force and abandons the rule of law, it also risks losing its hegemony.[255]

War and financial exploitation are the two dominant realities that have guided the US Global Empire in its effort to hold sway and dominion into the twenty-first century. This chapter's review of the *hidden politics of empire* has supplied sufficient evidence to make the case that it is past time for the citizens of the United States to join the rest of the citizens of the earth in principled opposition to the culture of militarism and desire for conquest that lies at the heart of the US Global Empire. Only through the unified effort of a domestic and international challenge to this colossus can humanity begin to put an end to the two dominant legacies of the US Global Empire—continuous war and a paradigm of continuous financial exploitation.[256] It is only by confronting and defeating this neoliberal/neoconservative assault on the majority of the human race that history can finally be reclaimed for the majority of the people of the world who now remain excluded. Only on a path that is supportive of a rising Global Community, in which a *post-Imperial America* plays a progressive, democratic, and inclusive role, can the future of humanity become fundamentally different from the recent past.[257]

REFLECTIONS ON THE FAILURES OF THE US GLOBAL EMPIRE

Had history moved in a different direction over the period of the last 40 years, it can be argued that the world could have developed a more mature Global Community. It would be more "mature" in the sense that its citizens and its elites would have been less afraid of diversity and more inclined toward achieving a peaceful resolution of conflicts through the UN and other international bodies. Instead, during the August 2005 congressional recess, President George W. Bush approved the appointment of John Bolton as US ambassador to the UN. That action stands as one more example of a right-wing trend that has been dedicated to removing all roadblocks to the imperial will of the US Global Empire.[258] It also is an action that allows the United States, with a revived imperial presidency, to act as a superpower that is ready to dictate what the world's agenda and goals should be—without consultation, without reference to real needs, without respect for other peoples' priorities. For example, in September 2005, the foreign policy establishment of the Bush-2 regime succeeded in editing, watering down, or just plain shredding the essence of the UN's Millennium Goals. It was the fulfillment of John Bolton's assignment to the UN. Bolton was ordered to begin a comprehensive deconstruction of the draft agreement for the 2005 Summit (which began on September 14, 2005).

Writing just a few days before the start of the summit, Julian Borger noted in *The Guardian Weekly* that: "The hundreds of deletions and insertions that Bolton's office has made to the draft represent a helpfully annotated map of administration thinking."[259] Bolton's red pen removed the substance behind the UN's Millennium goals of halving poverty in the Third World. In the US draft version, there was no discussion about the moral and political obligation of the industrialized nations giving 0.7 percent of their gross national product in aid to the developing world. Also expunged were all references to the Kyoto Treaty, taking concrete action against climate change, the ICC, and any reference to the word "disarmament" in the section on nuclear weapons. While endorsing those parts of the NPT that

would limit other countries from acquiring nuclear weapons, the Bush administration sought to reserve for itself the right to upgrade its own arsenal with the
addition of nuclear bunker-busting bombs.[260] World leaders simply caved in to US
pressure and came up with a watered-down compromise that was significantly less
than what UN Secretary General Kofi Annan had proposed just 6 months earlier.

Commenting on the aftermath of the UN fiasco, Stephen Schlesinger noted:
"The notoriously combative Bolton, despite being a late entrant into the fray,
demanded more than 700 changes to the document, including elimination of all
mention to the Millennium Development Goals the United States backed in 2000
to eradicate global poverty—the very reason for this summit—as well as all references to the Comprehensive Test Ban Treaty, the International Criminal Court,
global warming and enhancement of the General Assembly's power."[261] What
adds to the pathos of this outcome was that it was so utterly predictable. In early
August 2005, both *Asia Times*[262] and the *Common-Dreams New Center*[263]
bemoaned Bush's appointment of Bolton without US Senate approval as an
"embarrassment" that was receiving "a wholly predictable response from legislators and the foreign policy community."

The Bolton appointment to the UN is only a more recent example of what the
Bush-2 regime has been doing behind the scenes ever since seizing the presidency
through electoral fraud in the fall of 2000. It is further evident that the US Global
Empire, under the Bush-2 regime, had dedicated itself to essentially devastating
the Global Community in order to place it under the heel of a short-term effort to
realize imperial domination. Yet, the irony is that such a plan is ultimately doomed
to fail. As Professor Carl Boggs has noted: "Widespread chaos and disorder,
endemic to the ongoing cycle of militarism and terrorism, while no doubt favorable to *the power aspirations of a small circle of elites*, ultimately works against
the smooth functioning of the New World Order, including any system of consensual governance" (Italics are mine).[264]

The foregoing analysis serves to expose the soft underbelly of the US Global
Empire in its self-defeating mode. It is self-defeating because its policies and
practices offend friend and foe alike, undermine its own hegemonic ambitions by
reliance upon a doctrine of brutal militarism, and remove the possibility of developing a global politics of consensus and inclusion in both governance and the resolution of common problems that affect all of humanity. In light of the reality that
the policies currently being pursued by the US Global Empire are exclusionary
supportive of exclusionary policies for both First and Third World states—it has
placed itself in a position of practicing "democratic exclusion"—"because inclusionary practices do not automatically equate with the practice of democracy, in
either First or Third Worlds, it serves to underscore the point that mere labels are
not sufficient analytical substitutes."[265]

INCLUSIONARY GOVERNANCE VERSUS
PRO-CORPORATE GOVERNANCE

What matters most in assessing the degree of sociopolitical and socioeconomic
exclusion and/or inclusion is not what we label political practices, but rather how

certain political practices produce particular outcomes. For example, state power-lessness may be seen as a reflection of repression and exclusionary governance. The exclusionary state (ES) "is intolerant of classes and groups in the civil socie-ty that are not part of an elite pact. The ES promotes divisiveness, is elite-centered and beholden to certain select groups and parts of particular class interests … The ES engages in repression and coercion because it lacks moral authority and political legitimacy among broad segments of the population. In this context, then, the use of the term 'state power' is the wrong term to use, insofar as repression is actually an expression of 'state-powerlessness'."[266]

The United States under the Bush-2 regime as well as its foreign occupations of Iraq and Afghanistan are doomed to fail because of the administration's exclu-sionary policies. It also suffers from an inherent powerlessness due to its per-ceived lack of legitimacy both domestically and throughout most of the world. By virtue of its failure to change course and adopt an inclusionary agenda that would be supportive of inclusionary states (IS) and the Global Community at large, the elites of the Empire have sown the seeds of their own destruction. The Bush-2 regime is crippled by its own particularistic values and practices and is, by defini-tion, an exclusionary state (ES)—insofar as the construction and application of its policies are, in many respects, an attempt to use a neoliberal economic agenda and a neoconservative political agenda, in the hope of achieving virtual US hegemo-ny. Yet, these are the very policies that have undermined America's legitimacy in a world of sovereign states. The states and nations of the Global Community remain committed to the achievement of genuine national development—not a future of repression under imperial domination.

In a world of sovereign states, the opposition to any attempt of a superpower to play the role of a dominant hegemonic giant should be expected. The alternative to a scenario of endless wars, a perpetual reliance on US militarism as America's foreign policy, is found in realizing the global necessity for inclusionary politics, practices, and governance. Inclusionary governance is a form of governance that is ultimately guided by both universalistic principles and practices. These types of principles and practices would include: (1) eliminating weapons of mass destruction; (2) building a regional security regime for the Middle East; (3) engaging in confidence-building through regional education; (4) taking into account Russian and Chinese perspec-tives—not merely those of the US Global Empire; (5) re-emphasizing the value of diplomacy. As I have previously written,

> To be truly legitimate, a society, as well as its state, must evolve toward the recognition that particularistic values and practices lead back to anarchy and the state of nature. As Hobbes reminded us, it is essential to form a Commonwealth of mutual respect, where inclusionary practices foster inclusionary governance and lay the foundation for more universalistic principles and practices. In turn, these principles and practices support the long-run efficacy of inclusionary gov-ernance in the service of the Commonwealth as a whole."[267]

In the alternative, the hegemonic discourse emanating from the elites of the US Global Empire will probably continue to comfort large elements of the American public, but the fact remains "hegemonic discourses readily available to elites on the home front will be ineffective outside American borders, they will tend to subvert hegemony as the United States mobilizes its resources to shore up the foundations of its global supremacy."[268] Resistance to the US Global Empire will continue to grow in direct correspondence to its imperial hubris, its lack of fidelity to human rights, and its incapacity to create a place for social justice and inclusionary forms of governance within a viable democratic framework.

In the events leading up to the 2003 invasion of Iraq, the rather quick reversal of America's democratic traditions came about because of the development of a *war-making consensus*. In Congress, both the Democrats and Republicans discovered that a "war-making consensus depends on a high degree of patriotic or nonpartisan agreement, where doubts and ambiguities at both the elite and popular levels can be resolved or downplayed."[269] This is exactly what transpired between the Congress and the White House in the months leading up to the *"Second Gulf War."* A new version of America's political economy had begun to emerge with the Bush-2 regime. Since 2001, some scholars have argued that a distinctive Bush-fashioned political economy has emerged. It is composed of five key features:

1. Bush-2 regime aggressively put the interests of US corporations ahead of the concerns of the global capitalist class, even at the risk of serious disharmony.
2. Bush's political outlook is wary of any steps toward globalization that are not managed by the US government so as to ensure that the process does not dilute the economic power of the United States.
3. The Bush-2's inner-circle is deeply skeptical of multilateralism. Its members are fearful because even though multilateralism may promote the interests of the global capitalist class in general, it may, in many instances, go against particular US corporate interests.
4. For the Bush people, politics is key, not only in the sense of using state power to repay political favors to corporate interests but, even more important, in the sense that for them, strategic power is the ultimate form of power.
5. While the Bush-2 administration is dedicated to advancing the interests of US capital as a whole, it is especially concerned about what might be called the hard economy, which includes firms that are tied to government leaders by direct business connections—as is the case of the oil industry.[270]

Although it might seem that the Bush-2 agenda is inevitable or predetermined, the good news is that the imperial projects of the Bush-2 regime, like those of globalization, are *not historically inevitable*. Rather, they are historically conditioned projects. In fact, they reflect *a process constructed by government policy*. What is of central importance to historical change and global transformation is human agency.[271] Individual agency can change history and defy the most elegant of academic theories. For example, the birth of the Fifth Republic gave de Gaulle powers that the Fourth Republic had denied him. Shortly before the end of the Cold War, Gorbachev was able to outmaneuver hard-liners in the Politburo.[272] Against great odds, these men reshaped history because they were able to guide the circumstances of their times in a more humane and hopeful direction. It is a great testimony to the power of human agency to recognize that the choices these individuals made served to remake history.

MODERN EXTREMISM: MARKET THEOLOGY AND THE RISE OF THEOCRATIC STATES

The power of human agency, human choice, and human courage is a far more powerful influence than all the theories of the world put together. It is for this reason that the Bush-2 regime and its ideological doctrines are ultimately doomed to fail. As some critics of the Bush-2 regime have observed,

> this new American empire is not a classic imperial quest for control over territory, even though it is driven by the self-interest of an American corporate and financial elite. Rather, it reflects the use of political and military power on behalf of ideology—a radical pro-corporate, anti-government, free-market fundamentalism. In many ways, this ideology mirrors the archaic and dangerous fundamentalism of the erstwhile Taliban and al-Queda, a zealous quest for ideological empire that justifies violent means and tolerates no disagreement."[273]

The very zealotry of the Bush administration is more reminiscent of the crusades of the Middle Ages than of a post-Enlightenment America forged by a declaration of independence from the colonial rule of another King George. At the dawn of the twenty-first century, one transparent irony of American history is realizing that the United States started out with a constitutionally sanctioned separation of church and state, but it is now governed by a national administration that wants to breach that wall of separation so that it may install its own officially sanctioned brand of Christianity on the nation—as a matter of law. It is equally ironic that varieties of Islamic fundamentalism, currently at war with the Bush-2 regime, are so well represented in the United States by its virtual counterpart—a radical Christian fundamentalism. So as the US Global Empire wages a war against fundamentalism outside of its borders, within its borders a White House and a majority in Congress want to legally establish their own theocratic fundamentalism—as a matter of law. In response to these developments, we can certainly argue that what is most needed in both worlds is moderation. The role of moderation, with respect to the application of religious law and democratic governance, is to assist against all forms of extremism—whether of the right or the left. In so doing, moderates can make reasonable arguments for rejecting all theocratic forms of government.

On the matter of the role of religious law in Muslim democracy, most moderates not only reject the model of a theocratic government, they also "reject a model in which the state exists to enforce a Divine code of laws that is beyond human accountability or change."[274] In this regard, it is a little more than ironic that the foreign policy of the Bush-2 regime is so dramatically influenced by a president who acts more like a "Christian American Emperor." In various speeches, for example, Bush has announced that he is seeking to protect "God's people" from an "Axis of Evil." Similarly, on the domestic front, Bush seeks to remake the

US Supreme Court in his own image—with the assistance of lawyers "whose viewpoints will never change."

In the alternative, both Muslim and American moderates largely agree that, in matters of faith and the nature of the infinite, "divinity is too awesome and immutable to be represented by human institutions or a single individual."[275] Those who subscribed to the cult of the emperor, or those who endorsed the doctrine of the *Divine Right of Kings*, or the cult of the dictator, did not take much time to worry about the distinction between the finite and the infinite. They also did not take much time to ask themselves why they lived under tyranny—unless they believed themselves to be the beneficiaries of that tyranny.

It would probably be a safe bet to assert that the plutocracy of the American Establishment does not spend a great deal of time concerned about the extent of domestic and global tyranny that the US Global Empire employs. After all, the corporate CEOs do not see themselves as obligated to sharing the profits of their enterprises with their workers—the very labor that makes possible great profits and huge salaries in the first place. Also, given the way in which current law is written and practiced, we could assume that the corporate CEOs do not see themselves as obligated to the shareholders (who should be the true owners of the companies). Hence, with no real sense of obligation to anyone except their own self-defined concerns, it should be no surprise that the corporate titans of today's corporations do not see themselves as responsible to the advancement of the collective interest of their nation. Further, insofar as the majority of the CEOs corporate managers do not hold the development and collective advancement of Third World economies in any higher regard than they do their domestic labor force and shareholders, the entire human interests of billions of persons are sacrificed on the corporate altar of expediency. The reason for the sacrifice should be clear—there is no higher transcendent value to transfigure corporate behavior. Under these circumstances, there should be little wonder about the growth in corporate criminality and white-collar crime since the Bush-2 regime assumed office (WorldCom, Enron, Tyco, etc.).

Perhaps the adoption of such an uncritical viewpoint accounts for why a large number of American citizens supported and voted for George W. Bush. To hold such unreflective views implies that many average American citizens ignored the transfer of class power during the Reagan years. Reagan's two terms actually heralded a return to feudalism. It represented rule by a power elite of well-connected insiders—modern aristocrats. New manifestations of an aristocracy of wealth have created a newer form of corporate feudalism—otherwise called fascism. The modern Trojan horse of campaign contributions and the hidden influence of lobbyists opened the gates for the ministers of corporate capitalism to buy their way into the policy and decision-making centers of American government.

The new power elite operated through the mechanisms of cartel, oligopoly, and corporate executives (CEOs) aligned against labor. Clearly, the business sector of the power elite was not in search of ways to advance the general welfare, but was seeking to purchase the power of the State to crush their competitors as they advanced the interests of their particular industries. By undertaking this path, the rich and politically powerful have worked together to perpetuate privilege, often at the expense of the national interest and at the expense of the middle and lower classes.

In his political history of America's rich, *Wealth & Democracy*, Kevin Phillips warned: "As the twenty-first century gets underway, the imbalance of wealth and democracy in the United States is unsustainable, at least by traditional yardsticks." Phillips argues that market theology and the hidden forces of an un-elected leadership "have been displacing politics and elections. Either democracy must be renewed, with politics brought back to life, or wealth is likely to cement a new and less democratic regime—plutocracy by some other name."[276] Early in the nation's history, Alexander Hamilton worried about the destructive influence of heredity wealth matched to political privilege. In Hamilton's own day, he often pointed to the dangers to the nation that were produced by financial and market manipulation. He actively sought to contain those dangers with the policies he provided for President Washington. About 170 years later, President Kennedy's efforts to combat a modern version of the same dangers ended with his assassination.

What Kennedy shared with Hamilton was a genuine concern for advancing the general welfare—not private interests. An historical assessment of the Kennedy years shows that "at the center of his program was the attempt to make the investment process work on behalf of the general welfare. In the 1970s the investment process broke down. The oil-banking network treated the United States with little more regard than it showed for Third World nations. The interest rate and energy price shocks delivered to the US economy between the late 1960s and early 1980s, disrupted the investment process and brought economic progress in the United States and in the Third World to a halt."[277] Within the United States, both the middle and lower classes would suffer. It was no longer just the poor who couldn't make enough money to live at a decent level. The general welfare was crumbling in every major area of public concern: jobs, schooling, health care coverage, childcare, affordable housing, and being able to pay for a college education.[278] Under the auspices of the Bush-2 regime, the neoconservative agenda has effectively transformed both the domestic and foreign affairs of the nation. Following in the steps of its forefathers, the CPD,[279] the neoconservatives have emphasized and relied upon the doctrine of resurgent militarism to advance their cause.

RESURGENT MILITARISM AND THE US GLOBAL EMPIRE

Resurgent militarism remains the primary doctrine under which an imperial America operates. In large measure, it has foreclosed upon possibilities for the domestic renewal of the United States by ignoring the needs of the middle and lower classes, while ensuring that billions of dollars in tax breaks are sent upwards toward the top 3 percent of the US population. The investment decisions of many in the upper income brackets are centered upon profits to be derived from expanded investments in arms production, the privatization of war by corporations, and the depletion of funds that were originally designated for the general welfare. The elites who profit from resurgent militarism are members of an establishment that reflects the interests of a plutocracy of wealth. American cities are being decimated by the economic costs of resurgent militarism. For the US Congress to allow

this economic carnage to continue is a tragic demonstration of a collective violation of each member's oath to preserve, protect, and defend the Constitution and
to promote the general welfare. Instead, the majority inside congress have done
more to fund resurgent militarism and advance the cause of Global Empire than
to restrain or reject the imperial project. The line that divides a republic from an
empire has been crossed.

The formal exercise of democracy in congress has largely become an empty
ritual. Congressional funding of imperial ambitions has been largely accepted as
a foregone conclusion. The congressional abdication of its war power and power
of the purse has effectively severed a functional system of checks and balances
from any real system of accountability. In addition, the congressional abdication
of its constitutional responsibilities has resulted in the uncontested bankrolling of
resurgent militarism for the immediate future.

Part of the newly updated pattern involves the rise of a privatized military
industry. Breaking out of the guns-for-hire mold of traditional mercenaries,
corporations now sell skills and services that until recently only state militaries
possessed. Their products range from trained commando teams to advice from
generals. Hundreds of companies and thousands of employees encompass the
Privatized Military Industry. It is a business that generates billions of dollars in
revenue. Acting as either proxies or suppliers, this new industry has participated
in wars from Africa to Asia, from the Balkans to Latin America.[280]

By late 2003, it had become common knowledge that if Secretary of Defense
Donald Rumsfeld had his way, the vaunted US military of the future would be
transformed into what amounts to corporate owned units. Rumsfeld actually called
his plan "outsourcing." He even considered privatizing US military arsenals. As the
companies for these corporate warriors grow in size, so too does their tendency to
get involved in politics, making campaign contributions to members of congress,
and engaging in corporate lobbying. Under the Bush-2 regime, much of the US
military logistics have been farmed out to private companies—the most prominent
of which is Cheney's Halliburton subsidiary Kellogg, Brown and Root.[281]

The defense of constitutional government means that congress should retain its
war power as well as the power of the purse. To this end, the US Congress should
have constrained and restrained the power of the executive to go to war. Had the
concerns and priorities of a constitutional republic still mattered, then the
members of congress should have acted to cut off the funding for war(s) through
out the Middle East that are not in the nation's defense. In addition to the issue of
defense, wars should not be undertaken if they fail to promote the nation's real
security and violate its treaty and charter commitments under the UN and international law.[282] However, since 9/11 this has not been the case.

The congressional abdication of its constitutional role and responsibilities has
contributed to the effective erosion of what remained of a system of checks and balances. In the case of judicial appointments, the constitutional requirement of *advise
and consent* has been largely abandoned. In the matter of intelligence oversight, the
congress has failed to adequately investigate the CIA and Pentagon with regard to
officially sanctioned torture as a means by which the US-led *war on terror* was to
be conducted. The Bush-2 regime emitted a stream of lies regarding the danger

posed by Saddam Hussein and his alleged possession of weapons of mass destruction (WMD). A process of sanctioned distortions, disinformation, and outright falsehoods provided the path that led to war with Iraq in 2003. The process of deception necessitated an early end to the work of the UN weapons inspectors, as well as the manipulation of US intelligence agencies so that their work product could be used to deceive congress and the public. With respect to the dangers associated with the rebirth of an imperial presidency, most members of congress turned a blind eye to its excesses and its transparent employment of lies and deception—all designed to further advance the hidden agenda of the Establishment's empire builders.[283]

The injustices inflicted by global poverty and inequality, within and between nations, continue to plague the entire Global Community. These harsh realities were confronted before in our recent global history, as exemplified in the administration of John F. Kennedy, in the senatorial career and presidential campaign of Robert F. Kennedy, and in the public ministry of Martin Luther King, Jr., as well as those he inspired with his legacy of nonviolence, such as South Africa's Nelson Mandela.[284] Individually and collectively, they criticized and condemned the imperial mind-set. If anything, the Kennedy brothers, King, and Mandela called for accountability and spoke of the need to revive the human conscience in reference to a higher authority than that of the State.[285] As political and moral leaders, each of them recognized the need to build sustainable communities that would be capable of nurturing people who would be capable of guiding human institutions in a more humane and inclusive direction.[286] In this respect, they all worked to affirm their commitment to the creation of an alternative reality, beyond the world of power politics. Instead of merely allowing the future to be a repetition of the past, they understood the idea that humane visions and ideals transcend time and place. Therefore, they would argue that only by admitting its failures—or having its failures exposed and rejected—could the US Global Empire be dismantled and a *post-Imperial America* take its place.[287] Whether the proper channels for this process are tribunals, international courts, truth and reconciliation commissions, or a combination of all of them, it is essential to expose the nature and failures of the US Global Empire. If a rising Global Community is to unite with a *post-Imperial America*, then a process of national and global education is necessary to move beyond the rationales of imperial thinking and its justifications.

For the sake of a rising Global Community, it will be necessary to bring an end to the imperial enterprise and to move a *post-Imperial America* toward de-funding the elite groups, institutions, and lobbies, that all help to make resurgent militarism a possibility—research and development (R&D), defense industries in the service of arms and weapons production, and the continued basing of military forces around the globe that support the smooth functioning of the US Global Empire. The empire's hidden politics, hidden history, and hidden agendas need to be exposed, judged, and ultimately rejected. In its place, a *post-Imperial America* and the rest of humanity can evolve toward creating an international order that will no longer tolerate the presence of any would-be empire builders. Collectively, every nation can work through the already-existing human rights treaty structure in order to build more inclusive institutions, capable of sustaining the evolution of a rising Global Community. In this task, the abolition of global poverty and inequality should be the first order of business. After all, the US Global Empire currently presides over an international environment where hundreds of billions of dollars are spent every year on global arms sales and arms transfers[288] while, at the same time, the UN has estimated that over 2 billion people live on less than a dollar a day.

THE DOWNING STREET MEMO: EVIDENCE OF GEORGE W. BUSH'S SEARCH FOR A PRETEXT TO GO TO WAR

On May 1, 2005, a London *Sunday Times* article disclosed the details of a classified memorandum—also known as the *Downing Street Minutes* or *Downing Street Memo*. It recounted the minutes of a July 2002 meeting of Prime Minister Tony Blair that describes an American president already committed to going to war in the summer of 2002—despite contrary assertions to both the public and the congress. Additionally, the minutes also describe apparent efforts by highly placed Bush administration officials to manipulate intelligence data to justify the war.

The hidden politics of empire is clearly revealed in the *Downing Street Memo*. It clearly shows that President George W. Bush was not only committed to remove Saddam through military action, but also how the overriding concern in both the United States government and the British government was how to "fix" the intelligence. Without such a "fix" it was clear that the war could not be justified. The justification was in search of a pretext—a pretext for war. In this regard, the great value of the memo is that it reveals a conscious concern with creating a pretext for war and, at the same time, the existence of a clear hierarchy of decision making.[289] Both Bush and Blair were at the epicenter of the political decision to go to war.

In creating a pretext for war, the truth of the facts did not ultimately matter. What mattered was that the facts that were presented "fit" the official story line. The game of doctoring or fixing the intelligence was an integral part to initiating a war and a cover-up at the same time. In this sense, the approach to making a case for war against Iraq, used by the CIA and the Bush administration, began with an official story that used the events of 9/11 as its baseline.

Whether or not al-Queda was involved with Saddam and an emerging network of terrorist cells, it simply did not matter. What mattered was that the American public and world opinion would be provided with a plausible scenario for going to war. In this task, the work of the Bush-2 administration and the CIA was similar to that of the Warren Commission: start with the premise that Lee Harvey Oswald was the "lone assassin" of the president. If evidence of a conspiracy came to the surface, it was to be quashed, rejected, and dismissed.

The Warren Commission rejected the evidence of a conspiracy in the assassination of President Kennedy because it feared what it might find about a plot that was carried out in conjunction with certain government agencies—particularly the CIA and FBI. Interlocking directorships and corporate interests that united the interests of oil with the military-industrial-complex had a stake in the investigation's outcome. Therefore, some members of the Warren Commission were representatives of the economic and financial powers in the American Establishment. Both John McCloy and Allan Dulles were assigned that role. In addition, Dulles, the former CIA Director at the time of the Bay of Pigs fiasco, could cover for the agency. As the Warren Commission completed its work, these powerful financial and corporate interests would remain immune from examination or prosecution, as would the FBI and CIA. So too, in 2004, President George W. Bush would bestow on the then retired CIA Director, Mr. George Tenet, the highest civilian honor for his service—the Medal of Freedom. Mr. Tenet did his job and Bush and Blair got their war.

It was a going to be a war of choice, not a war of necessity. According to Mark Danner, "by July 2002 at the latest, war had been decided on: the question at issue now was how to justify it—how to 'fix', as it were, what Blair will later call 'the political context'."[290] Surprisingly, in July 2002, Bush had not even contemplated going to the UN or demanding that inspectors be sent into Iraq to determine whether or not there were weapons of mass destruction. The *Downing Street Memo* makes clear that the National Security Council—the senior security officials of the US government—had no patience with the UN route. Yet, in order to establish "the political context" for the war, as Blair put it, the United States would eventually discover that it could not bypass the UN.

According to Mark Danner,

> the British realized they needed "help with the legal justification for the use of force," because, as the attorney general pointed out, rather dryly, "the desire for regime change was not a legal base for military action." Which is to say, the simple desire to overthrow the leadership of a given sovereign country does not make it legal to invade that country; on the contrary. And, said the attorney general, of the "three possible legal bases: self-defense, humanitarian intervention, or [United Nations Security Council] authorization," the first two "could not be the base in this case." In other words, Iraq was not attacking the United States or the United Kingdom, so the leaders could not claim to be acting in self-defense; nor was Iraq's leadership in the process of committing genocide, so the United States and the United Kingdom could not claim to be invading for humanitarian reasons. This left Security Council authorization as the only conceivable legal justification for war. But how to get it?[291]

The answer came from Tony Blair himself—according to the *Downing Street Memo*:

> The *Prime Minister* said that it would make a big difference politically and legally if Saddam refused to allow in the UN weapons inspectors. Regime change and WMD were linked in the sense that it was the regime that was producing the WMD. There were different strategies for dealing with Libya and Iran. If the political context were right, people would support regime change. The two key issues were whether the military plan worked and whether we had the political strategy to give the military plan the space to work.[292]

In a much longer and widened context, it becomes possible to discover that the plan for regime change predated the Bush-2 presidency by about 10 years. It is a plan that goes back to his father, George Herbert Walker Bush. According to Scott Ritter, one of the UN's top weapons inspectors between 1991 and 1998, Ritter believed that his mission was to conclusively disarm Iraq, thereby enabling the UN to lift its sanctions. But what he discovered was that Washington was only ever interested in using inspections as a conduit to spy on Saddam's government and to effect *regime change*, not disarmament.[293]

In order to effectuate this end, Ritter asserts that the "CIA was designated as the principle implementer of this policy. Therefore, when one looks at the March 2003 invasion of Iraq and the subsequent removal from power of the government of Saddam Hussein, the only conclusion that can be reached is that the CIA accomplished its mission."[294] It is a mission that most recently can be traced back to the *Downing Street Memo*, "where we now know that both the US and the UK intelligence services had, by July 2002, agreed to 'fix the intelligence around policy'." However, the task of "fixing intelligence around policy" has been a practice of the US Global Empire since at least 1992 "when the decision was made to doctor the intelligence about Iraqi SCUD missile accounting, asserting the existence of missiles in the face of UNSCOM inspection results which demonstrated that there were none."[295]

To say that the CIA was *designated* as the principle implementer of this policy, is not to say that it was the source for the inspiration to do the "fixing." Rather, the source for ordering the CIA to do what it did came from the Executive branch. The Pentagon, acting on Bush's orders, found a willing fix-it-man in CIA Director George Tenet. After failing to find links between Iraq and al-Queda for years the CIA under Tenet's leadership began to play politics and arranged intelligence to tell the Pentagon what it wanted to hear. Tenet took the work of the CIA's key intelligence analysts and framed it in such a way that their conclusions would conform to the Pentagon's preconceived view.[296] Within the Pentagon itself a channel was opened up to collect intelligence from Iraqi exiles, using people off the books, including contractors. One inside observer said that it was "getting pretty close to an Iran-Contra type of situation."[297]

While officials at the highest levels of the Pentagon and CIA collaborated in fixing intelligence, the diplomatic offensive was gathering strength at the US State Department. Following the logic set out in the *Downing Street Memo*, it was thought that the inspectors would be introduced into Iraq as a means to create the legal justification for war. In other words, if the UN could be made to agree upon some kind of ultimatum that "Saddam accept inspectors, and if Saddam then refused to accept them, the Americans and the British would be well on their way to having a legal justification to go to war ... Thus, the idea of UN inspectors was introduced not as a means to avoid war, as President Bush repeatedly assured Americans, but as a means to make way possible."[298]

According to Hans Blix, the former director of the UN Inspection Commission,

> there was another option for the states that wish to take armed action against Iraq in the spring of 2003. They could have heeded the Council's request for more time for inspection. Support by the Security Council for preemptive

action would have given the armed action legitimacy. Instead, a greater price was paid for this action: in the compromised legitimacy of the action, in the damaged credibility of the governments pursing it, and in the diminished authority of the United Nations.[299]

We find in Blix's assessment there is some agreement with the prediction that Tony Blair made that July morning on Downing Street, when he noted that the "two key issues were whether the military plan worked and whether we had the political strategy to give the military plan the space to work." Specifically, Blair was proven right in the sense that "his political strategy only half worked: the Security Council's refusal to vote a second resolution approving the use of force left 'the UN route' discussed that day incomplete, and Blair found himself forced to follow the United States without the protection of international approval."[300]

   As to the military plan, it has turned out not to have "worked." Instead of a short and decisive war, Bush and Blair began an unending Iraqi insurgency accompanied by a toll of thousands of dead and wounded—American, British, and Iraqi soldiers and citizens. In a larger context, the military plan reveals the horror and illegality of the Bush-2 doctrine of preemptive war. From the beginning, the doctrine of preemption—in combination with the strategy labeled *shock and awe*— sought a long-term political, economic, and military objective: the permanent presence of the US in the Persian Gulf. The strategy chosen to realize this objective was a massive military operation that sought to conquer and occupy Iraq for an indefinite period of time. The strategy was not only a military strategy. It was a strategy designed to permanently usurp the integrity of international law and the effectiveness of the United Nations as a counterweight to superpower and non-superpower aggression. In a world of legally sovereign states, the US invasion and occupation of Iraq signified a new level of imperial indiscretion in the context of a *New World Order*. In this undertaking, it "was not a random act of raw power. It was the first salvo of a new and dangerous US doctrine, a doctrine which advocates the unprovoked invasion and occupation of sovereign nations."[301]

   Not since the decade of the 1930s has the world witnessed such planning and preparation for war as with the Bush-2 regime's build-up to war with Iraq. Not since the Nazis regime has a great power relied more upon such a combination of propaganda mixed with a right-wing ideology—as has been the case with the neo-conservatives in the Bush-2 regime. Not since the Nazi invasion of Eastern Europe has the world seen such a doctrine (the doctrine of preemptive war) placed into practice in the last 100 years.[302] Not since the Nuremberg Charter's legal admonitions against *planning and preparation for aggressive war* and its condemnation of *crimes against humanity* has a supposedly democratic nation or set of nations (the United States and UK) embarked upon such an illegal and immoral course in world affairs.[303] In this sense, the actions of the Bush-2 regime against Iraq are unprecedented in the history of the United States.[304]

IN THE SHADOW OF THE VIETNAM WAR

While the Vietnam War provides historical parallels to the involvement of the United States in Iraq and throughout the Persian Gulf, the main difference is that the invasion of Iraq in 2003 was not undertaken in the context of a Cold War paradigm. The nature of global struggles is, in large measure, determined by the nature and character of the combatants themselves. The Cold War paradigm was largely determined by the unique nature of the USSR, insofar as it embodied both the quality of being a *revisionist great power* (one concerned with revising the global distribution of power and prestige in its favor), and a *revolutionary great power* (the holy land of a messianic political religion with adherents in many counties).[305] Additionally, most of the rationales employed to justify the Cold War could not factually become the operative guiding principles for the US invasion of Iraq in 2003. This was the case because, first: the terrorist organization (al-Queda) is a *stateless* entity. It was not a sovereign state which a war could be declared upon. Second, while the US and USSR fought for *spheres of influence*, they could only do so through *low-intensity conflicts* or *proxy wars* because neither dare risk a head-to-head confrontation that would result in a nuclear war. In the case of al-Queda, the war was taken directly to the American homeland on 9/11. Third, with the demise of the USSR in 1990, policymakers in the US national security bureaucracy spent most the first decade after its demise looking for *rogue states* as an excuse to bolster the Pentagon's already-bloated post-Cold War budget.

There never was a clearly direct enemy to justify *a war on terror* or any other kind of war. The use of the events of 9/11 changed all of that for US policymakers in the Pentagon, CIA, FBI, and the White House. A fundamentally different element was at work in the case of the US/UK invasion of Iraq. The new element was determining how, in a post-Cold War world, the United States could possibly justify its desire for *another American Century* The combination of the 9/11 attacks, the historical dependence of the United States on Middle East oil for energy, the new struggle that the United States faced for global hegemony against a rising Europe and China, all combined to force US policymakers to develop a new paradigm for *another American Century*.[306] Still, the many parallels between the way in which the US Global Empire conducted the Vietnam War and now the war in Iraq are startling (see the table overleaf: *Shared Characteristics Between the Vietnam War and the Iraq War*).

The phrase *another American Century* is actually a code for the concept of hegemony. In order to pursue another century of maintaining global dominance, through the pursuit and maintenance of hegemony, the neoconservatives of the Bush-2 regime worked out a plan to rationalize the project by adopting a new long-term justification. The plan was inaugurated with the attacks on 9/11, when Bush declared that the United States would spend the rest of the twenty-first century in what would be an endless global *war on terrorism*. In reality, the *war on terrorism* was actually designed to secure energy resources while, at the same time, attempting to shore up America's declining hegemony.[307] The only way to sell the funding for the goal of the global domination by the US Global Empire was to disguise it as a defense of the US homeland through a global war on terror. When confronting the complexities of the new post-Cold War world, the president relied upon deception, rather than education.[308]

Looking beyond Iraq, it is difficult to see anything more to come out of the current US power structure than a US foreign policy bureaucracy at work that is

Shared Characteristics Between Vietnam War and Iraq War

Iraq	Vietnam	Shared characteristics
X (Weapons of Mass Destruction)	X (Gulf of Tonkin)	Administration misled Congress and the public to get US into the conflict
X	X	Frequent false claims of progress
X	X	War turns into a quagmire
X	X	Huge budgetary costs
X	X	Budget costs not paid—increasing deficit
X	X	Low-level US casualties at start of war
X	X	"Staying the course" justified by sacrifices
X	X	Insurgents motivated by foreign occupation
X	X	No historical understanding of other nation
X (Terrorism)	X (Communism)	War is framed in context of larger struggle
X	X	High number of "collateral" civilian deaths
X	X	US uncertain re-number of civilian deaths
X	X	Use of enemy body counts = "progress"
X	X	War used as an election issue
X	X	War undermines world opinion of the United States
X	X	Little support from US allies
X	X	War erodes fighting capacity of US military
X	X	Lowered standards for military recruitment
X	X	Failure to understand limits of high-tech war
X	X	Election results touted as progress
X	X	United States claims insurgents are isolated groups
X	X	Public support deteriorates into opposition
X	X	No exit strategy or timeframe for war's end

ultimately dedicated to finding a pretext for another war. In the world of the *Downing Street Memo*, as was the case in the covert world of Operation Northwoods, the planning/conspiracies/cover-ups for the 9/11 attacks and the Kennedy assassination; a nonexistent attack on US ships in the Gulf of Tonkin; and the road of deception and cover-ups that led to the Vietnam War, there is one common denominator: the US Global Empire's quest for hegemony and world domination. All of this leads to one dominant and overarching question which is derived from the school of Realist thought: "In a world of one superpower, how is that superpower going to be restrained from an excessive use of that power in a 'unipolar moment'—a moment in history where there is no true rival?"[309] As the United States contemplates making the twenty-first century *another American Century*, the answer to that question is of primary importance.

Unfortunately, the first priority for those who are the architects of the US Global Empire is—and always will be—the maintenance of its twentieth century hegemony into the future. Even though such a US-directed hegemony is already a lost project, the paradigm still being used by most in the American Establishment requires nothing less. In fact, if anything can truthfully be said about the rationale operating behind the *hidden politics of empire*, it should be that the use and employment of American power—in the twentieth and early twenty-first centuries—has been perpetually, purposefully, and intentionally guided in a direction that places human rights, national development, and humane/inclusive directions for governance at the bottom of the list of its priorities.

THE TEMPLATE OF CONSPIRACY AND COVER-UP: THE 9/11 COMMISSION AND WARREN COMMISSION AS MIRROR IMAGES

In the case of the 9/11 attacks, the 9/11 Commission failed to investigate the events of that time in an appropriately credible and critical manner. As was the case with the work of the Warren Commission,

> huge amounts of relevant historical and contemporary data have been ignored; irrelevant data and narratives have been used to construct an inaccurate chronology of 9/11 and its historical context; the embarrassing and damaging implications of ample evidence, including testimony presented to the Commission, have been overlooked; blatantly dishonest testimony contradicting well-documented facts has been uncritically accepted ... Ultimately, the Commission has served to veil the underlying truth behind the phenomenon of international terrorism in the post-Cold War period, of which 9/11 was a most terrifying manifestation.[310]

Behind the 9/11 Commission's cover-up of the truth there is a hidden strategy that the Empire uses to its advantage: convert the assertion of "a war on terrorism" into an excuse to expand American military power in order to maintain America's weakening hegemonic position. For example, some observers have noted "every twist in the war on terrorism seems to leave a new Pentagon outpost in the Asia-Pacific Region, from the former USSR to the Philippines. One of the lasting consequences of the war could be what amounts to a military encirclement of China."[311] The war on terrorism has served to open up a host of new enterprises and strategies for the empire. Among them is a strategy to ensure that no rival nation or coalition of nations emerge to challenge its current hegemonic dominance. Hence, what is actually behind this momentous shift in US policy toward China is the American fear that its twenty-first century supremacy could be eclipsed. At its root is the continuing influence of neoconservative strategists who have long championed a policy of permanent US military supremacy.

The fear of another global rival on the scale of the former USSR is what has driven US policy. Therefore, in this new century, the one that is supposed to be *another American century*—the threat to American supremacy can only come from China, insofar as no other potential adversary possesses a credible capacity to generate global power.[312] The preservation of American supremacy into "the far realm of the future," as the then-Governor George W. Bush put it in a 1999 campaign speech, required the permanent containment of China. As was the case with the Cold War strategy of *containment* with respect to the USSR, the national security bureaucracy and President George W. Bush seek to limit the capacity of any potential global rival to effectively compete with the United States for dwindling oil supplies around the globe. In what is supposed to be another century of American dominance, the US Global Empire seeks to contain China while it allows itself to endure an occupation of Iraq, generating an insurgency that has become a quagmire.

The neoconservative forces that assumed office with Bush in 2001 only needed a pretext in order to implement their ambitious plans to extend US power around the world. The attacks of 9/11 supplied that historical opening for launching *a war for American dominance*—euphemistically called the *war on terror*. The war on terror would be used to justify an illegal invasion and occupation of Iraq, as well as inaugurate a new containment strategy for China. Both these endeavors would be premised upon the foundation of a desire for American hegemony and its military capability to achieve "full spectrum dominance" over the globe and in outer space.

Conservatives in the national security bureaucracy had long championed the pursuit of a policy dedicated to permanent US military supremacy. It was expressed as recently as 1992 in the Defense Planning Guidance (DPG) report for fiscal years 1994–1999. The DPG was a master blueprint for US dominance in the post-Cold War era. It was prepared under the supervision of the then-Under Secretary of Defense Paul Wolfovitz—one of the neoconservative authors of a different document entitled, *Project for the Next American Century* (PNAC). Wolfovitz rose to prominence in the new Bush-2 regime. The events of 9/11 became the trip wire for the implementation of his views and that of the other neoconservatives.

The post-9/11 era would open up another chapter in what I have termed *a war for American dominance*. In the Cold War years a war for American dominance was carried out through a strategy of containment, designed to limit the military and economic reach of the USSR. In the post-9/11 years a war for American dominance is being carried out through a strategy of containment, designed to limit the military reach of China and its capacity to capture oil resources from areas currently under US control or with in easy access. In the Cold War years, an insurgency in Vietnam became a quagmire for US troops. In the post-9/11 years, an insurgency in Iraq has become a quagmire for US troops.

As was the case with the eventual American intervention in Vietnam,

> the impetus for the assertive use of military power in Vietnam came overwhelmingly from the national security bureaucracy itself, rather than from the presidency ... the policy making process on Vietnam became dysfunctional because of the refusal of national security advisors to accept a presidential policy that rejected the use of military force in defense of national security interests.[313]

In this respect, the main historical distinction that needs to be made in any comparison between President Kennedy and President Bush is that while President Bush concurred with his national security bureaucracy, President Kennedy did not agree with his. Yet, even that is putting it mildly. Kennedy had enraged the CIA and the Pentagon because of his policy of military restraint.[314]

Because Kennedy was genuinely committed to peaceful existence with the Soviets, there were many in his own government that perceived his policies as nothing less than treason. This is precisely why it was necessary for elite interests, in and out of government, to remove Kennedy by assassination. In fact, it was because so many in the CIA and Pentagon were considered traitors for "going soft on communism," and by starting to bring an end to the Cold War, it was easier for the conspirators to launch a successful cover-up and set the stage for the ratification of the assassination.[315] Kennedy did not agree with most in the American Establishment about how a military intervention in Asia—using American combat troops—was going to advance the "national interest." So, between Kennedy's decision to withdraw from Vietnam and his signing of the Nuclear Test Ban Treaty—both accomplished in October of 1963—the war-oriented hard-liners in the American power structure made the decision to set the assassination apparatus into immediate effect.[316]

President Kennedy's vision embraced a world of diversity, not a monolithic empire that would have to be maintained by American weapons of war. He endorsed cooperation between the superpowers, not continued hostility. He sought "a grand and global alliance, North and South, East and West," that would benefit all of humankind. In other words, he saw a *post-Imperial America* pursuing a *strategy of peace* within an interdependent Global Community. Kennedy's vision embraced an end to war and international disarmament. Why invest in arms "that can only destroy and never create?" Even in his inaugural address, Kennedy asked the Soviets to join the United States in a struggle against the real enemies of humankind: "tyranny, poverty, disease, and war itself." His enemies had a different world in mind. With America as the imperial heir to the British Empire, Kennedy's enemies all believed that the national interest and security of the United States required massive military forces.[317]

Kennedy's vision was best expressed in his *strategy of peace* commencement address, as proclaimed in June 1963 at American University. He saw the potential for a rising Global Community without seeking the establishment of a *Pax Americana*. However, the military-industrial-complex, the Pentagon, CIA, FBI, Texas oilmen, and the financial elites of the establishment did not agree with Kennedy's visionary approach.[318] Therefore, it was decided that Kennedy had to be removed and removed as quickly as possible. If too much time passed, Lyndon Johnson and his cohorts who had been involved in various illegal activities could face jail time. The 1964 tax bill that Kennedy had proposed might succeed in removing the oil depletion allowance. The schedule that Kennedy had already initiated for a phased withdrawal from Vietnam might be sped up if the situation in South Vietnam continued to deteriorate at an even faster pace. The October 1963 signing of the Nuclear Test Ban Treaty with the USSR and Great Britain might accelerate the Kennedy administration's call for cuts in the defense budget and a winding down of the Cold War. The Alliance for Progress was making headway in Latin America as more governments turned toward the democratic option and embraced a wide variety of social reforms from education to health care. The Alliance was also a threat to both American business interests and Latin American oligarchs who opposed land reform and the expansion of socioeconomic rights and opportunities for the lower classes. If the Alliance continued on its current course, elites in both North America and South America would see a diminishment in their profit margins and a bleak future without the assistance of repressive military dictatorships to protect their privileged positions. With all of these uncertainties hanging in the balance, it was decided that Kennedy had to be immediately removed—by assassination.

With Kennedy's assassination, none of his scenarios for a more peaceful world were allowed to materialize. Instead, the right-wing hawks in the Pentagon and CIA found that the door was now open for direct military force being applied in Vietnam. With a more compliant occupant in the Oval Office, the White House would once again become subservient to an elite vision that was based on permanent American dominance and global hegemony. President Lyndon Johnson believed in the strategic importance of Asia—especially Vietnam—for reasons that Kennedy did not.[319] Therefore, he helped to orchestrate the Gulf of Tonkin incident and turned it into a resolution for war.[320]

In the same manner, George W. Bush used the attacks on 9/11 to orchestrate a *war on terror*. Without evidence, without a concern for truth, a compliant media and a docile congress assisted the Johnson administration—and *all of the administrations that were to follow*—with an uncritical eye for the truth about the goals and aims of America's foreign policy. Whether it was the path to war in Vietnam or the way in which the symbolic attacks of 9/11 were used, a media composed largely of stenographers merely parroted the administration line.[321] Similarly, the majority of those in congress found it easier to abdicate their constitutional responsibilities with respect to the war power than to be faithful to their oath of office. Ultimately, the same outcome would obtain with regard to the passage of the USA Patriot Act. Without even reading the USA Patriot Act, a majority in congress would place the protections of the Bill of Rights on the altar of the national security state and expediency, sacrificing them in the name of a "war on terrorism."

In a damning critique of this outcome, historian Arthur M. Schlesinger, Jr., notes: "President Bush made a drastic change in the foreign policy of the United States, a change that deserved to be debated on its merits. No national debate preceded the Iraq War of a quality and seriousness that preceded most wars in American history. This represented a failure of the political process."[322] The same may be said of the aftermath of the Kennedy assassination and the road to Vietnam.[323] To underscore this point, it should also be added that the role of ideology is huge in undertaking the task of taking a nation to war. However, the effect of ideology upon the citizenry is not to enlighten, but to confuse. The media has acted as an advertising agency for the Bush-2 regime's hard-core ideological viewpoints (and lies) that supported road to war. Such an outcome is predictable when "ideologies can provide a comforting way of understanding a complex world and a guide to swift action. But even under the best of circumstances, they are likely to distort, to miss a great deal, and to inhibit adjustment to changing circumstances."[324] The reluctance and refusal of President Bush and his senior officials in the departments of Defense and State to consider a withdrawal of American troops from Iraq is testimony to their strict adherence to an ideological course of action.

The common denominator that lay behind both the Kennedy assassination and the 9/11 attacks was the American Establishment's desire to promote a *war for*

American dominance and global hegemony. Behind both events, the tentacles of the warfare state not only demanded a continuation of foreign wars abroad, but a more chaotic and fearful citizenry at home—incapable of mounting an effective opposition to the enterprises of the US Global Empire. Just 7 years after the assassination in Dallas, the District Attorney of New Orleans, Jim Garrison, observed:

> Just as the Cold War provides reasons for the existence of autocratic power, so does chaos within the nation operate as a source of power. As chaos continues, the population will tend to be less concerned about abridgment of individual rights and will more willingly grant to a strong centralized government such power it claims it needs."[325]

Such is the post-9/11 world, replete with the USA Patriot Act, the CIA freed to spy on Americans by Executive Order, a presidential lifting of the ban on assassination and torture as tools of American foreign policy in the so-called *war on terrorism*.

The US Global Empire is a warfare state. It demands its sacrifices. The elites that run the empire understand this basic principle and will only allow the American people to enjoy the appearance of democracy, not its substance. Ever since the Dallas assassination, it has become abundantly clear that democratic institutions, constitutional protections, and presidents were expendable when it came to realizing the elite's version of what constituted the *national interest*.[326] Under close examination, the true nature of the so-called national interest reveals the duplicity and hypocrisy of the warfare state and it cannot remain hidden under the thinly veiled disguise of ideology and propaganda. The Vietnam War years taught that lesson, and the war in Iraq is already providing another opportunity to revisit the lesson.

There comes a breaking point where the failures of empire can no longer be masked. Both the body counts and the escalating costs of war begin to effectively undermine the imperial project. Take, for example, the historical record of the Vietnam War where

> by mid-1967 Lyndon Johnson's scheme to finance the war painlessly had been torpedoed. He could no longer hide the high cost or the devastating impact upon the federal budget. The Defense Department estimates of expenditures to support US obligations in Southeast Asia by fiscal year were as follows: 1965, $103 million; 1966, $5,812 million; 1967, $20,133 million; 1968, $26,547 million; and 1969, $28,805 million. By mid-1967, the start of fiscal 1968, the number of troops in Vietnam peaked at 525,000; the cost topped out at $28.8 billion in 1969.[327]

The national interest had become the private property of the wealthy interests in the American Establishment—an establishment that derived the bulk of its wealth from Wall Street investments in the military-industrial-complex, aerospace, oil, global finance, and bank lending to Third World nations under the auspices of the IMF and World Bank. By the 1990s, this system would be governed by the draconian rules of the WTO. It is from this perspective—based upon these historical events and their consequences—that we can trace the template of conspiracy and cover-up that connects the work and purpose of the Warren Commission with that of the 9/11 Commission.

The Template of Conspiracy and Cover-up: The 9/11 Commission and the Warren Commission Follow Similar Paths on the Road to a Cover-up

In many crucial ways, the aftermath and official investigation of the 9/11 attacks fit the same template as the aftermath and official investigation of the assassination of President Kennedy:

—Within hours, despite a lack of real evidence, one man was blamed for the event, along with hints that he was connected to foreign enemies.

—Official pronouncements that were widely publicized were quietly admitted as errors later on.

—Although within the jurisdiction of the local authorities, the entire case was usurped by the FBI and CIA, both agencies under the control of a president who benefited from the tragedy.

—A group of specialists (medical in the JFK case and engineers in the WTC) was convened, but limited in what they could view and study, blocked from conducting an objective probe by federal officials.

—Evidence in the case was hastily removed and destroyed, forever lost to an impartial and meaningful investigation. The autopsy of President Kennedy, the quick rebuilding of the presidential car after the assassination, the alteration of photographs depicting the true nature of the president's wounds, are all a part of the history of cover-up of the assassination. As to 9/11, the remnants of the Twin Towers were hastily disposed of and never properly investigated. The actual causes of structural collapse could never be determined with certainty.

—More evidence was locked away in government files under the shield of "national security."

—Federal malfeasance was excused by claiming lack of manpower and resources, and no one was disciplined or fired. Federal agency budgets were increased.

—Any alternative to the official version of events was decried as a "conspiracy theory" and "unpatriotic." Evidence of conspiracy was either suppressed or destroyed.

—The federal government used the event to increase its own centralized power. After 9/11, the War Powers Resolution was rendered impotent by a compliant congress.

—Also, the passage of the USA Patriot Act opened the door for greater CIA/FBI intrusions into the private lives of American citizens. Domestic surveillance increased and the creation of the Department of Homeland Security added another layer of centralized governmental power to an already intrusive intelligence and spy apparatus.

—A foreign war (Vietnam in the aftermath of the Kennedy assassination—and Afghanistan and Iraq in the Bush-2 regime) was supported by a grieving population that would have otherwise opposed such foreign wars.

—Top government leaders (Lyndon Johnson from 1963 to 1968 and now George W. Bush) were propelled to new heights of power and popularity after having been formerly under suspicion for election fraud and corrupt business dealings.

—Many citizens were aware or suspected that the official version of events was incorrect or a cover-up of the truth, but were afraid to speak out. In the JFK case, those who did speak out often wound up as dead witnesses.

—A compliant mass media was content to merely repeat the official version of events without investigating the veracity of what they were being told and avoided asking hard questions that may have exposed the truth. With the exception of the Watergate scandal, most reporters in the national media have been little more than official stenographers for the White House.

The consequence of imposing this veil of secrecy and distortion has been to leave the actions and motivations of the US Global Empire unchallenged. By extrapolation, it can also be argued that this veil of secrecy and distortion has made an *exodus from empire* more difficult. It is more difficult because the truth about the true nature of this empire lies buried within a *hidden history* as well as a *hidden politics*. Only by revealing the true facts, motivations, and political history of the empire's elites can there be a movement toward accountability. Whether the search for truth ends up in the International Criminal Court, a Global Peoples Tribunal, or some other appropriate forum, it will represent a new beginning for the era of a rising Global Community. Only by exposing the determinative roles of economic and political elites in the US Global Empire can the empire's geostrategic imperatives and institutional agenda be opposed and ultimately be removed as a threat to a humane future and world peace. Only in these fundamental ways can an adequate challenge be mounted to empire that has the capacity to both reveal its hidden politics and, at the same time, lay the foundation for a path over which the United States and the world can finally embark upon an *exodus from empire*.

6
Claiming "A Right of Peace"

Moving Beyond the "Empire Syndrome"

The American superpower is an artificial construct, widely perceived as illegitimate, whatever the acquiescence it coerces in others. Its reign is therefore inherently unstable. Indeed, its reach for full-scale world domination marks the beginning of its decline. A large task for the world, and for Americans in particular, is the early recognition and humane management of that decline.[1]

Robert Jay Lifton

Among international scholars *there is support for **a right of peace** that should be accepted in international and local courts, or in the right of exodus*, which could be enforced against a warring state by citizens of that state against their respective government or the governments of other states. The **right of peace** would become part of the ensemble of rights that humanity now expects for itself, through legal, social, and political institutions and ultimately by its own actions. With **a right of peace**, the burden shifts away from the citizen to blindly follow the call to war, for the nation would be constrained in its activities by those who opt out of the war system ... The right to peace challenges the assumptions of national security and defense policy that have burdened the United States since the Second World War (*Bolding and Italics are mine*).[2]

Marcus G. Raskin

The first step in creating a more satisfactory basis for managing the interrelationships between security and sustainable development is to broaden our vision. Conflicts may arise not only because of political and military threats to national sovereignty; they may derive also from environmental degradation and the pre-emption of development options ... The global commons cannot be managed from any national center. The nation-state is insufficient to deal with threats to shared ecosystems. Threats to environmental security can only be dealt with by joint management and multilateral procedures and mechanisms.[3]

World Commission on Environment and Development

The United States does not fight wars to change regimes or impose new world orders. It fights to deter things from happening ... Deterrence did

260

not end with the Cold War. The nuclear stand-off kept the two super-powers at peace with each other for forty years. The difference today is that deterrence is taking the form of *dissuasion*, the relentless application of force 365 days a year. Deterrence is a very peculiar form of action: *it is what causes something not to take place*. It dominates the whole of our contemporary period, and it tends not to produce events but to cause something not to occur, while looking as though it is a historical event (Italics in the original).[4]

Christopher Coker

THE DETERRENCE OF DEVELOPMENT OPTIONS
FOR THE GLOBAL COMMUNITY BY THE
US GLOBAL EMPIRE

There is now general agreement among scholars, social activists, and many thoughtful political leaders around the world that the US Global Empire is in decline, despite its militarily dominant position. This is the assessment of many realist theorists who argue that America's relative power position has been slowly, but inexorably eroding for several decades. In attempting to address the problem of the erosion of its relative power, the architects of the US Global Empire have sought to shore up its declining hegemony by placing an even greater reliance on the use of military threat and force. However, by exercising this force, the US Global Empire has intentionally engaged upon a course of action leading to the deterrence of development options for the Global Community. This trend has been coupled with deepening military investments and widening sales in the global arms market.

A culture of war and armaments constitutes the predominant thrust of the US Global Empire's strategy for maintaining its hegemony. The sale of conventional arms and weapons has become an over $900 billion dollar annual plague on humanity. While claiming that it is concerned about nuclear proliferation, the Bush-2 regime did nothing to advance the work of those seeking to strengthen the Non-Proliferation Treaty at a United Nationals NPT Conference in May 2005. At the same time, the Bush administration has continued efforts to upgrade the nuclear capabilities of the US arsenal—including "bunker busters" to threaten Iran and North Korea. In fact, Bush has actively worked to undermine the NPT when, in early 2006, he agreed to share nuclear technology with India, thereby opening the door to even greater proliferation throughout Asia in an effort to contain China as a rising global power.

Despite its attempts to maintain global hegemony it may be that the enterprise will fail. The reasons for the failure are multifaceted, but what can be asserted is that a global culture of violence is not sustainable. The foreign policies of the US Global Empire have contributed dramatically to global violence. For example, it has undermined efforts of Third World nations and social movements throughout the global South to escape the financial domination of the WTO, IMF, and World Bank. In so doing, it has warped trade policies and its potential benefits to such a great degree that civil wars have erupted between the excluded and those who have positioned themselves in elite positions. As a consequence of civil war, coupled inequitable socioeconomic imbalances, and the effects of exclusionary governance, have led to more so-called *failed states*.

Certainly, there have been failed or incomplete democratic transitions. Key examples are Ethiopia, Pakistan, and Peru. In these states, the institutions needed for a successful transition to democracy were weak and democratization remained incomplete. Despite this reality, it did not halt the efforts of the governing elites of the US Global Empire from working through the WTO and IMF to impose economic programs that would contribute to an ever-widening gap between those groups and classes that held elite decision-making positions versus those who were excluded from an equitable sharing or distribution of the nation's wealth. In the decade of the 1990s, Latin America's negative growth rates and incomes inequalities worsened. Structural adjustment programs and their costs fell disproportionately on the middle- and low-income groups. Yet, the top 5 percent of the population retained or even increased its standard of living.

From this vantage point, the basic thrust of Realist theories is that "relations among the Western states will return to the patterns of the 1930s and early 1940s, in which the problems of anarchy dominated: economic rivalry, security dilemmas, arms races, hyper-nationalism, balancing alliances, and ultimately the threat of war."[5] Many of the predictions contained in Realist theories have already materialized. Europe and China have become economic rivals to the US Global Empire, threatening its role as a twenty-first century superpower that is capable of maintaining an unrivaled hegemony. Part of the reason for this trend transcends pure economics and political maneuvering. It reflects something about the world of ideas and how the idea of *another American Century* is not acceptable to the Global Community.

Yet, with Fukuyama-esque assurance mixed with neoconservative arrogance, Paul Wolfowitz argued that history had in fact ended, and that the world was left with "a single sustainable model for national success: freedom, democracy, and free enterprise."[6] Despite this imperial assumption, security dilemmas plague the empire's occupation of Iraq and Afghanistan, even as it seeks to buttress its collapsing position in the Middle East under the guise of a democracy crusade to liberate the Arab world from tyrannical regimes.[7]

Arms races and the development of a nuclear weapons capacity have been accelerating among various Third World states from Iran to North Korea. In the case of Iran as well as North Korea, the rationale for building a nuclear weapons capacity appears to be a reaction to the Bush-2 regime's proclivity for planning and preparation for aggressive wars—justified by the doctrine of preemption. Hence, it may be argued, that if these two states have engaged in building up their nuclear weapons programs, such a build-up has been undertaken in order to deter the US Global Empire from its apparent willingness to engage in preemptive wars.[8]

From the Nixon era to the Bush-2 regime, the US Global Empire has continued to invest hundreds of billions of dollars into military technologies that would allow it to deter major socioeconomic and sociopolitical change throughout the

Global Community. Believing that the American model should remain supreme, the architects of the US Global Empire have dedicated both national wealth and national security investments into military spending so as to guarantee such an outcome. This phenomenon constitutes the US Global Empire's actual doctrine of deterrence. The US Global Empire employs its vast military might to preserve this order and enforce its rules.[9] It is ultimately designed not to deter potential terror-ists, but to deter other countries from pursuing national development options that would reduce the profit margins of US-based corporations. While claiming to pursue its own security and fight terrorism, the empire's actual strategy has been increasingly premised upon creating and implementing policies that will ensure that change will not occur in the international order that would in any way threaten its current supremacy.

In order to maintain this supremacy, interventions by the US Global Empire throughout the global village have made the world a more violent place—ravaged by seemingly endless civil wars and armed conflicts. Even with the end of the Cold War the US Global Empire did not alter the nature of its conventional arms sales that became even more competitive and less accountable.[10] In terms of the buyers of these arms, there was no litmus test for whether the regimes that purchased the arms were developing states that supported human rights and democracy or authoritarian regimes that paid attention to neither.[11] In this respect, as well as others, the Bush-2 regime's war on terror has unleashed more terror on the world than it has either eliminated or contained.

Between 2003 and 2005, US military forces have inflicted casualties on the Iraqi civilian population that exceed 100,000 people and then call it "collateral damage." In 2003, various human rights charities noted that on average 500,000 people were killed each year by armed violence—roughly one victim a minute.[12] In this global environment approximately 300,000 children are fighting in conflicts around the world. The future of a rising Global Community is seriously compromised with the harsh realities of children placed into conflict as both armed combatants and victims. The new and un-addressed tragedy of the global commons is that the use of children as soldiers and as terrorists is one of the new aspects of twenty-first century warfare.[13]

The US Global Empire's logic of deterring global change through the sale of arms and conventional weapons may be seen as just one element in a larger picture of US attempts to engage blocking development options throughout the Global Community in order to retain its current hegemonic position. For example, as civil wars rage across the African continent, from Sudan to Niger, it is in the interest of US oil and mineral companies to support those social forces that are willing to accommodate US corporations by allowing access to and the exploitation of the nation's resources. At the close of a civil war, those who are the "winners" share in the spoils of war. In this way, a sociopolitical group that captures the state is the beneficiary of the civil war. Once in power, this sociopolitical group consti-tutes an elite that has succeeded in not only "state capture" but has also been posi-tioned to engage in a course of inequitable development. Those groups that are excluded suffer from human rights abuses and fail to enjoy an equitable share of the nation's wealth. Exclusionary states (ES) are supported by US business and military interests because they are able to guarantee US access to markets that would otherwise be denied to them.

The unsettling reality is that the logic of deterring global change has had a blowback effect within the homeland of the empire. Attempting to deal with this blowback effect also accounts for the spread of hypernationalism in the United States. As a result of foreign wars abroad the Bush-2 regime has defined many persons with a Middle Eastern background as potential enemies of the empire. Racial profiling of persons who are of Middle Eastern origin comes under increased scrutiny by both the FBI and CIA. On this basis, military tribunals have been set up to evade constitutional restrictions. The CIA has been empowered to engage in the techniques of torture. The CIA has also engaged in the kidnap of suspects in a process called *renditions*, and then taken these suspects to what are referred to as *black sites*.

The Bush-2 regime's domestic reaction to the events of 9/11 has wound up creating a near-fascist state of affairs. Certainly the passage of the USA Patriot Act offers substantial credence to such a proposition. Also, George W. Bush appointed an attorney general closely associated with the legalization of torture and nominated a UN ambassador who believes that there is no such thing as international law that constrains the United States from acting unilaterally.[14] Under Bush, an effort is being made to remake the global order subservient to the US Global Empire's designs. As a result, internationally, the empire's hypernationalism has furthered a global trend toward anarchy—as predicted by Realist theories.

At the present moment, given this record, there is little hope that there will be a humane management of the US Global Empire's decline. Rather, it appears that global conflicts will continue to be on the rise because of the empire's intention to engage in the preemption of development options for the majority of humankind. Threats to both global environmental security and human security grow as the US Global Empire resists the call to engage in multilateral procedures that could strengthen a rising Global Community.

A GLOBAL COMMUNITY REQUIRES
GLOBAL GOVERNANCE

In order to strengthen a rising Global Community, what is required involves the union of norms and institutions that are constitutive of global governance. Global governance should be understood to mean that there is a universally shared recognition of the need to support a process leading to fundamental social transformations. The necessity for global social transformations is the strongest argument for asserting that, at this point in history, humanity cannot afford a US policy of deterrence. A rising Global Community must be equipped to undertake fundamental and substantive social transformations. To maintain a US policy of deterrence to historical transformations is to promote a policy that runs counter to the dynamics of history, the aspirations of social movements for global justice, and the resource limitations of a planet already suffering from severe environmental degradation.

Properly understood, *global governance* "can be considered an institutional fact constituted by acting in accord with the norms that stress coordination and cooperation over unilateral actions."[15] Global governance is not a product of the individual actions of one state or nation. It cannot be the province of the US Global Empire acting alone. By definition, it must involve all nations as participating co-partners, dedicated to bringing an end to unnecessary conflicts and addressing the underlying causes of those conflicts. In the task of forging a new security order in the Persian Gulf, an alternative model to empire can be proposed. This alternative stands for the proposition that

> the road to Gulf security is not paved with programs for radical reshaping of other societies along lines reflecting US values and institutions. Nor will it be guaranteed by maintaining global military primacy. Instead, a peaceful Persian Gulf is one in which large regional powers such as Iran and Saudi Arabia coexist with all their smaller neighbors in a mutually beneficial set of relationships based on prosperity and respect rather than fear and domination. Only by jettisoning the failed strategies of local hegemony, global hegemony, armed victory and pure power politics can the United States help construct a new security order that is seen as equitable by all states in the region—ultimately to the benefit of US national security goals.[16]

Among the many causes of violent conflicts are environmental stresses, scarcities, and ensuing resource wars to capture dwindling resources. Already, there are wars and conflicts due to scarcities of such vital renewable resources as cropland, fresh water, and forests. By 2025, it has been projected that the earth's population will pass eight billion. In such a world, these environmental scarcities will have many profound social consequences—contributing to ethnic clashes, urban unrest, and other forms of civil violence and conflict in the developing world. If allowed to continue, these trends have the capacity to foreclose upon the dawn of a rising Global Community. Hence, the deterrence policies of the US Global Empire need to be re-routed from their present course—because the US Global Empire continues to pursue an anti-development agenda toward the Third World. In its attempt to maintain military supremacy and global economic domination, the United States has allowed its anti-development agenda to become a strategy that ultimately leads toward unsustainable development. Unsustainable development is not the product of good global governance, but rather the result of the empire's uncoordinated unilateral action.

After decades of study and experience, it should be clear that violent conflict can and should be seen as one of the major products of unsustainable development. In turn, arms competition and armed conflict are responsible for creating major obstacles to sustainable development. That is because arms competition and armed conflict "make huge claims on scarce material resources. They pre-empt human resources and wealth that could be used to combat the collapse of environmental support systems, the poverty, and the underdevelopment that in combination contribute to so much contemporary political insecurity."[17] There is a strong correlation between the economic waste due to channeling resources and wealth toward arms and weapons, and the corresponding realities of poverty and environmental degradation that so often lead to conflict and civil wars.

Eventually, the results of environmental degradation will foster other problems and these problems produce more violence.[18] Therefore, the real challenges facing human security in the twenty-first century revolve around environmental security, not a narrow focus on military security. The channeling of wealth and resources toward the already wealthy beneficiaries of the current system of US global dominance will pit the wealthy of the global economy against the billions of excluded. Such a situation can lead to ecological collapse, the derailment of growth, and social chaos. Such an outcome could constitute the next world war.[19]

The reality of increasing violent conflicts and civil wars reflects what transpires when the road to social transformation is blocked and needed resources are denied to excluded groups and classes. The role of elites who exclude the vast majority of people from the benefits of growth leads to a sense of subjugation, marginalized status, and a state of oppression. Extremist measures and the global growth of terrorism are testimony to the failure of elites who have sought to maintain their systems of exclusionary governance. Exclusionary forms of governance act to subject marginalized classes and groups to greater stresses as social and economic inequality increases. Widening gaps between excluded classes and groups create a world of inequality both within and between states. Further, greater degrees of socioeconomic and sociopolitical inequality have been exacerbated by the deterrence policies of the US Global Empire. When viewed in combination with the crushing weight of international debt (Africa, Asia, Latin America), the growing global energy crisis due to a narrow focus on oil as a primary source for energy, the reluctance of global elites to bring already discovered energy alternatives online (solar power, wind power, water power), it becomes apparent that the current global system of inequality is unsustainable.

Exclusionary forms of governance enhance inequality. In turn, rising levels of inequality simultaneously lead toward civil wars and violent conflicts. At the same time, widening patterns of inequality contribute toward widening levels of environmental degradation that compound the problems associated with resource scarcities and exclusionary patterns of unequal distribution. Marginalized classes and excluded groups become the breeding grounds for massive social discontent, political extremism, and terrorism. In order to break this cycle of violence, it is necessary to understand and address the predictable effects of socioeconomic exclusion.

THE PREDICTABLE EFFECTS OF SOCIOECONOMIC EXCLUSION

When basic social entitlements are denied to the excluded, the poor, and the oppressed, violent conflict is often the predictable result. In this regard, "during the 1990s, a decade marked by the increase in inequalities, 3.6 million people died in civil wars and ethnic violence more than sixteen times the number killed in wars between states."[20] This outcome is largely the result of exclusionary governance and the policies of ES. Within the ES the "haves" decide who gets what in the development process and seek to deny any kind of viable empowerment to the excluded, the poor, the marginalized, and the oppressed.[21] The inevitable outcome of exclusionary governance, in the context of inequality, is that "the vicious cycle of inequality, elite capture, and disempowerment can spiral out of control in the absence of a framework for equality and nondiscrimination in decision making. This framework, moreover, must be applied objectively with the rights and interests of the disadvantaged uppermost in mind."[22]

Clearly, the adoption creation of such a framework for nondiscrimination and equality would turn the ES on its head. By creating a new set of priorities that target the needs of the excluded, the poor, and the marginalized a long-term process of unsustainable development would be re-routed toward a path of long-term sustainable development. Acting in accordance with new priorities would mean that the inclusion or adoption of the concerns articulated by the voices of the poor and marginalized would bring these previously excluded social forces into the processes of decision making, thereby making them active participants in governance and agents in the creation of their own history.

Such a reversal of priorities is signified and embodied by what I have called *inclusionary governance*. For inclusive principles and norms contribute to building inclusive institutions that allow for increased political participation by the poor and previously excluded groups who make up the majority in most societies. Global governance, when viewed under the rubric of inclusion, requires clearly articulated human rights norms, on the one hand, and strong inclusive institutions, on the other. Under the rubric of inclusion, the promotion of human rights and human dignity builds the foundation for a sustainable future because it allows people to effectively address our most critical environmental problem—global poverty.

In order to address the problem of global poverty, it is necessary to look at the issue of how best to level the economic and political playing fields. Leveling the economic and political playing fields becomes the task of addressing equity. According to the authors of the World Bank's *World Development Report: 2006— Equity and Development*:

> We argue that an equity lens enhances the poverty reduction agenda. The poor generally have less voice, less income, and less access to services than most other people. When societies become more equitable in ways that lead to greater opportunities for all, the poor stand to benefit from a "double dividend." First, expanded opportunities benefit the poor directly, through greater participation in the development process. Second, the development process itself may become more successful and resilient as *greater equity leads to better institutions*, more effective conflict management, and a better use of all potential resources in society, including those of the poor. Resulting increases in economic growth rates in poor countries will, in turn, contribute to a reduction in global inequities (Italics are mine).[23]

However, the assertion that *greater equality leads to better institutions* is not entirely accurate. Insofar as it "puts the cart before the horse"—otherwise known as an issue of *sequencing*—I am maintaining that the proper sequence for undertaking the move toward a reduction in national and global inequalities, the problem of poverty, as well as the problem of exclusion, is to build strong inclu-sionary institutions. A society does not automatically become *more equitable*.

The realization of equity is the result of a combination of factors. These factors include the relationship between the state, the civil society, and the market. Usually, social movements that emerge from civil society have to make equitable claims upon the state. In turn, for a state to positively respond to claims that will result in greater equity, it must be willing to engage elites and the excluded groups, classes, and the poor into a bargaining process. This process requires of the state that it play a mediating role. The state must also have a long-term vision of the future that incorporates all major classes, interests, and groups into its cal-culus in order to advance a more politically and economically inclusive national interest.

THE LEGAL FOUNDATIONS FOR CLAIMING
A "RIGHT OF PEACE"

At the dawn of the twenty-first century, there must be a global transformation that removes poverty wherever possible and mitigates its effects as quickly as possi-ble. Undertaking this task will involve coupling the commitment to eliminate poverty with the commitment to begin a global transition to a clearly articulated and respected *right of peace*. With a *right of peace* citizens would be able to con-nect this right to an established ensemble of rights within international law, remove the burden from citizens to follow the call to war, and allow them to opt out of the war system. In short, a *right of peace* would provide the poor and excluded citizens of the globe with objective capabilities for freedom, democracy, and peace that have rarely been known for vast numbers of people throughout history.

The evolution of international law has already laid the foundations for claiming a *right of peace*. We can make this assertion because the crimes of rape, genocide, and pillage are predicates for the conclusion that people have a *right of peace*. While this right applies to everyone in the Global Community, it has particular salience for the poor, excluded, and oppressed because they have borne the greatest burden of global violence, wars, and inequalities.

Those who exercise control over the various forms of state-sponsored violence have used their power with indiscriminate ease. The architects of the US Global Empire and their proxy armies and puppet governments have historically con-signed the poor, excluded, and oppressed to the category of "collateral damage." Yet, such a relegation of human life to the realm of being expendable has not brought real security for anyone. Genuine security is the product of cooperation, a shared sense of mutual destiny, and fidelity to the norms of inclusive gover-nance and the institutional structures to protect and advance those norms. In order to realize a *right of peace* it is essential that a global and national consen-sus emerge that is supportive of the transition to a Global Community that is committed to enhancing the capabilities, assets, and human dignity of the poor and excluded.

CLAIMING A "RIGHT OF PEACE" REQUIRES
INCLUSIONARY GOVERNANCE

In order to achieve the transition to a sustainable Global Community, there is no question that both the assets and the capabilities of the poor must be expanded and enhanced. Under Amartya Sen's "capability" approach to poverty, poverty is defined as the absence of capabilities to realize certain freedoms that are themselves fundamentally valuable for minimal human dignity.[24] It should also be understood that it is not simply a matter of "ethics." Third World poverty contributes to cultural regression as well as an overwhelming sense of hopelessness. This growing sense of hopelessness in the Middle East has produced the phenomenon of suicide bombers and terrorists. It has hardened old resentments and contributed to new ones. In this respect, Third World poverty will also have an impact on the people of the First World in various and menacing ways. Among these consequences will be an increase in migrations and refugees, terrorism, and the continuation of authoritarian regimes and ES that can exacerbate all of these negative trends.

However, with the decline of the ES and a reversal of its priorities, the growth of the IS means that national and global governance will have to be dedicated to protecting and respecting the capabilities of the poor—as well as previously excluded groups and classes as a matter of legal right.[25] In an earlier publication, I have previously outlined the exact nature of the policies, practices, and goals of the IS that are designed to give priority to the needs of the poor and excluded. The policies, practices, and goals that I have outlined are represented in the following table.

The Policies, Practices, and Goals of the IS

I *Policies*

A Advance the "rule of law" and condemn the practice of "rule by law";

B Engage in the protection and extension of human rights in all realms;

C Promote tolerance, mutuality, and cooperation between all social classes by removing the roots of categorical inequality and the connections that preserve and reinforce it;

D Encourage the members of the civil society to increase popular participation in social movements that place claims upon the state to promote an agenda which reflects the claims of distributive justice and democratic inclusion;

E Maintain state integrity in decision making by removing practices that advance exploitation and opportunity hoarding;

F Advance an inclusionary agenda for inclusionary development that emphasizes material equalization by weakening the links and connections among the categories of exploitation and opportunity hoarding;

G Construct mediating institutions between the state and civil society.

II *Practices*

A Create, establish, and maintain an independent and impartial judiciary;

B Establish constitutionally protected human rights categories and channels for redress of grievances;

C Build state society linkages which promote negotiation, mediation, and arbitration in accord with the principles of an IS and inclusionary development;

D Make economic decisions in accord with the claims of distributive justice and advanced practices of equitable distribution, so that growth is not left isolated from distributional considerations;

E   Remove categories that protect and preserve exploitation and opportunity hoarding;
F   Bring the state back in to selectively regulate market mechanisms and remedy market failures
     that negatively affect the poor and excluded under the rubric of an IS and the criteria of an
     inclusionary development agenda; and
G   Incorporate the poor and excluded into a participatory framework of institution-building through
     mediating institutions that give voice, political empowerment, and legal force to their
     inclusionary and equitable claims.

III   *Goals*

A   Remove the threat of the exercise of arbitrary state power from old categories that reflect the
     values and priorities associated with class exploitation and opportunity hoarding;
B   Enforce and expand human rights protections through domestic and international bills of rights;
C   Strengthen state and civil society linkages and bonds for accommodating the articulation of new
     claims which advance inclusionary development and an IS;
D   Maintain a policy orientation and state practice which is directed toward the realization of the
     values, norms, and priorities that are embodied in the concept and practice of distributive justice;
E   Preserve the legitimacy of the IS through maintaining the integrity of its
     decision making and policymaking practices;
F   Eliminate absolute poverty by ensuring the meeting of basic human needs while, at the same
     time, working to expand the social, economic, and political space that is required for
     participatory inclusion and to eliminate the growth/equity trade-off and the liberty trade-off; and
G   Realize and institutionalize the newly gained rights of previously excluded groups.

Source: Terrence E. Paupp, *Achieving Inclusionary Governance: Advancing Peace and Development in First and Third World Nations*, Transnational Publishers, Inc., 2000, pp. 386–387.

By claiming a *right of peace* the process of inclusive norms and institutions can act to remove obstacles that block the realization of minimal human dignity. Further, by uniting the concerns of equitable development with the goal of eliminating gross inequalities, the contributions of the poor and excluded will become a part of the process of economic growth, social development, and human rights. In place of obstacles to human realization and fulfillment, the realm of human freedom can be extended by virtue of the expansion and enhancement of capabilities that were previously reserved for elites and the upper classes. As outlined above, the inclusive norms and institutions of an IS provide a viable framework for greater equality and nondiscrimination in decision making. Insofar as the IS framework can be placed into practice, I would argue that the recognition of the rights of the poor, the excluded, and the disadvantaged will take on new significance, for they will have become the agents of their own destiny. Such an accomplishment should go a long way toward eliminating civil wars and ethnic violence throughout the entire Global Community.

CENTRALIZING THE CLAIMS OF THE POOR AND EXCLUDED IN GLOBAL DEVELOPMENT

By centralizing the concerns and well-being of the poor and excluded within the developmental paradigm, this would provide a radical alternative to the priorities pursued by the US Global Empire. Such a framework would make it possible for the United States to move toward a *post-Imperial America*. No longer could military dominance be logically equated with national security or human security. Why? Because of the recognition that equity concerns and human development need to be placed together in a mutually interactive process that leads to greater socioeconomic and sociopolitical inclusion.

The incorporative features of inclusive norms that are actualized through the institutions of an IS have the capacity to remake the nation-states of the entire Global Community. At the national level, an IS can provide a disincentive to engage in planning and preparation for aggressive wars. At the international level, a world of nation-states committed to creating their own versions of inclusive states can more easily find alternatives to the global war system, the global trade in arms and weapons, and the prospect of endless civil wars. A world of nation-states committed to building their own version of an IS will be more equipped to settling disputes among nations or within nations. In so doing, it is possible to build a world that protects and respects the *right of peace*.

Significantly, the World Bank's own *World Development Report 2003, Sustainable Development in a Dynamic World: Transforming Institutions, Growth, and Quality of Life*, noted that "increased voice and major increases in substantive democratization" were essential if the Global Community was to have national communities ensure greater inclusion. The authors noted that "inclusiveness can be expanded through significant changes in governance that increase representation and accountability ... empowering groups excluded from decision-making— women, indigenous people, and other disadvantaged groups, who may be in the majority."[26]

The authors concluded:

This Report argues that the lack of assets, opportunity, and effective voice for large segments of the population blocks the emergence of general welfare-enhancing policies, impedes growth, and undermines the potential for positive change. At the national level, it robs us of the talents of those left out in society. And at the international level, it deprives us of the contribution poor countries can make to a more just and sustainable future.[27]

A similar emphasis upon the significance of inclusive norms and institutions for the Global Community was articulated in the Bank's own *World Development Report, 2000/2001: Attacking Poverty*. Its authors noted:

Empowering poor people is part of the broader agenda of sound governance and accountability of state institutions to their citizens. National empowerment of citizens can have important indirect effects on poor people, by influencing the quality and pace of economic and social development. But the outcome for poor people depends on the political and social structures within a society. Governments are often more responsive to the concerns of elites than to the needs of poor groups.[28]

This same theme was taken up by the UNDP in its *Human Development Report 2003, Millennium Development Goals: A compact among nations to end human poverty.* Its authors noted:

> economic growth alone is not enough. Growth can be ruthless or it can be poverty reducing—depending on its pattern, on structural aspects of the economy and on public policies. Poverty has increased even in some countries that have achieved overall economic growth, and over the past two decades income inequality worsened in 33 of 66 developing countries with data. All countries—especially those doing well on average but with entrenched pockets of poverty—should implement policies that strengthen the links between economic growth and poverty reduction.[29]

In preparation for the World Bank's *World Development Report 2000/20001*, comparative fieldwork involving interviews with over 60,000 people was undertaken. The goal of this fieldwork was to shed light on how poverty is experienced by the poor themselves. The findings were laid out in a World Bank publication entitled, *Voices of the Poor.* What these findings revealed was that poverty was experienced not merely as the absence of commodities and services to meet basic needs—it was the experience of disempowerment.

Commenting on this discovery, some scholars have noted: "When asked what was needed most to increase their freedom of choice and improve their lives, the answers read like the Universal Declaration of Human Rights (UDHR)."[30] The ten *assets and capabilities*—or, in human rights terms, constitutive and legally enforceable characteristics of human dignity and freedom—identified through these interviews are set forth in the following table.

The answers provided in the table give us a rather complete answer to two questions that were asked in 2001 by one of Latin America's leading social thinkers

"Voices of the Poor": Assets and Capability Examples Mentioned by Poor People to Increase Their Freedom of Choice and Improve Their Lives

Material assets	Employment, land, house, savings, ownership of productive assets
Bodily health	Freedom from hunger and disease; strong bodies
Emotional integrity	Freedom from anxiety and fear; love
Respect and dignity	Self-respect; respect from others and the community
Social belonging	Belonging to a collective; honor, respect, and trust within and across social groups
Cultural identity	Living in accordance with one's values; participation in rituals that give meaning; sense of cultural continuity
Imagination, inventiveness, information, and education	Informed and educated decision making, literacy; entrepreneurship; problem-solving capacity; expressive arts
Organizational capacity	Ability to organize and mobilize; participation in representative organizations
Political representation and accountability	Ability to influence those in power; accountability of those in power.

Source: Mac Darrow and Amparo Tomas, "*Power, Capture, and Conflict: A Call for Human Rights Accountability in Development Cooperation,*" *Human Rights Quarterly*, Vol. 27, No. 2, May 2005, p. 478.

and Brazil's finance minister in the early 1990s—Fernando Henrique Cardoso. After reviewing the impact of globalization on developing countries and the associated problems of inequality and structural unemployment, he asked: "How can we reinvent a sense of community on the international plane, so as to avoid social exclusion and segregation? How can we strengthen the social responsibility of the cultural and economic elites?"[31] He then proceeded to answer his own questions.

As if writing in anticipation of the new struggle against social, economic, and political exclusion, as well as global inequality, he stated:

> I have the conviction that the developing countries can contribute, perhaps even more than the developed countries, to this conceptual passage from the realm of the economy to the realm of values ... more than ever before, we have to exercise our creative capability of responding simultaneously to the challenges of the new reality and the overcoming of a social legacy which grieves and shames us. It is not a question of going back to the values of the past, reviving utopias which no longer explain the contemporary world nor mesh with the prevalence of democratic values and the market economy. *The solution to contemporary problems goes beyond national borders and demands universal mobilization* (Italics are mine).[32]

He not only rejects the models of the past, he also rejects neoliberal prescriptions for the market economy and a US-imposed definition of what constitutes democracy. The reason he rejects these two models is because of their inherently exclusionary nature. In practice, it is not enough to have the symbolic elements of democracy—such as elections—when the core distributional issues of national and international society are left un-addressed. Similarly, a capitalist market economy that is guided by a neoliberal doctrine of privatization and deregulation does not take into account the social needs of the entire society, but rather focuses on those groups and elites that are already well situated and secure. It does not address the needs of those millions of excluded and poor who remain vulnerable throughout the Global South.

When viewed in the context of North-South relations we discover that many North-South conflicts are rooted in profound asymmetries of power, and that political weakness and vulnerability are fundamental sources of Third World behavior. Professor Stephen Krasner has made this explicit point the main theme of his book, *Structural Conflict*. He notes:

> Vulnerability, not simply poverty, is the motivating force for the Third World's meta-power program for transforming international regimes. Those following basic human needs, liberal, and interdependence approaches have failed to comprehend the fundamentally political character of many Third World demands."[33] From his structural or realist approach to international relations, he maintains "the international system would be more stable and less conflictual if the North and South had less to do with each other. From a Northern as well as a Southern perspective collective self-reliance is preferable to greater interdependence.[34]

Again, the reason for asserting that collective self-reliance is preferable to greater interdependence is that "the defining characteristic of Third World politics is vulnerability. This vulnerability has not been reduced by economic growth."[35] It is for this reason that IMF/World Bank prescriptions for structural adjustment programs constitute a deadly prescription for societies across the global South. Further, as will be discussed later in this chapter, I am arguing for a *global counter-hegemonic alliance*—designed to oppose the intrusions and interventions of the US Global Empire—thereby reducing the vulnerabilities currently experienced throughout the global South.

DEVELOPMENT IS NOT ENOUGH: CREATING SOUTH-SOUTH LINKAGES TO REMOVE VULNERABILITY AND EXCLUSION

Just because Third World states achieved decolonization with a level of de jure and de facto control which "they could not have attained or defended through their national power capabilities" does not mean that there are not remaining "incongruities between underlying power capabilities and transnational principles and norms."[36] What this means is that the fact of juridical sovereignty is not enough for the global South to claim victory when the global North favors market-oriented regimes, funds, and creates international organizations (WTO, IMF, World Bank) that allow challenges to be voiced, but no real decision-making power is granted.[37]

In short, the sovereign nations of the global South can "attack and undermine existing international regimes but they cannot destroy or replace them." It is because of this paradox that there is a continuing tension and conflict between the North and South that "cannot be mitigated by economic development alone."[38] This is the case because economic development and growth by themselves do not address distributional inequities and the resulting inequalities that are produced by them. Distributional inequities and inequalities reinforce the power of ES and policies. In turn, these conditions often lead to internal conflict and civil war. In terms of North-South relations, economic development alone still leaves the North in a position of dominance. In order to maintain its dominance, the US Global Empire does not view the replacement of social, political, and economic exclusion in its long-term interests. Therefore, it has followed a course of deterring democracy and alternative developmental courses for Third World nations. In this fundamental respect, the US Global Empire has often acted as a counterrevolutionary force to socioeconomic and sociopolitical transformations throughout the course of the twentieth and early twenty-first centuries.

The basic point remains: *Economic development alone is not enough to either mitigate conflict between North and South or to bring socioeconomic justice and inclusionary governance to the national communities of the global South.* A compelling assessment of this reality is forcefully articulated by Walden Bello when he notes: "From the perspective of the southern governments, the founding of the

WTO and the acceleration of corporate-driven globalization marked a retreat from efforts at independent national development dating back to the 1970s."[39] Independent national development requires an end to exclusionary governance in all of its forms—social, political, and economic.

The reasons for eliminating exclusionary governance are varied and complex. However, two general observations should be made at the outset. First, exclusionary governance at the national levels allows for the continued domination and exploitation of the global South by the US Global Empire. Second, exclusionary governance is an inherently inequitable system of governance that serves elite interests at the expense of the majority. Therefore, exclusionary governance is antidemocratic and often leads to social violence, civil strife, and even civil war. Insofar as it severs equitable policies from the processes of development, exclusionary governance may be said to be anti-developmental as well as antidemocratic. In my earlier work entitled, *Achieving Inclusionary Governance*, I set forth the six constitutive factors or dimensions of what constitutes exclusionary governance. They are outlined in the following table.

The Dimensions of Exclusionary Governance

---

1. Weak States
2. Fragmented Civil Society
3. Shifting Political Coalitions
4. Short-Term Policies
5. Elite-Led Pacts
6. "Rule by Law" in place of "Rule of Law"

Source: Terrence E. Paupp, *Achieving Inclusionary Governance: Advancing Peace and Development in First and Third World Nations*, Transnational Publishers, Inc., 2000, p. 404.

The architects of the US Global Empire have historically resisted the pursuit of genuine national development in the global South insofar as it would bring an end to virtual US domination. Yet, if the nations of the South are to build an effective Global Community in which they are no longer vulnerable to the exigencies of empire, it will be necessary for them to create effective South-South linkages that empower their drive for independence from the US Global Empire. It will also be necessary for the nations of the South to finally overcome the problems of exclusionary governance—in all of its forms and manifestations.

In this regard, Cardoso has argued that in view of the comprehensive nature of the problems of the marginalized poor and politically excluded it will be necessary to understand the developmental challenge as one that encompasses more forms of exclusion that have not been addressed until recently. He explicitly lists several other forms of exclusion that need to be acknowledged if a comprehensive mobilization of peoples is to take place and result in the building of a truly Global Community. In his view, "there are several forms of exclusion: that of women, children, the elderly, the uneducated, the unemployed, the disabled, victims of violence, the landless, and those affected by pollution and environmental damage." In order to effectively deal with all of these forms of exclusion, he concludes: "all forms of exclusion must be politicized and in all these areas mobilization must be encouraged, organizations must be formed and the channels between such organizations and the State must be expanded."[40]

THE PRINCIPLES OF INCLUSIONARY GOVERNANCE

In order to promote efficiency and effectiveness in governance, the five principles of inclusionary governance—*consensus, consistency, congruence, cohesiveness, and coherence*—should be understood as mutually reinforcing principles. They should also be understood as mutually reinforcing aspects and expression of the IS in practice. The incorporation of the poor, marginalized, and excluded into the national life is essential not only for genuine national development, but for the sake of development with equity. If a nation fails to move toward realizing an equitable distribution of its resources, the human capital it needs for a viable and peaceful future will dissipate and disappear. In order that this not be the outcome, the IS has a particular role to play in ensuring that governments adhere to the responsibilities of sovereignty—by working to guarantee the security of fundamental rights, civil liberties, and securing the general welfare of their citizens and those under their domestic jurisdiction.

As the following table demonstrates, the principle of *consensus* serves to guide the IS toward striking bargains between social groups and makes the IS into a mediator—not merely a front for the elite. In turn, the principle of *consistency* strengthens the leadership and bureaucracy of the IS by mandating governmental compliance with established procedures, goals, and policies that ensure an equitable distribution of resources as well as an equitable sharing of sacrifices for the nation's long-term development. The principle of *congruence* demands that the IS not only cultivate the conditions for development, but also aids the state in its task to be a catalyst for development. The principle of *cohesiveness* refers both to the internal cohesiveness of the state's policies and practices as well as its linkages to civil society (thereby making it more democratic and accountable to the will of the people). Finally, the principle of *coherence* entails the guidance of the IS in developing linkages between the state, the civil society, and the market.

In combination, the principles and practices of the IS can serve to effectuate the national development of a social, political, and economic community that is equitable while, at the same time, create an environment that is conducive to the evolution of democratic principles and practices.[41] In such an environment, the poor and excluded should finally find the realization of their human rights, dignity and liberty without the fear of elite tyranny. Such an historical achievement can also become an historical trajectory toward a culture of peace. For, as some scholars have noted "while inequality by itself may not always be a sufficient condition to trigger violent conflict, the 'capture' of economic and political benefits associated with growing inequality may well be, particularly when it undermines the basic human entitlements of the excluded."[42] Such a conclusion is justified when various studies show how horizontal inequalities may lead to grievances that, in combination with other factors, may form the basis of group mobilization by conflict entrepreneurs, thus increasing a society's disposition toward violent conflict.[43]

While the international community remains the ultimate guarantor of universal human rights and humanitarian standards, the fact remains that national sovereignty has acquired a new meaning. The significance of the idea of sovereignty for a rising Global Community comes with the recognition that sovereignty's claim on governance works to impose a greater responsibility upon the state. Sovereignty can no longer insulate the state against external scrutiny insofar as

> it is increasingly postulated as a normative concept of responsibility, requiring a system of governance based on democratic citizen participation, constructive management of diversities, respect for fundamental rights, and equitable distribution of national wealth and opportunities for development. For a government or a state to claim sovereignty, it must establish legitimacy by meeting minimal standards of good governance or responsibility for the security and general welfare of its citizens and all those under its jurisdiction.[44]

Given this perspective, in order for a state to be viewed as taking all of the necessary steps to accomplish these things, I am arguing that the minimal standards of good governance—understood as meeting the general welfare requirements of its citizens—demands no less than the conscious adoption of the principles and practices of the IS. For if all those under the jurisdiction of the state are to be the beneficiaries of an equitable distribution of national wealth and opportunities, it should be clear that only the principles and practices of an inclusive framework of governance can actually provide the basis for such an outcome. To that end, the principles and practices of an IS are essential to realizing the general welfare of all citizens under the jurisdiction of such a sovereign. In outlining the elements of the IS approach to governance, I offer the following table:

The Principles of the IS and Their Expression in Practice

Principles	Practices
Consensus	Bargains, Negotiations, and Compromises
Consistency	Procedures, Goals, and Policies
Congruence	Solving Problems of Political, Social, Economic Displacement, and Transformation
Cohesiveness	State/Society Linkages
Coherence	State, Civil Society, Market

Source: Terrence E. Paupp, *Achieving Inclusionary Governance: Advancing Peace and Development in First and Third World Nations*, Transnational Publishers, Inc., 2000, p. 340.

By following the above principles and practices, in accordance with the proposed framework of an IS, there is a strong likelihood that violent conflict within a society can ultimately be avoided. However, while it is true that developmental perspectives on conflict frequently highlight the important role that respecting human rights plays in strategies to prevent violent conflicts, they often fail to recognize that woven into the fabric of human rights themselves are tensions between rights and responsibilities—tensions that may lead to conflict. In this regard, the fact remains that

> to the extent that development policies or programs disturb existing relations of power at the national level ... development may thereby create or exacerbate the scope for conflict at all levels—for example between sexes, between rural and urban areas, between sectors in the economy, between social groups, between ethnic groups or between generations. It is true, however, that progress in human development, when considerations of equity are factored in, minimizes the risk of violent conflict.[45]

Strong institutions emerge when the values and norms associated with equity become the governing standard, thereby ensuring distributional justice. In the alternative, the World Bank's own *World Development Report 2006, Equity and Development* warns that:

> Poor institutions will emerge and persist in societies when power is concentrated in the hands of a narrow group ... Such an elite may grant property rights to itself, but the property rights of most citizens will be unstable. There may be equality before the law for a particular elite group, but not for the majority of people. Government policies may favor such an elite, granting them rents and monopolies, but most people will be excluded from entering profitable lines of business. The education system may invest heavily in the children of such elites, but most will be excluded.[46]

The Report then concludes the thought by noting: "A society with greater equality of control over assets and incomes will tend to have a more equal distribution of political power ... In contrast, a society with greater inequality of assets will tend to have a less egalitarian distribution of power and worse institutions, which tend to reproduce the initial conditions."[47]

Given this assessment, in order to bring the excluded and voiceless into the mainstream of governance, it will be necessary to strike a balance between ideals and demands. The demands of the excluded and the ideal of inclusionary governance need to be processed through the *radicalization of democracy*. According to Cardoso, "the key to this balance that is central to the idea of the radicalization of democracy is the idea that the State must serve all citizens effectively. How is that possible?"[48] Previously, I laid out my own formulation of inclusionary governance with an eye to creating an IS that would prioritize the issues of equity and inequitable distribution. Yet, even prior to that determination, the IS is dedicated to giving a seat at the decision-making table to every major group, class, and interest in the nation. The IS stands for the proposition that if this is done, the *radicalization of democracy* is going to be inaugurated, then made a part of the political culture, and as it transitions through various phases of development it can then be consolidated. Now we turn to a discussion of the details of and challenges to the task of bridging the gap between the ideals and demands of the democratic process within the IS.

RADICALIZING DEMOCRACY: THE TASK OF BRIDGING
THE GAP BETWEEN IDEALS AND DEMANDS

Democracy is a fundamental theme in both political science and philosophy. In the twentieth century, it has been increasingly linked to economic considerations from the market to labor relations. This is necessarily the case because "it is a theme that is as provocative as it is inexhaustible, because it is basically linked to the permanent problem of defining what makes a good society."[49] In the world of the twenty-first century, it is a concept with even greater inexhaustible capacity because it has meaning for a rising Global Community of nations. Democracy has great relevance with respect to resolving the issues of equity and inequitable distribution, as well as the way in which economic development is carried forward and how its priorities are defined. Democracy is of critical concern with respect to the protection and promotion of human rights, as well as the accountability of a state to its citizens.

The UNDP published a 2004 report entitled, *Democracy in Latin America: Towards a Citizen's Democracy*.[50] Its authors continually stress the notion that democracy presents itself as a system of government that is always characterized by the lack of fulfillment and completion.[51] It is precisely because of democracy's unfulfilled potential and the ever-expanding list of issues that it is asked to address that it is now viewed as an approach to governance that makes it an integral part of the framework of political, civil, and social citizenship. Given this perspective, "the great challenge is to consolidate this emerging consensus and to turn it into support for reforms that will strengthen the democracies of Latin America."[52] This is a difficult task for it means taking the ideal of democracy, an ideal that is always being modified in some way, and using that ideal in connection with practical policies, institutions, and efforts to forge a society that reflects the qualities of a long historical search for freedom, justice, and material and spiritual progress.

In the case of Latin America, after two decades of differing forms of democratic transition and consolidation, the authors of the report acknowledge the reality that "today, renewing the content of democracy and giving impetus to a new phase is a much larger and more uncertain goal. In concrete terms, what does *striving for a democracy of citizenship* really mean? What conditions do we need to address them? Who are the new opponents of a deeper democracy?"[53] Twenty-five years ago, the challenges and the answers seemed to be much more straightforward. Twenty-five years ago there was no question but that the major tasks involved the effort to defeat dictatorships, end wars, and achieve democracy and peace. In short, no one questioned what the agenda for democracy was. Today, 25 years later, while the rules and institutions in Latin America are similar to those in countries where democracy is more mature, its societies are fundamentally different. While the region has undergone great changes by virtue of being organized under democratic government, "a new and unprecedented situation has emerged in Latin America: the coexistence of democracy, poverty, and inequality."[54] The current challenge is how to address Latin America's fundamental problem: the coexistence of political freedom alongside widespread material deprivation.

What is clear is that the development of democracy means much more than how to perfect the electoral system. The deeper crisis is one of politics that has resulted in not only inefficiency in government, but "deficits of citizenship."[55] On this matter, the authors of the report quote Charles Beitz and his observation:

> No theory of democracy that failed to give the egalitarian a central place could possibly yield a faithful representation of the extraordinary grip of democracy in the modern political imagination [...] We must keep in mind that historically a main goal of democratic movements has been to seek to redress in the political sphere for the effects of inequalities in the economy and society.[56]

As with the UNDP and World Bank Reports referred to earlier, the issue of inequity is seen as the great problem for both realizing genuine development and genuine democracy. The authors of this report state: "Between 1990 and 2002 ... in 15 of the 18 countries under consideration, one-quarter of the population lives below the poverty line, and in seven of these, more than 50 percent of the population is poor."[57] These numbers also reveal the problems faced by a region that has been subjected to IMF structural adjustment programs with their over-emphasis upon market forces, deregulation, and privatization. The neoliberal theories, derived from the Washington Consensus, failed to take into account the reality that "the possibility of greater equality is linked to the strength of democracy. Satisfaction of the social objectives of development, especially human development, cannot be achieved through market forces alone. The drive for equality does not come from the markets but from the promise implicit in democracy. Equality among citizens strengthens and consolidates democracy."[58]

A PRACTICAL STRATEGY FOR REALIZING EQUALITY AND CONSOLIDATING DEMOCRACY

At this point, we should specify what is meant by the term *equality*. If equality is a goal of human development, then it must be more than a rhetorical device and its realization demands that we give it substance. To that end, I want to begin with three thesis statements:

1. There can be no broad or long-term path of human development in a society that does not ensure equitable access to education, jobs, health care, decent wages, opportunities for investment, and wealth creation by even the economically poorest citizens (*especially the economically poorest citizens*). Therefore, the IS works to ensure that its implementation of human rights encompasses civil, political, social, economic, and cultural rights.
2. Genuine human development demands that every citizen be given the means and the opportunity to become a viable stakeholder in their society. That is what inclusion ultimately means.
3. To that end, it is the primary obligation of the IS to ensure that human development and equitable social progress for all major classes, groups, and interests is not left to market forces alone.

Now, I want to take these three statements and arrange them into a workable and practical program for the real world so that they can reach a point of convergence and find their ultimate expression in concrete ways. In order to accomplish this outcome, I suggest that we make the *indivisibility principle* of human rights as our primary guide in arranging these statements into a workable policy.[59] What the indivisibility principle means is that priority cannot be arbitrarily given to just one category of rights (i.e., civil and political) over and above another (economic, social, and cultural). This is a vitally important requirement insofar as it serves to protect the principle and practice of equitable distribution and equity in general.

Equity has social, economic, and cultural dimensions that are usually overlooked, ignored, or even rejected when a narrow framework of civil and political rights are made absolute. Therefore, in order to overcome this bifurcation of rights, it is essential to invoke the indivisibility principle so that there is a normative basis for citizens to challenge the decision-making processes of their government when they claim a right to considerations of equity. By juxtaposing the standard of equitable development next to the decisional outcomes of the state's bargaining processes, it is possible to more objectively evaluate whether or not the state has implemented an inclusive or exclusionary standard of governance. In so doing, it becomes possible to make corrections in accordance with inclusive claims based upon the principle of equity and the indivisibility principle.

From this principle it follows that the IS should work to incorporate all major classes, groups, and interests into its strategies for investment, budgetary decisions, and decisions for long-term economic growth in accordance with all of these rights (civil, political, social, economic, cultural). By governing in this incorporative/inclusive manner, the IS guarantees that human development and equitable social progress are not left to market forces alone (see: Thesis Number 3, above). By guaranteeing that each citizen be given access to employment and educational opportunities that are appropriate to their talents and abilities, each citizen can become a viable stakeholder in their society (see: Thesis Number 2, above).

By ensuring opportunities for investment and wealth creation by every citizen (a stakeholder), it becomes possible for the IS to chart a long-term path for human development that guarantees an equitable sharing of resources among equally valued stakeholders (citizens). Such an outcome is also premised upon a radicalized democracy that guarantees citizen access and input into the decision-making processes of governance and economic policymaking (see: Thesis Number 1, above). In this way, when we speak of equality, we can genuinely speak of the substantive realization of civil, political, social, economic, as well as cultural rights—and therefore, the realization of equality in all of these arenas serves to consolidate democracy. Further, we have also demonstrated how the *indivisibility principle* operates to ensure that "human rights of all kinds (*civil, social, economic, political, and cultural*) are of equal worth and validity, inextricably linked, and equally deserving of priority."[60]

In the above discussion, I have demonstrated how I intend to make use of the goal of equality (greater equitable distribution) and the indivisibility principle in reference to the IS. I have also begun to explain the way in which the realization of equality can lead to the consolidation and strengthening of social democracy. When speaking of democratic consolidation, I am pointing to the ideal embodiment of not just any kind of democracy, but a social democracy within an IS. The ideal to which I am referring is a social democracy because a social democracy centralizes and prioritizes human rights. Alternatively, when a democracy is divorced from broadly shared social goals and human rights norms, it will most likely move in a direction that relies on the market to further enrich elite classes, strike nondemocratic bargains, and accelerate the spiral of decision making toward an ES point. Such a result will have the consequence of creating greater degrees of inequality and an inequitable distribution of resources and opportunities. Such an inequitable outcome has usually been the result of governments surrendering their sovereign decision-making authority to the IMF and/or World Bank, thereby incurring large amounts of *odious* debt that the state is incapable of repaying (to be discussed in detail later in this chapter). As a consequence of this worsening condition of debt not only is default a predictable outcome but the hopes of the people for genuine national development are destroyed. Their condition of vulnerability has, at that point in time, been translated into a condition of subordination to the interests of international capital.

The long-term survival of a democracy that is dedicated to the indivisibility of human rights requires both the institutional mechanisms and a philosophical orientation to maintain an historical trajectory that does not merely rely on the market and works toward the realization of an inclusive social democracy. Therefore, the IS, as defined earlier in this chapter, should be understood as the institutional means through which the ideals of equality and human rights among citizens can be realized. In this way, we can sever the coexistence of political freedom from widespread material deprivation. The inherent incompatibility of these two realities throughout Latin America exposes the tenuous nature of neoliberalism as a policy that ostensibly promotes development.

As outlined above, the three thesis statements should be understood in reference to the *indivisibility principle*. The application of the indivisibility principle is necessary so as to ensure that the IS is not left on its own to determine how to guide the process of inclusion, but rather is both philosophically and practically equipped to undertake the task of implementing inclusive practices, policies, and goals. Further, I am arguing that once this linkage is established then the consolidation of a viable social democracy becomes more attainable. I also want to argue that in conjunction with the indivisibility principle, there are two other principles that other scholars have suggested as being significant in the process of realizing this broad-based approach to development. These scholars have argued that we need to incorporate the *principle of interrelatedness* and the *principle of interdependence*. In that regard, "the principle of inter-relatedness recognizes that all human rights are conceptually and functionally linked. Similarly, the principle of interdependence among the human rights requires that improvement in the realization of any one human right be a function of increased realization of all or at least some of the other human rights, in any context."[61]

In light of the discussion above, I am arguing that it is only in the context of an inclusive social democracy that it becomes possible to realize and achieve genuine

The Consolidation of a Viable Social Democracy in Conjunction with Human Rights

Social Democracy and the IS

1. The IS works to ensure equitable access to the full rights of citizenship.
2. Every citizen has the opportunity to become a stakeholder in the society.
3. The IS works to ensure equitable social progress for all major classes/groups.

Supportive Human Rights Principles

1. The indivisibility principle (rights cannot be arbitrarily prioritized because every category of rights needs to be simultaneously addressed).
2. The interdependence principle (improvement in one area requires a similar improvement in other areas of rights, or at least an approximation).
3. The interrelatedness principle (all human rights are conceptually and functionally linked).

The Co-Realization of Rights Produces a Viable Social Democracy

1. Full rights of citizenship.
2. Every citizen is a stakeholder in the society.
3. Equitable social progress is attainable by all major classes and groups.

---

inclusion, opportunity, and equity (*as defined by the principles of indivisibility, interdependence, and interrelatedness*). In turn, a viable social democracy derives its strength from a comprehensive realization of all human rights as they are actualized vis à vis the workings of an IS. It is the *co-realization* of political, civil, social, economic, and cultural rights that actually produces concrete results in the lives of people. Thus,

> it is futile to talk of the right to information in the absence of a certain minimal realization of the right to education; or it is meaningless to talk of the right to work in the presence of violations of the rights to participate and have equal access to public service and be considered as an equal on grounds of race, color, sex, language, or religion. Malnutrition retards a child's educational prospects, and low quality education increases child labor incentives. The right to vote is devalued without mutually supporting guarantees for access to information, freedom of association, educational guarantees, and underlying economic and social rights guarantees. Poor health diminishes capacities to perform productive employment, translating to lower income, and a corresponding greater vulnerability to violations of a range of other rights. The principles of indivisibility, interdependence, and inter-relatedness together make it necessary to see the realization of rights-based development as a process of co-realization of all human rights.[62]

GLOBALIZATION, POVERTY, AND INEQUALITY ARE RELATIONAL

Just as a process of *rights-based development* should be understood as a process of the co-realization of all human rights, so too, globalization should be understood as a *relational* process that leads to greater poverty and inequality. It has this effect because globalization is premised upon the economic prescriptions of neoliberal orthodoxy. Neoliberal orthodoxy demands independence from any kind of intervention or interference from the state that would ameliorate the influence of the market as the final arbiter of all things economic—including how to address the problems of poverty and inequality (which includes the political realm when the state seeks to dictate policies that contradict neoliberal orthodoxy about the primacy of the market). The ideological commitment to make the market the final and absolute arbiter of all things social, economic, and political is a commitment that is designed to safeguard the process of capital accumulation—as set forth by neoliberal doctrines, practices, and programs.

Neoliberal economic prescriptions and programs seek to limit investments in human capital. Its prescriptions and programs are designed to limit and severely reduce the realm of citizen participation in decision making, thereby reducing the agency of the poor, the workers, and those seeking to be engaged more directly in the decision-making processes of both national and international life. The neoliberal agenda demands not only structural adjustment throughout the nations of the South, but also the power to affect and/or eliminate the social power of labor markets and unions. The neoliberal agenda is also dedicated to the elimination of environmental laws and regulations that would have the effect of diminishing profits in the worldwide process of capital accumulation.

In practical terms, the greatest challenge that has to be confronted by development experts, national and international leadership, and national and global civil society is to rethink the developmental paradigm—examining what is considered in isolation and what needs to be inclusively considered. What this means is that it is time to address the fact that "social policy remains largely detached from economic policy, or it is seen as an add-on intended to mitigate the social costs of economic liberalization and structural adjustment."[63] That perspective is no longer good enough. It is not good enough because it looks at the developmental paradigm mainly from the perspective of neoliberal orthodoxy.

Neoliberal orthodoxy is mainly the product of the leading nation-states of the North. As such, since the early 1980s, neoliberal orthodoxy emphasized the control of inflation and sound public finance, but it virtually neglected altogether any serious attention being given to the issues of full employment and social protections as the primary goals of economic policy. In so doing, neoliberal economics would wind up giving next to no attention to the human crisis in the South where poverty, human rights violations, rising unemployment, and deepening inequalities have condemned billions of people to a life of unremitting poverty with no end in sight. Commenting upon this crisis, the authors of the UNRISD report, *Visible Hands: Taking Responsibility for Social Development* stressed: "The invisible hand of the market may be able to keep the global economy turning. But it takes the human hand to guide it in the most productive direction and to fashion a world that is *socially inclusive*, transparent and democratically anchored" (Italics are mine).[64]

For the liberalization agenda to have proceeded without giving attention to income distribution and poverty reduction throughout the South was to proceed in a reckless direction. Yet, that is precisely what has happened. In a study sponsored by the Inter-American Development Bank, the United Nations Economic Commission for Latin America and the Caribbean, and the World Bank, its authors observed:

> Rising skill-based earnings differentials hint at *insufficient human capital investment*, and financial opening in most countries preceded establishment of adequate regulatory frameworks and mechanisms to limit volatility in capital inflows. These issues, along with *a greater concern about income distribution and poverty reduction, are now surfacing as "second-stage reforms" on the liberalization agenda ... but clearly they ought to have been part of the reform process right from the start* (Italics are mine).[65]

Human capital investment is an economic term which, simply put, means investing in people. To invest in people means not only that people will be given a certain bundle of rights, but that they will be participants and agents in creating their own destiny. To invest in people is both an economic and a political act. It is not and either/or dichotomy that presents us with a choice between *either* an economic set of options for people, *or* a political set of options for people. Rather, human beings are supposed to be participants and agents in the shaping of their own destiny. As agents, people must be able to freely participate and "participation, to be considered effective, must ultimately be characterized by a genuine capacity to influence the economic and political agendas. It must mean more than merely participating as an economic unit, or *'consumer of public services'*." And so, most critical of all, "*collective participation in this very real sense must logically involve the capacity of people to determine the political and economic systems under which they live*, and whether economic and social models favored by development actors (in consultation with local elites or otherwise) are desirable or appropriate for the country concerned" (Italics are mine).[66]

However, neoliberalism deprives both the individual person and the collective group the kind of participation that would allow them to democratically determine what kind of political and economic system that they would wish to live under. Neoliberalism strips away the choice of being able to freely determine what kind of just society one would want to live under if one could make such a choice. Neoliberalism disallows choice, for it imposes its own predetermined conclusion of what kind of society one will have to accept. This is the case insofar as neoliberalism is guided by its own regime of "rights." These are the "rights of capital." Neoliberalism's regime of rights includes: (1) the independence from state interference (hence, deregulation and privatization under the rubric of a "free market"); (2) individual responsibility and liability; (3) equality of opportunity in the market and before the law; (4) rewards for entrepreneurial endeavor; (5) care for oneself and one's own; and (6) an open marketplace that allows for both the freedoms of contract and exchange.

In short, neoliberalism is a doctrine that means a person must either "accept or submit to that bundle of rights necessary for capital accumulation."[67] Under the rubric of neoliberal economics, capital accumulation has been put at odds with investments in human capital, concerns with poverty reduction, attempts to address widening gulfs of economic and political equality, and addressing the task of providing access to material resources and social opportunities needed to realize human rights claims. As a direct consequence of this stark choice, the objection to this neoliberal regime of rights is quite simple: "to accept it is to accept that we have no alternative except to live under a regime of endless capital accumulation and economic growth no matter what the social, ecological, or political consequences."[68] This definition of neoliberalism and its regime of rights constituted what was referred to as the *Washington Consensus*. According to one scholar, "it is a policy agenda which, in its ideal type, strips governments of the responsibility for and capability of influencing either the allocation of resources to promote and influence growth or the distribution of income."[69]

Yet, to accept this approach is to also be willing to accept a future centered around endless capital accumulation and a world in which this neoliberal regime of economic imperialism must be geographically expanded across the globe by violence (as with the Bush-2 regime's invasions of Afghanistan and Iraq). After all, the neoliberal regime of rights is in the service of the US Global Empire. As such, it is a regime of capitalist rights that is designed to accommodate the imperialist policies of the World Trade Organization, the IMF, and the World Bank. If *another American Century* is to be realized, it will be realized when the "inalienable rights of private property and the profit rate will be universally established. This is precisely what Bush means when he says the US dedicates itself to extend the sphere of freedom across the globe."[70] Such a path will never lead to an *exodus from empire* (at least not a voluntary exodus). Rather, such a path will allow market forces to preserve a process of globalization that is led by an ever-widening circular pattern of capital accumulation that creates an even more unequal world where poverty and inequality reign as the supreme reality for billions of people. This is necessarily the case because globalization, poverty, and inequality are relational.[71]

In order to demonstrate how globalization, poverty, and inequality are relational it would be helpful to expose how the system run by the US Global Empire allows for continuous transfers of wealth from the periphery of the system (the global South) to the center of the system (the global North). Contrary to the hype and propaganda created for public consumption in the North, the North is not trying to help the South with aid or launch a path to genuine national development. Rather, as acknowledged at the G-7 Summit in Naples in July 1994, former French president François Mitterrand declared: "Despite the considerable amounts spent on bilateral and multilateral aid, the flow of capital from Africa towards the highly industrialized countries is greater than that which flows towards the developing countries."[72]

The reality and actual functioning of the neoliberal system—as conducted under the auspices of the IMF and World Bank, as well as the WTO—allows for a massive transfer of social surplus created by salaried workers and small producers in the South toward the ruling classes of the industrialized and Third World countries. Nowhere is this transfer of wealth more graphically seen than in the cycle of Third World debt repayment. In 1980, according to the World Bank, the total external debt of the developing countries amounted to $580 billion. By the end of 2002, it came to about $2.4 trillion—a fourfold increased. Between 1980 and 2002, the developing countries repaid their creditors a little more than $4.5 trillion. Hence, the countries of the global South have repaid eight times the amount they owed, only to find themselves four times more indebted. Additionally, another way of conceptualizing this transfer of wealth is to recognize that between 1980 and 2002, the populations of the global South have sent the equivalent of 50 Marshall Plans to creditors in the North (with the capitalists and governments of the periphery skimming off their commissions on the way).[73] The proportional increase of debt per region during this period is staggering, as shown in the following table:

External Debt of Developing Countries by Region (in billions of dollars)		
	1980	2002
Southeast Asia and the Pacific	64.6	509.5
South Asia	37.8	166.8
Middle East and North Africa	102.5	317.3
Sub-Saharan Africa	60.8	204.4
Latin America and the Caribbean	257.4	789.4
Former Soviet Bloc	56.5	396.8

Source: Erich Toussaint, *Your Money [or] Your Life: The Tyranny of Global Finance, Updated Edition*, 2005, p. 149.

THE WASHINGTON/WALL STREET ALLIANCE: LEADING THE WAY TO GLOBAL POVERTY

The financial history of the United States from 1980 to the present should be centered upon the ideology and practices emanating from within the Washington/ Wall Street Alliance. A close examination of this alliance will contribute a great deal to comprehending how a small but strategically positioned financial and political elite has been leading the way to a deepening of global poverty for over two decades. In combination with the IMF, World Bank, the central banks of nation-states, commercial and investment banks (headquartered outside of Washington in commercial sites such as New York, Boston, London, Zurich, and Tokyo), the Washington/Wall Street Alliance is responsible for the economic policy of the banking world.[74]

During the Reagan and Bush-1 administrations, James A. Baker III and Richard Darman represented Wall Street and the interests within the military-industrial-complex. Baker served as secretary of the Treasury for President Reagan between 1985 and 1988, after working in the Houston, Texas law firm of Andrews and Kurth from 1957 to 1975. Darman served as assistant secretary of Commerce in the Ford administration and as deputy secretary of the Treasury for President Reagan (1985–1987). Both men were associated with the Carlyle Group—a private global investment firm that is intimately tied to the Pentagon and military-industrial-complex.[75] During the Clinton years, Robert E. Rubin and Lawrence

Summers represented Wall Street interests in their respective turns as secretary of the Treasury. Rubin had served as co-chairman of Goldman Sachs and Company (a Wall Street investment banking firm), and later became a director at Citigroup, with ties to Citibank, Solomon Smith Barney (an investment services company). Summers followed Rubin as secretary of the Treasury after having served as chief economist for the World Bank.[76] All of these men worked for the advancement of the interests associated with the *Washington/Wall Street Alliance*. It was primarily their task to help establish, protect, and reinforce a neoliberal policy regime that served to deregulate the world economy—in terms of nation-state intervention. Their primary legacy has been to open the way for US corporations to exploit the global South.

Other aspects of this exploitation include the trading of industrial commodities without interference, and the movement of capital assets across national boundaries. Evaluating the scope and nature of their respective accomplishments, some observers have lamented that "rather than a 'sound' global system, the result is a wild economy of colliding interests and immanent debt beyond the control of any particular interests or institution."[77] In summary, we discover that the international financial market is the meeting point at which all of the biases of these hidden elites collide. These elites literally gamble on whether the economic model adopted by a country— acting on advice from the IMF or World Bank—will actually produce interest, profit, and repayment, or not. This is the real world situation wherein the dominant and elite forces of finance and government come together in an attempt to formulate "economic rationality." Critics of this system ask: "This is the best that 'economic science' has been able to imagine for determining the livelihoods of billions of people? This is what the finest civilization ever known is organized by?"[78]

In answer to these questions, we can say one thing with certainty: *The neo-liberal model and capitalist world system is not adequate for either reducing poverty or conforming to the indivisibility principle for human rights-based development.* Rather, this system is best equipped to deny access to education, health care, and culture. With the rising cost of goods and services in the Third World, three or four dollars a day is not enough for decent food, housing, health care, or education. By setting the figure for determining the number of people who live in absolute poverty at one dollar per day, the World Bank deliberately under-estimates the real costs and burdens of absolute poverty. By deliberately mislead-ing through its underestimation of poverty, the World Bank has sought to create the impression that absolute poverty is marginal in the Third World. In fact, it affects the majority of the population throughout the global South.[79] As the following table indicates, the population living below the absolute poverty line shifts from the minority to the majority when two dollars a day is used as the measurement.

In addition to playing games with the numbers used to calculate absolute poverty, the World Bank has tarnished its reputation by allying itself with the IMF in order to place a positive face on structural adjustment. In the late 1980s, following the lead of officials at the IMF, the World Bank attempted to argue that what hindered structural adjustment was the whole process of policymaking, and the nature of relations between the private sector, the state, and large segments of civil society. In order to critique this process, the World Bank designated the term "governance"

Absolute Poverty Line

	Year of Survey	Population in absolute poverty (percent)	
		<$1 per day	<$2 per day
India	1999–2000	35	80
Indonesia	2000	7	55
Laos	1997–1998	26	73
Nigeria	1997	70	90
Pakistan	1998	13	66
Philippines	2000	15	46
Senegal	1995	26	68
Tanzania	1993	20	60
Vietnam	1998	18	64
Russia	2000	6	24
Ghana	1998	45	78
Egypt	2000	3	44
China	2000	16	47
Bangladesh	2000	36	83

Source: Erich Toussaint, *Your Money [or] Your Life: The Tyranny of Global Finance—Updated Edition*, Haymarket Books, 2005, p. 36.

as the primary problem for nations reaching their developmental goals. In 1989, the World Bank specifically singled out the African crisis as one of *governance*. Therefore, the World Bank would argue (in collusion with the IMF) that the pursuit of structural adjustment required the reform of the entire political framework—with special attention being given to the institutional contexts in which policies are designed as well as the channels through which they are to be implemented. By the beginning of the 1990s, the World Bank had reached the conclusion that the whole system of state and civil society relations was at stake.[80] The net effect of this shift, however, failed to substantially modify the goals of the Washington Consensus. Rather, "it was meant to *improve* the performance of structural adjustment programs by reshaping the state in accordance with the main tenets of an ideology of economic globalization and free trade."[81]

At first glance, it seemed as though the *governance agenda* was going to overcome all of the contradictions and internal tensions of the neoliberal model and a human rights centered process for development. The *governance agenda* did this by making the argument that all of these disparate elements could be effectively combined under the rubric of privatization, the commodification of services, and the opening of the global marketplace. However, in reality, the *governance agenda* "reflects the success of a strategy which sought to reframe the expansion of capitalist social relations as a force of emancipation and empowerment."[82] Nothing could have been further from the truth. Yet, this is the Big Lie that resides in the heart of the imperial project of the US Global Empire. It is the falsehood that "US leaders have, with considerable domestic public support projected upon the world [which is] the idea that American neo-liberal values of freedom are universal and supreme, and that such values are to die for."[83]

   The project of neoliberalism can be interpreted "either as a utopian project to realize a theoretical design for the reorganization of international capitalism or as a political project to re-establish the conditions for capital accumulation and to restore the power of economic elites." According to some scholars, "neo-liberalism has not been very effective in revitalizing global capital accumulation, but it has succeeded remarkably well in restoring, or in some instances (as in Russia and China) creating the power of an economic elite."[84] In the African context, the impacts of globalization and neoliberalism have been a disaster where the process of state building is still underway and the problems of poverty and social inequality are rampant. Hence, "a distinction needs to be drawn between the existing disarticulated state and a state that advances social interest."[85] In the case of Mexico, the drive to modernize and globalize the Mexican economy, pursuant to neoliberal prescriptions, has produced neither a higher level of economic growth nor a higher standard of living for the majority of the population. In the fact, "it could be argued that the liberalization process demanded by globalization has not fulfilled its promise because it has not also reduced poverty ... The rising tide of exports has not lifted all boats—the poor have been left stranded on the shore."[86]

   Throughout Africa, Russia, China, and Mexico, the neoliberal agenda has reinforced the growth of the ES. The spread of ES has become a necessity for governance whenever and wherever the neoliberal agenda is adopted. Yet, the unmanaged competition that takes place in ES that adopt a neoliberal agenda always marginalizes the poor, disadvantaged, and excluded groups and classes. As globalization spreads it takes with it a neoliberal agenda that reinforces exclusionary forms of capital accumulation and strengthens elite bastions of political and economic privilege. In so doing, genuine national development is foreclosed upon and national economic distortions become replicated throughout the Global Community. In turn, as economic distortions and exclusionary governance combine to defend this inherently inequitable status quo, it is virtually inevitable that the cleavages being made will further divide classes, groups, and ethnic minorities. In short, it is a prescription for civil war.

   From an Islamic perspective,

   in a world like this, totally unmanaged competition and absolutely unregulated liberalization can only be to the disadvantage of the poor and the under-privileged ... Unless there are safeguards for those who are weak and as such disadvantaged, globalization cannot but aggravate a process through which the poorer countries of the world will be further marginalized, if not decimated, in terms of economic and political influence on world affairs.[87]

Taken in combination, these perspectives from across the Global Community help to articulate the views of neoliberalism's critics—representing the unheard voices of billions of people regarding the ideology of neoliberalism and its rightwing elite.

   These critical voices from throughout the developing world reflect the reality that, in the eyes of millions of people,

   there is a consistent and coherent pattern: *the IMF-World Bank reform package constitutes a coherent program of economic and social collapse.* The austerity measures lead to the disintegration of the state, the national economy is remolded, production for the domestic market is destroyed through the compression of real earnings and domestic production is redirected towards the world market. These measures go far beyond the phasing-out of import-substituting industries. They destroy the entire fabric of the domestic economy (Italics are mine).[88]

By destroying the domestic economy, the net effect of structural adjustment programs is one where the interests of elites and popular sectors are reinforced while, at the same time, the participatory mechanisms of adjusting societies have been weakened—not strengthened. These programs also have a potentially negative long-term effect upon the capacity of the government to work any more closely with civil society and to manage their resources more effectively in the future.[89]

The destruction of the domestic economy is inevitable

when nations: (1) adopt an IMF structural adjustments program (SAP); (2) experiences "overcapacity" in all sectors of the economy—which also characterizes the world capitalist economy as a whole; (3) the market itself becomes a conduct for the destruction of the national economy—what Joseph Schumpeter called the market's "*creative destruction*"; (4) in the aftermath of this "*creative destruction*" the entire economy is restructured until the weak are eliminated and the cost of all the so-called factors of production are lowered, allowing the accumulation process to begin once more from a new foundation.[90]

This process is endemic to neoliberal globalization because of its commitment to a model of open economies, minimal government interventions, and free markets—including free global capital movements and "flexible" labor markets. However, even though it has been presented as the only effective policy approach in the new global economy, the reality is that this approach has generated injustice, insecurity, instability, and inefficiency.[91] In order to more clearly comprehend some of the critical differences between neoliberal globalization versus the inclusive approach of a human rights based development project, I offer the following table (overleaf).

The fundamental differences between neoliberal-driven globalization and an inclusive human rights based developmental agenda are so profound as to point toward the creation of two entirely different worlds. The world of human rights seeks a world in which there is freedom from want and deprivation—the basic human right to adequate food that guarantees basic health, nutrition, and wholeness.[92] The world of neoliberal globalization simply wants more: more profit, more power, and more economic growth for the few. Among the various rationalizations produced to justify neoliberal globalization is the promise they see in economic growth for the sake of growth. In order to account for massive divergences in performance between the West and the rest, the apologists of neoliberal-driven globalization assert "a large part of the answer is cumulative historical forces that go back centuries … At a certain point, economic growth has become routine. A positive

Neoliberal Globalization versus Inclusive Human Rights Based Development

Neoliberalism	Human Rights Based Development
"Good governance"	Inclusionary governance
Participation is limited	Participation is expanded
Priority is given to economic policy	Priority is given to social policy
Emphasis on controlling inflation, public finance	Full employment and social protections in reference to the principles of indivisibility, interdependence, and inter-relatedness
Capital accumulation at the center (North), exploitation of periphery (South)	Investments in human capital, poverty reduction, elimination of socioeconomic and sociopolitical disparities, providing access to material resources in order to achieve co-realization of human rights for all groups
Eliminate state interference	Bring IS back into the development process and build social democracies to widen participation in decision making
Equality of opportunity is limited to the sphere of the market	Equality of opportunity in all realms pursuant to the indivisibility principle of human rights based development
In the service of the US Global Empire and ES	In the service of the Global Community and a guide to IS
Adoption of IMF structural adjustment programs	Rejection of IMF structural adjustment programs
Countries in the global South are marginalized in the global economy as they are subordinated to the systemic demands and features of capitalism	Countries throughout the global South work toward socialism so that the systemic features of capitalism no longer define society

Sources: Terrence E. Paupp, *Achieving Inclusionary Governance: Advancing Peace and Development in First and Third World Nations*, Transnational Publishers, Inc., 2000; William F. Felice, *Taking Suffering Seriously: The Importance of Collective Human Rights*, State University of New York Press, 1996; William F. Felice, *The Global New Deal: Economic and Social Human Rights in World Politics*; Rowman & Littlefield Publishers, Inc., 2003.

cycle of reinforcement has then gone from the economy to polity and society, and back again."[93]

The above-cited argument ignores the effects of Western invasions, colonialism, and US-supported regimes and dictatorships from the Philippines under Marcos to Indonesia under Suharto. A Euro-centric vision distorts much of what is contained in the arguments of neoliberals. Perhaps this is why early twenty-first century neoliberal arguments present bold assertions in place of objective analysis and historical inquiry. For example, the cover story for *The Economist*, November 2005, declares: "Tired of Globalization—But in need of much more of it."[94] The editorial on the subject discusses what it calls "the case for selfish generosity." What is an example of "selfish generosity"? The editors assert: "[If] the rich world could gird itself to be more ambitious on agriculture the gains would be even greater for the poorest countries, making the rich look generous; better access to the biggest and richest developing countries for western companies; and a rise in global income in a decade's time of $300 billion a year (says the World

Bank), which would thus help everyone."[95] Well, not quite everyone. By their own admission, the "biggest and richest developing countries" are the target for Western companies seeking access to large markets. The truly poor countries in Africa and Asia are left out of the plans so that "selfish generosity" turns out to be just selfish.

From a more critical perspective, I argue that the analysis of the editors at *The Economist* fails to account for the fact that capitalist production is class-alienated and class-exploitative production. As a consequence of this oversight,

> they forget to consider the critical question of whether contemporary capitalist production ... is capable of achieving success in terms of the sustainable development of productive forces (human, social, ecological) on a global scale. This causes them to overlook the fact that the creative element of capitalism's "creative destruction" is now far outweighed by the destructive element, especially once one takes the global socio-economic and ecological "side effects" of national capitalist successes into account.[96]

Alternatively, a human rights based developmental strategy looks to different principles to guide the direction of economics by addressing international governance reform. Specifically, the UNDP, the UN Environment Program, the World Resources Institute, and even the World Bank all opined that it had become necessary to look at the "poverty-environment-governance nexus." In their jointly co-authored report, *World Resources (2002–2004): Decision for the Earth—Balance, Voice, and Power*, these institutions concur: "Progress in solving environmental problems can only be made if strategies to combat them are consistent with a priority objective of the international community and most countries: The eradication of poverty."[97] In other words, the rising voice and power of the emerging Global Community has begun to unite many people in both the global North and the global South. Collectively, the viewpoint from the Global Community is that:

> The political motivation for this posture is that dealing with poverty is a top priority for many developing countries and one of the main goals of development cooperation between North and South. Environmental decisions and actions that are consistent with this priority are likely to gain wider acceptance from governments and stakeholders. Conversely, when such decisions and actions are perceived to be "anti-development" or contrary to poverty reduction goals, resistance to their adoption is predictable.[98]

FROM REDESIGN TO REPLACEMENT OF THE NEOLIBERAL FRAMEWORK

Now, as we are confronted with alternative development paths, one primary question that needs to be answered is: *Should the global North and global South redesign the current neoliberal framework of international financial institutions or embark upon a replacement of them?* Insofar as the Washington/Wall Street Alliance remains committed to the historical policy prescriptions of the

IMF/World Bank/WTO/US Treasury-Complex, the answer to the question as to whether to redesign or replace the current system is obvious from the standpoint of progressives, social democrats, and the poor and excluded. It must be replaced. Why? Because, as outlined above, the very nature of capitalist development vis-à-vis these institutions, serving at the behest of the US Global Empire, has worked to corrupt the process of genuine national and human development throughout the global South. The kind of development that has been imposed on entire nations through IMF structural adjustment programs, neoliberal doctrines, and the requirements associated with loan conditionality constitutes an anti-development agenda. In this regard, Professor William Robinson has explained this phenomenon as one where " *development* as the modernization of structures as such does not necessarily involve meaningful improvement in the lives of majorities and can (indeed often does) entail a further relative or absolute deterioration of material and cultural life conditions as well as a widening of asymmetries in social power relations."[99]

Without the collective ability of social groups and classes to shape structures in their interests, they lack social power. They also lack the ability to realize fundamental human rights under these conditions. I have referred to this outcome as the product of *exclusionary governance*. It is an outcome that reflects the resistance of the US Global Empire, its agencies, and collaborator elites throughout the global South to adopt a human rights based approach that is grounded upon achieving inclusive forms of governance—guided by the application of the *indivisibility principle*. When the tasks of development and modernization allow for the division of rights between political and civil rights, on the one hand, and socioeconomic and cultural rights, on the other hand, we discover the bitter irony of human rights practice under the auspices of neoliberalism. This division of rights reveals the harsh reality that "the halting but ineluctable spread of the global economy is linked to an evolving human rights irony: *states become less able to help their citizens attain social and economic rights, even though they often retain their ability to violate human rights*. Even where reforms have led to the enjoyment of basic political rights, the implementation of neo-liberal economic policies can erode the right to freedom from want (Italics are mine)."[100]

In light of this reality, I am arguing that it would ultimately be in the best interest of the citizenry of the global North, to join with the citizenry of global South, in demanding and implementing a human rights based development agenda that unites the entire Global Community. Such a convergence of people and interest has the capacity to replace the failed policies of the past. Additionally, it should be a human rights based development agenda that postulates the emergence of a *post-Imperial America*. In short, it needs to be an agenda that reflects an American *exodus from empire*. At the most fundamental level, the *exodus from empire* will require an end to the present global system of capitalist accumulation as conducted by the IMF, World Bank, WTO, and the Washington/Wall Street alliance. Neither national societies nor the Global Community can be sustained under the rubric of neoliberal capitalist accumulation. Not only does this system truly exacerbate social conflict and social contradictions but it also accelerates systemic tendencies toward violence, civil war, and reliance upon military solutions to address what are fundamentally political and economic problems. Take, for example, what has happened throughout Central America (1970–2005). According to some scholars, "the most fundamental social contradiction in Central America and in global society is this: the model of polarized (flexible) accumulation does not resolve the social contradictions of capitalism, and cannot ... [It] tends to aggravate them. The problem therefore is the social structure of accumulation under global capitalism."[101]

Under the current system of global capital accumulation, increasing levels of global inequality lead to a new "politics of exclusion." In turn, social control through an antidemocratic and antidevelopmental policy state takes the place of social welfare. It is responsible for producing new forms of social apartheid both within nations and on a global basis. The failure to embark upon an *exodus from empire* and its system of capital accumulation tends to move humanity toward greater levels of global polarization. The rise in the number of *gated communities*, *enclaves*, *citadels*, and *fortresses* are all testimony to the new *politics of exclusion*. It is a politics that leaves the poor to fend for themselves even as the deceptive discourse of "community empowerment" goes forth, allowing a shift in the burden of responsibility for social reproduction from the state and society to the most marginalized communities themselves.[102] These are the realities that give clear evidence and testimony to why the reform and/or redesign of the current system of global capital accumulation and the US Global Empire is not sufficient for bringing an end to the abuses of neoliberalism and those of the US Global Empire. Rather, only a thorough and total replacement of the current global power structure— that has been premised upon continuing US hegemony and domination—can sustain a rising Global Community.

The historical record of cohesive-capitalist states has proven that economic growth, by itself, is not enough to sustain humane and inclusive forms of democratic governance. As one scholar has noted,

> What if this growth comes at the serious political cost of a repressive state that amasses and uses power well in some areas but also curtails the important urge of the many to participate politically and to control their own destinies? While not totalitarian, cohesive-capitalist states do resemble fascist states of the past. Can one then comfortably recommend such states as desirable on the ground that they are the most likely agents of rapid industrialization and economic growth?[103]

The World Bank and IMF make this recommendation all of the time. It is the basis of loan conditionality. Nigeria, South Korea, Brazil, and India, are all countries where this experiment has taken place. Out of these experiences, two normative implications arise:

> First, any assessment of economic success in such states as South Korea, Taiwan, military-ruled Brazil, or contemporary China must be weighed against the serious political costs paid by the citizens of these countries. Second, the somewhat lower economic growth rates achieved by such countries as India or

Malaysia ought not always to be judged harshly, at least not without a serious analysis of possible trade-offs.[104]

Too often, the trade-off for economic growth under IMF and World Bank direction has been the uncritical adoption of a right-wing authoritarian government—an ES.

Such states have remained amenable to the demands and requirements of the US Global Empire and its financial networks, but these exclusionary states have been hostile to human rights based development. This outcome has been, in part, the result of a willingness to uncritically adopt the IMF/World Bank mythology that democracy, equality, free markets, and rapid economic growth can all be achieved simultaneously throughout the global South.[105] The evidence presented in this chapter proves otherwise. There are alternatives to the US Global Empire's neoliberal model. The table below offers the outline of an alternative for the Global Community.

When viewed in combination, the factors associated with a human rights based development strategy that is linked to achieving inclusive forms of governance serve to provide the strongest and most viable alternative to the policies and practices of the IMF, World Bank, and the institutional forces and networks promulgated by the US Global Empire.[106] Still, the questions remain: "What social,

---

Replacing the Neoliberal Model of the US Global Empire with a Human Rights Based Development Strategy

---

When human development is conceived of as an *exodus from empire*, a rejection of the neoliberal model, and a refusal to follow IMF and World Bank guidelines, then a human rights based development agenda (*premised upon the indivisibility principle*) can be offered to provide the following results on a global basis:

1. Accelerate the democratization process by building strong and inclusive state institutions, policies, practices, and goals;
2. Move nations away from a culture of war and a culture of militarism;
3. Incorporate elites into the transition to democratic and inclusive forms of governance (as was the case in South Africa from 1990 to present);
4. Enable the process of consolidation for democratically inclusive nations (emerging from autocracy or dictatorship), to engage in building new institutions with mediating institutions designed to incorporate all major groups, classes, and the poor—thereby facilitating the evolution of a culture of peace (both within and between nations);
5. Reduce the dangers of war that are posed by the historical legacy of militarist and nationalist ideologies;
6. Reinforce a culture of peace by helping to remove the following antidevelopmental elements from the process of democratic consolidation: exclusionary nationalism, pressure group politics, logrolling among elite factions, weak brokerage of political bargains by the ruling elite, contradictory and unconvincing signaling in foreign affairs, the use of aggressive foreign policies by declining elites gambling for domestic political resurrection, the use of media dominance to promote nationalist ideology, and nationalist bidding wars between old elites and rising mass groups.

Sources: Terrence E. Paupp, *Achieving Inclusionary Governance: Advancing Peace and Development in First and Third World Nations*, Transnational Publishers, Inc., 2000; Edward D. Mansfield and Jack Snyder, *Electing to Fight: Why Emerging Democracies Go to War*, MIT Press, 2005.

economic, or political forces are available and prepared for the task of waging a popular war of resistance against neoliberalism and exclusionary governance?" Also: "Who will provide the leadership for the transformation of government and the economy, and from where and from whom will they derive their support for such an undertaking?" These are the questions that need to be examined and answered next.

THE CAPACITY OF SOCIAL MOVEMENTS TO CONFRONT THE US GLOBAL EMPIRE

In the absence of an emerging *post-Imperial America*, one of the greatest dangers to the United States and the world is that there will probably be an increased reliance by elites on nationalism as an ideology. Where social movements have arisen and are arising in opposition to the policies, allies, and institutions of the US Global Empire, there has been an ever-increasing consciousness of the need to seek alternatives to the status quo.

As discussed earlier, the crisis for the international order of capitalist accumulation has been breaking apart as the neoliberal model disintegrates around the world. Neoliberalism is economically dysfunctional, in social terms it is extremely exclusionary, and for both the short- and long-term it is politically unsustainable. Given this trend, it has generated destabilizing forces of resistance in the form of social movements against globalization, neoliberalism, and the resurgent militarism of the US Global Empire. The fact of neoliberalism's global failures throughout the 1980s and 1990s is what accounts for the Bush-2 regime's shift from emphasizing neoliberal economic approaches to a reliance on its strongest asset—the US military. Insofar as economic exploitation and its repressive consequences can only go so far in securing the interests of US and European capital, the US Global Empire has been forced to defend its declining economy and global hegemony through a resurgent culture of militarism dedicated to bringing about a colonization of strategic regions that are rich in oil and other natural resources, as well as markets for US goods.

In order to try to halt or defuse a global trend of the powerless to unite in social movements against the intrusions of the US Global Empire, elites associated with the current system of US power arrangements have employed the rhetoric of democratization and civil society. In so doing, the neoliberal elites of the North have sought to contract nonprofit voluntary associations (NGOs) and convert them into their agents as *strategic partners*. Why? Because they believe that they can recruit NGOs into their campaign for the development of "good governance." The problem with that strategy is that good governance has nothing to do with democracy or human rights. In reality, good governance is a set of policies designed to obtain consent from the oppressed. If the IMF and World Bank can build a counter-reform for bolstering their executive power and that of client governments who remain supportive of the neoliberal ideology, then the IMF and World Bank can engage in undermining radical social movements that are hostile to them.

Additionally, these same elites have sought to maintain their power by invoking patriotism and the ideology of nationalism into their public pronouncements.

In states with a democratic deficit or those that are in a weak position because their democratic transition has yet to be consolidated, the appeal of nationalism provides a convenient ideology for elites to maintain their power because it does not necessarily promise that the government should be strictly accountable to the average voter through democratic processes governed by the rule of law. The primary reason for such a result is that

> nationalism is an ideology that allows elites to exploit the rhetoric of popular sovereignty without submitting to its reality. It offers government for the people, but not necessarily by the people. Nationalism also offers a built-in justification for curtailing the civil rights of potential opponents. This doctrine inherently draws a line between one's own nation and other nations, between the nation's friends and its foes. From there, nationalists and their audiences have found it a short step to fingering and accusing "enemies" and "traitors" whose civic rights must be abridged in order to protect the nation.[107]

In the Cold War years this strategy worked well to set up dictatorships that were hostile to *communism* and the Soviet influence. For example, as revolutionary movements sought to defeat US-supported dictatorships in Chile, Argentina, El Salvador, Nicaragua, the dictators claimed that they were nationalists protecting their people against communist sympathizers while, at the same time, they were engaged in torturing dissidents who opposed the criminality of their respective regimes and sought relief for the poor, the unemployed in both urban and rural sectors, and protections of their civil and human rights.

In the post-9/11 era, the new excuse for the US Global Empire and its client regimes to repress social movements and dissent is the *war on terror*. However, within the periphery of the global South, governments that have chosen a neoliberal path are experiencing a growing crisis of legitimacy inside their respective countries. The ruling classes in these countries are, generally speaking, incapable of offering credible prospects for progress to the great majority of their citizens. That is precisely why the power of social movements is a power that is greater than ever before. Demands for an end to neoliberal governments and policies have the capacity to transform even the most seemingly intractable situations throughout the global South. In response to these movements, the right wing and reactionary forces within Argentina, Brazil, Ecuador, and Bolivia have continued to support their neoliberal benefactors in Washington and Europe. In this context, social movements have been forced to forego the electoral path to power insofar as it requires conformity to a game designed and played by members of the "political class." Instead, social movements generally take a confrontational approach to change and pursue a strategy of mass mobilization of the forces of resistance against the system and the political regime that supports it.

Such is the nature of global political life under the Bush-2 regime and its right-wing allies, collaborators, and adherents. In their respective attempts to shore up their position, the proponents and adherents of globalization, neoliberalism, militarists, and free-market advocates have all worked in concert to develop a strategy that is primarily designed to undermine the social movements coming against them. Not only have they invoked the ideology of nationalism, but they have also begun to redirect attention toward electoral politics, reformist social organizations, and the tasks of local development. All of these efforts are designed to demobilize social movements. In this task, many NGOs have been recruited "in dousing the fire of revolutionary ferment in the countryside."[108] For if social movements succeed in their radical opposition, there will not be a reform of the system, but rather a replacement of it.

The growing democratic social forces of a global army of poor, excluded, and oppressed multitudes is a rising force throughout the Global Community. Although the Bush-2 regime, as well as the repressive and exclusionary governments that serve in its network (such as Israel and neoliberal-friendly regimes throughout Latin America) will continue to argue that these movements are associated with terrorist groups, the reality of the situation is that the US Global Empire and its client regimes are being placed on the defensive by the aspirations of a rising Global Community. Working through social movements, they are people who are seeking the realization of their human rights, as guaranteed by the UN Charter and other human rights treaties. Certainly this is the case for the Palestinian people, the people of Columbia, the Philippines, and most of Latin America and Africa, that have borne some of the gravest injustices imaginable at the bidding of the US Global Empire and its clients, collaborators, and allies in these regions.

As the US Global Empire has promulgated its economic mythology about how it can be engaged in advancing democracy abroad while simultaneously advancing economic growth, the harsh realities of rising levels of global poverty, massive violations of human rights, and the lack of environmental sustainability that accompanies imperial endeavors have all combined to underscore the fallacies and failures that reside within the mythology. The present reality is that the hegemonic discourse of empire is in the process of unraveling. For while the Bush-2 regime has dedicated itself to a revival of resurgent militarism, the inevitable opposition to such force is creating a backlash of opposition not only throughout the world, but also in the United States itself. As the grim reality of the USA Patriot Act exposes the presence of a growing fascist state within the American homeland, all of the assurances of the Bush-2 regime regarding its crusade to bring democracy to the Middle East seem less viable and increasingly hollow. These harsh realities are accompanied by a declining US economy, the Bush-2 regime's reliance upon resurgent militarism, and the growth of a global culture of war (conducted in the name of fighting terrorism). To acknowledge this reality leaves the door open for workers and social movements in both the North and the South to join in a common struggle and work in combination with one another.

TOWARD A CONVERGENCE OF GLOBAL STRUGGLES: THE BASIS FOR A NORTH/SOUTH ALLIANCE AGAINST NEOLIBERALISM

Workers of the South need support from workers in the North if they are to obtain wage increases and the trade union rights that can pave the way for an overall improvement of their living conditions to levels of those that exist in the North. Such a victory could also lead to an end to the corporate practice of *outsourcing* jobs to impoverished labor markets in the South. If that kind of struggle by social movements could be undertaken and won, it would go a long way toward solidifying the peoples of the Global Community and open the doors to genuine national development. It would be possible because it would end the current international economic regime of dependency. For too long, the South has been made to be dependent upon capital investment from the North, but it is not a form of capital investment that advances national development. Rather, it is a form of capital investment that goes to a few elites who profit from the system while vast majorities are left with intolerable amounts of debt.

If it became possible for social justice movements in the North and South to join in common effort and in common cause, such an historical event would end a persistent sense of isolation—"one of the most cumbersome problems encountered by movements of resistance. One of the most pressing tasks for progressives is to break down these walls of isolation and work toward a convergence of struggles."[109] Recent history catalogs various examples of how social movements in the North and South have experienced convergence in their goals and struggles. Some examples are cited in the table below.

The task that confronts social movements in the twenty-first century is a multifaceted one. It cannot be reduced to one aspect of class struggle. It cannot be limited to one aspect of an economic crisis. It cannot be expressed through the political and/or economic agenda of just one particular group. Rather, social movements around the globe will have to pay attention to a wide array of concerns from a variety of social contexts. This means that the praxis (time, place, and

---

Examples of Social Movements in the Global North and the Global South Moving Toward a Convergence of Struggles

---

1. The struggle of landless peasants in Brazil is at one with the struggle of Volkswagen workers against their multinational company.
2. The struggle by Zapatista indigenous people for dignity in the rural areas of Mexico is at one with the strike of American UPS workers.
3. The struggle of hundreds of thousands of Indian farmers against the WTO is at one with the *sans papiers* (undocumented immigrants) movement in France and Spain.
4. The struggle by South Korean trade unions to defend their gains is at one with the campaign by grassroots African communities for the cancellation of the debt.
5. The struggle of the population of Honduras against the privatization of the health sector ties in with that of workers in France, Austria, and Brazil, as does the combat against the undermining of earned pension rights and the promotion of private pension funds.
6. The struggle of Algerian women is at one with the people's tribunals in Argentina that denounce the country's illegitimate debt.
7. The struggle of students in Nicaragua, Burkina Faso, Niger, and the United States against increases in tuition is at one with the campaigns of teachers in France and Peru.
8. Citizens in Bolivia (Cochabamba), South Africa (Soweto), and India fight water privatization just as those of Peru (Arequipa) and trade unionists in Senegal (at SENELEC) fight privatization of electricity.

Source: Erich Toussaint, *Your Money [or] Your Life: The Tyranny of Global Finance—Updated Edition*, Haymarket Books, 2005, pp. 416–417.

historical situation) of each community and nation has a special and particular relevance for determining how best to create local, national, and global alternatives to the status quo that are complementary. This is important so that a unified vision for the human future can be articulated in such a way that people are able to decide upon the best unified strategy for the achievement of short- and long-term goals.

For example, the economic crisis faced by Argentina from 2001 to 2003 highlights the great difficulties that are posed by international debt, neoliberal policies, and the particular structural and class arrangements that made the crisis possible. Some scholars who are also critics of the neoliberal strategy have noted:

in the short term Argentina will continue to "recover," based in part on the extraordinary boom in agro-exports, high petroleum prices, and the reactivation of industry from its cataclysmic decline between 1998 and 2002. But the underlying structural and ideological foundations, which produced the crisis and popular uprising, are still in place. Moreover, the tendency is for the government to move toward a greater accommodation with the elite foreign beneficiaries of the neo-liberal model.[110]

By the middle of 2004 new sets of economic contradictions were emerging, but what was also manifestly clear was the fact that the time for popular rebellion against the ruling political class had temporarily passed. In light of this result, "what emerges from the extended and massive popular rebellion is that spontaneous uprisings are not a substitute for political power."[111] In combination with the failure of Argentina's social movements to gain political power was the failure of these movements to address the development of an alternative socialist society. Given this failure, "the mass movement was easily manipulated into accepting microeconomic changes to ameliorate the worse effects of poverty and unemployment, without changing the structures of ownership, income, and economic power of bankers, agro-exporters or energy monopolies."[112]

The election of Nestor Kirchner to the presidency of Argentina led to a brief period of relief for millions of his fellow citizens, but the political changes that took place in his administration occurred "in a context of substantial continuities on socioeconomic structures and policies, which have had only slight impacts on the classes structure, including unemployment, incomes, and poverty."[113] President Kirchner's employment of political power "has revealed its structural weakness in the face of the energy, gas, and electrical crises provoked by the foreign-owned MNCs."[114] As a result of the MNC-induced "energy crisis" there came "layoffs and plant shutdowns (increasing unemployment and lowering wages) while increasing the number of impoverished households, who literally live in the cold."[115]

In the aftermath of this recent history, the resurgence of the mass class struggle in Argentina can benefit from having learned what the limitations really are. Among these lessons is the realization that mass class struggle must directly confront the structural problems of poverty, low salaries, and unemployment. In other words, it can begin to undertake a process of revolutionary transformation that opposes and resists the neoliberal attempt to convert the citizens of Argentina into little more than neoimperial colonial subjects. For those involved with mass class struggle, they can further benefit from the realization that "none of the basic problems will be solved by an 'alliance' with the national bourgeoisie, even a benign Kirchner version."[116]

In light of Argentina's travails, as well as the travails of the East Asian crisis, the critics of the IMF-bailouts—such as Joseph Stiglitz—have acknowledged the reality that "we cannot go back to the past. But neither should we fail to recognize the failures of the present. Reform has to be reformed."[117] Reformation is the least that needs to be done. Many critics, including myself, stand for the proposition that the IMF and World Bank need to be replaced after 20 years of imposing conditionalities that turned out to have catastrophic consequences for human rights. After all, the IMF and World Bank hold about $450 billion credits on indebted countries—and a large part of those debts fall into the *odious* category.[118]

THE ARGUMENT FOR RELIEF, REPARATIONS, AND THE FORGIVENESS OF DEBT

What constitutes "odious" debt? According to Alexander Sack (1927) who theorized the doctrine, "odious" debt can be defined as follows: *If a despotic power incurs a debt not for the needs or interests of the State, but to strengthen its despotic regime, to repress the population that fights against it, etc., this debt is odious for the population of all the State. This debt is not an obligation for the nation; it is a regime's debt, a personal debt of the power that has incurred it, consequently it falls with the fall of this power.*[119]

Certainly, the apartheid government of South Africa fits this description "odious" debt perfectly. The white apartheid system—inherently racist and anti-human rights—obligated itself to debts in order to further the power of the racist state. It was only after social movements for justice organized and put pressure on Washington and the rest of the international community that there was sufficient international support to begin to apply sanctions on South Africa. Through that international effort and the raising of global awareness about the apartheid system's injustices and abuses, the apartheid system was finally strangled by the ensuing boycotts and sanctions. Further, only with the democratic election of Nelson Mandela to the presidency of South Africa did the nation finally have the benefit of a truly legal regime. On the matter of a regime's legality, the same may be said of the lawful governments that followed the dictatorships of South America in the 1980s (in Argentina, Uruguay, Brazil, Chile, etc.). One of the many remaining challenges confronting all of these nations emerging from dictatorships, apartheid, and a legacy of human rights abuses is the reality that they are still trapped in a global financial system of debt peonage to the North's neoliberal bankers operating through the auspices of the IMF and World Bank.

Since 1912, several additions have been made to the definition of *odious* debt as formulated by Alexander Sack. At McGill University (Canada), The Center for International Sustainable Development (CISDL) has proposed the following definition: *Odious debts are those contracted against the interests of the population of a state, without its consent and with the full awareness of the creditors* (Italics are mine).[120]

Supplied with this definition, we can now offer some provisional answers to the two major questions raised at the beginning of this section on social movements:

1. What social, economic, or political forces are available and prepared for the task of waging a popular war of resistance against neoliberalism and exclusionary governance?
2. Who will provide the leadership for the transformation of the government and the economy, and from where and from whom will the forces seeking such a transformation derive their support in such an undertaking?

In answer to both the first and second questions, the answers are virtually the same. I am arguing that a *counter-hegemonic alliance*, composed of those classes of people who have been oppressed by the hegemonic policies of the US Global Empire (including the IMF, and the World Bank) are best equipped to wage a moral and legal war of principled resistance against all forms of neoliberal exploitation and exclusionary governance. Additionally, a North/South *counter-hegemonic alliance* would be in the best position to develop the kind of transformational leadership required for such an undertaking. With regard to the global South in particular, it is from within the ranks of the victims of neoliberalism and the US Global Empire that social justice movements derive their true inspiration.

All across the global South the victims of neoliberalism and the US Global Empire are perfectly situated—as citizens of the Global Community—to construct a *counter-hegemonic alliance*. Also, it is within the ranks of the oppressed, excluded, victimized, and the poor that we find the peoples who are best equipped to serve the primary source of social power for providing the necessary leadership to advance the transformation of their own nation's government and economy, as well as the liberation of the rest of the global South. Capable individuals from the affected areas and communities of the global South are uniquely qualified to coordinate a *counter-hegemonic alliance*—designed to bring about a widespread exodus from empire among those peoples and nations most adversely affected by decades of imperial abuse, financial exploitation, and political oppression.

Ultimately, once united in common cause and common effort with other victims of the US Global Empire's hegemonic policies, all of these individuals can strive to make collective claims against the US Global Empire and its financial network (especially the IMF and World Bank) for reparations and relief from odious debt. Through the establishment of People's Tribunals, TRC, as well as under the auspices of appropriate UN mechanisms and the ICC, this counter-hegemonic alliance of people from throughout the global South can begin to remake their own history as well as humanity's future.

After all, the victims of the US Global Empire's hegemonic policies constitute an injured and exploited class of persons. As members of this class, it is they who possess both the moral and the legal right to engage in making claims against the empire. In the efforts designed to seek redress for their legitimate grievances and losses, an emerging consensus of international law norms provides credence to the claims of the Third World's victims, thereby opening the door for relief from odious debt, a framework for granting reparations, and the means through which the empire's "crimes against humanity" can be lawfully adjudicated.

Through this globally constituted *counter-hegemonic alliance*, the peoples of the world can begin to confront a long pattern of systemic and structural abuses, wrongdoing by states and international finance, crimes against humanity, and an embedded structural pattern of hegemonic dominance that has resulted in the denial of the human rights of billions of people over many decades.

In the initial stages of this incipient *counter-hegemonic alliance*, the victims, their children, and their children's children will finally discover that they have the power and the ability to claim the right to be removed from the burden of "odious" debt. They may also discover that they have the right to claim their freedom from a long history of foreign intrusion by US-based corporations and multilateral banks that continue to extort debt payments, deny the rights of labor, and extract wage concessions from them (as a sovereign class of persons, whose citizenship has been relegated to the status of slaves, in violation of the UN Charter and all international treaties dealing with human rights). In this regard, it has been suggested that there are several examples of cases where the *doctrine of odious debt* should be applied. The following table cites some of these examples that are in line with the CISDL definition: *Odious debts are those contracted against the interests of the population of a state, without its consent and with the full awareness of its creditors.*

Examples of Where the Doctrine of Odious Debt Should Be Applied

---

1. Multilateral debts contracted by despotic regimes (dictatorships in South Africa, Latin America, and Asia that were supported by the IMF and World Bank) must be considered odious. The IMF and World Bank have no right to demand repayment from the democratic regimes that replace dictatorships.
2. Multilateral debts contracted by legal and legitimate regimes to repay debts contracted by despotic regimes are themselves odious and must not be repaid. This is the case for at least 30 countries (a non-exhaustive list).
3. Multilateral debts contracted by legal and legitimate regimes within the framework of structural adjustment policies detrimental to populations are also odious. This amounts to *dolus malus*, defrauding the borrowers and their populations. The loan contract concerned is null and void. The letters of intent that the governments of indebted countries are obliged to send to the IMF and World Bank are invented by these institutions to cover themselves in the eventuality of legal proceedings against them. The procedure is nothing but an artifice and has no legal value. Just as an individual does not have the *right* to be reduced to slavery (the contract whereby a person renounces his or her liberty has strictly no legal value), a government has no right to renounce the exercise of its country's sovereignty. The Bretton Woods Institutions cannot use this letter of intent to escape responsibility. They remain fully responsible for the wrongs done to populations through the application of the conditionalities.
4. The antidemocratic, despotic nature of the Bretton Woods Institutions themselves also needs to be recognized.
5. At the same time as actions are brought to cancel multilateral loans, the Bretton Woods Institutions must also be forced to make reparations to the populations who have suffered the human and environmental damage caused by their policies.
6. Finally, civil and criminal actions must be brought against the officials of those institutions, who should be held responsible for the violations of basic human rights they have perpetrated and still perpetrate by imposing structural adjustment and/or by ending support to despotic regimes.

Source: Eric Toussaint, *Your Money [or] Your Life: The Tyranny of Global Finance*, Haymarket Books, 2005, pp. 387–388.

The victims of the US Global Empire's hegemonic policies can and should join their supporters throughout the Global Community (North and South) in an effort to begin building an international *counter-hegemonic alliance*. The nature of such an alliance can and should be an international one. It should be designed so as to be equipped to engage in boycotts and arrange for sanctions against those corporate and banking interests of the US Global Empire that continue to exploit the human rights, the quality of the environment, and violate citizenship rights, as well as the rights to personal and national development. This general approach was employed as the general strategy used to overcome the abuses of the apartheid government of South Africa. Therefore, in light of this history, progressive social movements in the global North and global South (but especially the citizens and victims in the affected countries) have the sociopolitical means and moral authority to make ethical, moral, social, legal, economic, and political claims upon their oppressors in order to remove the burdens of *odious* debt.

When viewed this way, it becomes clear that national social movements have the capacity and the need to combine their efforts with those of an international social movement, thereby allowing a new trajectory of historical possibility for the twenty-first century. In following this new trajectory, we just might discover that there can be creative spaces within a rising Global Community for building a culture of peace and humane progress.

BUILDING A COUNTER-HEGEMONIC ALLIANCE ACROSS
THE GLOBAL COMMUNITY

So, what is a *counter-hegemonic alliance*? By definition,

> *counter-hegemony begins with the people oppressed by hegemonic policies:* in the food riots of the workers in structurally adjusted countries; with the peasants dispossessed of livelihoods by trade liberalization; among indigenous people whose organic knowledge becomes the intellectual property of pharmaceutical companies; by the victims of AIDS cut off from cheap drugs by the WTO. *Counter-hegemonic uprisings in the peripheries are represented by a diverse array of social movements and unions that, increasingly interlinked, are joined with student, environmental and worker movements on the inner fringes of the centers of power* (Italics are mine).[121]

The promise, power, and reality of a rising Global Community is predicated upon the emergence of such a *counter-hegemonic alliance* in opposition to the US Global Empire, its transnational corporations, and its multilateral financial institutions and banks.

The range and scope of political participation in social movements that are a part of this larger *counter-hegemonic alliance* is difficult to define, but only because it is necessary to expand the definition of what is exactly meant by the term *political*. It is more than merely citizen interaction related to a state or a political party. Some scholars maintain that it is preferable "to employ an extended definition and also view as political those activities which try to solve social problems, independent of whether this occurs in self-help initiatives or via direct contracts with the political authorities."[122] So, the term "political" needs to be understood within the broader context of human experience and meaning. That which is *political* must be capable of taking on and addressing the needs, aspirations, and concerns of the entire person.

Truly *political* action means the engagement of people with not only their individual lives and concerns, but also their collective life and concerns. That which is *political* should be understood as being incorporative—for political actions and political concerns incorporate the lives of individuals and groups in such a way that their agendas become inclusive, broad, and all encompassing. The normative aspects of one's life cannot afford to be artificially divorced from the structural realities of economic, social, and political life. When one *participates* in *political* life it becomes a form of action that makes a claim against the state, against privileged institutions of power, against elite interests, that are responsible for contributing to a human crisis in which the necessities of life are at stake—and, in this situation, it is only through collective action and public action that this denial of human needs and human rights can be adequately addressed.

In this regard, whatever the scope of action, what really matters most from the standpoint of a rising Global Community is that greater attention and organizational effort be given to the problems associated with serious social inequality and poverty. As noted earlier, the challenges associated with social inequality and poverty also comprise the source of other problems that are manifested in "uneven income distribution as well as poor provision of goods and services. In this perspective, *participation is political when it aims to overcome this lack of provision via collective and public activities* (Italics are mine)."[123] Relying upon this definitional standard, I am proposing a *counter-hegemonic alliance* that involves a reliance on more than just the traditional notion of state-society linkages. Rather, the nature of the *counter-hegemonic alliance* that I am proposing transcends the state-society relationship—without forgetting about it. As I envision the nature of this *counter-hegemonic alliance*, it is global in scope. It encompasses both the moral and legal mandates of human rights claims, duties, and responsibilities. In accordance with this definition, it is an alliance that is premised upon the idea that its claims, agenda, and purpose are universal (refer back to Chapter 4).

In the most practical sense, it is going to have to be an alliance that recognizes the fact that one nation cannot act alone and succeed in its struggle against the US Global Empire and its tentacles of financial manipulation, as embodied in the IMF, World Bank, and WTO. Rather, nations from across the global South will have to develop continental and cross-continental alliances against the policies of neoliberal elites, both within their own governments and at the helm of key leadership positions in the global North. Only in this manner can the global South begin to chart a course of independence from the North, reclaim the power of its own natural resources, and the control of decision-making processes that the global South can call its own.

By ascribing to this alliance a universal character it is possible to speak of degrees of progress with regard to how the Global Community manifests the claims, agenda, and purpose of this alliance. For example, to assert the universality of the alliance is not the same as claiming that it will have the power to transform every element of injustice within the world. Rather, the assertion of universality stands for the proposition that once its claims, agenda, and purpose are globally adopted to that of the Global Community, then the alliance can begin to mitigate the damage that has been done by the old economic and political order. In that sense, it is possible for the Global Community to begin to bring a halt to the growing global disparities, inequalities, and injustices that are suffered by over two-thirds of humankind. Once the alliance is in place and is demonstrating that it can produce concrete results it will be taken seriously by governments. The next stages toward global transformation can then be undertaken step-by-step under the auspices of newly designed international institutions (replacing the IMF, World Bank, and WTO), as well as multilateral agencies acting under the direction of a reformed UN (a UN that is more democratic than as it is currently constituted).

In answer to those who will say that my proposal for building a *global counter-hegemonic alliance* is nothing more than a utopian fantasy, I would remind them that there is an historical precedent for it. That historical precedent can be traced to the April 1955 Asian-African Conference in Bandung, Indonesia. The conference had its origins in an initiative taken by the leaders of five Asian states—Indonesia, India, Pakistan, Burma, and Sri Lanka. It is often remembered in the context of the global history of the times—a time in which a Third World group of states developed a conference that became the largest and most influential gathering of Third World leaders during the colonial era.[124] Historians in the early twenty-first century now argue that part of the overwhelming significance of the conference was its timing—"coming right after the French withdrawal from Indochina and at a time when several African countries seemed headed for independence."[125] This is the historical context in which "the conference caught the moment of greatest hope and expectation in the anti-colonial struggle."[126]

By extrapolation, I am arguing that the 2001 to 2008 period can be viewed in a similar manner. Given the breakdown of the US Global Empire's occupation of Iraq, the undisputed global failure of neoliberalism as an economic model for the global South (especially with the collapse of the "Washington Consensus"), the crumbling institutional legitimacy of the IMF, World Bank, and WTO, as well as the rising power of social movements across the Third World and within First World nations, the early twenty-first century can be seen as an era constitutive of a failed and declining US Global Empire. The response of the Bush-2 regime has been to rely on a global network of US military bases and friendly like-minded regimes so as to engage in what some scholars have called *state-sponsored terrorism*—violence and repression of social movements by right-wing states backed up by the US military. In Latin America, Mexico, Columbia, and Ecuador are now primary examples of nations whose governments have engaged in spreading waves of terror that consist of repression and violence (which are ultimately state sanctioned, notwithstanding the appearance of multiple sources). The phenomenon of state-sponsored terrorism is directed against all those who challenge structural inequalities and injustices. Social movements for change have become singular targets for this terror.

Yet, moving into this void, there seems to be emerging a *global counter-hegemonic alliance* of individuals, social justice movements, and peoples from vastly different socioeconomic classes and nations, who are ready to commit themselves to a revolution in political values and economic priorities—by working through a moral mandate for a fundamental change of current socioeconomic conditions that breed inequality and sociopolitical conditions that seek to repress social movements designed to oppose these inequalities. Further, many of these social movements are actively seeking reparations and relief from decades of *odious* debt—as well as political and economic independence from the structures of America's imperial dominance and hegemony. By claiming that the full force of human rights (both legal and moral) be recognized, that poverty alleviation go forward, that a global new deal take over from the wreckage of the policies of the past, this *global counter-hegemonic alliance* is pressing all of humanity toward an *exodus from empire*.[127]

Given this assessment of the nature and purpose of this emerging *global counter-hegemonic alliance* of peoples and nations, there is a great deal more to this alliance than an empty utopian fantasy. The above-cited historical events and the trends emanating from them are constitutive of a planetary acknowledgment of the need to strive for a global future that is sustainable, survivable, and worth living for. In this sense, the spirit of idealism that is embodied in this *global counter-hegemonic alliance* has already begun to demonstrate that it has the capacity to transcend the lies, rhetoric, and empty promises of the architects of the US Global Empire. When viewed from this perspective, there are a great many parallels between the April 1955 Asian-African conference in Bandung and the global situation of the early twenty-first century. Why? Because "at the heart of the efforts of the nativist leaders at Bandung lay an attempt to create some form of common ideology which, eventually, could supersede the Cold War system, at least as far as the Third World was concerned."[128]

In the early twenty-first century, with the failure of neoliberalism and the collapse of the Washington Consensus, resurgent US militarism, wars for natural resources (especially oil), and the nature of the international crisis of capital, there is a growing global acknowledgment that the great majority of the people on the planet would like to embark upon an exodus from empire. The failed imperial policies of empire have only brought a greater debt burden to nations already overburdened with the problems of poverty, a lack of economic growth, and the exploitation of their wealth by Multinational Corporations. As with the people who attended the conference in Bandung, there is a growing global aspiration throughout the Global Community for forms of national development and international solidarity that transcend the current arrangements of a declining world order.

Perhaps this aspiration for the development of a common ideology was most clearly embodied in the perspective announced by Sukarno of Indonesia. In his opening speech at the conference, Sukarno globalized his own aim of integrating nationalism, Islam, and Marxism into a new, moral ideology within Indonesia. He stated:

Perhaps now more than at any other moment in the history of the world, society, government and statesmanship need to be based upon the highest code of morality and ethics. And in political terms, what is the highest code of morality? It is the subordination of everything to the well-being of mankind. But today we are faced with a situation where the well-being of mankind is not always the primary consideration. Many who are in places of high power think, rather, of controlling the world.[129]

In Sukarno's view, the only way in which morality could be regained within international relations was through the efforts of the Third World, which, having suffered the indignities of colonialism, could understand such aims better than either the European societies or the United States. Yet, in the final analysis, such efforts demanded Third World unity (what I am calling a *global counter-hegemonic alliance*). Sukarno declared:

All of us, I am certain, are united by more important things than those which superficially divide us. We are united for instance, by a common detestation of racialism. And we are united by a common determination to preserve and stabilize peace in the world ... Relatively speaking, all of us gathered here today are neighbors. Almost all of us have ties of common experience, the experience of colonialism. Many of us have a common religion. Many of us have common cultural roots. Many of us, the so-called 'underdeveloped' nations, have more or less similar economic problems, so that each of us can profit from the others' experience and help. And I think I may say that we all hold dear the ideals of national independence and freedom. Yes, we have much in common. And yet we know so little of each other.[130]

At the dawn of the twenty-first century, there are historical changes that distinguish our worldview from that of Sukarno in 1955. Globalization has done more than any other international force to connect the planet. Common problems in socioeconomic relations from refugee problems emanating from civil wars to the issue of border crossings (as between the United States and Mexico) have begun to unite the disparate populations of the global North with the human rights concerns of the global South. As transnational corporations have circled the globe and solidified their hold on governments and their national policies, so too have the citizens of the North seen their jobs "outsourced" and taken abroad into Latin America and Asia, where the labor markets offer lower wages and trade barriers have been either removed or curtailed vis-à-vis the rule-making powers of a corporate-friendly WTO.

Yet, despite these particular differences that have emerged with the passage of time as well as the evolution of corporations, nation-states, and elite interests, there are certain enduring truths and realities from the time of the Bandung conference in 1955. For example, racism still persists throughout the world despite major efforts to combat it. While a postapartheid South Africa is a major victory against state-sanctioned racism, racism is a problem that remains as a source of division throughout the world. While the decade of the 1950s reflected a common experience under colonialism for the peoples of the Third World, the common experience of neoliberalism and structural adjustment policies have come to define the common experience of the US Global Empire throughout the global South from the 1970s through the first years of the twenty-first century. In many respects, neoliberalism is little more than an updated form of neocolonialism and neo-imperialism wrapped in the rhetoric of economic growth.

On a positive note, despite the events associated with 9/11, there is still a greater degree of convergence in perspective between the world's great religions than there is a *clash* or unbridgeable gulf. In making this observation, it is important to highlight a global trend that points to an emerging global culture that is not the product of any one nation or culture. Rather, it is an observation regarding a growing consciousness that values diversity. This consciousness of diversity and its importance is increasingly respected and relied upon as a source for normative guidance and reflection (refer back to Chapter 4). For example, the wisdom of native and indigenous peoples has resurfaced as an emergent source of insight for dealing with many of the contemporary problems that have resulted from unsustainable capital accumulation and the exploitation of nature. It is the product of all nations and the commingling of a diversity of perspectives in the service of the idea that humankind is increasingly understood as the ultimate constituency to which we must be held accountable. It is a perspective that removes us from the emptiness of nationalist claims, the narrow agenda of empire building, and fallacy of national superiority. As a consequence of this trend, there is greater attention being given to the problem of global poverty and the culpability of the North in this global crime.

Additionally, there is a growing global consciousness of the fact that many of the leading economic institutions of the North (the IMF, World Bank, WTO, and others) have imposed a global institutional order that regularly produces and reproduces poverty. By attempting to maintain this order, the North is upholding a system of radical inequality. Therefore, the call for a global economic revolution has become a moral mandate at the dawn of the twenty-first century, as it was for the majority of delegates at the Bandung conference who saw that the unfinished struggle for liberation would continue to form their future agenda.[131]

So it is today as over two-thirds of humanity, located throughout the global South, who still are committed and dedicated to their liberation from the bonds of poverty, disease, war, widening inequalities, and odious debt. In this regard, it would be well to remember that the main focus of the Bandung conference's final communiqué—passed by the 29 states represented—found its ultimate significance in the 10 basic principles listed at the end that were intended to govern the relations between Third World states.[132] The application of these principles would not only assist in the task of governing relations between Third World states, but also serve to act as a standard of accountability for the states of the global North. For example, by preserving respect for human rights, pursuant to the purposes and principles of the Charter of the UN, the enforcement of human rights norms could have the capacity to make the institutions of the global North more accountable to the peoples of the South when entering into trade agreements, when assessing the degree to which the North actually helps or hinders the challenge of widening inequalities, and the need for genuine national and international development. Sovereignty, security, and the advancement of mutual interests were then, and remain today, vitally important and relevant issues that need to not only be addressed, but also affirmatively acted upon. Only in this way can we begin to bring an end to both state-sponsored terror (from above) and terrorism as a political strategy (from below). For this reason, as well as for the sake of building a *twenty-first century counter-hegemonic alliance*, it is necessary to revisit the principles that emerged from the Bandung conference. Those principles are listed in the following table.

The 10 Basic Principles from the Bandung Conference's Final Communique

---

1. Respect for fundamental human rights and for the purposes and principles of the Charter of the UN.
2. Respect for the sovereignty and territorial integrity of all nations.
3. Recognition of the equality of all races and the equality of all nations large and small.
4. Abstention from intervention or interference in the internal affairs of another country.
5. Respect for the right of each nation to defend itself, singly or collectively, in conformity with the Charter of the UN.
6. (a) Abstention from the use of arrangements of collective defense to serve the particular interests of any of the big powers.
   (b) Abstention by any country from exerting pressures on other countries.
7. Refraining from acts or threats of aggression or the use of force against the territorial integrity or political independence of any country.
8. Settlement of all international disputes, by peaceful means, such as negotiation, conciliation, arbitration of judicial settlement as well as other peaceful means of the parties' own choice, in conformity with the Charter of the UN.
9. Promotion of mutual interests and cooperation.
10. Respect for justice and international obligations.

Source: Quoted from *Bandung* 1955 (Colombo: Government Press, n.d.) pp. 30–31. *Cited in:* Odd Arne Westad, *The Global Cold War: Third World Interventions and the Making of Our Times*, Cambridge University Press, 2005, p. 102.

THE ELEMENTS OF A NATIONAL/INTERNATIONAL
COUNTER-HEGEMONIC ALLIANCE

A viable twenty-first century *counter-hegemonic alliance* must comprise both national and international social forces and social movements. Between its national and international constituencies, a viable twenty-first century *counter-hegemonic alliance* must have the capacity to agree upon a common set of principles, practices, and policies. For without a common ground on which to stand and evolve there is always the danger that such an alliance could potentially self-destruct— going the way of many previous social movements. A practical approach to building both a national and international counter-hegemonic alliance to the US Global Empire and its tentacles of financial exploitation and repression must integrate all of the progressive local, national, regional, and international social movements and governments.

In making this argument, I am outlining what amounts to a dual strategy: *an alliance built from below* (social movements) and *an alliance built from above* (progressive governments that are responsive to the agenda outlined by social movements for change). This approach is practical insofar as it has the capacity to solidify a broad-based consensus around commonly shared norms. In this manner, such a counter-hegemonic alliance can avoid infighting among its members. At the same time, such a broad-based consensus has the capacity to embark upon the practice of inclusion—in ideas, between peoples and groups, and among various regional blocs. When viewed from this perspective, a *national and international counter-hegemonic alliance* embodies the power of the people to withdraw from a system of structural domination. It is able to do so because it empowers itself to do so vis-à-vis a strategy that unifies its normative (value) dimensions with a structural revolution (unification of purpose and action between social movements and governments at the local, national, regional, and international levels). This approach follows the basic lesson of all political struggle—unite friends and divide enemies.[133]

In practical terms, the nature of the political struggle means that a successful *national/international counter-hegemonic alliance* will attempt to break the cross-national solidarity of elites within the US Global Empire and in nations that are in service to its agenda. At the same time, this counter-hegemonic alliance will seek to build cross-national class solidarity with like-minded social movements (*from below*) and like-minded governments (*from above*). The hoped for result would be the interruption of alliances between the US Global Empire and its collaborators in the pursuit of imperial projects, thereby bringing to an end the ability of the empire to engage in any further repression of progressive movements and governments. Correspondingly, the other hoped for result is that while the power of the empire to dominate and manipulate declines, those progressive social movements and governments that have forged their solidarity in this alliance will be able to consolidate their victories at both the sociopolitical and socioeconomic levels simultaneously. What such a victory means is that the members of this counter-hegemonic alliance will be able to embark upon an *exodus from empire*. The exodus from empire through a counter-hegemonic alliance has three major elements. These elements are outlined in the following table.

Exodus from Empire through a Counter-Hegemonic Alliance

In order to accomplish an *exodus from empire* vis-à-vis a counter-hegemonic alliance, it needs to be emphasized that an inclusive normative agenda is developed to sustain the alliance's ideological needs. Therefore, in order to avoid the many dangers associated with political self-destruction, a *national-international counter-hegemonic alliance* can and should be conceived very broadly—encompassing normative, strategic, and structural dimensions.

1. The *normative dimensions* should be associated with inclusive and humane principles, practices, and policies. In this regard, greater attention should be given to the two most ideologically powerful global forces of our time: the teachings of the world's great religions and the progressive and evolving norms of customary international law.

2. The *strategic dimensions* of the alliance must involve social movements at the national and international levels—eventually being conjoined into a global alliance in opposition to the US Global Empire and its support network.

3. The *structural dimensions* of the alliance should involve the removal of odious debt, the rejection of the neoliberal economic model, and building a viable global opposition to national and international militarism. The international components for each of these goals are already in

place. A definition, legal strategy, and political strategy for renouncing "odious" debts—currently available. The debt forgiveness and reparations strategy of the Jubilee Movement exists. It presents its version of a plan that can be adapted to the needs and goals of a national and international counter-hegemonic alliance, or around which an international consensus can emerge. A global opposition to national and international militarism exists in the form of a Comprehensive Test Ban Treaty (CTBT), the NPT, the Nuremberg Charter, and other related international documents, charters, and treaties.

Source: Terrence E. Paupp, *Achieving Inclusionary Governance: Advancing Peace and Development in First and Third World Nations*, Transnational Publishers, Inc., 2000.

When viewed in combination, the normative, strategic, and structural dimensions of a *counter-hegemonic alliance* constitute the expression of global aspirations, but they are also expressions of the practical components of a larger national and international alliance of social movements and progressive governments to build a global movement that seeks to build approximations of a newer world—a world that is filled with vibrant alternatives that the present world order seeks to deny. In short, the normative, strategic, and structural dimensions of a *counter-hegemonic alliance* reflect a growing international consensus about what are to be considered the *political* concerns of all people, everywhere.

At the international level, it is important for regional groupings of states to gather together in a common forum to express their shared commitments, as well as their differences, for developmental paths that are independent of imperial dictates and preferences. In recent years, the OAS has charted new terrain in the defense and promotion of democracy. It intervened in Peru (2000) and in Venezuela (2002–2004). The OAS facilitated an intra-elite dialog roundtable. The nature and purpose of the OAS intervention in these two nations was to use the roundtable or forum involving key domestic political actors from government, opposition, and civil society in a sustained collective effort to negotiate a consensual and peaceful solution to the political crisis. In Peru, the *Mesa de Dialogo*, or dialog roundtable, filled the institutional vacuum caused by the polarization of political forces in Peru following the May 2000 elections. In Venezuela, the *Mesa de Negociacion y Acuerdos* (Forum for Negotiation and Agreement) performed a similar valuable service in keeping the lines of communication open between polarized government and opposition elites. It was something that might not have happened without the assistance of the OAS. The OAS missions in Peru and Venezuela, by placing dialog tables at their center, engaged in a softer mode of intervention: *intervention without intervening*. In this way, the OAS was able to insert itself into the domestic politics of these two countries without intruding in the political decisions.[134] The vital point to be stressed is that the OAS agents at the table were neutral, impartial dialog facilitators as opposed to mediators or arbiters with the authority to make decisions or recommendations.

Other examples abound where national differences are being resolved by regional bodies dedicated to assisting the parties in arriving at a consensus or resolution to their difficulties. The European Union, and the emerging effort to create an Arab League, as well as a Unified Africa, may be seen as expressions of movements and institutions—throughout the global North and the global

South—to forge an identity and a developmental path that is not at the mercy of the prerogatives of the financial elite of the US Global Empire. However, not all attempts to accomplish regional solidarity are immediately effective. Take, for example the collapse of the Arab League Summit in March 2004. Its cancellation dealt a blow to efforts to secure approval for the creation of an Arab-formulated free trade zone—designed to compete with other regional trading blocs in the emerging global economy. The proposed Arab Free Trade Area (known by the acronym AFTA) would link all 22 Arab League members—creating a single market of over 300 million consumers, with a combined Gross Domestic Product (GDP) of almost $700 billion. It represents a sweeping vision of the region's potential. Yet, it had fallen victim to conflicting views about just what role the Arab League should play in this arrangement and what policies it should promote. What is certain is that failure to act may prove very costly—compelling Arabs to accept American or European alternatives.[135] Were such a failure to take place, it would obviously compromise the ability of these 22 Arab League members to pursue their own developmental goals, reduce the number of countries capable of joining a counter-hegemonic alliance, and making next to impossible their capacity to undertake an *exodus from empire*.

In the case of Africa, November 13, 2005 marked an historic day for the advocates of a unified Africa. Seven of the most powerful leaders in Africa agreed that the continent should move toward becoming a single, unified state. The caveat was that it would be a slow and gradual process. In a joint statement, issued at the close of the meeting, they noted: "The necessity for eventual union is not in doubt. It is even characterized as an imperative."[136] The statement reflected a consensus view held by those in attendance: the president of Nigeria, Olusegun Obasanjo (who is also chairman of the African Union), President Thabo Mbeki of South Africa, President John Klufuour of Ghana, and President Abdoulaye Wade of Senegal.

In all of the above-cited examples, there is evidence of a growing conscious effort throughout the global South to find an independent path from the US Global Empire and its financial elites. Efforts to curtail violence and engage in a new forum of dispute resolution that does not surrender the integrity of the major parties has come under the purview of the OAS—acting as a regional body. Aspirations for making Africa into a unified state serve to represent strategic and normative choices, as well as needed structural changes, for many African leaders and their constituencies. In the Middle East, the adoption of AFTA, were it to be endorsed by the members of the Arab League, would have the potential to disengage over 300 million people throughout 22 Arab states from the hegemony of American and European elite interests.

In combination, these are examples that may be cited as the first rumblings of a socioeconomic and sociopolitical earthquake that is beginning to shake the global South loose from its historic subordination to the US Global Empire. As such, these examples may be seen as the beginning steps in a national, regional, and international *counter-hegemonic alliance*. As such, these developments point toward a new historical horizon for the people of the global South. This new horizon is not *the end of history*, but rather the start of an *exodus from empire*.

THE TRANSFORMATION OF LATIN AMERICA INTO
A NEW REGIONAL POWER

In the case of Latin America the growing phenomenon of mass movements serves to demonstrate the historical importance of resistance "from below." As the imposition of neoliberalism has taken its toll on the Latin American continent (privatization, labor flexibility, debt repayment, balanced budgets, and trade liberalization), there has come about a new emphasis upon the value of mass struggle. The most pronounced feature of the present period in Latin America is the reemergence of the masses—mass actors and forms of mass struggle. Take, for example the events of April 2005 in Bolivia. A coalition of factory workers, peasants, irrigators, coca growers, and neighborhood associations in Cochabamba, Bolivia, won a great victory against corporate globalization. After battling police for several days, this coalition was able to halt the privatization of water and ran the US-based transnational Bechtel Corporation out of the city. Since that time, struggles across Latin America have continued apace. The following table shows some recent examples of where mass direct action was used to block or halt privatization, defend the human rights of indigenous peoples, and protect labor and employment rights.

The Power of Mass Movements and Direct Action against the US Global Empire

Mass Direct Action	Results
2002	
Peru	Blocked the privatization of electric power
Paraguay	Halted the sell-off of state banks and social services
Bolivia	Defended the rights of coca farmers
Chile	Defended the rights of indigenous peoples
Uruguay	Protected small saving accounts and the security of employment
Venezuela	Venezuelans who defeated a US-led attempt to stage a palace coup against President Hugo Chavez
2003	
Bolivia	Roll back of an IMF-imposed tax increase
Bolivia	Social movements against the sale of natural gas and for recognition of the rights of the indigenous movement forced President de Lozada to resign
Central America	Throughout Central America there were intensified campaigns against the CAFTA
2004	
Argentina	Workers and middle-class sectors opposed the Kirchner government's policies of price increases, low wages, and continued high unemployment
Chile	Struggles over social security and unemployment led to 400 laid off miners blocking a highway to demand back pay and extension of unemployment insurance
Venezuela	President Hugo Chavez wins a clear victory in a recall referendum demanded by the country's right wing (also a defeat for the Bush-2 regime)
Uruguay	Leftist reformer Tabare Vasquez wins the office of president after voters reject the neoliberal policies of outgoing president Jorge Battle

Source: Tom Lewis, "Analysis of A Continent in Revolt: Latin America on Fire," *International Socialist Review*, November–December 2005, Issue No. 44, pp. 38–44.

After having briefly discussed the role of regional bodies, the power of mass movements, and mass direct action, I want to now turn to three aspects of what I believe are the essential elements for a *national/international counter-hegemonic alliance*: (a) the normative dimension of constitution writing at the national level; (b) the strategic dimension of how to address human needs at the national and international levels and; (c) the structural dimension of how to build inclusive forms of governance at the national as well as international levels.

The Normative Dimension of Constitution Writing

With the collapse of the Soviet Union, it became important at the nation-state level for the countries of Eastern Europe to forge their own new democratic identities. The same was the case for South Africa as it emerged from the bondage of an oppressive system of racial apartheid. A similar challenge confronted many Latin American countries that had replaced dictatorships with democratic experiments. A common requirement for all of them was the task of constitution writing.[137] At the nation-state level, constitutions and constitution writing for newly formed democratic regimes emerging from dictatorships were and are vitally important for every aspect of the nation's political future. This is especially the case for divided societies and also for deeply divided countries.[138] It is obvious that before a truly national and international counter-hegemonic alliance can be forged, those nations joining the alliance must be able to effectively deal with the twin challenges confronting many nations: the challenge of divided societies and the challenge of constitutional engineering.

At the dawn of the twenty-first century, there is a broad agreement among scholars on how to address the challenges associated with both divided societies and constitutional engineering. The three major points of agreement are as follows:

1. First, they agree that deep ethnic and other social divisions pose a grave problem for democracy and that it is more difficult to maintain democracy in divided rather than homogeneous societies;
2. The problem of ethnic and other deep divisions is greater in countries that are not yet democratic or not fully democratic than in the well-established democracies;
3. The two key ingredients for successful democracy in divided societies are the sharing of executive power and group autonomy. "Power sharing," means the participation of the representatives of all significant groups in political decision making, especially at the executive level; "group autonomy" means that these groups have authority to run their own internal affairs, especially in the areas of education and culture.[139]

These three areas of agreement about the nature of constitutional engineering in divided societies have great implications for building a national and international counter-hegemonic alliance in a divided world. These three areas of agreement have great relevance for ultimately addressing some overarching questions about the nature and structure of global-cosmopolitan governance. But, let us focus upon the challenge of building a counter-hegemonic alliance.

To begin with, many nations throughout the global South are in situations where their movement toward some sort of democratically organized constitutional government is not yet consolidated. Therefore, neither the needed practices nor processes of democratic decision making are fully institutionalized nor are the concerns of various groups (other than that of elite groups) being given the necessary access or inclusion to decision making that would make a consolidated inclusive social democracy possible. Therefore, it needs to be recognized that when social movements are excluded from having a voice in decision making regarding the effects of state-imposed neoliberal economic policies (i.e., upon workers, the environment, employment, the rights of indigenous peoples), then they are little more than victims of the hegemonic power of the US Global Empire (IMF, World Bank, WTO, and counterinsurgency strategies).

In order to liberate the majority of these social movements from the domination of local and US elites, it is essential that they develop the political capacity to democratize their own national governing structures so that an inclusive social democratic state can emerge that is equipped to better mirror their preferences. Insofar as their preferences are at odds with the agenda of neoliberalism, power-sharing arrangements can begin to forge linkages. In turn, these linkages can be used to build a national and international counter-hegemonic alliance to the US Global Empire. This approach involves "fresh counter-hegemonic strategies aimed at 'democratizing democracy'… to ensure that democratic structures at all levels address the concerns of the great mass of citizens and not merely those of political elites."[140]

There is a nexus between the ability of a nation to consolidate a viable social democracy at the national level and its ability to join in a counter-hegemonic alliance against the US Global Empire at the international level. In order to move into the status of a nation capable of joining other nations in a counter-hegemonic alliance against empire, it is essential for each nation in that alliance to purge itself of elite practices and politicians who are willing to give concessions to a Washington-based neoliberal elites, transnational corporations, and Western-based financial institutions that are hostile to genuine national development given their history of refusing debt relief to the most indebted and poverty-stricken populations on earth. Therefore, in order to consolidate an inclusive social democracy, the nations of the global South need to use their constitutional and institutional powers in such a way that progress can be made in resolving the problems associated with inequality in unequal societies. This is especially true in the situation of divided societies, such as South Africa. The problem of inequality in South Africa must be addressed even if it is not a matter of political structure because the problem of inequality has a constitutional status because "inequality is surely the one policy question that could de-legitimize a new regime, and it needs to be considered at the outset."[141]

I am arguing that whether a constitution addresses and incorporates socioeconomic rights and protections is ultimately just as important as the protections that are to be afforded civil and political rights. Constitutional protections involve normative, procedural, structural aspects—and even involve strategies for governance, such as balance-of-power arrangements. Yet, constitutional protections will be of little value if the structural dimensions of the state are still loyal to the same exploitative economic interests that worked through the previous dictatorship—as with the apartheid regime of South Africa.

Similarly, constitutional protections will be of little value if the strategic dimension of the state's leadership is hostile to social movements that arise in opposition to its economic programs (such as ones favorable to neoliberal elites). In other words, there are still a great many areas for contestation between competing interests. So, while there may be normative agreements within the constitutional design, the actual expression and manifestation of those normative understandings may be of little long-term value if they are nonbinding on the parties. Should that turn out to be the case then the great danger is that the strategies of the powerful will remain at odds with the aspirations and needs of the powerless. If the old alliance between the deposed dictatorship and Western neoliberal elites continues on into the future, affecting the newly elected leadership and democratic structures of a democratic state, then legitimacy of the new state will come into question—as well as its ability to embark upon a process of peaceful consolidation of power.[142]

From this perspective, I want to briefly address the case of South Africa and the role of socioeconomic constitutional protections. To begin with, it should be noted that the protection of social and economic rights is a major topic not only in South Africa's continuing constitutional and economic debate, but is gaining momentum in other parts of the world as well. The main difference between the proponents and opponents of the protection of social and economic rights centers on the following question: *Whether the state should have a passive and noninterventionist role in the protection of economic rights or whether the state should be under a justiciable legal obligation to adopt an active and interventionist role in order to address socioeconomic inequalities and disparities.*[143] What is at stake in these two propositions is the central question of whether or not the state *should* be placed under a legal obligation, or a political and moral obligation, in order to address these matters. I have previously set forth the proposition that addressing socioeconomic inequalities and disparities is the duty and the purpose of the inclusionary state. Addressing these issues and resolving them for billions of excluded people is at the heart of an inclusive social democratic project at both the national and international levels. Only by rejecting the traditional neoclassical and laissez-faire doctrines can progressive constitutions and charters emerge throughout the Global Community that are capable of sustaining and advancing an inclusive social contract.

The traditional Lockean approach to this question looks at the state's duty as a duty to refrain from interfering in the sphere of individual rights and freedoms. Hence, the Lockean formulation holds that the state is obliged to provide a framework within which the individual can enjoy maximum freedom from state action.[144] Alternatively, with the rise of the welfare state in the twentieth century, new approaches to the role of the state developed that led to having the state intervene in issues that involved poverty and the socioeconomic plight of the excluded. This approach characterized not only those in developing countries, but also those living in the poverty-stricken rural and urban areas in developed countries. Because of this shift in perspective, the twentieth century bore witness to a variety of efforts to extend the categories of justiciable rights for inclusion in human rights documents.[145] In light of this shift in thinking and practice, there are now three different categories of rights, often referred to as first, second, and third-generation rights.[146]

Additional developments in terms of the application of these different generations of rights may be seen in the work of the Organization of African Unity (OAU), which adopted the African Charter on Human and Peoples' Rights in 1981 (coming into force in 1986, after having been ratified by a majority of members of the OAU). The Charter contains various provisions relating to social and economic rights such as: (1) the right to work under equitable and satisfactory conditions as well as to receive equal pay for equal work; (2) the right to enjoy the "best attainable" state of health; (3) the right to education, participation in cultural life, and the "promotion and protection of morals and traditional values" by the state. In all of these examples, it is clear that the social and economic rights provided for in the African Charter are all (individually and collectively) geared toward development. The problem is that "the African Charter could be interpreted as non-binding in the that there are insufficient guarantees to the effect that states are legally obliged to uphold the rights and there is no express guarantee that the rights have to be protected by the states." Yet, despite these weaknesses, the African Charter "represents an important attempt to develop an African framework for the protection of rights and freedoms against the background of international experience."[147]

In light of this history, it is important to remember that the "background of international experience" remains foundational to the advancement of human rights embodied within the African Charter. Also, this background of international experience is reflective of the interrelated and converging forces of the teachings of the world's great religions in combination with the evolving norms of customary international law (see Chapter 4). Insofar as these teachings and norms reconfirm the right to self-determination, the right to genuine national development (free of the entrapments of debt bondage to the IMF and World Bank), and the realization of all three generations of human rights, it is possible to view the emergence of a counter-hegemonic alliance as a necessary step for the nations of the global South in undertaking an *exodus from empire*. Also, with the rise of more inclusive social democracies—based on pact making, but moving toward a more inclusive social contract—we may argue that the pursuit of these rights and the efforts to institutionalize them are increasingly understood as universally shared international goals which point the way toward an *exodus from empire*.

In the case of South Africa, it is important to note that the first phases of South Africa's transition to democracy were based on pact making. Writing on the eve of South Africa's new democratic experiment, Timothy Sisk observed that the democratization pact reached in 1993 represented a compromise

between the competing government and ANC preferences, respectively, for a founding pact and a founding election: when the constituent assembly is elected and convened, it will be limited by a prior agreement on constitutional principles and a considerable degree of detail. The institutions created by South Africa's democratization pact will be an experiment in power sharing.[148]

Still, the democratic experiment would not be completed or finalized with the establishment of a power-sharing arrangement. Rather, as Sisk noted: "after the agreed-upon government of national unity and the elected constituent assembly are in place, a South African democracy could form that goes beyond a transitional power sharing pact and become a true social contract."[149] In turn, a social contract would require "a new web of political institutions for the long run that guarantees basic human rights, reconciles majority rule with minority rights, ensures nondiscrimination and equality before the law, and promotes restitution and equal economic opportunity for the long-disenfranchised black majority."[150]

A new social contract would not be limited to political changes. It would also have to include a new set of economic institutions as well as the development of a new and invigorated civil society where interest groups could be formed that could transcend the racial and ethnic divisions that had either been created or exacerbated by apartheid.[151] Based upon this historical trajectory, I am arguing that nations throughout the global South can benefit from South Africa's national example. Across the global South as regional groupings of nations begin to establish their own South-South networks, a national and international counter-hegemonic alliance has the capacity to evolve. Through this alliance, nations that have adopted a more inclusive path to governance—in both the economic and political arenas—can begin to better affirm their autonomy, more effectively protect the rights of their peoples, and begin the task of undertaking an *exodus from empire*. With this general strategy in mind, we can now turn to an analysis of the strategic dimension of how the nations of the global South may begin to address and meet human needs, both nationally and internationally, without being subordinate to the US Global Empire.

The Strategic Dimension of How to Address Human Needs

A *counter-hegemonic alliance* that is dedicated to inclusive and humane forms of governance should be given a privileged *political* place (*broadly defined*) to address global human needs. This means that social movements, civil society, and cultures, must be able to oppose the re-imposition of IMF and World Bank financial control over their respective economies. Even if a state calls itself democratic, it must be held accountable to its people as they work to avoid a re-colonization of their lives, government, and economy by the neoliberal institutions and ideologies of the North. In this regard, a viable *counter-hegemonic alliance* should be able to accomplish this goal by giving primary attention and focus to the protection and expansion of socioeconomic human rights in both theory and practice. Such a policy focus would necessarily benefit the cause of environmental sustainability, the growth of social democratic states that exhibit inclusive traits, and promote efforts designed to realize the creation of a *political* public space that expands the realm of democratic discourse and participatory decision making.[152]

The cynics and the skeptics will no doubt ask: *Where on earth is such a system of governance possible?* And they will also probably ask: *Where has such a system been tried or implemented before anywhere on the globe?* My answer to both questions points to one of the best real-world models that can be cited from the last half of the twentieth century—a democratic South Africa. In many key respects, the evolution of a democratic South Africa combines the normative, strategic, and structural aspects of how it is possible to build inclusive forms of governance. With this result achieved at the national level, I will argue that the foundation is being laid for an international counter-hegemonic alliance.[153]

Yet, South Africa's victory is limited by its still lingering adherence to the dictates of the North's neoliberal financial elite.[154] Until South Africa is fully freed from the bondage of odious debt incurred by the apartheid regime, it cannot enjoy the full vindication of its political victory. Should it remain in bondage to the merchants of neoliberal debt, South Africa will have won the battle against apartheid, but lost the war for socioeconomic justice. For with the bondage of debt—especially *odious* debt—there continues the necessity of remaining trapped in a global financial order that does not allow for adequate investments in national development and the national economic capacity to meet human needs.[155] In this situation, an elite minority of capitalists and state managers in the South African government will maintain power through privatization, deregulation, and the surrender of the ability to affect the international terms of trade. Yet, addressing the social welfare concerns of the people, the need to invest in youth, the basics of life from sanitation to affordable water and housing, access to decent paying jobs, and the ability to form social movements and unions without fear of reprisal may all be lost if there is a failure of political will to build a truly inclusive state.[156] This is the main challenge that confronts South Africa. The outcome of this challenge will ultimately be determined by South Africa's ability to build a thoroughly inclusive economy in much the same manner it has already built a largely inclusive domestic political order.

At the dawn of the twenty-first century, South Africa's future under the leadership of Thabo Mbeki does not appear to be very promising. Under Mbeki,

> the South African neo-liberal state acts for foreign capital, within the interests of national capital, and, if necessary, against the development of its own domestic resources to meet popular needs. In so doing it fails to protect South Africa's resources against the rapacious short-term interests of international capital. It also resoundingly fails to meet popular socioeconomic aspirations, specifically those that require any increase in the social wage, as this drives up state expenditure and calls for the retention and even increase of state-owned resources and state intervention in the economy.[157]

This realization leads us to consider the structural dimensions of building inclusive forms of governance.

The Structural Dimension: Building Inclusive Forms of Governance

Breaking the bonds of a racist apartheid system based on white-minority control represents an amazing transformation. Many elements went into the victory—a five-decades long struggle by the African National Congress (ANC); an international boycott accompanied with sanctions; corporate disinvestments, designed to further economically undermine the apartheid state; a long transition process that relied upon the statesmanship and cooperation of the leader of the apartheid state, President De Klerk, and the leader of the ANC, Nelson Mandela. It was the combination of all of these factors that led to the political and human rights victory of the people of South Africa.[158] Yet, the lingering economic power of neoliberalism still continues to cripple South Africa's full embrace and realization of that victory.

Although South Africa has moved away from political repression to political democracy, it has yet to be fully freed from the financial influence and power of neoliberal elites in its own government, under the administration of President Thabo Mbeki, and the influence of imperial elites in the global North. This is the case because

> neoliberal orthodoxy ... requires a reconfiguration of political control. The political power of the state is shifted to those arenas controlled by capital, and specifically concentrated in those wings that are closest to the global economy, such as the ministries of trade and finance, and the central (Reserve) bank. The role of the executive is redefined so as to de-emphasize and disempower those areas of government with close ties to popular domestic interests, such as parliament, local government, and especially welfare and labor. This is accompanied by the increasing centralization of political decision-making in order to ensure ideological consistency and "policy harmonization." The streamlining of the executive and the drive for policy coordination under the Mbeki presidency fits in with this progression. Thus these aspects of an "imperial presidency" do not reflect Mbeki's persona, but rather his ideological conformity to neo-liberalism.[159]

To understand this reality is to also acknowledge that the next phases of South Africa's transformation are underway through its vibrant civil society, social movements, as well as a growing mass political opposition to the intrusions of the IMF and the World Bank. Therefore, while South Africa is not a perfect example of a socially democratic state, it still remains a good example of a nation that has moved toward an inclusive social democratic framework that allows for the representation of many different parties through a system of proportional representation. It is the legacy of Mandela's powersharing democracy arrangement. Political scientists use the formal term "consociational" to describe it.

A power-sharing arrangement means that government includes the representatives of all significant groups and revolves around inter-ethnic cooperation. Further, "minority rights are protected through minority vetoes."[160] In this regard, even previously marginalized groups and parties can have seats in the nation's Government of National Unity (GNU) by having secured a minimum percentage of votes in the general elections. It is a system that is not confined to the limitations of a *winner-take-all* electoral system. In light of the fact that South Africa now has the structural components of an inclusive political democracy—along with the societal capacity to generate social movements in opposition to IMF and

World Bank policies—is testimony to the historical reality that South Africa is demonstrating it has the potential for further transformations as the people make constitutional claims and demand changes in the socioeconomic arena.

Under President Nelson Mandela the Government of National Unity successfully accomplished the building of an inclusive system of political representation that far surpasses the limitations of the *winner-take-all* system employed in the United States. The GNU is both the product and result of a constitutional design that is better equipped to give attention to the task of realizing socioeconomic rights with the same degree of importance that is given to civil and political rights. In beginning to strike a balance between advancing the socioeconomic rights of the poor in conjunction with protecting civil and political rights, the GNU has laid the foundation for an inclusive government in South Africa. This is the historical reality and political promise that still remains active in the consciousness of millions of South Africans.

In the final analysis, "the social and economic restructuring of South Africa lies at the heart of the transformation process ... South Africa, as a developing country, may find it difficult to convince its millions of squatters and poverty-stricken people that the protection of civil and political rights is of value to them if they do not have the material, intellectual, and social ability and circumstances to make use of such rights."[161] The same may be said of every other nation throughout the global South. For as the US Global Empire attempts to shore up its financial domination over the globe with its program of *democracy promotion*, it is simultaneously allowing for the historical likelihood of global revolt against a partially realized democracy.

In combination with already desperate poverty and a general lack of hope in the current system, billions of people throughout the global South will be more than likely seek membership in social movements that are committed to a fundamental change of capital's status quo. The most obvious and odious institutional symbols for their anger and opposition are the IMF and World Bank, and the WTO. As they embark upon the search for more socially just alternatives, these billions of people will start to form an international constituency. It is this international constituency that lies at the heart of a rising Global Community.

It is a truly Global Community for it is ideologically committed in its opposition to the US Global Empire's financial hegemony and its ruthless attempt to impose that hegemony through the violence of resurgent militarism. In this respect, the strategic positioning of nations that are more politically inclusive, increasingly seeking alternatives to the neoliberal economic order, and even more committed to opposing resurgent militarism, will find new paths to build a national and international counter-hegemonic alliance.

OVERCOMING THE PAST

South Africa's greatest obstacle to developmental success and greater freedom is not merely an internal one. Rather, its greatest obstacle is found in the negative external economic effects of the IMF and World Bank. Even though civil and political rights have won the battle against apartheid, South Africa has yet to win the war for socioeconomic justice, distributional fairness, and a more equitable approach to governance that is capable of guaranteeing the affordability of the basics of life—water, sanitation, housing, and employment. Having said this, it is still possible to argue that postapartheid South Africa represents one of the best examples of a politically inclusive nation-state. Even though it is still a nation that is in a state of transition, it has dealt with confronting the truth about its past.

Emerging from the brutality of the apartheid system, South Africans established a TRC. The TRC was designed to elicit stories from both the victims and the executioners of the apartheid state. By granting amnesty for truth telling, the perpetrators of the violence could disclose a fuller version of the truth of what had transpired. In turn, the truths that were revealed served to provide the historical substance for an aggregated picture that could then be forged into a collective memory about the past. From these truths, the foundation was laid for social and personal reconciliation. In turn, it is believed that reconciliation can provide the political foundation for a transition to democratization.

The nature of this transition can best be conceptualized by viewing South Africa's truth and reconciliation process as "actually a mini-theory about the process of democratization, including an implicit causal model of how the truth and reconciliation process would contribute to the consolidation of democracy in South Africa. The theory posits that: *Amnesty>Truth>Reconciliation> Democratization.*"[162]

The great value of the TRC was to "produce a collective memory for South Africa." In so doing, the work of the TRC became more than just a chronicle of who did what to whom, "instead, it is an authoritative description and analysis of the history of the country. Was apartheid a crime against humanity? Was the criminality of apartheid due to the missteps of a few rogue individuals, or was apartheid criminal by its very ideology and through its institutions? These are questions for which the TRC provided unambiguous and, by its accounting, definitive answers."[163]

By extrapolation, I will argue that the emerging global counter-hegemonic alliance against the abuses of the US Global Empire needs to follow a similar path to the one taken by South Africa's TRC. For example, if we take the above-cited questions and substitute the word "apartheid" with the terms "US Global Empire" and "neoliberalism" there emerges an analytical truth. The truth is that nations with different cultural backgrounds still share a common historical experience with the crimes, ideology, and institutions of the US Global Empire. Insofar as the empire's neoliberal economic network of institutions has exacted a heavy price from nations that have been subjected to loan conditionality and structural adjustment programs—the nature and extent of this price can begin to be calculated. With these calculations it should become possible for nations throughout the global South to begin to confront the true nature of the exploitation to which they have been subjected, the psychological denial which some still remain trapped in, and identify the ideological chains which still bind most of them.

In reviewing the recent history of postapartheid South Africa, nations across the global South have an historic opportunity to assess not only their own history of abuse and victimization by the crimes of the US Global Empire, but also other national histories and experiences of it. If a *Global Truth Commission on Empire* (GTCE) can emerge—with representatives from over 70 nations throughout the global South—then it would be possible for a global conclusion to be reached about the harms done. Under the auspices of a GTCE the voices of the empire's victims could finally be heard. The establishment of such an historical record of US criminality could serve as the basis for a number of different outcomes, ranging from building evidentiary cases for the ICC, to calculating the nature and scope of harms inflicted by the policies and conduct of the Empire and its institutional network of collaborators.

From such a calculation of harms, nations throughout the global South could legitimately make moral and legal demands for reparations. The nature of these reparations could come in the form of money for actual damages (which is often hard to measure), debt forgiveness, and/or grants of financial aid without any strings attached. Further, with a calculation of imperial harms, nations throughout the global South would be better positioned to chart new national courses for their national development. No longer tied to dependence upon foreign aid packages, loan conditionality, and the incessant pressure of paying off impossible amounts of debt to a few Western bankers, the wealth of the global South could finally be reinvested in the global South.

At the same time, nations throughout the global South could begin to forge regional and international linkages with other similarly situated nation-states seeking to embark upon an *exodus from empire*. A common ideology could be constructed from these regional and international linkages that would serve to unite most if not all nations throughout the Global Community. In turn, such a common ideology would serve to cement relationships between nations and peoples in a *global counter-hegemonic alliance* to the Empire and its transnational financial networks. Alternatives that are more appropriate to the realities, needs, and challenges of the peoples of the global South, could be forged in the context of a new atmosphere of hope and understanding.

South Africa has already begun its own march in this direction. It is capable of great democratic transformations as long as its civil society is fully engaged with its national leadership in making joint decisions about the direction of the economy in meeting the needs of the most neglected and vulnerable. In so doing, South Africa can be seen as a nation that is dedicated to an eventual *exodus from empire*. It is also a nation that is in the process of becoming uniquely equipped to lead, in conjunction with other progressive nation-states throughout the Global Community, in a potential *counter-hegemonic alliance*. Following the example of the Nuremberg Tribunal, it will be necessary for the nations of the global South, to establish a tribunal on the crimes of the US Global Empire.

PLACING THE EMPIRE ON TRIAL: ESTABLISHING A TRIBUNAL ON THE CRIMES OF THE US GLOBAL EMPIRE

The World Tribunal on Iraq (WTI) held its culminating session in Istanbul, Turkey, July 24–27, 2005. It represented the last and most elaborate of 16 condemnations of the Iraq War held worldwide over a two-year period (2003–2005). The global scope of these tribunals included Barcelona, Tokyo, Brussels, Seoul, New York, London, and other cities. According to Professor Richard Falk, "the cumulative process, described by organizers as 'the tribunal movement,' is unique in history: Never before has a war aroused this level of protest on a global scale—first to prevent it (the huge February 15, 2003, demonstrations in eighty countries) and then to condemn its inception and conduct."[164]

In Falk's perspective, the WTI "expresses the opposition of global society to the Iraq War, a project perhaps best described as a form of 'moral globalization'."[165] Falk's concept of *moral globalization* frames one of the central aspects of what I am calling the *rise of Global Community*. Insofar as the power politics of empire building have historically been built upon violence, exploitation, and domination, it makes sense to refer to its antithesis as a rising Global Community in opposition to these forces of empire. Yet, at an even deeper level of meaning, the idea of *moral globalization* also serves to overcome many of the arguments that characterize the *class of civilizations* thesis.

The convergence of common aspirations and moral sentiments for the respect, dignity, and rights of the person constitutes a global pledge and commitment to remake and revolutionize the world. "Moral globalization" is an example of how and where there is a conscious convergence of peoples and cultures that transcends the particularities of history and tradition. Embodied within world tribunals and truth commissions there are the elements of a globally shared moral consciousness that is also at work in widening the scope of legal standards—such as universal jurisdiction. The phenomenon of universal jurisdiction exemplifies a convergence of moral and legal standards around the rights and duties of peoples around the globe. As such, universal jurisdiction is emerging—along with world tribunals and truth commissions—as one of the practical mechanisms for bringing the leaders of dictatorships and empires to judgment. We might even call this global trend the *Nuremberg moment* (my term). As I define it, the *Nuremberg moment* is that point in time where the legacy, principles, and standards of the Nuremberg Tribunal (1945–1946) find practical application in current historical situations. This is especially the case where crimes of aggression, war crimes, and crimes against humanity, are of such consequence that demands for justice, atonement, and reparations become impossible to ignore.

Further, by taking the phenomenon of *the tribunal movement* as an expression of *moral globalization* it then becomes possible to argue that an alternative standard of international legality and morality can be placed in opposition to the hegemonic claims of empire (refer to Chapter 4 on "universal jurisdiction"). We stand at an historical moment—the *Nuremberg moment*—where it is possible to argue that—at some point in the not too distant future—the actions, behaviors, and policies of empire will be judged by the courts, tribunals, and truth commissions of the Global Community. The reign of the US Global Empire cannot last forever—and it should not be allowed to abscond with impunity.

Historically, international law has evolved over the centuries making claims and judgments about the indiscretions and abuse of power by nation-states. In doing so, due in large measure to the increasing scope of international human rights law, it has at least progressed beyond the jurisdictional defenses that surround claims of sovereignty. It is a tribute to the work of the Nuremberg Tribunal that its principles were made into a charter that has universal scope and relevance with regard to the behavior of states and their agents.

Due to the claims embodied in the Nuremberg Charter the Global Community is equipped with the power to inaugurate the *Nuremberg moment*. We can make this claim because the international legal structure of the Global Community has evolved to a point of maturity where national and/or individual accountability is not delimited to either a nation or empire. The ICC and the ICJ are further examples of how the reach of international law and the moral claims of the Global Community have evolved to such an extent that national leaders can be called to account. This includes the leaders of empires. This trend also reflects the growing significance of *people power* or *citizen power*. In the context of the *tribunal movement* there is more of an emphasis upon citizen power and the claims of global citizens to be able to demand an evidentiary accounting of where, how, and by whom, critical abuses of power have taken place. In this regard,

> the ad hoc tribunals for the former Yugoslavia and Rwanda derive their author-
> ity from the widespread support of the international community. The same
> can ... also be said for the International Criminal Court, since the number of
> ratifying states rapidly increases. Some have gone so far as to argue that
> because of this these international tribunals should not be considered as foreign
> courts, but rather as "an extension of domestic courts."[166]

If we can take this claim literally—that these international tribunals are acting as *an extension of domestic courts*—then we can also argue that the Global Community itself is sitting in judgment in these forums. The legal standard for this judgment is predicated upon a globally developed and globally received history of international law and the evolving norms of customary international law. Yet, also contained within the standards, precedents, and norms of international law are moral and ethical components. These are some of the underlying values that the Global Community continually seeks to advance. Understood in this manner, "the support for international criminal justice is to a considerable degree based on the view that prosecution of international crimes will contribute to international peace and security ... The preamble to the ICC Statute also recognized that the commission of international crimes threatens international peace and security."[167] I am arguing that the "Nuremberg moment" allows for a greater expansion of ideas about criminality. With a more expansive concept of criminality, the crimes of empires can eventually be brought to global forums and judged by the Global Community.

When the work of tribunals can be viewed from this perspective, the significance of the WTI comes into sharper focus. For this perspective allows us to legitimately speak of the *crimes of empire*. Only by addressing the crimes of empire through world tribunals can we hope to overcome the institutional failure of both nation states and the UN to stop the US war on Iraq in 2003, as well as the ongoing suffering, torture, and human rights abuses that have resulted from the US occupation of Iraq. On this matter, according to Falk,

> the motivations of citizens to organize such a tribunal do not arise from uncertainty about issues of legality and morality but from a conviction that the institutions of the state, including the UN, have failed to act to protect a vulnerable people against such Nuremberg crimes as aggression, violations of the laws of war and crimes against humanity. It is only because of such institutional failures in the face of ongoing suffering and abuse in Iraq that individuals and institutions made the immense organizational effort to put together this kind of transnational civic tribunal.[168]

As the nations of the world move toward an *exodus from empire*, it will be necessary to establish world tribunals that are inclusive so that all nations may examine and expose all of the relevant issues pertaining to their victimization by the Empire and its collaborators. This means that the empire's imperial wars and "interventions" should not be the only subject on the list. Rather, the empire's crimes against the environment, its proclivity to entrap developing nations into debt bondage ("odious debt"), its failure to comply with the legal mandates of the ICJ, its failure to embark upon the abolition of nuclear weapons, rhetorical reliance on human rights as a means toward securing its global hegemony, its record of slavery and other historical injustices, are all examples of issues that should become the relevant subject matter of world tribunals and truth commissions.[169]

THE FUTURE OF GLOBAL GOVERNANCE

Global governance and the maintenance of peace and security around the world are the primary concerns that affect all humanity. Global governance cannot and should not be defined through the lens of one nation's perspective—even if it is a superpower (or, especially if it is a superpower). Rather, global governance demands and requires the inclusion of all nations and peoples in a process of building an era of mutual cooperation and growing individualism.[170] Emerging forms of global governance can be understood as manifestations of a new consciousness regarding the nature, content, and purpose of global unity and interdependence. Some scholars have recently attempted to differentiate the uniqueness of this new consciousness of global unity and interdependence as *World Culture*.[171]

There are many components to what these scholars mean by the term, "World Culture." Suffice it to say that the financial globalization of the world has demonstrated the possibility for societies to follow suit and build an interconnected Global Community. Such an achievement will be the product of not just new institutions, but a product of a new consciousness forged by global challenges. In this regard, there are many global challenges that can help to forge this new consciousness of global unity throughout the Global Community: the AIDS pandemic,[172] global warming and climate change,[173] the move from free trade to fair trade,[174] the control and eventual abolition of nuclear weapons,[175] and the search for alternatives sources of energy for the sake of ecological security.[176]

Insofar as the old paradigm of *balance-of-power* politics is antithetical to the rising force of the Global Community, it is incumbent upon the people of the United States to dismantle their empire, reclaim their democracy, and begin to live with the rest of the world as a *post-Imperial America*. In short, for the sake of global peace, security, international peace, and a sustainable future, both the United States and every other nation on the planet should embark upon an *exodus from empire*. In sum, this call to an exodus from empire is predicated on the growing conscious reality that seeking world domination is a failed enterprise of the past. Only cooperation, mutual cooperation, can sustain the human future. Further, such an assertion is no longer seen as utopian, in most responsible quarters.

In an age of still lingering nuclear weapons and the unresolved challenges of nuclear disarmament and nuclear abolition, it has become increasingly clear that even the US Global Empire cannot continue to seek further advances in nuclear weapons without effectively dismantling the Nuclear Non-Proliferation regime. Such a result could only encourage more nations to engage in a race for the bomb. Genuine global security can only emerge from the practice of mutual cooperation, dialog, and discourse. Global security will never be achieved as long as the imperial quest for world domination remains. Therefore, the hope that a rising Global Community offers is a hope that life-furthering values and practices can guide societies toward a new future while working to eclipse empires and the imperial mind-set

After all, there is no logical reason why societies cannot accomplish what commerce and finance have already achieved under the rubric of globalization. In this regard,

> discovering the unknown other—stripping away the ancient fears and accepting that humanity is now a shared enterprise—is perhaps the hardest struggle posed by the global system. Yet, many people have, in fact, already made this leap of consciousness, including many of the managers, engineers and financial analysts who are dispersed around the global marketplace. If business can see the world as a unified whole, then surely societies can do the same.[177]

"WE THE PEOPLE"—THE VOICE OF WORLD TRIBUNALS AND TRUTH COMMISSIONS

The pursuit of global governance and maintaining the peace and security of global society can now be reconceived as more than the consequence of a *balance-of-power* game. This insight is especially relevant at the dawn of the twenty-first century, when there is only one remaining superpower. In the conventional sense of the *balance-of-power* concept, there is no longer any one particular state or group of states for the US Global Empire to balance itself against. Rather, the new reality that global civil society itself has become "the world's other superpower." What makes global civil society different from its historical predecessors is that its superpower status is not derived from any notion of territoriality or nationality.

Global civil society exits beyond both because it is a truly transnational reality—reflective of an emerging world culture that is in the process of moving toward the realization of a Global Community. Aspects of this emerging global civil society can be seen in the establishment of world tribunals and truth commissions.

While the first tribunals and truth commissions have been limited to the boundaries of nation-states, there is now a trend to see the expansion of their jurisdiction both in terms of subject matter and geography. In this regard, the idea of a truth commission and related concepts, such as "forgiveness," could become relevant in the context of the global debt crisis. Already, many voices throughout the global South have campaigned for debt reduction, cancellation, or repudiation ("odious debt"). It is an emerging perspective that is allowing people to think outside the box. Hence, the historical or moral debt that the North has accumulated over the centuries of colonial and neocolonial rule is a debt that is coming due. In this respect, the growth and widening scope of human rights laws and treaties may be seen as promissory notes that are about to be called in by the global South. World tribunals and truth commissions may be incorporated into this quest by acting as the first internationally conceived mechanisms for such a day of reckoning.

The proposition that world tribunals and truth commissions can serve in demanding restitution of the riches extracted from the people of the global South and the payment of reparation is something that has already been contemplated and proposed at the International People's Tribunal on Debt in 2002. This new reality exposes the fact that global civil society is in the process of becoming the global counterbalance to the imperial legacy and current schemes of the US Global Empire. Operating through the mechanism of world tribunals, the Global Community has empowered itself to legally and morally act as a force of restraint upon an empire that is out of control.

Additionally, the establishment of world tribunals and truth commissions—as vehicles for accumulating evidence of crimes—plays a critical role in establishing world order. In this respect, we should also recall that the Nuremberg Tribunal's enduring contribution as not finding out whether the Nazi regime had committed the crimes alleged but documenting its criminality. This trend toward documenting the criminality of regimes and governments has been expanded with regard to US-backed regimes that engaged in massive human rights abuses—as was the case with Chile's dictatorship under the guidance of General Augusto Pinochet.[178] Since 1946, the international community has been paying greater attention to the phenomenon of state terror—terror that is unleashed by the state against its own citizens, sometime with the support of the architects of the US Global Empire. The twentieth century history of Latin America provides us with many examples of state-sponsored terror, supported by the United States. The various nation-states that subjected their own citizens to terror include: Nicaragua, El Salvador, Mexico, Guatemala, Honduras, Costa Rica, Columbia, Peru, Uruguay, and Argentina.[179]

From the experiences of South Africa under apartheid to Guatemala's reign of terror, truth commissions have come to be an essential component for documenting human rights in those particular societies.[180] They have also served to raise the consciousness of global civil society as well. Additionally, the creation of truth commissions has forced its participants and practitioners to contemplate the relationship between truth commissions and international courts—as in the case of Sierra Leone.[181] Yet, it is with respect to the issue of state terror that the most progress has been made in establishing justiciable norms on victims' rights in the criminal process. International law developments in this area of law have served to create new standards in both the arenas of universal jurisdiction and the universality of justiciable victims' rights.[182]

The subject matter for world tribunals and truth commissions on the crimes of the US Global Empire needs to be expanded. For example, the West's complicity in slavery, colonialism, and imperialism, is largely to blame for massive world poverty, inequality, and hunger. The entire Global Community has been affected by the policies of empire. Both the British and then the US Global Empire have inflicted tremendous harms upon billions of people throughout the global South. At the dawn of the 21st century, it is time to rectify the imbalances brought about through the historical legacy of imperial ambition. In fact, these imbalances lie at the heart of the failure of the US Global Empire.

THE FOOLISHNESS OF EMPIRE AND THE IMPERIAL PROJECT

In its drive to dominate the world, create spheres of influence, and play the balance-of-power game, the US Global Empire has done damage to the nations of the global South that cannot be undone by internal policies today—no matter how wise, just, or uncorrupted those policies may be.[183] These imbalances also point to another failure of the US Global Empire: a failure to recognize the fact that its own power will eventually diminish and it may soon experience a relative decline—as was the case with Rome and the British Empire. In order to deal effectively with such a potential—or eventuality—it has been suggested that

> a wise diplomacy would create global institutions now to protect humane values long after the United States will lack the power to protect itself by itself. One might expect officials to establish global guidance procedures for peaceful change, for assuring equitable sharing of resources, for respecting human rights and nature so that the descendents of Washingtonians will not suffer a plight similar to the one that the West inflicted on the rest of the world when imperialism flourished and industrial prosperity turned its back on overseas poverty.[184]

The European Union and European Parliament, acting in compliance with the European Convention on Human Rights have acted on the international stage with the same consistency with regard to the enforcement of rights as its does on its domestic stage. Why can't the United States demonstrate a similar fidelity to the protection and expansion of human rights? In part, it may be that the US Global Empire is still preoccupied with playing a "balance-of-power" game, with potential twenty-first century rivals, such as China. Perhaps it may also be in part because its foreign policy has been taken captive by a neoconservative ideology that is dedicated to world domination under the rubric of *another American century*. Whatever the reasons for its failure to abide by domestic and international human rights standards, the US Global Empire is certainly not engaged in wise diplomacy or efforts to create new global institutions to protect humane values and/or human rights.

Under these circumstances, a global effort is required to gather evidence and give voice to the claims of the entire Global Community. Such an effort will not only involve the challenge of giving voice to the victims of the crimes of the US Global Empire, but also of giving voice to the victims of massive material inequalities that are morally alarming. We can see the inequalities through the lens of aggregated data, but this too has its limitations.[185] Therefore, as the gap between rich and poor nations continues to widen, it is increasingly obvious that "any theory of justice that proposes political principles defining human entitlements ought to be able to confront these inequalities and the challenge they pose, in a world in which the power of the global market and of multinational corporations has considerable eroded the power and autonomy of nations." Hence, "any theory of justice that aims to provide a basis for decent life chances and opportunities for all human beings must take cognizance of both inequalities internal to each nation and of inequalities between nations, and must be prepared to address the complex intersections of these inequalities in a world of increased and increasing global interconnection."[186]

So far, there have been few economic theories put forward that explicitly show how to overcome the inequalities and imbalances that poorer countries face. However, Joseph Stiglitz, awarded the Nobel Prize in economics in 2001, has suggested one such approach in the area of trade liberalization and its effects on the poorer countries of the global South. He states:

> If the global gains from trade liberalization are as large as some researchers suggest—the World Bank estimates that further liberalization could yield an increase in real income by 2015 of more than US$500 billion—then it is reasonable to enshrine a principle of compensation whereby those countries that suffer significant adjustment costs relative to welfare gains should receive offsetting assistance.[187]

In correspondence with Nussbaum's admonition about the need for inclusive principles to be employed in any meaningful theory of global justice, Stiglitz demonstrates that it is possible to produce a just theory of trade that is designed to produce just outcomes. He notes:

> a principle of compensation is important for at least two reasons. First ... not only do adjustment costs fall particularly harshly on the poorest people in the world because they are least able to afford them, but the costs also consume resources that would otherwise be spent on alternative development priorities. For many people, the impact of trade reform will overwhelm the effects of other economic development programs. The second motivation for the provision of compensation for adjustment costs is the pragmatic need to win political support

for reform. High adjustment costs give some groups a vested interest in the status quo. Identifying and compensating those groups may be an effective way of removing impediments to welfare-improving global policy changes.[188]

Stiglitz's proposal of a principle of compensation satisfies the need to focus more on welfare-improving global policy changes. This proposal is one of many that are needed in order to create a more satisfactory basis for managing the inter-relationships between security and sustainable development. The World Commission on Environment and Development noted in 1987: "conflicts may arise not only because of political and military threats to national sovereignty; they may also derive from environmental degradation and the pre-emption of development options."[189] In this regard, Stiglitz's proposal may also be seen as a strategy for both enhancing development options and avoiding conflict within a society that already suffers from resource wars, the exploitation of natural resources, and issues about equitable distribution.

In the case of Africa,

many of Africa's wars are driven in part by the process of globalization: they are funded by the purchase of raw materials (diamonds, gold, coltan, timber, oil) and they are fueled by the sale of weapons, especially small arms, to the continent. The profits of war are often laundered through the wealthier nations' banking systems. Even where exploitation of natural resources is not linked to outright civil war, it has well-known negative effects on prospects for a healthy political economy based on democratic and accountable government.[190]

What the African example reveals is that the connection between security and sustainable development is multifaceted. Sustainable development and genuine economic and military security both require socially inclusive democratic institutions. Socially inclusive democratic institutions are needed to assure distributional equity, control and regulate the use of resources, manage potential conflicts within the civil society, and promote equitable economic development in accordance with just principles in all arenas of economic life—from external trade to internal programs designed to enhance the domestic welfare of the people.

A socially inclusive democratic regime will not allow the uncontrolled sale of small weapons and arms. Such investments threaten not only the security of the people, but their ability to forge a political economy that exemplifies a path of sustainable development. The sales of small arms and weapons destroy both lives and the potential of the nation to evolve toward a unified economic and political program that contains welfare enhancing programs. Further, the sales of small arms and weapons debilitate the economy itself by shifting valuable financial resources *from* health, education, job creation, and democratically accountable government *toward* a system that mainly profits Western banks and weapons dealers. The real costs associated with investments by nations that bankroll the small arms and weapons trade are costs that are borne by nations and groups that cannot afford them in the first place and can only lead to greater costs once hostilities are initiated. Such investments usually lead to civil war as various groups struggle to dominate the profits from the nation's natural resource base.

These civil wars are often avoidable. They are avoidable if the Global Community and individual nations do the following: (a) place a global ban on weapons sales; (b) introduce a UN-sponsored treaty against weapons sales; (c) develop a dialog around new principles that can redefine the meaning of "peace," "security," and "development"—with a nonmilitary focus; (d) centralize the human interest of persons (their dignity, rights, and needs) above the conventional reliance on military force and war to determine the outcomes of disputes. In the aftermath of civil war, the role that truth commissions play in resolving the long-term structural problems of nations and the international system will probably be of limited value if the above-cited structural changes are not inaugurated. Hence, it would be more appropriate for nations to invoke human rights principles from the outset. By doing this, nations can foreclose upon anti-development choices. Also, by centralizing the role of human rights concerns in the development and governing process, there is a greater likelihood that nations can better address not only the interconnected challenges posed by globalization, but also the link between security and sustainable development.

After that is accomplished, an already existent network of courts and treaties can be brought into alignment in assisting the entire Global Community—under the auspices of the UN—to bring the US Global Empire into compliance with the world's findings and mandates emanating from these tribunals and truth commissions. In this crucial respect, the work of world tribunals and global truth commissions may be seen as key components in advancing the rise of the Global Community and universalizing international law.[191]

The work of these world tribunals and truth commissions may also be understood as a means toward effectuating a global exodus from the violence, illegality, and the abuses and occupations of empire. After all, a Global Community knows no fixed territorial demarcations. Further, the work of tribunals and truth commissions can unlock a sense of global solidarity among and between people. In this regard, a Global Community is both a community of nation-states and individual persons.

From the standpoint of the individual, individuals can share membership in a variety of associations and organizations, as well as enjoy dual citizenship. Therefore, the realm of the individual is an expanding realm—both in accordance with evolving institutional and membership identities, as well as an enlarged area of protections afforded to the individual by virtue of human rights commitments. From the perspective of the Global Community, the reality of an increasingly inclusive *World Culture* affords both individuals and nations to benefit from new opportunities in light of the convergence and appreciation of traditions outside of one's own, adherence to commonly recognized legal norms, and the claims of global cultural norms in the service of human rights protections, economic opportunities, and the development of human capacities. Yet, this Global Community can only peacefully evolve if due attention is given to human rights in the context of sustainable development,[192] enforcing socioeconomic rights,[193] and reliance on others to be faithful to the task of achieving a sustainable order of justice through international law.[194]

THE EVOLVING NORMS OF A RISING GLOBAL COMMUNITY

A rising Global Community—properly configured—will ultimately emerge as the product of evolving norms of international law, human rights commitments, and inclusive forms governance at every level—local, national, regional, and international. It will be the result of the union of the theory and practice of global citizens working in concert toward a common good. At its most foundational level, the common good is a universal good that all peoples and nations share a common interest in attaining. Therefore, it is an idea in theory and practice that surpasses the claims of nationalist creeds and ideologies. Membership in the Global Community is best described by the phrase: "We the People." My use of the phrase "We the People" is employed in order to focus on the emerging reality of world citizenship in a *World Culture*. Further, the authority of this rising Global Community is derived from inclusive ideas, principles, traditions, and practices that highlight the centrality of *human cooperation, ethical reason*, and *sociability*.

The importance of these ideas for the rise of Global Community is that they combine in the Grotian idea that we are beings who have a common good and seek a "common life ... organized according to the measure of [our] intelligence." According to Nussbaum,

this intelligence is a moral intelligence. The three central facts about human beings that this moral intelligence apprehends are the dignity of the human being as an ethical being, a dignity that is fully equal no matter where humans are placed; human sociability, which means that part of a life with human dignity is a common life with others organized so as to respect that equal dignity; and the multiple facts of human need, which suggest that this common life must do something for us all, fulfilling needs up to a point at which human dignity is not undermined by hunger, or violent assault, or unequal treatment in the political realm.[195]

Far from being utopian notions, the articulation of these various aspects of human dignity have the capacity to be emulated by every nation in accordance with its own unique civilization and tradition (see Chapter 4). After all, every nation seeks to have its citizens live in conditions of peace and security for all of its citizens so that order is not undermined by hunger, violence, or inequality in the political realm. It is in this respect that the rise of Global Community can be comprehended in the establishment of legal systems that protect rights and secure the dignity of persons and groups, so that who participate in this order are able to discover a common life that does something beneficial for all concerned.

When viewed in combination, the three central facts about human beings—that Nussbaum places under the category of "moral intelligence"—have already played an historical role in the genesis and creation of the European Convention on Human Rights. The European Convention on Human Rights, which came into force in 1953—after signature in 1950, established the most effective system for the protection of human rights which has yet come into existence anywhere in the world. Since the collapse of communism it has come to be extended to the countries of Central and Eastern Europe. At the dawn of the twenty-first century some seven hundred million people live under its protection.[196]

The European Convention on Human Rights has legal force within 32 European states. Further, it has had a tremendous influence in shaping the European Parliament's 1989 Declaration on Fundamental Rights and Freedom. Unlike the ECHR the European Parliament's declaration was not legally binding—as with all declaratory bills of rights. Yet,

> such non-legal declarations have real practical significance not only as guidelines for internal institutional purposes, and symbolically in the context of EC citizenship, but also for the EU/EC's standing in the wider world and its dealings with individual foreign states.

The protection of human rights has come to play a leading role in international relations and is directly relevant to the work conducted under the EU pillar of foreign and defense affairs. It is highly advantageous, therefore, for the EU to possess its own document on human rights standards—agreed to by all its member states—to facilitate the closer integration of all its foreign policy work. If it insists upon a particular set of moral standards for other countries, without which it will refuse to conduct or allow normal relations, then the EU must very clearly show its own commitment to those same standards. Thus consistency between the internal and the external human rights policies of the EU underpins all its work.[197]

The main point that needs to be stressed is that the ECHR embodies in its principles and legal standard a basis for the enforcement and protection of human rights. As such, the ECHR reflects a universal human attribute—*moral intelligence*. Further, its principles and legal standards need not be bounded by either territorial or geographical limits. Rather, the principles and standards embody a global reach—universality. In this regard, *a rising Global Community finds itself as the beneficiary of this heritage*. It is the beneficiary of this heritage because the past history of the ECHR may now become prologue for new global institutions, a greater degree of accountability in the foreign policy of all nations to human rights principles, and ensure domestic accountability in the nation states of the global North and the global South. In other words, *both the principles and institutions of the ECHR—that serve as the basis for the European Union—may also serve as both legacy and vision for a Global Community that is in the process of embarking upon an exodus from empire*. For example, as world citizens look to the possibility of forging a democratic world parliament, they have the benefit of using the history of the European Parliament as a model and a guide.[198] As world citizens confront the challenge of remaking their national cultures and contemplate what kind of world culture that they wish to create, they have the benefit of examining the philosophical dimensions of human rights policies within Europe.[199] As world citizens confront the human rights abuses of multinational corporations, they have the benefit of looking to those examples of how the EU holds multinational corporations accountable.[200]

This brief outline of Europe's post-1950 political evolution is not intended to suggest that a "Euro-centric" model for development and governance be imposed on the nations or regional organizations of the global South. Rather, I am suggesting that Europe's recent history with respect to the formation of the European Union and the ECHR can be used as a template for the global South. After all, Europe has emerged from the end of the Cold War as virtually independent from US threats and its pressures. Europe has gained maturity and independence. In fact, it may also be seen as a major rival to the US Global Empire. The same cannot be said of most nations across the global South. Therefore, if the global South is to effectuate its own *exodus from empire*, as Europe has done, it must sever its political and economic bondage from the United States. In order to accomplish this, democratic elections have been increasingly used as the vehicle to send more leftist leaders to power.

Throughout the global South there has been a rising popular opposition to privatization and neoliberalism. As regional and nation-to-nation linkages are strengthened throughout the global South both an institutional and normative order for a rising Global Community is in the process of being forged. These linkages will serve as the basis for a *counter-hegemonic alliance* to the US Global Empire. That is because these linkages can make possible *an exodus from empire* throughout the global South. This trend has been developing throughout Latin America.

It is a trend that can be seen in the cooperative and ideologically cohesive political union between Venezuelan president, Hugo Chavez, and Cuban leader Fidel Castro. This trend has been further strengthened by the December 2005 presidential election that made Evo Morales, Bolivia's new president. As reported by *The New York Times*,

> on the campaign stump, Evo Morales liked to say that if he was elected president of Bolivia he would become America's nightmare. After his election ... a State Department official said essentially the same thing, calling Mr. Morales "potentially our worst nightmare." The Bush administration says it fears that Mr. Morales will follow through on his promise to join Hugo Chavez, the Venezuelan president, as an anti-American leftist leader.

The article went on to note. "Mr. Morales made an early strike on Tuesday when he told Al Jazeera television in an interview that President Bush was 'a terrorist' and that American military intervention in Iraq was 'state terrorism'."[201]

Just a few weeks before Morales' election, *The New York Times Magazine* ran a story on him entitled, *Che's Second Coming?* The article noted: "The Indian leader of a coca-growers' movement wants to make Bolivia the next domino in Latin America's revolt against globalization, neo-liberalism, and the Bush administration."[201] From this depiction of Morales, it is clear that his ideology fits well with what I have called a growing *counter-hegemonic alliance* to the US Global Empire. If the Morales candidacy was perceived in such a manner before the election, it has certainly been certified after the election. The architects of the US Global Empire feared that such an alliance was in the making. Already, Chavez

and Castro have cemented their alliance. By November 2005, as reported by
David Rieff: "If Bolivians who support Morales seem drawn to thinking in con-
spiratorial terms about the US, the mirror image of this attitude is found in
Washington. There is a powerful consensus in US government circles that Morales
is being bankrolled by Chavez."[202] By December 2005, Bolivia's new president
served notice on the Bush administration that Bolivia was about to embark upon
its own *exodus from empire*.

In his speech given on December 24, 2005 at the "In Defense of Humanity"
conference, Bolivia's newly elected president stated:

> What happened these past days in Bolivia was a great revolt by those who have
> been oppressed for more than 500 years. The will of the people was imposed
> this September and October, and has begun to overcome the empire's cannons.
> We have lived for so many years through the confrontation of two cultures: the
> culture of life represented by the indigenous people, and the culture of death
> represented by the West ... When we speak of the "defense of humanity," as we
> do at this event, I think that this only happens by eliminating neo-liberalism and
> imperialism. But I think that in this we are not so alone, because we see, every
> day that anti-imperialist thinking is spreading, especially after Bush's bloody
> "intervention" policy in Iraq. Our way or organizing and uniting against the
> system, against the empire's aggression toward our people is spreading, as are
> the strategies for creating and strengthening the power of the people.[203]

His speech was entitled: "I believe only in the Power of the People."[204] As the
gathering storm and force of a national/international counter-hegemonic
alliance to the US Global Empire grows, it appears that this is the theme that will
resonate the most passionately.

7
Conclusion

Emerging from Tribulations, Truths, and Tribunals

We're an empire now, and when we act, we create our own reality. And while you're studying that reality—judiciously, as you will—we'll act again, creating other new realities, which you can study too, and that's how things will sort out.[1]

An unnamed senior adviser to President Bush

Institutionalizing "criminal global justice" is, I admit, very different from bringing about "economic global justice," but the one may clear the way to the other in two ways: first, since in the field of international criminal law the problem of how to establish global institutions with universal jurisdiction is at least tentatively being resolved, these procedures might aid our understanding of how to develop more encompassing global institutions. Second, understanding the nature of international criminality will make clear that global justice should not aim at punishing international criminals only, but also at preventing criminality, requiring a careful description and understanding of the globalized world we are increasingly inhabiting.[2]

Thomas Merton

The affluent countries and their citizens are ... implicated in world poverty in two ways. We are implicated, first, because our great privileges and advantages as well as their extreme poverty and disadvantage have emerged through one historical process that was pervaded by unimaginable crimes. To be sure, we bear absolutely no moral responsibility for these crimes, even if we are direct descendants of people who do. Still, we are at fault for continuing to enforce extreme inequalities that emerged in the course of that deeply unjust historical process. Secondly, and independently, we are implicated because we are using our economic, technological, and military advantages to impose a global institutional order that is manifestly and grievously unjust ... By imposing this grievously unjust global order upon the rest of the world, the affluent countries, in collaboration with the so-called elites of the developing countries, are harming the global poor—to put it mildly. To put it

339

less mildly, the imposition of this global order constitutes the largest (though not the gravest) crime against humanity ever committed.[3]

Thomas Pogge

THE TRIBULATIONS OF GLOBALIZATION
AND THE CRIMES OF EMPIRE

Globalization is a concept that has been primarily discussed in economic terms. Globalization has often been placed in the context of economic strategies ranging from trade and commerce to neoliberal programs such as privatization and deregulation. Only secondarily has the concept of globalization been framed as a process that also has political consequences, such as a diminished role for the state and an increased reliance on the market. There is a strategic reason for the omission. The proponents of globalization and the architects of empire do not wish to discuss their vulnerabilities and weaknesses. Rarely do its adherents and/or proponents admit that globalization is a process that can be contested. In reality, it is not set in stone and it is not the product of divine predestination. Rather, as the previous chapters have demonstrated, it is a process that has been dominated and guided by the US Global Empire, Western systems of banking and finance, as well as predatory and repressive institutions such as the IMF, WTO, and World Bank.

The imposition of this global order has done more to promote poverty than to reduce it. Yet, globalization's adherents and proponents still cling to the myth that poverty will be eliminated if the market-oriented growth strategies—sponsored by these interests—are simply given more time. On the other hand, the critics of globalization are able to point to greater levels of criminality as corporations, governments, and financial institutions collude and conspire to advance the interests of their global empire at the expense of human rights and human well-being.

In sum, many of these descriptions constitute a standard list of globalization's economic strategies and institutions. Yet, they fail to address the full impact of globalization's political consequences across the global South. Neither do they do justice to any attempt to account for the covert role of the US Global Empire in undermining the economies of the global South. In short, very few of the aforementioned descriptions—whether taken individually or even collectively—approach the realities of the twenty-first century world. The realities produced by globalization and empire reveal the twin phenomena of economic integration on the one hand, and criminality on the other.

The NAFTA is a prime example of regional economic integration. It was passed on the condition that along with its voluminous trade conditions there would also be *side agreements* relating to the protection of labor and environmental rights. The problem was that neither of the side agreements was equipped with any kind of trigger mechanism to make them enforceable. What I have called the phenomenon of *criminality under the rubric of globalization* results from the destruction of labor rights and environmental protections, as well as the theft of a nation's natural resources. In this context, the criminality associated with the destruction of the environment accounts for a growing health crisis due to the pollution that comes out of unregulated industries in northern Mexico. The deadly effects of environmental contamination affect mainly the poor, but ultimately no one is immune. Additionally, the destruction of labor unions, restrictions on the right to organize, and the elimination of decent wages, all constitute an attendant human rights crisis.

These developments are testimony to violations of the UN Charter, as well as international human rights laws and covenants. The violation of human rights that transpires under the rubric of globalization amounts to what I have called *criminality*. Eventually, as the jurisdiction of the ICC expands and world tribunals expand their efforts and jurisdiction in gathering evidence, the crimes against humanity by both the warfare sector of states *and* the financial sectors of states will come under judgment. Yet, in the meantime, under the rubric of globalization and a narrowly defined notion of free trade, these violations are often accounted for as merely *the cost of doing business*. In response, the critics of globalization call such results the consequence of *unfair trade*. After all, the US Global Empire enjoys superior bargaining power and added leverage by virtue of its control of the WTO, IMF, and World Bank. In this context of power relationships and their effects on billions of people throughout the Global Community, the issue of fair or unfair terms of trade needs to be juxtaposed to a wider range of abuses engaged in by the US Global Empire and the corporations that it serves. In this regard, the unregulated sale of conventional arms and weapons—that amounts to more than $900 billion dollars annually—needs to be controlled, monitored, and eventually eliminated by international agreement and enforcement. If just a fractional amount of this $900 billion were to be applied to the global challenges of health, nutrition, disease, education, and poverty, there would be no real need for nations to become so grievously indebted to the IMF and World Bank in the first place. In fact, a new direction for investment and funding would do much to restore the sovereign equality of nations while, at the same time, removing much of the influence of the US Global Empire. This is another aspect of what is contemplated by the idea of embarking upon an *exodus from empire*.

It is clear that threats against the entire global South have been made by the managers of the US Global Empire in either the form of threats of military intervention or in the form of financial threats. For example, in an effort to expropriate resources in Third World nations, the institutions and bureaucrats of the IMF threaten these countries with calling in their debts, limiting their credit, and cutting off aid—all at the expense of the public welfare. Further, if the country in question is an energy-rich nation, then its oil, coal, and gas reserves may become a military target for acquisition by the US Global Empire. What cannot be obtained through unfair trade advantages and the snake oil of neoliberalism could simply be taken through the exercise of resurgent militarism and the use of American troops as a force of occupation—as in the case of Iraq.

The phenomenon of economic integration is largely the integration of elite interests. As such, *it is a form of integration that is highly exclusionary in economic, social, political, and cultural terms*. Capitalist integration under the guidance of elite interests uses terms of trade and treaties to undercut and dismember the human rights structure of international law and the principles set forth in the UN Charter. I would call this phenomenon *exclusionary integration* insofar as this form of globalization advances a very narrow profit-oriented agenda at the expense of billions of people throughout the Global Community. By setting up greater wage differentials and economic hierarchies within and between nations, *exclusionary integration* introduces new justifications and rationalizations for crimes against humanity that are condoned or covered up under the rubric of terms such as *creative destruction* and globalization. The consequence is the development of new forms of global apartheid.

In order to frame the challenge of globalization in its wider context it would be beneficial to try to understand the phenomenon by identifying its stated goals and then proceed to evaluate the effects of these goals in the real world. In order to move past the theoretical claims of globalization's proponents we must be able to move past the myths and ideological assertions that divert our attention from actual evidence of its harms. Hence, there are two main tasks we must undertake. First, an adequate description of globalization needs to be juxtaposed to a comprehensive list of its stated goals. Second, an adequate description of globalization should be juxtaposed to a comprehensive list of its effects—both predicted and unpredicted. In formulating these descriptions of globalization's goals and effects the Global Community will be engaged in the task of gathering evidence and testimony. Once this process is completed, we shall probably find that somewhere between the goals of globalization—as defined by global elites—and its effects upon the majority of humanity, lies a more accurate depiction of its nature. In between its claims and its consequences, its agenda and the effects of that agenda, lies the true nature of the world order (*or disorder*) that has emerged between the 1990s and the early twenty-first century.

Once the true nature of US-guided globalization becomes more grounded in evidence than in ideology, it will be possible to begin to chart its criminal nature and assess the damage that it has wrought on individuals and on nations. Only by assembling evidence and testimony will it become possible to establish world tribunals that are appropriately equipped to evaluate the collected evidence and testimony, and then proceed to make assessments about the crimes of globalization under the auspices of the US Global Empire and its allies (within international corporate networks and within collaborator states). At that point, the true costs and damages of globalization can be assessed. Theoretically, the final totals of these costs and damages could be calculated in reference to the Third World's debt, and then be subtracted from it. The net result might be that Third World debt could be wiped out by means of making debt forgiveness a form of reparations to the global South.

THE UNITED NATIONS' MILLENNIUM DEVELOPMENT GOALS: AN ALTERNATIVE PATH FOR GLOBALIZATION

There are alternatives to the directions established by globalization. For example, there exists a vast range of global issues that humanity needs to address, which lies beyond the scope and goals of the globalization project. This vast range of global issues is best summarized within the UN's *Millennium Development Goals*

(MDG). The MDGs consist of an alternative agenda for shaping world order in the twenty-first century. The MDG agenda is not the globalization agenda. Rather, the MDGs constitute an agenda for addressing the effects of globalization's criminality—the global health crisis, environmental degradation, and widening gulfs of inequality and poverty.

A comprehensive list of alternatives for a humane world order are set forth in the *Millennium Declaration of September 2000*. In the declaration, the UN articulated eight development goals for the international community to address and solve. These developmental goals involve more than just providing solutions to global socioeconomic problems. These goals constitute a mandate to effect global changes within a specified time frame so that current trends which threaten the Global Community may be reversed. The goals constitute the agenda of the Global Community. These goals include addressing and mitigating the following global challenges: poverty, hunger, illiteracy, gender, inequity, communicable diseases, and environmental degradation.

Eradicating poverty and hunger was made the first priority. The *Millennium Declaration* sought to inaugurate a global war on poverty. Sadly, the so-called *war on terrorism* has had a negative and debilitating effect upon the global war on poverty. Unfortunately, the *war on terrorism* has reinforced the power of those global elites that drive and shape the process of globalization. In fact, this is why the process of what I have called *exclusionary governance* has been growing while social movements and progressive seeking *inclusionary governance* have been placed in a more defensive mode. Yet, at the same time, offensive strategies are in the making by progressive social movements. These strategies include: (1) reclaiming the power of the state for the people; (2) advancing more people-oriented policies to serve the welfare of the previously excluded and poor; (3) legal calls for an end to "odious debt"; (4) opposition to resurgent militarism; (5) an international rejection of the neoliberal model of development; (6) the effort to construct more regional alliances as a means of withdrawing from the dictates of the US Global Empire; (7) laying the foundation for an international counter-hegemonic alliance to the US Global Empire.

By virtue of the power of propaganda, a small global elite—working through a corporate-driven media monopoly—has sought to simply label social movements against globalization and neoliberal policies as terrorist networks, in an effort to discredit them. Throughout global civil society a global elite has sought to label the poor, progressives, peasants, students, union members, and people from faith-based communities as terrorists just because they are members of social movements that are in the process of organizing against the excesses and injustices of globalization. In short, some aspects of the so-called *war on terror* serve to constitute a *war on the poor and oppressed*. In truth, the opposition of social movements to globalization and neoliberalism is a principled opposition. These movements are an expression of people's aspirations for a more just, inclusive, and humane world order throughout the Global Community. By opposing the world disorder that globalization has created, these social movements are also acting in opposition to the policies and practices of the US Global Empire. It is through their opposition that they see the possibility for embarking upon an *exodus from empire*.

"WE THE PEOPLE": THE RISE AND EMERGING
POWER OF GLOBAL CIVIL SOCIETY

The rise and newly emerging power of global civil society—as well as social movements across the global South—represent a direct challenge to the US Global Empire. With the rise of global civil society it becomes possible to argue that this global civil society has become the world's second superpower. For example, the worldwide opposition to the US invasion and occupation of Iraq signaled an emerging global consensus that has served to lay the foundation for a national and international counter-hegemonic alliance to the US Global Empire. With the exception of economic and political elites and some right-wing political parties and groups, the entire Global Community is opposed to the resurgent militarism of the US Global Empire. In large measure, this opposition is coupled with a growing global resistance to the US neoliberal model of development. By stressing deregulation and privatization this model has led entire nations into greater poverty, debt, and bankruptcy while, at the same time, the natural resources and endowments of nations and continents are being stolen under the auspices of US corporations, financial and banking interests, and a US-dominated trading system under the WTO. The response of most nations to this treatment is a growing resentment and resistance in the form of social movements, electing more left-wing governments, and demands for adherence to international law and the right of the nations of the global South to pursue their own development in regional alliances that are not tied to the tentacles of the empire. In short, a growing national and international counter-hegemonic alliance to the US Global Empire is evolving.

The beginning of this counter-hegemonic alliance was clearly visible in the fall of 2005 when President Bush was confronted with violent street protests, while he was attending the Summit of the Americas in Argentina. The Summit of the Americas became the venue where his hemispheric free-trade proposal was buried. Despite all of the corporate backing that President Bush enjoyed in advancing a neoliberal trade structure under the rubric of a *Free Trade for the Americas Agreement* (FTAA), it failed to inspire Latin American leaders who are more acutely attuned to the negative effects of corporate globalization and IMF-sponsored aid packages.

In addition to the burial of a hemispheric free-trade proposal, more political failures for the architects of the US Global Empire came into view in December 2005, when the people of Bolivia elected Evo Morales to the presidency. Throughout the region, the election of Morales assisted in building momentum for a resurgence of leftist and anti-US candidates throughout Latin America. By the beginning of 2006, Brazil, Mexico, Peru, and Ecuador had embraced progressive and leftist candidates. The makings of a Latin American counter-hegemonic alliance had been put into place by the effects of IMF policies. The heavy burden that corporate-driven globalization had on the poor and middle classes has continued to drive social movements which, in turn, effected a dramatic change in the region's electoral politics. Additionally, even though he was an announced enemy of the Bush-2 regime, the president of oil-rich Venezuela, Hugo Chavez, remained well entrenched—despite all previous Bush-2 administration attempts to either assassinate or overthrow him. Within this same time frame, more progressive and leftist leaders had toppled conservative governments in Uruguay and Honduras. When viewed in combination, all of these trends led some North American commentators to wonder whether or not there was a *Chavez effect*.

As 2006 began, Mexican presidential candidate Andre Manuel Lopez Obrador had become the front-runner to win the presidency in the presidential election scheduled for July 2006. In Peru, Ollanta Humala began 2006 in a virtual tie with the favorite candidate of the center-right. The virtual tie was due to a 10-point bounce that Humala received in light of Morale's victory in neighboring Bolivia. In Chile, on January 15, 2006, a socialist candidate, Michelle Bachelet won 53.5 percent of the vote, to 46.5 percent for her rival, Sebastian Pinera, conservative multimillionaire businessman. Ms. Bachelet became the first woman in South America to be elected president on her own merits and not as a relative of a beloved deceased male leader—as was the case in 1974 when Argentina's Isabel Peron was elected to fill the shoes of her late husband, Juan. What these twenty-first century candidacies demonstrate is that socialism, feminism, and an expansive human rights consciousness have been placed on the ascendancy throughout Latin America's civil society. A new and previously submerged hierarchy of values was beginning to take hold of political processes that had previously been the historical province of dictatorships and *death-squad democracies*—supported by Washington (i.e., El Salvador and Guatemala in the Reagan Years).

In many respects, the aspirations of Latin America's social movements and changes produced in the electoral arena reflected aspirations that were similar to those found in the UN's Millennium Development Goals. When viewed in combination, these new social movements and leftist candidacies are evidence of discomfort within Latin America's civil society that has had enough of watching one-third of their population try to live on less than $2 a day. The contradictions of life are compounded by the fact that economic and social justice eludes millions throughout Latin America despite the growth of electoral democracies throughout the region. Because these democracies have segregated political and civil rights from a broader conception of human rights as socioeconomic as well, social disparities and economic disparities are more evident. Despite a growing respect for human rights, under the rubric of democratic government, Latin Americans have witnessed even greater increases in social inequality and higher rates of unemployment. These trends have transpired as globalization has evolved over the 1990s and on into the twenty-first century.

The role of the US Global Empire has been closely associated with the work of the IMF in bringing about financial collapse in Argentina. It is now clear to billions of people that the processes of globalization, in combination with a neoliberal economic model, have done more to deepen poverty than act as an antidote to it. In many respects, emerging majorities throughout Latin America have come to think of the US Global Empire as both the sponsor of globalization and the source of their misery. The same viewpoint is held by billions of people throughout Africa, Asia, and the Middle East. It is for this reason that social movements, newly elected governments, and people of conscience throughout the Global Community are in the process of embarking upon an *exodus from empire*.

Notes

INTRODUCTION

1. David Anderson, *Histories of the Hanged: The Dirty War in Kenya and the End of Empire*, W.W. Norton & Company, 2005.
2. Caroline Elkins, *Imperial Reckoning: The Untold Story of Britain's Gulag in Kenya*, Henry Holt and Company, 2005.
3. Philippe Sands, *Lawless World: America and the Making and Breaking of Global Rules from FDR's Atlantic Charter to George W. Bush's Illegal War*, Viking, 2005.
4. James Risen, *State of War: The Secret History of the CIA and the Bush Administration*, Free Press, 2006. See also: Evan Thomas and Daniel Klaidman, "How Much Power Should They Have?—Spying In America: A New War Over the 'Imperial Presidency'," *Newsweek*, January 9, 2006, pp. 22–30; Benjamin Barber, "Neither Consent nor Dissent: Bush's Uncontested War," *The American Prospect*, November 4, 2002, pp. 25–27; Andrew Mack, "Containing Saddam," *The Nation*, December 16, 2002, pp. 4–5; Investigative Status Report of the House Judiciary Committee Democratic Staff, *The Constitution In Crisis: The Downing Street Minutes and Deception, Manipulation, Torture, Retribution, and Cover-ups in the Iraq War*, January 2006; Jeremy Brecher, Jill Cutler, and Brendan Smith, editors, *In the Name of Democracy: American War Crimes in Iraq and Beyond*, Metropolitan Books, 2005; Mark Leon Goldberg, "Bolton vs. World: In his first six months at the UN, John Bolton has offended allies, blocked crucial negotiations, undermined the Secretary of State—and harmed US interests. We expected bad; we didn't expect this bad," *The American Prospect*, January 2006, pp. 22–27; Center For Constitutional Rights, *Articles of Impeachment Against George W. Bush*, Melville House Publishing, 2006.
5. Gustavo Gutierrez, *A Theology of Liberation: History, Politics, and Salvation*, Orbis Books, 1973, p. 159. Gutierrez notes: "The Exodus experience is paradigmatic. It remains vital and contemporary due to similar historical experiences which the People of God undergo. As Neher writes, it is characterized 'by the twofold sign of the overriding will of God and the free and conscious consent of men'."
6. Alonzo Johnson, *Good News for the Disinherited: Howard Thurman on Jesus of Nazareth and Human Liberation*, University Press of America, 1997, pp. 93–114.
7. Walter E. Fluker, *They Looked For A City: A Comparative Analysis of the Ideal Community in the Thought of Howard Thurman and Martin Luther King, Jr.*, University Press of America, 1989, p. 144.
8. Ibid., p. 160.
9. People's Health Movement, *Global Health Watch: An Alternative World Health Report*, Zed Books, 2005; Jeffrey Kluger, "By Any Measure, Earth is at the Tipping Point," *TIME*, Special Report on Global Warming, April 3, 2006.
10. Makere Stewart-Harawira, *The New Imperial Order: Indigenous Responses to Globalization*, Zed Books, 2005, p. 244.
11. Chandra Lekha Sriram and Karin Wermester, editors, *From Promise to Practice: Strengthening UN Capacities for the Prevention of Violent Conflict*, Lynne Rienner Publishers, 2003.
12. Michael Bothe, Mary E. O'Connell, and Natalino Ronzitti, editors, *Redefining Sovereignty: The Use of Force After the Cold War*, Transnational Publishers, Inc., 2005. See also: Allen Buchanan, *Justice, Legitimacy, and Self-Determination: Moral Foundations for International Law*, Oxford University Press, 2004.
13. Paul Gready and Jonathan Ensor, *Reinventing Development? Translating Rights-Based Approaches From Theory Into Practice*, Zed Books, 2005. See also: *Dying for Growth: Global Inequality and the Health of the Poor*, edited by Jim Yong Kim et al., Common Courage Press, 2000.

14. John Boli and George Thomas, editors, *Constructing World Culture: International Non-Governmental Organizations Since 1875*, Stanford University Press, 1999.
15. James Bouvard, *Attention Deficit Democracy*, Palgrave Macmillan, 2005.
16. Odd Arne Westad, *The Global Cold War: Third World Interventions and the Making of Our Times*, Cambridge University Press, 2005.
17. John Gray, *False Dawn: The Delusions of Global Capitalism*, The New Press, 1998.
18. Nancy Soderberg, *The Superpower Myth: The Use and Misuse of American Might*, John Wiley & Sons, 2005.
19. Christopher Bayly and Tim Harper, *Forgotten Armies: The Fall of British Asia, 1941–1945*, Harvard University Press, 2005.
20. Michael A. Fitts, "The Paradox of Power in the Modern State: Why a Unitary, Centralized Presidency May Not Exhibit Effective or Legitimate Leadership," *University of Pennsylvania Law Review*, Vol. 144, No. 3, January 1996, pp. 845–846.
21. Zbigniew Brezinski, *The Grand Chessboard: American Primacy and Its Geostrategic Imperatives*, Basic Books, 1997, p. 3
22. Ibid., p. 215.
23. Terrence E. Paupp, *Achieving Inclusionary Governance: Advancing Peace and Development in First and Third World Nations*, Transnational Publishers, Inc., 2000.
24. Odd Arne Westad, *The Global Cold War: Third World Interventions and the Making of Our Times*, Cambridge University Press, 2005, pp. 99–109.
25. Ibid., pp. 99–102.
26. Anne Orford, "Globalization and the Right to Development," *People's Rights*, edited by Philip Alston, Oxford University Press, 2001, pp. 127–184.
27. Philip Alston, "People's Rights: Their Rise and Fall," *People's Rights*, edited by Philip Alston, Oxford University Press, 2001, p. 293.
28. Boaventura de Sousa Santos, "General Introduction—Reinventing Social Emancipation: Toward New Manifestos," *Democratizing Democracy: Beyond the Liberal Democratic Canon*, edited by Boaventura De Sousa Santos, Verso, 2005, p. xvii. See also: Henry Veltmeyer, James Petras, and Steve Vieux, *Neo-liberalism and Class Confliction in Latin America: A Comparative Perspective on the Political Economy of Structural Adjustment*, St. Martin's Press, Inc., 1997.
29. Orford, "Globalization and the Right to Development," p. 144. See also: Branko Milanovic, *Worlds Apart: Measuring International and Global Inequality*, Princeton University Press, 2005; Martin Khor, "The Main Issues in North-South Free Trade Agreements," *Third World Resurgence*, No. 182/183, Oct/Nov 2005, pp. 16–22.
30. Orford, "Globalization and the Right to Development," p. 150.
31. Ibid., p. 153.
32. Paupp, *Achieving Inclusionary Governance*. See also: Gerd Schonwalder, *Linking Civil Society and the State: Urban Popular Movements, the Left, and Local government in Peru, 1980–1992*, The Pennsylvania State University Press, 2002; Philip Oxhorn, *Organizing Civil Society: The Popular Sectors and the Struggle for Democracy in Chile*, The Pennsylvania State University Press, 1995.
33. Ihid., pp. 287–348.
34. John Gray, *False Dawn*, p. 21.
35. Bahram Ghazi, *The IMF, the World Bank Group and the Question of Human Rights*, Transnational Publishers, 2005, p. 311. See also: Beverly M. Carl, *Trade and the Developing World in the 21st Century*, Transnational Publishers, Inc., 2001.
36. Jeremy Gould, "Poverty, Politics, and States of Partnership," *The New Conditionality: The Politics of Poverty Reduction Strategies*, Zed Books, 2005, pp. 6–7.
37. Jose Correa Leite, *The World Social Forum: Strategies of Resistance*, Haymarket Books, 2005.
38. Walden Bello, "The International Architecture of Power," *Another World Is Possible: Popular Alternatives to Globalization at the World Social Forum*, edited by William F. Fisher and Thomas Ponnian, Zed Books, 2003, p. 285.
39. Ibid., p. 286.
40. Francois Polet, editor, *Globalizing Resistance: The State of Struggle*, Pluto Press, 2004.
41. David Solnit, *Globalize Liberation: How to Uproot the System and Build a Better World*, City Lights Books, 2004.

42. Amory Starr, *Global Revolt: A Guide to the Movements Against Globalization*, Zed Books, 2005; Amory Starr, *Naming the Enemy: Anti-Corporate Movements Confront Globalization*, Pluto Press, 2000; Sam Moyo and Paris Yeros, editors, *Reclaiming the Land: The Resurgence of Rural Movements in Africa, Asia and Latin America*, Zed Books, 2005; Peter H. Smith, *Democracy in Latin America: Political Change in Comparative Perspective*, Oxford University Press, 2005.

1   FROM PRECEDENCE WE COME

1. John H. Bodley, *The Power of Scale: A Global History Approach*, M.E. Sharpe, 2003, pp. 3–27. See also: Mark Cocker, *Rivers of Blood, Rivers of Gold: Europe's Conquest of Indigenous Peoples*, Grove Press, 1998.
2. Ellen M. Wood, *Empire of Capital*, Verso, 2003, p. 21.
3. Ibid., p. 21.
4. Amy Chua, *World on Fire: How Exporting Free Market Democracy Breeds Ethnic Hatred and Global Instability*, Doubleday, 2003, p. 21. See also: Ulrich Beck, *Power in the Global Age: A New Global Political Economy*, Polity, 2005, p. 147. Beck notes:

As economic globalization advances, the incidence of social and political conflicts and crises increases. This development may be driven forwards to a point where social upheavals are imminent or actually occur in various parts of the world—as was the case in the Southeast Asia of 1998–1999, as is in danger of occurring in Russia and Latin America, and has long since become everyday reality in sub-Saharan Africa. It is when this boiling point has been reached that the quietly dominant economistic hubris of 'managing' economic globalization by economic means alone is exposed. This means, conversely and paradoxically, that state power can be revitalized by the experience of political crisis.

5. Ibid., p. 175. See also: Beck, *Power in the Global Age*, p. 148. Beck notes: "global business requires the legitimatory force of a democratically organized transnational renewal of political, so that the disparities and anomic circumstances to which it gives rise can be regulated in a legitimate fashion."
6. Wood, *Empire of Capital*, p. x. See also: Francis Fukuyama, *America at the Crossroads: Democracy, Power, and the Neo-conservative Legacy*, Yale University Press, 2006; Perry Anderson, "Inside Man—With his new book, Fukuyama has defected from the neo-conservative movements, which once regarded him as an invaluable asset," *The Nation*, April 24, 2006, pp. 23–29; Isaac Chotiner, "The Neo-Neo-Conservative—In explaining how his movement went wrong, Francis Fukuyama all but embraces liberal internationalism," *The Washington Monthly*, May 2006, pp. 44–45; Beck, *Power in the Global Age*, p. 124. According to Beck:

state politics and the world of business have always been mutually intertwined ... Politics itself also acquires an enhanced image and significance as a response to the expansion of market power, not only by virtue of being the only legitimate form of dealing with social conflict but also through being capable of influencing and shaping globalization.

7. Immanuel Wallerstein, *After Liberalism*, The New Press, 1995, p. 161. See also: Samir Amin and Alie El Kentz, *Europe and the Arab World: Patterns and Prospects for New Relationship*, Zed Books, 2005, p. 136. The authors note:

The so-called European proposals for "Euro-Mediterranean partnership" also include an economic component about which the European institutions claimed to have made "new efforts" in qualifying their proposals as coming within the framework of "mutual development," "partnership," and "joint development," in place of "aid," a devalued term. An analysis of these "partnership" proposals shows that they are nothing of the sort. All these proposals come within the exclusive logic of globalized neo-liberalism (opening markets, creating "enabling" conditions for foreign investment, deregulating and defusing protections, etc.) as formulated by the United States, the WTO, the World Bank, and the IMF. Submission to the rules defined by these authorities, including the so-called Structural Adjustment Programs, is moreover formulated as a pre-condition for implementation of the European proposals. Here too, the real position of Europe is not different from that of the United States. In both their political and economic dimensions Europe's proposals currently form a part of a dominant twofold alignment: liberal globalization and United States hegemonism. The two elements are interrelated.

See also: Beck, *Power in the Global Age*, p. 256. Beck notes:

Global perception of the dangers facing humanity threatens to being about global delegitimization of the nation-state order—unless endangered nation-states set about rebuilding themselves into transnational states, into cosmopolitan states. The social contract can no longer be grounded in the anarchy of separate individual states. Instead, it needs to create an inter-state order that draws its cosmopolitan legitimacy from preventively combating the threat to humanity.

8. Immanuel Wallerstein, *The Decline of American Power: the US in a Chaotic World*, The New Press, ca. 2003, p. 41. See also: Reg Whitaker, "Drifting Away from the Edge of Empire: Canada in the Era of George W. Bush," *Empire's Law: The American Imperial Project and the "War to Remake the World*," edited by Amy Bartholomew, Pluto Press, 2006, p. 281. Whitaker notes:

Together with deep anxieties about the threat Bush's fiscal policies pose for the collapse of the US dollar, it is evident that a common capitalist front under US hegemony cannot be sustained forever. America First nationalism may have profound political resonance in "red state" America ... but it can only spawn counter-nationalist revolts among America's erstwhile alliance partners.

Similarly, see also: James Petras and Henry Velmeyer, *Empire With Imperialism: The Globalizing Dynamic of Neo-liberal Capitalism*, Zed Books, 2005; Jack Snyder, "Myths of Empire and Strategies of Hegemony," *Lessons of Empire: Imperial Histories and American Power*, edited by Craig Calhoun et al., The New Press, 2006, p. 282. Snyder notes in his conclusion:

These perspectives of the opportunities and costs of empire provide insights on the dilemmas that America may confront in a hegemonic effort to reshape world politics. They alert us to the rising costs of expansion and the need for some form of governance to coordinate collective action, the benefits of voluntarily institutionalized cooperation over hierarchical domination, and the catalytic role of culturally creative transnational networks in developing new sources of social power. Overall, these insights suggest that America needs to use its vast resources to organize global politics more successfully, but that a coercive attempt to roll up the system in the name of global liberal democracy will be self-defeating.

9. William I. Robinson, *Transnational Conflicts: Central America, Social Change, and Globalization*, Verso, ca. 2003, p. 235.
10. Andrew J. Bacevich, "The Real World War IV," *The Wilson Quarterly*, Winter 2005, p. 61.
11. Richard Falk, *On Humane Governance: Toward a New Global Politics*, The Pennsylvania State University Press, ca. 1995.
12. Paupp, *Achieving Inclusionary Governance*.
13. Samir Amin writes:

The globalized "liberal" economic order requires permanent war—military interventions endlessly succeeding one another—as the only means to submit the peoples of the periphery to its demands. The new-style Empire, on the contrary, is defined naively as a "network of powers" whose center is everywhere and nowhere, which thus dilutes the importance of the national state. This transformation moreover is essentially attributed to the development of the productive forces (the technological revolution). This is a shallow and simplistic analysis that isolates the power of technology from the framework of social relations within which it operates. Once again, we recognize here the propositions of the dominant discourse vulgarized by Rawls, Castells, Touraine, Rifkin, and others, in the tradition of North American liberal political thought. [Samir Amin, *The Liberal Virus: Permanent War and the Americanization of the World*, Monthly Review Press, 2004, p. 24.]

14. Immanuel Wallerstein, *Alternatives: The United States Confronts the World*, Paradigm Publishers, 2004, p. 159.
15. Corey Robin, *Fear: The History of a Political Idea*, Oxford University Press, 2004; Benjamin R. Barber, *Fear's Empire: War, Terrorism, and Democracy*, W.W. Norton & Company, 2003; Andrew Bard Schmookler, *Out of Weakness: Healing the Wounds That Drive Us to War*, Bantam Books, 1988; Carl Sagan, *The Dragons of Eden: Speculations on the Evolution of Human Intelligence* (1977 Common Reader Classic Bestseller), Texas Press, 2004.
16. Schmookler, *Out of Weakness*, p. 29. See also: Lawrence Harrison, *The Central Liberal Truth: How Politics Can Change a Culture and Save It from Itself*, Oxford University Press, 2006; Lawrence E. Harrison and Samuel P. Huntington, *Culture Matters: How Human Values Shape Progress*, Basic Books, 2000; *Many Globalizations: Cultural Diversity in the Contemporary World*, edited by Peter L. Berger and Samuel P. Huntington, Oxford University Press, 2002; The Human Security Center, *Human Security Report (2005): War and Peace in the 21ˢᵗ Century*, Oxford University Press, 2005; David Korten, *The Great Turning: From Empire to Earth Community*, Kumarian Press, 2006.

2   THE OCCUPATIONS OF EMPIRE

1. David Held, *Democracy and the Global Order*, Stanford University Press, 1995, pp. 119–120.
2. Richard Falk, *On Human Governance: Toward a New Global Politics*, The Pennsylvania State University Press, 1995, p. 111.
3. Paul Kennedy, *The Rise and Fall of Great Powers: Economic Change and Military Conflict from 1500 to 2000*, Random House, New York, 1987.
4. Roger Burbach and Jim Tarbell, *Imperial Overstretch: George W. Bush & the Hubris of Empire*, Zed Books, 2004, p. 13.
5. Thomas McCormick, "American Hegemony and European Autonomy, 1989–2003; One Framework for Understanding the War in Iraq," *The New American Empire: A 21st Century Teach-In on U.S. Foreign Policy*, edited by Lloyd Gardner and Marilyn B. Young, New Press, 2005, p. 110. On this matter, see also: Nicholas Guyatt, *Another American Century? The United States and the World Since 9/11*, Zed Books, 2003, pp. 114–176.
6. Robert Johansen, *The National Interest and the Human Interest: An Analysis of U.S. Foreign Policy*, Princeton University Press, 1980, p. 20.
7. Ibid., 20.
8. Ibid.
9. Michael T. Klare, *Blood and Oil: The Dangers and Consequences of America's Growing Dependency on Imported Petroleum*," Metropolitan Books, 2004, p. 23.
10. Ibid., p. 25.
11. Johansen, *The National Interest and the Human Interest*, p. 21.
12. Charles A. Kupchan, *The Vulnerability of Empire*, Cornell University Press, 1994, p. 51. On this matter, see also: Neil Smith, *The Endgame of Globalization*, Routledge, 2005, pp. 177–210.
13. Grant McConnell, *Private Power and American Democracy*, Vintage Books, 1966.
14. Wright Mills, *The Power Elite*, Oxford University Press, 1956.
15. Jonathan Kwitny, *Endless Enemies: The Making of an Unfriendly World*, Congdon & Weed, Inc., ca. 1984.
16. Marcus Raskin, *Liberalism: The Genius of American Ideals*, Rowman & Littlefield Publishers, Inc., 2004, p. 113, and also see, Walden Bello, *Dilemmas of Domination: The Unmaking of the American Empire*, Metropolitan Books, 2005, p. 126:

    Financial liberalization, like trade liberalization, was a fundamental tenet of the neoliberal doctrine that served as the ideology of corporate-driven globalization. Through financial liberalization, Third World nations were promised their private sectors would get the capital they needed for development, in exchange for a just return to foreign capital investors ... Many nations in the South bought this line. It did not take long for them to realize, however, that speculative investors were not interested in nurturing strategic sectors of the economy, like industry and agriculture. Rather, they were there to play the stock and real estate markets. Nor were they committed for the duration; they would take advantage of local hospitality only as long as the rates of return on their investments in a particular market were higher than in other markets and the political conditions more stable. Governments have liberalized their capital accounts with an eye to facilitating the entry of speculative capital, not recognizing that the same easy road in would be the easy road out once a market fell from favor or, worse, panic took hold. Then they stare disaster in the face.

17. Mills, *The Power Elite*, p. 353.
18. Ibid., p. 361.
19. Raskin, *Liberalism*, pp. 229–230.
20. Chalmers Johnson, *The Sorrows of Empire: Militarism, Secrecy, and the End of the Republic*, Metropolitan Books, 2004, p. 2.
21. Wm Roger Louis, *Imperialism At Bay: The United States and the De-colonization of the British Empire, 1941–1945*, Oxford University Press, 1978.
22. Robert Smith Thompson, *The Eagle Triumphant: How America Took Over the British Empire*, John Wiley & Sons, 2004, p. 213.
23. Steven Hugh Lee, *Outposts of Empire: Korea, Vietnam, and the Origins of the Cold War in Asia, 1949–1954*, McGill-Queen's University Press, 1995.
24. W. W. Brands, *The Wages of Globalism: Lyndon Johnson and the Limits of American Power*, Oxford University Press, 1995, p. 3. The reality of the situation was, of course, very different from the official line. On this matter, see: Melvyn P. Leffler, *The Specter of Communism: The United States and the Origins of the Cold War, 1917–1953*, Hill and Wang, 1994, p. 49, "The men who made US policy were anything but idealists. They cared little about human rights and personal freedoms inside the Soviet Union and the Soviet orbit. They were concerned with configurations of power in the international system and how these configurations affected US interests abroad and, more important, the American political economy at home."
25. Andrew J. Bacevich, *American Empire: The Realities & Consequences of US Diplomacy*, Harvard University Press, 2002, p. 3. The expansion of the American empire/imperium would come at a terrible cost. On this matter, see: Frank Kofsky, *Harry S. Truman and the War Scare of 1948: A Successful Campaign to Deceive the Nation*, St. Martin's Press, 1993, p. 9—"Truman deserves our condemnation for foisting upon the nation a permanent war economy that now serves primarily to accelerate the rate at which the quality of life in the United States declines." In the conclusion of Kofsky's book, entitled, "Of Presidents and Precedents," he writes of the Truman administration's penchant for "crisis politics." Crisis politics is also a good description of what President George W. Bush used with the WMD scare as a justification for the invasion and occupation of Iraq, starting in 2003. Yet, it would not be the first time in American history that this strategy was employed. As Kofsky notes of the Truman administration and subsequent administrations:

> Rather than encouraging a rational discussion of the issues by an informed electorate, the president and his chief lieutenants found it more convenient to proceed by deceit and manipulation, using, baseless claims of an impending Soviet military offensive to stampede Congress and the citizenry. Anyone who has lived through the years of the US war in Southeast Asia or, to take a more recent example, the 1991 war against Iraq, will not have to be told how readily later presidents have emulated the kind of chicanery practiced by the Truman administration in 1948" (p. 234).

> Other scholars have been drawn to a similar conclusion: John L. Harper, *American Visions of Europe: Franklin D. Roosevelt, George F. Kennan, and Dean G. Acheson*, Cambridge University Press, 1994; Jerry W. Sanders, *Peddlers of Crisis: The Committee on the Present Danger and the Politics of Containment*, South End Press, 1983; *Re-making Asia: Essays on the Uses of American Power*, edited by Mark Selden, Pantheon Books, 1974.

26. Ibid., p. 3. On this matter, see also: Melvyn E. Leffler, *A Preponderance of Power: National Security, the Truman Administration, and the Cold War*, Stanford University Press, 1992, p. 516. Speaking of the US leadership, Leffler writes:

> Between 1947 and 1952, these men integrated Western Europe, West Germany, and Japan into a US-led orbit. Through NATO, the contractual agreements with Germany, the security treaty with

Japan, and other supranational mechanisms of control, they created a configuration of power in the industrial core of Eurasia that comported with US security interests. By acting as financial hegemon, moreover, and by supporting multilateral trade, they helped promote unprecedented economic growth that reinforced the cohesion on which US geopolitical preponderance depended ... The Cold War, Truman and his advisors believed, could be won. And so it has been. But it has taken longer than expected and the costs have been high, higher than necessary. US officials exaggerated the importance of the periphery, misconstrued the relationships between the Kremlin and revolutionary nationalist leaders, and overestimated the gains that the Kremlin could derive from developments in the Third World ... Over time, moreover, these military expenditures and overseas commitments may have eroded America's margin of economic superiority and facilitated the rise of formidable competitors.

Other references to the Truman administration's policies on these matters are: *The Truman Presidency*, edited by Michael J. Lacy, Woodrow Wilson International Center for Scholars and Cambridge University Press, 1989; *The Truman Presidency: The Origins of the Imperial Presidency and the National Security State*, edited with Commentary and Introduction by Athan Theoharis, Earl M. Coleman Enterprises, Inc., Publishers, 1979; Arnold A. Offner, *Another Such Victory: President Truman and the Cold War, 1945–1953*, Stanford University Press, 2002; Michael J. Hogan, *A Cross of Iron: Harry S. Truman and the Origins of the National Security State, 1945–1954*, Cambridge University Press, 1998; Daniel Yergin, *Shattered Peace: The Origins of the Cold War and the National Security State*, Houghton Mifflin Company, 1977.

27. Johnson, *The Sorrows of Empire*, p. 291. For a more detailed discussion of Truman's leadership in this regard, see also: Offner, *Another Such Victory*, p. xii, pp. 456–470.
28. Ibid., p. 281. On this matter, see also: Bello, *Dilemmas of Domination*; Walter Russell Mead, *Mortal Splendor: The American Empire in Transition*, Houghton Mifflin Company, 1987.
29. Joseph S. Nye, Jr., *Bound To Lead: The Changing Nature of American Power*, Basic Books, Inc. 1990.
30. Richard A. Falk, *The Declining World Order: America's Imperial Geopolitics*, Routledge, 2004, p. 25.
31. Ibid., p. 25.
32. David Held, *Global Covenant: The Social Democratic Alternative to the Washington Consensus*, Polity, 2004, p. 74. See also: Russell Mead, *Mortal Splendor*, p. 311. On this matter, as early as 1987, Walter Russell Mead observed that:

Measures taken to promote capital formation—tax cuts, subsidies, and such, do not stimulate expansion of productive capacity in the United States in this brave new world. With excess capacity dogging almost every important productive industry in the country, new investment capital goes into anything other than new manufacturing capacity. Tax shelters, bonds, corporate takeovers within the United States; new factories and mines outside it—this is where the money goes ... There is a way out of this impasse, but like all answers to difficult situations, it is easier to describe than to implement. It can be stated simply: real wages in the Third World must rise. If the world has truly advanced to a condition in which wages seek a universal level, it is in the interests of everyone, and not just the workers, that those wages be high.

See also: Bello, *Dilemmas of Domination*, p. 20. As recently as 2005, Walden Bello commented that:

The formulation of a grand strategy in the United States is greatly influenced by the interplay between the economic and the political drives of an advanced capitalist society and the conflict among classes and interest groups ... The imperial enterprise is inherently fluid, unstable, and volatile. The drives for capitalist expansion, strategic dominance, and ideological enclosure operate with relative autonomy, sometimes in complementary fashion, sometimes in conflict with one another. Thus the imperial undertaking is a negotiated and conflict-ridden process in which various factions of the ruling elite, agencies of the bureaucracy, and contending intellectual forces develop competing strategies to achieve what they all claim to be in the national interest.

33. McCormick, "American Hegemony and European Autonomy, 1989–2003," p. 112.
34. Falk, *The Declining World Order*, p. 25.

35. Stefan Halper and Jonathan Clarke, *America Alone: The Neo-Conservatives and the Global Order*, Cambridge University Press, 2004, p. 230.
36. Rashid Khalidi, *Resurrecting Empire: Western Footprints and America's Perilous Path in the Middle East*, Beacon Press, 2004, p. 25.
37. Kupchan, *The Vulnerability of Empire*, pp. 493–495.
38. Halper and Clarke, *America Alone*, p. 14.
39. Ibid., p. 231.
40. Earl Shorris, "Ignoble Liars: Leo Strauss, George Bush, and the philosophy of mass deception", *Harper's Magazine*, June 2004, pp. 65–71. The Straussians who advise the Bush Administration have been described as a cabal. Given the results of their combined advice on Iraq, among other things, they would be better described as a ship of fools. Paul Wolfowitz and Richard Perle head the list. Here are a few more who have served the government: Leon Kass, director of the President's Council on Bioethics; Francis Fukuyama, member of the bioethics council and author of *The End of History and the Last Man*; Gary Schmitt, executive director of the Project for the New American Century; Alan Keyes, former assistant secretary of state; Douglas Feith, undersecretary of defense for policy; Stephen A. Cambone, undersecretary of defense for intelligence; Abraham Shulsky, Defense Department Office of Special Plans; Irving Kristol and William Kristol, journalists and nonconservative entrepreneurs—the father was an adviser to the Reagan Administration, and the son was Dan Quayle's chief of staff.
41. Mark Zepezauer, *Boomerang! How Our Covert Wars Have Created Enemies Across the Middle East and Brought Terror to America*, Common Courage Press, 2003.
42. Andrew Bacevich, "The Real World War IV," *The Wilson Quarterly*, Winter 2005, p. 43.
43. Mills, *The Power Elite*, p. 267.
44. Ibid., p. 267.
45. Joshua Micah Marshall, "Practice to Deceive: Chaos in the Middle East isn't the Bush-hawks' Nightmare Scenario—it's their Plan," *The Washington Monthly*, April 2003, pp. 28–34; Jim Lobe, "They're Back: Neocons Revive the Committee on the Present Danger, This Time against Terrorism," *Foreign Policy In Focus* (www.fpif.org), July 21, 2004; Halper and Clarke, *America Alone*; Guyatt, *Another American Century*; James Mann, *Rise of the Vulcans: The History of Bush's War Cabinet*, Viking, 2004; Craig R. Eisendrath and Melvin A. Goodman, *Bush League Diplomacy: How The Neo-Conservatives Are Putting The World At Risk*, Prometheus Books, 2004; Rahul Mahajan, *Full Spectrum Dominance: U.S. Power In Iraq and Beyond*, Seven Stories Press, 2003; Burbach and Tarbell, *Imperial Overstretch*; Ivo H. Daalder and James M. Lindsay, *America Unbound: The Bush Revolution In Foreign Policy*, Brookings Institution Press, 2003.
46. Cited in J. M. Jover, 1635, Historia de una polemica y semblanza de una generacion, Madrid 1949, p. 401, n. 26, and also in, Henry Kamen, *Empire: How Spain Became A World Power (1492–1763)*, HarperCollins Publishers, 2003, p. 381.
47. Kamen, *Empire*, p. 509.
48. Ward Churchill, *A Little Matter of Genocide: Holocaust and Denial in the Americas, 1492 to the Present*, City Lights Books, 1997, p. 250.
49. Ibid., p. 250.
50. Ward Churchill, *Struggle For The Land: Native North American Resistance To Genocide, Ecocide And Colonization*, City Lights Books, 2002.
51. Howard Zinn, *A People's History of the United States, 1492-Present*, HarperCollins Publishers, 1999, 2003; Howard Zinn and Anthony Arnove, *Voices of a People's History of the Untied States*, Seven Stories Press, 2004. On the matter of the dynamics of inclusion or exclusion with respect to citizenship rights at the nation-state level, see also: Anthony Marx, *Making Race and Nation: A Comparison of the United States, South Africa, and Brazil*, Cambridge University Press, 1998, p. 5. Marx writes:

Citizenship is a key institutional mechanism for establishing boundaries of inclusion or exclusion in the nation-state. It selectively allocates distinct civil, political, and economic rights, reinforcing a sense of commonality and loyalty among those included. But by specifying to whom citizenship applies, states also define those outside the community of citizens, who then live within the state as objects of domination. Even in formal democracies, some are not included nor have their interests served. Such imposed exclusion inadvertently may serve as a unifying issue, mobilizing the excluded group to seek inclusion in the polity as a central popular aspiration. Gradual expansion of citizenship is then gained through protracted contestation.

With respect to the dynamics of inclusion or exclusion with respect to self-determination and sovereignty at the international level, see: Bello, *Dilemmas of Domination*, p. 6. Bello writes: "Today a crisis of legitimacy pervades the multilateral system and the neo-liberal ideology that underpins it. Instead of promoting prosperity, as the major postwar financial institutions promised, corporate-drive globalization has proven destabilizing. It has increased [poverty and widened inequalities both within and between nations." On the dynamic interplay between national and international disparities, see also: Terrence E. Paupp, *Achieving Inclusionary Governance: Advancing Peace and Development in First and Third World Nations*, Transnational Publishers, Inc., 2000; Thomas Pogge, *World Poverty and Human Rights: Cosmopolitan Responsibilities and Reforms*, Polity, 2002; Walden Bello, *The Future in the Balance: Essays on Globalization and Resistance*, Food First Books, 2001; Alberto Alesina and Edward L Glaeser, *Fighting Poverty in the US and Europe: A World of Difference*, Oxford University Press, 2004.

52. Ward Churchill, *Perversions of Justice: Indigenous Peoples and Anglo-American Law*, City Lights Books, 2003.
53. Noam Chomsky, *World Orders—Old and New*, Columbia University Press, 1994, p. 271.
54. Martin Luther King, Jr., *Where Do We Go From Here: Chaos or Community?*, Bantam Books, 1968, pp. 101–102. On this matter, see also: Paul Joseph, *Cracks In The Empire: State Politics In The Vietnam War*, South End Press, 1981; Michael Parenti, *Against Empire*, City Lights Books, 1995; James Petras and Morris Morley, *Empire or Republic: American Global Power and Domestic Decay*, Routledge, 1995; Robert W. Tucker and David Hendrickson, *The Imperial Temptation: The New World Order and America's Purpose*, Council On Foreign Relations Press, 1992; Joshua S. Goldstein, *The Real Price of War: How You Pay For The War On Terror*, New York University Press, 2004; Seymour Melman, *Our Depleted Society*, Holt, Rinehart and Winston, 1965; Seymour Melman, *The Permanent War Economy: American Capitalism in Decline*, Simon and Schuster, 1974; Seymour Melman, *Profits Without Production*, Alfred A. Knopf, 1983; Victor Perlo, *Super Profits and Crises: Modern US Capitalism*, International Publishers, 1988; Robert Pollin, *Contours of Descent: US Economic Fractures and the Landscape of Global Austerity*, Verso, 2003; Chalmers Johnson, *Blowback: The Costs and Consequences of American Empire*, Metropolitan Books, 2000; Charles A. Kupchan, *The End of the American Era: US Foreign Policy and the Geopolitics of the Twenty-First Century*, Alfred A. Knopf, 2002; *American Power in the 21st Century*, edited by David Held and Mathias Koenig-Archibugi, Polity, 2004; The Brandt Commission, *Common Crisis North/South: Cooperation for World Recovery*, The MIT Press, 1983; Report of the Independent Commission on International Development Issues (Willy Brandt), *North/South: A Program For Survival*, The MIT Press, 1980.
55. *The Torture Papers: The Road to Abu Ghraib*, edited by Karen J. Greenberg and Joshua L. Dratel, 2005; *Torture: A Collection*, edited by Sanford Levinson, Oxford University Press, 2004; Seymour Hersh, *Chain of Command: The Road from 9/11 to Abu Ghraib*, HarperCollins Publishers, 2004; David Rose, *Guantanamo: The War on Human Rights*, The New Press, 2004; *The Abu Ghraib Investigations: The Official Reports of the Independent Panel and Pentagon on the Shocking Prisoner Abuse Scandal in Iraq*, edited by Steven Strasser, Public Affairs, 2004; Michael Ratner and Ellen Ray, *Guantanamo: What the World Should Know*, Chelsea Green Publishing Company, 2004; David Cole, *Enemy Aliens: Double Standards and Constitutional Freedoms in the War on Terrorism*, The New Press, 2003; Mark Danner, *Torture and Truth: America, Abu Ghraib, and the War On Terror*, New York Review Books, 2004; James Bovard, *Terrorism and Tyranny: Trampling Freedom, Justice, And Peace To Rid The World Of Evil*, Palgrave, 2003; Nigel S. Rodley, *The Treatment of Prisoners Under International Law, Second Edition*, Oxford University Press, 2000.
56. William F. Pepper, *An Act of State: The Execution of Martin Luther King*, Verso, 2003, p. 172. See also: Alejandro Reuss, "Ruling the Empire," *Dollars & Sense*, January/February 2003, p. 39; Thomas Frank, "Get Rich Or Get Out: Attempted Robbery with a Loaded Federal Budget," *Harper's Magazine*, June 2003, pp. 33–42.

57. Pollin, *Contours of Descent*, p. 193.

58. On this matter, see: *World Economic Order: Liberal Views*, edited by Ronald Clapham and Hans Kammler, N.P. Engler, Publisher, 1983; *Transnational Enterprises: Their Impact on Third World Societies and Cultures*, edited by Krishna Kumar, Westview Press, 1980; *Globalism Versus Realism: International Relations' Third Debate*, edited by Ray Maghroori and Bennett Ramberg, Westview Press, 1982; *The Challenges of South-South Cooperation*, edited by Breda Pavlic, Raul R. Uranga, Boris Cizelj, and Marjan Svetlicic, Westview Press, 1983; *The Non-Aligned Movement In World Politics*, edited by A. W. Singham, Lawrence Hill & Company, 1977; Charles A. Jones, *The North-South Dialogue: A Brief History*, St. Martin's Press, 1983; Jeffrey A. Hart, *The New International Economic Order: Conflict and Cooperation in North-South Relations, 1974–1977*, St. Martin's Press, 1983; *Latin America and the New International Economic Order*, edited by Ricardo French-Davis and Ernesto Tironi,. St. Martin's Press, 1982; Richard L. Jackson, *The Non-Aligned, The UN, and the Superpowers*, Praeger, 1983; *The New International Economic Order: Confrontation or Cooperation between North and South?*, edited by Karl P. Sauvant and Hajo Hasenpflug, Westview Press, 1977; Andre Gunder Frank, *Crisis: In The World Economy*, Holmes & Meier Publishers, 1980; Andre Gunder Frank, *Crisis: In The Third World*, Holmes & Meier Publishers, 1981.

59. Bello, *Dilemmas of Domination*, p. 8.

60. Thomas Bodenheimer and Roubert Gould, *Rollback: Right-wing Power in US Foreign Policy*, South End Press, 1989. See also: Henry Veltmeyer, James Petras, and Steve Vieux, *Neo-liberalism and Class Conflict in Latin America: A Comparative Perspective on the Political Economy of Structural Adjustment*, St. Martin's Press, Inc., 1977; Jeff McMahan, *Reagan and the World: Imperial Policy in the New Cold War*, Monthly Review Press, 1985; *The Politics of Intervention: The United States in Central America*, edited by Roger Burbach and Patricia Flynn, Monthly Review Press, 1984; James Petras and Morris Morley, *US Hegemony Under Siege: Class Politics and Development in Latin America*, Verso, 1990; James Petras and Fernando Ignacio Leiva with Henry Veltmeyer, *Democracy and Poverty in Chile: The Limits to Electoral Politics*, Westview Press, 1994; *Capital, Power, and Inequality in Latin America*, edited by Sandor Halebsky and Richard L. Harris, Westview Press, 1995; James F. Petras with A. Eugene Havens, Morris Morley, and Peter DeWitt, *Class, State, and Power in the Third World: With Case Studies on Class Conflict in Latin America*, Zed Press, 1981; Thomas Carothers, *In The Name Of Democracy: US Policy Toward Latin America In the Reagan Years*, University of California Press, 1991; *With Friends Like These: The Americas Watch Report on Human Rights & US Policy in Latin America*, edited by Cynthia Brown, Pantheon Books, 1985.

61. Bello, *Dilemmas of Domination*, p. 9.

62. William M. LeoGrande, *Our Own Backyard, The United States in Central America, 1977–1992*, The University of North Carolina Press, 1998, p. 478.

63. Lawrence E. Walsh, *Firewall: The Iran-Contra Conspiracy and Cover-up*, W.W. Norton & Company, 1987.

64. Bello, *Dilemmas of Domination*, p. 9. On this matter, see also: Gabriel Kolko, *Confronting The Third World: United States Foreign Policy, 1945–1980*, Pantheon Books, 1988; Joyce Kolko, *Restructuring The World Economy*, Pantheon Books, 1988.

65. Ibid., p. 9; see also: Duncan Green, *Silent Revolution: The Rise of Market Economies in Latin America*, Latin America Bureau, 1995.

66. Pollin, *Contours of Descent*. On the matter of the "Third Way," see also: Paupp, *Achieving Inclusionary Governance*.

67. Thom Hartman, *Unequal Protection: The Rise of Corporate Dominance and the Theft of Human Rights*, Rodale, 2002; John B. Judis, "Taking Care of Business: George W. Bush's Compassion for Corporations," *The New Republic*, August 16, 1999, pp. 24–29; David Moberg, "The War At Home: The Budget is the Latest Front in the Bush Administration's Global Battle on behalf of Corporations and the Very Rich," *In These Times*, March 17, 2001, pp. 12–14.

68. J.M. Coetzee, *Waiting for the Barbarians*, Penguin Books, 1980, p. 133.

69. Geoffrey Parker, *Success Is Never Final: Empire, War, and Faith in Early Modern Europe*, Basic Books, 2002, p. 6.

70. Jeffrey W. Taliaferro, *Balancing Risks: Great Power Intervention in the Periphery*, Cornell University Press, 2004.

71. Samir Amin, "Confronting the Empire," *Pax Americana: Exposing the American Empire*, edited by John B. Foster and Robert W. McChesney, Monthly Review Press, 2004, pp. 104–111.

72. Ibid., p. 110.

73. Carl Boggs, *Imperial Delusions: American Militarism and Endless War*, Rowman & Littlefield Publishers, 2005, p. 13. See also: *Masters of War: Militarism and Blowback in the Era of American Empire*, edited by Carl Boggs, Routledge, 2003.

74. John B. Foster, "The New Age of Imperialism," *Pax Americana: Exposing the American Empire*, edited by John B. Foster and Robert W. McChesney, Monthly Review Press, 2004, p. 174.

75. Raskin, *Liberalism*, p. 228.

3   WHEN THE "LAW OF THE LAND" BECOMES LAWLESS

1. Sheldon S. Wolin, *Politics and Vision: Continuity and Innovation in Western Political Thought—Expanded Edition*, Princeton University Press, 2004, p. 601.

2. Ibid., p. 591.

3. *Rule of Power or Rule of Law?: An Assessment of US Policies and Actions Regarding Security-Related Treaties*, edited by Nicole Deller, Arjun Makhijani, and John Burroughs, Lawyers' Committee on Nuclear Policy, The Apex Press, 2003, p. 138.

4. Terry Nardin, *Law, Morality, and the Relations of States*, Princeton University Press, 1983, p. 193.

5. John Ferling, *A Leap in the Dark: The Struggle to Create the American Republic*, Oxford University Press, 2003.

6. Robert Higgs, *Against Leviathan: Government Power and a Free Society*, The Independent Institute, 2004, p. 201.

7. Ibid., pp. 213–214.

8. Robert Higgs, *Crisis and Leviathan: Critical Episodes in the Growth of American Government*, Oxford University Press, 1987, p. 260.

9. William Blum, *Rogue State: A Guide to the World's Only Superpower*, Common Courage Press, 2000.

10. Thomas Donnelly, "What Is Within Our Powers?: Preserving American Primacy in the Twenty-First Century," *The Obligation of Empire: United States Grand Strategy for a New Century*, edited by James J. Hentz, The University Press of Kentucky, 2004, p. 87. See also: David J. Rothkopf, *Running the World: The Inside Story of the National Security Council and the Architects of American Power*, Public Affairs, 2005.

11. Michael Byers, "Introduction: The Complexities of Foundational Change," *United States Hegemony and the Foundations of International Law*, edited by Michael Byers and Georg Nolte, Cambridge University Press, 2003, p. 4.

12. David Hendrickson, *Peace Pact: The Lost World of the American Founding*, University Press of Kansas, 2003, pp. 22–23.

13. Ibid., p. 23.

14. Wolin, *Politics and Vision*, p. 591. On this matter, see also: Dale R. Herspring, *The Pentagon and the Presidency: Civil-Military Relations from FDR to George W. Bush*, University Press of Kansas, 2005; Amy B. Zegart, *Flawed by Design: The Evolution of the CIA, JCS, and NSC*, Stanford University Press, 1999; Peter D. Feaver, *Armed Servants: Agency, Oversight, and Civil-Military Relations*, Harvard University Press, 2003; William Bundy, *A Tangled Web: The Making of Foreign Policy in the Nixon Presidency*, Hill and Wang, 1998; Randall Bennett Woods, *Quest for Identity: America Since 1945*, Cambridge University Press, 2005, James Mann, *Rise of the Vulcans: The History of Bush's War Cabinet*, Viking, 2004; Larry Everest, *Oil, Power, and Empire: Iraq and the US Global Agenda*, Common Courage Press, 2004; Rothkopf, *Running the World*.

15. Ibid., p. 591. Wolin insightfully captures the nature of a Superpower when he states:

Superpower might be described in Freudian terms as ego driven by id (basic power drive) with only mild remonstrance from a weak superego (norms or conscience). Superpower flaunts its ego in a cavalier disregard for its allies, renounces treaty obligations when it finds them confining, refuses to enter into international agreements or to join international agencies and tribunals when they impose limitations on its freedom of action (sovereignty), and asserts its right to invade or wage war against any country that it deems dangerous.

On this matter, see also: Harold Hongju Koh, *The National Security Constitution: Sharing Power After the Iran-Contra Affair*, Yale University Press, 1990; Alexander DeConde, *Presidential Machismo: Executive Authority, Military Intervention, and Foreign Relations*, Northeastern University Press, 2000; Stephen Toope, "Powerful but unpersuasive?—The Role of the United States in the Evolution of Customary International Law," *United States Hegemony and the Foundation of International Law*, edited by Michael Byers and Georg Nolte, Cambridge University Press, 2003, pp. 287–316; Nico Krisch, "More Equal Than the Rest?—Hierarchy, Equality, and US Predominance in International Law," *United States Hegemony and the Foundations of International Law*, edited by Michael Byers and Georg Nolte, Cambridge University Press, 2003, pp. 135–175; Brad R. Roth, "Bending the Law, Breaking it, or Developing it?—The United States and the Humanitarian Use of Force in the post-Cold War Era," *United States Hegemony and the Foundations of International Law*, edited by Michael Byers and Georg Nolte, Cambridge University Press, 2003, pp. 232–263; John F. Murphy, *The United States and the Rule of Law in International Affairs*, Cambridge University Press, 2004; Terrence Edward Paupp, "The Nuclear Crucible: The Moral and International Law Implications of Weapons of Mass Destruction," *In Democracy's Shadow: The Secret World of National Security*, edited by Marcus G. Raskin and A. Carl LeVan, Nation Books, 2005, pp. 73–95; William Michael Treanor, "The War Powers Outside The Courts," The *Constitution in Wartime: Beyond Alarmism and Complacency*, edited by Mark Tushnet, Duke University Press, 2005, pp. 143–160.

16. *Rule of Power or Rule of Law?—An Assessment of US Policies and Actions Regarding Security Related Treaties*, edited by Nicole Deller, Arjun Makhijani, and John Burroughs, The Apex Press, 2003, p. xiii; Peter J. Spiro, "Realizing Constitutional and International Norms in the Wake of September 11," *The Constitution in Wartime: Beyond Alarmism and Complacency*, edited by Mark Tushnet, Duke University Press, 2005, pp. 198–215.

17. Wolin, *Politics and Vision*, p. 591. See also: Dominic D. P. Johnson, *Overconfidence and War: The Havoc and Glory of Positive Illusions*, Harvard University Press, 2004; Andrew J. Bacevish, *The New American Militarism: How Americans Are Seduced By War*, Oxford University Press, 2005; Carl Boggs, *Imperial Delusions: American Militarism and Endless War*, Rowman & Littlefield Publishers, Inc., 2005; Gareth Porter, *Perils of Dominance: Imbalance of Power and the Road to War in Vietnam*, University of California Press, 2005.

18. Robert Jay Lifton, *Super Power Syndrome: America's Apocalyptic Confrontation with the World*, Nation Books, 2003, p. 187.

19. Ibid., p. 188. For an even broader discussion of this phenomenon, see also: Wilhelm Reich, *The Mass Psychology of Fascism*, Pocket Books, 1976; Geoffrey Hodgson, *The World Turned Right Side Up: A History of the Conservative Ascendancy in America*, Houghton Mifflin Company, 1966; Bob Altermeyer, *The Authoritarian Specter*, Harvard University Press, 1996; John Pilger, "Iraq: The Unthinkable Becomes Normal," *The New Statesman*, Monday 15 November 2004 Edition; *Towards A Critical Theory of Society—Herbert Marcuse—Collected Papers of Herbert Marcuse, Volume Two*, edited by Douglas Kellner, Routledge, 2001.

20. Ibid., p. 188. See also: Bundy, *A Tangled Web*; Milan Vesely, "Debunking the Domino Theory," *The Middle East*, May 2003, pp. 10–11.

21. Ibid., p. 188. In the complete context of his analysis, Lifton writes:

The symptoms are of a piece, each consistent with the larger syndrome: unilateralism in all-important decisions, including those relating to war-making; the use of high-technology to secure the ownership of death and history; a sense of entitlement concerning the right to identify and destroy all those considered to be terrorists or friends of terrorists, while spreading "freedom" and virtues seen as preeminently ours throughout the world; the right to decide who may possess weapons of mass destruction and who may not, and to take military action, using nuclear weapons if necessary, against any nation that has them or is thought to be manufacturing them; and underlying these symptoms, a righteous vision of ridding the world of evil and purifying it spiritually and politically.

For a more detailed discussion of these matters, see also: Craig R. Eisendrath and Melvin A. Goodman, *Bush League Diplomacy: How The Neoconservatives Are Putting The World At Risk*, Prometheus Books, 2004; John Micklethwait and Adrian Wooldridge, *The Right Nation: Conservative Power In America*, The Penguin Press, 2004; Stefan Halper and Jonathan Clarke , *America Alone: The Neo-Conservatives And The Global Order*, Cambridge University Press, 2004, *Unilateralism and US Foreign Policy: International Perspectives*, edited by David M. Malone and Yuen Foong Khoong, Lynne Rienner Publishers, 2003; T. D. Allman, *Rogue State: America At War With The World*, Nation Books, 2004, pp. 375–376.

22. Hendrickson, *Peace Pact*, pp. 260 and 274.
23. Wolin, *Politics and Vision*, p. 595.
24. Terrence E. Paupp, *Achieving Inclusionary Governance: Advancing Peace and Development in First and Third World Nations*, Transnational Publishers, Inc., 2000.
25. Brian Loveman, *For La Patria: Politics and the Armed Forces in Latin America*, A Scholarly Resources Inc. Imprint, 1999. Loveman notes: "Defending la patria (the nation, or fatherland) against internal and external threats is the historical mission claimed by Latin American armed forces" (p. xi). Also,

    Latin American constitutions almost always define a broad obligation and authority for the military: external defense, internal security, upholding the laws, and protecting the constitution and national institutions ... Typically ... the armed forces have constitutional status much like the congress, presidency, and judicial branch. This constitutional mission reinforces the armed forces' perceived historical role and legitimizes actions taken to protect, defend, and conserve la patria (p. 232).

    While the US Constitution makes the president the "commander-in-chief" of the armed forces, the presidency of George W. Bush has taken the entire nation in a militarist direction. In this respect, the US has been placed into a "state of siege" set of conditions that can be likened to the "state of emergency" situations in Latin America where constitutional protections are withdrawn to ostensibly protect the nation. In this respect, Loveman notes: "Regimes of exception are the result, in constitution-making, of a priori philosophical, moral, and political decisions that, at times, 'human rights' must be subordinated to 'protecting la patria." (p. 233). In short, the juridical model of a "state of siege" results in a situation where "military intelligence agencies seek the whereabouts of the enemy; interrogating prisoners is one way to locate and destroy enemy resources and combatants. The distinction between interrogation, abuse, and torture may become blurred." (p. 233). Hence, the analogy can be made to the prisoner abuse scandal at Abu Ghraib.

26. See: Michael Tonry, *Malign Neglect—Race, Crime, and Punishment in America*, Oxford University Press, 1995; Ted Gest, *Crime & Politics: Big Government's Erratic Campaign for Law and Order*, Oxford University Press, 2001; Franklin E. Zimring, Gordon Hawkins, and Sam Kamin, *Punishment and Democracy: Three Strikes and You're Out in California*, Oxford University Press, 2001; William J. Chambliss, *Power, Politics, and Crime*, Westview Press, 1999; Joel Dyer, *The Perpetual Prisoner Machine: How America Profits from Crime*, Westview Press, 2000.
27. John Dinges, *The Condor Years: How Pinochet and His Allies Brought Terrorism to Three Continents*, The New Press, 2004; Peter Kornbluh, *The Pinochet File: A Declassified Dossier on Atrocity and Accountability*, The New Press, 2003; Robert Johansen, *The National Interest and the Human Interest: An Analysis of US Foreign Policy*, Princeton University Press, 1980, pp. 196–281.
28. Ivo H. Daalder and James M. Lindsay, *America Unbound: The Bush Revolution in Foreign Policy*, Brookings Institution Press, 2003; Andrew J. Bacevich, *American Empire: The Realities and Consequences of US Diplomacy*, Harvard University Press, 2002; Francis A. Boyle, *Destroying World Order: US Imperialism in the Middle East Before and After September 11*, Clarity Press, Inc., 2004; Everest, *Oil, Power And Empire*; William D. Hartung, *How Much Are You Making On the War, Daddy?—A Quick and Dirty Guide to War Profiteering in the Bush Administration*, Nation Books, 2003.
29. Terrence E. Paupp, "Between the Arrows and the Olive Branch: The Tortured Path of the War Powers Resolution in the Reagan Years," *The Journal of Contemporary Legal Issues*, Vol. 1, No. 1, The University of San Diego School of Law, 1987.

30. Richard J. Barnet, *The Rockets' Red Glare: When America Goes To War—The Presidents and the People*, Simon and Schuster, 1990; John Hart Ely, *War and Responsibility: Constitutional Lessons of Vietnam and its Aftermath*, Princeton University Press, 1993; Fred Anderson and Andrew Cayton, *The Dominion of War: Empire and Liberty in North America, 1500–2000*, Viking, 2005; Stephen Graubard, *Command of Office: How War, Secrecy, and Deception Transformed the Presidency from Theodore Roosevelt to George W. Bush*, Basic Books, 2004.

31. Nancy Chang and the Center for Constitutional Rights, *Silencing Political Dissent: How Post September 11 Anti-Terrorism Measures Threaten Our Civil Liberties*, Seven Stories Press, 2002; David Cole and James Dempsey, *Terrorism and the Constitution: Sacrificing Civil Liberties in the Name of National Security*, The New Press, 2002; David Cole, *Enemy Aliens: Double Standards and Constitutional Freedoms in the War on Terrorism*, The New Press, 2003; *The War on Our Freedoms: Civil Liberties in an Age of Terrorism*, edited by Richard Leone and Greg Anrig, Public Affairs, 2003; Nat Hentoff, *The War on the Bill of Rights and the Gathering Resistance*, Seven Stories Press, 2003; Samuel Dash, *The Intruders: Unreasonable Searches and Seizures from King John to John Ashcroft*, Rutgers University Press, 2004; Elaine Cassel, *The War on Civil Liberties: How Bush and Ashcroft Have Dismantled the Bill of Rights*, Lawrence Hill Books, 2004; Amitai Etzioni, *How Patriotic is the Patriot Act?—Freedom Versus Security in the Age of Terrorism*, Routledge, 2004; *Lost Liberties: Ashcroft and the Assault on Personal Freedom*, edited by Cynthia Brown, The New Press, 2003; Charles Tiefer, *Veering Rights: How the Bush Administration Subverts the Law for Conservative Causes*, University of California Press, 2004; James Bovard, *The Bush Betrayal*, Palgrave, 2004; James Bovard, *Terrorism and Tyranny: Trampling Freedom, Justice, and Peace to Rid the World of Evil*, Palgrave, 2003; Raneta Mack and Michael J. Kelly, *Equal Justice in the Balance: America's Legal Responses to the Emerging Terror Threat*, The University of Michigan Press, 2004; Eric Alterman and Mark Green, *The Book on Bush: How George W. (Mis)leads America*, Viking, 2004; Geoffrey R. Stone, *Perilous Times: Free Speech in Wartime—From the Sedition Act of 1798 to the War on Terrorism*, 2004; David Corn, "The Fundamental John Ashcroft," *Mother Jones*, March/April, 2002; Nancy Gibbs, "Believe Him or Not—Does Bush Have A Credibility Gap?," *Time Magazine*, February 16, 2004; Curt Anderson, "Ashcroft Condemns Judges Who Question Bush," *The Associated Press*, November 13, 2004; Jeffrey Rosen, "John Ashcroft's Permanent Campaign," *The Atlantic Monthly*, April 2004, pp. 68–82.

32. Wright Mills, *The Power Elite*, Oxford University Press, 1956, 2000, p.296. See also: Matthew Josephson, *The Robber Barons: The Great American Capitalists, 1861–1901*, Harcourt Brace Jovanoich, 1962; Matthew Josephson, *The Politicos: 1865–1896*, Harcourt, Brace & World, Inc., 1938, 1966; *The President Makers: The Culture of Politics & Leadership in an Age of Enlightenment, 1896–1919*, Matthew Josephson, *A Capricorn Book*, G. P. Putnam's Sons, 1940, 1979.

33. *The Breakdown of Democratic Regimes*, edited by Juan J. Linz and Alfred Stepan, The Johns Hopkins University Press, 1978; *Transitions from Authoritarian Rule: Prospects for Democracy*, edited by Guillermo O'Donnell, Philippe Schmitter, and Laurence Whitehead, The Johns Hopkins University Press, 1986; *The Failure of Presidential Democracy*, edited by Juan J. Linz and Arturo Valenzuela, The Johns Hopkins University Press, 1994; *Constructing Democratic Governance: Latin America and the Caribbean in the 1990s*, edited by Jorge Dominguez and Abraham F. Lowenthal, The Johns Hopkins University Press, 1996; *Decentralization, Democratic Governance, and Civil Society in Comparative Perspective: Africa, Asia, and Latin America*, edited by Philip Oxhorn, Jospeh S. Tulchin, and Andrew D. Selee, The Johns Hopkins University Press, 2004; *Politics in Developing Countries: Comparing Experience With Democracy*, edited by Larry Diamond, Juan J. Linz, and Seymour Martin Lipset, Lynne Rienner Publishers, 1995.

34. Charles Lewis and The Center For Public Integrity, *The Buying of the Congress: How Special Interests Have Stolen Your Right to Life, Liberty, and the Pursuit of Happiness*, Avon Books, Inc., 1998; Donald L. Bartlett and James B. Steele, "Big Money & Politics: Who Gets Hurt," *Time Magazine*, February 7, 2000; John B. Judis, *The Paradox of American Democracy: Elites, Special Interests, and the Betrayal of Public Trust*, Pantheon Books, 2000; Matt Taibbi, "The Secret History of the Most Corrupt Man in Washington," *Rolling Stone*, April 6, 2006, pp. 38–44, pp. 76–77.

35. Adam Yarmolinsky, *The Military Establishment: Its Impact on American Society*, Harper & Row, Publishers, 1971; David Dickson, *The New Politics of Science*, Pantheon Books, 1984.

36. Michael Hart, with Bill Dymond and Colin Robertson, *Decision at Midnight: Inside the Canada-US Free-Trade Negotiations*, UBC Press, 1994.

37. *The Political Economy of North American Free Trade*, edited by Ricardo Grinspun and Maxwell A. Cameron, St. Martin's Press, 1993.

38. Beth Mintz and Michael Schwartz, *The Power Structure of American Business*, The University of Chicago Press, 1985. See also: Jomo K. S., "Imperialism is Alive and Well: Globalization and East Asia after September 11," *Lessons of Empire: Imperial Histories and American Power*, edited by Craig Calhoun et al., The New Press, 2006, pp. 253–268.

39. Thomas Ferguson and Joel Rogers, *The Hidden Election: Politics and Economics in the 1980 Presidential Campaign*, Pantheon Books, 1981; Scott R. Bowman, *The Modern Corporation and American Political Thought: Law, Power, and Ideology*, The Pennsylvania State University Press, 1996; David Vogel, *Kindred Strangers, The Uneasy Relationship Between Politics and Business in America*, Princeton University Press, 1996; David Vogel, *Fluctuating Fortunes: The Political Power of Business in America*, Basic Books, Inc., 1989; Joel Bakan, *The Corporation: The Pathological Pursuit of Profit and Power*, Free Press, 2004; Marjorie Kelly, *The Divine Right of Capital: Dethroning the Corporate Aristocracy*, Berrett-Koehler Publishers, Inc., 2001; William Greider, *One World, Ready or Not: The Manic Logic of Global Capitalism*, Simon & Schuster, 1997; Dan Briody, *The Halliburton Agenda: The Politics of Oil and Money*, John Wiley & Sons, Inc., 2004.

40. William Blum, *Killing Hope: US Military and CIA Interventions Since World War II—The Updated Edition*, Common Courage Press, 2004; Blum, *Rogue State*; Gregory F. Treverton, *Covert Action: The Limits of Intervention in the Postwar World*, Basic Books Inc., 1987; Michael McClintock, *Instruments of Statecraft: US Guerrilla Warfare, Counter-Insurgency, Counter-Terrorism, 1940–1990*, Pantheon Books, 1992; D. Michael Shafer, *Deadly Paradigms: The Failure of US Counterinsurgency Policy*, Princeton University Press, 1988; John Jacob Nutter, *The CIA's Black Ops: Covert Action, Foreign Policy, and Democracy*, Prometheus Books, 2000; L. Fletcher Prouty, *The Secret Team: The CIA and its Allies in Control of the World*, Ballantine Books, 1973; Jonathan Marshall, Peter Dale Scott, and Jane Hunter, *The Iran Contra Connection: Secret Teams and Covert Operations in the Reagan Era*, South End Press, 1987.

41. Peter Dale Scott, *Drugs, Oil, and War: The United States in Afghanistan, Columbia, and Indochina*, Rowman & Littlefield Publishers, Inc., 2003; Paupp, "Between the Arrows and the Olive Branch: The Tortured Path of the War Powers Resolution in the Reagan Years (1981–1987);" Michael T. Klare and Peter Kornbluh, *Low Intensity Warfare: Counterinsurgency, Proinsurgency, and Antiterrorism in the Eighties*, Pantheon Books, 1988; Ted Galen Carpenter, *Bad Neighbor Policy: Washington's Futile War on Drugs in Latin America*, Palgrave, 2003; Alfred W. McCloy, *The Politics of Heroin: CIA Complicity in the Global Drug Trade—Afghanistan, Southeast Asia, Central America, Columbia*, (Revised Edition), Lawrence Hill Books, 2003; Dan Russell, *Drug War: Covert Money, Power & Policy*, Kalyx,com., 2000; *Transnational Crime in the Americas: An Inter-American Dialogue Book*, edited by Tom Farer, Routledge, 1999; David Jordan, *Drug Politics: Dirty Money and Democracies*, University of Oklahoma Press, 1999; Alexander Cockburn and Jeffrey St. Clair, *White Out: The CIA, Drugs, and the Press*, Verso, 1998; Peter Dale Scott and Jonathan Marshall, *Cocaine Politics: Drugs, Armies, and the CIA in Central America*, University of California Press, 1991; Gary Webb, *Dark Alliance: The CIA, the Contras, and Crack Cocaine Explosion*, Seven Stories Press, 1998; R. T. Naylor, *Wages of Crime: Black Markets, Illegal Finance, and the Underworld Economy*, Cornell University Press, 2002.

42. Nafeez Mosaddeq Ahmed, *Behind The War on Terror: Western Secret Strategy and the Struggle for Iraq*, New Society Publishers, 2003; Tariq Ali, *Bush in Babylon: The Recolonisationn of Iraq*, Verso, 2003; Stephen Pelletiere, *America's Oil Wars*, Praeger, 2004; Stephen Pelletiere, *Iraq and the International Oil System: Why America Went to War in the Gulf*, Maisonneuve Press, 2004; Michael T. Klare, *Blood and Oil: The Dangers and Consequences of America's Growing Dependency on Imported Petroleum*, Metropolitan Books, 2004; Michael T. Klare, "Beyond the

Rogues' Gallery: What's A Superpower To Do?—Some Credible Threat Has To Justify Military Spending," *The Nation*, May 26, 1997, pp. 22–26; Michael Klare, *Rogue States and Nuclear Outlaws: America's Search for a New Foreign Policy*, Hill and Wang, 1995; Michael T. Klare, *With Without End: American Planning For The Next Vietnams*, Vintage Books, 1972.

43. Chalmers Johnson, *Blowback: The Costs and Consequences of American Empire*, Metropolitan Books, 2000.

44. Sheldon Wolin, "Inverted Totalitarianism—How the Bush Regime Is Effecting the Transition to a Fascist-Like State," *The Nation*, May 19, 2003, pp. 13–15. See also: Jayan Nayar, "Taking Empire Seriously: Empire's Law, People's Law and the World Tribunal on Iraq," *Empire's Law: The Imperial Project and the 'War to Remake the World*,' edited by Amy Bartholomew, Pluto Press, 2006, pp. 313–339.

45. Aaron L. Friedberg, *In the Shadow of the Garrison State: America's Anti-Statism and Its Cold War Grand Strategy*, Princeton University Press, 2000, p. 65.

46. Wolin, "Inverted Totalitarianism," p. 13.

47. Ibid.

48. Ibid., p. 14.

49. *The Other Davos: The Globalization of Resistance to the World Economic System*, edited by Francois Houtart and Francois Polet, Zed Books, 2001; Maude Barlow and Tony Clarke, *Global Showdown: How the New Activists Are Fighting Global Corporate Rule*, Stoddart, 2001; Alan Tonelson, *The Race To The Bottom: Why a Worldwide Worker Surplus and Uncontrolled Free Trade Are Sinking Living Standards*, Westview, 2002; Claude E. Barfield, *Free Trade, Sovereignty, Democracy: The Future of the World Trade Organization*, The AEI Press, 2001; Walden Bello, *Dilemmas of Domination: The Unmaking of the American Empire*, Metropolitan Books, 2005, pp. 155–178.

50. Bello, *Dilemmas of Domination*, p. 76.

51. Richard Falk, *The Declining World Order: America's Imperial Geopolitics*, Routledge, 2004, p. 166. Commenting on the aftermath of the September 11, 2001 attacks, Falk notes:

The attacks give rise to a strengthened marriage of economic and state power—taking the unprecedented form of a non-territorial, counter-terrorist crusade, that wields its interventionary authority throughout the world and seeks to perpetuate and extend this role to global security through the exercise of monopoly control over the militarization of space and oceans. Only the great world's religions have the credibility, legitimacy, and depth of understanding to identify and reject the idolatry that seems to lie at the core of this American project of planetary domination.

52. Bello, *Dilemmas of Domination*, p. 217. With promise of a different future, of the power of the inclusive principles of Global Community supplanting the claims of Global Empire, Bello notes:

the crisis of the empire bodes well not only for the rest of the world. It may also benefit the people of the United States. It opens up the possibility of Americans relating to other peoples as equals and not as masters. Failure of the empire is, moreover, a precondition for the reemergence of a democratic republic. That was the American promise before it was hijacked by imperial democracy.

See also: *Globalize Liberation: How to uproot the system and build a better world*, edited by David Solnit, City Lights Books, 2004; Susan George, *Another World Is Possible If …*, Verso, 2004; *Another World is Possible: Popular Alternatives to Globalization at the World Social Forum*, edited by William F. Fisher and Thomas Ponnian, Zed Books, 2003.

53. Marcus G. Raskin, *Liberalism: The Genius of American Ideals*, Rowman & Littlefield Publishers, Inc., 2004, p. 74.

54. Sheldon Wolin, "Inverted Totalitarianism," pp. 14–15.

55. Lou Dobbs, *Exporting America: Why Corporate Greed is Shipping American Jobs Overseas*, Warner Books, 2004; William Bonner and Addison Wiggin, *Empire of Debt: The Rise of an Epic Financial Crisis*, John Wiley & Sons, Inc., 2006.

56. Robert P. Abele, *A User's Guide to the USA Patriot Act and Beyond*, University Press of America, Inc., 2005.

57. Michael J. Klarman, *From Jim Crow to Civil Rights: The Supreme Court and the Struggle for Racial Equality*, Oxford University Press, 2004.

58. Walter Williams, *Reaganism and the Death of Representative Democracy*, Georgetown University Press, 2003.

59. *Disaffected Democracies: What's Troubling The Trilateral Countries?*, edited by Susan J. Pharr and Robert D. Putnam, Princeton University Press, 2000.

60. *Why People Don't Trust Government*, edited by Joseph S. Nye, Philip D. Zelikow, and David King, Harvard University Press, 1997.

61. G. William Domhoff, *Who Rules America?—Power and Politics in the Year 2000, Third Edition*, Mayfield Publishing Company, 1998.

62. Jeffrey Isaac, *Democracy in Dark Times*, Cornell University Press, 1998, p. 196.

63. Jeff Gates, *Democracy at Risk: Rescuing Main Street from Wall Street—A Populist Vision for the Twenty-First Century*, Perseus Publishing, 2000, p. 180.

64. Murphy, *The United States and the Rule of Law in International Affairs*, p. 8.

65. Ibid., p. 355.

66. On this matter, see: Anthony W. Marx, *Lessons of Struggle: South African Internal Opposition, 1960–1990*, Oxford University Press, 1992; Patti Waldmeir, *Anatomy of a Miracle: The End of Apartheid and the Birth of the New South Africa*, W.W. Norton & Company, 1997; Timothy D. Sisk, *Democratization in South Africa: The Elusive Social Contract*, Princeton University Press, 1995; Robert I. Rotberg, *Ending Autocracy, Enabling Democracy: The Tribulations of Southern Africa, 1960–2000*, Brookings Institution Press and the World Peace Foundation, 2002; David Ottaway, *Chained Together: Mandela, De Klerk, and the Struggle to Remake South Africa*, Times Books, 1993.

67. William Greider, *Who Will Tell The People: The Betrayal of American Democracy*, Simon & Schuster, 1992; William Greider: *The Soul of Capitalism: Opening Paths to a Moral Economy*, Simon & Schuster, 2003; Greider, *One World, Ready or Not*.

68. Edward Luttwak, *Turbo-Capitalism: Winners and Losers in the Global Economy*, HarperCollins Publishers, 1999, p. 236.

69. Alan Crawford, *Thunder on the Right: The 'New Right' and the Politics of Resentment*, Pantheon Books, 1980; Russ Bellant, *Old Nazis, the New Right, and the Republican Party*, South End Press, 1991; *Eyes Right!—Challenging the Right Wing Backlash*, edited by Chip Berlet, South End Press, 1995; Harvey Cox, "The Warring Visions of the Religious Right," *The Atlantic Monthly*, November 1995, pp. 59–69; Michael Parenti, *America Besieged*, City Lights Books, 1998; Frances Fox Piven, *The War At Home: The Domestic Costs of Bush's Militarism*, The New Press, 2004.

70. Michael Parenti, *Blackshirts & Reds: Rational Fascism and the Overthrow of Communism*, City Lights Books, 1997, pp. 1–22; Carl Boggs, *The End of Politics: Corporate Power and the Decline of the Public Sphere*, The Guilford Press, 2000, pp. 161–165; Michael Parenti, *Dirty Truths: Reflections on Politics, Media, Ideology, Conspiracy, Ethnic Life and Class Power*, City Lights Books, 1996, pp. 32–43; Bertram Gross, *Friendly Fascism: The New Face of Power in America*, South End Press, 1980; Michael Mann, *Fascists*, Cambridge University Press, 2004; Robert O. Paxton, *The Anatomy of Fascism*, Alfred A. Knopf, 2004.

71. Robert F. Kennedy, Jr., *Crimes Against Nature: How George W. Bush and His Corporate Pals Are Plundering the Country and Hijacking Our Democracy*, HarperCollins Publishers, 2004, pp. 193–194.

72. Ibid., p. 195. See also: Evaggelos Valliantos, *This Land is Their Land: How Corporate Farms Threaten the World*, Common Courage Press, 2006; Patrick Hossay, *Unsustainable: A Primer for Global Environmental and Social Justice*, Zed Books, 2006; Mike Davis, *Planet of Slums*, Verso, 2006; *The Quest for Environmental Justice: Human Rights and the Politics of Pollution*, edited by Robert D. Bullard, Sierra Club Books, 2005; *Unequal Protection: Environmental Justice and Communities of Color*, edited by Robert D. Bullard, Sierra Club Books, 1994; Kristin Shrader-Frechette, *Environmental Justice: Creating Equality, Reclaiming Democracy*, Oxford University Press, 2002.

73. Michael T. Klare, *Resource Wars: The New Landscape of Global Conflict*, Metropolitan Books, 2001, p. 3. On this issue of US security concerns with respect to the control of resources, Klare notes:

The strategic nature of American interest in the Caspian region was first articulated by the Department of State in an April 1997 report to Congress. As a major consumer of oil, the report indicated, the United States has a direct interest in "enhancing and diversifying" world energy supplies. Such diversification is important not only in economic terms—to provide an additional source of energy for American industries and transportation systems—but also as a security measure, to build a hedge against supply disruptions elsewhere. Accordingly, it has become US policy "to promote rapid development of Caspian energy resources' in order to 'reinforce Western energy security."

See also: V. G. Kiernan, *America: The New Imperialism—From White Settlement to World Hegemony*, Verso, 2005.

74. Ibid., p. 6. On the matter of US determination to secure US access to overseas supplies of critical resources, Klare notes:

As the American economy grows and US industries come to rely more on imported supplies of critical materials, the protection of global resources flows is becoming an increasingly prominent feature of American security policy. This is evident not only in the geographic dimensions of strategy—the growing emphasis on military operations in the Persian Gulf, the Caspian, and other energy-producing areas—but also in its operational aspects. Whereas weapons technology and alliance politics once dominated the discourse on military affairs, American strategy now focuses on oil-field protection, the defense of maritime trade routes, and other aspects of resource security.

75. Ibid., p. 9. On this matter, see also: Dana Priest, *The Mission: Waging War and Keeping Peace with America's Military*, W.W. Norton & Company, 2003, p. 73. Priest notes: "Like the European colonialists who divided up Asia and Africa, the Defense Department draws and redraws the CinCdoms every two years as part of its biannual review of the unified Command Plan. The chairman of the Joint Chiefs of Staff recommends to the president and the defense secretary changes guided by the size and geopolitical importance of individual countries." On this matter, see also: Michael T. Klare, *War Without End: American Planning For the Next Vietnams*, Vintage Books, 1972, p. 320. Klare notes:

Evidently the military planners in the Pentagon realize the necessity for a continued US presence, for despite promises of US troop withdrawals from Asia following the cessation of hostilities in Vietnam, the Defense Department has made it quite clear that it will maintain a military establishment in the area for an indefinite period. Thus, in its annual budget report to Congress, the Pentagon states in 1969 that it "will be necessary for the United States to continue some form of military presence in the region for some time," and that this "presence" will require "appropriate basing arrangements."

76. Jayan Nayar, "Taking Empire Seriously: Empire's Law, People's Law and the World Tribunal on Iraq," p. 314. See also: Alex Callinicos, *The New Mandarins of American Power: The Bush Administration's Plans for the World*, Polity, 2003, chapter 3; Paul Rogers, *A War On Terror: Afghanistan and After*, Pluto Press, 2004, pp. 81–84; Christian Reus-Smit, *American Power and World Order*, Polity, 2004; Amartya Sen, *Identity and Violence: The Illusion of Destiny*, W.W. Norton & Company, 2006; Robert Higgs, *Resurgence of the Warfare State. The Crisis Since 9/11*, The Independent Institute, 2005; Charles S. Maier, *Among Empires: American Ascendancy and Its Predecessors*, Harvard University Press, 2006; Philippe Sands, *Lawless World: America and the Making and Breaking of Global Rules from FDR's Atlantic Charter to George W. Bush's Illegal War*, Viking, 2005; Morris Berman, *Dark Ages America: The Final Phase of Empire*, W.W. Norton & Company, 2006.

77. J. M. (Mac) Destler, "The United States and a Free Trade Area of the Americas: A Political-Economic Analysis," *Integrating The Americas: FTAA and Beyond*, edited by Antoni Estevadeoral, Dani Rodrik, Alan Taylor, Andres Velasco, Harvard University Press, 2004, p. 413. On this matter, see also: Walden Bello, *Dark Victory: The United States and Global Poverty—New Edition*, Food First Books, 1999; *Free Trade and Economic Restructuring in Latin America—A NACLA Reader*, edited by Fred Rosen and Deidre McFayden, Monthly Review Press, 1995; Robin Paul Malloy, *Law and Market Economy: Reinterpreting the Values of Law and Economics*, Cambridge University Press, 2000; Charles E. Lindbloom, *The Market System: What it is, How it Works, and What to Make of it*, Yale University Press, 2001; David Vogel, *Trading*

Up: Consumer and Environmental Regulation in a Global Economy, Harvard University Press, 1995; Erich A. Schultz, *Markets and Power: The 21ˢᵗ Century Command Economy*, M.E. Sharpe, 2001; George Tsogas, *Labor Regulation in a Global Economy*, M.E. Sharpe, 2001.

78. Mark Barenberg and Peter Evans, "The FTAA's Impact on Democratic Governance," *Integrating the Americas: FTAA and Beyond*, edited by Antioni Estevadeoral et al., Harvard University Press, 2004, p.780. See also: *Governance for Sustainable Development: A Foundation for the Future*, edited by Georgina Ayre and Rosalie Callway, Earthscan, 2005; Marie-Claire Cordonier Segger and Ashfaq Khalfan, *Sustainable Development Law: Principles, Practices, and Prospects*, Oxford University Press, 2004; Guillermo de la Dehesa, *Winners and Losers in Globalization*, Blackwell Publishing, 2006; James Petras and Henry Veltmeyer, *Empire With Imperialism: The Globalizing Dynamics of Neo-liberal Capitalism*, Zed Books, 2005; George F. DeMartino, *Global Economy, Global Justice: Theoretical Objections and Policy Alternatives to Neo-liberalism*, Routledge, 2000.

79. Tom Barry, *Zapata's Revenge: Free Trade and the Farm Crisis in Mexico*, South End Press, 1995, p. 55. A similar crisis emerged in Chile after the adoption of neoliberal policies. On this matter, see also: *Victims of the Chilean Miracle: Workers and Neo-liberalism in the Pinochet Era, 1973–2002*, Duke University Press, 2004.

80. Ibid., p. 55.

81. Ibid., p. 117. The sacrifice of other rights came in the following forms:

the granting to ejidatarios of the rights to sell, rent sharecrop, or mortgage their individual parcels and to enter into joint ventures and contracts with private (including foreign) investors and stockholding companies; the collective right of ejidatarios to dissolve the ejido and distribute the property among members; and the elimination of the requirement that ejidatarios had to work their land to retain control. [Note: "ejido" is a category of land tenure that grants use-rights to agrarian reform communities in which there are usually individual parcels and common lands].

82. Ibid., p. 127.

83. Ibid., p. 128.

84. Paupp, *Achieving Inclusionary Governance*.

85. As quoted in: Peter H. Smith, *Talons of the Eagle: Dynamics of US-Latin American Relations, Second Edition*, Oxford University Press, 2000, p. 283. On this matter, see also: Holly Sklar, "Trilateralism: Managing Dependence and Democracy—An Overview," *Trilateralism: The Trilateral Commission and Elite Planning for World Management*, South End Press, edited by Holly Sklar, 1980, p. 52. Sklar notes:

The Western capitalist prescription for development is a model which always leaves intact the dynamic of exploitation and the machinery of repression—regardless of what concessions or reforms may be instituted. It is a model which sees human labor as one more resource to be exploited (as cheaply as possible). It is a model which ties people to a treadmill of conspicuous consumption, warping the promise of human potential. It is a model which is built upon competition and advocates cooperation only in the self-interest of the most powerful. It is a model of development which buys stability for business at the price of shattered and stunted lives; offering people a t-shirt, a pair of sneakers, plastic dishes, maybe a radio or a watch, in place of freedom.

86. Callinicos, *The New Mandarins of American Power*, p. 94. Callinicos notes:

The Cheney report highlighted the growing dependence of the US on imported oil. Fifty two percent of America's net oil needs were met by imports in 1999. US oil consumption is expected to rise by 33 percent by 2020, when declining domestic output would cover less than 30 percent of the country's oil consumption. These trends would place the US in what the Cheney team called "a condition of increased dependency on foreign powers that do no always have America's interests at heart." Accordingly, "energy security must be a priority of US trade and foreign policy." The report recommended diversifying US sources of supply: Canada, Saudi Arabia, Venezuela and Mexico produced nearly 55 percent of US oil imports in 2000.

See also: Chesa Boudin, Gabriel Gonzalez, and Wilmer Rumbos, *The Venezuelan Revolution: 100 Questions—100 Answers*, Thunder's Mouth Press, 2006.

87. Klare, *Blood and Oil*, p. 115.

88. Ibid., p. 115.

89. Ibid., p. 121. See also: Jeff Goodell, "The Fake Solution: For all the president's talk about our addiction to foreign oil, his much-hyped energy initiative does nothing to address, the real causes of the looming crisis," *Rolling Stone*, February 23, 2006. p. 37.

90. Krisch, "More Equal Than the Rest?—Hierarchy, Equality, and US Predominance in International Law," p. 149. On this point, other scholars have noted:

> Empire under capitalism is inherently unstable, forever devoid of a genuine world state and pointing to greater and potentially more dangerous wars. Its long-term evolution is towards barbarism—armed with ever more fearsome weapons of mass destruction. What hope remains under these dire circumstances lies in the building of a new world peace movement that recognizes what ultimately must be overcome is not a particular instance of imperialism and war, but an entire world economic system that feeds on militarism and imperialism. The goal of peace must be seen as involving the creation of a world of substantive equality in which global exploitation and the geopolitics of empire are no longer the principal objects (John Bellamy Foster, "The New Geopolitics of Empire," *Monthly Review*, January 2006, p. 16).

See also: Ivan Eland, *The Empire Has No Clothes: US Foreign Policy Exposed*, The Independent Institute, 2004; Jack L. Goldsmith and Eric A. Posner, *The Limits of International Law*, Oxford University Press, 2005; Claes G. Ryn, *America the Virtuous: The Crisis of Democracy and the Quest for Empire*, Transaction Publishers, 2004.

91. Kirsch, "More Equal Than the Rest? Hierarchy, Equality and US Predominance in International Law," p. 147. See also: Thomas Pogge, *World Poverty and Human Rights: Cosmopolitan Responsibilities and Reforms*, Polity, 2002.

92. Ibid., p. 153. See also: *Changing Paths: International Development and the New Politics of Inclusion*, edited by Peter Houtzager and Mick Moore, University of Michigan Press, 2003.

93. Ibid., p. 153. See also: Julie A. Merus, *Bait and Switch: Human Rights and US Foreign Policy*, Routledge, 2004; *People Out of Place: Globalization, Human Rights, and the Citizenship Gap*, edited by Alison Bryusk and Gershon Shafir, Routledge, 2004; David Macarov, *What The Market Does to People: Privatization, Globalization and Poverty*, Clarity Press, Inc., 2003; Jay R, Mandle, *Globalization and the Poor*, Cambridge University Press, 2003; *Pox Americana: Exposing the American Empire*, edited by John Bellamy Foster and Robert W. McChesney, Monthly Review Press, 2004; Amy L. Chua, "The Paradox of Free Market Democracy: Rethinking Development Policy," *Harvard International Law Journal*, Vol. 41, No. 2, Spring 2000, pp. 287–379; Jeffrey D. Sachs, *The End of Poverty: Economic Possibilities for our Time*, The Penguin Press, 2005; Jeffrey D. Sachs, "The Development Challenge," *Foreign Affairs*, March/April, 2005, pp. 78–90; Waldon Bello, "The Meaning of Cancun," *Yes!—A Journal of Positive Futures*, Winter 2004, pp. 46–48; Gene Sperling and Tom Hart, "A Better Way to Fight Global Poverty: Broadening the Millennium Account," *Foreign Affairs*, March/April, 2003, pp. 9–14; Kevin Watkins, "Countdown to Cancun," *Prospect*, August 2003, pp. 28–33; James E. Mahon, Jr., "Good-Bye to the Washington Consensus?," *Current History*, February 2003, pp. 58–64.

94. Department of State, Policy Planning Study (PPS)- 23 Foreign Relations of the United States (FRUS), 1948, vol. I, (part 2), February 24, 1948, p. 23. On this matter, see also: Bruce Kuklick, *Blind Oracles: Intellectuals and War from Kennan to Kissinger*, Princeton University Press, 2006; Glenn Palmer and T. Clifton Morgan, *A Theory of Foreign Policy*, Princeton University Press, 2006; David A. Welch, *Painful Choices: A Theory of Foreign Policy Change*, Princeton University Press, 2005.

95. William I. Robinson, *Promoting Polyarchy: Globalization, US Intervention, and Hegemony*, Cambridge University Press, 1996, p. 1. Maintaining high levels of privilege and power, befitting a Superpower, the rationale for opposing nationalist movements and special concern over the future of Southeast Asia after World War II, laid the groundwork for US strategic planning. Nowhere was this more evident than in Washington's buildup to American intervention in Vietnam (beginning with full commitment and intensity in 1964). In reviewing this history, see also: Jonathan Marshall, *To Have and Have Not: Southeast Asian Raw Materials and the Origins of*

the Pacific War, University of California Press, 1995, p. 186. Marshall notes: Even as World War II brought the United States into a new position of preeminence in the region, it unleashed forces of revolutionary change, triggering responses from Washington toward communism and nationalism reminiscent of the Roosevelt administration's response to Imperial Japan. In May 1947, for example, Secretary of State George Marshall warned of the "danger that nationalist movements" could upset an area "of greatest economic importance," thus giving the United States "special concern" for the future of Southeast Asia. In July 1949, the National Security Council concluded that in pursuing control of Southeast Asia "the Kremlin is, of course, motivated in part by a desire to acquire SEA's resources and communications lines, but its immediate and perhaps even greater desire is to deny them to us." The State Department warned in 1951 that "the fall of Indochina to communism would also pave the way for aggression against Indochina's neighbors," who supplied "80 percent of the free world's supply of natural rubber and half of its tin." The loss of these resources would be serious to the free world and would enormously increase the military capabilities of the Communist bloc.

96. Paupp, *Achieving Inclusionary Governance*. The drive of the US for hegemony, regardless of the human cost, represents a drive that is diametrically opposed to the United Nations Millennium Project to end poverty by 2025. On this matter, see: Sachs, *The End of Poverty*. Regarding the costs of attempting to maintain Global Empire and hegemony, the primary mechanism through which this will be accomplished is the National Security State. On this matter, see: Raskin, *Liberalism*, p. 217. Raskin notes:

World capitalism presents itself as a hegemonic system, and since the defeat of state socialism in large part at its own hand, there is no organized, comprehensive challenge to it. In the twenty-first century the challenge must come from the weakness of this hegemony and its incapacity to solve problems of war, the environment, hunger, and disease. Its method to ameliorate these conditions through the national security state (continuous small wars) and the control of local economies (the work of uncontrolled and unaccountable international corporations), merely adds to the human tragedy, the evisceration of other cultures that are now to become appendages of the aggressive international military and corporate system.

For a more extended discussion of this process, see: Paupp, "The Nuclear Crucible: The Moral and International Law Implications of Weapons of Mass Destruction," pp. 73–95. Related studies on these issues include: *The Politics of Empire: Globalization in Crisis*, edited by Alan Freeman and Boris Kagarlitsky, Pluto Press, 2004; James Petras and Henry Veltmeyer, *System in Crisis: The Dynamics of Free Market Capitalism*, Zed Books, 2003; Michael Chossudovsky, *War and Globalization: The Truth Behind September 11*, Global Outlook, 2002; *Implicating Empire: Globalization and Resistance in the 21st Century World Order*, edited by Stanley Aronowitz and Heather Gautney, Basic Books, 2003.

97. David Harvey, *The New Imperialism*, Oxford University Press, 2003, p. 74. See also: Ulrich Beck, *Power in the Global Age: A New Global Political Economy*, Polity, 2005, Frances Fukuyama, *America at the Crossroads: Democracy, Power, and the Neo-Conservative Legacy*, Yale University Press, 2006; Saul Landau, *The Pre-Emptive Empire: A Guide to Bush's Kingdom*, Pluto Press, 2003.

98. Jack Manno, *Arming The Heavens: The Hidden Military Agenda for Space, 1945–1995*, Dodd, Mead & Company, 1984, p. 7. On this matter, see also: Christopher Simpson, *Blowback: America's Recruitment of Nazis and Its Effects on the Cold War*, Weidenfeld & Nicolson, 1988; Christopher Simpson, *The Splendid Blond Beast: Money, Law, and Genocide in the Twentieth Century*, Grove Press, 1993; Bob Ward, *Dr. Space: The Life of Wernher von Braun*, Naval Institute Press, 2005.

99. Ibid., p. 157. For an in-depth look at the relationship between Edward Teller and the Reagan administration on the issue of star wars, see: Frances Fitzgerald, *Way Out There In The Blue: Reagan, Star Wars, and the End of the Cold War*, Simon & Schuster, 2000, pp. 121, 127–129, 131–137, 140–141, 194, 196, 199, 200, 202, 206, 208, 210–211, 278, 376, 380; Sanford Lakoff and Herbert F. York, *A Shield in Space?—Technology, Politics, and the Strategic Defense Initiative (How the Reagan Administration Set Out to, Make Nuclear Weapons 'Impotent and Obsolete' and Succumbed to the Fallacy of the Last Move)*, University of California Press, 1989; Daniel Wirls,

Buildup: The Politics of Defense in the Reagan Era, Cornell University Press, 1992; Paul Lettow, *Ronald Reagan and His Quest to Abolish Nuclear Weapons*, Random House, 2005; Richard Butler, *Fatal Choice: Nuclear Weapons and the Illusion of Missile Defense*, Westview Press, 2001; *Rocket's Red Glare: Missile Defenses and the Future of World Politics*, edited by James J. Wirtz and Jeffrey A. Larsen, Westview Press, 2001; Gordon R. Mitchell, *Strategic Deception: Rhetoric, Science, and Politics in Missile Defense Advocacy*, Michigan State University Press, 2000.

100. Ibid., p. 157 On this matter, see also: Christopher Simpson, *National Security Directives of the Reagan and Bush Administrations: The Declassified History of US Political and Military Policy, 1981–1991*, Westview Press, 1995, pp. 5–6, 74, 233, 370, 421, 439, 422, 449–50, 460, 634, 646, and 734.

101. Rupert Cornwell, "The Real Star Wars: Bush Revives Missile Defense Plan," *The Independent UK*, May 30, 2005; at: www.truthout.org/docs 2005/0531051, shtml; William D. Hartung and Michelle Ciarrocca, "Star Wars II: Here We Go Again," *The Nation*, June 19, 2000, pp. 11–20; William D. Hartung and Micelle Ciarrocca, "Star Wars, Continued: The Boondoggle that Won't Stop, and the Corporate Money that Keeps it Going," *Multinational Monitor*, October 2000 (the article identifies the four major companies that benefit from NMD investment as—Boeing, Lockheed Martin, Raytheon, and TRW); Jonathan Schell, "The New Nuclear Danger," *The Nation*, June 25, 2001; Jack Hitt, "Battlefield Space—Space-based warfare used to seem pure fantasy. Now, to the delight of war planners, and to the dismay of many civilians, it's closer to reality than you'd think," *The New York Times Magazine*, August, 2001; Geov Parrish, "The Pentagon's Trojan Horse: Theater Missile Defense," *In These Times*, July 21, 2001; T. Christian Miller, "Bush Pushes for Missile Defense for All 50 States," *The Los Angeles Times*, May 24, 2000, A-4; Tony Benn, "A Complete Fraud: The New Democracy According to Bush, Blair, Bombs and Business," *Covert Action*, April-June 2001; Michael Wines, "Still Time to Negotiate Missile Defense, US Envoy Says," *The New York Times*, August 23, 2001; Jason Vest, "Darth Rumsfeld: Don Rumsfeld developed his foreign policy in the early 1970s, under President Gerald Ford. It was bad then. It's worse now," *The American Prospect*, February 26, 2001; Morton Mintz, "Two Minutes to Launch: Will President Bush take our missiles off 'hair-trigger' alert—or keep us on the brink of nuclear disaster with a misguided missile defense?," *The American Prospect*, February 26, 2001; Karl Grossman, "Space Corps: The dangerous business of making the heavens a war zone," *Covert Action*, April–June 2001; Elaine Lafferty, "Bush Signals Determination to Abandon ABM Treaty: Appointment of Gen. Myers seen as victory for 'Star Wars' lobby," *Irish Times*, August 25, 2001; Noam Chomsky, "Militarizing Space: 'To Protect US Interests and Investment'," *International Socialist Review*, August–September, 2001; Charles L. Glasser and Steve Fetter, "National Missile Defense and the Future of US Nuclear Weapons Policy," *International Security*, Vol. 26, No. 1, Summer 2001, pp. 40–92; *National Missile Defense: What Does It All Mean?—A CDI Issue Brief*, Center For Defense Information, September 2000; Bruce M. DeBlois, Richard L. Garwin, R. Scott Kemp, and Jeremy Marwell, "Space Weapons: Crossing the US Rubicon," *International Security*, Fall 2004, Vol. 29, No. 2, pp. 50–84.

102. John Pike, "The Military Uses of Outer Space," *SIPRI Yearbook 2002—Armaments, Disarmament and International Security*, Stockholm International Peace Research Institute, Oxford University Press, 2002, p. 654.

103. Ibid., p. 654.

104. DeBlois, Garwin, Kemp, and Marwell, "Space Weapons," *International Security*, Vol. 29, No. 2, Fall 2004, p. 51.

105. Ibid., p. 83.

106. Ibid., p. 84. The authors note:

An aggressive campaign to prevent the deployment of weapons by other nations might best be implemented as a US commitment not to be the first to deploy or test space weapons or to further test destructive anti-satellite weapons. A unilateral US declaration should be supported by a US initiative to codify such a rule, first by parallel unilateral declarations and then perhaps in a formal treaty. A treaty would have the added benefit of legitimizing the use of sanctions or force against actions that would imperil the satellites of any state.

Other progressive initiatives include proposals to take Russian and US nuclear missiles off "hair trigger alert." Such a move would satisfy all reasonable requirements of deterrence while greatly alleviating the more urgent problem of operational safety. Such a move would also complement the efforts to put constraints on national antiballistic missile defenses. A comprehensive discussion of both initiatives is addressed in: *The Nuclear Turning Point: A Blueprint for Deep Cuts and De-Alerting of Nuclear Weapons*, edited by Harold A. Feiveson, Brookings Institution Press, 1999. In terms of understanding the actual capacity of the Russian nuclear arsenal, about the best reference source is: Steven J. Zaloga, *The Kremlin's Nuclear Sword: The Rise and Fall of Russia's Strategic Nuclear Forces, 1945–2000*, Smithsonian Institution Press, 2002. For state of the art studies on what directions the United States could take toward both nuclear security and a less dangerous world, the following studies are recommended: Steven Lambakis, *On The Edge of Earth: The Future of American Space Power*, The University Press of Kentucky, 2001; Michael A. Levi, *The Future of Arms Control*, Brookings Institution Press, 2005; *Transparency in Nuclear Warheads and Materials: The Political and Technical Dimensions*, edited by Nicolas Zarimpas, SIPRI/Oxford University Press, 2003; *Nuclear Disarmament: Obstacles to Banishing the Bomb*, edited by Jozef Goldblat, I.B. Tauris Publishers—in association with, The Toda Institute for Global Peace and Policy Research, 2000.

107. Gary Dorrien, *Imperial Designs: Neo-conservatism and the New Pax Americana*, Routledge, 2004, Gary Dorrien, *The Neo-Conservative Mind: Politics, Culture, and the War of Ideology*, Temple University Press, 1993; Mann, *Rise of the Vulcans*; Rothkopf, *Running the World*; Everest, *Oil, Power And Empire*, pp. 216–217.

108. Andrew J. Bacevich, *The New American Militarism: How Americans Are Seduced by War*, Oxford University Press, 2005, p. 87. See also: Jack Snyder, "Myths of Empire and Strategies of Hegemony," *Lessons of Empire: Imperial Histories and American Power*, edited by Craig Calhoun et al., The New Press, 2006, p. 276.

109. Trial of the Major War Criminals before the International Military Tribunal (Nuremberg, 1947, p. 223, as quoted in: Telford Taylor, *Nuremberg and Vietnam: An American Tragedy*, Bantam Books, 1971, p. 84. See also: Michael Byers, *War Law: Understanding International Law and Armed Conflict*, Grove Press, 2005.

110. Toope, "Powerful but Unpersuasive?—The Role of the United States in the Evolution of Customary International Law,", pp. 292–293.

111. Mel Hurtig, *Rushing to Armageddon: The Shocking Truth About Canada, Missile Defense, and Star Wars*, McClelland & Stewart, Ltd., The Canadian Publishers, 2004. See also: Lloyd Axworthy, "Open Letter to Condoleezza Rice," *The Progressive*, June 2005, Volume 69, Number 6, pp. 30–31, (originally published on March 3, 2005 in the *Winnipeg Free Press*).

112. Rothkopf, *Running the World*, p. 468. See also: Andre J. Bacevich, "Trigger Man: In Paul Wolfowitz, messianic vision meets faith in the efficacy of force," *The American Conservative*, June 6, 2005, Vol. 4, No. 11, pp. 11–14.

113. Nafeez Mosaddeq Ahmed, *Behind the War on Terror*, p. 29.

114. Ibid., p. 244. The author also observes:

it is crucial to note that the transition of the imperial system from a colonial to a surrogate method of organization—although rehabilitating and consolidating that system—certainly signified that system's inevitable decline due to its intrinsic contradictions, evidenced by the massive almost simultaneous unrest and uprisings against colonialism. Such a brutal system of unashamed repression and profiteering was thus unsustainable, and de-colonization allowed the basic social, political, and economic structures of colonial states to be essentially maintained through Western alliances with regional surrogates (Ibid., p. 244).

115. Bello, *Dilemmas of Domination*, p. 198.

116. Ibid., p. 199.

117. Everest, *Oil, Power and Empire*, p. 21.

118. Boggs, *Imperial Delusions*, p. 195. Boggs notes: "Widespread chaos and disorder endemic to the ongoing cycle of militarism and terrorism, while no doubt favorable to the power aspirations of a small circle of elites, ultimately works against the smooth functioning of the New World Order, including any system of consensual governance."

4 CLASH OR CONVERGENCE?: THE EMERGING
UNITY OF RELIGIONS AND CIVILIZATIONS

1. Richard A. Falk, *The Declining World Order: America's Imperial Geopolitics*, Routledge, 2004, p. 166.
2. Fritjof Capra, *The Turning Point: Science, Society, and the Rising Culture*, Simon and Schuster, 1982, p. 296.
3. William S. Waldron, "Common Ground, Common Cause: Buddhism and Science on the Afflictions of Identity," *Buddhism & Science: Breaking New Ground*, edited by B. Alan Wallace, Columbia University Press, 2003, p. 165.
4. The Universal Declaration of Human Rights was approved and proclaimed by the General Assembly of the UN on December 10, 1948, as resolution 217 A (III).
5. Roger Burbach and Jim Tarbell, *Imperial Overstretch: George Bush and the Hubris of Empire*, Zed Books, 2004, p. 85. See also: Michael W. Doyle, *Ways of War and Peace: Realism, Liberalism, and Socialism*, W.W. Norton & Company, 1997, pp. 499–500. Doyle notes:

> Our modern identities are pluralistic, found in individual identity, nation, and class (whether ideal or real) as well as religion, race, and gender (which states have yet to embody). We cannot escape multiplicity's entering our policy choices, nor, if we want to be true to ourselves, should we try to. Given a world of diverse moral identities within and between human beings, we need an ethics of statesmanship capable of accommodating our diverse moralities. Each of our visions of morality has a legitimate sway on our identities, interests, and duties. The tug of national solidarity, global human rights, and class identity and a commitment to the liberation of the disadvantaged poor: Each carries weight, as it should, in our complex moral world.

6. Robert Johansen, *The National Interest and the Human Interest: An Analysis of US Foreign Policy*, Princeton University Press, 1980, p. 21.
7. Burbach and Tarbell, *Imperial Overstretch*, p. 85.
8. Michael Chossudovsky "Global Poverty in the Late Twentieth Century," *Devastating Society: The Neo-Conservative Assault on Democracy and Justice*, edited by Bern Hamm, Pluto Press, 2005, p. 255.
9. Terrence E. Paupp, *Achieving Inclusionary Governance: Advancing Peace and Development in First and Third World Nations*, Transnational Publishers, Inc., 2000.
10. Ibid., p. 256.
11. Thomas Pogge, *World Poverty and Human Rights: Cosmopolitan Responsibilities and Reforms*, Polity, 2002, p. 166. See also: Charles S. Maier, *Among Empires: American Ascendancy and its Predecessors*, Harvard University Press, 2006, p. 145. Maier notes:

> American ascendancy was based in part upon a 'Fordist' organization of economic activity as well as on possession of weapons of mass destruction. Earlier British ascendancy was built on the cotton mills of Lancashire as well as on naval power. Behind the key industrial processes were social arrangements that facilitated stability at home and the capacity to project power abroad. Both societies were wealthy enough to sanction the inequality needed to mobilize financial surpluses. They could finance friends abroad and in so doing make their own monetary system a further component of world power. We cannot really understand the structural ordering of domestic and international politics apart from each other.

12. Chossudovsky, "Global Poverty in the Late Twentieth Century," *Devastating Society*, p. 259. See also: Doyle, *Ways of War and Peace*, p. 488. Doyle notes: "The semi-periphery needs strong states in order to mobilize savings into investment into growth and thereby onto a path that is equalizing rather than one that perpetuates and reinforces global capitalist hierarchy. Capitalism develops unevenly, and capitalist growth is the product of forcible extraction and class warfare." American "economic civilization" has had a distorting influence on the lives of its citizens and its foreign policy. On this matter, see: Liah Greenfeld, *The Spirit of Capitalism: Nationalism and Economic Growth*, Harvard University Press, 2001; Jeffrey A. Frieden, *Global Capitalism: Its Fall and Rise in the Twentieth Century*, W.W. Norton & Company, 2006.
13. Chossudovsky, p. 259.

14. Chossudovsky, p. 259.
15. Ibid.
16. Ibid., p. 259. Waldon Bello, *Dilemmas of Domination: The Unmaking of the American Empire*, Metropolitan Books, 2005, p. 9. Bello notes:

    Reagan did chart new territory ... launching comprehensive counterinsurgency campaigns to undermine those state-assisted capitalist regimes that had served as the base for such challenges as the New International Economic Order. The right-wing foreign policy circle of the Reagan regime wanted to transform these nations into free-market economies. Trade wars were waged to open up more advanced economies of the South, like Taiwan and South Korea, which were making the transition from developing to developed countries. More decisive, though, were the structural adjustment programs, inaugurated by the IMF, which promoted trade liberalization, deregulation, and privatization. They served as the principal mechanisms for disciplining the economic aspirations of the South.

    See also, John Mason Hart, *Empire and Revolution: The Americans in Mexico since the Civil War*, University of California Press, 2002, pp. 433–434. Hart notes:

    In general, US capital flowed into the underdeveloped world during the 1980s and 1990s in response to opportunities that resulted from trade liberalization, privatization, less regulation of stock markets, and tighter international controls over the monetary policies of Third World nations ... In 1989, in response to a panic among investors, President Ronald Reagan announced the Brady Plan. Countries that were deep in arrears could restructure their commercial bank debt by issuing Brady bonds, which would be guaranteed by the US Treasury Department. The first Brady bonds were issued by the Mexican government in 1990.

    See also: *Neo-liberalism: A Critical Reader*, edited by Alfredo Saad-Filho and Deborah Johnston, Pluto Press, 2005; John Gray, *False Dawn: The Delusions of Global Capitalism*, The New Press, 1998.
17. Burbach and Tarbell, *Imperial Overstretch*.
18. Capra, *The Turning Point*, p. 298. On this matter, see also: *A World-Systems Reader: New Perspectives on Gender, Urbanism, Cultures, Indigenous Peoples, and Ecology*, edited by Thomas D. Hall, Rowman & Littlefield Publishers, Inc., 2000; *Culture and Public Action*, edited by Vijayendra Rao and Michael Walton, Stanford University Press, 2004; *Culture, Ideology, and World Order*, edited by R.B.J. Walker, Westview Press, 1984; Theodore Roszak, *Where The Wasteland Ends: Politics and Transcendence in Postindustrial Society*, Anchor Books, Doubleday & Company, Inc., 1973; Daniel Singer, *Whose Millennium?—Theirs or Ours?*, Monthly Review Press, 1999; *Buddhism & Science: Breaking New Ground*, edited by B. Alan Wallace, Columbia University Press, 2003.
19. Alex Callinicos, *The New Mandarins of American Power: The Bush Administration's Plans for the World*, Polity, 2003.
20. Ibid., pp. 129–130.
21. Samuel P. Huntington, *The Clash of Civilizations and the Remaking of World Order*, Simon & Schuster, 1996. p. 29. Huntington's central thesis is that:

    the post Cold War world is a world of seven or eight major civilizations. Cultural commonalities and differences shape the interests, antagonisms, and associations of states. The most important countries in the world come overwhelmingly from different civilizations. The local conflicts most likely to escalate into broader wars are those between groups and states from different civilizations. The predominant patterns of political and economic development differ from civilization to civilization. The key issues on the international agenda involve differences among civilizations. Power is shifting from the long predominant West to non-Western civilizations.

22. Ibid., p. 29.
23. Peter Ackerman and Jack DuVall, *A Force More Powerful: A Century of Nonviolent Conflict*, St. Martin's Press, 2000.

24. Christopher Chase-Dunn and Bruce Podobnik, "The Next World War: World System Cycles and Trends," *The Future of Global Conflict*, edited by Volker Bornschier and Christopher Chase-Dunn, SAGE Studies in International Sociology 49, 1999, p. 52.

25. Ibid.

26. Jean L. Cohen and Andrew Arato, *Civil Society and Political Theory*, The MIT Press, 1994, p. ix.

27. On this matter, see: Richard Falk, *Religion and Humane Global Governance*, Palgrave, 2001, p. 68. Falk notes:

Samuel Huntington's notorious 'clash of civilizations' assessment gives a deterministic spin to these developments from a Western and hegemonic perspective, positing intercivilizational conflict and warfare as the inevitable wave of the future, which will give rise to an embattled West doing its best to withstand the challenges posed by Islamic and other non-Western peoples. In this scenario, the West and Islam are pictured as locked in a mortal combat that can only be resolved by the defeat of one by the other. In some important sense, the resonance of the Huntington thesis arises from his recognition that the era of sovereign states is past and that the future belongs to the political outcomes of this religious resurgence, which he associates with spatially distinct regions. This insight is diminished by his treatment of civilizations as geographic wholes, ignoring the important intermingling of civilizations that is itself a major byproduct of globalization. Huntington also neglects reconciliation possibilities, including the unifying impact of environmental and cultural challenges that are planetary in scale and the hybrid multicultural realities associated with intercivilizational migration patterns. The impact of globalization is contradictory, both generating a kind of homogenized world civilization that ignores civilizational particularities and revitalizing the traditional ethnic and religious identities that give renewed potency to civilizational categories. The homogenizing impact is partly decried by traditionalists and representatives of the global South as a thinly disguised Western (or American) project for global hegemony. The backlash is decried by globalists as a descent into a self-defeating primitivism that hurts those who are currently most economically disadvantaged.

28. Jayan Nayar, "Taking Empire Seriously: Empire's Law, People's Law, and the World Tribunal on Iraq," *Empire's Law: The American Imperial Project and the 'War to Remake the World*, edited by Amy Bartholomew, Pluto Press, 2006, p. 314.

29. Ibid., p. 319.

30. Falk, *The Declining World Order*, p. xi. See also: Richard Falk, *The End of World Order: Essays on Normative International Relations*, Holmes & Meier, 1983.

31. Falk, *The Declining World Order*, p. xi.

32. William Difazio, "Time, Poverty, and Global Democracy," *Implicating Empire: Globalization and Resistance in the 21st Century World Order*, edited by Stanley Aronowitz and Heather Gautney, Basic Books, 2003, p. 171.

33. Paupp, *Achieving Inclusionary Governance*.

34. Michael Chossudovsky, "Global Poverty in the Late Twentieth Century," *Devastating Society: The Neo-Conservative Assault on Democracy and Justice*, edited by Bernd Hamm, Pluto Press, 2005, p. 260. He notes:

The inauguration of the WTO in 1995 marks a new phase in the evolution of the postwar economic system. A new "triangular division of authority" among the IMF, the World Bank, and the WTO has unfolded. The IMF has called for more effective "surveillance" "of the developing countries" economic policies and increased coordination among the three international bodies, signifying a further infringement on the sovereignty of national government.

See also: *Sovereignty under Challenge: How Governments Respond*, edited by John D. Montgomery and Nathan Glazer, Transaction Publishers, 2002; *The Political Economy of Imperialism: Critical Appraisals*, edited by Ronald H. Chilcote, Rowman & Littlefield Publishers, Inc., 2000; Albert Szymanski, *The Logic of Imperialism*, Praeger, 1981.

35. Andrew Austin, "War Hawks and the Ugly American: The Origins of Bush's Central Asia and Middle East Policy," *Devastating Society: The Neo-Conservative Assault on Democracy and Justice*, edited by Bernd Hamm, Pluto Press, 2005, pp. 47–66.

36. Stefan Halper and Jonathan Clarke, *America Alone: The Neo-Conservatives And The Global Order*, Cambridge University Press, 2004, *Unilateralism and US Foreign Policy: International Perspectives*, edited by David M. Malone and Yuen Foong Khoong, Lynne Rienner Publishers, 2003.

37. Marjorie Cohn, "Bolton Nominated to Destroy UN," Truthout Editorial, April 4, 2005. http://www.truthout.org/docs_20005/040405B.shtml. See also: Paul Richter, "Bolton Faces Stiff Fight over UN Nomination," *The Los Angeles Times*, March 31, 2005.

38. Eva Golinger, "US Aggression Towards Venezuela: The Rise of Black Propaganda and Dirty War Tactics," at: www.truthout.org/docs_2005/040105N.shtml. See also: Christian Parenti, "Hugo Chavez, Petro Populist," *The Nation*, April 11, 2005.

39. Bruce Cummings, Ervand Abrahamian, and Moshe Mz'oz, *Inventing the Axis of Evil: The Truth about North Korea, Iran, and Syria*, The New Press, 2004.

40. Roszak, *Where The Wasteland Ends: Politics and Transcendence in Postindustrial Society*, Anchor Books, 1973, pp. 222–223. Roszak notes:

Science ... participates in the technocracy because it, like all else, has been caught up in the evolution of industrial society. It too yields to the imperatives of the artificial environment ... Ethical rhetoric and not statistics is the language of politics; action not analysis is its culmination, and its resolutions can never be neatly rounded out. Frustration, imprecision, and impermanence are of the essence of political life. Necessarily so, because people consciously engage in politics with more of themselves than scientists feel professionally obliged to take with them into research.

41. Ramsey Clark, *The Fire This Time: US War Crimes in the Gulf*, Thunder's Mouth Press, 1992.

42. Roszak, *Where the Wasteland Ends*, p. 224.

43. Edward W. Said, "The Clash of Ignorance," *The Nation*, October 22, 2001, p. 13.

44. Other members of the World Order Models Project (WOMP) included Saul H. Mendlovitz, Rajni Kothari, Richard Falk, and Johan Galtung. They produced a series of books under the general theme of, "Preferred Worlds for the 1990s."

45. Ali A. Mazrui, *A World Federation of Cultures: An African Perspective*, The Free Press, 1976, p. 61.

46. Ibid.

47. Ibid.

48. Ibid., p. 63.

49. Chossudovsky, "Global Poverty in the Late Twentieth Century," p. 261. See also: Maier, *Among Empires*, pp. 139–140. Maier notes:

Does empire produce more violence or less violence, more uprooting or less, than alternative principles of political organization? Such a determination remains out of reach; only the particular possibilities can be soberly taken into account. Like all programs that allow us to construct a collective political life or a social order, empire comes with a set of rationalizations, intellectualizations within intellectualizations: onion layers of ideological justification, including those stressing historical antecedents, national splendor, and social rationality. None should ever be taken at face value.

50. Robert Johansen, *The National Interest and the Human Interest: An Analysis of US Foreign Policy*, Princeton University Press, 1980, p. 377.

51. Pogge, *World Poverty and Human Rights*, p. 144. A more updated and detailed proposal along these lines is found in: Jeffrey D. Sachs, *The End of Poverty: Economic Possibilities For Our Time*, The Penguin Press, 2005; Jeffrey D. Sachs, "The Development Challenge," *Foreign Affairs*, March/April 2005, pp. 78–90.

52. Oswaldo De Riverso, *The Myth of Development: The Non-Viable Economies of the 21ˢᵗ Century*, Zed Books, 2001; Waldon Bello, *De-globalization: Ideas for a New World Economy*, Zed Books, 2002; Graham Dunkley, *Free Trade: Myth, Reality and Alternatives*, Zed Books, 2004; *Beyond Bretton Woods: Alternatives to the Global Economic Order*, edited by John Cavanagh, Daphne Wysham and Marcos Arruda, Pluto Press, 1994; Wim Dierckxsens, *The Limits of Capitalism: An Approach to Globalization Without Neo-liberalism*, Zed Books, 2000; *Law and Poverty: The*

Legal System and Poverty Reduction, edited by Lucy Williams, Asbjorn Kjonstad, and Peter Robon, Zed Books, 2003; *Views From The South: The Effects of Globalization and the WTO on Third World Countries*, edited by Sarah Anderson, Food First Books, 2000.

53. Daniel Little, *The Paradox of Wealth and Poverty: Mapping the Ethical Dilemmas of Global Development*, Westview Press, 2003, pp. 94–95.

54 *Reinventing the World Bank*, edited by Jonathan R. Pincus and Jeffrey A. Winters, Cornell University Press, 2002, p. 198. See also: Robert Biel, *The New Imperialism: Crisis and contradictions in North-South Relations*, Zed Books, 2000; Stephen D. Krasner, *Structural Conflict: The Third World Against Global Liberalism*, University of California Press, 1985; Samir Amin, *The Liberal Virus: Permanent War and the Americanization of the World*, Monthly Review Press, 2004; *Global Trade and Global Social Issues*, edited by Annie Taylor and Caroline Thomas, Routledge, 1999; Alternatives to Economic Globalization: A Better World Is Possible—A Report of the International Forum on Globalization, edited by John Cavanagh and Jerry Mander, Berrett-Koehler Publishers, Inc., 2002; *Dying for Growth: Global Inequality and the Health of the Poor*, edited by Jim Yong Kim et al., Common Courage Press, 2000; Arthur Mitzman, *Prometheus Revisited: The Quest for Global Justice in the Twenty-first Century*, University of Massachusetts Press, 2003; *Democratizing the Global Economy: The Battle Against the World Bank and the IMF*, edited by Kevin Danaher, Common Courage Press, 2001; Eric Toussaint, *Your Money or Your Life!— The Tyranny of Global Finance*, Pluto Press, 1999; Kevin Watkins, *The Oxfam Poverty Report*, Oxfam, 1995; Lorie Wallach and Patrick Woodall, Public Citizen, *Whose Trade Organization?— A Comprehensive Guide to the WTO*, The New Press, 2004; Lori Wallach and Michelle Sforza, *Whose Trade Organization?—Corporate Globalization and the Erosion of Democracy*, Public Citizen, 1999; *Beyond Economic Liberalization in Africa: Structural Adjustment and the Alternatives*, edited by Kidane Mengisteab and B. Ikubolajeh Logan 2000; Biplad Dasgupta, *Structural Adjustment, Global Trade and the New Political Economy of Development*, Zed Books, 1998; *50 Years Is Enough: The Case Against the World Bank and the IMF*, edited by Kevin Danaher, South End Press, 1994; *The IMF and the South: The Social Impact of Crisis and Adjustment*, edited by Dhara Ghai, Zed Books, 1991; James Raymond Vreeland, *The IMF and Economic Development*, Cambridge University Press, 2003; Bruce Rich, *Mortgaging the Earth: The World Bank, Environmental Impoverishment, and the Crisis of Development*, Beacon Press, 1994; Noreen Hertz, *The Debt Threat: How Debt is Destroying the Developing World*, Harper Business, 2004; Noreen Hertz, *The Silent Takeover: Global Capitalism and the Death of Democracy*, The Free Press, 2001; Belinda Coote, *The Trade Trap: Poverty and the Global Commodity Markets*, Oxfam, 1992; *Global Capitalism*, edited by Will Hutton and Anthony Giddens, The New Press, 2000; Joseph E. Stiglitz, *Globalization and Its Discontents*, W.W. Norton & Company, 2002.

55. Anuradha Mittal, "The South in the North," *Views From The South: The Effects of Globalization and the WTO on Third World Countries*, Food First Books, 2000, p. 172.

56. Mazrui, *A World Federation of Cultures*, p. 65.

57. Amartya Sen, "Civilizational Imprisonments: How to Misunderstand Everybody in the World," *The New Republic*, June 10, 2002. p. 28.

58. Roszak, *Where The Wasteland Ends*, p. 227.

59. Marcos Arruda, *External Debt: Brazil and the International Financial Crisis*, Pluto Press, 2000, p. 43. Arruda notes:

The IMF today is a failed institution. It faces major criticisms: it lacks a neutral international reserve currency (the international currency is a nation currency: the US dollar); it lacks mechanisms for stabilizing exchange rates and for macroeconomic guidance of the global system; it lacks a lender of last resort; its decision-making structure is undemocratic; it lacks social participation and is excessively confidential; it is powerless and asymmetrical when dealing with the imbalances between the hemispheres; it uses medium-term loans as if they were long-term; it duplicates the activities of the World Bank; and special drawing rights (the IMF currency) are poorly distributed.

60. Roszak, *Where The Wasteland Ends*, p. 228. Roszak notes:

Reductionism flows from many diverse sources: from an overweening desire to dominate, from the hasty effort to find simple, comprehensive explanations; from a commendable desire to deflate the pretentious obscurantism of religious authority; but above all from a sense of human estrangement from nature which could only increase inordinately as western society's commitment to single vision grew ever more exclusive. In effect, reductionism is what we experience whenever sacramental consciousness is crowded out by idolatry, by the effort to turn what is alive into a mere thing.

61. Ibid., p. 231.
62. Stephen Toope, "Powerful But Unpersuasive?—The Role of the United States in the Evolution of Customary International Law," *United States Hegemony and the Foundations of International Law*, edited by Michael Byers and Georg Nolte, Cambridge University Press, 2003, p. 288.
63. Ibid., p. 289.
64. Terry Nardin, *Law, Morality, and the Relations of States*, Princeton University Press, 1983, pp. 18–19.
65. Toope, "Powerful But Unpersuasive?," p. 290,
66. Ibid., p. 291.
67. Ibid., p. 289.
68. Ibid., p. 303.
69. Ibid., p. 313.
70. Ibid., p. 316.
71. Terry Nardin, *Law, Morality, and the Relations of States*, Princeton University Press, 1983, p. 19.
72. M. Cherif Bassiouni, "The History of Universal Jurisdiction and its Place in International Law," *Universal Jurisdiction: National Courts and the Prosecution of Serious Crimes Under International Law*, edited by Stephen Macedo, University of Pennsylvania Press, 2004, p. 42. See also: Harold James, *The Roman Predicament: How the Rules of International Order Create the Politics of Empire*, Princeton University Press, 2006, pp. 141–149.
73. Ibid., p. 43.
74. Richard A. Falk, "Assessing the Pinochet Litigation: Whither Universal Jurisdiction?," *Universal Jurisdiction: National Courts and the Prosecution of Serious Crimes under International Law*, edited by Stephen Macedo, University of Pennsylvania Press, 2004, pp. 97–120.
75. Johansen, *The National Interest and the Human Interest*, pp. 196–281.
76. Bassiouni, "The History of Universal Jurisdiction and its Place in International Law", p. 47.
77. Johansen, *The National Interest and the Human Interest*, p. 19. See also: Robert S. McNamara, "Apocalypse Soon," *Foreign Policy*, May/June 2005, pp. 29–35; Robert J. Lifton and Greg Mitchell, *Hiroshima In America: Fifty Years of Denial*, G.P. Putnam's Sons, 1995; Terrence E. Paupp, "The Nuclear Crucible: The Moral and International Law Implications of Weapons of Mass Destruction," *In Democracy's Shadow: The Secret World of National Security*, edited by Marcus Raskin and A. Carl LeVan, Nation Books, 2005, pp. 73–95; *International Law, The International Court of Justice And Nuclear Weapons*, edited by Laurence Boisson De Chazournes and Philippe Sands, Cambridge University Press, 1999; Michael Krepon, *Cooperative Threat Reduction, Missile Defense, and the Nuclear Future*, Palgrave-Macmillan, 2003; Dinshaw Mistry, *Containing Missile Proliferation: Strategic Technology, Security Regimes, and International Cooperation in Arms Control*, University of Washington Press, 2003; Campbell Craig, *Glimmer of a New Leviathan: Total War in the Realism of Niebuhr, Morganthau, and Waltz*, Columbia University Press, 2003; *At the Nuclear Crossroads: Choices about Nuclear Weapons and the Extension of the Non-Proliferation Treaty*, edited by John B. Rhinelander and Adam M. Scheinman, University Press of America, Inc., 1995; *Nuclear Proliferation and the Legality of Nuclear Weapons*, edited by William M. Evan and Ved P. Nanda, University Press of America, Inc., 1995; G. Weermantry, *Nuclear Weapons and Scientific Responsibility*, Longwood Academic, 1987; *Nuclear Weapons After the Comprehensive Test Ban: Implications for Modernization and Proliferation*, edited by Eric Arnett, SIPRI and Oxford University Press, 1996; *1995—A New Beginning for the NPT?*, edited by Joseph Pilat and Robert Pendley, Plenum Press, 1995.
78. James Gustave Speth, *Red Sky at Morning: America and the Crisis of the Global Environment*, Yale University Press, 2004, p. 141. See also: Gareth Porter et al., *Global Environmental Politics, Third Edition*, Westview Press, 2000.

79. Paupp, *Achieving Inclusionary Governance*.
80. Bassiouni, "The History of Universal Jurisdiction and Its Place in International Law," p. 45.
81. Ibid., pp. 21–25. Principle 1-Fundamentals of Universal Jurisdiction; Principle 2-Serious Crimes Under International Law; Principle 3-Reliance on Universal Jurisdiction in the Absence of National Legislation; Principle 4-Obligation to Support Accountability; Principle 5-Immunities; Principle 6-Statutes of Limitations; Principle 7-Amnesties; Principle 8-Resolution of Competing National Jurisdictions; Principle 9-Double Jeopardy; Principle 10-Grounds for Refusal of Extradition; Principle 11-Adoption of National Legislation; Principle 12-Inclusion of Universal Jurisdiction in Future Treaties; Principle 13- Strengthening Accountability and Universal Jurisdiction; Principle 14-Settlement of Disputes.
82. Ibid., p. 63.
83. A. Hays Butler, "The Growing Support for Universal Jurisdiction in National Legislation," *Universal Jurisdiction: National Courts and the Prosecution of Serious Crimes under International Law*, edited by Stephen Macedo, University of Pennsylvania Press, 2004, p. 67. See also: M. Cherif Bassiouoni, The Legislative History of the International Criminal Court, Volume 1—Introduction, Analysis, and Integrated Text of the Statute, Elements of Crimes and Rules of Procedure and Evidence, Volume 2—*An Article-by-Article Evolution of the Statute from 1994–1998, Volume 3—Summary Records of the 1998 Diplomatic Conference*, Transnational Publishers, Inc., 2005; *The Rome Statute of the International Criminal Court: A Commentary, Volumes 1–3*, edited by Antonio Cassese et al., Oxford University Press, 2002; *The International Criminal Court: Elements of Crimes and Rules of Procedure and Evidence*, edited by Roy S. Lee, Transnational Publishers, Inc., 2001; Bruce Broomhall, *International Justice and the International Criminal Court: Between Sovereignty and the Rule of Law*, Oxford University Press, 2003; Dorothy Jones, *Toward A Just World: The Critical Years in the Search for International Justice*, The University of Chicago Press, 2002; Mauro Politi and Giuseppe Nesi, *The International Criminal Court and the Crime of Aggression*, Ashgate, 2004.
84 *America's Disappeared: Detainees, Secret Imprisonment, and the "War on Terror"*, edited by Rachel Meetropol, Seven Stories Press, 2005; Neil Macmaster, "Torture: From Algiers to Abu Ghraib," *Race & Class: A Journal on Racism, Empire, and Globalization*, October–December 2004, Vol. 46, No. 2, pp. 1–21; *Crimes of War—Iraq*, edited by Richard Falk et al., Nation Books, 2006.
85. David Cole and James Dempsey, *Terrorism and the Constitution: Sacrificing Civil Liberties in the Name of National Security, 2006, pp. 190-193; The Torture Debate in America*, edited by Karen Greenberg, Cambridge University Press, 2006, pp. 317–360; *In the Name of Democracy: American War Crimes in Iraq and Beyond*, Metropolitan Books, 2005; *Human Rights in the 'War on Terror'*, edited by Richard A. Wilson, Cambridge University Press, 2005; Alfred W. McCoy, *A Question of Torture: CIA Interrogation, from the Cold War to the War on Terror*, Metropolitan Books, 2006; Stephen John Hartnett, *Globalization and Empire: The US Invasion of Iraq, Free Markets, and the Twilight of Democracy*, The University of Alabama Press, 2006; Noam Chomsky, *Failed States: The Abuse of Power and the Assault on Democracy*, Metropolitan Books, 2006.
86. Butler, "The Growing Support for Universal Jurisdiction in National Legislation," p. 76.
87 Telford Taylor, *Nuremberg and Vietnam: An American Tragedy*, Bantam Books, 1971, p. 83. See also: Arieh J. Kochavi, *Prelude To Nuremberg: Allied War Crimes Policy and the Question of Punishment*, The University of North Carolina Press, 1998; Telford Taylor, *The Anatomy of the Nuremberg Trials—A Personal Memoir*, Alfred A. Knopf, 1992.
88. Ibid., p. 13. See also, Nikolaus Wachsmann, *Hitler's Prisons: Legal Terror in Nazi Germany*, Yale University Press, 2004.
89. Ibid., pp. 206–207.
90. Ibid., p. 207.
91. Francis Cardinal Arinze, *Religions For Peace: A Call For Solidarity To The Religions Of The World*, Doubleday, 2002, pp. 78–79.
92. James W. Douglas, *The Non-Violent Cross: A Theology of Revolution and Peace*, The Macmillan Company, 1969, p. 8.
93. Elsa Tamez, *The Bible of the Oppressed*, Orbis Books, 1982, p. 41.
94. Ibid., p. 42.
95. Ibid.

96. Elsa Tamez,, p. 53.

97. Jose Miranda, *Communism in the Bible*, translated from the Spanish by Robert R. Barr, Orbis Books, 1982, p. 74.

98. Ibid., p. 74. Miranda goes on to ask the following questions:

Would it be more violent to shoot them than to prevent them from eating? Where did this definition of violence come from? The aggression is right here, right now, in the form of genocide, and it is constant. By what prodigies of doctrinal immorality are its victims denied the right of legitimate defense? How can anyone think that it is less aggressive systematically to reduce the life and vitality of a human being than to cut it off suddenly?

99. Robin Wright, "Two Visions of Reformation," *World Religions and Democracy*, edited by Larry Diamond, Marc F. Plattner, and Philip J. Costopoulis, The Johns Hopkins University Press, 2005, p. 181. See also: Diarmaid MacCulloch, *The Reformation*, Viking, 2003.

100. Ibid., p. 181. Robin Wright also notes: "Only a few groups, such as the Wahabi in Saudi Arabia, are in fact fundamentalist. This term, coined in the early twentieth century to describe a movement among Protestant Christians in the United States, denotes passive adherence to literal reading of sacred scripture."

101. Ibid., pp. 181–182.

102. John Bellamy Foster and Brett Clark, "Empire of Barbarism," *Monthly Review*, December 2004, pp. 1–15.

103. Mitzman, *Prometheus Revisited*.

104. Wright, "Two Visions of Reformation," p. 182. See also: Mehran Kamrava, *Cultural Politics in the Third World*, Routledge, 1999; Mehran Kamrava, *Politics and Society in the Developing World*, Routledge, 1993; Mehran Kamrava, *Understanding Comparative Politics: A Framework for Analysis*, Routledge, 1996; Mehran Kamrava, *The Modern Middle East: A Political History since the First World War*, University of California Press, 2005.

105. Ibid., p. 183.

106. Ibid., p. 191.

107. Harun Yahya, "Only Love Can Defeat Terrorism," *Islamica Magazine*, Issue 12, Spring 2005, p. 87.

108. Ibid., p. 87.

109. Ibid., pp. 92 and 95.

110. Esther Kaplan, *With God On Their Side: How Christian Fundamentalists Trampled Science, Policy, And Democracy In George W. Bush's White House*, The New Press, 2004; David Domke, *God Willing?—Political Fundamentalism in the White House, The 'War On Terror,' and the Echoing Press*, Pluto Press, 2004; Kevin Phillips, *American Theocracy: The Peril and Politics of Radical Religion, Oil, and Borrowed Money in the 21st Century*, Viking, 2006; Michael Lerner, *The Left Hand of God: Taking Back Our Country From The Religious Right*, HarperCollins, 2006; Jim Wallis, *God's Politics: Why the Right Gets It Wrong and the Left Doesn't Get It*, HarperCollins, 2005.

111. Yahya, "Only Love Can Defeat Terrorism," pp. 92–93.

112. Emran Qureshi and Michael A. Sells, "Introduction: Constructing the Muslim Identity," *The New Crusades: Constructing the Muslim Enemy*, edited by Emran Qureshi and Michael A. Sells, Columbia University Press, 2003, p. 29.

113. Ibid., p. 129.

114. Waldron, "Common Ground, Common Cause: Buddhism and Science on the Afflictions of Identity."

115. Terence E. Fretheim, " 'I was only a little angry': Divine Violence in the Prophets," *Interpretation: A Journal of bible and Theology*, Vol. 58, No. 4, October 2004, p. 367.

116. Ibid., p. 368.

"Israel's (and the world's) long story of successful resistance to God's will for non-violence has had deep effects on every aspect of life and the resultant violent reality complicates God's working possibilities in the world. Because of God's committed relationship to the world, no resolution will be simple, no 'quick fix' available, even for God. The enemies of God cannot be overcome with a flick of the wrist. One might wish that God would force compliance and stop the violence, but, because of the genuine relationship, God's efforts to that end will entail constraint and restraint in the use of power. And so, with continued resistance to the will of God for non-violence, laments will continue and suffering will go on for both the world and God.

See also: Richard Horsley, *Jesus and Empire: The Kingdom of God and the New World Disorder*, Fortress Press, 2003.

117. Martin Luther King, Jr., "Facing the Challenge of a New Age (1957)," *I Have a Dream: Writings and Speeches that Changed the World*, edited by James M. Washington, Harper San Francisco, 1986, 1992, p. 15.
118. Ibid., p. 23.
119. Ibid., p. 67.
120. UNDP, *Human Development Report (2003)—Millennium Development Goals: A Compact Among Nations to end Human Poverty*, Oxford University Press, 2003, p. 145.
121. Martin Luther King, Jr., *Where Do We Go From Here: Chaos or Community?* Bantam Books, 1968, p. 221.
122. William F. Pepper, *An Act of State: The Execution of Martin Luther King*, Verso, 2003, p. 172. Pepper notes of King that:

> He said that concerning certain values and practices of the existing social order, and in particular the growth of militarism, he was proud to be maladjusted and he called upon all people to become maladjusted. He said he refused to adjust to a socio-economic order, which deprived the many of the necessities and allowed luxuries for the few. He refused to adjust to the madness of militarism and the self-perpetuating use of violence in the development of the American empire. He refused to adjust to an economic system in which people had become objects—things used in pursuit of riches by others and disposed of when no longer needed. Long before globalization was in mode he knew that a global system, dreamed of by corporate imperialists, would harmonize standards across the globe down to the lowest common element. Social responsibility would be regarded as inefficient and a global free market and demands for a living wage would be a targeted source of inefficiency and purged wherever possible.

123. King, Jr., *Where Do We Go From Here*, p. 221.
124. Ibid., pp. 221–222.
125. Samir Amin, "Confronting the Empire," *Pox Americana: Exposing the American Empire*, edited by John B. Foster and Robert W. McChesney, Monthly Review Press, 2004, p. 205.
126. Ibid., p. 205. Some scholars have argued that globalization has undermined national policies to raise the living standards and enhance the opportunities of the poor. Alternatively, other scholars have suggested that globalization does not preclude social insurance and egalitarian redistribution—but it does change the mix of policies that can accomplish these ends. On this point, see: *Globalization and Egalitarian Redistribution*, edited by Pranab Bardham et al., Russell Sage Foundation/Princeton University Press, 2006. The role of law in the movements for social justice signals the emergence of a subaltern cosmopolitan law movement and politics that call for new social and legal theories capable of capturing the potential and tensions of counter-hegemonic globalization. On this point, see: *Law and Globalization from Below: Towards a Cosmopolitan Legality*, edited by Boaventrua de Sousa Santos et al., Cambridge University Press, 2005; *Democratizing Democracy Beyond the Liberal Democratic Canon*, edited by Boaventura de Sousa Santos, Verso, 2005.
127. Paul Kowert and Jeffrey Legro, "Norms, Identity, and Their Limits: A Theoretical Reprise," *The Culture of National Security: Norms and Identity in World Politics*, edited by Peter J. Katzenstein, Columbia University Press, 1996, pp. 451–497.
128. Ibid., p. 451.
129. Ibid., p. 458. See also: *Promoting the Rule of Law Abroad: In Search of Knowledge*, edited by Thomas Carothers, Carnegie Endowment for International Peace, 2006.
130. Ibid., p. 458.
131. Ibid., pp. 458–459.

132. Michael T. Klare, "The Intensifying Global Struggle for Energy," *Tom Dispatch*, May 9, 2005. See also, Michael T. Klare, "Imperial Reach: The Pentagon's New Basing Strategy," *The Nation*, April 25, 2005.

133. Robert D. Kaplan, "How We Would Fight China," *The Atlantic*, June 2005, Vol. 295, No. 5, pp. 49–64.

134. Ibid., p. 62.

135. Ethan B. Kapstein, "Does Unipolarity Have a Future?" Unipolar Politics: Realism and State Strategies After the Cold War, edited by Ethan B. Kapstein and Michael Mastanduno, Columbia University Press, 1999, p. 486. Kapstein noted:

balancing against the United States is not a likely outcome, since in economic terms there is no good alternative to the American order, while in military terms it spends as much on defense as the rest of the world combined. From all this, once can only conclude that the American century has just begun. How long it endures will be a function of whether an alternative form of political economy emerges that is capable of mobilizing widespread support.

136. Richard J. Barnet, *Roots Of War: The Men And Institutions Behind US Foreign Policy*, Penguin Books Inc., 1971.

137. Ibid., p. 340.

138. Ibid., p. 341. Barnet writes: "We can have a chance for a generation of peace only if the American people demand it and are prepared to build a society rooted in the politics of peace."

139. Daniel Deudney and G. John Ikenberry, "Realism, Structural Liberalism, and the Western Order," *Unipolar Politics: Realism and State Strategies After the Cold War*, edited by Ethan B. Kapstein and Michael Mastanduno, Columbia University Press, 1999, p. 104.

140. Ibid.

141. Michael Fortmann, T. V. Paul, and James J. Wirtz, "Conclusion: Balance of Power Theory at the Turn of the New Century," *Balance of Power: Theory and Practice in the 21st Century*, edited by T. V. Paul, James Wirtz, and Michael Fortmann, Stanford University Press, 2004, p. 371.

142. Ibid., p. 372.

143. Josef Joffe, "Defying History and Theory: The United States as the 'Last Remaining Superpower'," *America Unrivaled: The Future of the Balance of Power*, edited by G. John Ikenberry, Cornell University Press, 2002, p. 178.

144. Paul Farmer, *Pathologies of Power: Health, Human Rights, and the New War on the Poor*, University of California Press, 2003.

145. Ibid., p. 219.

146. Ibid.

147. Ibid. See also: Mike Davis, *Planet of Slums*, Verso, 2006.

148. Ibid., p. 244.

149. William I. Robinson, *Promoting Polyarchy: Globalization, US Intervention, and Hegemony*, Cambridge University Press, 1996, p. 385. For some concrete examples on how to democratize global society, see: Jody Heymann, *Forgotten Families: Ending the Growing Crisis Confronting Children and Working Parents in the Global Economy*, 2006, pp. 195–222. After listing seven myths that feed inaction, she concludes noting:

"there is nothing about the race to the bottom that is inherent in globalization. In fact, the results of globalization are up to us. Increased social and economic relations across countries can just as readily lead to widely shared economic gains as they can to a downward spiral toward worse working conditions ... We need to put in place universal standards for minimum decent working conditions" [p. 222].

150. Robert Jackson, *The Global Covenant: Human Conduct in a World of States*, Oxford University Press, 2000, p. 31. See also: S. Neil MacFarlane and Yeun Foong Khong, *Human Security and the UN: A Critical History*, Indiana University Press, 2006; Peter Rogers et al., *An Introduction to Sustainable Development*, Harvard University Press, 2006; Geert Demuijnck *Real World Justice: Grounds, Principles, Human Rights, and Social Institutions*, edited by Andreas Follesdal and Thomas Pogge, Springer, The Netherlands, 2005; *Reinventing Development? Translating Rights-Based Approaches from Theory into Practice*, edited by Paul Gready and Jonathan Ensor, Zed Books, 2005.

151. Ibid., p. 371.
152. Ibid., p. 400.
153. Ibid., p. 408.
154. Ibid.
155. Ibid., pp. 408–409.
156. Ibid., p. 409.
157. Ibid., p. 410.
158. Ibid.
159. Ibid.
160. Peter J. Katzenstein, "Conclusion: National Security in a Changing World," *The Culture of National Security: Norms and Identity in World Politics*, edited by Peter J. Katzenstein, Columbia University Press, 1996, p. 515. Katzenstein elaborates on this view noting:

> The principle of unquestioned state sovereignty never triumphed. Instead, the practice of intervention, before and after 1648, has left state sovereignty deeply problematic, and with it the sharp distinction between international and domestic levels of analysis. Economic, social and environmental issues that increasingly permeate state boundaries reinforce that trend.

See also: *US Hegemony and International Organizations: The United States and Multilateral Institutions*, edited by Rosemary Foot et al., Oxford University Press, 2003.

161. Philip Allott, *The Health of Nations: Society and Law Beyond the State*, Cambridge University Press, 2002, p. 150. See also: Jennifer Van Bergen, *The Twilight of Democracy: The Bush Plan for America*, Common Courage Press, 2005.
162. Ibid., p. 151. See also: *US Hegemony and International Organizations: The United States and Multilateral Institutions*, edited by Rosemary Foot et al., Oxford University Press, 2003.
163. Ibid., p. 151. On this matter, see also, Nardin, *Law, Morality, and the Relations of States*, pp. 17–18. Nardin writes:

> Where ... the political community is understood as an association of individuals united by a common law, that is, as a kind of practical association, the common good is recognized not as a set of aims to be achieved through cooperation among those moved by a common wish to achieve them but as a set of values defined by common laws. The precise content of the common good, thus defined, depends upon the circumstances of particular communities and is a matter for the statesman and the citizen to determine. But it can be specified roughly as having to do above all with peace, justice, protected liberty and guaranteed rights, clearly defined and circumscribed by law, and perhaps also with provisions for the education of the members of the community and for certain minimum standards of well being, not as ends in themselves but as conditions for the public order for the community. The common good, however specified, consists of ends that are immanent in the idea of the political community as an association of citizens united not in the joint pursuit of particular purposes but because they fall under the authority of a common body of laws.

164. Ibid., pp. 418–421.
165. Paupp, *Achieving Inclusionary Governance*.
166. Harsh Mander, "Rights as Struggle—Towards a more Just and Humane World," *Reinventing Development?—Translating Rights-Based Approaches from Theory into Practice*, Zed Books, 2005, pp. 233–253.
167. Falk, *The Declining World Order*, p. 158. See also: Geert Demuijnck, "Poverty as a Human Rights Violation and the Limits of Nationalism," *Real World Justice: Grounds, Principles, Human Rights, and Social Institutions*, Springer, 2005.
168. Phillip Allott, "The Concept of International Law," *The Role of Law in International Politics: Essays in International Relations and International Law*, edited by Michael Byers, Oxford University Press, 2000, p. 88.
169. Ibid., p. 88.
170. Ibid., p. 89.
171. Frantz Fanon, "The Algerian War and Man's liberation," *El Moudjahid*, No. 51, November 1, 1958, as quoted in, *Toward The African Revolution (Political Essays)*, by Frantz Fanon, Grove Press, 1967, p. 144.
172. Ibid., p. 145.

173. Frantz Fanon, *The Wretched of the Earth*, Grove Press, 1963, p. 245.
174. Ibid., p. 246.
175. Ibid.
176. BBC Focus On Africa, "The United States of Africa," *BBC Focus On Africa*, April–June 2005, Vol. 16, No. 2, pp. 10–13.
177. Kwame Nkrumah, *Consciencism: Philosophy and Ideology for Decolonization*, Monthly Review Press, 1964, p. 102.
178. Julius K. Nyerere, *Man and Development*, Oxford University Press, 1974, p. 73.
179. Bello, *Dilemmas of Domination*, p. 126.
180. Ibid.
181. Ibid.
182. Ibid., p.128.

5   THE HIDDEN POLITICS OF EMPIRE: FROM THE NEW FRONTIER TO THE FINAL FRONTIER

1. Giovanni Arrighi, "The Social and Political Economy of Global Turbulence," *New Left Review*, March/April 2003, p. 71.
2. Toby Shelley, *Oil: Politics, Poverty and the Planet*, Zed Books, 2005, p. 197.
3. Nafeez Mosaddeq Ahmed, *The War on Truth: 9/11, Disinformation, and the Anatomy of Terrorism*, Olive Branch Press, 2005, p. 370.
4. Gerald D. McKnight, *Breach of Trust: How the Warren Commission Failed the Nation and Why*, University Press of Kansas, 2005, p. 361.
5. Hans J. Morgenthau and revised by Kenneth W. Thompson, *Politics Among Nations: The Struggle for Power and Peace, Sixth Edition*, Alfred A. Knopf, 1985, p. 52.
6. Ibid., p. 52. See also: Walter A. Davis, *Death's Dream Kingdom: The American Psyche Since 9–11*, Pluto Press, 2006; James Bouvard, *Terrorism and Tyranny: Trampling Freedom, Justice, and Peace to Rid the World of Evil*, Palgrave, 2003.
7. Nafeez Mosaddeq Ahmed, *The War On Truth:*, p. 348. See also: Carl Davidson and Jerry Harris, "Globalization, Theocracy, and the New Fascism: The US Right's Rise to Power," *Race & Class: A Journal on Racism, Empire and Globalization*, Volume 47, No. 3, January-March 2006, pp. 47–67; James Petras and Henry Veltmeyer, *Empire with Imperialism: The Globalizing Dynamics of Neo-liberal Capitalism*, Zed Books, 2005.
8. Ibid., p. 348.
9. Matthew Smith, *Conspiracy: The Plot to Stop the Kennedys*, Citadel Press, 2005, p. 50. Smith writes:

Having shackled the Pentagon, Kennedy was showing he was not prepared to unleash US military power to achieve political ends. Any lingering doubts on this were sealed by the Cuban missile crisis. The Pentagon advised the president to blast the missile installations out of existence, but he chose eyeball-to-eyeball tactics instead. Therefore, the generals had a lot to be unhappy about. They headed the most powerful military force in the world, and yet they were prevented from as much as flexing their muscles by the new president. The success of the president's peaceful approach to the Cuban missile crisis was applauded the world over, but his means of obtaining it was seen as weakness by many nearer to home. The "knock-on" effect of Kennedy's policies was that, quite apart from those industries directly affected by a reduced need for armaments, many 'feeder' industries, such as steel and plastics, and many servant industries who depended on contracts from the 'big boys' for survival, saw an uncertain future if Kennedy was allowed a second term and time to develop his fresh new way in politics. The oil millionaires were disturbed for other reasons, also. President Kennedy had been looking at the oil depletion allowances that had made them rich and were calculated to make them richer. This was a form of tax exemption established when the oil giants were being pressed to invest and reinvest in new drillings. It was a huge bonus that was long outdated and Kennedy was planning revisions to bring the oil producers into line with other industries.

Some of the leading sources which offer a more detailed analysis of this Kennedy trend in leadership are: L. Fletcher Prouty, *JFK: The CIA, Vietnam, and the Plot to Assassinate John F. Kennedy*, A Birch Lane Press Book, 1992; James Hepburn, *Farewell America: The Plot to Kill JFK*, Penmarin Books, 2002, originally published in 1968 by Frontiers Publishing Company, Vaduz, Liechtenstein; Peter Dale Scott, *Deep Politics and the Death of JFK*, University of California Press, 1993.

10. Donald Gibson, *Battling Wall Street: The Kennedy Presidency*, Sheridan Square Press, 1994; Donald Gibson, *The Kennedy Assassination Cover-Up*, Nova Science Publishers, Inc., 2000; John M. Newman, *JFK and Vietnam: Deception, Intrigue, and the Struggle for Power*, Warner Books, 1992; Michael Calder, *JFK vs. CIA: The Central Intelligence Agency's Assassination of the President*, West LA Publishers, 1998; Irving Bernstein, *Promises Kept: John F. Kennedy's New Frontier*, Oxford University Press, 1991; Robert Dallek, *An Unfinished Life—John F. Kennedy (1917–1963)*, Little Brown and Company, 2003; Robert J. Groden and Harrison Edward Livingstone, *High Treason: The Assassination of President John F. Kennedy—What Really Happened*, The Conservatory Press, 1989; Howard Jones, *Death of a Generation: How the Assassinations of Diem and JFK Prolonged the Vietnam War*, Oxford University Press, 2003; Arthur M. Schlesinger, Jr., *Robert Kennedy and His Times*, Houghton Mifflin Company, 1978.

11. Steve Brouwer, *Robbing Us Blind: The Return of the Bush Gang and the Mugging of America*, Common Courage Press, 2004; William D. Hartung, *How Much Are You Making On The War, Daddy?: A Quick and Dirty Guide to War Profiteering in the Bush Administration*, Nation Books 2003; *Devastating Society: The Neo-Conservative Assault on Democracy and Justice*, edited by Bernd Hamm, Pluto Press, 2005; *The Politics of Empire: Globalization in Crisis*, edited by Alan Freeman and Boris Kagarlitsky, Pluto Press, 2004.

12. Joel Bainerman, *The Crimes of a President: New Revelations on Conspiracy & Cover-Up in the Bush and Reagan Administrations*, SPI Books, 1992.

13. Nafeez Mosaddeq Ahmed, *The War On Freedom: How and Why America was Attacked, September 11th, 2001*, A Media Messenger Book, 2002; Nafeez Mosaddeq Ahmed, *The War On Truth*; Nafeez Mosaddeq Ahmed, *Behind The War on Terror: Western Secret Strategy and the Struggle for Iraq*, New Society Publishers, 2003.

14. Geoff Simons, *Future Iraq: US Policy in Reshaping the Middle East*, SAQI Books, 2003; Larry Everest, *Oil, Power & Empire: Iraq and the US Global Agenda*, Common Courage Press, 2004; Michael Ruppert, *Crossing The Rubicon: The Decline of the American Empire At the End of the Age of Oil*, New Society Publishers, 2004.

15. Walter M. Brasch, *America's Unpatriotic Acts: The Federal Government's Violations of Constitutional and Civil Rights*, Peter Lang, 2005; Stephen J. Schulhofer, *Rethinking the Patriot Act: Keeping America Safe and Free*, A Century Foundation Report, 2005; Howard Ball, *The USA Patriot Act*, ABC-CLIO, Inc., 2004; Peter Irons, *War Powers: How the Imperial Presidency Hijacked the Constitution*, Metropolitan Books, 2005; *Challenging US Human Rights Violations Since 9/11*, edited by Ann Fagan Ginger, Prometheus Books, 2005.

16. David Ray Griffin, *The New Pearl Harbor: Disturbing Questions about the Bush Administration and 9/11*, Olive Branch Press, 2004; David Ray Griffin, *The 9/11 Commission Report: Omissions and Distortions*, Olive Branch Press, 2005.

17. Jeffrey E. Garten, "The Global Economic Challenge," *Foreign Affairs*, January/February 2005, p. 39. See also: Andrew Kydd, "In America We (Used to) Trust: US Hegemony and Global Cooperation," *Political Science Quarterly: The Journal of Public and International Affairs*, Winter 2005–06, pp. 619–636. Kydd notes: "Most striking in light of the Soviet experience in the Cold War, the percentage thinking that the United States wishes to 'dominate the world' is 53% in France, 46% in Germany, 44% in Russia, 61% in Turkey, 55% in Pakistan, 61% in Jordan, and 60% in Morocco. This is approximately where US public opinion about the Soviet Union stood in early 1946, after the imposition of the iron curtain in Eastern Europe."[p. 635].

18. Everest, *Oil, Power, and Empire*, p. 241.

19. Ibid., p. 243. See also: Noam Chomsky, *Power and Terror: Post-9/11 Talks and Interviews*, Seven Stories Press, 2003; Scott McConnell, "From Kennan to Wolfowitz: The Intellectual Collapse of American Foreign Policy," *The American Conservative*, Vol. 4, No. 11, June 6, 2005, pp. 7–10.

20. Janice J. Terry, *US Foreign Policy in the Middle East: The Role of Lobbies and Special Interest Groups*, Pluto Press, 2005.

21. *Civil Rights in Peril: The Targeting of Arabs and Muslims*, edited by Elaine Hagopian, Pluto Press, 2004. See also: John S. Friedman, "Spying on the Protestors," *The Nation*, September 19, 2005. Friedman notes: "The protection of American citizens from unwarranted surveillance and spying now squarely rests with independent groups like the ACLU, the Bill of Rights Defense Committee and the Center for Constitutional Rights."

22. Richard Falk, "State Terror versus Humanitarian Law," *War And State Terrorism: The United States, Japan, and the Asia-Pacific in the Long Twentieth Century*, edited by Mark Seldon and Alvin So, Rowman & Littlefield, 2004, pp. 41–61. See also: CCN, "Rights Group Leader Says US Has Secret Jails," at: www.truthout.org/docs_2005/060605Z.shtml; Jim Lobe, "Jailhouse Rock," Inter Press Service, June 2, 2005, at: www.truthout.org/docs_2005/060205C.shtml; William Schultz, *Tainted Legacy: 9/11 and the Ruin of Human Rights*, Thunder's Mouth Press, 2003.

23. Ibid., p. 57. See also: Noam Chomsky, *Failed States: The Abuse of Power and the Assault on Democracy*, Metropolitan Books, 2006.

24. Michael Parenti, *Democracy for the Few, Sixth Edition*, St. Martin's Press, 1995, pp. 14–15. See also: John Kelly, "Who Counts?—Imperial and Corporate Structures of Governance, Decolonization and Limited Liability," *Lessons of Empire: Imperial Histories and American Power*, edited by Craig Calhoun et al., The New Press, 2006, pp. 157–174; James Petras and Henry Veltmeyer, *Empire with Imperialism: The Globalizing Dynamics of Neo-liberal Capitalism*, Zed Books, 2005; Chomsky, *Failed States*.

25. Nafeez Mosaddeq Ahmed, *Behind the War on Terror*, p. 29. See also: Amy Bartholomew, "Empire's Law and the Contradictory Politics of Human Rights," *Empire's Law: The American Imperial Project and the 'War to Remake the World,'* edited by Amy Bartholomew, Pluto Press, 2006, pp. 161–189.

26. Mark Curtis, *The Great Deception: Anglo-American Power and World Order*, Pluto Press, 1998, p. 112. See also: *The New Conditionality: The Politics of Poverty Reduction Strategies*, edited by Jeremy Gould, Zed Books, 2005.

27. Andre Gunder Frank, *Crisis: In The World Economy*, Holmes & Meier Publishers, 1980, p. 320.

28. Henrik Spruyt, *Ending Empire: Contested Sovereignty and Territorial Partition*, Cornell University Press, 2005, p. 26.

29. Robert Dallek, *An Unfinished Life—John F. Kennedy—(1917–1963)*, Little, Brown and Company, 2003, p. 443.

30. Ibid., p. 445.

31. Ibid., p. 450.

32. Ibid., p. 452.

33. Ibid., p. 435.

34. Ibid., p. 454. Kennedy's insight and wisdom about Indochina was lost on Lyndon Johnson, Walt Rostow, or the Joint Chiefs. Except for Kennedy, none of them could admit that they were deeply involved in a civil war in Vietnam. JFK knew that the regime in Saigon could not be saved unless it had popular support. Popular support would not come from an American escalation. That is why Kennedy had begun the withdrawal of US Marines just before his death. On this point, see: Gerard Colby with Charlotte Dennett, *Thy Will Be Done: The Conquest of the Amazon—Nelson Rockefeller and Evangelism in the Age of Oil*, HarperCollins Publishers, 1995, p. 583.

35. Lawrence Freedman, *Kennedy's Wars: Berlin, Cuba, Laos, and Vietnam*, Oxford University Press, 2000, p. 304.

36. John M. Newman, *JFK and Vietnam: Deception, Intrigue, and the Struggle for Power*, Warner Books, 1992, p. 163.

37. Ibid., p. 453.

38. Gareth Porter, *Perils of Dominance: Imbalance of Power and the Road to War in Vietnam*, University of California Press, 2005, p. 266,

39. Ibid., p. 261.

40. Ibid., p. 274. This point is critical insofar as Kennedy's approach to the Vietnam question was informed by his understanding of contemporary history and his own experience. Kennedy's views

placed him into constant conflict with his own government. As L. Fletcher Prouty notes in his book, *JFK: The CIA, Vietnam, and the Plot to Assassinate John F. Kennedy*, A Birch Lane Press Book, 1992, pp. 313–314:

Kennedy had learned much from his own experiences in Indochina since the beginning of our military/OSS involvement there in September 1945. He had seen that the billions of dollars of military aid provided to the French had been ineffectual in preventing their humiliating defeat by the Vietminh at Dien Bien Phu in 1954. He knew that during the Eisenhower administration, three US Air Force fighter aircraft armed with tactical-size nuclear weapons had been deployed to an air base in Thailand, just across the river from Laos, for potential use against North Vietnamese forces that had been observed marching into eastern Laos. He knew that these aircraft had been recalled because wiser heads had prevailed and had persuaded Eisenhower that the use of such massive weapons against guerrilla forces could not have altered the course of that insurrection and might have ignited superpower retaliation and the conflagration of the Earth.

41. Michael T. Klare, *War Without End: American Planning for the Next Vietnams*, Vintage Books, 1972, p. 9. Klare's analysis is well supported by the history of American plundering and war profiteering engaged in by the Rockefeller brothers and LBJ and his closest friends. On this point, Gerard Colby and Charlotte Dennett in their book, *Thy Will Be Done: The Conquest of the Amazon—Nelson Rockefeller and Evangelism in the Age of Oil*, HarperCollins Publishers, 1995, p. 562, note that:

The vision of Nelson and his brother went far beyond the immediate war profiteering enjoyed by some of Johnson's closest friends among Texas nouveau riche. The Rockefellers were talking about bigger things, like changing the landscape of the entire subcontinent. There were, to be sure, short-term profits to be made. Rockefeller family investments scored well in blue-chip defense contractors, such as Standard Oil of California, Standard Oil of New Jersey, Boeing, and General Motors—which took in more than $1.3 billion in military contracts in 1968 alone.

42. Peter Dale Scott, "The Vietnam War and the CIA-Financial Establishment," *Remaking Asia: Essays on the American Uses of Power*, edited by Mark Seldon, Pantheon Books, 1974, pp. 91–154,

43. Carl Boggs, *Imperial Delusions: American Militarism and Endless War*, Rowman & Littlefield Publishers, Inc., 2005, p. 83.

44. Spruyt, *Ending Empire*, pp. 26–27.

45. James R. Arnold, *The First Domino: Eisenhower, the Military, and America's Intervention in Vietnam*, William Morrow and Company, Inc., 1991.

46. David Kaiser, *American Tragedy: Kennedy, Johnson, and the Origins of the Vietnam War*, Harvard University Press, 2000, p. 20. Other historical studies have traced US commitments to Vietnam back to the late 1940s. In a book by Mark Atwood Lawrence entitled, *Assuming The Burden: Europe and the American Commitment to War in Vietnam*, University of California Press, 2005, he explores the process by which the Western powers set aside their disagreements over colonialism and extended the Cold War fight into the Third World. He also discusses the reasons why Eisenhower made a decision in 1950 to send military equipment and economic aid to bolster France in its war against the revolutionaries. That decision, in his view, marked America's first definitive step toward engagement in Indochina.

47. Ibid., p. 20. This was not only the American position under Eisenhower, because it was shared by Great Britain as well. In fact, Britain encouraged Kennedy to follow a military track in Vietnam in order to safeguard the Commonwealth's interests in Southeast Asia. On this matter, see: Peter Busch, *All The Way with JFK?—Britain, the US, and the Vietnam War*, Oxford University Press, 2003.

48. F. Gregory Gause III, "Can Democracy Stop Terrorism," *Foreign Affairs*, September/October 2005, p. 62.

49. Ibid., p. 63.

50. Ibid. On this matter, see: Adam Hanieh, "Palestinian Elections," *Z-Magazine*, March 2006, p. 4. Hanieh notes:

Hamas's landslide victory in the January 25 elections for the 132-seat Palestinian Legislative Council (PLC) is an unprecedented turning point for politics in both Palestine and the broader

Middle East. Arguably, for the first time since the establishment of Israel in 1948, an official administrative power in the West Bank and Gaza Strip has strong popular support and is not directly beholden to Israeli or Western interests.

Even after a democratic election placed Hamas in power, the Bush administration refused to recognize it because it was radical, extremist, and violent. Yet, as Chomsky notes "the organization is hardly alone in this stance." [Chomsky, *Failed States*, pp. 260–261.]

51. Ibid., p. 73.
52. Mark Levine, "Echoes of Oslo: Iraq's New Constitution Won't Change Lives Unless the Conditions of Occupation Change With It," *In These Times*, September 19, 2005, p. 20.
53. Ibid., p. 270.
54. Ibid., p. 272.
55. Ibid., p. 248.
56. Ibid., p. 251.
57. John M. Newman, *JFK and Vietnam: Deception, Intrigue, and the Struggle for Power*, Warmer, 1992, p. 393.
58. Ibid., pp. 403 and 453. With regard to the issue of JFK's position on introducing combat troops into Vietnam and his battle with the Pentagon and CIA, as well as his own advisors, Howard Jones in his study, *Death of a Generation: How the Assassinations of Diem and JFK Prolonged the Vietnam War*, Oxford, 2003, p. 1, notes:

What strikes anyone reading the veritable mountain of documents relating to Vietnam is that the only high level official in the Kennedy administration who consistently opposed the commitment of US combat forces was the president. Numerous staff studies and White House discussions of South Vietnam's troubles from 1961–1963 demonstrate his acute understanding of the issues.

59. Ibid., p. 456. Regarding JFK's planning for withdrawal through National Security Action Memoranda, see: Peter Dale Scott, "Vietnamization and the Drama of the Pentagon Papers," *The Senator Gravel Edition—The Pentagon Papers—Critical Essays Edited by Noam Chomsky and Howard Zinn and an Index to Volumes One-Four—(Volume V)*, Beacon Press, 1972, pp. 211–247.
60. Howard Jones, *Death of a Generation: How the Assassinations of Diem and JFK Prolonged the Vietnam War*, Oxford University Press, 2003, p. 452.
61. Ibid., pp. 454 and 456. Peter Dale Scott's discussion of NSAMs 263 and 273 is in his essay, "Vietnamization and the Drama of the Pentagon Papers," p. 231. A more detailed account of the differences between Kennedy's policy regarding withdrawal from Vietnam versus those of Johnson are in Chapter 2 of Scott's book entitled, *Deep Politics and the Death of JFK*, pp. 24–37.
62. Ibid., p. 452. An even more detailed account of Johnson's actions and behavior in the post-assassination period is provided by David Kaiser in his book, *American Tragedy: Kennedy, Johnson, and the Origins of the Vietnam War*, Harvard University Press, 2000, pp. 289–290. Kaiser notes:

Johnson's behavior with respect to Vietnam in 1964–1965 confused his subordinates, the press, and the public, and it has continued to confuse many historians. Largely because the president was moving on very different tracks privately and publicly, he left behind evidence that can support almost any interpretation. Only gradually did his beliefs and plans become apparent and because he instinctively told people what they wanted to hear, one must in the end focus upon what Johnson did, rather than what he said, to determine his real beliefs. Johnson clearly did not eagerly seek war in Southeast Asia, but he never questioned the need for the United States to resist the Communist threat to Vietnam by any necessary means. He certainly wanted to avoid war before the November elections, but he always seems to have been ready to undertake it should the situation become critical enough and he never seriously considered the alternatives of neutralization and withdrawal. Johnson, in short, accepted the premises of the policies that had been developed under Eisenhower—premises whose consequences Kennedy had consistently refused to accept for three years. And under Johnson the government decided quickly … in principle to implement some version of those plans to save South Vietnam.

The developing historical record on the war also points toward the fact that the war was not "inevitable," as some have claimed. On this point, H. R. McMaster in his book, *Dereliction of*

Duty: Lyndon Johnson, Robert McNamara, The Joint Chiefs of Staff, and the Lies that Led to Vietnam, HarperCollins Publishers, 1997, p. 323, noted:

The Americanization of the Vietnam War between 1963 and 1965 was the product of an unusual interaction of personalities and circumstances ... Much of the literature on Vietnam has argued that the "Cold War mentality" put such pressure on President Johnson that the Americanization of the war was inevitable. The imperative to contain Communism was an important factor in Vietnam policy, but neither American entry to the war nor the manner in which the war was conducted was inevitable. The United States went to war in Vietnam in a manner unique in American history. Vietnam was not forced on the United States by a tidal wave of Cold War ideology. It slunk in on cat's feet.

A similar conclusion was reached by Fredrik Logevall in his book, *Choosing War: The Lost Chance for Peace and the Escalation of War in Vietnam*, University of California Press, 1999.

63. McKnight, *Breach of Trust*, p. 354.
64. Scott, *Deep Politics and the Death of JFK*, p. 223. In his later writing, Professor Scott expanded his analysis of this period to include a discussion of the role of oil interests and other elite groups in organizing support for American military intervention in Vietnam, contrary to the policies laid out by President Kennedy. In keeping with the central thesis of my chapter on the "hidden politics of empire," Professor Scott lays out essential facts about the influence of hidden corporate interests and planning for the Vietnam War in his book, *Drugs, Oil, and War: The United States in Afghanistan, Columbia, and Indochina*, Rowman & Littlefield Publishers, Inc., 2003, p. 11. He notes:

Those who controlled the most secret intelligence sources (electronic and communications intelligence) allowed them to be manipulated to influence policy outcomes as well as to deceive Congress. Those who feared that the war would be lost through negotiations, (rather than on the battlefield) repeatedly applied pressure to prevent the threat of diplomatic peace. Oil interests aware of untapped reserves in the South China Sea lobbied vociferously and successfully for an increased US commitment in Indochina, well in advance of the nation's nominal decision makers. Powerful lobbies like the American Security Council veiled, in patriotic rhetoric, cases for intervention and escalation that in fact masked the budget priorities of their corporate subscribers.

65. Robert Dreyfuss, "Persian Gulf—or Tonkin Gulf: Illegal 'no-fly zones' could be war's trip wire,' *The American Prospect*, December 30, 2002, p. 10.
66. Zbigniew Brzezinski, *The Grand Chessboard: American Primacy and Its Geostrategic Imperatives*, Basic Books, 1997.
67. Nafeez Mossadeq Ahmed, *The War on Truth*, p. 336.
68. Michael Chossudovsky, *War and Globalization: The Truth Behind September 11*, Global Outlook, 2002, pp. 66–67.
69. Ibid., p. 71.
70. Ibid., p. 72.
71. Ibid., p. 77.
72. Brzezinski, *The Grand Chessboard*, p. 194.
73. Ibid., p. 214.
74. Nafeez Mosaddeq Ahmed, *The War On Truth*, p. 157.
75. Ibid., p. 158.
76. Ibid., p. 159.
77. Ibid., pp. 161–164.
78. Ibid., p. 167.
79. Ibid., p. 183.
80. Ibid., p. 210.
81. Ibid., p. 217.
82. Ibid.
83. Ibid., p. 247.
84. Ibid., pp. 262–263. On this matter, see also: Walter E. Davis, "September 11 and the Bush Administration: Compelling Evidence for Complicity," *Devastating Society: The Neo-Conservative*

Assault on Democracy and Justice, edited by Bernd Hamm, Pluto Press, 2005, pp. 67–87; Barrie Zwicker, "The Great Conspiracy: The 9/11 News Special You Never Saw," *Global Outlook*, Issue 9, Fall 2004/Winter 2005, pp. 7–20; David Ray Griffin, *The 9/11 Commission Report: Omissions and Distortions*, Olive Branch Press, 2005; David Ray Griffin, *The New Pearl Harbor: Disturbing Questions about the Bush Administration and 9/11*, Olive Branch Press, 2004; Ian Henshall and Rowland Morgan, *9/11 Revealed: The Unanswered Questions*, Carroll & Graf Publishers, 2005; Douglas Kellner, *Media Spectacle and the Crisis of Democracy: Terrorism, War, and Election Battles*, Paradigm Publishers, 2005; Douglas Kellner, *From 9/11 to Terror War: The Dangers of the Bush Legacy*, Rowman & Littlefield Publishers, Inc., 2003.

85. Ibid., p. 366.

86. Ibid.

87. Ibid., p. 367.

88. Scott, *Drugs, Oil, and War*, p. 16.

89. James Hepburn, *Farewell America: The Plot to Kill JFK*, Penmarin Books, 2002, originally published in 1968 by Frontiers Publishing Company, Vaduz, Liechtenstein. It is really the work of French intelligence officers, filled with restricted information about US intelligence agencies, the White House, global business, and the hidden politics of military and political affairs. See also: *The Assassinations: Probe Magazine on JFK, MLK, RFK and Malcolm X*, edited by James DiEugenio and Lisa Pease, Feral House, 2003; Philip H. Melanson, *The Robert F. Kennedy Assassination: New Revelations on the Conspiracy and Cover-Up, (1968–1991)*, Shapolsky Publishers, Inc., 1991; William Klaber and Philip H. Melanson, *Shadow Play: The Murder of Robert F. Kennedy, the Trial of Sirhan Sirhan, and the Failure of American Justice*, St. Martin's Press, 1997; David S. Lifton, *Best Evidence: Disguise and Deception in the Assassination of John F. Kennedy*, Macmillan Publishing Co., Inc., 1980; Lamar Waldron with Thom Hartmann, *Ultimate Sacrifice: John and Robert Kennedy, the Plan for a Coup in Cuba, and the Murder of JFK*, Carroll & Graf Publishers, 2005.

90. McKnight, *Breach of Trust*, pp. 355–356. The author notes:

> The Secret Service and FBI agents who were present at the Bethesda Hospital morgue and witnessed the Kennedy autopsy were never able to reconcile the official version of the shooting with the wounds they saw on the president's body. The most stunning and puzzling disconnect derived from the X-ray of JFK's head revealing on the order of thirty to forty dust-like particles that showed up on the light screen like the "Milky Way" (Agent Roy Kellerman's characterization). The immediate reaction from both the FBI and Secret Service onlookers was that Kennedy's massive lacerated head wound had been caused by a dum-dum bullet, that is, a hollow nosed ammunition that explodes when it enters the body. Although not conclusive, this speculation about an exploding bullet was consistent with the FBI's firearms expert Robert Frazier's diagrams of the distribution of bullet fragments, blood, brain matter, and tissue in the presidential limousine. Frazier's report noted the scattering of blood and JFK's brain matter in front of and behind the right visor and more importantly, on the hood of the car. All of this indicated that the bullet or bullets that had struck the president in the head had exploded upon impact.

> On this matter, see also: Groden and Livingstone, *High Treason*,; Harrison Livingstone, *The Radical Right and the Murder of John F. Kennedy: Stunning Evidence in the Assassination of the President*, The Conservatory Press, 2004; The Committee to Investigate Assassinations under the Direction of Bernard Fensterwald, Jr., *Coincidence Or Conspiracy*, Zebra Books, 1977.

91. L. Fletcher Prouty, *JFK: The CIA, Vietnam and the Plot to Assassinate John F. Kennedy*, A Birch Lane Press Book, 1992, pp. 315–316.

92. Michael Parenti, *The Assassination of Julius Caesar: A People's History of Ancient Rome*, The New Press, 2003, pp. 82–83; See also: Chalmers Johnson, "The Scourge of Militarism: Rome and America," *TomDispatch,com*, at: www.truthout.org/doc_2005/061005M.Shtmil.

93. Gibson, *Battling Wall Street*.

94. Gibson, *The Kennedy Assassination Cover-Up*, pp. 247–248. For a wider context and expanded historical perspective on Gibson's claims and analysis, see also: Richard N. Goodwin, *Promises*

To Keep: A Call for a New American Revolution, Times Books, 1992; Seymour Melman, *After Capitalism: From Managerialism to Workplace Democracy*, Alfred A. Knopf, 2001; Robert Scheer, *America After Nixon: The Age of Multinationals*, McGraw-Hill Book Company, 1974; *Leviathans: Multinational Corporations and the New Global History*, Cambridge University Press, 2005; Richard J. Barnet and Ronald E. Muller, *Global Reach: The Power of the Multinational Corporations*, Simon and Schuster, 1974; Richard J. Barnet and John Cavanagh, *Global Dreams: Imperial Corporations and The New World Order*, Simon & Schuster, 1994; Samuel Bowles and Herbert Gintis, *Democracy and Capitalism: Property, Community, and the Contradictions of Modern Social Thought*, Basic Books, 1986; Edwin Amenta, *Bold Relief: Institutional Politics and the Origins of Modern American Social Policy*, Princeton University Press, 1998; David M. Gordon, *Fat and Mean: The Corporate Squeeze of Working Americans and the Myth of Managerial "Downsizing,"* The Free Press, 1996; Michael J. Sandel, *Democracy's Discontent: America in Search of a Public Philosophy*, Harvard University Press, 1996; David Plotke, *Building A Democratic Political Order: Reshaping American Liberalism in the 1930s and 1940s*, Cambridge University Press, 1996; Jonathan Bell, *The Liberal State on Trial: The Cold War and American Politics in the Truman Years*, Columbia University Press, 2004.

95. James Bamford, *Body of Secrets: Anatomy of the Ultra-Secret National Security Agency From the Cold War Through the Dawn of a New Century*, Doubleday, 2001, p. 82.

96. Ibid.

97. Ibid., p. 83. See also: *Bay of Pigs Declassified: The Secret CIA Report on the Invasion of Cuba*, edited by Peter Kornbluh, The New Press, 1998.

98. Ibid., p. 85.

99. Ibid., p. 87.

100. Ibid., p. 88.

101. Ibid., p. 89.

102. Ibid., p. 90. On this matter and its connection to the events of 9/11, see: Nafeez Mosaddeq Ahmed, *The War On Truth*, pp. 385–390; Nafeez Mosaddeq Ahmed, *The War On Freedom*, pp. 322–328.

103. Ibid., p. 91. Bamford notes:

> Now ... in light of the Operation Northwoods documents, it is clear that deceiving the public and trumping up wars for Americans to fight and die in was the standard approved policy at the highest levels of the Pentagon. In fact, the Gulf of Tonkin seems right out of the Operation Northwoods playbook: "We could blow up a US ship in Guantanamo Bay and blame Cuba ... casualty lists in US newspapers would cause a helpful wave of indignation." One need only replace "Guantanamo Bay" with "Tonkin Gulf." And "Cuba" with "North Vietnam."

> See also: Robert B. Stinnett, *Day of Deceit: The Truth About FDR and Pearl Harbor*, Touchstone, 2000.

104. McKnight, *Breach of Trust*, p. 331. See also: Livingstone, *The Radical Right and the Murder of John F. Kennedy*. See also: Morris H. Morley, *Imperial State and Revolution· The United States and Cuba, 1952–1986*, Cambridge University Press, 1987. The most recent discussion of covert CIA planning, hidden even from the Kennedy brothers, indicates that the CIA-Mafia plots against Castro continued despite assurances being given to the President and Attorney General Robert Kennedy—by the CIA—that they had ended. In a recently published study by Lamar Waldron with Hartmann, *Ultimate Sacrifice*, p. 428, the authors note:

> Even Rosselli's work for the CIA on the CIA-Mafia plots to kill Castro didn't give Rosselli any leverage with Bobby, since the plots had begun before JFK was elected and the CIA had assured Bobby and CIA Director McCone that the plots had ended; however, CIA officials at the level of Richard Helms, William Harvey, and David Morales were continuing the plots to kill Castro with Rosselli in the spring, summer, and fall of 1963.

105. Scott, "Vietnamization and the Drama of the Pentagon Papers," p. 230.

106. Ibid., p. 230.

107. Scott, "Vietnamization and the Drama of the Pentagon Papers," p. 230.

108. Ibid., p. 231.

109. Terrence E. Paupp, "The Nuclear Crucible: The Moral and International Law Implications of Weapons of Mass Destruction," *In Democracy's Shadow: The Secret World of National Security*, edited by Marcus G. Raskin and A. Carl LeVan, Nation Books, 2005, pp. 73–95. See also: Charles Tiefer, *Veering Right: How the Bush Administration Subverts the Law for Conservative Causes*, University of California Press, 2004; Cass R. Sunstein, *Radicals In Robes: Why Right-Wing Courts Are Wrong for America*, Basic Books, 2005; Chris Mooney, *The Republican War On Science*, Basic Books, 2005; Walter Williams, *Reaganism and the Death of Representative Democracy*, Georgetown University Press, 2003; Ronald Brownstein and Nina Easton, *Reagan's Ruling Class: Portraits of the President's Top 100 Officials*, The Presidential Accountability Group, 1982; Eric Alterman and Mark Green, *The Book on Bush: How George W. (Mis)leads America*, Viking. 2004; Bruce Montgomery, "Congressional Oversight: Vice President Richard B. Cheney's Executive Branch Triumph," *Political Science Quarterly: The Journal of Public and International Affairs*, Vol. 120, No. 4, Winter 2005–06, pp. 581–617.

110. Laurence H. Shoup, "Bush, Kerry, and the Council on Foreign Relations," *Z-Magazine*, October 2004, pp. 27–34; Laurence H. Shoup and William Minter, *Imperial Brain Trust: The Council on Foreign Relations & United States Foreign Policy*, Monthly Review Press, 1977; Laurence H. Shoup, *The Carter Presidency and Beyond: Power and Politics in the 1980s*, Ramparts Press, 1980.

111. Amy Gutman and Dennis Thompson, *Why Deliberative Democracy?* Princeton University Press, 2004.

112. Nancy Bermeo, *Ordinary People in Extraordinary Times: The Citizenry and the Breakdown of Democracy*, Princeton University Press, 2003.

113. Terrence E. Paupp, "Between The Arrows and the Olive Branch: The Tortured Path of the War Powers Resolution in the Reagan Years (1981–1987)," *The Journal of Contemporary Legal Issues*, Vol. 1, No. 1, Fall 1987, p. 67. See also: John Hart Ely, *War and Responsibility: Constitutional Lessons of Vietnam and its Aftermath*, Princeton University Press, 1993; Richard J. Barnett, *The Rocket's Red Glare: When America Goes To War—The Presidents and the People*, Simon and Schuster, 1990; *The Constitution and the Conduct of American Foreign Policy*, edited by David Gray Adler and Larry N. George, University Press of Kansas, 1996; Christopher N. May, *In The Name of War: Judicial Review and the War Powers since 1918*, Harvard University Press, 1989.

114. Peter Irons, *War Powers: How the Imperial Presidency Hijacked the Constitution*, Metropolitan Books, 2005, pp. 234–235. See also: Andrew Rudalevige, *The New Imperial Presidency: Renewing Presidential Power after Watergate*, The University of Michigan Press, 2005, pp. 192–221.

115. James Bouvard, *Terrorism and Tyranny: Trampling Freedom, Justice, and Peace, to Rid the World of Evil*, Palgrave, 2003, p. 80. See also: James Bouvard, *The Bush Betrayal*, Palgrave, 2004; John Podesta, "Bush's Secret Government: Using fear and national security to hide information from the public," *The American Prospect*, September 2003, pp. 44–46.

116. Geoffrey R. Stone, *Perilous Times: Free Speech in Wartime—From the Sedition Act of 1798 to the War on Terrorism*, W.W. Norton & Company, 2004, p. 557. See also: Coleen M. Rowley, "Civil Liberties and Effective Investigation," *Patriotism, Democracy, and Common Sense: Restoring America's Promise at Home and Abroad*, edited by Alan Curtis, The Milton S. Eisenhower Foundation and Rowman & Littlefield Publishers, Inc., 2004, pp. 349–364; Thom Hartmann, *What Would Jefferson Do?—A Return to Democracy*, Harmony Books, 2004.

117. Michael Ratner, "Moving Toward a Police State (Or Have We Arrived?)", *Global Outlook*, No. 1, 2002, p. 35. See also: Michael Chossudovsky, *War and Globalization: The Truth Behind September 11*, Global Outlook, 2002, p. 9; Rudalevige, *The New Imperial Presidency*, pp. 241–248.

118. Stephen R. Shalom, "V-J Day: Remembering the Pacific War," *Z-Magazine*, July/August 1995, p. 76; See also: Chossudovsky, *War and Globalization*, pp. 10–13; John W. Dean, *Worse Than Watergate: The Secret Presidency of George W. Bush*, Little Brown and Company, 2004,

pp. 103–104. See also: Rudalevige, *The New Imperial Presidency*, p. 226. Rudalevige notes:

A permissive set of rules governing interrogation was approved by the president, allowing the CIA to set up secret detention centers abroad; for high-level terror suspects, reportedly, the order allowed treatment on the edge (or over the edge) of torture—for example, techniques like "water barding," where a bound prisoner is held underwater to the brink of drowning. Other detainees were sent to third countries with few constraints on outright torture or kept as unofficial "ghosts" in army facilities. A series of memos from the CIA's general counsel and the Justice Department's Office of Legal Counsel (OLC) claimed for the agency wide custodial and interrogation powers that in some cases overrode the Geneva Conventions governing the treatment of prisoners and civilians during wartime and occupation. OLC argued that, "to facilitate interrogation," formal charges should not be brought against potential suspects, as this would trigger Geneva protections preventing detainees from being moved to other countries.

119. Steve Coll, *Ghost Wars: The Secret History of the CIA, Afghanistan, and Bin Laden, From the Soviet Invasion to September 10, 2001*, The Penguin Press, 2004. See also: William Blum, *Killing Hope: US Military and CIA Interventions Since World War II (Updated Edition)*, Common Courage Press, 2004.

120. Ibid., pp. 21–353. See also, Chossudovsky, *War and Globalization*, pp. 18–34; Paul Thomason and the Center for Cooperative Research, *The Terror Timeline—Year By Year, Day By Day, Minute By Minute: A Comprehensive Chronicle of the Road to 9/11—and America's Response*, Regan Books, 2004.

121. Dilip Hiro, "Fallout From the Afghan Jihad," Inter Press Services, November 21, 1995. See also: Scott, *Drugs, Oil, and War*, pp. 39–58.

122. "An Underlying Impetus for Soviet Invasion," *Business Week*, September 29, 1980, p. 62.

123. Chossudovsky, *War and Globalization*, pp. 24–25.

124. As quoted in Jonathan Marshall, *To Have And Have Not: Southeast Asian Raw Materials and the Origins of the Pacific War*, University of California Press, 1995, p. 1.

125. Ibid., p. 1.

126. Ibid., p. 7.

127. Ibid., p. 16.

128. Ibid., p. 186.

129. Porter, *Perils of Dominance*, p. 255.

130. Ibid., p. 255. Porter states:

The fear of neutralism was not limited to Southeast Asia but was part of the global perspective inherited by the national security bureaucracy from Eisenhower. The CIA reflected that perspective in its "Estimate of the World Situation" a few days before Kennedy took office, learning that, unless reversed, the trend toward neutralism already underway in the developing world "will become so strong that it will draw away from the West some of those nations now associated with it." That was a trend that national security officials strongly resisted wherever possible.

The historical record demonstrates that Kennedy's approach to neutralism in the Third World was positive, especially given the constraints of the Cold War and opposition from his national security officials. See, for example: Dennis Merrill, *Bread and the Ballot: The United States and India's Economic Development, 1947–1963*, The University of North Carolina Press, 1990, pp. 183–186; Robert J. McMahon, *The Cold War on the Periphery: The United States, India, and Pakistan*, Columbia University Press, 1994; Richard D. Mahoney, *JFK: Ordeal In Africa*, Oxford University Press, 1983. For an extended discussion of American fears regarding the growing Non-Aligned Movement from the Eisenhower presidency through 1964, see: Odd Arne Westad, *The Global Cold War: Third World Interventions and the Making of Our Times*, Cambridge University Press, 2005, pp. 73–109.

131. Dale R. Herspring, *The Pentagon and the Presidency: Civil-Military Relations from FDR to George W. Bush*, University Press of Kansas, 2005, pp. 148–149.

132. Porter, *Perils of Dominance*, pp. 178–179. See also: Robert S. McNamara, James Blight, Robert Brigham, Thomas Biersteker, and Col. Herbert Schandler, *Argument without End: In Search Of Answers to the Vietnam Tragedy*, Public Affairs, 1999, p. 402. As of 1999, Vietnam still remained

an "argument without end." In assessing new perspectives on what was and was not inevitable, a collection of participants in shaping those events came to an important conclusion: "The confrontation leading to war, between Washington and Hanoi need not have occurred if each had correctly understood the other's perception of the evolution of the Cold War in Asia and the other's role in that evolution."

133. Chossudovsky, *War and Globalization*, p. 14. See also: Douglas B. Lee, Jr. and John W. Dyckman, "Economic Impacts of the War in Indochina: A Primer," *Cambodia: The Widening War In Indochina*, edited by Jonathan S. Grant et al., Committee of Concerned Asian Scholars, Washington, Square Press, 1971; Julian E. Barnes, "Investigative Report—Profiteers Of War: How Some of America's Biggest Companies are Making Millions Off the Defense Buildup Since 9/11," *US News & World Report*, May 13, 2002, pp. 20–34; Joshua S. Goldstein, *The Real Price of War: How You Pay For The War On Terror*, New York University Press, 2004; Seymour Melman, *Our Depleted Society*, Holt, Rinehart and Winston, 1965.

134. Joe Klein, "Saddam's Revenge: The Secret History of U.S. Mistakes, Misjudgments and Intelligence Failures that let the Iraqi Dictator and his Allies Launch an Insurgency now Ripping Iraq Apart," *Time*, September 26, 2005, p. 52. See also: Gareth Porter, "The Third Option in Iraq: A Responsible Exit Strategy," *Middle East Policy*, Volume XII, Fall 2005, Number 3, pp. 29–45.

135. Ibid., p. 52.

136. Robert Buzzanco, *Masters of War: Military Dissent and Politics in the Vietnam Era*, Cambridge University Press, 1996, p. 273; See also: Lloyd Gardner, *Pay Any Price: Lyndon Johnson and the Wars for Vietnam*, Ivan R. Dee, 1995.

137. Gregory Douglas, *Regicide: The Official Assassination of John F. Kennedy*, Monte Sano Media, 2002; Harrison E. Livingstone, *Killing Kennedy And the Hoax of the Century*, Carroll & Graf Publishers, Inc., 1995; Harold Weisberg, *Never Again: The Government Conspiracy in the JFK Case*, Carroll & Graf Publishers, 1995; *Assassination Science: Experts Speak Out on the Death of JFK*, edited by James H. Fetzer, Catfeet Press, 1998; *The Great Zapruder Film Hoax: Deceit and Deception in the Death of JFK*, edited by James H. Fetzer, Catfeet Press, 2003; John Prados, *Keepers Of The Keys: A History of the National Security Council from Truman to Bush*, William Morrow and Company, Inc., 1991.

138. McKnight, *Breach of Trust*, p. 357.

139. Ibid., p. 352.

140. Ibid., p. 357. For a detailed account of the second Cuban invasion scenario and its linkage to the JFK assassination, see also: Matthew Smith, *JFK: The Second Plot*, Mainstream Publishing, 1992; Anthony Summers, *Conspiracy*, McGraw-Hill Book Company, 1980.

141. Ibid., p. 357.

142. Matthew Smith, *Say Goodbye to America: The Sensational and Untold Story Behind the Assassination of John F. Kennedy*, Mainstream Publishing, 2001; James DiEugenio, *Destiny Betrayed: JFK, Cuba, and the Garrison Case*, Sheridan Square Press, 1992; Alexsandr Fursenko and Timothy Naftali, *"One Hell Of A Gamble"—Khrushchev, Castro & Kennedy (1958–1964)*, W.W. Norton & Company, 1997; Sheldon M. Stern, *Averting "The Final Failure"—John F. Kennedy and the Secret Cuban Missile Crisis Meetings*, Stanford University Press, 2003; Warren Hinckle and William W. Turner, *Deadly Secrets: The CIA-Mafia War Against Castro and the Assassination of JFK*, Thunder's Mouth Press, 1992; McKnight, *Breach of Trust*, 2005.

143. Porter, *Perils of Dominance*, p. 266.

144. Ibid., p. 265.

145. Ibid.

146. Ibid.

147. Scott, *Deep Politics and the Death of JFK*, p. 222. See also: Mark Lane, *Plausible Denial: Was the CIA Involved in the Assassination of JFK?*, Thunders' Mouth Press, 1991, pp. 91–114; Gaeton Fonzi, *The Last Investigation*, Thunder's Mouth Press, 1993; Noel Twyman, *Bloody Treason: The Assassination of John F. Kennedy*; Laurel Publishing, 1997.

148. McKnight, *Breach of Trust*, 2005.

149. Gibson, *The Kennedy Assassination Cover-Up*, pp. 248–249.

150. Ibid., p. 253. See also: Gibson, *Battling Wall Street*.

151. Seymour M. Hersh, *The Price of Power: Kissinger in the Nixon White House*, Summit Books, 1983; Anthony Summers, *The Arrogance of Power: The Secret World of Richard Nixon*, Viking, 2000; Anthony Summers, *Official and Confidential: The Secret Life of J. Edgar Hoover*, G.P. Putnam's Sons, 1993; Tad Szulc, *The Illusion of Peace: Foreign Policy in the Nixon Years*, The Viking Press, 1978; Jeffrey Kimball, *The Vietnam War Files: Uncovering the Secret History of Nixon-Era Strategy*, University Press of Kansas, 2004; Jeffrey Kimball, *Nixon's Vietnam War*, University Press of Kansas, 1998; Larry Berman, *No Peace, No Honor: Nixon, Kissinger, and Betrayal in Vietnam*, The Free Press, 2001; Robert S. Litwak, *Détente and the Nixon Doctrine: American Foreign Policy and the Pursuit of Stability, 1969–1976*, Cambridge University Press, 1984; *Open Secret: The Kissinger-Nixon Doctrine in Asia*, edited by Virginia Brodine and Mark Selden, Perennial Library/Harper & Row, Publishers, 1972.

152. McKnight, *Breach of Trust*. See also: Harrison Edward Livingstone, *High Treason (2)—The Great Cover-Up: The Assassination of President John F. Kennedy*, Carroll & Graf Publishers, Inc., 1992; Harrison E. Livingstone, *Killing The Truth: Deceit and Deception in the JFK Case*, Carroll & Graff Publishers, Inc., 1993.

153. Robert Engler, *The Politics of Oil: Private Power and Democratic Directions*, The University of Chicago Press, 1961, First Phoenix Edition (1967). Engler notes:

"In the name of prosperity and technology, the industry has been able to destroy competition and limit abundance. In the name of national interest it has received privileges beyond those accorded to other industries. In the name of national security, oil has influenced and profited from a foreign policy that has supported the chauvinism of a few rather than generosity to the aspirations of many in the underdeveloped areas. In the name of private enterprise, it has contributed to the attenuation of vital portions of democratic life, from education to civic morality. In the name of the right of representation, it has so entrenched itself within the political processes that it becomes impossible to distinguish public from private actions. In the name of freedom, the oil industry has received substantial immunity from public accountability.

See also: Vijay Prashad, *Fat Cats & Running Dogs: The Enron Stage of Capitalism*, Common Courage Press, 2003; Michael Waldman and the staff of Public Citizen's Congress Watch, *Who Robbed America?—A Citizen's Guide to the S & L Scandal*, Random House, 1990.

154. Michael T. Klare, *Blood And Oil: The Dangers and Consequences of America's Growing Petroleum Dependency*, Metropolitan Books, 2004, p. 57.

155. Ibid., p. 57.

156. Ibid., pp. 58–66. See also: John Bacher, *PetroTyranny*, Science for Peace Dundurn Press, 2000; John Vidal, "Coming Oil Crisis Feared: Expert Warns that price may soar to $100 a barrel and spark economic collapse," *The Guardian Weekly*, April 29–May 5, 2005, Vol. 172, No. 19; Richard Heinberg, *The Party's Over: Oil, War and the Fate of Industrial Societies*, New Society Publishers, 2003; Stephen Pelletiere, *Iraq and the International oil System: Why America Went To War in the Gulf*, Maisonneuve Press, 2004; Dan Briody, *The Halliburton Agenda: The Politics of Oil and Money*, John Wiley & Sons, Inc., 2994; Paul Sperry, *Crude Politics: How Bush's Oil Cronies Hijacked the War On Terrorism*; WND Books, 2003; Paul Roberts, *The End of Oil: On the Edge of a Perilous New World*, Houghton Mifflin Company, 2004.

157. Ibid., p. 67.

158. Ibid.

159. Nafeez Mosaddeq Ahmed, *The War On Truth*, p. 319.

160. Alan M. Dershowitz, *Supreme Injustice: How the High Court Hijacked Election 2000*, Oxford University Press, 2001; Daniel Lazare, *The Velvet Coup: The Constitution, the Supreme Court, and the Decline of American Democracy*, Verso, 2001; Howard Gillman, *The Votes That Counted: How The Court Decided The 2000 Presidential Election*, The University of Chicago Press, 2001; Vincent Bugliosi, *The Betrayal of America: How the Supreme Court Undermined the Constitution and Chose our President*, Thunder's Mouth Press, 2001.

161. Robert Bryce, *Cronies: Oil the Bushes, and the Rise of Texas, America's Super-State*, Public Affairs, 2004.

162. Michael Lind, *Made In Texas: George W. Bush and the Southern Takeover of American Politics*, Basic Books, 2003; Kevin Phillips, *American Dynasty: Aristocracy, Fortune, and the Politics of*

Deceit in the House of Bush, Viking, 2004; Daniel Altman, *Neoconomy: George W. Bush's Revolutionary Gamble with America's Future*, Public Affairs, 2004.

163. Andrew J. Bacevich, "The Real World War IV," *The Wilson Quarterly*, Winter 2005, pp. 36–61; Andrew J. Bacevich, *The New American Militarism: How Americans Are Seduced by War*, Oxford University Press, 2001; Andrew J. Bacevich, *American Empire: The Realities and Consequences of US Diplomacy*, Harvard University Press, 2002; *The War System: An Interdisciplinary Approach*, edited by Richard A. Falk and Samuel S. Kim, Westview Press, 1980; *The Obligations of Empire: United States' Grand Strategy for a New Century*, edited by James J. Hentz, The University Press of Kentucky, 2004; *The Use of Force: Military Power and International Politics, Fifth Edition*, edited by Robert J. Art and Kenneth N. Waltz, Rowman & Littlefield Publishers, Inc., 1999.

164. Martin Meredith, *The Fate of Africa: From the Hopes of Freedom to the Heart of Despair—A History of Fifty Years of Independence*, Public Affairs, 2005; Richard Falk, *Predatory Globalization: A Critique*, Polity Press, 1999; Fred Rosen, "Introductory Essay: Empire and Dissent," *NACLA Report on the Americas*, Vol. 39, No. 2, September/October 2005,

165. Alan Knight, "Empire, Hegemony and Globalization in the Americas," *NACLA Report on the Americas*, Vol. 39, No. 2, September/October 2005.

166. Robert F. Kennedy, *To Seek A Newer World*, Doubleday & Company, Inc., 1967, p. 80.

167. Gibson, *Battling Wall Street*, p. 84.

168. Gerard Colby with Charlotte Dennett, *Thy Will Be Done: The Conquest of the Amazon—Nelson Rockefeller and Evangelism in the Age of Oil*, HarperCollins Publishers, 1995, p. 536.

169. Ibid., pp. 534–535.

170. Ibid., p. 538.

171. Ibid., p. 539.

172. Clara Nieto, *Masters Of War: Latin America and United States Aggression from the Cuban Revolution Through the Clinton Years*, Seven Stories Press, 2003, p. 95. See also: Lester D. Langley, *The Americas in the Modern Age*, Yale University Press, 2005, pp. 189–223; Jeff Shesol, *Mutual Contempt: Lyndon Johnson, Robert Kennedy, and the Feud That Defined a Decade*, W.W. Norton & Company, 1997; Sean J. Savage, *JFK, LBJ, and the Democratic Party*, State University of New York Press, 2004.

173. Ernest Feder, "Counter-reform," *Agrarian Problems And Peasant Movements In Latin America*, edited by Rodolfo Stavenhagen, Anchor Books, Doubleday & Company, Inc., 1970, pp. 205–206. This view has taken on new importance in the late 1990s and early years of the twenty-first century. On this matter, see: William Easterly, "The Political Economy of Growth without Development: A Case Study of Pakistan," *In Search of Prosperity: Analytic Narrative on Economic Growth*, edited by Dani Rodrik, Princeton University Press, 2003, pp. 460–461. In his study of growth without development in Pakistan, economist William Easterly asked: "Why didn't Pakistani growth result in social and political development? Why is the social crisis so pronounced in Pakistan for its level of income?" Easterly notes that

> Pakistani economist Ishrat Husain put forward a persuasive formulation of the effects of elite dominance: "The ruling elites found it convenient to perpetuate low literacy rates. The lower the proportion of literate people, the lower the probability that the ruling elite could be displaced" ... Landowners have been prominent in virtually all Pakistani government coalitions ... Landowners have formed an alliance with the military leadership, who have in turn played a prominent role in Pakistani politics.

174. Ibid., p. 208.

175. Ibid., p. 214.

176. Ibid., p. 223.

177. L. Ronald Scheman, *Greater America: A New Partnership for the Americas in the Twenty-First Century*, New York University Press, 2003, p. 68.

178. Ibid., p. 77.

179. Schlesinger, Jr., *Robert Kennedy And His Times*, p. 689.

180. Ibid., p. 690.

181. Ibid.

182. Gibson, *The Kennedy Assassination Cover-Up*, p. 255.

183. Ibid., p. 256.

184. Brian Dooley, *Robert Kennedy: The Final Years*, St. Martin's Press, 1996, p. 101.

185. *IMF Conditionality*, edited by John Williamson, Institute for International Economics, 1983; Robin Broad, *Unequal Alliance: The World Bank, the International Monetary Fund, and the Philippines*, University of California Press, 1988; Robert E. Wood, *From Marshall Plan To Debt Crisis: Foreign Aid and Development Choices in the World Economy*, University of California Press, 1986; Robert E. Wood, "The World Bank and the Third World: Towards a Politics of Aid," *Socialist Review*, No. 73, Vol.14, No. 1, January/February 1894, pp. 123–138; James Petras and Howard Brill, "The IMF, Austerity, and the State In Latin America," *Third World Quarterly*, April 1986, Vol. 8, No. 2, pp. 425–448; *The Politics of International Debt*, edited by Miles Kahler, Cornell University Press, 1986; *Global Finance: New Thinking on Regulating Speculative Capital Markets*, edited by Walden Bello, Nicola Bullard, and Kamal Malhotra, Zed Books, 2000; Kavaljit Singh, *The Globalization of Finance: A Citizen's Guide*, Zed Books, 1999; Michael Chossudovsky, *The Globalization of Poverty: Impacts of IMF and World Bank Reforms*, Zed Books, 1997; Susan George, *The Debt Boomerang: How Third World Debt Harms Us All*, Westview Press, 1992; Susan George, *A Fate Worse Than Debt: The World Financial Crisis and the Poor*, Grove Press, 1988; *Debt Disaster?—Banks, Governments, and Multilaterals Confront the Crisis*, edited by John F. Weeks, New York University Press, 1989; Catherine Caufield, *Masters of Illusion: The World Bank and the Poverty of Nations*, Henry Holt and Company, 1996; Shahrukh Rafi Khan, *Do World Bank and IMF Policies Work?*, St. Martin's Press, Inc., 1999; Jackie Roddick, *The Dance of the Millions: Latin America and the Debt Crisis*, Latin America Research Bureau, 1988; Graham Hancock, *Lords of Poverty: The Power, Prestige, and Corruption of the International Aid Business*, The Atlantic Monthly Press, 1989; *The Poverty of Nations: A Guide to the Debt Crisis—from Argentina to Zaire*, Elmar Alvater et al. editors, Zed Books, 1991; *The IMF and the Debt Crisis: A Guide to the Third World's Dilemma*, edited by Peter Korner et al., Zed Books, 1986.

186. Gibson, *The Kennedy Assassination Cover Up*, p. 256. See also: *Reinventing the World Bank*, edited by Jonathan R. Pincus and Jeffrey A. Winters, Cornell University Press, 2002; David Woodward, *Debt, Adjustment and Poverty in Developing Countries, Volume I, National and International Dimensions of Debt and Adjustment in Developing Countries*, Pinter Publishers (London) in association with Save the Children, 1992.

187. Ibid., p. 256.

188. Joseph E. Stiglitz, "Development Policies in a World of Globalization," *Putting Development First: The Importance of Policy Space in the WTO and IFIs*, edited by Kevin P. Gallagher, Zed Books, 2005, p. 19. See also: Joseph E. Stiglitz, *Globalization And Its Discontents*, W.W. Norton & Company, 2003; Biplab Dasgupta, *Structural Adjustment, Global Trade and the New Political Economy of Development*, Zed Books, 1998; Robert Biel, *The New imperialism: Crisis and Contradictions in North-South Relations*, Zed Books, 2000; Bruce Rich, *Mortgaging the Earth: The World Bank, Environmental Impoverishment, and the Crisis of Development*, Beacon Press, 1994.

189. Ibid., p. 15. See also: *After The Washington Consensus: Restarting Growth and Reform in Latin America*, edited by Pedro-Pablo Kuczynski and John Williamson, Institute for International Economics, 2003; Jeffrey A. Friedman, *Debt, Development, and Democracy: Modern Political Economy and Latin America, 1965–1985*, Princeton University Press, 1991.

190. Ibid., p. 23.

191. Ibid., p. 32. See also: *Fault Lines of Democracy in Post-Transition Latin America*, edited by Felipe Aguero and Jeffrey Stark, North-South Press Center, 1998; Herman E. Daly, *Beyond Growth: The Economics of Sustainable Development*, 1996; Robert Brenner, *The Boom and the Bubble: The US in the World Economy*, Verso, 2002; *The Role of the World Trade Organization in Global Governance*, edited by Gary P. Sampson, United Nations University Press, 2001; Oswaldo de Rivero, *The Myth of Development: Non-Viable Economics of the 21st Century*, Zed Books, 2001; Michael D. Yates, *Naming the System: Inequality and Work in the Global Economy*, Monthly Review Press, 2003; Graham Dunkley, *The Free Trade Adventure: The WTO, the Uruguay Round and Globalism—A Critique*, Zed Books, 1997; Noreen Hertz, *The Debt*

Threat: How Debt is Destroying the Developing World, Harper-Business, 2004; Noreen Hertz, *The Silent Takeover: Global Capitalism and the Death of Democracy*, The Free Press, 2001; Joseph E. Stiglitz, *The Roaring Nineties: A New History of the World's Most Prosperous Decade*, W.W. Norton & Company, 2003.

192. Gibson, *Battling Wall Street*, p. 113. See also: *Global Trade and Global Social Issues*, edited by Annie Taylor and Caroline Thomas, Routledge, 1999; Remarks of Chairman of the Federal Reserve Board, Alan Greenspan, before the Annual Convention of the American Society of Newspaper Editors, Washington, DC, April 2, 1998, in a speech entitled: "The Ascendance of Market Capitalism," at: www.bog.frb.us/boarddoc/speeches/19980402.htm. For some contrary perspectives on Greenspan's views, see also: Martin Meyer, *The Fed: The Inside Story of How the World's Most Powerful Financial Institution Drives the Markets*, The Free Press, 2001; Ravi Batra, *Greenspan's Fraud: How Two Decades of His Policies Have Undermined the Global Economy*, Palgrave, 2005; Lou Dobbs, *Exporting America: Why Corporate Greed Is Shipping American Jobs Overseas*, Warner Books, 2004; Mark Curtis, *The Great Deception: Anglo-American Power and World Order*, Pluto Press, 1998; Dan Briody, *The Iron Triangle: Inside the Secret World of the Carlyle Group*, John Wiley & Sons, Inc., 2003; Grant McConnell, *Private Power and American Democracy*, Vintage Books, 1970.

193. Ibid., p. 116.

194. Ibid.

195. Bernd Hamm, "Introduction," *Devastating Society: The Neo-Conservative Assault on Democracy and Justice*, edited by Bernd Hamm, Pluto Press, 2005, p. 11. See also: Lori Wallach and Patrick Woodall, Public Citizen, *Whose Trade Organization?—A Comprehensive Guide to the WTO*, The New Press, 2004.

196. Ronald W. Cox and Daniel Skidmore-Hess, *US Politics and the Global Economy: Corporate Power, Conservative Shift*, Lynne Rienner Publishers, 1999, p. 165.

197. Ibid. See also: Ann Markusen, Peter Hall, Scott Campbell, and Sabrina Deitrick, *The Rise of the Gunbelt: The Military Re-mapping of Industrial America*, Oxford University Press, 1991; Ann Markusen and Joel Yudken, *Dismantling The Cold War Economy*, Basic Books, 1992; Ivan Eland, *The Empire Has No Clothes: US Foreign Policy Exposed*, The Independent Institute, 2004; Michael Mann, *Incoherent Empire*, Verso, 2003; Bertram Gross, *Friendly Fascism: The New Face of Power in America*, South End Press, 1980; Robert Sherrill, *The Oil Follies of 1970–1980: How the Petroleum Industry Stole the Show (And Much More Besides)*, Anchor Press/Doubleday, 1983.

198. Trevor Evans, "The Vulnerabilities of an Economic Colossus," *Devastating Society: The Neo-Conservative Assault on Democracy and Justice*, edited by Bernd Hamm, Pluto Press, 2005, p. 111.

199. Ibid., pp. 111–112.

200. Ibid., p. 122. See also: Juliet B. Schor, *The Overspent American: Upscaling, Downshifting, and the New Consumer*, Basic Books, 1998; Juliet B. Schor, *The Overworked American: The Unexpected Decline of Leisure*, Basic Books, 1991; James K. Galbraith, *Created Unequal: The Crisis in American Pay*, The Free Press, 1998; Thomas I. Palley, *Plenty of Nothing: The Downsizing of the American Dream and the Case for Structural Keynesianism*, Princeton University Press, 1998.

201. Kevin Phillips, *Boiling Point: Republicans, Democrats, and the Decline of Middle-Class Prosperity*, Random House, 1993.

202. Steven V. Roberts, "Workers Take It on the Chin," *US News & World Report*, January 22, 1996, pp. 44–46. See also: John Greenwald, "A Tilt Toward the Rich?—A TIME Forum debates the impact of the Republican spending cuts on an already polarized economy," *TIME*, October 30, 1995, pp. 62–63.

203. Kevin Phillips, *Arrogant Capital: Washington, Wall Street, and the Frustration of American Politics*, Little Brown and Company, 1994.

204. Ibid., p. 97.

205. Ibid., p. 99.

206. David Cay Johnston, *Perfectly Legal: The Covert Campaign to Rig Our Tax System To Benefit The Super Rich—And Cheat Everybody Else*, Portfolio, 2003.

207. James MacGregor Burns and Georgia J. Sorenson, *Dead Center: Clinton-Gore Leadership and the Perils of Moderation*, A Lisa Drew Book/ Scribner, 1999, p. 137.

208. For a thorough economic discussion of these points, see: Thomas I. Palley, *Plenty of Nothing: The Downsizing of the American Dream and the Case for Structural Keynesianism*, Princeton University Press, 1998.

209. Ibid., p. 99. For an excellent economic history of this trend and where it has led, see: Michael A. Bernstein, *A Perilous Progress: Economists and Public Purpose in Twentieth-Century America*, Princeton University Press, 2001.

210. Robert Pollin and Stephanie Luce, *The Living Wage: Building A Fair Economy*, The New Press, 1998.

211. *Unfinished Work: Building Equality and Democracy in an Era of Working Families*, edited by Jody Heymann and Christopher Beem, The New Press, 2005.

212. Stanley Aronowitz and William DiFazio, *The Jobless Future: Sci-Tech and the Dogma of Work*, University of Minnesota Press, 1994.

213. Jeremy Rifkin, *The End of Work: The Decline of the Global Labor Force and the Dawn of the Post-Market Era*, A Jeremy P. Tarcher/Putnam Book published by G. P. Putnam's Sons, 1995.

214. David Bollier, *Silent Theft: The Private Plunder of our Common Wealth*, Routledge, 2002.

215. Matthew A. Crenson and Benjamin Ginsberg, *Downsizing Democracy: How America Sidelined It's Citizens and Privatized Its Public*, The Johns Hopkins University Press, 2002.

216. Michael Chossudovsky, "Global Poverty in the Late Twentieth Century," *Devastating Society: The Neo-Conservative Assault on Democracy and Justice*, Pluto Press, 2005, p. 260.

217. Ibid.

218. Martin Khor, "WTO Pressures Will Build On Developing Countries From September," *Third World Resurgence*, July 2005, No. 179, p. 6.

219. Chossudovsky, "Global Poverty in the Late Twentieth Century," p. 261.

220. Daniel Yergin and Joseph Stanislaw, *The Commanding Heights: The Battle Between Government and the Marketplace that is Remaking the Modern World*, Simon & Schuster, 1998, p. 11.

221. Ibid., p. 12.

222. Noam Chomsky, *Deterring Democracy*, Hill and Wang, 1992, p. 348.

223. Ibid. See also: Russell Mokhiber and Robert Weissman, *On the Rampage: Corporate Predators and the Destruction of Democracy*, Common Courage Press, 2005.

224. Meg Greenfield, "When the Budget is Colonized: Cutting a program is like bombing a settlement," *Newsweek*, May 22, 1995, p. 78.

225. Frances Fox Piven and Richard A. Cloward, *The Breaking of the American Social Compact*, The New Press, 1997, p. 377.

226. "Rewriting the Social Contract," the editors of *Business Week*, November 20, 1995, pp. 120–134.

227. Ibid., p. 182.

228. Donald L. Barlett and James B. Steele, *America: What Went Wrong?*, Andrews and McMeel, 1992.

229. Donald L. Barlett and James B. Steele, *America: Who Stole the Dream?*, Andrews and McMeel, 1996.

230. Derek Bok, *The State of the Nation: Government and the Quest for a Better Society*, Harvard University Press, 1996.

231. Wolfgang Beck, Laurent van der Maesen, Alan Walker, editors, *The Social Quality of Europe*, Kluwer Law International, 1997. See also: Theda Skocpol, *Social Policy in the United States: Future Possibilities in Historical Perspective*, Princeton University Press, 1995; Margaret Weir, *Politics and Jobs: The Boundaries of Employment Policy in the United States*, Princeton University Press, 1992.

232. Ibid., p. 102.

233. Katherine McFate, Roger Lawson, and William Julius Wilson, editors, *Poverty, inequality, And The Future of Social Policy in the New World Order*, Russell Sage Foundation, 1995. See also: Alberto Alesina and Edward L. Glaeser, *Fighting Poverty In the US and Europe: A World of Difference*, Oxford University Press, 2004; Joel F. Handler and Yeheskel Hasenfeld, *We the POOR People: Work, Poverty, and Welfare*, Yale University Press, 1997; *The New Poverty*

Studies: The Ethnography of Power, Politics, and Impoverished People in the United States, edited. by Judith Goode and Jeff Maskovsky, New York University Press, 2001; Alice O'Connor, *Poverty Knowledge: Social Science, Social Policy, and the Poor in Twentieth-Century US History*, Princeton University Press, 2001; Sheldon H. Danziger and Robert H. Haveman, editors, *Understanding Poverty*, Russell Sage Foundation and Harvard University Press, 2001; Benjamin I. Page and James R. Simmons, *What Government Can Do: Dealing with Poverty and Inequality*, The University of Chicago Press, 2000.

234. Gar Alperovitz, *America Beyond Capitalism: Reclaiming Our Wealth, Our Liberty, and Our Democracy*, John Wiley & Sons, Inc., 2005, p. 239. See also: *America Needs Human Rights*, edited by Anuradha Mittal and Peter Rosset, Food First Books, 1999; *The Wealth Inequality Reader*, edited by Dollars & Sense and United for a Fair Economy, Dollars & Sense—Economic Affairs Bureau, 2004; Thad Williamson, David Imbriscio, and Gar Alperovitz, *Making A Place For Community: Local Democracy In A Global Era*, Routledge, 2002; *Reclaiming Prosperity: A Blueprint for Progressive Economic Reform*, edited by Todd Schafer & Jeff Faux, Economic Policy Institute, M.E. Sharpe, 1996; Robert D. Putnam and Lewis M. Feldstein, *Better Together: Restoring the American Community*, Simon & Schuster, 2003: Senator Edward M. Kennedy, *America Back on Track*, Viking, 2006.

235. Williamson, Imbroscio, and Alperovitz, *Making A Place for Community*, p. 34.

236. David Bacon, *The Children of NAFTA: Labor Wars on the US/Mexico Border*, University of California Press, 2004.

237. Jennifer Gordon, *Suburban Sweatshops: The Fight for Immigrant Rights*, Harvard University Press, 2005.

238. Mae M. Ngai, *Impossible Subjects: Illegal Aliens and the Making of Modern America*, Princeton University Press, 2004.

239. Williamson, Imbroscio, and Alpterovitz, *Making A Place for Community*, pp. 37–42.

240. Donald Bartlett and James B. Steele, *The Great American Tax Dodge: How Spiraling Fraud and Avoidance Are Killing Fairness, Destroying the Income Tax, and Costing You*, Little, Brown and Company, 2000; Donald Barlett and James B. Steele, "Special Investigation—Big Money & Politics: Who Gets Hurt," *TIME*, February 7, 2000; Jonathan Chait, "Tax Fraud: Why the Bush Administration Doesn't Want Real Reform." *The New Republic*, January 17, 2005, pp. 17–19; Charles Lewis, Bill Allison, and the Center for Public Integrity, *The Cheating of America: How Tax Avoidance and Evasion by the Super Rich Are Costing the Country Billions—and What You Can Do About It*, William Morrow, 2001; Bob Williams and Jonathan Werve, and the Center for Public Integrity, "Gimme Shelter (from Taxes)," *Truth Out—Issues*, July 16, 2004, US Oil and Gas Companies Have 882 Subsidiaries in Tax Haven Countries, at: www.truthout. org/docs_04/072104E.shtml.; Robert McIntyre, "President George W. McKinley?—Bush waxes nostalgic for robber baron-era policies," *The American Prospect*, December 16, 2002, p. 21; Robert McIntyre, "Standing Up Against America—An army of mercenaries has enlisted to defend the Bermuda tax loophole," *The American Prospect*, November 4, 2002.

241. Williamson, Imbroscio, and Alperovitz, *Making A Place for Community*, p. 43. See also: Walden Bello, *Dilemmas of Domination: The Unmaking of the American Empire*, Metropolitan Books, 2005, p. 132. Bello notes: "From the perspective of the southern governments, the founding of the WTO and the acceleration of corporate driven globalization marked a retreat from efforts at independent national development dating back to the 1970s."

242. Ibid., pp. 46–47.

243. Ibid., p. 48.

244. Bello, *Dilemmas of Domination*, p. 133. On this matter, see also: Michael Goldman, *Imperial Nature: The World Bank and Struggles for Social Justice in the Age of Globalization*, Yale University Press, 2005, p. 88. Goldman notes:

The bank's long string of loans helped fuel a dramatic increase in the South's foreign debt, which grew at an average annual rate of 20 percent between 1976 and 1980 … By the 1980s, much of what the World Bank was lending did not go for bricks and mortar, seeds and tractors, or even research and training: most went to pay the interest on national budget deficits … The twin effects of massive borrowing to rural industrialization and the linking of Southern food and agricultural sectors to the consumption of Northern-based capital goods and farm inputs, contributed heavily to the net flow of capital out of the South and into the North.

Another study argues that although the forces of globalization and neo-liberalism dominate contemporary society and may seem irreversible, the possibility for a different kind of world still exists. On this matter, see also: Arthur Mitzman, *Prometheus Revisited: The Quest for Global Justice in the Twenty-first Century*, University of Massachusetts Press, 2003. Walter Isaacson and Evan Thomas, *The Wise Men: Six Friends and the World They Made*, Simon and Schuster, 1986, pp. 428–429.

245. David North, *The Crisis of American Democracy: The Presidential Elections of 2000 and 2004*, Mehring Books, 2004. See also: Jennifer Van Bergen, *The Twilight of Democracy: The Bush Plan for America*, Common Courage Press, 2005.

246. Brian Loveman, *For la Patria: Politics and the Armed Forces in Latin America*, A Scholarly Resources Inc. Imprint, 1999, p. 233.

247. Ibid. On this point, see: Terry Nardin, *Law, Morality, and the Relations of States*, Princeton University Press, 1983, p. 276. Nardin writes:

To speak of rights is to invoke the considerations of a moral or legal practice in such a way as to emphasize the point of view of those toward whom one has a duty or obligation. To fail in that duty or obligation would be an injustice to them. It is the most basic and general of these duties, such as the duty to avoid interfering arbitrarily with the liberty of individuals to live, think, worship, and associate as they choose, that we point to when we speak of human rights. To insist on respect for human rights is to demand that the policies and laws of a community reflect the principles of impartiality with respect to persons and their ends inherent in the idea of practical association. It is to judge these policies and laws not according to their relation to the achievement of particular substantive purposes or goods but in terms of their relation to the common good of the community. And this common good is not an aggregate of substantive benefits to be distributed but simply the totality of these conditions, embodied in the common rules of the community, for the pursuit by its members of their own self-chosen ends.

On the issue of treaties, see also: Pierre Klein, "The Effects of US Predominance on the Elaboration of Treaty Regimes and on the Evolution of the Law of Treaties," *United States Hegemony and the Foundations of International Law*, edited by Michael Byers and Georg Nolte, Cambridge University Press, 2003, p. 384.

248. Laurence W. Britt, "Fascism Anyone? *Free Inquiry Magazine*, Vol. 23, No. 2, Spring 2003, at: http://secularhumanism.o/library/fi/brit_23_2.htm. For a more detailed examination of American war crimes in Iraq and elsewhere, see also: *In The Name of Democracy: American War Crimes In Iraq and Beyond*, edited by Jeremy Brecher, Jill Cutler, and Brendan Smith, Metropolitan Books, 2005.

249. Bello, *Dilemmas of Domination*, p. 212. Bello notes:

America will continue to decline economically because the global framework for transnational capitalist cooperation to which the WTO is central is eroding. Bilateral and regional trade agreements are likely to proliferate. But the most dynamic hookups may not be those that integrate weak economies with one superpower, like the United States or the European Union. Regional economic collaboration among Third World countries—or, in the parlance of development economics, 'South-South cooperation'—is the wave of the future.

On this matter, see also: Ankie Hoogvelt, *Globalization and the Postcolonial World: The New Political Economy of Development—Second Edition*, The Johns Hopkins University Press, 2001; Paul Street, *Empire and Inequality: America and the World Since 9/11*, Paradigm Publishers, 2004; Marc Williams, *Third World Cooperation: The Group of 77 in UNCTAD*, Pinter Publishers and St. Martins Press, 1991; *Globalization, the Third World State and Poverty-Alleviation in the Twenty-First Century*, edited by B. Ikubolajeh Logan, Ashgate, 2002; Erich Toussaint, *Your Money [or] Your Life: The Tyranny of Global Finance—Updated Edition*, Haymarket Books, 2005, p. 404. Toussaint writes:

Can the IMF and the World Bank be reformed? There is every reason to doubt it. In my opinion, these institutions should be abolished and replaced by other global institutions. They should be abolished because their property-based constitutions, their allegiance to a very limited number of countries (of which only one, the United States, has the veto on any decision it may wish to block, even if all 183 other members want it to go forward), and the distribution of power within their ranks are incompatible with any truly democratic reform.

250. *The Progressive Manifesto: New Ideas for the Center-Left*, edited by Anthony Giddens, Polity, 2003; Anthony Giddens, *The Third Way: The Renewal of Social Democracy*, Polity Press, 1998; Anthony Giddens, *The Third Way and its Critics*, Polity Press, 2000; *The Global Third Way Debate*, edited by Anthony Giddens, Polity, 2001; Alex Callinicos, *Against the Third Way: An Anti-Capitalist Critique*, Polity, 2001.

251. Jan Knippers Black, *Inequity in the Global Village: Recycled Rhetoric and Disposable People*, Kumarian Press, 1999; Bob Sutcliffe, 100 *Ways of Seeing an Unequal World*, Zed Books, 2001; Branko Milanovic, *World's Apart: Measuring International and Global Inequality*, Princeton University Press, 2005; William Ryan, *Equality*, Pantheon Books, 1981; *Demanding Accountability: Civil-Society Claims and the World Bank Inspection Panel*, edited by Dana Clark, Jonathan Fox, and Kay Treakle, Rowman & Littlefield, Publishers, Inc., 2003; Sebastian Mallaby, *The World's Banker: A Story of Failed States, Financial Crises, and the Wealth and Poverty of Nations*, The Penguin Press, 2004.

252. William Felice, *The Global New Deal: Economic and Social Human Rights in World Politics*, Rowman & Littlefield Publishers, Inc., 2003, p. 208. See also: Anne F. Bayefsky, *The UN Human Rights Treaty System: Universality at the Crossroads*, Transnational Publishers, 2001. See also: Balakrishnan Rajagopal, *International Law From Below: Development, Social Movements, and Third World Resistance*, Cambridge University Press, 2003; *Governing for Prosperity*, edited by Bruce Bueno De Mesquita and Hilton L. Root, Yale University Press, 2000; Lawrence A. Hamilton, *The Political Philosophy of Needs*, Cambridge University Press, 2003; *Globalization and Change: The Transformation of Global Capitalism*, edited by Berch Berberoglu, Lexington Books—A Division of Rowman & Littlefield Publishers, Inc., 2005; Luis Cabrera, *Political Theory of Global Justice: A Cosmopolitan Case for the World State*, Routledge, 2004; David Held, *Democracy And The Global Order: From the Modern State to Cosmopolitan Governance*, Stanford University Press, 1995.

253. Ibid., p. 208.

254. Ralph Nader, "How to Curb Corporate Power: Seven Steps to Reclaim the Principle that Companies Should Serve the Public Good," *The Nation*, October 10, 2005, pp. 20–24. See also: Mark Zepezauer, *Take the Rich Off Welfare—New Expanded Edition*, South End Press, 2004; Victor Perlo, *Super Profits and Crises: Modern US Capitalism*, International Publishers, 1988; Andrei Cherny, *The Next Deal: The Future of Public Life in the Information Age*, Basic Books, 2000; *The Next Agenda: Blueprint for A New Progressive Movement*, edited by Robert L. Borosage and Roger Hickey, Westview, 2001; *What We Stand For: A Program for Progressive Patriotism—The New Democracy Project*—edited by Mark Green, Newmarket Press, 2004; John Gray, *False Dawn: The Delusions of Global Capitalism*, The New Press, 1998; Thom Hartmann, *Unequal Protection: The Rise of Corporate Dominance and the Theft of Human Rights*, Rodale, 2002; Jeff Gates, *Democracy At Risk: Rescuing Main Street from Wall Street—A Populist Vision for the Twenty-First Century*, Perseus Publishing, 2000; John B. Judis, "Taking Care of Business: George W. Bush's Compassion for Corporations," *The New Republic*, August 16, 1999, pp. 22–29.

255. Geoff Simons, *Future Iraq: US Policy in Reshaping the Middle East*, SAQI, 2003; Michael Mann, "The First Failed Empire of the Twenty-First Century," *American Power in the Twenty-First Century*, edited by David Held and Mathias Koenig-Archibugi, Polity, 2004, p. 57; *The New American Empire: A Twenty-First Century Teach-In on US Foreign Policy*, edited by Lloyd Gardner and Marilyn B. Young, The New Press, 2005.

256. David Rieff, *At The Point Of a Gun: Democratic Dreams and Armed Intervention*, Simon & Schuster, 2005, p. 179. Rieff notes: "Still, the current neo-conservative vision is very different in scope, and to some degree in substance, from traditional American exceptionalism. In particular, its faith in unilateral military action goes very much against the American grain." See also: *American Exceptionalism and Human Rights*, edited by Michael Ignatieff, Princeton

University Press, 2005; Warren I. Cohen, *America's Failing Empire: US Foreign Relations since the Cold War*, Blackwell Publishing, 2005; Michael Mann, *Incoherent Empire*, Verso, 2003.

257. Gates, *Democracy at Risk*, p. xi.

258. Julian Borger, "Bolton Tramples Over UN Dreams," *The Guardian Weekly*, September 2–8, 2005, p. 8.

259. Ibid.

260. Ibid.

261. Stephen Schlesinger, "The Perils of UN Reform," *The Nation*, October 10, 2005, pp. 6–8.

262. William Fisher, "Ambassador Bolton to take the UN floor/s," at: www.atimes.com/atimes/printN.Htmel, August 4, 2005.

263. John Nichols, "The Bolton Embarrassment," *Common Dreams New Center*, August 2, 2005, at: www.commondreams.org/views05/0802-31/htm.

264. Boggs, *Imperial Delusions*, p. 195. See also: Joseph S. Nye, Jr., "Does Increasing Democracy Undercut Terrorists?"—*Christian Science Monitor*, September 22, 2005, at: www.csmonitor.com/2005/0922/p09s02-coop.htm.; Andrew J. Bacevich, "Robert Kaplan: Empire Without Apologies," *The Nation*, September 26, 2005, at: www.thenation.com/docprint.mhtml?I=20050926&s=bacevich; Ivan Eland, "Democratic Hallucinations in Afghanistan and Iraq," *Common Dreams New Center*, September 20, 2005, at: www.commondreams.org/view05/0920-30.htm.; Ivan Eland, *The Empire Has No Clothes: US Foreign Policy Exposed*, The Independent Institute, 2004.

265. Terrence E. Paupp, *Achieving Inclusionary Governance: Advancing Peace and Development in First and Third World Nations*, Transnational Publishers, 2000, p. 167. See also: *Managing The Global: Globalization, Employment And Quality of Life*, edited by Donald Lamberton, L.B. Tauris Publishers—in association with The Toda Institute for Global Peace and Policy Research, 2002.

266. Ibid., p. 183.

267. Ibid., p. 275. See also: *Bridging A Gulf: Peace-Building in West Asia*, edited by Majid Tehranian, I.B. Tauris, The Toda Institute for Global Peace and Policy Research, 2003.

268. Boggs, *Imperial Delusions*, p. 195.

269. Carl Boggs, *The End of Politics: Corporate Power and the Decline of the Public Sphere*, The Guilford Press, 2000, p. 226.

270. Bello, *Dilemmas of Domination*, pp. 180–181.

271. Ronald W. Cox and Daniel Skidmore-Hess, *US Politics and the Global Economy: Corporate Power, Conservative Shift*, Lynne Rienner Publishers, 1999, p. 219.

272. Spruyt, *Ending Empire*, 2005, p. 274.

273. David Moberg, "The War at Home," *In These Times*, March 17, 2003, pp. 12–13. See also: Michael Gross, "Killing Civilians Intentionally: Double Effect, Reprisal, and Necessity in the Middle East," *Political Science Quarterly: The Journal of Public and International Affairs*, Winter, 2005–06, pp. 555–579; Charles S. Maier, *Among Empires: American Ascendancy and its Predecessors*, Harvard University Press, 2006, p. 64. Maier notes:

> Liberal imperialists will always deplore killing and beating, imprisoning and humiliating civilians, burning their homes, and torturing suspects as aberrant and counterproductive. But if empire is to be maintained, the soldiers assigned the dirty work know that it is sometimes necessary even at the price of the later disavowal and disgrace. Ultimately a mix of secrecy or "deniability" must be developed if leaders are not prepared to renounce the imperial project. Hypocrisy is the tribute imperialism pays to democracy. Certainly the revelations of journalist Seymour Hersh point to the veracity of Maier's conclusion. In the aftermath of the Abu Ghraib/Guantanamo prison scandals and the endless denials of Bush, Rumsfeld, Rice, and Cheney, one can only conclude that the "chain of command" in the Bush-2 regime not only authorized torture and abuse, but actively condoned it.

274. Khaled Abouel Fadl, *The Great Theft: Wrestling Islam from the Extremists*, HarperSanFrancisco, A Division of HarperCollins Publishers, 2005, p. 196.

275. Ibid.

276. Kevin Phillips, *Wealth and Democracy: A Political History of the American Rich*, Broadway Books, 2002, p. 422.

277. Gibson, *Battling Wall Street*, p. 127.

278. Peter Edelman, *Searching for America's Heart: RFK and the Renewal of Hope*, Houghton Mifflin Company, 2001, p. 179.

279. Jerry E. Sanders, *Peddlers of Crisis: The Committee on the Present Danger and the Politics of Containment*, South End Press, 1983.

280. P. W. Singer, *Corporate Warriors: The Rise of the Privatized Military Industry*, Cornell University Press, 2003; P. W. Singer, "Outsourcing War," *Foreign Affairs*, March/April 2005, pp. 119–132.

281. James Ridgeway "Rumsfeld Watch," *The Village Voice*, December 4, 2003. Also found at: www.truthout.org/docs_03/120603F.shtml. The emphasis upon technology and advancements in the area of technological design are also intrinsically important to the managers of a far-flung global Empire. On this matter, see: Michael Adas, *Dominance by Design: Technological Imperatives and America's Civilizing Mission*, Harvard University Press, 2006.

282. *The United Nations and a Just World Order*, edited by Richard Falk, Samuel Kim, and Saul Mendlovitz, Westview Press, 1991; *International Law: A Contemporary Perspective*, edited by Richard Falk, Friedrich Kratochwil, and Saul Mendlovitz, Westview Press, 1985; *Toward A Just World Order*, edited by Richard Falk, Samuel Kim, and Saul Mendlovitz, Westview Press, 1982.

283. John Prados, *Hoodwinked: The Documents That Reveal How Bush Sold Us A War*, The New Press, 2004; James Bamford, *A Pretext For War: 9/11, Iraq, and the Abuse of America's Intelligence Agencies*, Doubleday, 2004; Mark Crispin Miller, *Cruel and Unusual: Bush/Cheney's New World Order*, W.W. Norton & Company, 2004; Scott Ritter, *Iraq Confidential: The Untold Story of the Intelligence Conspiracy to Undermine the UN and Overthrow Saddam Hussein*, Nation Books, 2005; Hans Blix, *Disarming Iraq*, Pantheon Books, 2004; C. G. Weeramantry, *Armageddon or Brace New World?—Reflections on the Hostilities in Iraq, Second Edition*, A Publication of the Weeramantry International Center for Peace Education and Research, 2005; John Bonifaz, *Warrior-King: The Case for Impeaching George W. Bush*, Nation Books, 2003.

284. Arthur M. Schlesinger, Jr., *A Thousand Days: John F. Kennedy in the White House*, Houghton Mifflin Company, 1965, p. 663. With regard to President John Kennedy, Schlesinger notes: "Many of the legislative measures of the New Frontier may have been left over from the new Deal. But the generational perception was new and original. It reinforced the President in his determination to transform a wealthy society into a civilized community and gave his program its distinctive design and theme. American politics would never be the same again." See also: Peter Edelman, *Searching for America's Heart: RFK and the Renewal of Hope*, Houghton Mifflin Company, 2001, p. 19. With regard to Robert Kennedy, Edelman writes:

> The new progressivism that I derive from Robert Kennedy emphasizes a fair measure of government responsibility in a world where too many see little or no role for public policy. It means a mixed economy based in the market but holding corporate predators to account. And it also means a robust role for the civic sector in solving our pressing problems, not instead of government but along with government. It is both/and, not either/or.

> With regard to King and Mandela, see: Robert K. Massie, *Loosing The Bonds: The United States and South Africa in the Apartheid Years*, Doubleday, 1997, pp. 191–198. Massie writes:

> As King's vision moved beyond the boundaries of the South and roamed across the national horizon, he became more and more unhappy with the behavior of American corporations and of the American government abroad, particularly in South Africa ... [p. 191] ... By 1966, Martin Luther King, Jr. and Robert F. Kennedy were among a small but influential group of persons who were growing disenchanted with the direction of Lyndon Johnson's foreign policy ... [p. 194].

285. William F. Pepper, *An Act of State: The Execution of Martin Luther King*, Verso, 2003.

286. Robert F. Kennedy, "On Rebuilding a Sense of Community," Worthington, Minnesota, September 17, 1966, as quoted in, *RFK: Collected Speeches*, edited and introduced by Edwin O. Guthman and Richard Allen, Viking, 1993, pp. 211–212.

287. Robert F. Kennedy, Issues & Answers, (ABC-TV), June 17, 1967, as quoted in, *Robert F. Kennedy: Apostle of Change: A Review of his Public Record with Analysis by Douglas Ross*, Pocket Books, 1968, pp. 536–537.

288. SIPRI (Stockholm International Peace Research Institute), *The Arms Trade with the Third World*, Humanities Press, Inc., 1971.

289. Mark Danner, "The Secret Way to War," *The New York Review of Books*, June 9, 2005, p. 70. See also: Mark Danner, *The Secret Way to War: The Downing Street Memo and the Iraq War's Buried History*, New York Review of Books, 2006; James Risen, *State of War: The Secret History of the CIA and the Bush Administration*, Free Press, 2006.

290. Ibid., p. 70.

291. Ibid., pp. 70–71.

292. Text of the Downing Street Memo, as printed in—*The New York Review of Books*, June 9, 2005, p. 71.

293. Ritter, *Iraq Confidential*.

294. Ibid., p. 291.

295. Ibid.

296. Robert Dreyfuss, "The Pentagon Muzzles the CIA: Devising bad intelligence to promote bad policy," *The American Prospect*, December 16, 2002, pp. 26–29.

297. Ibid., p. 28.

298. Mark Danner, "The Secret Way to War," *The New York Review of Books*, June 9, 2005, p. 71.

299. Hans Blix, *Disarming Iraq*, Pantheon Books, 2004, p. 274.

300. Danner, "The Secret Way to War," p. 73.

301. Bonifaz, *Warrior-King*.

302. Richard J. Evans, *The Third Reich in Power (1933–1939)*, The Penguin Press, 2005. See also: David Corn, *The Lies of George W. Bush: Mastering the Politics of Deception*, Crown Publishers, 2003.

303. Paupp, *Achieving Inclusionary Governance*, p. 74. See also: Bob Woodward, *Plan Of Attack*, Simon & Schuster, 2004; Chomsky, *Failed States*, p. 83; Elizabeth Holtzman, "The Impeachment of George W. Bush," *The Nation*, January 30, 2006, pp. 11–18; Lewis H. Lapham, "The Case for Impeachment: Why We can no Longer Afford George W. Bush," *Harper's Magazine*, March 2006, pp. 27–35; Charles S. Maier, *Among Empires*; Alan M. Dershowitz, *Preemption: A Knife That Cuts Both Ways*, W.W. Norton & Company, 2006; Center for Constitutional Rights, *Articles of Impeachment Against George W. Bush*, Melville House Publishing, 2006.

304. *Hijacking Catastrophe: 9/11, Fear and the Selling of American Empire*, edited by Sut Jhally and Jeremy Earp, Olive Branch Press, 2004.

305. Michael Lind, *Vietnam: The Necessary War—A Reinterpretation of America's Most Disastrous Military Conflict*, The Free Press, 1999, p. 269.

306. Emmanuel Todd, *After The Empire: The Breakdown of the American Order*, Columbia University Press, 2002.

307. Ibid., p. 202. See also: Craig Unger, *House of Bush, House of Saud: The Secret Relationship Between The World's Two Most Powerful Dynasties*, Scribner, 2004; James Moore, *Bush's War For Reelection: Iraq, The White House, And The People*, John Wiley & Sons, Inc., 2004.

308. Eric Alterman, *When Presidents Lie: A History of Official Deception and its Consequences*, Viking, 2004, p. 307.

309. Porter, *Perils of Dominance*, p. 275. Porter notes:

> Realist theory generally asserts that the tendency of the strongest state to extend its power and influence continues until it is checked by external forces or by sociopolitical forces at home that weaken its ability to do so. Until the end of the Cold War, realists generally did not apply this general principle to the United States, but in the present "unipolar moment", the issue of how to restrain the excessive use of US power is unavoidable.
>
> It has now become part of the debate over the advantages and disadvantages to the United States and to the world of US dominance of the international system."

310. Nafeez Mosaddeq Ahmed, *The War On Truth*, p. 351.

311. Ibid., p. 367.

312. Michael T. Klare, "Revving Up the China Threat," *The Nation*, October 24, 2005. Also available at: www.thenation.com/docprint.mhtml?I=20051024&s=klare. See also: Fred Bergsten et al., *China: The Balance Sheet: What the World Needs to Know Now About the Emerging Superpower*, Public Affairs, 2006; John Mearsheimer, "China's Un-peaceful Rise," *Current History: A Journal of Contemporary World Affairs*, April 2006, pp. 160–162; Michael T. Klare, "Fueling the Dragon: China's Strategic Energy Dilemma," *Current History: A Journal of Contemporary World Affairs*, April 2006, pp. 180–185.

313. Porter, *Perils of Dominance*, p. 275.

314. Jim Garrison, *On The Trail of the Assassins: My Investigation and Prosecution of the Murder of President Kennedy*, Sheridan Square Press, 1988, p. 293. Garrison asserts:

Actually, Kennedy seems to have had very little real support in Washington for the policy of military restraint to which he had come by 1963. His own secretary of defense, Robert McNamara, acknowledged in 1984 that as late as 1965 he was convinced that the United States would win in Vietnam. Dean Rusk, President Kennedy's secretary of state, made a similar acknowledgment. One has to wonder just who in the US government in 1963 did support Kennedy's lonely decision against our continued military involvement in Southeast Asia.

315. Ibid., p. 282. Garrison notes:

With the cover-up such a stunning success, the stage was now set for the ratification of the assassination. The surviving elements of the new government—from Lyndon Johnson, J. Edgar Hoover, and Earl Warren on down—were quick to see the advantages of supporting the scenario that no coup d'etat had occurred and that our democracy was safely intact, that a lone malcontent had murdered the President in a meaningless, random act of violence. And they were quick to understand the message of those who had engineered the assassination—that there was a forceful consensus that wanted the Cold War resumed at its pre-Kennedy intensity ... Motivated in some instances by self-preservation and in others by a belief that Kennedy had brought the assassination on himself by compromising too often with the Soviets, the remainder of the government—from high elected officials to heads of departments and agencies—lined up to add their solemn voices to the growing chorus chanting the great lie.

316. Ibid., p. 293. Garrison notes: "To the hard-line, war-oriented elements of the American power structure, for whom the CIA operations directorate had been created and for whom it functioned, this was nothing less than 'selling out to the communists'."

317. Irving Bernstein, *Guns Or Butter: The Presidency of Lyndon Johnson*, Oxford University Press, 1996, p. 331. Bernstein notes:

The mission of the Establishment was to shape and execute American foreign and defense policy to fit the goals of peace and international stability as well as the free flow of capital and trade between nations ... With the decline of Britain in the twentieth century, the Establishment saw America as heir to these policies by maintaining peace in Europe and by resisting aggression, notably by Germany in both World Wars, by Imperial Japan in the second, and by Soviet and Chinese Communism after World War II. Such a role required massive military forces.

A modern version of Kennedy's vision may be found in two books by Senator Gary Hart: *The Shield and the Cloak: The Security of the Commons*, Oxford University Press, 2006, and, *The Fourth Power: A Grand Strategy for the United States in the Twenty-First Century*, Oxford University Press, 2004.

318. Ibid., p. 331. Bernstein notes:

The core of the Establishment consisted of gentlemen of breeding, privileged education, wealth and power, who concentrated at the foot of Manhattan Island in investment banking and corporate law with tentacles reaching out to Washington and Boston. Overwhelmingly Republican, they included several notable Democrats and they willingly served Democratic Presidents, usually at substantial financial cost to themselves.

319. Ibid., p. 542. Writing of LBJ and his worldview, Bernstein notes:

With contempt he called North Vietnam a "piss-ant" sixth-rate or "raggedy-ass" fourth rate nation. With the legitimacy he had won in the election, he need not consult the Congress, or, for that matter, even let the Congress or the American people in on his secret. In the Greek sense, this was the arrogance that aroused the anger of the gods and caused them to inflict disaster upon the one who went to war. As with Pericles and Athens, the preference for guns over butter would bring calamity to Lyndon Johnson and to the United States.

320. Garrison, *On the Trail of the Assassins*, p. 295. Garrison notes:

Promptly following the congressional resolution, American planes began their first bombardment of North Vietnam. The US Pacific Command was ordered to prepare for combat. In 1965, more than 200,000 American troops poured into South Vietnam. In 1966 and 1967, upwards of 300,000 more followed. By the time the US signed the Paris Peace Agreement in January 1973, more than 55,000 Americans and millions of Vietnamese were dead.

321. Paul Rutherford, *Weapons of Mass Persuasion: Marketing the War Against Iraq*, University of Toronto Press, 2004. See also: Phyllis Bennis, *Before & After: US Foreign Policy and the September 11th Crisis*, Olive Branch Press, 2003; Walter Clemens, Jr., and illustrations by Jim Morin, *Bushed: An Illustrated History of What Passionate Conservatives Have Done to America and the World*, Outland Books, 2004.

322. Arthur M. Schlesinger, Jr., *War and the American Presidency*, W.W. Norton & Company, 2004, p. 81.

323. Ibid., p. 138. "Ignorance is no pathway to success; and Iraq seems likely to end as a repetition of Vietnam."

324. Robert Jervis, "Why the Bush Doctrine Cannot Be Sustained," *Political Science Quarterly: The Journal of Public and International Affairs*, Vol. 120, No. 3, Fall 2005, p. 374. On the matter of changing circumstances, see also: Francis A. Boyle, *Bio-warfare and Terrorism*, Clarity Press, Inc., 2005; Stephen Brooks, *Producing Security: Multinational Corporations, Globalization, and the Changing Calculus of Conflict*, Princeton University Press, 2005.

325. Jim Garrison, *A Heritage of Stone*, Putnam, 1970, p. 216. On this matter, see also: David Cole, Ronald Dworkin, Laurence Tribe et al., "On NSA Spying: A Letter to Congress," *The New York Review of Books*, February 9. 2006, pp. 42–44; David Cole "NSA Spying Myths," *The Nation*, February 20, 2006, pp. 5–6; Robert Dreyfuss, "The Pentagon's New Spies: The military has built a vast domestic-intelligence network to fight terrorism—but it's using it to track students, grandmothers and others protesting the war," *Rolling Stone*, April 20, 2006, pp. 38–42.

326. Ibid., p. 217. Garrison notes:

If we cannot have the truth once and for all about the government's murder of John F. Kennedy, if the warfare interests in our government are so powerful that they cannot be questioned about such things, then let us have an end to the pretense that this is a government of the people. If the American people choose to do nothing about what was done to John Kennedy and about the subtle conversion of their country from a democracy into a thinly disguised version of the warfare state, then the republic is lost and we shall never see it again in our time. In any event, we need no longer pretend that there is any mystery left about the assassination of John Kennedy. The Cold War was the biggest business in America, worth eighty billion dollars a year as well as tremendous power to the men in Washington. The president was murdered because he was genuinely seeking peace in a corrupt world.

327. Bernstein, *Guns Or Butter*, p. 359.

6   CLAIMING "A RIGHT OF PEACE": MOVING BEYOND THE "EMPIRE SYNDROME"

1. Robert Jay Lifton, *Super Power Syndrome: America's Apocalyptic Confrontation with the World*, Thunder's Mouth Press/Nation Books, 2003, pp.191–192.

2. Marcus G. Raskin, *Liberalism: The Genius of American Ideals*, Rowman & Littlefield Publishers, Inc., 2004, p. 230.

3. The World Commission on Environment and Development, *Our Common Future*, Oxford University Press, 1987, pp. 300–301.

4. Christopher Coker, "The United States and the Ethics of Post-modern War," *Ethics and Foreign Policy*, edited by Karen E. Smith and Margot Light, Cambridge University Press, 2001, p. 162.

5. Daniel Deudney and G. John Ikenberry, "Realism, Structural Liberalism, and the Western Order," *Unipolar Politics: Realism and State Strategies After the Cold War*, Columbia University Press, 1999, p. 104.

6. James P. Pinkerton, "The Next War?: Averting a Collision with China," *The American Conservative*, November 7, 2005, pp.7–15.

7. Vassillis K. Fouskas, *Zones of Conflict: US Foreign Policy in the Balkans and the Greater Middle East*, Pluto Press, 2003.

8. Bruce Cummings, Ervand Abrahamian, and Moshe Ma'oz, *Inventing the Axis of Evil: The Truth about North Korea, Iran, and Syria*, The New Press, 2004. See also: Christopher Layne, "Iran: The Logic of Deterrence," *The American Conservative*, April 10, 2006, pp. 7–11; Seymour M. Hersh, "The Secret Iran Plans—How Far Would Washington Go to Stop Tehran from Getting the Bomb?," *The New Yorker*, April 17, 2006, pp. 30–37; Michael T. Klare, "Defusing the Iran Crisis," *The Nation*, March 20, 2006, pp. 4–5; Hans Blix, "Interview with the Chairman of the WMD Commission," *The Fletcher Forum of World Affairs*, Winter 2006, Vol. 30:1, pp. 81–91; Sean Rayment, "Government in Secret Talks About Strike Against Iran," *The Telegraph UK*, April 2, 2006, also cited at: www.truthjout.org/docs_2006/040206A.Shtml.

9. William D. Hartung, *And Weapons For All*, Harper Perennial, 1994. See also, Vassilis K. Fouskas and Bulent Gokay, *The New American Imperialism: Bush's War on Terror and Blood for Oil*, Praeger Security International, 2005.

10. William W. Keller, *Arm in Arm: The Political Economy of the Global Arms Trade*, Basic Books, 1995.

11. Michael T. Klare, *Supplying Repression: US Support for Authoritarian Regimes Abroad*, Institute for Policy Studies, 1977. See also: Michael T. Klare, *American Arms Supermarket*, University of Texas Press, Austin, 1984; *Cascade of Arms: Managing Conventional Weapons Proliferation*, edited by Andrew J. Pierre, Brookings Institution Press/The World Peace Foundation, 1997; John Tirman, *Spoils of War: The Human Cost of America's Arms Trade*, The Free Press, 1997.

12. Owen Bowcott and Richard Norton-Taylor, "War On Terror Fuels Small Arms Trade," *The Guardian*, October 10, 2003.

13. P. W. Singer, *Children at War*, Pantheon Books, 2005.

14. Philippe Sands, *Lawless World: America and the Making and Breaking of Global Rules from FDR's Alliance Charter to George W. Bush's Illegal War*, Viking, 2005.

15. Raimo Vayrynen, "Norms, Compliance, and Enforcement in Global Governance," *Globalization and Global Governance*, edited by Raimo Vayrynen, Rowman & Littlefield Publishers, Inc., 1999, p. 30.

16. Michael Ryan Kraig, "Forging a New Security Order for the Persian Gulf," *Middle East Policy*, Vol. XIII, No. 1, Spring 2006, p. 101. See also: Vilmos Cserveny et al., *Building a Weapons of Mass Destruction Free Zone in the Middle East: Global Non-Proliferation Regimes and Regional Experiences*, (UNIDIR) United Nations Institute for Disarmament Research, Geneva, Switzerland, 2004, United Nations; Lyle Goldstein, *Preventive Attack and Weapons of Mass Destruction: A Comparative Historical Analysis*, Stanford University Press, 2006; Thomas F. Homer-Dixon, Environment, *Scarcity, and Violence*, Princeton University Press, 1999.

17. The World Commission on Environment and Development, *Our Common Future*, p. 294.

18. Nancy Lee Peluso and Michael Watts, editors, *Violent Environments*, Cornell University Press, 2001.

19. Roy Woodbridge, *The Next World War: Tribes, Cities, Nations, and Ecological Decline*, University of Toronto Press, 2004; Jared Diamond, *Collapse: How Societies Choose to Fail or Succeed*, Viking, 2005. See also: Annalisa Zinn, "Theory Versus Reality: Civil War Onset and Avoidance in Nigeria Since 1960," *Volume 1: Africa—Understanding Civil War: Evidence and Analysis*, edited by Paul Collier and Nicholas Sambanis, The World Bank, 2005, pp. 89–121; Stephen J.

Hartnett and Laura A. Strengrim, *Globalization and Empire: The US Invasion of Iraq, Free Markets, and the Twilight of Democracy*, The University of Alabama Press, 2006.

20. Mac Darrow and Amparo Tomas, "Power, Capture, and Conflict: A Call for Human Rights Accountability in Development Cooperation," *Human Rights Quarterly: A Comparative and International Journal of the Social Sciences, Humanities, and Law*, Vol. 27, No. 2, May 2003, p. 476.

21. Terrence E. Paupp, *Achieving Inclusionary Governance: Advancing Peace and Development in First and Third World Nations*, Transnational Publishers, Inc., 2000.

22. Darrow and Tomas, "Power, Capture, and Conflict: A Call for Human Rights Accountability in Development Cooperation," pp. 476–477. See also: Paupp, *Achieving Inclusionary Governance*, 2000.

23. The World Bank, *World Development Report, 2006—Equity and Development*, Oxford University Press, 2005, p. 9. See also: Jack M. Hollander, *The Real Environmental Crisis: Why Poverty, Not Affluence, is the Environment's Number One Enemy*, University of California Press, 2003.

24. Amartya Sen, *Development as Freedom*, Anchor Books, 1999.

25. Paupp, *Achieving Inclusionary Governance*, pp. 386–387.

26. The World Bank, *World Development Report 2003, Sustainable Development in a Dynamic World: Transforming Institutions, Growth, and Quality of Life*, Oxford University Press, 2003, p. 191.

27. Ibid., p. 197.

28. The World Bank, *World Development Report 2000/2001: Attacking Poverty*, Oxford University Press, 2001, p. 39.

29. UNDP, *Human Development Report 2003, Millennium Development Goals: A Compact among Nations to End Human Poverty*, Oxford University Press, 2003, p. 5.

30. Darrow and Tomas, "Power, Capture, and Conflict: A Call for Human Rights Accountability in Development Cooperation," p. 478.

31. Fernando Henrique Cardoso, *Charting a New Course: The Politics of Globalization and Social Transformation*, Rowman & Littlefield Publishers, Inc., 2001, p. 269.

32. Ibid., p. 269.

33. Stephen D. Krasner, *Structural Conflict: The Third World Against Global Liberalism*, University of California Press, 1985, p. 27.

34. Ibid., p. 30.

35. Ibid., p. 313.

36. Ibid.

37. Ibid., pp. 313–314. See also: Walden Bello and Shalmali Guttal, "The Limits of Reform: The Wolfensohn Era at the World Bank," *Race & Class*, Vol. 47, No. 3, January–March 2006, pp. 68–81.

38. Ibid., p. 314.

39. Walden Bello, *Dilemmas of Domination: The Unmaking of the American Empire*, Metropolitan Books, 2005, p. 132. See also: John Barton et al., *The Evolution of the Trade Regime: Politics, Law, and Economics of the GATT and the WTO*, Princeton University Press. 2006; Joseph Stiglitz and Andrew Charlton, *Fair Trade For All: How Trade Can Promote Development*, Oxford University Press, 2005; *Reality Check: The Distributional Impact of Privatization in Developing Countries*, edited by John Nellis and Nancy Birdsall, Center for Global Development, 2005.

40. Cardoso, *Charting a New Course*, p. 288.

41. Paupp, *Achieving Inclusionary Governance*, pp. 339–341.

42. Darrow and Tomas, "Power, Capture, and Conflict: A Call for Human Rights Accountability in Development Cooperation," p. 489.

43. Ibid., p. 489.

44. Frances M. Deng, "Beyond Cultural Domination: Institutionalizing Equity In the African State," *Beyond State Crisis?—Postcolonial Africa and Post-Soviet Eurasia in Comparative Perspective*, edited by Mark R. Beissinger and Crawford Young, Woodrow Wilson Center Press, 2002, p. 361.

45. Darrow and Tomas, "Power, Capture, and Conflict: A Call for Human Rights Accountability in Development Cooperation," p. 491.

46. The World Bank, *World Development Report—2006, Equity and Development*, p. 107.

47. Ibid., p. 108.

48. Cardoso, *Charting a New Course*, p. 286.

49. Ibid., p. 284.

50. UNDP, *Democracy in Latin America: Towards a Citizen's Democracy*, United Nations Development Program, 2004.

51. Ibid., p. 35.

52. Ibid., p. 47.

53. Ibid., p. 44.

54. Ibid., p. 39.

55. Ibid., p. 51.

56. Ibid., p. 54.

57. Ibid., p. 124.

58. Ibid., p. 125.

59. Darrow and Tomas, "Power, Capture, and Conflict: A Call for Human Rights Accountability in Development Cooperation," pp. 502–503. Both authors further note:

Human dignity is indivisible; denying one part of it affects the whole. The indivisibility principle is deeply entrenched in the form and structure of the UDHR, even if post-World War II geo-political and ideological differences resulted in bifurcation and entrenchment within two separate instruments: the International Covenant on Civil and Political Rights (ICCPR) and International Covenant on Economic, Social, and Cultural Rights (ICESCR)—along with a certain residual double standard in terms of their manifestation within national constitutional arrangements.

60. Ibid., pp. 502–503.

61. Ibid., p. 504.

62. Ibid., pp. 504–505.

63. United Nations Research Institute for Social Development (UNRISD), *Visible Hands: Taking Responsibility for Social Development*, A UNRISD Report, 2000, p. iii.

64. Ibid.

65. United Nations Economic Commission for Latin America and the Caribbean (ECLAC), *Beyond Reforms: Structural Dynamics and Macroeconomic Vulnerability*, edited by Jose Antonio Ocampo, Stanford University Press and the World Bank, 2005, p. 139.

66. Darrow and Tomas, "Power, Capture, and Conflict: A Call for Human Rights Accountability in Development Cooperation," p. 507.

67. David Harvey, *A Brief History of Neo-liberalism*, Oxford University Press, 2005, p. 181.

68. Ibid.

69. Raphael Kaplinsky, *Globalization, Poverty and Inequality: Between a Rock and a Hard Place*, Polity, 2005, p. 240.

70. Harvey, *A Brief History of Neo-liberalism*, p. 182.

71. Kaplinsky, *Globalization, Poverty and Inequality*, p. 240.

72. Erich Toussaint, *Your Money [or] Your Life: The Tyranny of Global Finance, Updated Edition*, Haymarket Books, 2005, p. 148.

73. Ibid., pp. 148–149.

74. Richard Peet, *Unholy Trinity: The IMF, World Bank, and WTO*, Zed Books, 2004, p. 207.

75. Ibid., p. 208.

76. Ibid., pp. 208–209.

77. Ibid., p. 211.

78. Ibid., p. 212.

79. Toussaint, *Your Money [or] Your Life*, p.36. See also: Joyce Kolko, *Restructuring the World Economy*, Pantheon Books, 1988, pp. 267–268. Kolko notes:

Programs that offer the same solution to every situation have generally led to recession, de-industrialization, inflation, aggravated imbalances of trade, unemployment, further concentration of income, and political repression. The enforced cutbacks in what economists call human capital formation—education and training—seriously undermine future developments of any sort. The examples are endless and readily found in the now vast literature on these institutions. Whether intentionally or not, the IMF has effectively de-capitalized the recipient countries ... The IMF's strategy is totally incompatible with economic development.

80. Nicolas Guilhot, *The Democracy Makers: Human Rights and International Order*, Columbia University Press, 2005, p. 213.

81. Ibid., p. 214. See also: Kolko, *Restructuring the World Economy*, pp. 270–271. Kolko notes:

> Earlier charitable rhetoric concerning basic needs and the eradication of poverty has receded and been supplanted by more protection of private banks through co-financing and cross-default loans as well as by the promotion of export-oriented policies. Project loans have become increasingly loaded with blatant policy conditions designed to move economies toward a reliance on "market criteria." In order to maximize its influence, the World Bank also engages in "dialogue" with government officials to build a consensus for the policy the bank deems desirable. "Policy changes are sometimes the condition for project appraisal, approval, or disbursement," a bank official observed, and reluctance to accept the bank's advice has frequently put the entire lending program in jeopardy. By co-financing projects with governments or requiring "matching funds," the bank can also determine how a government spends its own money.

82. Ibid., p. 221.

83. Harvey, *A Brief History of Neo-liberalism*, p. 206.

84. Ibid., p. 19.

85. Kidane Mengisteab, "Does Globalization Advance or Hinder Democratization in Africa?" *Globalization, the Third World State and Poverty-Alleviation in the Twenty-First Century*, edited by Ikubolajeh Logan, Ashgate, 2002, pp. 72–73.

86. Carlos Rozo, "Trade Liberalization and Economic Development in Mexico: A Case for Globalization?" *Globalization, the Third World State and Poverty-Alleviation in the Twenty-First Century*, edited by Ikubolajeh Logan, Ashgate, 2002, p. 123.

87. Khurshid Ahmad, "Globalization: Islamic Perspectives, Challenges and Prospects," *Poverty in Muslim Countries and the New International Economic Order*, edited by Munawar Iqbal and Habib Ahmed, Palgrave, The Islamic Research and Training Institute and the International Association for Islamic Economics, 2005, p. 19. See also: Scott Sernau, *Worlds Apart: Social Inequalities in a New Century*, Pine Forge Press, 2001; Paul Street, *Empire and Inequality: America and the World Since 9/11*, Paradigm Publishers, 2004; Michael Goldman, *Imperial Nature: The World Bank and Struggles for Social Justice in the Age of Globalization*, Yale University Press, 2005; *Challenges to the World Bank and IMF: Developing Country Perspectives*, edited by Ariel Buira for the G24 Research Program, Anthem Press, 2003; Kevin Bates, *Understanding Global Slavery: A Reader*, University of California Press, 2005; *Putting Development First: The Importance of Policy Space in the WTO and IFIs*, edited by Kevin P. Gallagher, Zed Books, 2005; *Just Sustainabilities: Development in an Unequal World*, edited by Julian Agyeman, Robert Bullard, and Bob Evans, The MIT Press, 2003; *Beyond Bretton Woods: Alternatives to the Global Economic Order*, edited by John Cavanagh, Daphne Wysham, and Marcos Arruda, Pluto Press, 1994; Patrick Bond, *Against Global Apartheid: South Africa Meets the World Bank, IMF and International Finance*; University of Capetown Press, 2001.

88. Michael Chossudovsky, *The Globalization of Poverty: Impacts of IMF and World Bank Reforms*, Zed Books, 1997, p 69.

89. David Reed, "Conclusions: Impacts of Structural Adjustment on the Sustainability of Developing Countries," *Structural Adjustment, the Environment, and Sustainable Development*, edited by David Reed, Earthscan Publications, 1996, p.346.

90. Kolko, *Restructuring the World Economy*, p. 248.

91. Ute Pieper and Lance Taylor, "The Revival of the Liberal Creed: The IMF, the World Bank, and Inequality in a Globalized Economy," *Globalization and Progressive Economic Policy*, edited by Dean Baker, Gerald Epstein, and Robert Pollin, Cambridge University Press, 1998, pp. 37–63.

92. George Kent, *Freedom From Want: The Human Right to Adequate Food*, Georgetown University Press, 2005.

93. Martin Wolf, *Why Globalization Works*, Yale University Press, 2004, p. 314.

94. Editorial, *The Economist*, "Tired of Globalization: But in need of much more of it," November 5–11, 2005, pp. 11–12.

95. Ibid.

96. Martin Hart-Landsberg and Paul Burkett, *China and Socialism: Market Reforms and Class Struggle*, Monthly Review Press, 2005, p. 116. See also: William I. Robinson, *Transnational Conflicts: Central America, Social Change, and Globalization*, Verso, 2003, p. 246. Robinson notes:

> Austerity programs and adjustment policies led to escalating poverty rates in the 1990s in many developing regions. In Latin America, the number of people living in poverty went from 118 million in 1980, or about a third of the regions total population, to 196 million in 1990, representing nearly half of the population. Alarmed over the social unrest resulting from neo-liberal reforms—the infamous "IMF riots"—the IFIs began to encourage governments implementing structural adjustment to launch externally funded social programs to give a "human face" to the reforms ... But to be managed by these programs was considered in the conception of the "new social policy" to be a pathology, not a consequence of the economic system itself. "Hence it isolates poverty from the process of capital accumulation and economic development," according to Carlos Villas. "Social policy is reduced to a limited series of measures intended to compensate the initial negative effects of structural adjustment among certain sectors of the population." These programs have not been able to ameliorate the spread of poverty and deprivation. They operate within the logic of the neo-liberal model largely as temporary relief to those marginalized by the model, without modifying the structural causes of that marginalization.

97. United Nations Development Program, United Nations Environment Program, The World Bank, The World Resources Institute, *World Resources' (2002–2004): Decisions for the Earth—Balance, Voice, and Power*, The World Resources Institute, 2003, p. 169.
98. Ibid.
99. Robinson, *Transnational Conflicts*, p. 307. See also: William K. Tabb, *Economic Governance in the Age of Globalization*, Columbia University Press, 2004, p. 3. Tabb notes:

> Neo-liberalism is widely understood by even many mainstream economists and policy wonks to have failed in terms of its announced goals. It has not brought more rapid economic growth, reduced poverty, or made economies more stable. In fact, over the years of neo-liberal hegemony growth has slowed, poverty has increased, and economic and financial crises have plagued most countries of the world economy. The data on all of this are overwhelming. Neo-liberalism has, however, succeeded as the project of the most internationalized factions of capital. In its unannounced goal it has increased the dominance of transnational corporations, international financiers, and sectors of local elites.

> See also: Kevin Danaher, *10 Reasons to Abolish the IMF and World Bank, 2nd Edition*, Seven Stories Press, 2004.

100. Paul Farmer, *Pathologies of Power: Health, Human Rights, and the New War on the Poor*, University of California Press, 2003, p. 243.
101. Robinson, *Transnational Conflicts*, p. 308.
102. Ibid., p. 314.
103. Atul Kohli, *State-Directed Development: Political Power and Industrialization in the Global Periphery*, Cambridge University Press, 2004, p. 421.
104. Ibid.
105. Fantu Cheru, *The Silent Revolution in Africa: Debt, Development, and Democracy*, Zed Books, 1989, p. 164. Cheru notes:

> In the final analysis, the struggle for emancipation from debt bondage can come about only through concerted political action by Africans themselves for greater democratization of the political system and participation in decision-making in all matters that directly affect them. This requires grassroots education and mass mobilization of workers, peasants, and students in the broader struggle for self-determination and social justice. Wholesale acceptance of establishment solutions, be they African or European in origin, can only lead to permanent bondage.

106. Paupp, *Achieving Inclusionary Governance*. See also: Robert Gilpin, *The Challenge of Global Capitalism: The World Economy in the 21st Century*, Princeton University Press, 2000, p. 355.

Gilpin notes:

Cooperation between the United States and the industrializing economies is possible only if the United States becomes more tolerant of differences in national economies ... in the IMF-American rescue efforts in East Asia and in American policy toward Japan, the United States has frequently attempted to impose its own economic policies and institutions on the rest of the world ... Many countries, however, have strong reservations about the social costs of the Anglo-Saxon model of market capitalism.

107. Edward D. Mansfield and Jack Snyder, *Electing To Fight: Why Emerging Democracies Go To War*, MIT Press, 2005, p. 62.
108. James Petras and Henry Veltmeyer, *Social Movements and State Power: Argentina, Brazil, Bolivia, Ecuador*, Pluto Press, 2005, p. 9.
109. Toussaint, *Your Money [or] Your Life*, p. 416.
110. Petras and Veltmeyer, *Social Movements and State Power*, p. 39. See also: James Petras and Henry Veltmeyer, *System In Crisis: The Dynamics of Free Market Capitalism*, Fernwood Publishing, Inc., 2003, p.69. The authors note: "failed neo-liberal states such as Argentina confront three alternatives: (1) to convert citizens of the country into neo-imperial colonial subjects; (2) to embark on a neo-structuralist project; or (3) to undertake a process of revolutionary transformation."
111. Ibid., p. 53.
112. Ibid., p. 54.
113. Ibid., p. 29.
114. Ibid., p. 56.
115. Ibid., p. 57.
116. Ibid., p. 59.
117. Joseph E. Stiglitz, "Development Policies in a World of Globalization," *Putting Development First: The Importance of Policy Space in the WTO and IFIs*, edited by Kevin P. Gallagher, Zed Books, 2005, p. 32.
118. Toussaint, *Your Money [or] Your Life*, p. 387.
119. Ibid., p. 382.
120. Ashfaq Khalfan, Jeff King, and Bryan Thomas, "Advancing the Odious Debt Doctrine," 2002, Working Paper for KAIROS: Canadian Ecumenical Jubilee Initiatives, February 28, 2002, Center for International Sustainable Development Law—Document No. COM/RES/ESJ/2001-07.
121. Richard Peet et al., *Unholy Trinity: The IMF, World Bank and WTO*, Zed Books, 2004, p. 219.
122. Norbert Kersting and Jaime Sperberg, "Political Participation," *Poverty and Democracy: Self-Help and Political Participation in Third World Cities*, edited by Dirk Berg-Schlosser and Norbert Kersting, Zed Books, 2003, p. 154.
123. Ibid., p. 154.
124. Odd Arne Westad, *The Global Cold War: Third World Interventions and the Making of Our Times*, Cambridge University Press, 2005, p. 99.
125. Ibid., p. 99.
126. Ibid.
127. On the issue of human rights as both a moral and a legal claim, see: Thomas Pogge, *World Poverty and Human Rights: Cosmopolitan Responsibilities and Reforms*, Polity, 2002, p. 53. Pogge notes:

This acknowledgment bears stressing because the distinction between moral and legal human rights is rarely drawn clearly. Many are therefore inclined to believe that our human rights are whatever governments agree them to be. This is true of legal human rights. But it is false, as these governments have themselves acknowledged, of moral human rights. Governments may have views on what moral human rights there are—their (not legally binding) endorsement of the UDHR expresses such a view—but even all of them together cannot legislate such rights out of existence.

On this matter, it is interesting to recall that in his inaugural address of January 1961, President John F. Kennedy addressed this point when he said: "the rights of man come not from the generosity of the state, but from the hand of God." See also: Marjorie Mayo, *Global Citizens: Social Movements and the Challenge of Globalization*, Zed Books, 2005. See also: Robert Higgs, *Resurgence of the Warfare State: The Crisis Since 9/11*, The Independent Institute, 2005; Robert Pinkney, *The Frontiers of Democracy: Challenges in the West, the East and the Third World*, Ashgate, 2005; *Globalization, the Third World State and Poverty-Alleviation in the Twenty-First Century*, Ashgate, 2002; Bob Sutcliffe, *100 Ways of Seeing an Unequal World*, Zed Books, 2001; Todd Landman, *Protecting Human Rights: A Comparative Study*, Georgetown University Press, 2005; William F. Felice, *The Global New Deal: Economic and Social Human Rights in World Politics*, Rowman & Littlefield Publishers, Inc., 2003; William F. Felice, *Taking Suffering Seriously: The Importance of Collective Human Rights*, State University of New York Press, 1996; Jan K. Black, *Inequity in the Global Village: Recycled Rhetoric and Disposable People*, Kumarian Press, 1999; Michael Goodhart, *Democracy As Human Rights: Freedom and Equality in the Age of Globalization*, Routledge, 2005; *Fighting For Human Rights*, edited by Paul Gready, Routledge, 2004; *Democratizing Global Governance*, edited by Esref Aksu and Joseph A. Camilleri, Palgrave Macmillan, 2002.

128. Westad, *The Global Cold War*, p. 99.
129. Ibid., p. 100. In expanding upon the definition and idea of what constitutes the highest dose of morality for humankind, there are scholars who argue that the citizenry of those who reside in the North is to begin to protect the victims of any injustice to which those who reside in the North contribute. On this matter, see: Thomas W. Pogge, *World Poverty and Human Rights: Cosmopolitan Responsibilities and Reforms*, Polity, 2002, p. 211. Pogge notes:

We are not merely distant witnesses of a problem unrelated to ourselves, with a weak, positive duty to help. Rather we are, both causally and morally, intimately involved in the fate of the poor by imposing upon them a global institutional order that regularly produces severe poverty and/or by effectively excluding them from a fair share of the value of exploited natural resources and/or by upholding a radical inequality that evolved through a historical process pervaded by horrendous crimes. We can realistically end our involvement in their severe poverty not by extricating ourselves from this involvement, but only by ending such poverty through economic reform. If feasible reforms are blocked by others, then we may in the end be unable to do more than mitigate some of the harms we also help produce. But even then a difference would remain, because our effort would fulfill not a duty to help the needy, but a duty to protect victims of any injustice to which we contribute.

130. Ibid., p. 100.
131. Ibid., p. 101. Perhaps we should ask why the same level of concern for human liberation from poverty, mounting inequality, and violations of human rights does not exist in the minds of many individuals in the world of the twenty-first century. Some scholars have raised the questions with great precision and attempted to offer an answer. For example: Pogge, *World Poverty and Human Rights*, pp. 2–3. Pogge notes:

Inequality continues to mount decade after decade as the affluent get richer and the poor remain at or below the subsistence minimum. Over a recent, closely studied five-year period, real growth in the global average per capita income was a respectable 5.7 percent. The top quintile (fifth) of the world's population got all of the gain—and then some: real incomes declined in all other income segments. "The bottom five percent of the world grew poorer, as their real incomes decreased between 1988 and 1993 by one-fourth while the richest quintile grew richer. It gained 12 percent in real terms, that is it grew more than twice as much as mean world income (5.7 percent)." This juxtaposition of great progress in our moral norms and conduct with a rather catastrophic moral situation on the ground raises two questions: (1) How can severe poverty of half of humankind continue despite enormous economic and technological progress and despite the enlightened moral norms and values of our heavily dominant Western civilization? (2) Why do we citizens of the affluent Western states not find it morally troubling, at least, that a world heavily dominated by us and our values gives such very deficient and inferior starting positions to so many people? Answers to the second question help answer the first. Extensive severe poverty can continue, because we do not find its eradication morally compelling. And we cannot find its eradication morally compelling until we find its persistence and the relentless rise in global inequality troubling enough to warrant serious moral reflection.

132. Ibid., p. 102.
133. Kevin Danaher, *In Whose Interest?—A Guide to US-South African Relations*, Institute for Policy Studies, 1984. Writing on the eve of South Africa's transition from apartheid to a democratic state, Danaher notes:

Historically, US elites have maintained a de facto alliance with South African elites, to the detriment of the South African and American people. They have been relatively successful in fighting off attempts to break their cross-national class solidarity. The general goal of the antiapartheid movement should be to build solidarity between progressive forces in South Africa and those outside, while interrupting cross-national elite collaboration.

134. Andrew F. Cooper and Thomas Legler, "A Tale of Two Mesas: The OAS Defense of Democracy in Peru and Venezuela," *Global Governance: A Review of Multilateralism and International Organization*, Vol. 11, No. 4, October–December 2005, 425–444.
135. Josh Martin, "Arab League Collapse," *The Middle East*, May 2004, pp. 29–31.
136. *The New York Times*, November 14, 2005.
137. Cass R. Sunstein, *Designing Democracy: What Constitutions Do*, Oxford University Press, 2001; Gerald W. Scully, *Constitutional Environments and Economic Growth*, Princeton University, 1992; Ziyad Motala, *Constitutional Options For A Democratic South Africa: A Comparative Perspective*, Howard University Press, 1994; Donald L. Horowitz, *A Democratic South Africa?—Constitutional Engineering in a Divided Society*, University of California Press, 1991.
138. Arend Lijphart, "The Wave of Power-Sharing Democracy," *The Architecture of Democracy: Constitutional Design, Conflict Management, and Democracy*, edited by Andrew Reynolds, Oxford University Press, 2002, p. 37.
139. Ibid., pp. 38–39.
140. Robin Luckham, "Are There Alternatives to Liberal Democracy?" *The Democratic Developmental State: Politics and Institutional Design*, edited by Mark Robinson and Gordon White, Oxford University Press, 1998, p. 315. See also: Samir Amin, "The Millennium Development Goals: A Critique from the South," *Monthly Review*, Vol. 57, No. 10, March 2006, pp. 1–15. Amin notes:

The legitimacy of governments has disappeared. Thus conditions are ripe for the emergence of other social hegemonies that make possible a revival of development conceived as it should be: the … combination of social progress, democratic advancement, and the affirmation of national independence within a negotiated multi-polar globalization. The possibility of these new social hegemonies is already visible on the horizon.

141. Horowitz, *A Democratic South Africa? Constitutional Engineering in a Divided Society*, p. 231.
142. Timothy D. Sisk, *Democratization in South Africa: The Elusive Social Contract*, Princeton University, 1995, p. 249. Sisk notes:

South Africa will continue to experience deep and enduring conflicts after apartheid. Above all, there will be conflicts over minority rights and majority prerogatives, deep class differences, ethnic and racial intolerance, and keen competition for resources under conditions of scarcity. Conflicts along these lines will be manifested at the national, regional, and local level. The critical questions, however, are whether South Africans can nonviolently channel these conflicts into legitimate, broadly inclusive, and accountable democratic political institutions, whether a companion economic pact is possible to ameliorate poverty, achieve reconstruction, development, and growth, and whether a vigorous integrated civil society will emerge to protect newly won democratic rights.

143. Bertus De Villiers, "Social and Economic Rights," *Rights And Constitutionalism: The New South African Legal Order*, edited by Dawid van Wyk et al., Clarendon Press/Oxford University Press, 1995, pp. 599–600.

144. Ibid., p. 602.

145. Ibid., pp. 602–603.

146. Ibid., p. 603.

147. Ibid., p. 610.

148. Sisk, *Democratization in South Africa*, p. 249.

149. Ibid., p. 250.

150. Ibid.

151. Ibid.

152. Patrick Bond, *Unsustainable South Africa: Environment, Development, and Social Protest*, University of Natal Press, 2002, pp. 421–422.

153. Robert Kinloch Massie, *Loosing the Bonds: The United States and South Africa in the Apartheid Years*, Doubleday, 1997.

154. Bond, *Against Global Apartheid*, 2001.

155. Neville Alexander, *An Ordinary Country: Issues in the Transition from Apartheid to Democracy in South Africa*, University of Natal Press, 2002. Alexander notes: "there is a fundamental contradiction between the classical raison d'etre of the national state, that is, to protect and promote the interests of is own citizens, and the objective functions which the state has come to perform on behalf of global finance capital."

156. Ibid., p. 152. Alexander notes: "There is no doubt that the South African government is placing its faith in the international capitalist class rather than in the social movements of the common people, the workers, peasants, women and other oppressed strata of the world, to bring about the reform and/or the undermining of the system."

157. Sahra Ryklief, "Does the Emperor Really Have no Clothes?: Thabo Mbeki and Ideology," *Thabo Mbeki's World: The Politics and Ideology of the South African President*, edited by Sean Jacobs and Richard Calland, University of Natal Press, 2002, p. 112.

158. Patti Waldmeir, *Anatomy of a Miracle: The End of Apartheid and the Birth of the New South Africa*, W.W. Norton & Company, 1997; *Business in the Shadow of Apartheid: US Firms in South Africa*, edited by Jonathan Leape et al., Lexington Books, 1985; *Launching Democracy in South Africa: The First Open Election, April 1994*, edited by, R.W. Johnson and Lawrence Schlemmer, Yale University Press, 1996; Massie, *Loosing the Bonds*, Doubleday, 1997.

159. Ryklief, "Does the Emperor Really Have no Clothes?: Thabo Mbeki and Ideology."

160. Andrew Reynolds, *Electoral Systems and Democratization in Southern Africa*, Oxford University Press, 1999, p. 106.

161. De Villiers, "Social and Economic Rights," p. 621.

162. James L. Gibson, *Overcoming Apartheid: Can Truth reconcile A Divided Nation?*, Russell Sage Foundation, 2004, p. 6. Gibson goes on to note:

That is, the framers of the TRC accepted the hypothesis that when gross human rights violators are granted amnesty, they will come forward and tell the truth about their deeds. If a condition for receiving amnesty for gross human rights violations is full disclosure, South Africa could learn something about the black holes in its past by making amnesty available. Many believe that amnesty did indeed produce specific evidence of past transgressions that would have never come to light otherwise. These truths were then aggregated into a collective memory about the past.

163. Ibid., p. 7.

164. Richard Falk, "The World Speaks on Iraq," *The Nation*, August 1/8, 2005, p. 8.

165. Ibid.

166. Goran Sluiter, "Legal Assistance to Internationalized Criminal Courts and Tribunals," *Internationalized Criminal Courts And Tribunals: Sierra Leone, East Timor, Kosovo, and Cambodia*, edited by Cesare P. R. Romano et al., Oxford University Press, 2004, pp. 384–385.

167. Ibid., p. 385.

168. Falk, "The World Speaks on Iraq," p. 8.

169. Heikki Potomaki and Teivo Teivainen, *A Possible World: Democratic Transformation of Global Institutions*, Zed Books, 2004, p. 131. These authors note:

It is also possible to apply the mechanisms of truth commissions to look at other kinds of historical injustice. We can think of commissions of inquiry working on issues such as historical patterns of slavery or Third World debt crises. This approach may be more suitable for expanding the emerging truth commission approach to broader issues of world politics and North-South relations.

170. Thomas M. Franck, *The Empowered Self: Law and Society in the Age of Individualism*, Oxford University Press, 1999, p. 279. Franck writes:

Individualism has proved contagious, spreading under propitious circumstances of industrialization, economic development, the emergence of an urban middle class, universal and higher education, political democratization, and revolutions in person access to information and communications. These exogenous factors, over time, are universally replicable and the human rights they tend, however incidentally, to foster are increasingly supported by the laws and mores of an emerging international system.

171. Frank J. Lechner and John Boli, *World Culture: Origins and Consequences*, Blackwell Publishing, 2005, pp. 25–29.

172. Greg Behrman, *The Invisible People: How the US Has Slept Through the Global AIDS Pandemic, the Greatest Humanitarian Catastrophe of Our Time*, Free Press, 2004; Geraldine Sealey, "An Epidemic Failure: President George Bush is Breaking his promise to spend $15 billion fighting AIDS in Africa—and by placing religion over science, he's actually making things worse," *The Rolling Stone*, National Affairs, June 16, 2005, pp. 45–48; Michael Vatikiotis and Shawn W. Crispin, Special Report—AIDS in Asia: It's About to Get A Lot Worse, *Far Eastern Economic Review*, July 15, 2004, pp. 32–51; Christine McMurray and Roy Smith, *Diseases of Globalization: Socioeconomic Transitions and Health*, Earth Scan Publications, 2001; Anne-Christine D'Adesky, *Moving Mountains: The Race to Treat Global AIDS*, Verso, 2004; Eileen Stillwaggon, *AIDS and the Ecology of Poverty*, Oxford University Press, 2006.

173. Committee on the Science of Climate Change, Division on Earth and Life Studies, National Research Council, *Climate Change Science: An Analysis of Some Key Questions*, National Academy Press, 2001; The Editors—Review of the Month—"The Pentagon and Climate Change," *Monthly Review: An Independent Socialist Magazine*, May 2004, pp. 1–13; Global Warming—Planetary Emergency, The *Rolling Stone*, November 17, 2005, pp. 72–102; Timothy Wirth, "Hot Air Over Kyoto: The United States and the Politics of Global Warming," *Harvard International Review*, Winter 2002, pp. 72–77; James Gustave Speth, *Red Sky At Morning: America and the Crisis of the Global Environment—A Citizen's Agenda For Action*, Yale University Press, 2004; Paul Ehrlich and Anne Ehrlich, *One With Nineveh: Politics, Consumption, and the Human Future*, Island Press, 2004; Diamond, *Collapse*; Jennifer Clapp and Peter Dauvergne, *Paths to a Green World: The Political Economy of the Global Environment*, The MIT Press, 2005; Daniel Esty and Maria Ivanova, editors, *Global Environmental Governance: Options and Opportunities*, Yale School of Forestry and Environmental Studies, 2002; Ken Conca and Geoffrey Dabelko, editors, *Green Planet Blues: Environmental Politics From Stockholm To Johannesburg, Third Edition*, Westview Press, 2004.

174. Stiglitz and Charlton, *Fair Trade For All*; Michael B. Brown, *Fair Trade: Reform and Realities in the International Trading System*, Zed Books, 1993; Charles Derber, *People Before Profit, The New Globalization in an Age of Terror, Big Money, and Economic Crisis*, St. Martin's Press, 2002; Robert Kuttner, *The End of Laissez-Faire: National Purpose and the Global Economy After the Cold War*, Alfred A. Knopf, 1991; Robert Kuttner, *Everything For Sale: The Virtues and Limits of Markets*, Alfred A. Knopf, 1997.

175. Charles J. Moxley, Jr., *Nuclear Weapons and International Law in the Post Cold War World*, Austin & Winfield, 2000; Ved P. Nanda and David Krieger, *Nuclear Weapons and the World Court*, Transnational Publishers, Inc., 1998; Joseph F. Pilat and Robert E. Pendley, *1995—A New Beginning for the NPT?* Plenum Press, 1995; *Nuclear Weapons After the Comprehensive Test*

Ban: Implications for Modernization and Proliferation, edited by Eric Arnett, SIPRI and Oxford University Press, 1996; C.G. Weeramantry, *Nuclear Weapons and Scientific Responsibility*, Longwood Academic, 1987; *Nuclear Proliferation and the Legality of Nuclear Weapons*, edited by William M. Evan and Ved P. Nanda, University Press of America, Inc., 1995; *At The Nuclear Crossroads: Choices About Nuclear Weapons and Extension of the Non-Proliferation Treaty*, edited by John B. Rhinelander and Adam M. Scheinman, University Press of America, Inc, and The Lawyer's Alliance for World Security, 1995; Francis A. Boyle, *The Criminality of Nuclear Deterrence*, Clarity Press, Inc., 2002.

176. Dennis Pirages and Theresa M. DeGeest, *Ecological Security: An Evolutionary Perspective on Globalization*, Rowman & Littlefield, Publishers, Inc., 2004.

177. William Greider, *One World, Ready or Not: The Manic Logic of Global Capitalism*, Simon & Schuster, 1997, p. 469.

178. Irwin Cotler, editor, *Nuremberg Forty Years Later: The Struggle against Injustice in Our Time—* International Human Rights Conference, November 1987—Papers and Proceedings and Retrospective 1993, McGill-Queens University Press, 1995. See also: Naomi Roht-Arriaza, *The Pinochet Effect: Transnational Justice in the Age of Human Rights*, University of Pennsylvania Press, 2005; Mark Ensalaco, *Chile Under Pinochet: Recovering the Truth*, University of Pennsylvania Press, 2000; Peter Kornbluh, *The Pinochet File: A Declassified Dossier on Atrocity and Accountability*, The New Press, 2003.

179. Cecilia Menjivar and Nestor Rodriguez, *When States Kill: Latin America, the US, and Technologies of Terror*, University of Texas Press, Austin, 2005.

180. Joanna R. Quinn and Mark Freeman, "Lessons Learned: Practical Lessons Gleaned from Inside the Truth Commissions of Guatemala and South Africa," *Human Rights Quarterly*, Vol. 25, No. 4, November 2003, pp. 1117–1149.

181. William A. Schabas, "The Relationship Between Truth Commissions and International Courts: The Case of Sierra Leone," *Human Rights Quarterly*, Vol. 25, No. 4, November 2003, pp. 1035–1066.

182. Raquel Aldana-Pindell, "An Emerging Universality of Justiciable Victims' Rights in the Criminal Process to Curtail Impunity for State-Sponsored Crimes," *Human Rights Quarterly*, Vol. 26, No. 3, August 2004, pp. 605–686. See also: Donald W. Schriver, Jr., *Honest Patriots: Loving a Country Enough to Remember Its Misdeeds*, Oxford University Press, 2005.

183. Martha Nussbaum, *Frontiers of Justice: Disability, Nationality, Species Membership*, Harvard University Press, 2006, p. 240. Nussbaum observes:

Even if we ignore the damage done by colonialism both to resources and to the economic and political culture of many contemporary nations, we should acknowledge the fact that the international economic system, and the activities of multinational corporations, create severe, disproportionate burdens for poorer nations, which cannot solve their problems by wise internal policies alone.

184. Robert Johansen, *The National Interest and the Human Interest: An Analysis of US Foreign Policy*, Princeton University Press, 1980, p. 402.

185. Nussbaum, *Frontiers of Justice*, p. 224. See also: Richard G. Wilkinson, *The Impact of Inequality: How to Make Sick Societies Healthier*, The New Press, 2005; Ichiro Rawachi and Bruce P. Kennedy, *The Health of Nations: Why Inequality is Harmful to Your Health*, The New Press, 2002; Finis Welch, editor *The Causes and Consequences of Increasing Inequality*, The University of Chicago Press, 2001; Paul Mosley and Elizabeth Dowler, *Poverty and Social Exclusion in North and South: Essays on Social Policy and Global Poverty Reduction*, Routledge, 2003; Branko Milanovic, *Worlds Apart: Measuring International and Global Inequality*, Princeton University Press, 2005; Scott Sernau, *Global Problems: The Search for Equity, Peace, and Sustainability*, Pearson, 2006; Laurie Wermuth, *Global Inequality and Human Needs: Health and Illness in an Increasingly Unequal World*, Pearson, 2003.

186. Ibid., p. 225. See also: *Global Sustainable Development in the Twenty-First Century*, edited by Keeok Lee, Alan Holland, and Desmond McNeill, Edinburgh University Press, 2000; Heikki Patomaki and Teivo Teivainen, *A Possible World: Democratic Transformations of Global*

Institutions, Zed Books, 2004; Don Kalb et al., editors, *The Ends of Globalization: Bringing Society Back In*, Rowman & Littlefield, Publishers, Inc., 2000.

187. Stiglitz and Charlton, *Fair Trade For All*, p. 205.

188. Ibid.

189. The World Commission on Environment and Development, *Our Common Future*, pp. 300–301.

190. Bronwen Manby, "The African Union, NEPAD, and Human Rights: The Missing Agenda," *Human Rights Quarterly*, Vol. 26, No. 4, November 2004, p. 1011. See also: Ernest Aryeetey et al., editors, *Asia and Africa in the Global Economy*, United Nations University Press, 2003; Paul Collier and Nicholas Sambanis, editors, *Volume 2: Europe, Central Asia, and Other Regions—Understanding Civil War: Evidence and Analysis*, The World Bank, 2005; Paul Collier and Nicholas Sambanis, editors, *Volume 1: Africa—Understanding Civil War: Evidence and Analysis*, The World Bank, 2005; Paul Collier et al., *Breaking The Conflict Trap: Civil War and Development Policy*, A World Bank Policy Research Report, 2003; Philip G. Roeder and Donald Rothchild, editors, *Sustainable Peace: Power and Democracy after Civil Wars*, Cornell University Press, 2005; Martin Meredith, *The Fate of Africa: From the Hopes of Freedom to the Heart of Despair—A History of Fifty Years of Independence*, Public Affairs, 2005.

191. G. Weeramantry, *Universalizing International Law*, Martinus Nijhoff Publishers, 2004.

192. Justice N. J. McNally, "Human Rights in the Context of Sustainable Development," *Sustainable Justice: Reconciling Economic, Social, and Environmental Law*, edited by Marie-Claire Cordinier Segger and G. Weeramantry, Martinus Nijhoff Publishers, 2005, pp. 73–81. See also: Marie-Claire Cordonier Segger and Ahfaq Khalfan, *Sustainable Development Law: Principles, Practices, and Prospects*, Oxford University Press, 2004.

193. Justice A. Sachs, "Enforcing Socio-Economic Rights," *Sustainable Justice: Reconciling Economic, Social, and Environmental Law*, edited by Marie-Claire Cordinier Segger and G. Weeramantry, Martinus Nijhoff Publishers, 2005, pp. 57–71.

194. Judge G. Weeramantry, "Achieving Sustainable Development through International Law," *Sustainable Justice: Reconciling Economic, Social, and Environmental Law*, edited by Marie-Claire Cordinier Segger and G. Weeramantry, Martinus Nijhoff Publishers, 2005, pp. 15–32.

195. Nussbaum, *Frontiers of Justice*, p. 274.

196. A. W. Brian Simpson, *Human Rights and the End of Empire: Britain and the Genesis of the European Convention*, Oxford University Press, 2001.

197. Robert Blackburn, "Current Developments, Assessment, and Prospects," *Fundamental Rights in Europe: The European Convention on Human Rights and its Member States, 1950–2000*, edited by Robert Blackburn and Jorg Polakiewicz, Oxford University Press, 2001, pp. 93–94.

198. Reinhard Rack and Stefan Lausegger, "The Role of the European Parliament: Past and Future," *The EU and Human Rights*, edited by Philip Alston et al., Oxford University Press, 1999, pp. 801–858.

199. Klaus Gunther, "The Legacies of Injustice and Fear: A European Approach to Human Rights and their Effects on Political Culture," *The EU and Human Rights*, edited by Philip Alston et al., Oxford University Press, 1999, pp. 117–144.

200. Menno T. Kamminga, "Holding Multinational Corporations Accountable for Human Rights Abuses: A Challenge for the EC," *The EU and Human Rights*, edited by Philip Alston et al., Oxford University Press, 1999, pp. 553–569.

201. Joel Brinkley, "US Keeps a Wary Eye on the Next Bolivian President," *The New York Times*, December 21, 2005, p. A-3.

202. David Rieff, "Che's Second Coming?" *The New York Times Magazine*, November 20, 2005, pp. 72.

203. Ibid., p. 76.

204. Evo Morales, "I Believe Only in the Power of the People," from the text of a speech given on December 24, 2005, at the "In Defense of Humanity" conference at: www.counterpunch.org/morales12302005.html. See also: Noam Chomsky, "Latin America at the tipping point," *International Socialist Review*, March–April 2006, pp. 10–11; Tom Lewis, "Will Evo Morales end Neo-liberalism?," *International Socialist Review*, March–April 2006, pp. 16–21; Ben Dangl and Mark Engler, "Bolivia and the Progressive Mandate in Latin America," *Z-Magazine*, March

2006, pp. 20–27; Nadia Martinez, "Political Upheaval: Latin America challenges the Washington Consensus," *In These Times*, April 2006, pp. 20–24; Noam Chomsky, *Failed States: The Abuse of Power and the Assault on Democracy*, Metropolitan Books, 2006, pp. 256–257. According to Chomsky:

In a further blow to Washington's energy policies, the leading oil exporter in the hemisphere, Venezuela, has forged probably the closest relations with China of any Latin American country, and is planning to sell increasing amounts of oil to China as part of its effort to reduce dependence on the openly hostile US government. Latin America as a whole is increasing trade and other relations with China, with some setbacks, but likely expansion, in particular for raw materials exporters like Brazil and Chile ... Some analysts have suggested that Cuba and Venezuela might even unite, a step towards further integration of Latin America in a bloc that is more independent of the United States [pp.256–257].

7 CONCLUSION

1. See, Ron Suskind, "Without a Doubt," the *New York Times Magazine*, October 17, 2004.
2. Thomas Mertens, "International or Global Justice? Evaluating the Cosmopolitan Approach," *Real World Justice: Grounds, Principles, Human Rights, and Social Institutions*, edited by Andreas Follesdal and Thomas Pogge, Springer, (the Netherlands), 2005, p. 102.
3. Thomas Pogge, "The First UN Millennium Development Goal: A Cause for Celebration?" *Real World Justice: Grounds, Principles, Human Rights, and Social Institutions*, edited by Andreas Follesdal and Thomas Pogge, Springer (the Netherlands), 2005, pp. 333–334.

Index

abuses of empire, 29, 32, 41, 51–4, 56, 76
affliction of identities, 150
African Charter on Human and Peoples'
    Rights, 319
African National Congress (ANC), 81,
    319, 321
    see also Mandela, Nelson
African Union (AU), 163, 314, 415n 190
Alliance for Progress, 213–20
Allott, P., 160
Alperovitz, G., 229
Alternative Eight, 88, 91
American Civil Liberties Union (ACLU), 83,
    177, 382n 21
American Empire, 10, 23, 31, 41–3, 49, 50, 54,
    56, 60, 76, 82, 169, 203, 242, 350n 5, 350n
    16, 351n 25, 352n 28, 356n 71, 356n 73,
    356n 74, 358n 28, 361n 43, 361n 49, 365n
    93, 390n 16, 377n 122, 377n 124, 381n 14,
    392n 163, 396n 241, 398n 255, 401n 304,
    405n 39
American National Security State (NSS), 67
American Revolution, 209
Amin, S., 60, 153, 348n 7, 349n 13, 356n 71,
    373n 54, 377n 125, 411n 140
Amnesty International, 80, 177
Anan, General Kofi, UN General Secretary, 239
Anti-Ballistic Missile Treaty (ABM), 31, 50, 70,
    68, 93, 94, 114, 367n 101
Apartheid, 4, 19, 24, 29, 79, 81, 91, 109, 110,
    137, 142, 167, 168, 170, 295, 302, 305,
    309, 316, 319, 320, 324, 330, 342, 362n
    66, 400n 284, 407n 87, 411n 133, 411n
    142, 412n 153, 412n 154, 412n 155,
    412n 158, 412n 162
Arab League, 411n 135
    Arab Free Trade Area (AFTA), 313, 314
    collapse of summit, 314
Axis of Evil, 90, 114, 201, 242, 243, 253, 256,
    372n 39, 404n 8

Bacevich, A.J., 49, 349n 10, 351n 25, 358n 28,
    368n 108, 392n 163
Bamford, J., 196, 387n 95, 387n 103, 400n 283
Barlett, D.L., Pulitzer Prize Winner, 226, 227,
    394n 228, 395n 229, 396n 240
Barnett, R., 155, 388n 113

Beitz, C., 280
Bello, W., 77, 162, 164, 165, 274, 374n 38,
    350n 16, 352n 16, 352n 32, 354n 51, 355n
    59, 355n 64, 361n 49, 361n 52, 363n 77,
    365n 93, 368n 115, 370n 16, 372n 52,
    380n 179, 393n 185, 396n 241, 396n 244,
    397n 249, 399n 270, 405n 37, 405n 39
Bill of Rights Act, 9, 62, 64, 76, 200, 231, 256,
    336, 359n 31, 383n 21
Biological Weapons Convention (BWC), 68
Blair, Tony, Prime Minister, 81, 235, 247,
    248, 250
Blix, Hans, Fomer Director, UN Inspection
    Commission, 249, 250
blow back effect of foreign policy, 202, 203, 205
Boggs, C., 182, 239, 356n 73, 357n 17, 362n
    70, 383n 43, 399n 269
Bok, D., President Emeritus, Harvard
    University, 227, 395, 230
Borger, J., 238, 399n 258
Britt, L.W., 234, 397n 248
Burbach, R., 31, 350n 4, 353n 45, 355n 60,
    369n 5, 369n 7, 370n 17
Bush, President George W., 179, 200,
    234, 238
    see also "axis of evil"; NEPDG
Bush, Sr., George H.W., President, 80,
    175, 249

capital/capitalist
    classes, 20
    empire, 20, 56
    integration, 341
    market, 20, 21, 115, 273
    regimes, 57, 370n 16
Capra, F., 100, 116, 369n 2, 370n 18
Cardoso, H., 273, 275, 278, 405n 31, 405n 40,
    405n 48
Carter, Jimmy, President, 48, 190, 212
    Brezinski, Z., National Security
        Advisor, 212
categorization, 128,
    of destruction, 129–31
Center for International Sustainable
    Development (CISDL), 302, 304
Central American Free Trade Agreement
    (CAFTA), 183, 223, 315

417

Central Intelligence Agency (CIA), 2, 144, 173,
    180, 181, 184, 202, 203, 207, 245, 247,
    249, 251, 254–6, 264
  failure, 192, 193, 196
  Pakistan ISI, 203
  sponsored guerilla training, 203
Chavez, H., 87
  see also Venezuela
Churchill, W., 54
clash of civilizations, 105, 109, 110, 113–16,
    118–20, 122, 124, 126, 128, 130, 136, 144,
    158, 164, 165, 202, 371n 27
clash of ignorance, 115, 116, 118, 149, 372n 43
  see also Said, E.
clash thesis, 102, 105, 111, 118, 119, 129, 136,
    139, 148, 156, 158, 167
Clinton, President Bill., 80, 222
Cloward, R.A., 226, 396n 225
Coalition Provisional Authority (CPA), 36
Coetzee, J.M., 58, 59, 355n 68
Cold War, 7, 11, 12, 25, 38, 42, 45, 66, 67, 70,
    71, 78, 80, 90, 94, 96, 110, 112, 115, 118,
    123, 155, 175, 188, 193, 204, 206, 208,
    209, 241, 250, 253–5, 257, 263, 298, 311,
    337, 346, n 12, 347n 16, 347n 24, 351n 23,
    352n 26, 355n 60, 355n 15, 361n 45, 366n
    98, 370n 21, 375n 85, 378n 135, 378n 138,
    381n 17, 385n 62, 387n 94, 389n 130,
    390n 132, 394n 197, 399n 256, 401n 309,
    402n 315, 403n 326, 404n 4
  strategy of containment, 253–5
collateral damage, 15, 20, 44, 51, 117, 118,
    129, 234, 263, 268
  policies, 67
commanding heights, 81, 225, 395n 220
Committee on the Present Danger (CPD),
    220, 244
Common Aero Vehicle (CAV), 93
community of nations, 5, 33, 155, 156, 279
Comprehensive Test Ban Treaty (CTBT), 68,
    70, 94, 113, 138, 239, 313
convergence of civilizations, 101, 102, 103
convergence thesis, 148
  analysis, 165
  normative, 168
Council of Foreign Relations (CFR), 174, 176,
    189, 190, 199
Counter-hegemonic alliance, 303, 304, 306,
    307, 308, 312, 314, 319, 325, 337
crisis of legitimacy, 52, 54, 95, 96, 125, 174,
    298, 354n 51
Cuban Missile Crisis, 66, 138, 181, 206, 380n 9,
    390n 142

Danner, M., 247, 248
Defense Planning Guidance (DPG), 254

democracy
  consolidating, 280
  promotion, 64, 90, 98, 121, 184, 185,
    186, 323
  radicalizing, 279
  social, 282, 283
democracy and justice, 127, 128, 175, 369n 8,
    371n 34, 369n 35, 381n 11, 386n 84, 394n
    195, 394n 198, 395n 216
democratic despotism, 71–3
Democratic Leadership Council (DLC), 81, 235
democratization, 30, 90, 217, 262, 271, 296,
    297, 319, 320, 321, 363n 66, 407n 85,
    408n 105, 411n 142, 412n 148, 412n 160,
    413n 170
  of Global community, 165–7
Dewey, J., 71
domino theory, 39, 181, 357n 20
Downing Street Memo, 247–9, 252

Eldredge, N. E., 59
Empire Syndrome, 13, 14, 60, 260, 403
Enron, 45, 80, 175, 179, 182, 211, 212, 243,
    391n 153
Equality
  goal of, 281
  realization of, 281
European Convention on Human Rights
    (ECHR), 336, 337
exceptionalism, 99, 398n 256
exclusionary governace, 72, 105, 113, 162,
    240, 262, 266, 275, 290, 294, 297,
    303, 343
Exclusionary State (ES), 15, 41, 87, 140, 161,
    166, 240, 263, 266, 267, 269, 274,
    290, 296
expansionism, 76, 84, 86

facism, 234
  see also Britt, L.W.
Falk, R., 116, 160, 161, 326
Fanon, F., 162, 163, 164, 379n 171, 380n 173
Farmer, Dr., P., 155, 378n 144, 408n 100
Federal Bureau of Investigation (FBI), 7, 62, 63,
    72, 202, 233, 247, 248, 251, 255, 258, 264,
    386n 90
Federal principle, 64, 66, 67
Foreign Intelligence Surveillance Act (FISA), 63
free market, 16, 21, 50, 57, 84, 97, 115, 125,
    129, 176, 242, 285, 291, 296, 298, 348n 4,
    365n 93, 366n 96, 370n 16, 375n 85, 377n
    122, 405n 19, 409n 110
  principles and policies, 58, 155, 188, 193,
    reforms, 225
Free Trade Area of the Americas (FTAA), 86,
    87, 344, 363n 77, 364n 78

Freedom of Information Act, 201
Free World, 11, 12, 13, 42, 66, 138, 205, 366n 95
Fukuyama, F., 112, 115, 262, 348n 6, 353n 40, 366n 97
full spectrum dominance, 8, 31, 91, 92, 93, 97, 114, 115, 126, 254, 353n 45
fundamentalism, 112, 150, 213, 242, 376n 110
  Christian, 149
fundamentalists, 63, 149, 203, 376n 110
  ideological agenda, 149

GAO, 211
General Trade on Trade and Tariffs (GATT), 156, 183, 405n 39
Geneva Convention, 3, 29, 50, 53, 63, 64, 80, 82, 120, 121, 130, 144, 389n 118
genocide, 23, 27, 52, 60, 120, 135, 137, 147, 169, 176, 211, 248, 268, 353n 48, 353n 50, 366n 98, 376n 98
  see King, Jr., Martin Luther
global
  climate change, 109, 121
  community, 68, 69, 77, 78, 81, 82, 89, 219, 228–30, 235, 236, 238, 239, 246, 255, 259, 263, 268, 270, 275, 279, 280, 293, 296, 299, 300, 303, 305, 306, 308, 317, 328, 329–31, 334, 335, 342, 343
  consciousness, 5, 66, 135, 139, 310' metonia,' 122
  Empire, 69, 77, 81, 82, 84, 85, 86, 88, 89, 95
  ethic, 121, 135, 165
global governance 119, 144, 160, 264
  hegemony, 13, 31, 70, 176, 228, 251, 256, 261, 265, 297, 328, 371n 27
  justice, 124, 128, 134, 159, 161, 229, 264, 332, 339, 364n 78, 373n 54, 397n 245, 398n 252, 416n 2
  policy, 69, 170, 333
  poverty, 33, 103, 121, 127, 140, 224, 239, 246, 267, 287, 299, 310, 363n 77, 365n 93, 369n 8, 369n 12, 371n 34, 372n 49, 395n 216, 395n 219, 414n 185
  resistance, 31, 40, 60, 91, 142, 344
  resistance movements, 77, 140
  security, 50, 69, 100, 117, 329, 361n 51
  system, 33, 54, 56, 125, 132, 266, 288, 294, 329, 373n 59, 377n 122
  violence, 123, 166, 167, 261, 268
  see also Falk R
globalization, 110, 139, 153, 230, 286, 290, 298, 309, 333, 337, 340, 342, 345
  on developing countries, 273
  economic, 155

  increase global inequality, 232
  progress of 157, 159
Global Truth Commission on Empire (GTCE), 325
Gould, S.J., 59, 347n 36, 355n 60, 382n 26
Government Accounting Office (GAO), 211
Government of National Unity (GNU), 322, 323
Graduated Reciprocation in Tension Reduction (GRIT), 181
Gross Domestic Products (GDP), 314
group think, 22
Guantanamo Bay, Cuba, 63, 80
Gulf of Tonkin (1964), 65, 191, 196, 197, 198, 252, 256, 387n 103

Habermas, J., 174
Hamilton, A., 244
Harvey, D., 91, 366n 47, 406n 67
healing of civilizations, 120, 121, 122
human rights, 2, 3, 5, 6, 11–3, 16–7, 19, 21, 34, 38, 42, 43, 46, 50, 144, 159, 241, 277, 334–6
  charities, 263
  development agenda, 291, 293
  liberation, 144
  protection, 8
Huntington, S., 101, 108, 109, 111, 113, 115, 118, 124, 129, 156, 350n 16, 370n 21, 371n 27
Hussein, Saddam, 246, 249
  see also Downing Street Memo; Weapons of Mass Destruction (WMD)

Imperial Dynamic, 55, 56
  overstretch, 30, 31, 59, 107, 350n 4, 353n 45, 369n 5, 369n 7, 370n 17
  plutocracy, 32, 34, 35
  presidency, 65, 72, 137, 200, 207, 209, 238, 246, 322, 346n 4, 352n 26, 381n 15, 388n 114, 388n 117
inclusionary governance, 27, 72, 140, 161, 166, 167, 240, 269, 270, 274, 275–8, 292, 296, 31, 343, 347n 23, 347n 32, 349n 12, 354n 51, 355n 66, 358n 24, 364n 84, 366n 96, 369n 9, 371n 33, 375n 79, 379n 165, 399n 265, 401n 303, 405n 20, 405n 25, 405n 41, 408n 106
Inclusionary State (IS), 15, 41, 140, 161, 166, 240, 267, 269, 270, 271, 277, 278, 280, 281, 283
  achieving IS, 275
  principles of IS, 276
inequality factor, 33
international anarchy, 60, 70
International Court of Justice (ICJ), 138, 169, 327, 328

International Criminal Court (ICC), 68, 114,
143, 144, 169, 229, 235, 239, 259, 300,
325, 327, 341
International Labor Organization (ILO), 105
International Law, 3, 6, 8, 9, 10, 12, 14, 15, 22,
25, 31, 37, 43, 50, 57, 60, 64, 65, 69, 72,
80–82, 85, 86, 89, 90, 93, 95, 99, 101–3,
107, 111, 114, 116, 126, 128, 130, 131–3,
135–7, 139, 157, 167, 170, 174, 229, 250,
268, 303, 312, 319, 326, 334, 346n 12,
354n 55, 356n 11, 357n 15, 365n 90, 366n
96, 368n 109, 374n 62, 374n 72, 374n 74,
374n 76, 374n 77, 375n 80, 375n 81, 375n
83, 379n 168, 388n 109, 397n 247, 398n
252, 400n 282, 413n 175, 415n 191,
415n 194
affairs, 89
standards, 133
International Monetary Fund, (IMF), 6, 13, 15,
16, 21, 27, 33, 37, 55, 57, 77, 91, 97, 106,
107, 113, 126, 127, 129, 132, 156, 159,
173, 174, 202, 218, 220, 224, 225, 230,
231, 325, 237, 257, 261, 274, 282, 286–8,
290, 294–7, 302, 303, 307, 319, 320, 322,
323, 340, 345, 347n 35, 348, 370n 16,
373n 54, 373n 59, 393n 185, 397n 249,
406n 74, 406n 79, 407n 87, 407n 88, 407n
90, 408n 96, 408n 99, 409n 106, 409n 121,
loan conditionality, 218, 220, 224, 225, 230
structural adjustment programs, 237, 280, 291
International People's Tribunal, 330
International Relations (IR), 15, 40, 72, 102,
124, 157, 230, 273, 309, 336, 355n 58,
371n 30, 379n 168
International Tribunal at Nuremberg, 95, 145,
177, 325
Inter Services Intelligence (ISI), 203
inverted totalitarianism, 75, 76, 78, 79, 80, 82,
83, 84, 361n 44, 361n 46, 361n 54
Iraq
SCUD Missiles, 249
war, 256, 257
Islamic Reformation, 148

Johansen, R., 33, 126, 139, 142, 350n 6, 350n
11, 358n 27, 369n 6, 374n 75, 374n 77,
414n 184
Johnson, Lyndon, B., President, 64, 65, 188,
206, 207, 209, 213, 215, 217, 221,
232, 255–7
Judeo-Christian tradition, 151, 152, 154

Kagan, R., 94, 95
Kaplan, R.D., 154, 155, 378n 133, 399n 264
Kellogg, Brown and Root, 245

Kennan, G., 90, 91, 351n 25, 365n 94,
381n 19
Kennedy, P., 30, 59, 350n 3
Kennedy, President, John F., 138, 174, 179, 181,
198, 213, 381n 152, 410n 127
Alliance for Progress, 213, 216, 217
Assassination of, 174, 191, 195, 205–8,
Bay of Pigs, 205,
Cuban Missile Crisis, 205
see also Warren Commission
Kennedy, Robert, 84, 193, 197, 213, 215, 217,
218, 381n 10, 386n 89, 387n 104, 392n
172, 392n 179, 393n 184, 400n 284
nationalization, 214
King, Jr, Dr Martin Luther, 151, 246
Klare, M.T., 154, 350n 9, 360n 41, 360n 42,
361n 42, 362n 73, 362n 75, 378n 132,
383n 41, 391n 154, 402n 312, 404n 8
Krasner, S., 273
Krisch, N., 89, 357n 15
Kupchan, C.A., 47, 48, 350n 12, 353n 37,
354n 54
Kwitny, J., 36, 350n 15

lawless twenty-first American Century, 61–99
lawlessness, 72, 73, 74–6, 79, 82
definition and dimensions, 68
Liberation theology, 3, 146–8
Latin American, 147
Lifton, R.J., 65, 70, 260, 357n 18, 403n 1

MacGregor Burns, J., 223, 395n 207
Mandela, Nelson, 246, 302, 322, 323
see also ANC, GNU
market dominant minorities, 22
Mazrui, A., 124, 125, 128
McCormick, T., 33, 350n 5, 352n 33
Mexico, 26, 42, 45, 55, 74, 86, 87, 88, 123, 215,
216, 218, 231, 290, 300, 307, 309, 330, 340,
344, 364n 79, 364n 86, 370n 16, 396n 236,
407n 86
Mexican constitution, 87
Salinas, President, 87
might-makes right principle, 51, 108
Millenium Development Goals (MDG), 239,
342, 343
Moltmann, J., 146
Multinational Corporations (MNC), 301
See also, Transnational Corporations

narcotics, international trade in, 204
Nardin, T., 61, 160, 356n 4, 374n 64, 374n 71,
397n 247
NASA Apollo Spacecraft, 92
nation of laws, 55

National Energy Policy Development Groups (NEPDG), 211, 212
National Labor Relations Board (NLRB), 221
National Liberation Army (ELN), 114
National Missile Defense (NMD), 8, 31, 68, 92, 93, 94, 95, 130, 211, 367n 101
   See also, Strategic Defense Initiative (SDI)
National Security Action Memorandum (NSAM), 39, 180, 187, 198, 209, 384n 61
National Security Agency (NSA), 9, 223, 387n 95
National Security State (NSS), 7, 10, 38, 39, 42, 67, 74, 78, 138, 140, 176, 256, 352n 26, 366n 96
nationalistic fervor, 28, 237
native americans, 53
Nazis, 77, 83, 109, 130, 137, 169, 202, 250, 330, 362n 69, 366n 98, 375n 88
   holocaust, 90, 330
   lebensraum, 91, 93, 97
   Wernher von Braun, 92
Neo-liberal/ism, 290, 297, 337
   failure of, 307
   and its regime of rights, 286
   Washington consensus, 286
network society, 28
New International Economic Order (NIEO), 11, 56, 57, 124
New World Order, 19, 54, 55, 79, 91, 164, 199, 205, 206, 239, 250, 260, 354n 54, 368n 118, 387n 94, 395n 233, 400n 283
Nicaragua
   see World Court
Nixon, President Richard, 175, 200, 232
   Watergate affair, 175
Nkrumah, K., 162, 163, 164, 380n 177
No-Fly Zone (NFZ), 189, 385n 65
Non-Aligned Nations Movement (NAM), 90, 163, 164, 184, 355n 58, 389n 130
Non-Government Organizations (NGO), 6, 7, 44, 50, 88, 161, 229, 297, 299
nonviolent strategies, 112, 142
North American Free Trade Agreement (NAFTA), 20, 45, 74, 86–7, 123, 183, 223, 231, 340, 396n 236
   Atlantic, 183, 223
North Treaty (NATO), 42, 48, 72, 84, 85, 102, 156, 351n 26
NSAM 39, 111, 180, 187, 198, 209, 263, 273
Nuclear Non-Proliferation Treaty (NPT), 8, 68, 70, 94, 138, 229, 238, 261, 313, 374n 77, 413n 175
nuclear weapons, 68, 94, 137–40, 144, 152, 169, 238, 262, 367n 99, 367n 101,

368n 106, 374n 77, 383n 40, 413n 175, 414n 175
Nuremberg Charter, 4, 89, 90, 137, 144, 169, 250, 313, 327
Nye, J.S., 44, 352n 29, 362n 59, 399n 264
Nyerere, J.K., 162, 164, 380n 178

OAS
   Peru-*Mesa de Dialogo*, 313, 314
   Venezuela-*Mesa de Negociacion y Acuerdos*, 313, 314
Office of Strategic Services (OSS), 67
Operation Mongoose, 197
Operation Northwoods, 193, 197, 252, 387n 103
   see also Kennedy, President J.F.
Organization for Economic Cooperation and development (OECD), 156
Organization of African Unity (OAU), 163, 319, 368n 107
Outer Space Treaty, 92, 93, 94

Parker, G., 59, 355n 69
Pathologies of power vs the Affirmation of human dignity, 155, 156
   see also Farmer, Dr. P.
Pax Americana, 40, 41, 65, 206, 255
Pentagon, 8, 31, 38, 39, 40, 51, 64, 67, 74, 75, 85, 92, 93, 97, 108, 116, 129, 138, 144, 170, 177, 179, 180, 182, 186, 188, 191, 195, 196, 202, 205, 206, 209, 211, 221, 241, 245, 249, 251, 245, 249, 251, 253–6, 287, 354n 55, 356n 14, 363n 75, 367n 101, 378n 132, 380n 9, 384n 58, 384n 59, 384n 61, 387n 103, 387n 105, 388n 107, 389n 131, 401n 296, 403n 325, 413n 173
Phillips, K., 221, 222, 244, 376n 110, 391n 162, 391n 201, 391n 203, 400n 276
Piven, F. F., 226, 362n 69, 395n 225
Pogge, T., 126, 340, 354n 51, 365n 91, 369n 11, 378n 150, 409n 127, 416n 2, 416n 3
policy goals, 43, 210
post-imperial America, 231, 235–8, 246, 255, 270, 294, 297, 329
Privatized Military Industry
   see Kellogg, Brown and Root
Project for the new American Century (PNAC), 5, 10, 31, 62, 65, 81, 94, 101, 115, 189, 220, 254

al-Qaeda, 187
   Abu Ghraib Prison, 202
   Bin Ladan, Osama, 191
   links with Iraq, 249, 251
   Taliban, 202, 205, 242, 247, 381n 10
   terrorist, 187, 192, 203

radical unilateralism, 67
Raskin, M., 38, 40, 60, 78, 350n 16, 374n 77
Reagan, President Ronald, 80, 212, 243,
    370n 16
  administration, 204
  Iran/Contra Affair, 175
Red Cross, 7, 80
Republican Party, 83, 235, 362n 69
Revolution in Military Affairs (RMA), 31
Revolutionary Armed Forces of Columbia
    (FARC), 114
Rieff, D., 338
Ritter, Scott, UN Weapon Inspector, 249
Robinson, W.I., 26, 90, 294, 349n 9, 365n 95,
    379n 149, 408n 96
Robust Nuclear Earth Penetrator (RNEF), 93
Rockfeller, David and Nelson, 213, 217
Roosevelt, President, administration, Revised
    Industrial Mobilization Plan, 205
Roszak, T., 370n 18
  objectivity, 117

Sack, A., 302
Said, E., W., 118, 372n 43
Schlesinger, Jr., A.M., 256
Schlesinger, S., 239
Scott, P.D., 182, 360n 40, 360n 61, 381n 9,
    383n 42, 384n 59, 384n 61
Sen, A., Nobel Prize Winner, Economics, 1998,
    129, 162
September 11th
  See also, war on terror
Sisk, T., 319
Sliglitz, J., Nobel Prize Winner, Economics,
    2001, 332, 333
social injustice
  within civilizations, 124
social justice, 81
social movements, 127, 298
South Africa, 318
  inequality in, 317
  racial apartheid, 316, 324
spheres of influence, 66,
  see also Cold War
Steele, J., 225, Pulitzer Prize Winner,
    226, 227
Stone, G., 201
Strategic Defense Initiative (SDI), 31, 92,
    366n 99
  See also, National Missile Defense (NMD)
Structural Adjustments program (SAP), 291
Superpower Syndrome, 4, 64, 65, 70
Swedish International Development Cooperation
    Agency (SIDA), 6

Taliaferro, J. W., 59, 356n 70
Tamez, E., 146, 375n 93, 376n 96
Tarbell, J., 31, 350n 4, 353n 45, 369n 5, 369n 7,
    370n 17
terrorism, 5, 9, 34, 44, 54, 60, 75, 81, 82, 97,
    107, 108, 110, 120, 130, 131, 148–50, 170,
    171, 177, 184, 196–7, 202–3, 234, 239,
    251, 253, 256, 257, 266, 269, 299, 307,
    311, 337, 343, 350n 15, 353n 45, 354n 55,
    385n 27, 359n 31, 360n 40, 368n 118,
    375n 85, 376n 107, 367n 111, 380n 3,
    380n 6, 382n 22, 383n 47, 386n 84, 388n
    115, 388n 116, 391n 156, 403n 324,
    403n 325
Thatcher, M., (Former British Prime Minister),
    28, 225, 236
Theater Missile Defense (TMD), 31, 94
Third way politics, 235
Third World, 310
Tillich, P., 115
Transnational Corporations (TNC), 13, 20, 37,
    83, 159, 305, 309, 317, 408n 99
Truman, President Harry S., 44, 65, 352n 26
Truth and Reconciliation Commission (TRC),
    101, 120, 121, 168, 303, 324, 412n 162
turbo capitalism, 83, 362n 68
  see also inverted totalitarianism

Union of Soviet Socialist Republics (USSR), 7,
    8, 64, 92, 175, 184, 188, 196, 204, 251,
    253, 254, 255
United Nations Charter, 3, 82, 85, 133, 229,
    304, 310, 341, 342
  violations of, 341
United Nations Development Program (UNDP),
    6, 271, 279, 280, 293, 377, 405n 29,
    406n 50
United Nations Research Institute for Social
    development (UNRISD), 284, 406n 63
Universal Declaration of Human Rights
    (UDHR), 103, 272 406n 59, 409n 127
universal empire, 66, 70, 71
universal jurisdiction, 134, 136, 137, 143, 144,
    326, 331, 339, 374, 375
USA Patriot Act, 7, 9, 44, 48, 62–4, 72, 73, 79,
    81, 82, 130, 131, 174, 175, 177, 201, 202,
    233, 256, 258, 299, 359n 31, 361n 56,
    381n 15
US Bankruptcy Code
  revision of, 79
US Global Empire, 2–8, 10–27, 29, 31–3, 35,
    37, 38–1, 43–6, 50, 53–6, 58, 60, 64, 69,
    70, 72, 77, 78, 81–6, 88–1, 92, 94, 99,
    112–20, 122, 123, 125–8, 140–2, 145, 148,

US Global Empire – *continued*
149, 151–6, 158, 160, 162, 163, 265, 269,
170, 171, 173, 174, 176, 178, 182–4, 186,
189, 191, 195, 196, 202, 207, 208, 213,
219, 220, 228, 232, 234, 237–9, 242–7,
252, 254, 259, 261, 263–6, 268, 270, 274,
275, 289, 294, 296–9, 303, 305–08, 314,
317, 319, 323–6, 329–2, 340, 343, 337–8,
340–5, 361n 52, 366n 96, 400n 281

Venezuela, 88, 114, 140, 313, 337, 344, 364,
372n 37, 411n 134, 416n 204
Vietnam
Buddhist Revolution, Thich Quang Duc, 186
war, 4, 5, 7, 31, 36, 42, 75, 90, 123, 138, 182,
188, 193, 206, 211, 217, 2221, 232, 250,
251, 252, 257, 381n 10, 383n 42, 383n
46, 383n 47, 384n 58, 384n 60, 384n 62,
385n 64, 391n 151

Waldron, W. S., 100, 116, 369n 3, 376n 114,
386n 89, 387n 104
war on terror/terrorism, 5, 9, 44, 73, 97, 108,
110, 115, 120, 133, 171, 184, 203, 251,
253, 256, 257, 298, 343, 354n 55, 359n 31,
388n 116, 391n 156
War Powers Act, 72
War powers Resolution, 200, 202, 258, 358n 29,
360n 41, 388n 113
Warren Commission, 172, 191, 193, 196, 199,
209, 210, 212, 247, 248, 253, 258, 350n 4
Washington/Wall Street Alliance
interests of, 288
Weapons of Mass Destruction (WMD), 64, 98,
246, 248, 351n 25, 404n 8

Wolfowitz, P., 31, 94, 262, 353n 40, 368n 112,
381n 19
Wolin, W. S., 62, 69, 71, 76, 79, 356n 1
see also inverted totalitarianism,
Wood, E., 393n 185
World Bank, 97, 106, 107, 113, 126, 127, 132,
156, 173, 202, 224, 225, 230, 232, 235,
237, 257, 261, 274, 289, 290, 293–7,
302, 303, 306–08, 317, 319, 320, 322,
323, 340, 341
World Court, 57, 413n 175
World Order Models Project (WOMP), 124,
372n 43
world order values, 6, 34, 35, 37, 40, 46,
50, 82
World Social Forum, 17, 18, 77, 347n 37, 347n
38, 361n 52
World Trade Center (WTC), 22, 62, 149, 191
World Trade Organization (WTO), 77, 106, 113,
126, 127, 132, 156, 173, 202, 220, 224,
225, 230, 232, 237, 238, 261, 274, 286,
294, 306–09, 317, 323, 340, 341
World Tribunal on Iraq (WTI), 325–7
World War I, 124
World War II, 2, 7, 8, 11, 12, 23, 41, 42,
67, 90, 144, 173, 193, 203, 205, 210,
221, 226, 229, 235, 360n 40, 365n 95,
366n 95, 389n 119, 402n 317,
406n 59
World War III, 208
World War IV, 349n 10, 353n 42, 392n 163
Wright Mills, C., 36, 38, 49, 50, 73, 81, 183,
350n 14, 359n 32

Yahya, H., 148, 376n 107

About the Author

Terrence E. Paupp

Terrence E. Paupp holds a Master of Theological Studies from the Lutheran School of Theology at Chicago and a juris doctor in law from the University of San Diego School of Law. He has taught philosophy, international law, and political science at Southwestern College and National University. He has served as National Chancellor of the United States for the International Association of Educators for World Peace (IAEWP). Currently, he is vice-president of the Association of World Citizens (AWC) and works as a senior research associate for the Council on Hemispheric Affairs (COHA). He is the author of, *Achieving Inclusionary Governance: Advancing Peace and Development in First and Third World Nations*. He has written numerous articles on human and civil rights and has contributed chapters to a number of books dealing with nuclear weapons and the struggle for their abolition.